# G. K. Chesterton

## A Reappraisal

# G. K. Chesterton

A Reappraisal

By Denis J. Conlon

Methuen

Published by Methuen & Co

Methuen & Co
35 Hospital Fields Road
York YO10 4DZ

www.methuen.co.uk

First published 2015

1

Typeset by SX Composing DTP, Rayleigh, Essex
Printed and bound by CPI Group (UK) Ltd, Croydon, CR0 4YY

ISBN: 978-0-413-77768-3

A CIP catalogue record for this book is
available from the British Library

For Hendrika

Owl by GK Chesterton early 1890s

# CONTENTS

# PREFACE

This study has developed into a sort of common-place book based on Chesterton's life. There was obviously no real point in going over ground covered in his *Autobiography*, when it was possible to use other accounts by the Chestertons, their relatives and their friends, thus viewing events from a different perspective or time. Consideration of Gilbert Chesterton as an artist had also been possible by including examples of his graphic work. By going back to original sources, it is hoped that many misleading accretions have been stripped away, not the least of which are the allegations of his anti-semitism. In this regard a complete mini-anthology of Chesterton's writings on Jewish matters has been included, thus establishing a more balanced picture of what he really did stand for.

# ACKNOWLEDGEMENTS

As so much original material was destroyed by Dorothy Collins at Frances Chesterton's request or lost in incendiary bombing raids by the Luftwaffe, I must begin by acknowledging a debt to the late Maisie Ward's *Gilbert Keith Chesterton* and *Return to Chesterton* which have now become the only source of many important documents. As ever I am in debt to Dr Richard Christophers of the British Library Department of Manuscripts for his help and guidance over many years and especially for my use of his magisterial *British Library Catalogue of Additions to the Manuscripts (The G.K. Chesterton Papers)*. Likewise Geir Hasnes has continued to be lavish with his advice and in particular supplied me with an invaluable copy of his as yet unpublished monumental Bibliography of Chesterton's works. He also consented to read and correct a rough copy of my typescript.

I owe a particular debt to the Nicholl family, above all to the late Mrs Joan Huffer (née Nicholl), Gilbert Chesterton's friend, for her help and hospitality, together with Frances Huffer, her daughter, who shepherded me through the streets of Paris and across the fields of France to her mother's home. I must record an equal debt to Philip and Caroline Morgan-Smith, Barbara Nicholl's son-in law and daughter, who opened up for me their treasure trove of photographs and GKC's poems and sketches. Peter Cockerill, Dorothy Nicholl's son, was instrumental in putting me in touch with his aunt and cousins.

This book would have been a far punier thing had it not been for the agreement and co-operation of Cdr. David Braybrooke, LVO, R.N., of Mr Giles

Darvill and Mrs Juliet Marks (Miss Collins' nephew and niece), of Mrs Nancy Dixon (Freda Spencer's daughter), of Miss Judith Lea (Miss Collins' friend) together with Mr Ronnie Sonnebord, of Bevis Hillier, of Sean Hawkins, of James Morris and of Rev'd Francis Thompson.

I am also grateful for the ongoing support of Dale Ahlquist, Ann Farmer, Rev'd Bob Hughes KHS, Aidan Mackey and Dr William Oddie. Dr William Griffiths's medical expertise has been invaluable. I must also mention the staff of the Swalecliffe branch of the Kent County Library, in particular Fiona Bainbridge who has provided me with a service far beyond the call of duty. Keighley Public Library kindly supplied me with details of Chesterton's visits to their area and to Ilkley in 1903. Any imperfections, infelicities or omissions are to be laid at my door rather than theirs.

Denis J. Conlon
Whitstable, December 2014

# PHOTOGRAPHS

1. Birdie (Beatrice Chesterton, (1870–78) aged 7 with her dog
   By permission of the Marion E. Wade Center, Wheaton college, Wheaton, Illinois.

2. Edward and Marie-Louise Chesterton with Gilbert aged five, 1879
   By permission of the Marion E. Wade Center, Wheaton college, Wheaton, Illinois.

3. Marie-Louise with Gilbert aged 6 and Cecil, 1880
   By courtesy of Sean Hawkins.

4. Gilbert and Cecil c1881
   By courtesy of Sean Hawkins.

5. Campden Hill Water-tower
   The Royal Borough of Kensington and Chelsea Libraries and Arts Service.

6. Gilbert Chesterton aged about 10, c1885

7. Gilbert aged about 16, c1890

8. The Junior Debating Club, 1890

9. Gilbert in art studio pose, possibly at Calderon's Art School, 1892

10. The Junior Debating Club, 1893

11. Gilbert with Frances Blogg during their engagement

12. Frances about the time of her marriage, c1901

13. The Great Wheel at Earl's Court
    Earls Court Limited.

14 Gilbert beginning to put on weight, c1905

15. Gilbert with Michael Braybrooke and Winkle, 1909

16. GKC with Father O'Connor
    By permission of the John M. Kelly Library, St Michael's College, University of Toronto.

# ILLUSTRATIONS

# PART ONE

# 1.

## UNDER THE GREAT GREY WATER-TOWER

It sometimes happens that a public or quasi-historical figure enters into the realm of folklore and that folklore figure then takes on a life of its own (Robin Hood, Guy Fawkes and Hereward the Wake spring to mind). Similar developments can take place within families, and it would seem that among the Chestertons a semi-fabulous *Enfances Gilbert* preceded the later adventures of the fat man in the brigand's hat and desperado's cape. When the subject of legend has confessed, as he did, that he spent most of his early life until the age of eighteen dissimulating what was really passing through his mind, it is easy to see that those of his relations who knew him at the time and later his wife and others (who did not) may have fallen unwarily into the trap of propagating and then continuing a colourful background story because it was indeed colourful and perhaps convenient. Perhaps the linchpin of the legend is the backward boy who did not learn to speak until he was three and did not learn to read at all until he was eight or nine (accounts vary), although at the same age of three Gilbert dictated a story to his Aunt Rose:

### The History of Kids

*The Birth of Kids*. Kid's father heard a trumpet's blast which seemed to say there was some boars and dragons and giants in a forest near there, and the King (Kid's father) went out to fight them, and the first thing he met was a large dragon, the next thing he met was a large giant, and when he came home 'Kids' was born. Then there was a fairy and she kept waving her wand, and a little sprite appeared, and the sprite kept growing prettier and prettier until at last he was a boy, and his name was Valimal. Then a prince appeared, and then the fairy waved her wand and the prince appeared like a Roman soldier. Then she waved her wand again and a horse appeared. Then the Roman soldier saw some Ancient Britons coming along in the distance, and the fairy said to the Roman Soldier: 'That horse is yours.' So the Roman Soldier jumped on the horse – he had just gone about 100 miles when he saw a giant before him, so he drew his dagger and struck the giant on his head, and the giant caught hold of his long sword – so the King (Kids' father) said: 'Run, run and get one more.' But the Roman Soldier wouldn't, but drew his short dagger and fought for the long one, and when he'd fought he got it, and killed the giant. When the King saw the wounded giant he said: 'The Soldier had won.' And so he had. This is the end of the birth of Kids.

*The Boyhood of Kids.* He was dressed up for fun in armour, with a short dagger by his side, and his father thought it would be only for fun, but Kids marched off and you could not see him except like a little speck a 100 miles off in the army. He fought and conquered. Kids' uncle was out at sea, his name was 'Waldimus', and there was a storm, and he was saved by the same Roman Soldier, who fought for Kids when he was a baby. So when the uncle came to land he wondered who that boy was, and he thought he was very like another boy he knew – and when the Queen came rushing up, she cried out: 'It's my son, my son.' Then 'Occradamus' came up, he was 4 years older than Kids, and Waldimus said: 'Is this little boy brother to Occradamus?' And the Roman Soldier who had saved him said: 'Is this the boy I fought for? What has he been doing, he is dressed in armour?' Then the same fairy came in who brought the horse when Kids was a baby and turned the Roman Soldier into the prince he was when Kids was born. All of them saw a great cloud of smoke in a doorway and a snake . . .
  Written by Aunt Rose, from dictation. G[ilbert] aged 3.[1]

Obviously a fair effort from a child who had only just learnt to speak. In like fashion, there is ample evidence of Gilbert Chesterton's ability to write (albeit with boyish spelling mistakes) and even compose stories and poems from a much earlier age than nine:

> Captain Sword and Dr Gunn
> Sail the sea beneath the Sun:
> All fantastical they stand
> Quaint as fishes on the land.
> Captain Sword with sparkling luck
> Like a sword-fish flashed and struck,
> Dr Gunn with peal on peal,
> Exploded like a conger-eel[2]

Perhaps Educational Psychologists should decide whether it is possible to write before being able to read, but it is always as well to be on one's guard when in Chestertonland, as GKC himself, knowing the value of a good story,

neither denied nor confirmed, the 'Am in Market Harborough. Where should
I be?' telegram, to which his wife replied 'Home!' However, he did tell us: 'And
it is also recorded of me that, at the age of six or seven, I tumbled down in the
street in the act of excitedly reciting the words,

> Do not for ever with thy veilèd lids
> Seek for thy noble father in the dust,

at which appropriate moment I pitched forward on my nose.'[3]

Later in his life, those whose acquaintanceship with GKC dated from after
1905 found it difficult to visualize a very tall slim young man who, although
at times ungainly and never overly athletic, had a collection of Maori fighting
sticks and Australian boomerangs[4] and did indulge in rowing, tennis, croquet,
golf, fencing and ice-skating[5] among other activities: we must never forget his
advice that 'If a thing is worth doing, it is worth doing badly,'[6] and give him
credit for practising what he preached.

It might well be thought impertinent to undertake any sort of biography of
the subject of one of the great autobiographies, but Gilbert Chesterton dutifully
deferred to his wife's request that he leave her out of his account, a request also
honoured by subsequent biographers for whom Frances Chesterton and later
Dorothy Collins were in turn the primary sources of information after much
original material had been destroyed. One purpose of this book is to try to fill
in the gaps left by design or default.

### 'The only right way of telling a story is to begin at the beginning,' (Introduction, *William Blake*, 1910)

Gilbert Keith Chesterton was born on May 29th, 1874 to Edward Chesterton
(1841–1922), an estate agent, and his wife Marie-Louise, née Grosjean (1844–
1932).[7] The family, already including a daughter Beatrice (1869–78), resided at
14 (later after a renumbering scheme 32) Sheffield Terrace (off Campden Hill,
Holland Park in West London, not too far from Kensington High Street and
Notting Hill underground station). This was overshadowed by the 'great grey
water tower' which, looming at the end of the road (see photograph), was to
prove an icon for the young Gilbert:

> I merely believe upon authority that I was baptized; I believe, merely by logical inference,
> that I was born. I'm glad to believe that I was baptized at St. George's Church, and that
> I was born in the neighbourhood of the Waterworks Tower opposite the church . . . in

the street outside there were remarkable things for the creative curiosity of childhood, which is too creative to be critical. There was a sham ruin covered with real ivy almost opposite the house, which was on Campden Hill. In the immediate neighbourhood was a house with a highly modern turret overhanging the fall of steep streets and bearing the rather too romantic name of Tower Crecy. High above it, high as the Tower of Babel to my childish eyes, and taking hold on heaven like a water-spout, rose the Tower of the Waterworks. It dominated my dreams so much that I afterwards tried to reproduce one of those pleasant nightmares in a novel called *The Napoleon of Notting Hill.*[8]

Edward Chesterton (Mr Ed.), while nominally heading the family firm of estate agents, now Chesterton Humberts, in fact, possibly on account of a slight heart condition, left everyday running of the business to his younger brother Sidney, and so had much free time to devote to his artistic and literary interests,[9] especially to the toy theatres with which he entertained and impressed his children, now nicknamed Birdie (Beatrice) and Diddie (Gilbert). This idyllic situation was tragically disrupted when Beatrice died of typhoid fever at the age of eight. Edward Chesterton, distraught, reacted morbidly by turning Beatrice's picture to the wall and never mentioning her name again; Gilbert's only recollection of Beatrice was of her riding a rocking-horse, a confused memory that half suggested to him that she had died in a riding accident. Within two years and shortly after the birth of a second son, Cecil Edward (1879–1918), he moved his family to 11 Warwick Gardens, the other side of Kensington High Street not far from the present Earl's Court Exhibition Centre, where, in the words of Annie Firmin, a childhood friend: 'the little boys were never allowed to see a funeral. If one passed down Warwick Gardens, they were hustled from the nursery window at once.'[10] And yet, despite the attempt to forget Beatrice's existence, some member of the family, presumably her mother, saved a pair of the girl's slippers which were found among GKC's effects after his death in 1936: 'I had a little sister who died when I was a child. I have little to go on; for she was the only subject about which my father did not talk. It was the one dreadful sorrow of his abnormally happy and even merry existence; and it is strange to think that I never spoke to him about it to the day of his death.'[11] The new house was described some time later by Ada Jones (Mrs Cecil Chesterton):

> The Chestertons' house . . . stood out from its neighbours. As you turned the corner of the street you had a glimpse of flowers in dark green window boxes and the sheen of paint the colour of West Country bricks, that seemed to hold the sunshine. The setting of the home never altered. The walls of the dining-room renewed their original shade of bronze green year after year. The mantel board was perennially wine colour, and the tiles of the hearth, Edward Chesterton's own design, grew more and more mellow.

Books lined as much of the wall space as was feasible and the shelves reached from floor to ceiling in a phalanx of leather. The furniture was graceful, a slim mahogany dining-table, a small sideboard, generously stocked with admirable bottles, and deep chairs . . .

The dining-room centred the interests of G.K. and Cecil all through their schooldays . . . On party nights wide folding doors stood open and through the vista of a warm yet delicate rose-coloured drawing-room you saw a long and lovely garden, burgeoning with jasmine and syringa, blue and yellow iris, climbing roses and rock plants. The walls were high, and tall trees stood sentinel at the far end . . . On special occasions Edward Chesterton . . . would hang up fairy lamps in absurd and ravishing loops among the flowers and trees.[12]

The birth of his younger brother, greeted by Gilbert with the remark: 'Now I shall always have an audience,' did eventually provide him with a debating partner as the brothers indulged in endless argument: 'I was always arguing. I was always arguing with my brother, and he was always arguing with every-body. When I was not arguing with my brother I was arguing with myself, and most things I have done have been the outcome of those well-balanced con-tests.'[13] In the early years the elder brother read and even wrote fairy stories for the younger. Many of those stories are now incomplete, lacking a beginning or an end, but that is perhaps testimony to their popularity; they are certainly to be commended for their ingenuity.

### THE WILD ROSES[14]

Once upon a time a little girl named Gertrude lived with her old grandmother in a little cottage at the foot of a mountain, and Gertrude liked to wander about in the evening to pick the wild roses that grew all around, to peep into the little dark fir-wood that sloped down the hill and to look at the single blue star-spark that hung at night just above the dark peak of that mountain. And one evening as she was straying just outside the house, to her astonishment she saw that the star had grown to about four times its usual size and had taken the form of a blue fantastic imp, with a blue gleaming spear and a blue flashing crown, hovering like a great blue will-o'-the-wisp over the peak. And beneath him the peak was crowned with a dimly flashing ring of goblin dancers whirling round and round like a blue Catherine wheel, and there were three other rings of dancers at intervals down the mountain. Faster and faster they flew round, looking like one continuous ring of light till at the height of their speed the lowest ring broke, and an imp figure flew like a blue meteor far over the world.

Far away Gertrude could see him wildly wandering, a weird grey figure wandering blindly, madly, aimlessly, over the dark expanse of moor like a ghost that has lost his way in the daytime, for a goblin is helpless and aimless when alone on the upper earth. For thousands and millions of ages he might have wildly traversed that little heath had not he in one of his blind aimless dashes thrown himself bang against Gertrude. The thin, pale weird imp fixed his wild blue eyes on the gentle beautiful face and long auburn tresses of the little girl, gave a strange moaning cry, and grovelled at her feet. He seemed so wild and miserable that Gertrude pitied him and spoke kindly to him and led him into the kitchen.

Her grandmother, who was a respectable old lady, would not, had she been at home, have permitted the misguided Gertrude to bring into the house a youth of the singular appearance and airy costume depicted in the illustrations, but respectability was gone to market and so compassion and hospitality had a chance. The imp regarded the busy preparations made for him by his kind little hostess with respectful but considerably mystified interest. Cakes, teapots, chairs were unknown luxuries to the elf whose meals consisted of moonshine and fossils and whose only resting place was a mushroom. He was, however, soon reconciled to these foreign elegances, and a stool on one side of the fire and a bowl of porridge made him quite cheerful and talkative in a quaint reflective way. Gertrude found his humorous philosophy and his marvellous stories very amusing, and they were soon close friends, if not more.

They strayed outside together and looked at the wild roses that straggled thick all around the edge of the fields. Gertrude leant over the stile and picked one and gave it to the elf. As she did, a flash of blue lightning from the mountain peak was followed by a peal of thunder. The elf turned to Gertrude, 'My time is up' he said, 'good-bye, and do not forget me,' and he sank down into the earth and vanished. Gertrude sank down on the grass and cried bitterly till she cried herself to sleep. Now a great nobleman of the court, Lord Bamboozle, happened to be riding by with a grand train of vassals on his way to the palace and, seeing that the little girl was very beautiful, he took it into his head to propose her as a wife for the young king, in order to rival an ambitious lady who was his enemy. So he bade his squires lift the sleeping girl and put her on his horse before him. And when Gertrude woke up she found herself to her astonishment robed in crimson and ermine and lying on a gorgeous state couch in the palace.

Now meanwhile the little elf, whose name was Flickerflash, had gone back to the grim, dark underground toils of the goblin miners. In the low, dark caverns and tunnels under the earth the goblins sowed tares and weeds and thistles that grew up among men's corn above and destroyed it. But Flickerflash had not forgotten little Gertrude, and he treasured up the sprig of rose tree she had given him, and, while the other elfins grew destructive plants and whispered dark, horrible words over them to make them grow, when no-one was looking he would sow a seed from the wild rose and, as the plant shot upwards, he would kneel down and gently whisper a prayer that it might reach Gertrude and remind her of him. And these rose trees he set growing in all parts of the underground kingdom from the various seeds of the roses she had given him.

And Gertrude, who was now a grand princess of the court expected as a matter of course to marry the handsome young monarch, every time she had almost agreed to wed him was certain to catch sight of the creepers of wild rose that grew all about the palace, no-one knew how, and she thought of the little elf she had talked to long ago, and forgot her royal suitor. A rose creeper grew up under her window, wild roses choked all the flowers in the garden, lined all the avenues in the park, and grew up in every flower-pot on the balcony. And Lord Bamboozle who, though not at all understanding anything else of it, had come to understand that there was something in the sight of wild roses that marred his matchmaking plan, took measures to prevent their appearance. Thousands of gardeners were employed all over the palace grounds to destroy all evidences of the mysterious growth, but all in vain. The rose blossoms increased and the chances of the King and Lord Bamboozle decreased in proportion.

Meanwhile Flickerflash had resolved to escape from the goblins. Just as he had grown one of his rose trees in a cavern that opened onto the side of the hill, he saw that no-one was near, and seizing his rose branch, he rushed out into the cool, clean starlight. After wandering for several hours on the dark, desolate moor, he saw a grim, dark monastic building in the middle of the fen, with blue light burning on each turret. Weary and starving, he made his way to the gate that was opened by a tall pale-robed monastic figure with a blue-burning torch in his hand. He was ushered into a bedroom and shown a bed with a single white sheet over it. No sooner had he lain down in it than several white-robed ghostly monks advanced, lifted up the bed on poles and sallied out as a funeral procession, the figure in front ringing a large funeral bell, while the rest carried weird blue lights and sang a funeral chant. For the moment he seemed dazed and unable to speak or move, but of a sudden he caught sight of the rose sprig that lay red and bright on the cold, white winding sheet. He started up and cried out, 'Stop! I live!' and the whole procession, with a shriek, vanished into darkness, like a dream. As he strode boldly out he passed under a ruined, moss-grown gothic arch over which was written: 'Thou hast woken from the Nightmare, which is superstition and the death and burial of the Soul.' Glad indeed he was and merry to be able to reach out into the free, fresh open air and watch the crests of the pine forest tossing like a dark ocean in the wind, and the countless black rooks flapping over the yellow fields. Being, however, rather sleepy he sought and soon found a tree which he climbed with the intention of sleeping among the branches. No sooner had he seated himself in a crook of a bough than a red hairy squirrel appeared with a pair of acorns from part of one side of the trunk, part of a house where he was busy sitting philosophically contemplating his own tail. Flickerflash apologised and requested him to tell him where he could get a night's shelter. The hospitable squirrel immediately welcomed him, gave him a good supper from his well-stored granary in the hollow of the tree and prevailed on him to lie down to sleep, apologizing as he did so for the periodic hammering on the bark of the tree. 'It's the woodpecker,' he observed, scratching himself with his forepaw, 'a good enough neighbour normally, but eccentric, decidedly eccentric, and given to these nocturnal rappings and, I don't know what to say, is actually known to eat what it finds, ugh!' and the prejudiced rodent wrinkled his cold nose and made a face. Flickerflash was soon fast asleep despite the tapping of the woodpecker and the chattering of the squirrel and the distant but distinct musical hum which came from the heavens. The Elf spent some years among the wild creatures of the wood till he became a sort of king over them, and they brought him in procession offerings of nuts and fruit and grain and other provisions, and he settled their disputes and helped them out of their difficulties and told them long and wonderful stories about the goblins and dragons of his home. And one day the animals, headed by the squirrel and the skylark, came to King Flickerflash and told him how terribly they were annoyed by the wild beasts that prowled on the outskirts of the forest, lions, wolves, eagles, bears, stags and many others. And King Flickerflash waited till nightfall, and bade all the animals go up into the trees and watch. Just as the last gleam of red sunset died away in the darkness the howls and the moans of the wild beasts echoed through the forest gloom. Then one by one, swift, dark and silent they bounded up, so terrifying an elderly maiden rabbit that she was with difficulty kept quiet by the squirrel and the woodpecker. In the centre under the elm stood Flickerflash with the wild rose branch in his hand, round him closed a ring of glaring green eyes followed by dark shadowy forms. A big, reddish lion advanced on him, lowering and bellowing. The fearless imp struck him on the forehead with the thorny rose sprig, and the lion tossed his mane and grumbled and crouched at his feet. One after another, a great grey wolf, a white bear, a golden eagle, and a huge stag with a hundred antlers, each struck by the magic rose-rod, crouched at his feet and whined and under his guidance finished up with an extraordinary dance. But while Flickerflash was ruling his little kingdom he had not forgotten Gertrude whose gift had given him this strange power, and of this there soon appeared a wondrous proof. Gertrude, at this time, having by repeated refusals frustrated the schemes of the ambitious Lord Bamboozle, had made in him a cunning and vindictive enemy. And he resolved to have her accused of witchcraft for which purpose he brought down a certain Dr Hocus Pocus, a famous witchfinder, learned in all the useful sciences of astrology, demonology, etc. about which he knew a variety of cheerful facts which were extremely forcible and interesting if true. And when he arrived at the castle accompanied by several wagons carrying his reference library and technical authorities on the subject, by dint of long and studious scientific labours he discovered what decision it was to his interest to give, and accordingly accused Gertrude of witchcraft. The repulsed King was sullen and angry, the Lord Bamboozle was cunning and cruel, Dr Hocus Pocus was learned and impressive, and poor Gertrude had no-one to stand by her. The Chief Justice, Lord Wagnoddle, solemnly gave sentence against her to please the King, for he had a loyalty to the kingly office and likewise an eye to the main chance, and handed her over to Hackblock, the Chief Executioner, to be burnt at the stake as a witch. Poor little Gertrude cried all night till the faint stealing rosy tint of dawn and the clarion of the herald's golden trumpet announced the day of doom.

A stake was set up in the market place, and a raised throne was made for the king, and Lord Bamboozle came up followed by his retainers all carrying faggots, and then came Lord Wagnoddle and all the judges in scarlet robes, and Dr Hocus Pocus with a black robe and a grin, and then Hackblock the Executioner, hooded and masked, followed by a file of guards with flashing halberds, leading in their midst a sorrowful, beautiful young girl dressed in white, with long tresses streaming down to her waist. Her executioners bound her to the stake, while the vindictive nobleman's retainers heaped up the faggots at her feet. But the people watching the proceedings did not share in the feelings of his Lordship or his Lordship's suite and pitied the beautiful and lonely girl, against whose fate they had already begun to protest in murmurs, when a singular event occurred. Just as Lord Bamboozle's squire was about to fire the heaped-up fuel, a cry of astonishment went up from all. The mysterious flower magic was again at work and the very stake was breaking into spray and leaf and bud of rose till it glittered like a laden rose tree with bright green leaves and bright red blossoms.

'Miracle!' shouted the people.

'Sorcery!' shouted the retainers.

Gertrude saw the well remembered flowers thickening round her, flushed with pleasure with a strange smile and a strange look in her eyes.

'She is a witch!' yelled the retainers.

'She is a saint!' roared the populace.

Just at this moment a new cause of astonishment appeared. A skylark had appeared aloft in the sky and circling round and round downwards alighted on Gertrude's brows, and laid among her auburn tresses a spray of wild rose twisted into a crown and, resting on her head like a living crest, flapped its wings thrice.

'A blessed angel!' said the populace.

'A familiar spirit!' cried the retainers.

Gertrude looked wildly but joyously up, first at the feathered messenger, then at the wild rose crown and said something in a quick whisper.

'A cabalism!' growled the irate retainers.

'A prayer!' gasped the awe-struck townsfolk.

It was not exactly either, for the word Gertrude had whispered was 'Flickerflash!' The next moment a strange roar shook the marketplace, and the attention of everyone was turned to a very curious procession that entered it. The portion of the procession that had the most unusual interest for the spectators in general consisted of a lion, a bear, a wolf, an eagle and a boa-constrictor, animals which inspired an interest which though considerable did not take the form of a general desire for close vicinity or prolonged inspection. But to the principal actor in the preparing ceremony another figure inspired considerably greater interest. Gertrude, as the head of the procession appeared, had burst her bonds with a sudden strength and sprung to Flickerflash's side, while the wild beasts formed a ring around the pair.

'What does this mean?' thundered Lord Bamboozle, advancing at the head of a group of the principal planners of the execution, 'Do you dare to protect a condemned criminal with a menagerie of wild beasts?', and drawing his sword he advanced onto the other group. With the greatest composure the lion advanced, snapped the sword with his teeth, pulled the baron's nose with one paw, smacked him on the head with another, and punched him in the chest with a third, and finally knocked him down and sat on him. Meanwhile, the other animals had been busy with the other executioners. The bear with a smug smile had embraced the Lord Chief Justice and hugged him tight till he kicked and yelled, and then hugged him tighter. The boa-constrictor had wound his coils round and round the long person of the Executioner with his lifted head towering above and glaring down on the horrified upturned countenance of the finisher of the law. The big grey wolf had startled and put to flight the terrified squire of Lord Bamboozle and was now hunting the unhappy man at lightning speed round and round the market-place. Lastly, the great eagle had seized the collar of Dr Hocus Pocus and lifted him kicking and bellowing into the air, and then amused itself by soaring up and dropping him from great heights, which did not improve his equanimity or his personal appearance.

While these ceremonies were pretty well taking all spirit of resistance out of the subordinates, the haughty and angry monarch, descending from his throne, had strode up to Gertrude, seized her by the wrist and attempted to drag her away. Flickerfash struck him with the rose-twig across the face and with such suddenness and violence that he staggered, lost his balance and fell full-length on the earth. He started to his feet and calling his squire to bring his steed and armour, challenged the rebel to mortal combat. Both rivals assumed mad horses and lances and took their places at each end of the market-place.

The lion gave a roar as the signal and the combatants charged, but aiming somewhat vaguely they passed each other about five yards apart and, turning round, at a given signal charged again. They met with a clash that made the sparks fly, shivered both lances to the grasp and hurled both their steeds back on their haunches, but the result being again indecisive. They sternly backed and charged once more. The third time they rushed together there was a bang, a chaos of arms and legs and then a cloud of obscuring dust which, clearing away, revealed two confronting horses rubbing their noses together in an amicable manner, and behind each a bewildered warrior sitting on the ground with his lance lying ten yards off. Two heralds immediately rushed forward to assist them to rise, but before they could interfere, both combatants had leapt up backwards with a suddenness and violence that knocked their respective heralds down, and brandishing their swords closed up in terrific and resounding conflict. It would be useless for the humble chronicler to attempt to describe that awful and complicated conflict, of which his recollections are indeed vague, in as much as when he, with his harp, was present at the recorded passage of arms, he took every opportunity to be out of their way. Suffice it to say that after three hours of hacking, stabbing, slashing, lunging, battering and banging that drove red sparks from brand and helmet, the king made a gigantic lunge at Flickerflash's heart who however, dodging it, the monarch stumbled forward, and the Elfin Knight with one terrific backhanded blow levelled him gasping on the earth. Flickerflash stood over him in silence for some time, and then threw down his sword and turned away. The people shouted, and the retainers trembled and dared not interfere. The assembly broke up and formed itself into two processions, the first a long line of the fallen officials, headed by the king, all with melancholy faces and dingy and bedraggled appearance, straggled away in a long line up to the Town Hall. The other procession was headed by Flickerflash with Gertrude leaning on his arm, followed by the wild beasts, several knights, burghers and halberdiers, with the rear brought up by the populace, shouting and hooraying like mad. They made their way up to the little church on the hill and they passed in and knelt before the priest. He was an old man with white flowing beard and tresses, with a cross on his breast. He was robed in white, like the monks of the Nightmare Convent, but whereas their robes were pale and misty and dim like the moonlight, his were pure and dazzling and bright like the untrodden snow in the sunlight. He led them up the long, grey-blue fretted aisle, gleaming with windows stained with bright red and green and blue and violet to the altar with tapers burning. There Flickerflash and Gertrude were married. And as they passed out the people plucked the wild roses and strewed them under their feet. And they begged Flickerflash to stay and be their King, but he thanked them and refused, and out of the city gates they passed alone together, and over the hills in the dying glow of the evening till they came to the spot where Gertrude had plucked the rose. And there they built them a castle and dwelt.

## 2.

## A LUMP OF WHITE FAT

The neighbourhood dominated by the great water-tower had been exchanged for one dominated by the Earl's Court Exhibition Centre with its constantly changing displays. There was much to explore in Kensington streets but also in the Chestertons' walled garden into which the children of relatives and neighbours alike were invited. There Gilbert played Cowboys and Indians with the two Firmin sisters, with Henry Vivian and his three sisters, Ida, Nina and Violet, among others: 'The Vivians lived in the same street or rather "gardens" as ourselves . . . I was very much elated to have the family, or at least the three eldest girls who represent it to the neighbourhood, standing once more on the well-rubbed lawn of our old garden, where some of my earliest recollections were of subjecting them to treatment such as I considered appropriate to my own well established character of robber, tying them to trees to the prejudice of their white frocks, and otherwise misbehaving myself in the funny old days, before I went to school and became a son of gentlemen only. "What old memories this garden calls up," said Nina, "I remember so well coming here in a new pink frock when I was a little girl. It wasn't so new when I went away." '[1]

Carefree days under his father's tutelage, interspersed by frequent holidays,[2] were to come to an end when Gilbert was enrolled at Colet Court (better known as Bewsher's after the name of the two brothers who were its first principals), a new (1883) preparatory school for St Paul's School on the Hammersmith Road. There it was that he began the process of 'being instructed by somebody I did not know, about something I did not want to know,'[3] and it was in fact at

Bewsher's that Mr Alexander was waspishly to remark 'You know, Chesterton, if we could open your head, we should not find any brain but only a lump of white fat!'[4] The target of that remark recalled that:

> . . . he was sent to Mr Bewsher who gave him desks and copy-books and Latin grammars and atlases to draw pictures on. He was far too innately conscientious not to use these materials to draw on. To other uses, asserted by some to belong to these objects, he paid little heed. The only really curious thing about his school life was that he had a weird and quite involuntary habit of getting French prizes. They were the only ones he ever got and he never tried to get them. But though the thing was quite mysterious to him, and though he made every effort to avoid it, it went on, being evidently a part of some occult natural law.[5]

Home in Warwick Gardens was not far away and so Gilbert walked to school often accompanied by other boys who later recalled that, although he was taller than most men, his mother still clad him in sailor suits. In January 1887 at the age of twelve Gilbert moved over to the senior school where, placed in the second form, he met a remarkable group of boys, most of whom were to be his friends for life. Sitting at the back of the class-room (the usual refuge for the shy and the awkward) he did impress himself on their memories:

> Laurence Solomon: 'Sleepy and indifferent in manner but able to master anything when he cared to take the trouble – as he very seldom did.'

> Edward Fordham: 'We thought him the most curious thing that ever was, apparently muttering poetry, breaking into inane laughter . . . I can see him now, very tall and lanky, striding untidily along Kensington High Street, smiling and sometimes scowling as he talked to himself, apparently oblivious of everything he passed; but in reality a far closer observer than most, and one who not only observed but remembered what he had seen.'

> E.C. Bentley: 'GKC, when I knew him first, was an unusually tall, lanky boy with a serious, even brooding, expression that gave way very easily to one of laughing happiness. He was by nature the happiest boy and man I have ever known; even in the adolescent phase of morbid misery that so many of us go through, and that he has described so thoroughly, laughter was never far away, in my recollection.'[6]

Repeated references to a scowling or brooding expression, often caught in photographs later in life, are evidence for an unfocussed gaze when he was not wearing spectacles to correct his myopia. The short-sighted boy did, however, have the insight to recall:

For the first half of his time at school he was very solitary and futile. He never regretted the time, for it gave him two things, complete mental self-sufficiency and a comprehension of the psychology of outcasts.

But one day, as he was roaming about a great naked building land [Bedford Park?] which he haunted in play hours, rather like an outlaw in the woods, he met a curious agile youth with hair brushed up off his head. Seeing each other, they promptly hit each other simultaneously and had a fight. Next day they met again and fought again, These Homeric conflicts went on for many days, till one morning in the crisis of some insane grapple, the subject of this biography quoted, like a war-chant, something out of Macaulay's *Lays*. The other started and relaxed his hold. They gazed at each other. Then the foe quoted the following line. In this land of savages they knew each other. For the next two hours they talked books. They have talked books ever since. The boy was Edmund Clerihew Bentley. The incident just narrated is the true and real account of the first and deepest of our hero's male connections. But another was to ensue, probably equally profound and far more pregnant with awful and dazzling consequences. Bentley . . . being seized with a peculiar desire to learn conjuring, he had made the acquaintance of an eerie and supernatural young man, who instructed him in the Black Art; a gaunt Mephistophelian sort of individual, who our subject half thought was a changeling. Our subject has not quite got over the idea yet, though for practical social purposes he calls him Lucian Oldershaw . . .

These three persons soon became known through the length and breadth of St. Paul's School as the founders of a singular brotherhood. It was called the J.D.C. [Junior Debating Club]. No one, we believe, could ever have had better friends than did the hero of this narrative . . . Bertram, who seemed somehow to have been painted by Van Dyck, a sombre and stately young man, a blend of Cavalier and Puritan, with the physique of a military father and the views of an ethical mother and a soul of his own which for sheer simplicity is something staggering. Vernède with an Oriental and inscrutable placidity varied every now and then with dazzling agility and Meridithian humour. Waldo d'Avigdor who masks with complete fashionable triviality a Hebraic immutability of passion tried in a more ironical and bitter service than his father Jacob. Lawrence and Maurice Solomon, who show another side of the same people, the love of home, the love of children, the meek and malicious humour, the tranquil service of a law. Salter who shows how beautiful and ridiculous a combination can be made of the most elaborate mental cultivation and artistic sensibility and omniscience with a receptiveness and a humility extraordinary in any man. These were his friends.[7]

Many school exercise books and jotters survive to show that, alongside basic school work, the dreamy boy was sketching illustrations for poems and for all types of stories from fairy tales to Stevensonian-type novellas, stories very often based on backgrounds absorbed during the holiday trips the Chesterton family made to the Essex coast, Thanet, Northumberland and Scotland but then infused with a traditionally Whig version of history presumably picked up both at home and at school:

'Do you not know me?' said the stranger in a low, musical but yet strangely terrifying voice. 'I am the Black Crow.'

'Guy – Devil!' was the hoarse exclamation of the pious and respectable lady. 'Lord Guy, I have lived twenty years in your foul castle, as wife, wife of your brother Ralph, and I know, and you know, Guy de Corbeau, how you treated me, aye and God Almighty knows, and let Him judge between you and me' . . . 'But I am not your brother's wife,' cried Elizabeth wildly. 'I was separated, divorced – in the chaos of the Civil War, you remember, – mad with the misery and cruelty that oppressed me, I fled – fled to the feet of Cromwell – Cromwell – and he, rebel and usurper as he was, yet ever heard the voice of justice, and he declared me free. Aye, thou rememberedst it, Guy, and I too. – the scene in the camp when you feared him, the only living man you ever feared – and he said, "This woman is no longer your brother's wife – Go, and the Lord be witness between us." Would that he were alive this day.'

'Why, you elderly Roundhead,' said the visitor, laughing, 'are you becoming a Cromwellite in your old age?'[8]

Eventually essays appear alongside the poems and the tales, most of a quality that gainsays the content of his master's reports:[9]

*December 1887.* Too much for me: means well by me, I believe, but has an inconceivable knack of forgetting at the shortest notice, is consequently always in trouble, though some of his work is well done, when he does remember to do it. He ought to be in a studio not at school. Never too troublesome, but for his lack of memory and absence of mind.

> [CROMWELL]
> He the man, the mighty soldier,
> He the ruler whose remains
> Hang there as a feast for ravens,
> Clanking in the gallows' chains.
> He had chased all Holland's navy
> Back into the Zuyder Zee,
> As he smote the Papist tyrant
> On the Spaniard's native sea. (1886)

*July 1888.* Wildly inaccurate about everything; never thinks for two consecutive moments to judge by his work; plenty of ability, perhaps in other directions than classics.

*December 1888.* Fair. Improving in Neatness. Has a very fair stock of general knowledge.

> SUFFERING
> Though pain be stark and bitter
> And day in darkness creep,
> Not to that depth I sink me
> That asks the world to weep.

*July 1889.* A great blunderer with much intelligence.

*December 1889.* Means well. Would do better to give his time to 'Modern' subjects.

*July 1890.* Can get up any work, but originates nothing.

### THE GERM
Meadow, Father, though thine eyes
  Shine with hoary mysteries,
Canst thou tell what in the heart
  Of a cowslip blossom lies?

Secret as the inmost sea,
  Tiny to infinity,
Stands a little house of seeds
  Like an elfin's granary.

Speller of the stones and weeds,
  Skilled in Nature's crafts and creeds,
Tell me what is in the heart
  Of the smallest of the seeds.

God Almighty and with Him
  Cherubim and seraphim,
Filling all eternity.
  Adonai Elohim.

*December 1890.* Takes an interest in his English work, but otherwise has not done well.

*July 1891.* He has a decidedly literary aptitude, but does not trouble himself enough about school work.

### PARABLES
A raven flapped o'er the rich man's roof,
O'er golden turrets and white walls proof.
And the rich man looked on the blackening sign
From his drowsy lamp and his fiery wine:
And he thought of the red blood, fierce with sin,
That gleamed in the cup and the wine therein;
He thought of the mad tears gathered up
To fill the glory that filled the cup.
He thought of the dim wine's secret red,
And the men that struggle and scream for bread,
And he gazed and murmured the bird to see:
'God feeds the raven. but men feed me.'
Reigns and revels are gone and past,
Shall not the good time come at last? (1891)

*July 1892.* Not on the same plane with the rest: composition quite futile, but will translate well and appreciate what he reads. Not a quick brain, but possessed by a slowly moving tortuous imagination. Conduct always admirable.

### THE KINGDOM OF HEAVEN

Said the Lord God, 'Build a house,
 Build it in the gorge of death,
Found it in the throats of Hell
 Where the last sea muttereth,
Fires and whirlwinds, build it well.

Laboured sternly flame and wind,
 But a little and they cry,
'Lord, we doubt of this Thy will,
 We are blind and murmur why.'
And the winds are murmuring still.

Said the Lord God, 'Build a house,
 Cleave its treasure from the earth,
With the jarring powers of Hell
 Strive with formless might and mirth,
Tribes and war-men, build it well.'

Then the raw red sons of men
 Brake the soil and lopped the wood,
But a little and they shrill,
 'Lord, we cannot view Thy good.'
And the wild men clamour still.

Said the Lord God, 'Build a house,
 Smoke and iron, spark and steam,
Speak and vote and buy and sell;
 Let the new world throb and stream.
Seers and makers, build it well.'

Strove the cunning men and strong,
 But a little and they cry.
'Lord. mayhap we are but clay,
 And we cannot know the why.'
And the wise men doubt today.

Yet though worn and deaf and blind,
 Force and savage, king and seer
Labour still, they know not why

At the dim foundation here;
Knead and plough and think and ply.

Till at last, mayhap hereon,
   Fused of passion and accord,
Love its crown and peace its stay,
   Rise the city of the Lord
That we darkly build today.

Chesterton in his last year at St. Paul's School was already taking a broader literary sweep, 'I really think that my own political and social tendencies were always touched with those first local impressions: of little London streets lifted up, as it were, upon something that seemed like the peak of a mountain. The waterworks tower still overshadowed me; and I had begun to imagine *The Napoleon of Notting Hill* while I was still going to school at St. Paul's School along the road to Hammersmith. I think I went through my schooldays in a sort of trance or sleep of sloth, dimly tracing those first fancies and refusing to put away childish things.'[10]

To his schoolmasters it must have come as a bolt from the blue when in the Spring term of 1892 Gilbert Chesterton submitted a poem in Spenserian stanza for the competition for the Milton[11] Prize which he then won, but the book presented when he also won the French Prize was another sign that all was not what it seemed.

ST. FRANCIS XAVIER
The Apostle of the Indies

He left his dust, by all the myriad tread
Of yon dense millions trampled to the strand,
Or 'neath some cross forgotten lays his head
Where dark seas whiten on a lonely land;
He left his work, what all his life had planned,
A waning flame to flicker and to fall,

Mid the huge myths his toil could scarce withstand,
And the light died in temple and in hall,
And the old twilight sank and settled over all.
He left his name, a murmur in the East,
That dies to silence amid older creeds,
With which he strove in vain: the fiery priest
Of faiths less fitted to their ruder needs . . .

Chesterton must have known what type of work was expected for the Milton Prize, but usually he was able to adopt less stiff and opaque styles; nonetheless, he did on occasion tend to return to the malign influence of Macaulay and others. And yet the Milton Prize had indeed been awarded to the dunce of Form 6B with F.W. Walker, the High Master, posting a notice that henceforth *G.K. Chesterton to rank with the Eighth* [or senior form].[12] That triumph was capped soon after he had left school when on December 17th, 1892 his first published work appeared in *The Speaker*:

### THE SONG OF LABOUR

A light, a glimmer outlines the crest of the mountain walls,
Starlike it broadens and brightens, and day o'er the valley falls;
It waketh the prince to praise, and it waketh the fool to mirth,
And it waketh a man to his toil and his place on the ordered earth.

There are uplands cloudlet-shadowed and mountains thunder-browed,
There are wastes of wood untravelled, and leagues of land unploughed,
Swamp-worlds heavy with poison, worlds grey and chill,
And I go, a clearer and builder, the voice of the human will.

God has struck all into chaos, princes and priests down-hurled,
But He leaves the place of the toiler, the old estate of the world.
In a season of doubt and of wrangle, in the thick of a world's uproar,
With the new life dark in wrestle, with the ghost of a life that is o'er,
When the old Priest fades to a phantom, when the old King nods on his throne,
The old, old hand of Labour is mighty and holdeth its own . . .

# 3.

# THE WHEEL OF STARS

The volte-face in GKC's fortunes is more easily understood when account is taken of a group of boys who on July 1st, 1890 met at Lucian Oldershaw's house in Talgarth Road to found the Junior Debating Club, no doubt influenced by the fact that membership of the St. Paul's School debating club known as The Union was restricted to the eighth form. The fourteen to sixteen year olds were unaware that the JDC would not only absorb their energies for the next four years, but also become a dominating influence over them for the rest of their lives: 'The little literary club, which in the hands of Bentley and myself had become an ethical brotherhood, a sort of Round Table whose groups knew nothing better than talking far into the night on all the things in heaven and earth and under the earth.'¹ That remark is perhaps less than fair, as the organizing genius behind the whole project was its secretary, Lucian Oldershaw, who was also to edit, produce, print and sell *The Debater*. The boys met at each other's houses where they were provided with tea and buns while solemnly reading papers and discussing diverse literary, historical and philosophical topics: "A penny bun of the sticky order caressingly stung the chairman's honoured cheek, sped on its errand of mercy by the unerring hand of Mr Fordham." I may remark that I was the chairman; and that I was generally honoured in that way. But the printer avenged me for he rendered the missile as "A peony of the stick order" . . . It was the beginning of a long career of martyrdom from misprints.'² It was remarkable not only that boys of their ages should contribute to a printed magazine but that they should have the nous to choose the sleepy class dunce as their chairman, and yet they were no doubt very well aware that 'Nobody who knows anything of the English schoolboy at that date will imagine that there was at the moment any pleasure in such prominence or distinction. We were all hag-ridden with a horror of showing off, which was perhaps the only coherent moral principle we possessed . . . I can remember running to school in sheer excitement repeating militant lines of *Marmion* with passionate emphasis and exultation; and then going into class and repeating the same lines in the lifeless manner of a hurdy-gurdy, hoping that there was nothing whatever in my intonation to indicate that I distinguished between the sense of one word and another.'[3]

Indeed, it was away from the classroom that a great deal of pleasure was taken in prominence and distinction by one of the ablest groups of boys ever to grace St. Paul's School:

Gilbert Keith Chesterton (nickname Geke), 1874–1936, Chairman of the Junior Debating Club.

Lucian Robert Frederick Oldershaw, 1876–1951, Secretary of the JDC, later President of the Oxford Union and OUDS, economist, and journalist. Mayor of Maidenhead on two occasions. He married Ethel Blogg and so became Chesterton's brother-in-law.

Edmund Clerihew Bentley, 1875–1956, librarian of the JDC, later journalist (*Daily News*, *Daily Telegraph*), author (*Trent's Last Case*, etc.) and creator of the Clerihew. Married Violet Boileau.

Francis George Lawder Bertram, 1875–1938, later Director of Civil Aviation, Air Ministry.

Digby Charles Henry d'Avigdor, 1876–1953. Born in New York, at some point a gas engineer. He spent time in India and the Far East, but he returned to become a medical administrator at Queen Charlotte's Hospital and King's College Hospital, contributing articles to the *British Medical Journal*. Married Miss. Stott.

Waldo d'Avigdor, 1877–1947. Born in Germany, took British nationality in 1901, later director Alliance Insurance Co. Married Mildred Wain.

Edward Wilfrid Fordham, 1875–1956, later a barrister.

Bernard Noel Langdon-Davies, 1876–1952, later President of the Cambridge Union, lecturer, publisher and politician.

Leonard Arthur Magnus, 1879–1924, later Russian linguist and author of *Heroic Ballads of Russia* (1921) and other works. Younger son of Sir Philip Magnus (1842–1933), the prominent Jewish educator.

Herbert Arthur Sams, 1875–1957, later Director-General of the Indian Post Office. The only member of the JDC to be knighted (1931). In his later years Bursar of Selwyn College, Cambridge.

Frederick Gurney Salter, 1876–1969, later Chesterton's solicitor (Salter & Lees).

Lawrence Solomon, 1876–1940, later senior tutor at University College, London.

Maurice Solomon (nickname Grey), 1878–1954, later director of the General Electric Company.

Robert Ernest Vernède, 1875–1917, poet, died in battle.

The membership varied little in numbers, adding only a few as the years passed; rules were strictly enforced and fines imposed for non-attendance without good reason. Among many other poems and songs[4] Chesterton wrote *Chant of the Junior Debating Club* :

> ...... Then pass the cup, Debaters all,
> And fill the tea-pot high,
> And in the joy of wild debate
> May hours like moments fly.
> As critics quiet and composed,
> As brothers kind and free,
> Join hand in hand the tea-pot round,
> Joy to the J.D.C.

Bentley also contributed a chant to be sung to the tune of *O My Darling Clementine* on all possible occasions much to the annoyance of Marie-Louise Chesterton among others:

> In the neighbourhood of Kensington where the bird sings on the tree
> Live the members of a society, which is called the J.D.C.
> I'm a member, I'm a member, member of the J.D.C.,
> I belong to it for ever; don't you wish that you were me?

Despite the inanity of Bentley's song, the influence of the JDC was strong enough to ensure that they were bound together for life, meeting at least for an annual dinner until the 1950s, one meeting in 1948 at the Great Western Hotel [now Hilton Paddington] being the occasion for the presentation of a bust of Chesterton to the Alma Mater, a bond only broken when the passage of time took its toll.

Much of Chesterton's early fiction was based on the characters of his JDC friends who appear loosely disguised in tales such as *The Human Club*. He also took pains to draw up an expanded version of the rulebook which transformed the JDC into some sort of semi-medieval confraternity:

### The Valiant Yet Judicious Order of The Long Bow

I.     The General Assembly of the Order shall occur at least once a fortnight – on Saturday Afternoon.

II.    On Each Such Occasion a Grand Master or HOLY UNCLE of the Order shall be elected, who shall rule the Order until the next General Assembly.

III.   That the HOLY UNCLE shall be absolute during the assembly and until the next assembly, when he may be impeached.

IV.      That Each Knight be provided with one helmet, with visor suitable for fencing mask, one wooden sword blunt at the end, one shield with blazon chosen by himself, one bow and eight arrows.

V.       That all such purchases be made by the HOLY UNCLE for the time being.

VI.      That the HOLY UNCLE for the time being have Charge of the Banner of the Order – the Book of the Order, in which these papers be included, and a Sceptre or staff indicative of his office.

VII.     That any one breaking any of these rules, or any of the rules of Knighthood, and being so judged by the HOLY UNCLE, may be disbarred from the sport at the next assembly, to the full Council of Knights, when his wrongs, if any, shall receive compensation.

VIII.    That any one disobeying the HOLY UNCLE in the exercise of rights herein stated, may be suspended as above, having the same right of appeal.

IX.      That Ladies, if willing, be admitted as Ladies of the Order of the Long Bow.

X.       That not less than two thirds of the Order be present, to legally constitute a general assembly.

XI.      That Elections to the Order be made by the Members.

XII.     That the HOLY UNCLE have at no time power over the direction of votes – and that otherwise he be supreme.

Daring with Domesticity. Its methods are:

(1).     Trials of Archery – or the First Use of the Long Bow.

(2).     The Invention and Introduction of such methods of sham fight as shall be innocuous to the knights themselves and to the Windows of their Parents.

(3).     Single Combat with Swords, under the restrictions thereinafter mentioned.

(4).     The Telling of Stories on Rainy Days – or the Second Use of the Long Bow – under no restrictions at all.

The Following are the Oaths of Knighthood: drawn from the Authentic Mediaeval Sources.

(See Guizot's History)

I.       Not to fight in Companies against one.

II.      In Tourney or Sportive Contest, not to use the point of the Sword.

III.     To abjure all tricks and artifices.

IV.      To touch no other Knight's Arms without his leave and take not that which is another's.

V.       To injure no one maliciously.

VI.      To wear but one sword.

VII.     Never to engage in Single Combat with Swords, except the vizors of both combatants be lowered. [+]

VIII.    Never to shoot with arrows at a mark unless all persons be standing well away from that mark. [+]

IX.      To Keep promises inviolably – and to defend the rights and advantages of comrades when they are absent.

X.       To obey always the Captain or the Master of the Game who is lawfully elected.

XI.     To be bound always to serve and escort all ladies.

XII.    On returning home or to the Court of our Sovereign to render only a true account of our adventures, even though we have been worsted – to the King and to the Registrar of the Order.

+ The Two marked thus have been inserted to meet modern social conditions. The rest are genuine Oaths of Chivalry. [In fact no such marks are to be found, although we have so marked the two most likely, Ed.]

To all above oaths of the Valiant yet Judicious Order of the Long Bow, I solemnly subscribe,

Gilbert Keith Chesterton.

As it had always been an unofficial grouping, the JDC left St. Paul's along with its original members, although they continued to appear as a group at school reunions, and it was at a meeting held on June 16th 1894, a year after Gilbert Chesterton had left school, that an innocent enquiry as to the intended careers of the members produced a series of fanciful projections in *Our Future Prospects*, in which it would seem that the intention was for each member to supply a chapter leaving the next contributor with a dilemma he had then to resolve. All went well until the manuscript was passed to E.C. Bentley who only returned it some twelve years later in 1906,[5] and so the project never came to fruition. Nonetheless, amongst what there is of it there is one story of biographical interest:

'Here Geke! Let me introduce you, Mr Chesterton, to Miss Dorothy Grey, Miss Gertrude Grey.' Mr Chesterton shakes hands with two young ladies, one dark and the other indescribably chestnut-haired, who proceed to make some very witty remarks about the weather . . .

We must now change the scene of our scattered and complicated drama to a room in St. Petersburg, where Gilbert Chesterton and his wife were sitting, or to speak more accurately, his wife was sitting and he was prowling up and down. On the table lay a letter from Sir Leonard Magnus, the new Member of Parliament for Bayswater, which they were discussing . . .

'Where do the people Magnus helps live?' asked the wife suddenly, raising her head on which the chestnut hair burnt like a red fire in the light of the embers. The husband named the place with some surprise.

'I can go to them,' she said, rising quickly.

'You! No, thank God, you can't, while I'm here.'

'Why no?' she cried, stamping her foot. 'It must be done. I will go.'

'But they are suspected.'

She drew herself up, showing her tall figure, hidden generally in her strange coiled and crouching attitudes, and pushed back her flaming hair. 'Do you think I am afraid?' she said . . .

'No . . . you are not afraid: I know you well, Gertrude.'

The thrust of the narrative of *Our Future Prospects* is, of course, nonsense, but its account of the meeting, love affair and marriage of Gilbert Chesterton and a red-haired cousin of E.C.Bentley's by the name of Gertrude Grey shows that the JDC were familiar with *Basil Howe*, Chesterton's first novel written in 1893–4 in which the eponymous hero, a tall shy young man, woos and marries Gertrude Grey. Ada Chesterton, Gilbert's sister-in-law and colleague, noted that 'the fugitive heroines who occasionally flit through his stories are inevitably red-headed . . . red hair signified to Gilbert beauty and romance.' Ada had also heard from Cecil that Gilbert was really in love with a girl called Gertrude, the name being misconstrued by Maisie Ward to be that of Gertrude Blogg, a situation which she then refuted in an appendix to her 1944 biography. But in the early 1890s Gilbert Chesterton does seem to have been fascinated by a red-haired girl:

A PORTRAIT
Her hair is as a floating fire,
    The glory of the world's desire,
Her visage sweet yet gaunt and free,
    Elvish and broken startlingly,
Her garb is green and climbs and clings,
    Her arm is weighted of strange rings,
Her eyes are brown and dreamy, mild
    Making the elfin to a child,
Childish she is, and quick and hot.
    Her heart is sealed: we know her not. (1892)

Who was the mysterious young lady who had claimed Gilbert's heart and who would appear to have moved away from Kensington?:

There is a heart within a distant town
Who loves me more than treasure or renown.
Think you it strange and wear it as a crown.
Is not the marvel here: that since the kiss
And dizzy glories of that blinding bliss,
One grief has ever touched me after this? (ca. 1893)

One group of young women who indeed did move away from Warwick Gardens to a convent boarding school in Norwood for at least a time was the Vivian sisters, the youngest of whom was 'Violet, a veritably delightful child with a temper as formless and as erratic as her tempest of red hair.'[6]

Could Violet Vivian, to whom, as V.V., Gilbert addressed poems, be disguised as Gertrude Grey (G.G.) in *Our Future Prospects* and in his first novel, *Basil Howe*, in 1894? Little is now known of what happened to the Vivian sisters; at the time when it would have been possible to find out there was no need to do so, as everybody probably knew. We are left with a possible clue in a love poem from the mid-1890s, a poem so full of nostalgia and of separation in love that it suggests some insurmountable barrier between a young man yet to make his way in the late Victorian world and the young woman whom he was in no financial position to ask for her hand in marriage:

### AGAIN

Like the wind on the sands she was in the flare of her sand-wild hair,
Like to a gull in the foam she was, like to a rushing of air;
Billowed and brake her flaming locks 'gainst the dreaming blue of the sea,
Like to a dash of a sudden rain, like to a flood went she.

And I, I followed fleetly, how could I follow but fleet,
For the sea went by in her great wild eyes, and the sea-wind in her feet,
And the long wave rose as an elfin wall and bent as a flickering crown,
And a russet cloudland barred the night when the broad red sun went down.

Many a maiden lingers, with poppy-fans at her feet,
When the swallows dapple the yellow dome, and the slopes are ribbed with wheat,
But at her feet, jaggèd and fiery only the starfish lay,
And above her head with a clamour the hoarse gull rushed astray.

She looked on the cliff and the shingles, she stood by the surfs and me,
She moved 'twixt the rock and the raucous wave, a very child of the sea.
The morning wasted the shorelands, one morning emptied the grot;
Morning she came unto me; one morning came she not.

Life went on with its duties, gatherings, questions, strife,
On through the long year's roaring; and she sank out of my life.
And I sealed up my heart with portals, walls without crevice or mark,
But within my heart lay an ocean whose pulses throbbed in the dark.

And some hour of the year, in the darkness whose sun was barred in a grave,
Would break with a sudden thunder a long white desolate wave.
And the good friends gathered round me, the true, the tender, the strong,
The brave old band of comrades I have loved so well and long,

And they trod my heart as a meadow, a windy wandering heath,
And the young-eyed daisies showed not the old earth-grave beneath.

One morning a word fell vaguely: she was coming, perchance was nigh.
How lightly the chance was taken on the lips of others than I!

A knocking: a door half-opened, a shape – and from that hour down
A dazzling fire and a fragrance: a sudden secret crown.
In the grey of a parlour twilight mine eyes could but heavily see –
If God's strong world be not as a dream – it was not a dream, but she

With her high head low for a greeting, her proud cheeks fair with a flame,
Speaking clear in the gloaming, simply saying my name.
After the long years, fruitful, strong, after the love gains won,
After the slow births, mighty and new, that now seemed little and done,

After the broad lands, noisy and thronged, that lay 'twixt me and the sea,
God, who forgets not what he has willed, looked on us, I and she.
She sat yet again beside me; a fire sang in my head;
We said things childish, frantic. Who knows what things we said

In jest and story and rhyming, memory, fancy, game?
I looked on her great eyes ever to find them ever the same.
She went to a drear piano, laughing dreamily slow,
And she played the old song, senseless, sweet, that she sang to me long ago.

And I scarce spake, vaguely deeming rankèd angels looking on,
That I might do nought unworthy of the great thing God had done.
We had our smile and we parted. I held her hand and she went,
But my heart had wakened within me with meaning and high intent:

It was not ended in childhood; it was not buried in sand.
God spake and set us there once again, for a moment, hand in hand.
It may be God shall will me lost love and a lonely chair:
God works no woe of the dusty world that a brave man may not bear.

But thorns be crowns or roses, loss be in lot or gain,
The old sea-dream was something. I have lived to see her again.[7]

It is idle to speculate how far this poem and *Basil Howe* are based on reality and how far they are an exercise in wish fulfilment, but an unhappy outcome to a first love affair might have helped to plunge Chesterton into the gloomy solipsism which dogged him soon after leaving St. Paul's School; inspired to write a romantic novel by the intensity of first love, the loss of that love could well have induced a reaction of equal intensity. He would never quite do the same dance of the seven veils again, for in future at least one veil was always in place to hide his emotional life, and yet always peeping through came the lost love's red hair which in story after story, carrying its Celtic connotation of fairy magic, bedecked those men and women deemed to be the inspiration of life.

An aphorism entitled *To My Lady* found in a notebook dating from 1894–96, before Lucian Oldershaw had taken his friend to Bedford Park to introduce him to the Blogg household, is apparently amended to indicate that it is addressed to Frances Blogg,[8] although the initials V.V. are on the next page:

> God made you very carefully
> He set a star apart for it
> He stained it green and gold with fields
> And aureoled it with sunshine –
> He peopled it with kings, peoples, republics
> And so made you, very carefully.
>
> All nature is God's book, filled with his rough sketch for you.

*The Nunnery* also predated the first meeting with Frances Blogg, although again the poem was revised and retitled *Dedicated* after that encounter, raising the intriguing possibility that Violet Vivian may have at least in jest considered the possibility of becoming a nun:

> THE NUNNERY
> Dark were the walls as books on dusty shelves
> Where war and love and tears and laughter cease,
> Crypts where the sexless slanderers of themselves
> Eat darkly the forbidden fruit of peace.
> Walls that behold the crowned pride of Eve
> Cleansed in the unclean pools of shame and fear.
> She turned that face which they that see, believe,
> And laughed, in passing, 'Shall I enter here?'
>
> Little I said: only in every vein
> My father Adam moved in ancient might,
> And on my body, bone and blood and brain
> Came the dark strength of that primeval night
> When sex was cried aloud to weed and worm
> In seven thunders from the hidden throne,
> The night when germ cried darkly unto germ:
> 'It is not well for man to be alone.'

The strength of Chesterton's feelings on the cloistered life is confirmed in *The Nun*, a poem written about the same time:

> The maid for whom through pictured panes alone God's sunlight
>     gleams,
> Who feeds a sexless tortured soul and mad ecstatic dreams,
> Whose cheek must never flush to words spoke in a lonely dell,

But pale to saintly glories and to tempting shades of Hell.
Oh, can her gloomy sacrifice by God be felt as good,
Who sears out her blinded soul the flower of womanhood?

At the end of Summer term 1892 at the age of eighteen Gilbert Chesterton finished at St. Paul's School, leaving his friends to continue there for a further year. Although he was fully occupied for most of the time, in some ways he took what we now call a gap-year, starting with a family holiday in North Berwick where, as he informed Bentley:

> I am enjoying myself very much down here, though our time is growing to a close. One of the nicest things about it is the way you mix with strangers and the absence of the cursed class feeling which makes me feel as if we were all humbugs. Whenever I feel tired of writing the novel [*Basil Howe*?], I sally out in the evenings and play with children on the sands: coastguards' and visitors' children alike, except that the coastguards' are rather the more refined.[9]

Later in the year he travelled fairly widely with his father in France and then on as far as Italy, all the while keeping Bentley in the picture:

> Hotel New York, Florence (undated)
>
> Throughout this tour, in pursuance of our theory of travelling, we have avoided the guide: he is the death-knell of individual liberty. Once only we broke through our rule and that was in favour of an extremely intelligent, nay impulsive young Italian in Santa Maria Novella, a church where we saw some of the most interesting pieces of mediaeval painting I have ever seen, interesting not so much from an artistic as from a moral and historical point of view. Particularly noticeable was the great fresco expressive of the grandest mediaeval conception of the Communion of Saints, a figure of Christ surmounting a crowd of all ages and stations among whom were not only Dante, Petrarca, Giotto, etc., etc., but Plato, Cicero, and best of all, Arius. I said to the guide, in a tone of expostulation, 'Heretico!' (a word of impromptu manufacture). Whereupon he nodded, smiled, and was positively radiant with the latitudinarianism of the old Italian painter.[10]

It may have been on this trip that Gilbert found inspiration for his poem on Leonardo da Vinci in which he toys with the idea of the same model being used for both Jesus and Judas:

LEONARDO DA VINCI

Talk we hear of higher natures, starry spirits proud and sure,
Yet methinks the nameless tempter has his foot in every door,
Deep in all the soils of nature lie the seeds of good or ill.
Hear the tale of Leonardo, as the Romans tell it still:

In a lamplit Roman chamber, Leonardo sat apart,
Father of a thousand painters in his mellowing dawn of art,

In his hand his chalk and brushes, by his side a Bible set,
And in front a virgin canvas stared upon him like a debt.
But from out the gilded missal, like a message dark and dumb,
Burnt one word out of the pages: *Friend and wherefore art thou come?*
Then he grasped his brush and colours, all his tools and things of worth,
And in curves and shade and colours that one little text went forth:
First about a dusky garden, crowned by olives, glimmering high
Gathered slow and swarthy moonset where the dragon clouds crawled by.
Then [. . .]

Through the loud and motley city went the artist up and down,
Found no brow of prince or Kaiser worthy of the thorny crown,
Found no limb of knight or noble worthy of the cross of shame,
Till one sunset in a byeway on a man of men he came,
Moving homeward in the evening, all his daily labours done,
Haloed hair and eyes as meteors walked the thought of Mary's son;
And the artist drew him nearer to that presence pale and rare,
Binding in a half-illusion as if Christ indeed were there,
Asked his boon whereto the stranger answered in a calm divine:
'I am Angelo Romano, Leonardo's will is mine.'
Day by day the young man sat there for the artist's eye to scan,
In his dark young eyes were dreaming all the burning dreams of man.
And the watchful painter laboured till at last one milling morn
Christ red-robed rose o'er the Judas with the fiery tears of scorn.
And the figure done and ended, curiously the painter said:
'Who art thou, my art's assistant, like a Christ out of the dead?'
And, his royal brows uplifting, said the stranger courteously:
'I am Angelo Romano and an artist like to thee.'
With the parting of the young man went a sunshine from the room;
Silence fell round Leonardo like the darkness of a tomb,
And he wearied of his picture and at last he let it be,
And long years went o'er its memory, and to power and fame rose he.

[. . .]

Struggling through the humming market went the artist passing by,
Found no lips well-firmed and fashioned for the kiss that was a lie,
Searched the noisiest nests of vipers, pierced the alleys drear and dim,
All he found a shag-haired sharper nodding o'er a flagon brim.
And the artist marked the visage teemed with hunger and desire,
Saw the champing jaws tough-bearded, watched the shifting eyes of fire,
Marked the brazen beak and cheek-bone, forehead barred with scar and
    line,
Muttered, 'I had known that presence if the devil drank the wine.'

Called the ruffian coolly to him, threw him money for his pain,
Muttered, 'If the dead could help me, Judas walks the earth again.'
Day by day the dusky model filled the canvas by degrees,
Still his eyes in shadow fallen gleamed with horrid memories,
Till the picture was done and finished, Vinci cried, 'Answer to me.
Crawling wreck of evil passions, tell me what are, what were ye?'
Gnawing hard his beard and scowling, convulsed, slow, the sodden soul
    replied,
Showing in his eyes a moment one low gleam of sullen pride:
'What am I? I am your Judas. What was I? Too much between.
I am Angelo Romano: I have been where I have been.'
Sprang aloft the trembling painter, in his eyes an awful flame,
Gazed and cried aloud upon him, 'And by God it is the same!
Speak, but how?' The stranger stopped him: 'Rapid is the soul's decline.
I have run the race I willed to: dice and daggers, lust and wine;
They have found me where I once was, they have left me where you see,
I am Angelo Romano. If you know me, let me be.'
Dashed the muttering maniac past him, shrieked aloud a maudlin song,
And the mighty Leonardo sat in silence late and long.

What man we ask? And know yet this thing we hardly know:
Straight and simple seems the pathway 'twixt the highest and most low,
Still as near through all the ages comes the [borne] of Heaven and Hell:
Man is Jesus, man is Judas: thou and I may know it well. (1893)

Chesterton may have seen several paintings by Leonardo during his tour, including *The Last Supper* in the refectory of the Dominican friary of Santa Maria delle Grazie in Milan, but strangely does not refer to it in a further communication with Bentley:

Grand Hotel de Milan (undated)
I write you a third letter before coming back, while Venice and Verona are fresh in my mind. Of the former I can only really discourse *viva voce*. Imagine a city, whose very slums are full of palaces, whose every other house wall has a battered fresco, or a gothic bas-relief, imagine a sky fretted with every kind of pinnacle from the great dome of the Salute to the Gothic spires of the Ducal Palace and the downright arabesque orientalism of the minarets of St. Mark's; and then imagine the whole flooded with a sea that seems only intended to reflect sunsets, and you will still have no idea of the place I stopped in for more than 48 hours. Thence we went to Verona, where Romeo and Juliet languished and Dante wrote most of 'Hell'. The principal products: (1) tombs: particularly those of the Scala, a very good old family with an excellent taste in fratricide. Their three tombs (one to each man I mean: one man, one grave) are really glorious examples of three stages of Gothic: of which more when we meet. (2) Balconies: with young ladies

hanging over them; really quite a preponderating feature. Whether this was done in obedience to local associations and in expectation of a Romeo, I can't say. I can only remark that if such was the object, the supply of Juliets seemed very much in excess of the demand. (3) Roman remains: on which, however, I did not pronounce a soliloquy beginning, 'Wonderful people . . .' which is the correct thing to do.[11]

Edward Chesterton had always regretted not himself taking up a career as an artist and, noting that his son was for ever drawing pictures in books, he had gone out of his way to encourage him. It would be wrong to suggest that pressure was brought to bear but, given that Gilbert was manifestly unsuited to enter the family firm of auctioneers and estate agents (a two week trial confirming it[12]). Having been taken on a 'grand tour' by his father, Chesterton returned to follow art classes at the St. John's Wood Art School founded at 9 Elm Tree Road by the Peruvian Abelardo Alvarez-Calderon (1856–1911) and later known as Leigh & Hatherley's when Calderon returned to Peru in the 1890s; not to be confused, as it has been, with the St. John's Wood Clique, a loosely associated group led by the Franco-Spaniard Philip-Hermogenes Calderon, Keeper of the Royal Academy. Teachers at the St. John's Wood Art School included Thomas Benjamin Kennington (1856–1916) and John William Waterhouse (1849–1917); John Byam Shaw (1872–1919), who had gone there on Millais' advice, was a fellow student of GKC's.

Gilbert still had ample time to continue to write poetry, stories and to finish his first novel, as well as co-operating with Edmund Clerihew Bentley and other members of the JDC on *The Dictionary of Biography*,[13] the first volume of Clerihews, a then new free verse form invented by Bentley, but not exclusively written by him. Gilbert and others including Edward Chesterton made occasional contributions, and Gilbert illustrated each clerihew and provided further illustrations and decorative borders when the volume was produced; he continued to do so when further volumes were published in later years, but the original passed into the hands of Grey (Maurice Solomon) until, upon his death in 1954, it was bequeathed to St. Paul's School. In later volumes Bentley forgot who had written what, but the original illustrations incorporated identifications by symbol.[14] Among Gilbert Chesterton's contributions was the following:

> The people of Spain think Cervantes
> Equal to half a dozen Dantes;
> An opinion resented most bitterly
> By the people of Italy.

The Junior Debating Club had debated its own future as far back as December 16th, 1892 'as members were already beginning to leave St. Paul's and in a year or so would be scattered over different parts of the world.'[15] Gilbert Chesterton was in favour of its continuing, but there were problems to do with funding *The Debater* and the last printed copy appeared in February 1893, although a further handwritten issue edited by GKC himself was circulated later in 1893–94, after which time he set about creating *The Human Club*, a series of fictional stories with characters based on his JDC friends, some of whom would use the name for their group when they met during their years up at Oxford. Frequent meetings continued, and as the other members were also acquiring lady friends, the names of Mildred Wain, the generally admired object of Waldo D'Avigdor's affections, and Violet Boileau, Bentley's, and others, began to appear in GKC's verse:

OUR LADY OF WAIN
Low eyelids that cloud like a prison,
Grey eyes full of shimmer and shower,
And the tremulous mouth and the risen
Pale face like a luminous flower;
Pale face of its own mirth bewild'rèd
What shall fix it at last, what remain?
O anything but sombre Miss Mildred,
Our Lady of Wain . . .

Another ten stanzas completed this parody of Swinburne's *Dolores*, while in her turn Violet Boileau received a *Ballade des Boileaux*. There were also adventures of a theatrical nature, with Chesterton providing the libretto for *Shipwrecked off Fairyland*, a musical comedy for a group led by Mildred Wain.[16]

The Chestertons were still faced with the dilemma as to what should be done with Gilbert. Marie-Louise, who always gave money to pavement artists as she feared that was how her son would end up, had consulted the High Master of St. Paul's for advice on a future career for Gilbert. F.W. Walker responded with 'Six foot of genius. Cherish him, Mrs Chesterton, cherish him.' As she was only present there because she did cherish him, this was hardly helpful advice for a worried mother. A subsequent visit to the doctor for a check-up elicited the opinion that her son's brain was large and sensitive: 'A genius or an idiot.' The St. John's Wood Art School now announced that, despite their best efforts, they had had little effect on Gilbert's artistic style, and so the ball was back in the Chestertons' court. As the cause of the anxiety had nothing particular in mind, Edward eventually decided that Gilbert would train as a book illustrator at University College, London: 'I went to an art school; having the presumptuous hope of learning to illustrate books, before I fell back in despair upon the lighter task of writing them.' He bade farewell to his 'first art-school in St. John's Wood'[17] with a triumphant *St John's Wood March* (1893):

> Let it be so, and so farewell
> Since God hath willed, and it must be so.
> The thing you leave you need not think,
> And the thing I leave you will never know.
>
> I never have known of friends as you,
> Have never known, nor shall ever know,
> And you grow coldly; best then [part]
> Since God has willed, and it must be so . . .

# 4.

# BETWEEN THE DEVIL AND THE GKC

G ilbert Chesterton was matriculated into University College, London, registering on October 6th, 1893 for courses in Latin, English, French with just one course in Fine Art at the adjacent Slade School. His Latin tutor was A.E. Housman whom he did not find a congenial influence either as a tutor or as a poet: 'The song of the cheerful *Shropshire Lad* I consider a perfectly horrid song,'[1] and after the first year he dropped Latin along with Fine Art, replacing them, perhaps under the influence of Robert Blatchford, with History and Political Economy for the 1894–95 academic year. He seems to have enjoyed French (in which he once again does seem to have done well in an examination)[2] and especially English. Fine Art at the Slade as of 1893 was under the control of Professor Frederick Brown and Professor Tonks, both strongly influenced by George Moore:

> . . . the centre of gravity of my existence had shifted from what we will (for the sake of courtesy) call Art to what we will (for the sake of courtesy) call Literature. The agent in this change of intention was, in the first instance, my friend Ernest Hodder Williams, afterwards the head of the well-known publishing firm [Hodder & Stoughton] . . . I joined him in following the English course; and for this reason I am able to boast myself among the many pupils who are grateful to the extraordinarily lively and stimulating learning of Professor W.P. Ker. Most of the other students were studying for examinations; but I had not even that object in this objectless period of my life. The result was that I gained an entirely undeserved reputation for disinterested devotion to culture for its own sake; and I once had the honour of constituting the whole of Professor Ker's audience. But he gave as thorough and thoughtful a lecture as I have ever heard given, in a slightly more colloquial style; asked me some questions about my

reading; and, on my mentioning something from the poetry of Pope, said with great satisfaction: 'Ah, I see you have been well brought up.' Pope had much less than justice from that generation of the admirers of Shelley and Swinburne.[3]

## The particular reasons for the dropping of the Fine Art course were because:

For some reason I have never understood, there is nothing that is so definitely dated as art and art schools. Artists are almost the only people who are still so retrograde as to believe in progress. There is art and art criticism of a certain date as there are hats and bonnets of a certain date; they are taken seriously as long as they are thought dressy; they are dismissed as lightly when they are thought dowdy. I should not find Latin taught at Oxford or Logic taught at Cambridge very differently from the way in which they were taught in the last generation. But if I went back to an art school, I should probably find myself in a new world. I belonged to the period of the Impressionists; their sons had not yet grown up to be Post-Impressionists; just as their grandsons are only now preparing to appear as Post-Post-Impressionists. Impressionism was, I think, an expression of scepticism. In teaching a man to paint his uncle as an arrangement in grey and purple, it insisted that these patches of tinted shade were all we actually saw of an uncle; and to prove this the artists would screw up their eyes till they could see nothing at all. But underneath it all was the old mad metaphysical question: 'What do I know but sense impressions?' And that was why the age which talked of the art of Whistler also talked of the philosophy of Schopenhauer. The chief educational effect of most schools that I went to was to teach me to play truant. But towards this school in its intellectual sense I began to find myself in the uncomfortable position of a mutineer rather than the more cheerful condition of a deserter. I began to argue with young artists because they were young pessimists. I found myself committed to the alarming task of defending the broad daylight and the breath of life. I had to do my best with desperate paradoxes; and nerved myself to declare firmly that grass is green. Hence I was not content with the philosophy which dissolved the uncle into grey and purple; I felt the need of believing in an uncle of clearer outline and more vivid colour; an uncle really existing elsewhere than on the retina of the eye. I did not know how ancient were the disputes I stirred; or how in the depths of my muddled mind St. Bernard rose against Abelard. But when a friend and fellow-student, now Sir Ernest Hodder-Williams, gave me some art books to review for The Bookman, I wrote down the arguments instead of reviewing the books.[4]

## This oversight of his first year at UCL is described a little differently in a letter to Bentley:

(undated, but probably 1894)

Inwardly speaking, I have had a funny time. A meaningless fit of depression, taking the form of certain absurd psychological worries, came upon me, and instead of dismissing it and talking to people, I had it out and went very far into the abysses, indeed. The result was that I found that things, when examined, necessarily *spelt* such a

mystically satisfactory state of things, that without getting back to earth, I saw lots that
made me certain it is all right. The vision is fading into common day now, and I am
glad. The frame of mind was the reverse of gloomy, but it would not do for long. It is
embarrassing, talking to God face to face, as a man speaketh to his friend.[5]

That funny time is perhaps summed up in The Poet's Vision (c1892):

'O why can visions never more
To mortal eyes be given?
O let me tread the mystic way
Through vales of Hell and Heaven.'

A rushing wind within his ears,
A shadow closing round,
And in the horrid worlds of pain
He trod the smoking ground.

A fearful cry, a crawling shape
Clung o'er the black abyss,
A lurid flash, a ghastly sight,
The face was like to his!

Pale spirits gibbered in their pain
In gleam or twilight shown,
They roared in shade, they tossed in fire,
And every face his own.

Wild sobbers clung about his feet,
Each face the face he bore;
Live corpses writhing in his way
That well-known feature wore.

In the dark shadows of the rocks
With fire-eyes weird and fell
With iron crown and awful wings,
The fallen Prince of Hell,

He peered into the Prince's face
Within the shadowed lair;
He broke, all ashen pale, away –
He knew the face was there!

He gave a cry: the thronging shades
Like bats and owls flew out;

Again, again the endless eyes
Were thickening all about.

'O let those eyes be closed,
This hideous dream be riven,
O lift me in a purer air,
The endless fields of Heaven.'

He rose aloft: the heaven shook
With stars on every side.
He stood before the radiant gate
That, rolling, opened wide.

Within the gateway of the place
An angel stood alone:
The crown was stars, the wings were flame,
The face was like his own.

He looked: in lily-starred lanes
The spirits went and came,
With every robe a varied hue,
And every face the same.

In every garden space and nook,
With palm and missal page,
The pallid face, all dreaming, broke
The golden foliage.

Soft talkers in some open courts
O'erlooked a sunset sea;
The dreamer looked on every face
And a low cry gave he:

'Behold the inmost ring of crowns,
Behold the inmost throne.'
The pallid dreamer hid his face
And groaned a fearful groan.

'O nought behold I but myself
In vales of peace or pain.
Let me not seek the form of God
And see that face again.'

Later in 1907 in the dedication to *The Man Who Was Thursday* Chesterton
would assure Bentley that:

> 'This is a tale of those old fears, even of those emptied hells,
> And none but you shall understand the true thing that it tells,
> Of what colossal gods of shame could cow men and yet crash,
> Of which huge devils hid the stars, yet fell at a pistol's flash.'

And later still in his *Autobiography* he defines what seems to have been a severe bout of solipsism:

I am not proud of believing in the Devil. To put it more correctly, I am not proud of knowing the Devil. I made his acquaintance by my own fault; and followed it up along lines which, had they been followed further, might have led me to devil-worship or the devil knows what . . . I had thought my way back to thought itself. It is a very dreadful thing to do; for it may lead to thinking that there is nothing but thought. At this time I did not very clearly distinguish between dreaming and waking; not only as a mood, but as a metaphysical doubt, I felt as if everything might be a dream. It was as if I had myself projected the universe from within, with all its trees and stars; and that is so near to the notion of being God that it is manifestly even nearer to going mad. Yet I was not mad, in any medical or physical sense; I was simply carrying the scepticism of my time as far as it would go. And I soon found it would go a great deal further than most of the sceptics went . . . And as with mental, so with moral extremes. There is something truly menacing in the thought of how quickly I could imagine the maddest, when I had never committed the mildest crime. Something may have been due to the the atmosphere of the Decadents, and their perpetual hints of the luxurious horrors of paganism; but I am not disposed to dwell much on that defence; I suspect I manufactured most of my morbidities for myself. But anyhow, it is true that there was a time when I had reached that condition of moral anarchy within, in which a man says, in the words of Wilde, that 'Atys with the blood-stained knife were better than the thing I am.' I have never indeed felt the faintest temptation to the particular madness of Wilde; but I could at this time imagine the worst and wildest disproportions and distortions of more normal passion; the point is that the whole mood was overpowered and oppressed with a sort of congestion of imagination.[6]

Seemingly coming close to defying St. Michael's battle-cry of 'Who is like to God?' some further account of the particular state of mind is given in a short story, *Apotheosis or The House of Stars*:

'I am the beginning and the end. I am before you and after. Your face is but one of the myriad masks through which I proclaim the mighty monologue of my everlasting pride. I do not destroy you to conquer you. In that day I create you, I conquer you.' The fear of me was on all the angels, as it is upon all the worlds . . . The woodcutter's blue eyes stood from his head, eyeing me with an unbearable quietness. What was that new, mild, merciless light that I had never seen? It was pity. At the same moment he had turned to those around and said, 'How long has he been mad?' . . . The next moment the illumination was lost, and I was once more Almighty God, unchanged from everlasting to everlasting (c1895).[7]

Some years later in 1921 in *The Crime of Gabriel Gale*, Chesterton gave a retrospective definition of what may have been his own experience:

A very large number of young men nearly go mad. But nearly all of them only nearly do it; and normally they recover the normal. You might almost say it's normal to have an abnormal period. It comes when there's a lack of adjustment in the scale of things outside and within . . . The inside gets too big for the outside . . . mind and self seem to be colossal and cosmic and everything outside them small and distant. In another way the world is much too big; and thoughts are fragile things to be hidden away. Now in that dangerous time, there's a dreadfully dangerous moment; when the first connexion is made between the subjective and the objective: the first real bridge between the brain and real things . . . Materialists are all right; they are at least near enough to heaven to accept the earth and not imagine they made it . . . The dreadful doubts, the deadly and damnable doubts, are the doubts of the idealist . . . the real sceptic who doubts matter and the minds of others and everything except his own ego. I have been through it myself . . . I also dreamed that I had dreamed of the whole creation. I had given myself the stars for a gift; I had handed myself the sun and the moon. I had been behind and at the beginning of all things; and without me nothing was made that was made. Anybody who has been in that centre of the cosmos knows that it is to be in hell . . . I was God once; for about fourteen hours. But I gave it up. I found it was too much of a strain.[8]

Resolution is finally found in *The Mirror of Madmen*:

I dreamed a dream of heaven, white as frost,
The splendid stillness of a living host;
Vast choirs of upturned faces, line on line,
Then my blood froze, for every face was mine.

Spirits with sunset plumage throng and pass,
Glassed darkly in the sea of gold and glass,
But still on every side, in every spot,
I saw a million selves, who saw me not.

I fled to quiet wastes, where on a stone,
Perchance, I found a saint, who sat alone;
I came behind; he turned with slow sweet grace,
And faced me with my happy, hateful face.

I cowered like one that in a tower doth bide,
Shut in by mirrors upon every side;
Then I saw, islanded in skies alone
And silent, one that sits upon a throne.

His robe was bordered with rich rose and gold,
Green, purple, silver out of sunsets old;
But o'er his face a great cloud edged with fire,
Because it covereth a world's desire.

But as I gazed, a silent worshipper,
Methought the cloud began to faintly stir;
Then I fell flat, and screamed with grovelling head,
'If thou hast any lightning, strike me dead!'

'But spare a brow where the clean sunlight fell,
The crown of a new sin that sickens hell.
Let me not look aloft and see mine own
Feature and form upon the Judgement-throne.'

Then my dream snapped; and with a heart that leapt
I saw across the tavern where I slept,
The sight of all my life most full of grace,
A gin-damned drunkard's wan half-witted face. (mid 1890s)

Chesterton's emergence from solipsism, if that be what it was, can be dated to about the end of his first year at UCL, when there took place an incident about which he reminisced thirteen years later:

What I have now to relate really happened . . . It was simply a quiet conversation which I had with another man. But that quiet conversation was by far the most terrible thing that has ever happened to me in my life . . . The thing befell me in the days when I was at an art school. An art school is different from almost all other schools or colleges in this respect: that, being of new and crude creation and of lax discipline, it presents a specially strong contrast between the industrious and the idle. People at an art school either do an atrocious amount of work or do no work at all. I belonged, along with other charming people, to the latter class; and this threw me often into the society of men who were very different from myself, and who were idle for reasons very different from mine. I was idle because I was very much occupied; I was engaged about that time in discovering, to my own extreme and lasting astonishment, that I was not an atheist. But there were others also at loose ends who were engaged in discovering what Carlyle called (I think with needless delicacy) the fact that ginger is hot in the mouth . . . In those small groups devoted to a drivelling dissipation, there is almost always one man who seems to have condescended to his company; one man who, while he can talk a foul triviality with his fellows, can also talk politics with a Socialist, or philosophy with a Catholic.

It was just such a man whom I came to know well. It was strange, perhaps, that he liked his dirty, drunken society; it was stranger still, perhaps, that he liked my society. For hours of the day he would talk with me about Milton or Gothic architecture; for hours of the night he would go where I have no wish to follow him, even in speculation. He was a man with a long ironical face, and close red hair; he was by class a gentleman, and could walk like one, but preferred, for some reason, to walk like a groom carrying two pails. He looked like a sort of Super-jockey; as if some archangel had gone on the Turf. And I shall never forget the half-hour in which he and I argued about real things for the first and the last time.

Along the front of the big building of which our school was a part ran a huge slope of stone steps,[9] higher, I think, than those that lead up to St. Paul's Cathedral. On the black wintry evening he and I were wandering on these cold heights, which seemed as dreary as a pyramid under the stars. The one thing visible below us in the blackness was a burning and blowing fire; for some gardener (I suppose) was burning something in the grounds and from time to time the red sparks went whirling past us like a swarm of scarlet insects in the dark. Above us also it was gloom; but if one stared long enough at that upper darkness, one saw vertical stripes of grey in the black and then became conscious of the colossal façade of the Doric building, phantasmal, yet filling the sky, as if Heaven were still filled with the gigantic ghost of Paganism.

The man asked me abruptly why I was becoming orthodox. Until he said it, I really had not known that I was; but the moment he had said it I knew it to be literally true. And the process had been so long and full that I answered him at once, out of existing stores of explanation.

'I am becoming orthodox,' I said, 'because I have come, rightly or wrongly, after stretching my brain till it bursts, to the old belief that heresy is worse even than sin. An error is more menacing than a crime, for an error begets crimes. An Imperialist is worse than a pirate. For an Imperialist keeps a school for pirates; he teaches piracy disinterestedly and without an adequate salary. A Free Lover is worse than a profligate. For a profligate is serious and reckless even in his shortest love; while a Free Lover is cautious and irresponsible even in his longest devotion. I hate modern doubt because it is dangerous.'

'You mean dangerous to morality,' he said in a voice of wonderful gentleness. 'I expect you are right. But why do you care about morality?'

I glanced at his face quickly. He had thrust out his neck as he had a trick of doing; and so brought his face abruptly into the light of the bonfire below, like a face in the footlights. His long chin and high cheek-bones were lit up infernally from underneath; so that he looked like a fiend staring into the flaming pit. I had an unmeaning sense of being tempted in a wilderness; and even as I paused a burst of red sparks broke past.

'Aren't those sparks splendid?' I said.

'Yes,' he replied.

'That is all I ask you to admit,' said I. 'Give me those few red sparks and I will deduce Christian morality. Once I thought like you, that one's pleasure in a flying spark was a thing that could come and go with that spark. Once I thought that the delight was as free as the fire. Once I thought that red star we see was alone in space. But now I know that the red star is only on the apex of an invisible pyramid of virtues. That red fire is only the flower on a stalk of living habits, which you cannot see. Only because your mother made you say 'Thank you' for a bun are you now able to thank Nature or chaos for those red stars of an instant or for the white stars of all time. Only because you were humble before fireworks on the fifth of November do you now enjoy any fireworks that you chance to see. You only like them being red because you were told about the blood of the martyrs; you only like them being bright because brightness is a glory. That flame flowered out of virtues, and it will fade with virtues. Seduce a woman, and that spark will be less bright. Shed blood, and that spark will be less red. Be really bad, and they will be to you like spots on a wallpaper.'

He had a horrible fairness of the intellect that made me despair of his soul. A common, harmless atheist would have denied that religion produced humility or humility a simple joy; but he admitted both. He only said, 'But shall I not find in evil a life of its own? Granted that for every woman I ruin one of those red sparks will go out: will not the expanding pleasure of ruin . . .'

'Do you see that fire? I asked, 'If we had a real fighting democracy, someone would burn you in it; like the devil-worshipper that you are.'

'Perhaps,' he said, in his tired, fair way. 'Only what you call evil I call good.'

He went down the great steps alone, and I felt as if I wanted the steps swept and cleaned. I followed later, and as I went to find my hat in the low, dark passage where it hung, I suddenly heard his voice again, but the words were inaudible. I stopped, startled: then I heard the voice of one of the vilest of his associates saying, 'Nobody can possibly know.' And then I heard those two or three words which I remember in every syllable and cannot forget. I heard the Diabolist say, 'I tell you I have done everything else. If I do that I shan't know the difference between right and wrong.' I rushed out without daring to pause; and as I passed the fire I did not know whether it was hell or the furious love of God.

I have since heard that he died: it may be said, I think, that he committed suicide; though he did it with tools of pleasure, not with tools of pain. God help him, I know the road he went; but I have never known, or even dared to think, what was that place at which he stopped and refrained.[10]

The man with the long ironical face and close red hair was long dead when Chesterton wrote in 1907, and so far he has not been identified. The description and timing could well fit Aubrey Beardsley (1872–1898) who is known to have taken Professor Frederick Brown's classes at Westminster College of Art in 1892, and could have followed him to the Slade in 1893. Beardsley is alleged to have had an incestuous relationship with his elder sister Mabel whom he got pregnant, although she later miscarried. However, Beardsley was supposed to have died from tuberculosis, although rumour may have implied otherwise.

An earlier self-assessment led to a slightly different conclusion: 'He went for a time to an Art School. There he met a great many curious people. Many of the men were horrible blackguards; he was not exactly that: so they naturally found each other interesting. He went through some rather appalling discoveries about human life and the final discovery was that there is no Devil – no, not even such a thing as a bad man.'[11]

Chesterton may well have been occupied discovering that he was not an atheist, but he was far from discovering what he in fact was. The Chesterton family were nominally Unitarians, and Gilbert's baptism in an Anglican church no doubt took place because it was at the end of the road and so convenient, and his subsequent journey towards his own form of orthodoxy took him along most unorthodox paths as well:

> I dabbled in Spiritualism without having even [taken] the decision to be a spiritualist. Indeed I was, in a rather unusual manner, not only detached but indifferent. My brother and I used to play with planchette, or what the Americans call the ouija board; but we were among the few, I imagine, who played in a mere spirit of play. Nevertheless I would not altogether rule out the suggestion of some that we were playing with fire; or even with hell-fire. In the words that were written for us there was nothing ostensibly degrading, but any amount that was deceiving. I saw quite enough of the thing to be able to testify, with complete certainty, that something happens which is not in the ordinary sense natural, or produced by the normal and conscious human will. Whether it is produced by some subconscious but still human force, or by some powers, good, bad, or indifferent, which are external to humanity, I would not myself attempt to decide. The only thing I will say with complete confidence, about that mystic and invisible power, is that it tells lies . . . I have sometimes fancied since that this practice, of the true psychology of which we know so little, may possibly have contributed towards the disturbed or even diseased state of brooding and idling through which I passed at that time. I would not dogmatise either way; it is possible that the whole thing was merely mechanical or accidental. I would leave planchette with a playful farewell, giving her the benefit of the doubt: I would allow that she may have been a joke or a fancy or a fairy or anything else; with the proviso that I would not touch her again with a barge-pole.[12]

Still armed with the Whig version of History he had absorbed at school together with his great admiration for Oliver Cromwell, he journeyed on through Theosophy, the Salvation Army and Christian Socialism of the William Morris sort, always seeking his own philosophical position. When on April 20th, 1895 Blatchford's socialist *The Clarion* published *Easter Sunday* Chesterton was displaying a strong anti-clerical streak:

The Christ is risen the preachers say:
   'Cry, for today is Easter Day'.
Yes, if the dead might rise; then
   He Might rise for one thing verily.
He has not heard the mouths that moved
   The faint and fallen that he loved,
The wheels that rack, the lips that rave:
   Stern is God's guard upon the grave.
Peace – for the priests in gold array –
   Peace – for today is Easter Day.
The bannered pomp; the pontiffs wise
   (Great God – methinks He might arise,
Might break for once from death's eclipse
   To smite these liars on the lips).

Along his way he left UCL in 1895 without a degree (degrees at that time often being of interest only to those thinking of entering the Church, the Civil Service or the teaching profession), but armed with a distinctive italic hand-writing he had adopted. He had found employment with Redway's, a publisher specialising in the occult and spiritualism, whose office was situated close by UCL and the British Museum:

> (To E.C. Bentley, undated but 1895)
> I am beastly busy, but there is something exciting about it . . . To give you some idea of what I mean. I have been engaged in 3 different tiring occupations and I enjoyed them all. (1) Redway says, 'We've got too many MSS; read through them, will you and send back those that are too bad at once.' I go slap through a room full of MSS, criticising deuced conscientiously, with the result that I post back some years of MSS to addresses, which I should imagine, must be private asylums . . . (2) Redway says, 'I'm going to give you entire charge of the press department, sending copies to Reviews, etc.' Consequence is, one has to keep an elaborate book and make it tally with other elaborate books, and one has to remember all the magazines that exist and what sort of books they'd crack up. I used to think I hated responsibility: I am positively getting to enjoy it. (3) There is that confounded 'Picture of Tuesday' which I have been scribbling at the whole evening, and have at last got presentable . . . I can't imagine anything more idiotic than what I've just finished.[13]

Chesterton was obviously working a 'nine hour's ramp' at Redway's and then returning home to do his own literary work, *A Picture of Tuesday* being part of an early version of *The Man Who Was Thursday* which was drafted at various times as a story or a play or a novel. It is likely that here Chesterton is referring to the story version which later appeared in 1896 in the first issue of a Slade

Art School magazine called *The Quarto*,[14] followed two years later by *A Crazy Tale* in the third issue:

## A PICTURE OF TUESDAY

Oscar Plumtree was a rising artist, who painted his general impressions of his intimate friends, and belonged to a sketching club which met every Tuesday. He was a small square man with masses of black hair, and stood with his hands in his pockets, a little too conscious that his head was against a green curtain.

'How decorative Plumtree is,' said Noel Starwood, symbolist, to Patrick Staunton, realist. 'I never noticed that his colour was so arbitrary. But like all the works of God, you have to see him twenty times before you see him for the first time.'

'If you can suggest any course likely to result in seeing him for the last time,' said Staunton, lighting a pipe, 'I shall be more gratified. So he looks decorative, does he?'

'So flat,' murmured Starwood, dreamily. 'So admirably flat. He looks as if he had just come out of a panel by Albert Moor.'

'Yes,' said Staunton; 'I wish he'd go back again.'

Patrick Staunton was a large young man with a handsome passive face, that looked *blasé* but was only sleepy. He was very young, it is true, but not quite young enough to have grown weary of the world. He was, in fact, the average young man, with the average young man's two admirable qualities, a sense of humour and an aversion to egoists. This was why he disliked Plumtree. Noel Starwood, a slight, fiery-haired, fiery tinted type, like a high-spirited girl, was a visionary, the painter of a series of 'Seven Dreams of Adam before the creation of Eve.' He did not dislike Plumtree. He said it was the great test and trial of true Christian philosophy not to dislike Plumtree.

He moved off, and another member came up to Staunton.

'Do you know it is Plumtree's turn to give out a subject for the sketches?' he said. 'These subject days are generally rather a lark. Do you remember the first time Starwood was asked for one? There was a silence, and then such a gentle, plaintive little voice said, 'The Resurrection of Cain.' But then he's a mystic, don't you know, and pities the Devil.'

'Well, well,' said Staunton charitably. 'I heard Plumtree was going to the devil the other day, and since then I rather pitied the devil myself.'

'But the joke of the thing is,' continued the other, 'that Plumtree is for ever telling us that the artistic mind cares no more for the subject of a picture, than for its weight in avoirdupois. He was immensely proud of his last picture, because three eminent art-critics looked at it the wrong way up.'

A small crowd had already gathered round Plumtree, and were pressing him for a subject.

'What do you want with a subject?' he said contemptuously. 'I don't want a subject, I want a picture. Won't anything do?'

'The primal enigma, anything,' said Starwood thoughtfully. 'A fine conception. Something bizarre, hasty, fantastic. Some wild, low shape of life, to symbolise the germ-fact, the indestructible minimum, the everlasting Yea. After all, it is but a superficial philosophy which is founded on the existence of everything. The deeper philosophy is founded on the existence of anything.'

'Well, we won't have that,' said Plumtree abruptly. 'You fellows don't seem to understand that art—'

Staunton cut him short hastily. 'I say, Plumtree, I asked for bread and you gave me a piece of india-rubber. Thanks. You were saying that the subject—'

'Oh, take anything you like: what does the subject matter? What's the day of the week? Tuesday; very well.' He turned to the throng and said in a clear voice, 'The subject for the sketches will be Tuesday.'

'I beg your pardon,' said Staunton politely.

'Tuesday,' repeated Plumtree. 'A picture of – Tuesday.'

Patrick Staunton lifted his full six feet two from the bench, and formally announced that he was relegated to a state of spiritual reprobation.

Only four members of the club exhibited sketches on this singular subject. The group consisted of Plumtree, Staunton, Starwood, and one Middleton, who had before him a lucrative career in virtue of an inexhaustible output of corpulent and comic monks.

The uncovering of his picture was received with loud cheers and laughter. It represented six monastic gentlemen of revolting joviality tossing pancakes. Thus it suggested Shrove Tuesday. Plumtree's was an admirable little suggestion of gaslight in the early morning. It might just as well be Tuesday morning as any other morning.

Staunton annoyed him very much by elaborately describing the noble thoughts that the picture suggested to him. His own was a study of his mother's at-home day, which occurred on Tuesday, in which he introduced all the uncles who had told him things for his own good.

Starwood's picture was the largest. When it was unveiled it seemed to fill the room. It was a dark picture, dark with an intricate density of profound colours, a complex scheme of sombre and subtle harmonies, a kind of gorgeous twilight. Plumtree, who was far too good an artist to let cynicism rob him of the gift of wonder, followed the labyrinth of colour keenly and slowly.

Suddenly he gave a little cry and stepped back.

The whole was a huge human figure. Grey and gigantic, it rose with its back to the spectator. As far as the vast outline could be traced, he had one hand heaved above his head, driving up a load of waters, while below, his feet moved upon a solemn infinite sea. It was a dark picture, but when grasped, it blinded like a sun.

Above it was written 'Tuesday,' and below, 'And God divided the waters that were under the firmament from the waters that were above the firmament: and the evening and the morning were the second day.'

'It is certainly very good,' he said, 'like creation. But why did you reckon Tuesday the second instead of the third day of the Jewish week?'

'I had to reckon from my own seventh day: the day of praise, the day of saying 'It is good,' or I could not have felt it a reality.'

'Do you seriously mean that you, yourself, look at the days of the week in that way?'

'The week is the colossal epic of creation,' cried Starwood excitedly. 'Why are there not rituals for every day? The Day of the creation of Light, why is it not honoured with mystic illuminations—'

'Do you Transcendentalists only wash once a week?' asked Staunton.

'The Day of the Earth – what a fire of flowers and fruit; the Day of Birds, what a blaze of decorative plumage; the Day of Beasts, what a—'

'What a deuced lot of nonsense,' said Middleton, who was getting a trifle tired of all this. 'If it comes to religion, and quotations from the Bible, what is there for us, Staunton? Can you think of a text for an at-home day?'

Staunton suggested, 'And Job lifted up his voice and cursed his day.'

But Plumtree was still staring at the picture of Tuesday.[15]

The technique of writing poems, short stories and playlets later to be redrafted into novels and plays seems to have become Chesterton's usual manner of working. The 1890s were to prove the most prolific period of his life in which he provided himself with enough material to draw on for many years, plus much else that was put aside and long forgotten. However, his career as a journalist had been launched on June 22nd, 1895 when his first review of *The Ruskin Reader* appeared unsigned. and unpaid in *The Academy*. He was to stay at Redway's for over a year before moving on November 1st, 1896 to be reader and illustrator at T. Fisher Unwin's, a larger publishing house situated at 11 Paternoster Row within sight of St. Paul's Cathedral, where he was to remain in the middle of the publishing world until 1900:

> Come hither, Fisher Unwin,
>   And leave your work a while,
> Uplooking in my face a span
>   With bright adoring smile.
> All happy leaping publishers
>   Round Paternoster Row,
> Gay Simpkin, dreamy Marshall
>   And simple Samson Low,
> Come round, forgetting all your fears,
>   Your hats and dinners, too . . .
>     (Lines to Waterloo Station. 1898)

It is likely that the new job was that sort of apprenticeship where a sum of money was paid (in this case by Edward Chesterton) to cover the costs of training, and the young employee received only a nominal amount as salary from the employer; this is confirmed by Edward Chesterton's involvement some years later when Gilbert was seeking an increase in salary with a view to marriage. As a reader at T. Fisher Unwin's Chesterton read thousands of books, all of which he was reputed to remember, and it is to be presumed that he recommended Somerset Maugham's first novel, *Liza of Lambeth*, for publication in 1897. By then Gilbert Chesterton was already using T. Fisher Unwin stationery to draft his own diverse literary work, among which was 'a new kind of novel, approximately defined as the romantically inclined philosophic: i.e. a story in which modern thoughts are typified, not by long arguments but by rapid symbolic incidents – an allegorical comedy . . .' Whether the synopsis was ever shown to T. Fisher Unwin or some other publisher is unclear. It went through many revisions under the title of *The Man With Two Legs*,[16] even having a slip-case designed for it, before being put aside only for parts of it to be resurrected years later in *The Club of Queer Trades* (1903) and *Manalive* (1912). Early versions with illustrations of *The Napoleon of Notting Hill*, *The Ball and the Cross* and *The Man Who Was Thursday* also appear in notebooks alongside many other projects, marked by a style which was to become all too recognizable: 'Marjory Dent was a dark and remarkably beautiful woman, but that her grey eyes were stale and her manner dreary and restless, like one with an incurable hunger. She was clad in nameless colours, in the aesthetic scheme, and had a way of entering a room as if she were appearing to her descendants.'[17] There were also plans for a new magazine (a revamped version of *The Speaker*) and indignant submissions to Captain Dreyfus' Court Marshall, for Chesterton was a committed Dreyfusard who would condemn France in *To a Certain Nation*, and commend in *Picquart* one of the few officers to speak out on Dreyfus' behalf.[18]

Other stories from the mid-1890s such as *Child Street* and *A Fable in Bricks and Mortar*[19] were based upon building works taking place to the west of Kensington at Bedford Park which Chesterton called 'The Fantastic Suburb':

> One day I had turned my aimless steps westward, through the tangle of Hammersmith Broadway and along the road that goes to Kew, when I turned for some reason, or more likely without a reason, into a side street and straggled across the dusty turf through which ran a railway, and across the railway one of those disproportionately high bridges which bestride such narrow railway-lines like stilts. By a culmination of futility, I climbed up to this high and practically unused bridge; it was evening, and I think it was then I saw in the distance of that grey landscape, like a ragged red cloud of sunset, the queer artificial village of Bedford Park . . . That sort of manufactured quaintness is now hardly even quaint, but at that time it was even queer. Bedford Park did look like what it partially professed to be; a colony for artists who were almost alien; a refuge for persecuted poets and painters hiding in their red-brick catacombs or dying behind their

red-brick barricades, when the world should conquer Bedford Park. In that somewhat nonsensical sense, it is rather Bedford Park that has conquered the world.[20]

This first of the so-called garden suburbs situated to the north of Chiswick featured in Norman Shaw's architectural designs a mixture of half-timbering and red-brick chimneys set along tree-lined roads, with the whole district centred on the Church of St. Michael and All Angels, a public house called The Tabard Inn and a sort of communal centre known as the Tower House where fancy-dress and other balls were held. The area attracted such avant-garde figures as the painters Camille and Lucien Pisarro and the poet W.B. Yeats together with several members of the Golden Dawn. The speculative builder behind the scheme was Jonathan Comyns-Carr, bankrupted by the project and left to live in one of his own villas with, so it was said, a bailiff as his butler. An anonymous rhyme published in *The St. James's Gazette* in 1881 described the undertaking:

### THE BALLAD OF BEDFORD PARK

In London town there lived a man
   a gentleman was he
Whose name was Jonathan T. Carr
   (as has been told to me).

'This London is a foggy town'
   (thus to himself said he),
'Where bricks are black, and trees are brown,
   and faces are dirtee.

'I will seek out a brighter spot,'
   continued Mr Carr.
'Not too near London, and yet not
   what might be called too far.

'Tis there a village I'll erect
   with Norman Shaw's assistance
Where men may lead a chaste correct
   aesthetical existence'.

With that a passing 'bus he hailed
   (so gallant to be seen)
Upon whose knife-board he did ride
   as far as Turnham Green.

'Oh, here we are,' said Mr Carr,
'no further will I roam;
This is the spot that fate has got
to give us for our home.'

Chesterton seems to have known the development from its earliest days, describing it in *Child Street* as 'a low line of unfinished red-brick villas . . . gaping like monstrous gaping heads in a pantomime, with window eyes rubbed with disks of white, each house like the huge, infantile mask for the man who was to live within. They ran, slightly downward along the brink of a fall of ground, forming one side of an unmade street. There is no poem so refreshing as the brick and sawdust of that row of doll's houses: reminding us that man is still a child playing with bricks.'[21] He was to continue to take great interest in the area recreating it as 'The suburb of Saffron Park [which] lay on the sunset side of London, as red and ragged as a cloud of sunset. It was built of bright brick throughout; its skyline was fantastic, and even its ground plan was wild. It had been the outburst of a speculative builder, faintly tinged with art, who called its architecture sometimes Elizabethan and sometimes Queen Anne, apparently under the impression that the two sovereigns were identical.'[22] He also recalled 'the grand and grotesque occasion on which I rode a bicycle for the first and last time; attired in the frock-coat and top hat of the period, on the tennis lawn at Bedford Park. Believe it or not . . . but it is true that I rode round and round the tennis-court with a complete natural balance, only disturbed by the intellectual problem of how I could possibly get off; eventually I fell off; I did not notice what happened to my hat, but then I seldom did.'[23] Once again, it must be underlined this recollection was that of the lean youth of the 1890s and not the GKC of later years, the vision of whom atop a bicycle of those days would have provided a grotesque sight indeed.

# 5.

## THE SATISFACTION OF SATAN

So it was into familiar territory that Lucian Oldershaw took his friend sometime in December 1896 for a meeting of the I.D.K. Debating Club at 8 Bath
Road, the home of the Blogg family who had helped to found it and each of
whose children in turn fulfilled the function of its secretary. The Bloggs claimed
to be of Huguenot extraction and it was thought that they had anglicized their
French family name of *de Blogue*; many Huguenots were, however, from the
Low Countries where the family name could have been De Blog, De Blogge or
even De Blok, a speculation supported by George William Blogg having been
a jeweller and diamond merchant who plied his trade at 4 Albemarle Street
off Bond Street. Although the Bloggs had long been separated[1] his demise in
1883 from a stroke suffered in Harley Street had changed the family fortunes
and his widow Blanche (née Keymer) was left to care for three daughters,
Frances Alice (1869–1938), Ethel Laura (1872–1953) and Gertrude Colborne
(1875–1899), and a son, Knollys [pronounced Knowles] (1871–1908). Two other
daughters, Helen Colborne (1873–1875) and Rachel Margaret (1878–1881) had
died in infancy, and there had been a son stillborn in 1876. Although their
father had left over £4,000, eventually the three girls had had to find secretar-
ial work to earn their living, Frances working at Murray House for the Parents'
National Educational Union, Gertrude being a secretary to Rudyard Kipling
at Rottingdean, and Ethel employed at the Royal Free Hospital by a group
of lady doctors, themselves something unconventional at that time; despite
their genteel poverty, there was always enough to cover frequent continental
holidays. Knollys never seems to have done very much other than occasional

tutoring and writing one or two articles for *The Girls' Realm* and *The Parents' Review*. The best description of Knollys is given by Mrs Cecil Chesterton:

> The Secretary of the society [I.D.K.], Noel [*sic*] Blogg, brother of Mrs G.K., had a queer memory, of the kind that simmers in a sea of perpetual doubt. He never knew whether or no he had read the minutes at the previous meeting, and usually tried to re-read them to make sure . . . That evening . . . poor Blogg went back to the records of months previously and read and read on solemnly for well over an hour . . . We went to no more meetings of the I.D.K., which I always felt symbolically described the secretary . . .[2]

Gilbert, however, enjoyed the I.D.K.:

> There was a debating-club in Bedford Park . . . It was frightful fun. It was called the 'I.D.K.'; and an awful seal of secrecy was supposed to attach to the true meaning of the initials. Perhaps the Theosophists did really believe that it meant India's Divine Karma. Possibly the Socialists did interpret it as 'Individualists Deserve Kicking'. But it was a strict rule of the club that its members should profess ignorance of the meaning of its name . . . The stranger, the mere intruder into the sacred village, would ask, 'But what does I.D.K. mean?' and the initiate was expected to shrug his shoulders and say, 'I don't know', in an offhand manner; in the hope that it would not be realised that, in a seeming refusal to reply, he had in fact replied.[3]

Lawrence Solomon told Maisie Ward that Marie-Louise, Gilbert's mother, did not like the rather arty-crafty atmosphere of Bedford Park and did not approve of her son's friendship with the Bloggs, having her eye on a girl [Annie Firmin] she considered ideal for him: 'Very open air, not booky, but good at games and practical.'[4] Gilbert, however, was soon to be taking his affections elsewhere. Gertrude Blogg was engaged to Reginald [Rex] Brimley Johnson the publisher, Ethel was being courted by Oldershaw whom she later married, and Frances, the eldest, was unattached. Gilbert himself also seems to have been unattached at that time, the Vivians no longer looming large after their move to Norwood, but it was only on his second visit that he was introduced to and seated next to Frances, at twenty-seven five years his senior. His reactions were immediate: 'If I had anything to do with this girl, I should go down on my knees to her; if I spoke with her she would never deceive me; if I depended on her she would never deny me; if I trusted her, she would never go back on me; if I remembered her, she would never forget me. I may never see her again. Goodbye. It was all said in a flash: but it was all said . . .'[5] It can never be known whether Gilbert was on the rebound or falling in love with love, but it is indisputable that it was love at first sight.

His reception as a suitor was far from guaranteed, as his income of twenty-five shillings a week was woefully inadequate for any consideration of marriage, and Mrs Blanche Blogg thought him at best 'a self-opinionated scarecrow.' The obvious way to improve the position was to make a name and income for himself by publication and debating. He was known in Bedford Park where he encountered W.B. Yeats among others, but he now frequented the Moderns, the Pharos Club and the Fabian Society, and poured his energies into poetry, prose and drama. Frequent references to a novel are hard to tie down because he worked on several of them, but an historical novel, *The Adventurous Abbot Stephen*, set in the reign of Henry III was certainly finished, and *The Man With Two Legs* reached the stage of a fair copy of several chapters being shown to Edward Garrett at T. Fisher Unwin's; whether they were published or serialized or not, and under what titles, are moot points. *The Adventurous Abbot Stephen* had a prefatory note:

'Two notes are required to this story, one general and the other touching a detail. There are two kinds of historical romance: one historic in essence, the other romantic: this is one of the latter. The first kind should be a serious reconstruction of a dead century, a work quite as philosophical and much more difficult than writing a modern problem story. And in the second the dead century is merely a saturnalia, a sort of imaginative holiday which permits of more varied and dubious events than our time. That this story is in no faintest sense historical can be gathered from the fact that it takes place within a stone's throw of the three most interesting characters in English history, Grosteste of Lincoln, Simon de Montfort and Edward I, and two appear only casually and the third only in his youth. Touching the detail, I have constantly pursued the principle of translation from Norman French languages: the man I have named 'Brassface' would have been called 'Front d'Airain'. G.K.C.[6]

By 1896–97 two collections of poetry were circulating, together with a tongue-in-cheek self-critique,[7] among friends, and stories, poems and reviews began to appear in *The Parents' Review*, *The Speaker* and *The Bookman*, the latter run by Ernest Hodder Williams, Gilbert's friend from UCL.

The morality of the times did not allow those romantically linked to stay under the same roof, so Gilbert continued to take holidays, usually in East Anglia, with his family. During Frances' frequent absences abroad, he lamented her departure while lunching in the ABC tea-shop in Ludgate Circus:

> Few are the dreams whose sickly gleams
> Have cheered my blighted path,
> But if some visions soothed awhile

My anguish and my wrath,
(It is a very curious thing
  – It will occur again)
They always, always went away
  To Caudebec on the Seine.

In vain anigh the window high
  The lady doctors wait,
The Parents of the world relapse
  Into the savage state,
The books remain unedited,
  The books remain unbound,
And I, in Ludgate Circus here,
  Lie groaning on the ground.

Lay by, lay by my waistcoat pink,
  My coat of satin blue,
They're going from Victoria,
  My visions always do.
I never loved a dear gazelle
  To charm me with its glance,
It packed its bag, that quadruped,
  And went away to France.

Me vainly calls to roistering halls
  The maddening ABC,
On twelve poached eggs I sadly lunch,
  But what are eggs to me?[8]

Frances returned to find another spoof musical comedy based on the PNEU, a story, *Gods: a Prehistorical Novel* in *The Speaker* on October 9th, 1897, and a ballad recounting his daily life, *The Satisfaction of Satan*, awaiting her:

The son of man, that is a worm,
  Rose up and searched his suits,
Assumed his wistful waistcoat,
  His sad and subtle boots.

He fell to work – (no Trifler he)
  His time is quickly given,
To sternly lying on the floor
  Till twenty past eleven.

Some fellows would (such labours o'er)
    Some moments rest have planned;
This indefatigable man
    Began to read 'The Strand',

But study wore his shaken health,
    Life seemed a weary level;
The son of man that is a worm
    Exclaimed 'I'll be the devil.'

This plan – abhorred by worthy chaps –
    Is seldom entertained,
And in that state of public views
    May need to be explained.

We learn from Mr Montefiore,
    That cultivated Jew
Whose fifteen volumes folio
    You take to bed with you,

That, wearied of the enforced praise
    Of all things made that are,
God made a critic of Himself
    Crowned with the 'Morning Star'.

(You will not find in Montefiore
    Upon the bookcase shelf
That happy phrase about 'The Star'.
    I made it up myself).

God flung the worlds before His feet
    To praise or to condemn,
(That 'flung the worlds' is quite beyond
    The powers of Mr M.)

Weighing the mountain in a scale
    The nameless angel stood,
And he alone of all things made
    Knew that the world was good.

Your painful language at this point
    Surprises all who knew you
'Well – What the Devil is, you tell,
    But why the devil do you?'

Twixt Bedford Park and Westminster
   Oft would a Lady hurry;
Inside she was divine and deep,
   And outside green and furry.

The golden armoury of God
   In truth was round her buckled.
– The son of man that is a worm,
   He blew his nose and chuckled.

His hat from out the coal scuttle
   He resolutely caught.
'Hast thou beheld my servant Job?'
   – 'Doth Job fear God for naught?'

For weary weeks and maddening months
   In sunny days and shady
That amateurish Satan bored
   That green and brown young lady.

For though not good or wise or strong,
   Save, like a plague, to cling –
For like an illness he was Long –
   And also Lingering.

Yet he was Patriot to the World,
   Proud of his brother-clod,
The swaggerer for the meanest star.
   The swashbuckler of God.

And he would slay the cynic thought
   That whispered 'Ver non semper
Viret' – the spring will lose its crown,
   And she will lose her temper.

'I rate her higher – there a niche
   Must be for all things mortal,
Where shall the orphan spirits go
   If her heart close the portal?'

'Therefore I thunder at the door
   (Not literally, Madam)
Vague, noisy, wearisome, not less
   Prince of the House of Adam.'

Within the low white wall of Heaven
   The lonely lady stood:

Round her like flowers the sun unfurled
   ('The sun unfurled' is good).

She saw the plumage round her flame,
   The splendour round her shed,
And Dr Schofield – cherub now
   With nothing but a head.

Was fluttering among the flowers
   With holy blessing shriven,
And Mr Hankin,[9] robed in white
   With all his sins forgiven.

Under the far low chaos-cloud
   Below the last sad stars,
In lost creations, wasted worlds
   Of moonshine and cigars.

While clear in heavenly paeon rose
   From angels in array
The Satan in life's lumberland
   Was happier than they.

Then at last in Summer 1898 Gilbert took the plunge, proposed, and was accepted: 'It happened in St. James's Park; where they keep the ducks and the little bridge . . . I admit that I crossed that bridge in undeserved safety; and perhaps I was affected by my early romantic vision of the bridge leading to the princess's tower. But . . . the bridge of St. James's Park can frighten you a good deal.'[10]

That adventure was described in *Kakkopodescatrixandrometrupatyphusi-satox*:

Fear not, fear not, my children,
   The last weird embers fade,
Blue corpses through the windows peer,
   But still you seem afraid:
Perhaps there's something in the room.
   Whatever would you do
If I were not among you now
   To cheer and comfort you?

Heed not that pale thing in the door,
It smiles so like a skull,
You hear hoarse spectres scream and clank,
You find the evening dull?

Then let me tell a merry tale
Of dear old days of yore,
About a dragon of the wastes
That drank of human gore.
It dwelt among untrodden ways
And ate the plaintive dove,
A dragon there were few to praise
And very few to love.
(I use this piece of Wordsworth
To show how much I know)
Uproariously popular
It was, as dragons go.

If I could only paint the thing!
Just imitate its wink.
All you five infants, one by one,
Would rise and take to drink:
Or roll in death-pangs on the floor,
And lie there choked and blue.
O how I wish I could describe
This animal to you.

Some swore its fur was bushy brown,
Some swore that it was green,
With savage eyes of bluish grey:
Some swore that they had seen
In coils upon a sofa wreathed
It, writhing as in pangs,
And tearing Bovril chocolate
With huge, abhorrent fangs.
Some said that far to eastward
They saw it, garbed in grey,
Standing upon a platform
And bellowing all day.
Some said that far to northward,
Through all the white snow-wreath,
They saw it, white and wolfish,
With half-a-million teeth.

When skies were blue with summer
It glittered, bright and blue,
And once, the stricken wanderer
In screaming terror flew,

For on the shining tableland
White gauze did round it glance,
And with one rose to crown it
He saw the dragon dance.

The witless youth in wonder
Sat lank upon a stone,
His hat was monumental,
Its secret – all his own.
The Sage was mild and hoary
And skilled in Wisdom's page,
The youth sat meek (as always)
And to him spoke the Sage.

'Go not to smite the Dragon
That wasteth field and fen,
Around her reeking cavern
Are strewn the hearts of men;
But youth is foolish: You, Sir,
Are singularly so –
So learn her horrid habits
At least, before you go.

'If you would raise her bristles up
And set her eye in flames,
Then seek the Hankin-Pankin
And read the Jenry-James;
Go with a train of spiders huge
With all their treads and thrums
From ledgers all declaiming
Interminable sums . . .

But would you see the awful smile,
And soften down the Eye,
Then fetch the Stompy-Steinthal
And bring the Rompy-Rye;
And choirs of ladies tall and proud
With all one kind of nose,
And bucketsful of flowers,
And basketsful of clothes.

The witless youth spake straitway
Albeit his thought was slow,
'If forth I go to meet it,

Thus, as I stand, I go –
To tempt the darkest wrestle,
To tread the inmost place,
With lifted head and empty hands
My folly on my face.

'If in my cap one feather,
If on my lute one string –
Would send me forth to triumph,
God keep me from this thing:
I go to ask a question,
Its answer Yes or No,
And if I go to ask it,
Thus, as I stand, I go –

*L'Envoy*
Princess, I know but one thing,
One word I say or sing
That slaying fiery dragons was
A very easy thing.'

Informing the two families of their new situation was not quite so easy. It is said[11] that Mrs Blogg tried to put Gillbert at his ease by asking his opinion of her new wallpaper, whereupon he took some coloured chalks from his pocket and drew a sketch of Frances upon it. Mrs Blogg then considered it as well not to announce the engagement too widely but to keep it to the immediate family. Her motivation was no doubt predicated on Gilbert's prospects being far from promising with his income still tied at twenty-five shillings, but perhaps she also had in mind that somebody, anybody, else might turn up. Nonetheless, the Bloggs were all too well aware that Frances was twenty-nine years old and facing being 'on the shelf', so swallowing her pride, Mrs Blogg accepted the situation while asking Lucian Oldershaw to have a word with a view to smartening up her prospective son-in-law; when approached, Gilbert thought that, as Frances had accepted him as he was, it would not be right to change. However, Frances herself must have made some attempt to change his image, for in his letters he began to tease her:

(postmark: July 9th, 1899)

. . . I am clean. I am wearing a frockcoat, which from a superficial survey seems to have no end of buttons. It must be admitted that I am wearing a bow-tie; but on careful research I find that these were constantly worn by Vikings. A distinct allusion to them is made in that fine fragment, the Tryggvhessa Saga, where the poet says, in the short alliterative lines of early Norse Poetry:

Frockcoat folding then
Hakon Hardrada
Bow-tie buckled
Waited for war.
(Brit. Mus. MSS CCCLXIX, lines 99981–99985)

I resume. My appearance, as I have suggested, is singularly exemplary. My boots are placed, after the fastidious London fashion, on the feet: the laces are done up, the watch is going, the hair is brushed, the sleeve-links are inserted, for such is the Kingdom of Heaven.[12]

Indeed Frances was extremely proud of the stand she had made:

### A BALLADE OF PAST DAYS: TO GKC

Oh where is the fearful wild hair
That once I used to abhor,
And the socks that were not a pair
That I without ceasing went for,
And the paper in pieces you tore?
They have gone to the shadowy land
And will never return any more.
    You know I have made my stand.

That remarkable coat and rare
My soul rejected of yore,
The hat you once used to wear,
The boots you held in such store,
They have been and are not: no more
Can you hold them fast in your hand;
Their departure I let you deplore.
    You know I have made my stand.

Where the shirt that made people stare,
Where the button I asked to restore,
Where the hateful expression 'Don't care!',
Where the tone I used to implore
You never to mention the war?
Where the chalks, the matches, the sand
You ceaselessly dropped on the floor?
    Gone, for I have made my stand.

    *Envoy*
They have gone to the limitless shore
In the manner in which I had planned;
They will never return any more.
You know I have made my stand.

Gilbert acknowledged Frances had made her point:

### BALLADE OF A STAND

Yes you have made your stand: I know
Growing are all the things you planned.
Horrible links at my wristbands grow,
Terrible ties on my chest expand,
Hats and boots of a novel brand
Seized and held me from heel to crown.
You were woman and I unmanned;
    You were standing and I sat down.

Let it continue, even so –
I need stir neither foot nor hand.
I can think about Ivanhoe,
Whitman, Tolstoy, war and the Rand,
God and pigs and Better Land,
While you settle my neckties down.
I am simple and still and bland:
    You are standing and I sit down.

Thunder may come and storm and snow,
Lightening leap over sea and land.
I shall sit though the torrents flow,
I shall sit though the world is banned,
I shall sit and admire you and
See you are wearing a quite new gown.
Wonder is best by a stillness fanned;
    You are standing and I sit down.

   *Envoy*
Yea, Princess, but when God's own band
Rise and shout at the great command,
Never I grudge the higher crown;
    You are standing and I sit down.

A more immediate problem was the fact that Gilbert had not yet broken the news to his own parents, perhaps because Marie-Louise had not taken to Frances, and because, in Annie Firmin's words, 'Aunt Marie was a bit of a tyrant in her own family.' Deciding that discretion was the better part of valour, Gilbert waited until late July when the family took their annual holiday in Felixstowe, but again could not quite grasp the nettle and, rather than speak out openly, wrote her a letter:

1 Rosebery Villas,
Granville Road,
Felixstowe. [1898]

My Dearest Mother,

You may possibly think this is a somewhat eccentric proceeding. You are sitting opposite me and talking – about Mrs Berline. But I take this method of addressing you because it occurs to me that you might possibly wish to turn the matter over in your mind before writing or speaking to me about it.

I am going to tell the whole of a situation in which I believe I have acted rightly, though I am not absolutely certain, and to ask for your advice on it. It was a somewhat complicated one, and I repeat that I do not think I could rightly have acted otherwise, but if I were the greatest fool in the three kingdoms and had made nothing but a mess of it, there is one person I should always turn to and trust. Mothers know more of their sons' idiocies than other people can, and this has been peculiarly true in your case. I have always rejoiced at this, and not been ashamed of it: this has always been true and always will be. These things are easier written than said, but you know it is true, don't you?

I am inexpressibly anxious that you should give me credit for having done my best, and for having constantly had in mind the way in which you would be affected by the letter I am now writing. I do hope you will be pleased.

About eight years ago you made a remark – this may show you that if we 'jeer' at your remarks, we remember them. The remark applied to the hypothetical young lady with whom I should fall in love and took the form of saying 'If she is good, I shan't mind who she is.' I don't know how many times I have said that over to myself in the last two or three days in which I have decided on this letter.

Do not be frightened; or suppose that anything sensational or final has occurred. I am not married, my dear mother, neither am I engaged. You are called to the council of chiefs very early in its deliberations. If you don't mind, I will tell you, briefly, the whole story.

You are, I think, the shrewdest person for seeing things whom I ever knew: consequently I imagine that you do not think that I go down to Bedford Park every Sunday for the sake of the scenery. I should not wonder if you know nearly as much about the matter as I can tell in a letter. Suffice it to say, however briefly (for neither of us care much for gushing: this letter is not on Mrs Ratcliffe lines), that the first half of my time of acquaintance with the Bloggs was spent in enjoying a very intimate, but quite breezy and Platonic friendship with Frances Blogg, reading, talking and enjoying life together, having great sympathies on all subjects; and the second half in making the thrilling, but painfully responsible discovery that Platonism, on my side, had not the field by any means to itself. That is how we stand now. No one knows, except her family and yourself.

My dearest mother, I am sure you are at least not unsympathetic. Indeed we love each other more than we shall either of us ever be able to say. I have refrained from sentiment in this letter – for I don't think you like it much. But love is a very different thing from sentiment and you will never laugh at that. I will not say that you are sure to like Frances, for all young men say that to their mothers, quite naturally, and their mothers never believe them, also, quite naturally. Besides, I am so confident, I should like you to find her out for yourself. She is, in reality, very much the sort of woman you like, what is called, I believe, 'a Woman's Woman,' very humorous, inconsequent and sympathetic and defiled with no offensive exuberance of good health.

I have nothing more to say, except that you and she have occupied my mind for the last week to the exclusion of everything else, which must account for my abstraction, and that in her letter she sent the following message: 'Please tell your mother soon. Tell her I am not so silly as to expect her to think me good enough, but really I will try to be.'

An aspiration which, considered from my point of view, naturally provokes a smile. Here you give me a cup of cocoa. Thank you.

Believe me, my dearest mother,

Always your very affectionate son,

GILBERT[13]

There was certainly an element of prevarication: 'I am not married, my Dear Mother, neither am I engaged,' and it appears that her reaction was expected to be unfavourable. It was indeed far from enthusiastic, for, as Lawrence Solomon indicated, Marie-Louise had had other plans for her elder son.

The even tenor of life was rudely shattered in late June 1899. Gertrude who had taken a few days off from her work for Kipling in Sussex, had gone out on her bicycle only to be run down by a horse omnibus and die of her injuries within a few days. It is hard to establish when the accident took place, given that Frances' letters and most of Gilbert's letters were later destroyed by Dorothy Collins on the instructions of Frances, but Gertrude died on 2nd July 1899, and had been buried before Gilbert wrote on 8th July 1899 to cheer up his devastated fiancée:

(Postmark 8 July 1899)

I am black but comely at this moment: because the Cyclostyle has blacked me. Fear not. I shall wash myself. But I think it my duty to render an accurate account of my physical appearance every time I write: and shall be glad of any advice and assistance . . . I like the Cyclostyle ink; it is so inky . . . I will not ask you to forgive this rambling levity. I, for one, have sworn, I do not hesitate to say it, by the sword of God that has struck us, and before the beautiful face of the dead, that the first joke that occurred to me I would make, the first nonsense poem I thought of I would write, that I would begin again *at once* with a heavy heart at times, as to other duties, to the duty of being perfectly silly, perfectly extravagant, perfectly trivial, and as far as possible, amusing. I have sworn that Gertrude should *not* feel, wherever she is, that the comedy has gone out of our theatre. This, I am well aware, will be misunderstood. But I have long grasped that whatever we do we are misunderstood – small blame to other people; for, we know ourselves, our best motives are things we could neither explain nor defend. And I would rather hurt those who can shout than her who is silent.

You might tell me what you feel about this; but I am myself absolutely convinced that gaiety that is the bubble of love, does not annoy me: the old round of stories, laughter, family ceremonies, seems to me far less really inappropriate than a single moment of forced silence or unmanly shame . . .'[14]

No doubt that Gilbert, always shielded from any contact with death, was finding it difficult to deal with the situation. At Gertrude's funeral his wreath of bright orange and scarlet flowers had stood out from the white of all the other wreaths, but the humour with which he attempted in their almost daily exchange of letters to comfort the inconsolate Frances was singularly inappropriate. Nonetheless, Frances replied immediately (in those times when it was possible to send a letter and receive a reply the same day), as did Gilbert in his turn:

> 11 Warwick Gardens (Postmark: 9th July 1899)
> . . . If there were such a thing as *blue*-hot iron, it would describe the sky tonight. I cannot help dreaming of some wild fairy-tale in which the whole round cosmos should be a boiling pot, with the flames of Purgatory under it, and that soon I shall have the satisfaction of seeing such a thing as boiled mountains, boiled cities, and a boiled moon and stars. A tremendous picture. Yet I am perfectly happy as usual. After all, why should we object to be boiled? Potatoes, for example, are better boiled than raw – why should we fear to be boiled into new shapes in the cauldron? These things are an allegory.
>
> I am so glad to hear you say . . . that, in your own words 'it is good for us to be here' – where you are at present. The same remark, if I remember right, was made on the mountain of the Transfiguration. It has always been one of my unclerical sermons to myself, that that remark which Peter made on seeing the vision of a single hour, ought to be made by us all, in contemplating every panoramic change in the long Vision we call life – other things superficially, but this always in our depths. 'It is good for us to be here – it is good for us to be here,' repeating itself eternally. And if, after many joys and festivals and frivolities, it should be our fate to have to look on while one of us is, in a most awful sense of the words, 'transfigured before our eyes': shining with the whiteness of death – at least, I think, we cannot easily fancy ourselves wishing not to be at our post. Not I, certainly. It was good for me to be there.[15]

Daily life resumed its course:

> (Postmark: 11th July 1899)
> . . . The novel, after which you so kindly enquire, is proceeding headlong. It received another indirect stimulus today, when Mr Garnett insisted on taking me out to lunch, gave me a gorgeous repast at a restaurant . . . and made me promise to send him some chapters of it . . . Excuse me for talking about these trivialities . . .

I have made a discovery: or I should say seen a vision. I saw it between two cups of black coffee in a Gallic restaurant in Soho: but I could not express it if I tried.

But this was one thing it said – that all good things are one thing. There is no conflict between the gravestone of Gertrude and a comic-opera tune played by Mildred Wain. But there is everlasting conflict between the gravestone of Gertrude and the obscene pomposity of the hired mute: and there is everlasting conflict between the comic-opera tune and any mean or vulgar words to which it may be set.[16]

(Postmark: 14th July 1899)

. . . costume slightly improved. The truth is that a mystical and fantastic development has taken place. My clothes have rebelled against me. Weary of scorn and neglect, they have all suddenly come to life and they dress me by force every morning. My frockcoat leaps upon me like a lion and hangs on, dragging me down. As I struggle my boots trip me up – and the laces climb up my feet (never missing a hole) like snakes or creepers. At the same moment the celebrated grey tie springs at my throat like a wild cat.

I am told that the general effects produced by this remarkable psychical development are superb. Really the clothes know best. Still it is awkward when a mackintosh pursues me down the street.[17]

These lines seem to have been sent immediately prior to the Chesterton family's summer holiday, as the next letter was from:

Felixstowe (undated)

. . . I have, as you see, arrived here. I have done other daring things, such as having my hair shampooed, as you commanded, and also cut. The effect of this is so singularly horrible that I have found further existence in London impossible. Public opinion is too strong for me . . . There are many other reasons I could give for being pleased to come: such as that I have some time for writing the novel; that I can make up stories I don't intend to write . . . that there are phosphorescent colours on the sea and a box of cigarettes on the mantlepiece.

Some fragments of what I felt (about Gertrude's death) have struggled out in the form of some verses[18] which I am writing out for you. But for real strength (I don't like the word 'comfort' for real peace, no human words are much good except perhaps some of the unfathomable, unintelligible, unconquerable epigrams of the Bible.

. . . 'Precious' – we could not say that Gertrude's death is happy or providential or sweet or even perhaps good. But it is something. 'Beautiful' is a good word – but 'precious' is the only right word.

It is this passionate sense of the *value* of things: of the richness of the cosmic treasure: the world where every star is a diamond, every leaf an emerald, every drop of blood a ruby, it is this sense of *preciousness* that *is* really awakened by the death of His saints. Somehow we feel that even their death is a thing of incalculable value and mysterious sweetness: it is awful, tragic, desolating, desperately hard to bear – but still 'precious' . . . Forgive the verbosity of one whose trade it is to express the inexpressible.[19]

At last there is a sense that Gilbert has begun to come to terms with his first experience of death and is now able to be of some comfort to his fiancée, especially in the seven poems written in her sister's memory. Frances had been on or over the verge of a nervous breakdown and her younger brother, Knollys, was never really to recover from the circumstances of Gertrude's death. A holiday abroad was prescribed and by September Gilbert was aware that:

(Postmark: 29th September, 1899)

all this world soliloquy will be poured into the soul of one wise and beautiful lady sitting far away beyond seas and rivers and cities under the shadow of an alien Cathedral . . . I do not know what Gertrude's death was – I know that it was beautiful, for I saw it. We do not feel that it is so beautiful now – why? Because we do not *see* it now. What we see now is her absence: but her Death is not her absence, but her Presence somewhere else. That is what we *knew* was beautiful, as long as we could see it. Do not be frightened, dearest, by the slow inevitable laws of human nature, we shall climb back into the mountain of vision: we shall be able to use the word, with the accent of Whitman. 'Disembodied, triumphant, dead.'[20]

Four days later he passes on the latest news concerning his career prospects:

3rd Oct. 1899

. . . My father again is engaged in the crucial correspondence with Fisher Unwin, at least it has begun by T.F.U. stating his proposed terms – a rise of 5/- from October, another rise possible but undefined in January, 10 per cent royalty for the Paris book and expenses for a fortnight in Paris. These, as I got my father to heartily agree, are vitiated to the bone as terms by the absence of any assurance that I shall not have to write 'Paris', for which I am really paid nothing, *outside* the hours of work for which I am paid 25/-. In short, the net result would be that instead of gaining more liberty to rise in the literary world, I should be selling the small liberty of rising that I have now for five more shillings. This my father is declining and asking for a better settlement. The diplomacy is worrying, yet I enjoy it: I feel like Mr Chamberlain on the eve of war. I would stop with T.F.U. for £100 a year [an increase of £35] – but not for less. Which means, I think, that I shall not stop at all.

But all these revolutions, literary, financial, and political fade into insignificance compared with the one really tremendous event of this week. It will take place on Saturday next. The sun will stand still upon Leicester Square and the Moon on the Valley of Wardour St. For then will assemble the Grand Commemorative Meeting of the Junior Debating Club . . . When this gorgeous function is over, you must expect a colossal letter . . .[21]

11 Warwick Gardens, W.

. . . This is the colossal letter . . . I cannot make out exactly whether I did or did not post a letter I wrote to you on Saturday. If I did not, I apologise for missing the day. If I did, you will know by this time one or two facts that may interest you, the chief of which is that I am certainly leaving Fisher Unwin, with much mutual courtesy and goodwill.

This fact may interest you, I repeat: at the moment I am not sure whether it interests me. For my head, to say nothing of another organ, is filled with the thundering cheers and songs of the dinner on Saturday night . . .[22]

There follow five pages of writing on the reunion dinner 'because I am a victim of the prejudice, common I trust to all mankind, that no one ever had such friends as I had.' How reassuring the news was to Frances is a matter of doubt, for it meant that *ipso facto* and willy-nilly Gilbert was out of a job and reliant on what he could earn as a journalist, even though to him that was of secondary importance in comparison with the JDC dinner. His journalistic earnings were to be rooted in 1899 in his reviews and articles for *The Bookman* and, after 1901, his weekly article or review in *The Daily News*. To these could be added whatever royalties came from his book of comic verse, *Greybeards at Play*, published in 1900 by Gertrude's ex-fiancé, Rex Brimley Johnson, and later in the same year of *The Wild Knight*, more solemn poetry published by Grant Richards with a generous subsidy from his father. By Easter 1900 when he answered a questionnaire from Frances matters had not progressed much further:

Good Friday, 1900

(1) How am I? I am in excellent health. I have an opaque cold in my head, cough tempestuously and am very deaf. But these things I count as mere specks showing up the general blaze of salubrity. I am getting steadily better and I don't mind how slowly. As for my spirits a cold never affects them: for I have plenty to do and think about indoors. One or two little literary schemes – trifles doubtless – claim my attention . . .

(5) Alas! I have not been to Nutt. There are good excuses, but they are not real ones. I will write to him now. Yes: now.

(6) Does my hair want cutting? My hair seems pretty happy. You are the only person who seems to have any fixed theory on this. For all I know it may be at that fugitive perfection which has moved you to enthusiasm. Three minutes after this perfection, I understand, a horrible degeneration sets in: the hair becomes too long, the figure disreputable and profligate: and the individual is unrecognised by all his friends. It is he that wants cutting then, not his hair.

(7) As to shirt-links, studs, and laces, I glitter from head to foot with them . . .

(9) I have got a really important job in reviewing – the *Life of Ruskin* for the *Speaker*. As I have precisely 73 theories about Ruskin it will be brilliant and condensed. I am also reviewing the *Life of the Kendals*, a book on the Renaissance and one on Correggio for the *Bookman* . . .

(11) Really and truly I see no reason why we should not be married in April if not before. I have been making some money calculations with the kind assistance of Rex, and as far as I can see we could live in the country on quite a small amount of regular literary work . . .[23]

Back in December 1898 Gilbert had answered a similar questionnaire:

> 5th. The Book for Nutt, which has reached its worst stage, that of polishing up for
> the eye of Nutt, instead of merely rejoicing in the eye of God. Do you know this is the
> only one of the lot about which I am at all worried. I do not feel as if things like the Fish
> poem ['The Dangers Attending Altruism on the High Seas] are really worth publishing.
> I know they are better than many books that are published, but Heaven knows that is
> not saying much. In support of some of my work, I would fight to the last. But with
> regard to this occasional verse I feel a humbug. To publish a book of my nonsense
> verses seems to me exactly like summoning the whole of the people of Kensington to
> see me smoke cigarettes . . .
> 6th. The collection of more serious poems of which I spoke to you. You shall have a
> hand in the selection of these when you get back.
> 7th. The Novel – which though I have put it aside for the present, yet has become
> too much a part of me not to be constantly having chapters written – or rather growing
> out of the others.
> And all these things, with the exception of the last one, are supposed to be really
> urgent, and to be done immediately . . . [24]

'The Novel', as ever, is tantalisingly untitled, and, if it was ever published by
David Nutt, remains untraced. A much more specific reference followed
(Postmark: 24 July 1899):

> My darling, I feel very much annoyed at not having been able to write to you for
> the last forty-eight hours: but not so guilty as I might feel, because this delay has been
> due to a violent attack of industry, under the influence of which (I say it with legitimate
> pride) I have written half a novel in three days, plus Fisher Unwin . . . It is not very good:
> but it has a really good conception (it is the recast Pistol one) and it is better than two
> novels I have just recommended Mr Fisher Unwin to publish. So if only there is another
> reader as lenient . . . [25]

The Pistol story had been part of *The Human Club* before being absorbed
in *The Man With Two Legs* and eventually reused yet again in *Manalive* in
1912. Another more immediate problem was that Francis Yvon Eccles, literary editor of *The Speaker*, had for some unaccountable reason decided that
Chesterton's italic handwriting, so painstakingly adopted, was proof positive
that he was Jewish, and at first rejected everything that Oldershaw's 'Jewish
friend' submitted. By the end of 1900 Chesterton, no longer the butt of Eccles's
anti-semitism, received from him a favourable review of *The Wild Knight*:

> Mr Gilbert Chesterton is a poet whose sincerity is, so to speak, in the first degree; who
> speaks directly, from soul to soul, of the things that preoccupy all men, who applies a
> spontaneous and cultivated lyrical talent not to the adornment of given themes, but

to the representation of the world he sees, divines and desires. Intent upon essentials, impelled to express an intimate and organic attitude, which is infinitely more than a bundle of opinions on love and life and death, he scorns to be impersonal.[26]

The *Manchester Guardian* on March 12th, 1901 also reacted very positively:

> *The Wild Knight and Other Poems*, by Gilbert Chesterton, is a small volume of virile, strenuous, and frankly personal poetry, full of fraternity and chivalry, and almost always thoroughly accomplished in rhythm and diction. The author has the courage, rarer among cultivated writers than among the ingenuously incompetent, to be himself – to show an unassumed contempt for the cant of sophistication and the cant of simplicity, a glowing faith in the supremacy of love, human and divine, and a conviction, abundantly and quaintly illustrated, of the vanity of human condemnations.'

Other reviewers were in general favourable, although James Douglas in *The Star* (January 5th, 1901) sprang to the conclusion that 'I have never heard of "Gilbert Chesterton." Is it a pseudonym? If so, I think I can identify the author. Surely "Gilbert Chesterton" is Mr John Davidson ... But I could quote poem after magnificent poem to prove that Mr John Davidson's voice betrays him, and that in this volume he has given us better than his very best.'[27] John Davidson was quick to disown 'such frantic rubbish.' It would have been interesting to have been the fly on the wall when some time later Douglas, Davidson and Chesterton found themselves seated together at a literary dinner. The immediate effect was to make GKC's name and launch him as a reviewer and bring him up against the realities of life:

> (Postmark: February 8th, 1901)
> ... The *Daily News* have sent me a huge mass of books to review, which block up the front hall. A study of Swinburne – a book on Kipling – the last Richard Le Gallienne – all very interesting. See if I don't do some whacking articles, all about the stars and the moon and the creation of Adam and that sort of thing ...
>
> Another rather funny thing is the way in which my name is being spread about. Belloc declares that everyone says to him 'Who discovered Chesterton?' and that he always replies, 'The genius Oldershaw.' This may be a trifle Gallic, but Hammond has shown me more than one letter from Cambridge dons and such people demanding the identity of G.K.C. in a quite violent tone. They excuse themselves by offensive phrases in which the word 'brilliant' occurs.[28]

> (Postmark: February 19th, 1901)
> I am, for the first time in my life, thoroughly *worried*, and I find it a rather exciting and not entirely unpleasant sensation. But everything depends just now, not only on my sticking hard to work and doing a lot of my very best, but on my thinking about it, keeping wide awake to the turn of the market, being ready to do things not in half a week, but in half an hour; getting the feelings and tendencies of other men and

generally living in work . . . I cannot express to you what it is to feel the grip of the great wheel of real life on you for the first time. For the first time I know what is meant by the word 'enemies' – men who deliberately dislike you and oppose your career – and the funny thing is I don't dislike them at all myself. Poor devils – very likely they want to be married in June too . . .

I am a Socialist, but I love this fierce old world and am beginning to find a beauty in making money (in moderation) as in making statues.[29]

(Postmark: March 4th, 1901)

. . . I have delayed this letter in a scandalous manner because I hoped I might have the arrangements with the *Daily News* to tell you; as that is again put off, I must tell you later. The following, however, are grounds on which I believe everything will turn out right this year. It is arithmetic. The *Speaker* has hitherto paid me £70 a year, that is £6 a month. It has now raised it to £10 a month, which makes £120 a year. Moreover they encourage me to write as much as I like in the paper, so that assuming that I do something extra (poem, note, leader) twice a month or every other number, which I can easily do, that brings us to nearly £150 a year, So much for the *Speaker*. Now for the *Daily News*, both certainties and probabilities. Hammond (to whom you will favour me by being eternally grateful) pushed me so strongly with Lehmann for the post of manager of the literary page that it is most probable that I shall get it [He didn't] . . . If I do, Hammond thinks they couldn't give me less than £200 a year. So that if this turns out right, we have £350, say, without any aid from *Bookman*, books, magazine articles or stories.

Let us, however, put this chance entirely on one side and suppose that they can give me nothing but regular work on the *Daily News*. I have just started a set of popular fighting articles on literature in the *Daily News* called 'The Wars of Literature'. They will appear at least twice a week, often three times. For each of these I am paid about a guinea and a half. This makes about £3 a week which is £144 a year. Thus with only the present certainties of *Speaker* and *Daily News* we have £264 a year, or very likely (with extra *Speaker* items) £288, close on £300. This again may be reinforced by all sorts of miscellaneous work which I shall get now my name is getting known . . . The only conclusion of this letter is that, on any calculation whatever, we ought to have £300 a year, and be on the road to four in a little while.[30]

An undated letter to his mother, probably given her by hand, titivates the situation even more:

Burley. Hants.

. . . There is a subject we have touched on once or twice that I want to talk to you about, for I am very much worried in my mind as to whether you will disapprove of a decision I have been coming to with a very earnest belief that I am seeking to do the right thing. I have just had information that my screw from the *Speaker* will be yet further increased from £120 a year to £150, or, if I do the full amount I can, £190 a year. I have also had a request from the *Daily News* to do two columns a week regularly, which [is] rather over £100 a year, besides other book reviews. My other sources of income which should bring the amount up to nearly £150 more, at any rate, I will speak of in a moment.

There is something, as I say, that is distressing me a great deal. I believe I said about a year ago that I hoped to get married in a year, if I had money enough. I fancy you took it rather as a joke: I was not so certain about it myself then. I have however been coming very seriously to the conclusion that if I pull off one more affair – a favourable arrangement with *Reynolds' Newspaper*, whose editor wants to see me at the end of this week, I shall, unless you disapprove, make a dash for it this year. When I mentioned the matter a short time ago, you said (if I remember right) that you did not think I ought to marry under £400 or £500 a year. I was moved to go into the matter thoroughly then and there, but as it happened I knew I had one or two bargains just coming off which would bring me nearer to the standard you named, so I thought I would let it stand over till I could actually quote them. Believe me, my dearest mother, I am not considering this affair wildly or ignorantly: I have been doing nothing but sums in my head for the last months. This is how matters stand. The *Speaker* editor says they will take as much as I like to write. If I write my maximum I get £192 a year from them. From the *Daily News*, even if I do not get the post on the staff which was half promised me, I shall get at least £100 a year with a good deal over for reviews, outside 'The Wars of Literature.' That makes nearly £300. With the *Manchester Sunday Chronicle* I have just made a bargain by which I shall get £72 a year. That makes £370 a year altogether. The matter now, I think, largely depends on *Reynolds' Newspaper*. If I do, as is contemplated, weekly articles and thumbnail sketches, they cannot give me less than £100 a year. This would bring the whole to £470 a year, or within £30 of your standard. Of course I know quite well that this is not like talking of an income from a business or a certain investment. But we should live a long way within this income, if we took a very cheap flat, even a workman's flat if necessary, had a woman in to do the laborious daily work and for the rest waited on ourselves, as many people I know do in cheap flats . . . I have, as I say, what seems to me a sufficient income for a start.

. . . I am terribly worried for fear you should be angry or sorry about all this. I am only kept in hope by the remembrance that I had the same fear when I told you of my engagement and that you dispelled it with a directness and generosity that I shall not forget. I think, my dear Mother, that we have always understood each other really. We are neither of us very demonstrative: we come of some queer stock that can always say least when it means most. But I do think you can trust me when I say that I think a thing really right, and equally honestly admit that I can hardly explain why. To explain why I know it is right would be to communicate the incommunicable, and speak of delicate and sacred things in bald words. The most I can say is that I know Frances like the back of my hand and can tell without a word from her that she has never recovered from a wound and that there is only one kind of peace that will heal it.

I have tried to explain myself in this letter: I can do it better in a letter, somehow, but I do not think I have done it very successfully. However, with you it does not matter and it never will matter, how my thoughts come tumbling out. You at least have always understood what I meant.

Always your loving son,
GILBERT'[31]

Gilbert's ability to look on the bright side was not justified by events, as he did not become manager of the *Daily News'* literary page, nor did his negotiations with *Reynolds' News* and the *Manchester Sunday Chronicle* bear any fruit, for none of his work appeared therein. Whatever she thought of her son's financial arrangements, Marie-Louise who, according to Annie Firmin, had 'always disliked Frances' can hardly have been comforted by the knowledge that her son was marrying Frances in order to help heal the wound inflicted by the death of her sister. Arrangements for a June wedding went ahead. It would have been natural to presume that, as the son of an estate agent, Gilbert would have had no difficulty finding somewhere to live, but neither Mr Ed. nor Gilbert seems to have given the matter any thought until the last minute when they were lent a 'charming little house in Edwardes Square, an oasis of good architecture and repose in the roar of the High Street and within a stone's throw of Warwick Gardens,'[32] by Mr and Mrs Boore, old friends of Frances. On a portico at the back of the garden Gilbert soon enjoyed himself by producing what Bentley recalled as 'flaming frescos done in vivid crayons, of knights and heroes and divinities' and the latter thought the Boores might have 'charged for them as dilapidations at the end of the tenancy.' Gilbert does seem to have expressed his appreciation for the kindness of the Boores by writing a ballade in French of which only the last stanza and the envoy survive:

> . . . Cyrano, allez aux chiens
>   Héro de l'art, l'amour, la guerre,
> Son nez à elle est moins que le sien,
>   Mais c'est pour moi plus grande affaire.
> Ah! c'est fâcheuse, cette manière,
>   Je m'ennuie de ces [becs] si courts,
> Elle n'est poète, cette Boore la mère.
>   Qu'elle est heureuse, cette Madame Boore.
>
>   l'Envoy
> Princesse la vie, la vie coûte cher,
>   Tout Roi tombe, chacun à son tour,
> Il n'y a qu'une belle chose sous l'éclair,
>   Qu'elle est heureuse cette Madame Boore.

With the wedding day almost upon them and presents beginning to arrive, Gilbert told Annie Firmin that, like the rich young man of the Gospels, he felt 'sorrowful, because I have great possessions.' He also presented his bride to be with *The Legend of Good Women*:

I did not see thy shadow fall
Through gap of hedge or chink of wall.
God gave His whole wide world to me
Before I gave myself to thee.

I came not from the heartless fête,
From loves more low than any hate,
To smirch you with my drear defence
And my polluting penitence.

Nor ever failed I to believe
The honour of the house of Eve.
A mighty sisterhood I knew
Bringing their empress, two and two:

My mother in whose soul abide
Perversity and secret pride
In all she loves: no toils control
Her humorous mutiny of soul.

And yours – as tremulous as steel
And yet as strong: who still could feel
Through seven heavens piled on her
The burden of the grasshopper.

Ethel, a despot by decree
Of her own great simplicity,
A great earth-angel shorn of wings,
The sister of all living things.

Elsie fulfilled of charities,
With the gold breadth of Veronese,
Made soft and strange (I know not why)
With all a woman's tragedy.

Mildred, the pale and laughing one,
Whom God made happier than the sun.
It did the old skies good to see
The ribbons of her bravery.

And Violet, like her sires of yore
High-coloured, keen, alert: when more
Than Ireland's mirth might mingled be
With more than France's chivalry.

Mabel your friend, mid grass and bloom
Alone: like one in an old room
Set by an old harp as to sing,
But still and vibrant as its string.

And she – your friend with whom you dwell,
Who loved the wreath of roses well,
The richest wines, the rosiest morns,
Only loved more the crown of thorns.

And she again, Earth's friend and yours,
The wind upon her Northern moors
That blows the robes about her feet
Is not more mighty – or more sweet.

And Lizzie with her tangled sense
And dazzling inconsequence,
And mixed a million jests among
The sadness of an Irish song.

Annie: with still eyes full of truth
Above my childhood and my youth:
Like Nature's face her face is hung,
Who was before me, yet is young.

And Leila, straight and sane and strong,
Who let not vigils late or long
Nor toils, nor any lesson wise
Make dark the laughter of her eyes.

And she: even she whom none forget,
Who well I know remember yet
Even from her smile as she passed by
Upon her road to victory.

Dearest: I boast one good indeed,
The loneliest star, the smallest weed,
The littlest growth of good I blessed,
Therefore it was I knew the best.

# 6.

# LUCIFER MEETS HIS MATCH

The wedding took place on 28th June 1901 (Frances' 32nd birthday) not in Bedford Park as the Bloggs had moved,[1] but at St. Mary Abbots, the Kensington Parish Church, with Conrad Noel,[2] their friend from the Christian Social Union, as celebrant. No photos of the wedding survive, if indeed there were any, save for one of Gilbert dressed for a wedding, although it may not have been his own. Frances' bridesmaids were her eleven-year old cousin, Rhoda Bastable, and eight-year old Doris Child to whom Frances tossed her bouquet. The little girl, already loaded down with flowers, gloves and a prayer book, did not realize the significance of the gesture and felt put upon by having to carry the bride's bouquet as well. Her assessment of the happy couple, the 6ft 3in Gilbert and the frail 5ft 2in Frances, was 'They don't match a bit.' Gilbert's best man was Lucian Oldershaw who seems to have had a trying time, for the groom had not only forgotten his tie but still had the price tag on his shoes. Annie Firmin's and Marie-Louise's eyes meeting, they began to giggle uncontrollably. The reception was remembered chiefly for the fact that Cecil and Gilbert for once in their lives did not get embroiled in an argument.

The honeymoon consisted of a few days spent at Coltishall on the Norfolk Broads, but once again no details have survived as to whether it was on water[3] or on land. The first wedding night was to be at the Great White Horse Inn in Ipswich. Lucian Oldershaw went ahead to Liverpool Street Station with the heavy baggage, loaded it on the train and waited, and waited increasingly feverishly. The train left, as did another, before at last the happy couple arrived to reveal that Gilbert had insisted on stopping at a dairy in Kensington High

Street: 'I stopped at that particular dairy because I had always drunk a glass of milk there when walking with my mother in my infancy. And it seemed to me a fitting ceremonial to unite the two great relations of a man's life.'4 A second stop had been made at a gunsmiths to purchase a revolver for Gilbert to protect his new wife against any pirates they might encounter on the Norfolk Broads.

Arriving very late on a slow train, they booked into the Great White Horse Inn. Gilbert decided to take a stroll, strode away from the hotel through the town until he reached the countryside; completely lost, he had to ask where he was and how to return to his bride. There are two accounts of the next stage of the honeymoon, one a poem by Gilbert, the other a story of the wedding night which Cecil Chesterton told to Ada, who published it in 1941:

### CREATION DAY

Between the perfect marriage day
   And that fierce future proud, and furled,
I only stole six days – six days:
   Enough for God to make the world.

For us is a creation made:
   New moon by night, new sun by day;
That ancient elm that holds the heavens
   Sprang to its stature yesterday –

Dearest and first of all things free,
   Alone as bride and queen and friend,
Brute facts may come and bitter truths,
   But here all doubts shall have an end.

Never again with cloudy talk
   Shall life be tricked or faith undone;
The world is many and is made,
   But we are sane and we are one.
      Coltishall, July 1901.

The opening chapters of the married life of Gilbert and Frances had gone strangely, pathetically awry. He was fathoms deep in love, and in that first transcendent moment of their honeymoon when, far beyond time and space, they found themselves utterly, unbelievably alone, he must have heard the sun, the moon and the stars singing together. And then the whole world went crash. The woman he worshipped shrank from his touch and screamed when he embraced her. A less sensitive or more experienced man would have regarded the affair as distressing though by no means irremediable, but he

was haunted by the fear that his brutality and lust had frightened the woman he would
have died to protect. He dared not even contemplate a repetition.

He went to Cecil, quivering with self-reproach and condemnation. His young
brother took a completely rationalistic view of the contretemps, and suggested that
some citadels must be taken by storm, while others yield only to long siege. Anyway, he
insisted, nothing had happened that could not be put right; they could both be happy
and have lots of children. But the mischief had been done. Gilbert hated himself for
what had happened, and Frances could not reconcile herself to the physical realities
of marriage. Temperamentally ascetic, physically sickly through spinal disease, the
experience must have shocked her profoundly. Her tragedy was that desiring children,
she shrank from sex. The final adjustment between them seems never to have been
made, and Gilbert, young and vital, was condemned to a pseudo-monastic life, in
which he lived with a woman but never enjoyed one.

For there was that about the Chestertons which would not let them be unfaithful. It
was a family idiosyncrasy, apart from religion, belief or social tradition. Once married,
they were dedicated for life.[5]

It is probably best to accept that there were some problems. What is certain
is that Frances was later (about 1904 or 1905) to have an operation to enable
her to have children, the exact nature of which is a matter of speculation;[6]
she certainly began to keep a diary at that time to help her overcome her
feeling 'flat or tired or dull.' Gilbert in *Orthodoxy* (1908) made the point that
he was not a practitioner of celibacy: 'I have not myself any instinctive kinship
with that enthusiasm for physical virginity, which has certainly been a note of
historic Christianity. It takes all sorts to make a church; she does not ask me
to be celibate . . . Celibacy is one flower in my father's garden, of which I have
not been told the sweet or terrible name.'

The return to London and to the task of earning a living with his pen
coincided with the publication of the first collections of Gilbert's articles, *The
Defendant* and *Twelve Types*, a sort of book that brought his critical talents to
a wider audience and was to be the mainstay of his income over the years. A
more permanent residence was acquired at 60 Overstrand Mansions, a block
of flats overlooking Battersea Park where they were to stay until 1909 with
only one move to No. 48. In Belloc's words:

> Frances and Gilbert have a little flat
> At eighty pounds a year and cheap at that,
> Where Frances, who is Gilbert's only wife,
> Leads an unhappy and complaining life;
> While Gilbert who is Frances' only man,
> Puts up with it as gamely as he can.

At some point the Chestertons acquired a cook who was to remain in their employ and transfer with them to Beaconsfield in 1909; unfortunately the lady concerned seemed to specialise in dishes based on potatoes, which allied with the poached eggs and pies and burgundy of Fleet Street soon had an effect on Gilbert's figure. This was not helped by a sedentary life now that he no longer went for walks with Cecil, and within a couple of years his slim silhouette at the time of his marriage had spread so much that by 1903 he was referred to as 'a fat humorist'; worse was to follow and in 1906 Bernard Shaw could compare him to Gulliver in Lilliput: 'Chesterton is our "Quinbus Flestrin", the young Man Mountain, a large abounding gigantically cherubic person who is not only large in body and mind beyond all decency, but seems to be growing larger as you look at him – "swellin' wisibly", as Tony Weller puts it.' In short Chesterton was well on the way to becoming the familiar figure of the caricatures and was soon disposed or obliged to take a hansom cab for even the shortest of journeys, even of a hundred yards. It was no doubt the underlying strength of his constitution which enabled him to go on for many years before the combined effects of increasing weight, dropsy and possibly the onset of type 2 diabetes eventually took their toll in 1914. In the meantime, his development from Gilbert Chesterton into the instantly recognizable GKC probably did him no harm in his Fleet Street career.

## A Singular Suicide

On December 31st, 1904 Frances noted in her diary 'Our poor Knollys very ill'. Her younger brother had still not got over his sister Gertrude's death in 1899; always of a nervous disposition, his behaviour had become more and more erratic to a point where at GKC's expense he became a patient at the Holloway Sanitorium near Egham. A particular crisis, perhaps the incident later alluded to at the inquest, seems to have occurred in the course of 1904–05 when Gilbert was to suddenly abandon work for *The Bystander, The Pall Mall Magazine, The Fortnightly Review*, cut short mid-chapter the serialisation of his novel *The Ball and the Cross* in *The Commonwealth* and terminate his Stevensonian-type novella, *Dead Man's Drum*; Frances abandoned her diary at the same time. Gilbert's subsequent interest in the care of mental patients may reflect the fact that Knollys had been committed, and his claim that *The Man Who Was Thursday* had been found useful in the treatment of such patients may have had some foundation. Knollys' health improved in 1906 and after being released he dedicated to GKC a book of essays, *Ledgers and Literature*, in which he gave a light-hearted account of his business life and his stay in the

Sanitorium. Under his pseudonym of George Knollys two articles were published in *The Girls' Realm*: 'Mr Gilbert Chesterton and his toy theatre' (Vol.10,
no.106, June 1907) and a posthumous 'A Humorist and his dolls: Mr Gilbert
Chesterton and his Japanese playthings' (Vol.11, no.121, November 1908). At
some point Knollys had become a Roman Catholic: 'We are all Catholics
now,'[7] as Syme said.

*The East Sussex News* for Friday, August 28th, 1908, under the heading
'Singular Suicide: Westdean. A Tutor's body found in the Cuckmere,' gives
details of an inquest held at Seaford on Monday, August 24th, 1908: Jesse
Fowler, a shepherd, gave evidence that on Friday, August 21st he had spotted
a body floating in the River Cuckmere at Exceat Bridge [where the A 259
now crosses the river], and that he had passed a message to a motorist to
be reported to the Seaford police. On the body the police had found some
money and two left-luggage tickets relating to two packages at Seaford
station. Dr W.P. Morgan believed the body had been in the water for five to six
days before it was discovered. He had found clearcut wounds on the throat,
dividing the jugular vein. In his opinion the wounds were self-inflicted and
probably fatal, but not instantaneously so; Knollys Blogg would have been
able to stagger a few steps before he collapsed, and this, rather than drowning
was the actual cause of death. The body was unrecognisable, but a ring and
other articles on it indicated it to be that of George Knollys Blogg who had
recently been living at Rye, and earning a living as a tutor, with one pupil
[unidentified]. Lucian Oldershaw, Knollys' brother-in-law, who attended
the inquest, had also identified the body by a previously broken leg and
elbow, injuries sustained earlier in an attempt to escape from or to commit
suicide while detained at the Holloway Sanitorium. Oldershaw further gave
evidence that 'while in business in London [George Knollys Blogg] had a
severe breakdown in health, which affected his mind and he had to go to the
Holloway Sanitorium. He had left that institution for about three years and
seemed to have recovered perfectly with the exception that he was at times
somewhat despondent . . . his brother-in-law had been staying at Westdean
and was intending to leave there to visit him in Maidenhead on 15th August.'
The story was taken up in the evidence of John Henry Lomas, steward of
the Hampshire House Club in Hammersmith, London, a working class
temperance club which held a summer holiday at West Dean Farm every year.
Knollys Blogg had helped at the previous year's holiday, and had joined them
again in 1908, arriving on July 31st and staying on for a second week, when he
had given recitations at the Thursday evening concert and had seemed well,

if somewhat quiet and studious. It had apparently been Knollys' intention to leave on Saturday, 15th August, first at 3.00 pm but then at 5.30 pm by a faster train in order to visit the Oldershaws. [An anomaly is that trains left Seaford for Lewes at 1.55 pm and 5.38 pm on Saturday, 15th August, and at 1.50 pm on Sunday, 16th August.] Knollys then had a further change of plan, saying he had received a letter which caused him to defer his departure until the Sunday at about 2.00 pm. He sent his luggage [the two packages?] to Seaford station, intending to ride his bicycle to catch the train. Henry Lomas had seen him at about 6.00 pm on the evening of the 15th and had felt Knollys resented being asked why he had not left: Lomas did not see him again and assumed that he had eventually left for Maidenhead. Lucian Oldershaw gave further evidence that he had not sent a letter asking for Knollys' visit to be delayed, and had indeed been expecting him; when there was no news by the middle of the next week [say 18th/19th August?] he had telegraphed his sister [presumably Knollys' sister Frances Chesterton] in Lowestoft asking if Knollys was by any chance there. The alarm was then raised in Westdean and the police were informed, so the finding of the body two or three days later was not unexpected by them. It appears that no-one else from his family, other than Oldershaw, attended the inquest. The Chestertons, spending the annual family holiday in Lowestoft, would (pace Mr Ed.) hardly have dared react to a suspicious death and subsequent funeral. The coroner's verdict was 'death due to a haemorrhage from wounds, and suicide while suffering from melancholia,' and that Knollys was insane at the time.[8]

Several mysteries remain, for how did Knollys come to have the left-luggage tickets on his person if he had not himself gone to the station; what had happened to his bicycle; what weapon had been used to inflict his wounds and what had become of it? Above all, what had happened to the mysterious letter, and had all the delay been due to Knollys' usual dithering or so as to meet somebody? Where did he spend the Saturday night, if not at West Dean Farm, if, as Frances was to claim, he did attend Mass on the Sunday? The nearest Roman Catholic churches in 1908 were in Newhaven and Eastbourne. Frances implied that Knollys had been drowned at sea but, although the Cuckmere is tidal in its lower reach, Exceat Bridge is a mile and a half from the sea. Given the proximity of the Seven Sisters and even the none too distant Beachy Head, it seems strange that Knollys should try to hack himself to death.

On August 25th, 1908, the day after the inquest, Frances wrote to Father John O'Connor (see Chapter 9) in Heckmondwike: 'I have to write in great trouble. My dear brother was found drowned at Seaford a few days ago. It is a terrible shock to us all – we were so happy about him . . . he seemed to have quite recovered from his terrible illness, but he sought his own death.'[9] She added that he had gone to Mass on the Sunday morning, and had apparently drowned himself on the same evening. Frances was quite naturally devastated, but there are inconsistencies in her account. Despite claims by previous biographers,[10] there is nothing to suggest that Frances hurried from Lowestoft to attend the inquest, so her insistence that Knollys had heard Mass on the day he died, a detail which did not emerge at the inquest, is somewhat strange, the last reported sighting of Knollys having been by Henry Lomas at 6.00 pm on August 15th. It is, of course, possible that Oldershaw had learnt something at Westdean, but why was this later sighting not revealed to the inquest? Again, it is possible that Oldershaw was trying to comfort Frances in her distress, but would he have gone so far as to hide the real cause of death? Her distress was indeed extreme, for now Frances had lost both a sister and a brother. As ever, she fell into a deep depression which lasted for well over a year, for Gilbert in turn wrote to Father O'Connor (Postmark: July 3rd, 1909) cancelling a proposed visit to Heckmondwike: 'I would not write this to anyone else . . . I don't mind suggesting the truth to you. Frances has just come out of what looked bad enough to be an illness, and is just going to plunge into one of her recurrent problems of pain and depression. The two may be just a bit too much for her and I want to be with her every night for a few days – there's an Irish Bull for you!'[11] What had looked bad enough to be an illness was particularly horrifying for Gilbert, for Frances in her grief had been seeking the comfort offered through a spiritualist medium, just the sort of practice against which he had reacted so strongly in the 1890s. His bitter disapproval springs forth from every line of the poem he wrote after finding her consulting spirits through a crystal ball:

THE CRYSTAL

I saw it; she lay as one in dreams,
    And round that holy hair, round and beyond
My Frances, my inviolable, screamed
    The scandal of the dead men's demi-monde.

Close to that face, a window into heaven,
    Close to the hair's brown surf of broken waves
I saw the idiot face of the ghosts
    That are the fungus, not the flower, of graves.

You whom the pinewoods robed in sun and shade,
　　You who were sceptred with thistle's bloom,
God's thunder! What have you to do with these
　　The lying crystal and the darkened room?

Leave the weird queens that find the sun too strong
　　To mope and cower beneath Druidic trees,
The still, sweet gardens of the dastard's dream.
　　God's thunder! What have you to do with these?

Low fields and shining lie in crystal land,
　　Peace and strange pleasure: wonder-lands untrod,
But not plain words, nor love of open things,
　　Truth, nor strong laughter, nor the fear of God.

I will not look: I am a child of earth,
　　I see the sun and wood, the sea, and grass.
I only saw one spirit. She is there
　　Staring for spirits in a lump of glass.

The remedy for Frances' morbidity was to accede to a wish she had made many times before: to leave London. Ada thought she knew the reason:

'She hated Fleet Street with an ice-cold detachment, unmitigated by her husband's meteoric journalistic success or the unstinted praise which applauded his work, or even the considerable income he made by it.

　　It is a world, I admit, full of irritation and disappointment to the average housewife. Hours are erratic, leisure uncertain, and whereas the business man leaves his home at a stated time and usually returns to schedule, the journalist is inevitably irregular and unpunctual. But it was not irregularity alone which affronted Frances. The whole atmosphere of the Street was alien to her. The bars and wine shops, the desultory meetings, queer associates, the perpetual, never-ending talk – why the sea is boiling hot, or whether pigs have wings – the impecuniosity, extravagance, strange championships, wild crusades: all the mean and shabby, the generous and immortal things that make up the Fleet Street world . . . Newspapers did not interest her, and this not because of their particular shade of politics. Frances disliked the press as such, and really only cared for small journals and parish magazines to which she contributed her quite charming verse. But she had literally no use for any of the dailies, and would, I think, have preferred to hear of world events through the medium of the town crier rather than read about them in cold print.'[12]

That judgement had earlier been confirmed by Frances herself: 'If I have a horror greater than any other, it is that I might be persuaded to publish

something . . . I loathe print. Perhaps I have too much of it, but it is a dangerous business always. "May the Cross of Christ be between me and harm," as
Elodie Belloc expresses it."[13]

And so it was that by the autumn of 1909 the Chestertons had upped sticks
and moved to Beaconsfield to Overroads on the corner of Station Road and
Grove Road, a none too large house into which they were to cram not only
themselves, their servants, but also many of Frances' relations, for Frances
had a multiplicity of cousins, among whom were the Braybrookes, with the
inevitable result that responsibility for the school fees of the children, as ever,
fell upon Gilbert. One boy, Michael Knollys Braybrooke, was to spend all his
weekends and vacations at Overroads until he was old enough in 1917 to leave
St. Paul's School and to join the Royal Naval Air Service in the First World
War, and after the Armistice, GKC continued to pay the costs of him attending
medical school. Michael often appears in photographs taken at the time and is
featured in *The Ballade of the Three Michaels*:

> On one tall crag in Normandy
>     A mighty church sits like a toy;
> You'll find there cider and the sea
>     And walls unscaleable as Troy.
> And omelettes that you'll enjoy
>     Until you call for the account,
> But do not let such things annoy;
>     For this is Michael on the Mount.
>
> Where England sinks south-westerly
>     Her last cliffs draggle and deploy;
> One cliff stands lonely as a tree,
>     Begirt by herring-boat and hoy,
> Lone as a fortress for Rob Roy
>     (But don't let my description count –
> I never saw it . . . I am coy . . .)
>     For this is Michael on the Mount.
>
> Norman and Cornish coast we flee
>     To find the scenes that never cloy;
> Only in BEACONSFIELD can be
>     The perfect glimpse of human joy:
> There is a bike. There is a boy
>     That vaults it like a catamount
> – No other sights your soul decoy –
>     For this is Michael on the Mount.

Envoy
Prince, though his wheels your roads destroy,
    Though mud spout upward like a fount,
Cry 'Yip! Yaddy! Yoicks! Ahoy!'
    For this is Michael on the Mount.

Gilbert obviously delighted in somewhat rowdy high spirits and seems to have
had a ready empathy with all young people, unlike Frances who, although she
adored babies, was not always comfortable in the company of teenagers.

# 7.

## TOWARDS A SLOVENLY AUTOBIOGRAPHY

It was not as a poet nor a novelist that Chesterton launched his journalistic career but as an essayist and a book reviewer, trades that were to provide the mainstay of his income throughout his lifetime. He had started regular work for *The Speaker* in April 1900 with his articles in *The Daily News* then appearing from January 1901 (his own by-line starting on May 31, 1901),[1] so Chesterton had had hardly more than eighteen months to establish himself as a literary critic when in December 1901 John Morley, General Editor of Macmillan's *English Men of Letters* series, offered him the chance to write a volume on Robert Browning. Chesterton accepted with alacrity, then decided that he had better head for the British Museum Library to read up his subject. At the time he was being paid by the piece, so when he decided to suspend his work for *The Daily News* from February until July 1902 he had nothing to rely on save his articles for *The Speaker* together with royalties from collected essays published as *The Defendant* in December 1901. It is from this period that we have stories of a hungry GKC drawing sketches of himself starving to elicit financial contributions from acquaintances in the British Museum Reading Room; it has been presumed that this was an hilarious instance of GKC leaving his purse at home, but there is a fair chance that the need was real. Once the back of the work had been broken by July he could resume his regular articles and the income that went with them. Now the proofs went to Macmillans where Chesterton's habit of quoting from memory caused consternation as the instances of misquotations and even invented lines multiplied; Stephen Gwynn who had recommended Chesterton in the first place, found the senior partner in a white fury: 'I wrote to Chesterton saying that the firm thought that the book was going to disgrace them. His reply was like the trumpeting of a crushed elephant. But the book was a huge success.'[2] When the book did appear in May 1903 it was well received:

> Mr Chesterton has done his work admirably, and has produced a really charming and delightful little volume.
>
> Henry Murray, *The Sunday Sun*, May 31st, 1903.

> Though the experiment of entrusting the 'English Men of Letters' monograph on Robert Browning to a young writer of such quaint originality and such recently acquired distinction was undoubtedly a bold one, the result has justified Mr John Morley's editorial courage and perspicacity . . . Mr Chesterton's essay is an able achievement, and one that must still further enhance his growing literary and critical reputation.
>
> *World*, June 2nd, 1903.

> This new volume of the 'English Men of Letters' is one of the most refreshing in that admirable series. It is a gay, confident, common-sense, extravagant, thoughtful, and diffuse apology for Browning; not a work of art, but something like the talk of an honest, generous, and combative man who discusses every point with an imaginary opponent.
>
> *The Athenaeum*, June 13th, 1903.

> There have been some misfits in the new series of 'English Men of Letters,' but Mr Chesterton's brilliant essay on Browning is not one of them. It was a delicate feat of imaginative wit on the part of Mr John Morley to choose him for this task, not only because he brings out the best in Browning, but also because Browning brings out the best in him.
>
> James Douglas, *The Bookman*, July 1903.

> This little book may be called the first definite pronouncement of the twentieth century upon the man, the poet and the thinker Robert Browning. It is wonderfully fresh, recalling in its vividness, its buoyancy, its gaiety and assurance, its alert play of mind the exuberant youth of Browning himself.
>
> *Manchester Guardian*, August 12th, 1903.

> [A] strong, live piece of work, a study of Browning that will rank high among the many studies that have been written.
>
> *Westminster Gazette*, September 15th, 1903.

His reputation considerably enhanced, Chesterton was now courted by *The Bystander, Pall Mall Gazette, The Fortnightly Review*, and many others; the world and the ball at his feet he could offer work without fear of rejection.

However, not every path opened smoothly before him, for John J. Sullivan's unpublished notes to his *Chesterton Bibliography* (1958) indicate a plan to publish *The Napoleon of Notting Hill* with 48 illustrations by the author under the Elkin Mathews imprint in 1902. Correspondence between Percy Muir of Elkin Mathews and Ben Abramson of Argus Books Inc. of New York refers to a threatened lawsuit on the grounds that copyright in Chesterton's sketches (catalogued as illustrations to the book even though they were never to appear in it) had been assigned to the plaintiff. Abramson offered to repurchase the drawings, but nothing further appears to have transpired. How the rights to the drawings came to be sold in the USA is unclear, but Chesterton is known to have sold work outright in the early years of his career. If true, this incident explains the mystery of why Chesterton, trained and working as a book illustrator, gave way to W. Graham Robertson for his own book. It may also give an indication as to why GKC's sketches[3] were not used for *The Ball and the Cross* and *The Man Who Was Thursday*. *The Man With Two Legs* and *The Adventurous Abbot Stephen* may also have disappeared into oblivion over the Atlantic. A highly variant contents list does suggest that the text of *The Napoleon of Notting Hill* might have been rewritten so no copyright was being infringed when the book finally appeared in March 1904:

**Earlier Version**

Prologue. Campden Hill

Book I.    Chapter 1. The Street of a Century
           Chapter 2. The Lost Patriot
           Chapter 3. Nonsense
           Chapter 4. The Coronation of King Auberon

Book II.   Chapter 1. An Episode of Notting Hill
           Chapter 2. The Charter of the Cities
           Chapter 3. The Problem of Pump Street
           Chapter 4. Enter a Lunatic

Book III.  Chapter 1. The Origin of Adam Wayne
           Chapter 2. Four Shops
           Chapter 3. Mark Turnbull
           Chapter 4. How the King's Champagne bottle was upset

Book IV.   Chapter 1. At the Office of the Court Journal
           Chapter 2. The Battle of the Lamps

Chapter 3. The Battle of the Tower
Chapter 3. (sic) The Office of the Court Journal

Book V.  Chapter 1. The New Songs
         Chapter 2. The Revolt
         Chapter 3. The Last Battle
         Chapter 4. Voices in the Dark

**1904 Version**

Book I.   Chapter 1. Introductory Remarks on the art of Prophecy
          Chapter 2. The Man in Green
          Chapter 3. The Hill of Humour

Book II.  Chapter 1. The Charter of the Cities
          Chapter 2. The Council of the Provosts
          Chapter 3. Enter a Lunatic

Book III. Chapter 1. The Mental Condition of Adam Wayne
          Chapter 2. The Remarkable Mr Turnbull
          Chapter 3. The Experiment of Mr Buck

Book IV.  Chapter 1. The Battle of the Lamps
          Chapter 2. The Correspondent of the Court Journal
          Chapter 3. The Great Army of South Kensington

Book V.   Chapter 1. The Empire of Notting Hill
          Chapter 2. The Last Battle
          Chapter 3. Two Voices

## Chesterton's debut in print as a novelist was fairly well-received:

It is impossible not to feel that the best tribute to this book would be to persuade some of those enthusiasts who have lately revived ancient dances to go to Mr Chesterton's house and there elaborate some intricate measure as an appreciative homage . . . For, in this novel GKC has found himself. The form of fiction gives free scope to the fantastic in his art; while the reader is wooed to pay more attention to old truths in new guise than when they are presented in the more personal form of the essay, by which Mr Chesterton has hitherto been chiefly known. To begin with, the workmanship of the book is far better than we should have expected from an author of Mr Chesterton's exuberant fancy and headlong turn for ideas; as a story it is far better than most stories of the future, which in form it challenges . . . Mr Chesterton shows himself a master of that most difficult of arts, plain, elemental tale-telling.

*Pall Mall Gazette*, March 22nd, 1904.

If the test of the success of any book is the pleasure it gives in the reading, this first novel[4] of Mr Chesterton must be pronounced a veritable triumph.

C.F.G. Masterman, *The Daily News*, March 22nd, 1904.

Mr Gilbert Chesterton has done a wonderful thing; out of the dull drab ore of modernity he has struck a new vein of romance. There is much else no doubt in this book of his; it may be called a farcical fantasy, a burlesque forecast, a nonsensical satire, a preposterous joke, and quite rightly, for it is all of these. But after all its essence, that without which not even its perpetual stream of audacious humour could keep it fresh and attractive, is its discovering the old beauty of the strange, the picturesque and the romantic in a sphere that might have seemed depressing and unpromisingly new and tame.

F.G. Bettany, *The Sunday Times*, March 27th, 1904.

[S]imple people, like the insignificant person who writes this article, have, at last, found something of Mr Chesterton's that they can unreservedly admire. For he has done what few men dare do, he has got on top of his imagination, and let it carry him whithersoever it happened to will. The result is the simplest, sanest and most stimulating book that has appeared for ages.

Arthur Ransome, *The Week's Survey*, May 7th, 1904.

But not everyone was so enraptured:

I have read *The Napoleon of Notting Hill*, and I am bound to say that I do not know what it means and that I find it all very foolish and irritating. I think that it is just a straining after effect of a writer trying to be funny, possessed but of a moderate amount of humour, and a great capacity for being tiresome. I know that my judgement must be wrong on this as on other books he has produced. The 'Life of Browning' was pronounced by some of the leading critics of the day – some for whose judgement I have the very greatest respect – the very best biography . . . So far from being the best, I thought it the worst book in the series in which it appeared. The same impression was made upon me by the volume of essays called *Twelve Types*. Here were papers on Byron, Charlotte Brontë, Pope and other literary subjects, all of them lacking, in my judgement, any salient idea and containing nothing that had not been better said before. There were people in the days when Charles Dickens was writing who did not realise how great he was; they wrote all the spiteful things about him that . . . I am now writing about Mr Chesterton, and they were wrong. Perhaps I am equally wrong, but I do not think so. I have said that I do not think Mr Chesterton has the faintest talent either as a novelist, a literary critic. or a literary biographer, but I do credit him with a talent in the direction of art . . . Mr Chesterton's *Watts* seems to be a very clever book, written with genuine sympathy.

C.K. Shorter, *The Sphere*, April 9th, 1904.

Cecil Chesterton, writing in *Vanity Fair* on April 7th 1904, lets us into his insider knowledge with 'Take the confident suggestion that Mr Chesterton, whose tale deals with a time a century hence, is "satirising" the copious crop of novels about the future that we have today. The fact is that this story was cast and, in essence, completed before Mr H.G. Wells (say) had published his first story, and years before the boom in social futures began . . . Its introductory chapter . . . is a dozen years younger than the book itself.'

What the favourable reception of Chesterton's *Browning* had done was to make him a saleable prospect in the publishing world, so that he was able to put forward the material he had been unable to place over the last several years. The first fruit of this development was the appearance of a series of stories that had been doing the rounds of publishers since the mid-1890s; revamped as *The Club of Queer Trades* six of them were serialised from December 1903 in the American *Harper's Weekly* followed a little later in Britain in *The Idler*,[5] and then collected for publication in book form in both countries in 1905. Chesterton had much to hand beside *The Napoleon of Notting Hill, The Ball and the Cross,* and *The Man Who Was Thursday*, and it would be put to use over many years. However, he also had the articles and reviews he was publishing weekly in *The Speaker,* the *Daily News* and from 1905 on in *The Illustrated London News*, and some of these were now revised for inclusion in *Heretics*, a volume dedicated to his father, which showed that Gilbert Chesterton was prepared to stand apart in opinion from most of his contemporaries. Early in 1903 Chesterton had reacted against the influence that one of his heroes, Robert 'Nunquam' Blatchford (1851–1943), had exercised over him since he had read Blatchford's articles on socialism in *The Clarion* (later in 1893 collected in book form as *Merrie England*). Blatchford now in 1903, after an enthusiastic review of Ernst Haeckel's *Riddle of the Universe*, invited Christians to respond. Chesterton did indeed respond in the *Daily News*, thus beginning a bruising exchange of views spread over two years which GKC was later to describe in his *Autobiography* as 'a landmark in my life', at the end of which he had more or less defined his religious position as Christian Socialist and Anglo-Catholic by indicating with what and with whom he was in profound disagreement, in other words whom he considered heretics and whom orthodox:

> Nothing more strangely indicates an enormous and silent evil of modern society than the extraordinary use which is made nowadays of the word 'orthodox'. In former days the heretic was proud of not being a heretic. It was the kingdoms of the world and the police and the judges who were heretics. He was orthodox. He had no pride in having rebelled against them; they had rebelled against him. The armies with their cruel security, the kings with their cold faces, the decorous processes of the state, the

reasonable processes of the law – all these like sheep had gone astray. The man was proud of being orthodox, was proud of being right. If he stood alone in a howling wilderness he was more than a man; he was a church. He was the centre of the universe; it was round him that the stars swung. All the torture torn out of forgotten hells could not make him admit that he was heretical. But a few modern phrases have made him boast of it. He says, with a conscious laugh, 'I suppose I am very heretical', and looks round for applause. The word 'heresy' not only means no longer being wrong; it practically means being clear-headed and courageous. The word 'orthodoxy' not only no longer means being right; it practically means being wrong. All this can mean one thing and one thing only. It means that people care less for whether they are philosophically right. For obviously a man ought to confess himself crazy before he confesses himself heretical. The Bohemian, with a red tie, ought to pique himself on his orthodoxy. The dynamiter, laying a bomb, ought to feel that, whatever else he is, at least he is orthodox.

It is foolish, generally speaking, for a philosopher to set fire to another philosopher in Smithfield Market because they do not agree in their theory of the universe. That was done very frequently in the last decadence of the Middle Ages, and it failed altogether in its object. But there is one thing that is infinitely more absurd and unpractical than burning a man for his philosophy. That is saying that his philosophy does not matter, and this is done universally in the twentieth century, in the decadence of the great revolutionary period. General theories are everywhere contemned; the doctrine of the Rights of Man is dismissed with the doctrine of the Fall of Man. Atheism is too theological for us to-day. Revolution itself is too much of a system; liberty itself is too much of a restraint. We will have no generalisations. Mr Bernard Shaw has put the view in a perfect epigram: 'The golden rule is that there is no golden rule.' We are more and more to discuss details in art, politics, literature. A man's opinion on tramcars matters; his opinion on Botticelli matters; his opinion on all things does not matter. He may turn over and explore a million objects, but he must not find that strange object, the universe; for if he does he will have a religion, and be lost. Everything matters – except everything.

Examples are scarcely needed of this total levity on the subject of cosmic philosophy. Examples are scarcely needed to show that, whatever else we think of as affecting practical affairs, we do not think it matters whether a man is a pessimist or an optimist, a Cartesian or a Hegelian, a materialist or a spiritualist. Let me, however, take a random instance. At any innocent tea-table we may easily hear a man say, 'Life is not worth living.' We regard it as we regard the statement that it is a fine day; nobody thinks that it can possibly have any serious effect on the man or on the world. And yet if that utterance were really believed, the world would stand on its head. Murderers would be given medals for saving men from life; firemen would be denounced for keeping men from death; poisons would be used as medicines; doctors would be called in when people were well; the Royal Humane Society would be rooted out like a horde of assassins. Yet we never speculate as to whether the conversationalist pessimist will strengthen or disorganise society; for we are convinced that theories do not matter.

That was certainly not the idea of those who introduced our freedom. When the old Liberals removed the gags from all the heresies, their idea was that religious and philosophical discoveries might thus be made. Their view was that cosmic truth was so important that everyone ought to bear independent testimony. The modern idea is that cosmic truth is so unimportant that it cannot matter what anyone says. The former freed inquiry as men loose a noble hound; the latter frees inquiry as men fling back into the sea a fish unfit for eating. Never has there been so little discussion about the nature of men as now, when, for the first time, anyone can discuss it. The old restriction meant that only the orthodox were allowed to discuss religion. Modern liberty means that nobody is allowed to discuss it. Good taste, the last and vilest of human superstitions, has succeeded in silencing us here where all the rest have failed. Sixty years ago it was bad taste to be an avowed atheist. Then came the Bradlaughites, the last religious men, the last men who cared about God; but they could not alter it. It is still bad taste to be an avowed atheist. But their agony has achieved just this – that now it is equally bad taste to be an avowed Christian. Emancipation has only locked the saint in the same tower of silence as the heresiarch. Then we talk about Lord Anglesey and the weather, and call it the complete liberty of all the creeds.

But there are some people, nevertheless – and I am one of them – who think that the most practical and important thing about a man is still his view of the universe. We think that for a landlady considering a lodger, it is important to know his income, but still more important to know his philosophy. We think that for a general about to fight an enemy, it is important to know the enemy's numbers, but still more important to know the enemy's philosophy. We think the question is not whether the theory of the cosmos affects matters, but whether, in the long run, anything else affects them. In the fifteenth century men cross-examined and tormented a man because he preached some immoral attitude; in the nineteenth century we feted and flattered Oscar Wilde because he preached such an attitude, and then broke his heart in penal servitude because he carried it out. It may be a question which of the two methods was the more cruel; there can be no kind of question which was the more ludicrous. The age of the inquisition has not at least the disgrace of having produced a society which made an idol of the very same man for preaching the very same things which it made him a convict for practising.

Now, in our time, philosophy or religion, our theory, that is, about ultimate things, has been driven out, more or less simultaneously, from two fields which it used to occupy. General ideals used to dominate literature. They have been driven out by the cry of 'art for art's sake.' General ideals used to dominate politics. They have been driven out by the cry of 'efficiency,' which may be roughly translated as 'politics for politics' sake.' Persistently for the last twenty years the ideals of order or liberty have dwindled in our books; the ambitions of wit and eloquence have dwindled in our parliaments. Literature has purposely become less political; politics have purposely become less literary. General theories of the relations of things have thus been extruded from both; and we are in a position to ask, 'What have we gained or lost by this extrusion? Is literature better, is politics better, for having discarded the moralist and the philosopher?'

When everything about a people is for the time growing weak and ineffective, it begins to talk about efficiency. So it is that when a man's body is a wreck he begins, for the first time, to talk about health. Vigorous organisms talk not about their processes, but about their aims. There cannot be a better proof of the physical efficiency of a man than that he talks cheerfully of a journey to the end of the world. And there cannot be a better proof of the practical efficiency of a nation than that it talks constantly of a journey to the end of the world, a journey to the Judgement Day and the New Jerusalem. There can be no stronger sign of a coarse material health than the tendency to run after high and wild ideals; it is the first exuberance of infancy that we cry for the moon. None of the strong men in the strong ages would have understood what you meant by working for efficiency. Hildebrand would have said that he was working not for efficiency, but for the Catholic Church. Danton would have said that he was working not for efficiency, but for liberty, equality, and fraternity. Even if the ideal of such men were simply the ideal of kicking a man downstairs, they thought of the end like men, not of the process like paralytics. They did not say, 'Efficiently elevating my right leg, using, you will notice, the muscles of the thigh and calf, which are in excellent order, I—' Their feeling was quite different. They were so filled with a beautiful vision of a man lying flat at the foot of the staircase that in that ecstasy the rest followed in a flash. In practice, the habit of generalizing and idealizing did not by any means mean worldly weakness. The time of the big theories was the time of big results. In the era of sentiment and fine words, at the end of the eighteenth century, men were really robust and effective. The sentimentalists conquered Napoleon. The cynics could not catch De Wet. A hundred years ago our affairs for good or evil were wielded triumphantly by rhetoricians. Now our affairs are hopelessly muddled by strong, silent men. And just as this repudiation of big words and big visions has brought forth a race of small men in politics, so it has brought forth a race of small men in the arts. Our modern politicians claim the colossal licence of Caesar and the Superman, claim that they are too practical to be pure and too patriotic to be moral; but the upshot of it all is that a mediocrity [Charles Thomson Ritchie] is Chancellor of the Exchequer. Our new artistic philosophers call for the same moral licence, for a freedom to wreck heaven and earth with their energy; but the upshot of it all is that a mediocrity [Alfred Austin] is Poet Laureate. I do not say that there are no stronger men than these; but will anyone say that there are any men stronger than those men of old who were dominated by their philosophy and steeped in their religion? Whether bondage be better than freedom may be discussed. But that their bondage came to more than our freedom it will be difficult to deny.

The theory of the unmorality of art has established itself firmly in the strictly artistic classes. They are free to produce anything they like. They are free to write a *Paradise Lost* in which Satan shall conquer God. They are free to write a *Divine Comedy* in which heaven shall be under the floor of hell. And what have they done? Have they produced in their universality anything grander or more beautiful than the things uttered by the fierce Ghibbeline Catholic, by the rigid Puritan schoolmaster? We know that they have produced only a few roundels. Milton does not merely beat them by his piety, he beats them at their own irreverence. In all their little books of verse you will not find a finer defiance of God than Satan's. Nor will you find the grandeur of paganism felt as that fiery christian felt it who described Faranata lifting his head as in disdain of hell. And the reason is very obvious, blasphemy is an artistic effect, because blasphemy depends upon a philosophical conviction. Blasphemy depends upon belief, and is fading with it. If anyone doubts, let him sit down seriously and try to think blasphemous thoughts about Thor. I think his family will find him at the end of the day in a state of some exhaustion.

Neither in the world of politics nor that of literature, then, has the rejection of general theories proved a success. It may be that there have been many moonstruck and misleading ideals that have from time to time perplexed mankind. But assuredly there has been no ideal in practice so moon struck and misleading as the ideal of practicality. Nothing has lost so many opportunities as the opportunism of Lord Rosebery. He is, indeed, a standing symbol of this epoch – the man who is theoretically a practical man, and practically more unpractical than any theorist. Nothing in this universe is so unwise as that kind of worship of worldly wisdom. A man who is perpetually thinking of whether this race or that race is strong, of whether this cause or that cause is promising, is the man who will never believe in anything long enough to make it succeed. The opportunist politician is like a man who should abandon billiards because he was beaten at billiards, and abandon golf because he was beaten at golf. There is nothing which is so weak for working purposes as this enormous importance attached to immediate victory. There is nothing that fails like success.

And having discovered that opportunism does fail, I have been induced to look at it more largely, and in consequence to see that it must fail. I perceive that it is far more practical to begin at the beginning and discuss theories. I see that the men who killed each other about the orthodoxy of the Homoousian[6] were far more sensible than the people who were quarrelling about the Education Act. For the Christian dogmatists were trying to establish a reign of holiness, and trying to get defined, first of all what was really holy. But our modern educationists are trying to bring about a religious liberty without attempting to settle what is religion and what is liberty. If the old priests forced a statement on mankind, at least they took some trouble to make it lucid. And it has been left for the modern mobs of Anglicans and Nonconformists to persecute for a doctrine without even stating it.

For these reasons, and for many more, I for one have come to believe in going back to fundamentals . . . I wish to deal with my most distinguished contemporaries, not personally or in a merely literary manner, but in relation to the real body of doctrine which they teach. I am not concerned with Mr Rudyard Kipling as a vivid artist or a vigorous personality; I am concerned with him as a Heretic – that is to say, a man whose view of things has the hardihood to differ from mine. I am not concerned with Mr Bernard Shaw as one of the most brilliant and one of the most honest men alive; I am concerned with him as a Heretic – that is to say, a man whose philosophy is quite solid, quite coherent, and quite wrong. I revert to the doctrinal methods of the thirteenth century, inspired by the general hope of getting something done.

Suppose that a great commotion arises in the street about something, let us say a lamp-post, which many influential persons desire to pull down. A grey-clad monk, who is the spirit of the Middle Ages, is approached upon the matter, and begins to say, in the arid manner of the Schoolmen, 'Let us first consider, my brethren, the value of light. If light be itself good –' At this point he is somewhat excusably knocked down. All the people make a rush for the lamp-post, the lamp-post is down in ten minutes, and they

go about congratulating each other on their unmediaeval practicality. But as things go
on they do not work out so easily. Some people have pulled the lamp-post down because
they wanted the electric light; some because they wanted old iron; some because they
wanted darkness, because their deeds were evil. Some thought it not enough of a lamp-
post, some too much; some acted because they wanted to smash municipal machinery;
some because they wanted to smash something. And there is war in the night, no man
knowing whom he strikes. So gradually and inevitably, to-day, to-morrow, or the next
day, there comes back the conviction that the monk was right after all, and all depends
on what is the philosophy of Light. Only what we might have discussed under the gas-
lamp, we now must discuss in the dark.

Heretics, London (Bodley Head) 1905, pp. 3 seq.

This book of essays was an immediate *succès de scandale* to further boost
his burgeoning career:

One must preface any remarks one has to make upon Mr Gilbert Chesterton with
admission that he is the most nimble-witted, the most brilliant, the most irresponsible
journalist of his years now writing in England. One must praise him for all that he is.
One can only blame him because, being what he is, he is not half-a-dozen times better.
In *Heretics*, his latest volume of essays, he is constantly girding at the artists and literary
men, and declaring that in literature, as such, he has very little interest. The result of
his heretical attitude is clearly seen in Mr Chesterton's own work . . . he jumps rapidly
to theories, and afterwards sets to thinking how best to make facts square with them.
In other words he is a casuist – a casuist, if such a thing be possible, on the side of the
angels. If he would only take the trouble to be a literary artist as well, what a boon
he would be to contemporary letters. Mr Chesterton, like Mr Kipling seems to me to
belong to the school of the ultra-decadents. They are the last fruits of the neurotic school
of poets and prose-writers who, from the Bodley Head, echoed the general despair of
nervous people at the close of the nineteenth century. Oscar Wilde and the aesthetic
decadents worshipped abnormal things, logically enough, because they thought that
abnormal things alone were worthy to be worshipped. Mr Kipling, Mr Chesterton,
and the unaesthetic decadents have extended the definition of the abnormal so as to
include the normal, and consequently have based their work on what I hold to be an
eternal, artistic, and philosophic falsehood. 'I found nought common on Thy earth' is
Mr Kipling's unashamed confession to his Maker; and Mr Chesterton, with as few signs
of blushing, declares that 'there is no such thing on earth as an uninteresting subject.'
The eye that can see nothing common or uninteresting in the world will, I fear, be hard
put to it to discover what is passionately interesting, what is goldenly rare . . . If one
wastes the limited number of one's raptures on lamp-posts and motor-cars and Crystal
Palace fireworks, one will find oneself without any to spare for God and the stars of
harvest and seas restless in moonlight.

(R.W.L.: 'The Ultra-Decadent', Black and White, July 8th, 1905).

The interest of this book lies in the judgements it contains – of a distinctly yet sympathetic and informed mind – on such men as Mr Rudyard Kipling, Mr Bernard Shaw, Mr H.G. Wells, Mr George Moore and Whistler, and on the literary or political cults they represent. The 'smart' novelists and the 'slum' novelists, the 'yellow' journalists and the Celtophiles, the aesthetes and the lovers of the simple life are treated with unfailing humour and insight. Mr Chesterton is as convinced and consistent as ever. He is consistent, of course, in the sense – the only intelligible sense – that all his conclusions come naturally out of a fundamental philosophy. And indeed, the whole book is based on the theory that the only thing about a man that really matters is his philosophy of life, his attitude to the cosmos.

(*Literary World*, July 1905).

Of course, anyone who has read much of Mr Chesterton's work knows that he cannot speak in any other manner than by paradox: he sees everything from a different point of view to most people: he says that home-life is a broad experience and that an excursion into your neighbour's garden is more prolific of adventure than a voyage round the world. He goes in for the 'Great Fundamentals'; and his blind critics, seeing only so far as their narrow judgment will permit, do not read the philosophy underlying all the paradoxical phraseology. There is quite a tirade against Humbug (Carlyle's bugbear) to be discovered by a discerning eye or an inquiring mind, and a whole world of experience of the human character is displayed beneath Mr Chesterton's disapproval of artistic or literary methods. 'Heretics' is decidedly a good book, but it will in no way appeal to the thoughtless, because it is a collection of essays written by a man with a thinking brain for men and women of intelligence.

(*Yorkshire Herald*, July 21st, 1905).

Bracing is the right word to apply to this book. It comes like a gale of wind into a stuffy room. Mr Chesterton is in a chronic state of mental uproar. He plunges about among the furniture, dancing in his glee, turning the chairs and tables upside down, flinging any piece of crockery out of the window which he happens to consider superfluous or in bad taste . . . He should remember before it is too late that this inversion of common platitudes is really an invention of those decadents whom he handles with such severity . . . [that] there is a moment when constant repetition causes it to jar, and at that moment the reader may get annoyed and tell Mr Chesterton that he has found him out. This would be a great mistake, for Mr Chesterton is really hard to find out. His inverted platitudes generally lead up to a thought which is deep and delicate and charmingly expressed. But in writing, as in all other arts, it is of great importance not to repeat the same effect too often.

(*Books of Today*, July 1905).

In 'Heretics' Mr Chesterton says many things that needed to be said. What we wish is that we could escape from the feeling that all the time we are looking at a troupe of performing truths. They come before us, we feel, not because they are truths, but because they can perform. In all the book contains twenty essays, each one brilliant, epigrammatic – in a word, Chestertonian. Yet there is something wanting, a something which only added, would give to Mr Chesterton that place which long ago we had expected him to fill. And that something is dignity.

(F.W. Elias, 'A Lack of Dignity', *The Bookman*, July 1905).

In 1904 Chesterton's growing reputation was such that he was approached by Sir Oliver Lodge (1851–1940) inviting him to submit an application for the inaugural Chair of English Literature in the University of Birmingham. GKC's ambitions did not lie in that direction (no doubt Knollys' illness was also a distraction) so he failed to respond; the Chair went to John Churton Collins (1848–1908) already dubbed by Tennyson 'a louse on the locks of literature'. Oddly enough, Chesterton was indeed immersing himself in literary criticism, this time in Charles Dickens as a mythologist and chronicler of the grotesqueness of the poorer classes, a truly popular writer in the sense that Dickens wrote about the people: 'He called to the people. He was popular in a sense of which we moderns have not even a notion. In that sense there is no popularity now . . . The old popularity was positive; the new is negative. There is a great deal of difference between the eager man who wants to read a book, and the tired man who wants a book to read. A man reading a Le Queux mystery wants to get to the end of it. A man reading the Dickens novel wished that it might never end . . . In short, the Dickens novel was popular, not because it was an unreal world, but because it was a real world; a world in which the soul could live.'[7] The book was generally well received and, if anything, its reputation has grown over the years:

> As a critic, Mr Chesterton has never sparkled better, or to more purpose. Naturally, no other Dickens devotee will agree with all he says. Does he always agree with himself? But then towards the end he half admits that he has been attempting the impossible, since criticism of genuine creation is so immensely difficult . . . The obvious defects of Dickens, and some that do not hit every reader in the eye, are fairly dwelt upon. But he holds at last that Dickens is like to be our one enduring nineteenth-century novelist. He created and his creations do not depend upon fidelity to a passing period.
>
> *Pall Mall Gazette*, August 30th, 1906.

> Mr Chesterton's monograph on Browning was one of the most stimulating books of its kind written within recent years . . . [I]f only because of its treatment of the matrimonial crisis in Browning's life, it commands the respect of even the most profound student of the poet. Mr Chesterton's latest book shows a great advance on its predecessor . . . In this study of Dickens he gives us of his best. It may be the line of Dickens' development from a precocious childhood of admiration in the family circle, through a slough of despond, to a maturity in the sunshine of popular applause; and in the result we have a vivid picture of the man as well as the novelist . . . This study of Dickens marks

the definitive entry of its author into the serious walks of literature. Henceforth Mr Chesterton must be taken seriously as a critic who achieves most because he can do his work laughingly, with a bright face and a cheery outlook. He is creative as well as critical. Wherefore he is helpful where most critics fail to do aught but weaken or crush the creative instinct in others.

Public Opinion, September 7th, 1906.

A book about Dickens is like a book about the Bible. It is almost impossible to say anything new about either . . . But one kind of critic Dickens has hitherto lacked, the critic as humorist . . . Far be it from me to belittle the genius of Dickens. I will even accept without demur Mr Chesterton's prediction that, as time goes on, Dickens' place as a novelist in nineteenth century England will not only be high, but altogether the highest. At the same time, I think Mr Chesterton is uncritical in weighing Dickens against Scott and Thackeray and Charlotte Brontë. They are not only not in the same genus, they are not in the same species . . . It is impossible to describe the riotous humour which Mr Chesterton has poured into this book. Dickens, he says, makes the flesh creep; he does not, like the decadents, make the flesh crawl. This is so witty that it would be stupid to point out that Dickens does not make the flesh creep . . . In his use of illuminating metaphor Mr Chesterton is as brilliant as ever, as in this retort to those who charged Dickens with plagiarism: 'To claim to have originated an idea in Dickens is like claiming to have contributed a glass of water to Niagara.' This book swarms with these good things, one of the best being the remark that Dickens had 'the key of the street.' It is this ability to make poleaxe judgements that links Mr Chesterton with Dr Johnson. You can easily smash a fallacy, but you cannot so easily smash a graven image. Mr Chesterton's graven images stand a good deal of battering.

James Douglas, The Throne, September 8th, 1906.

His book on Dickens seems to me to be the best essay on that author that has ever been written.

T.S. Eliot, The Tablet, June 20th, 1936.

Chesterton's views as expressed in *Heretics* were challenged so they were followed up within three years with further explanation:

When some time ago I published a series of hasty but sincere papers, under the name of 'Heretics,' several critics for whose intellect I have a warm respect (I may mention specially Mr G.S. Street) said it was all very well for me to tell everybody to affirm his cosmic theory, but that I had carefully avoided supporting my precepts with example. 'I will begin to worry about my philosophy,' said Mr Street, 'when Mr Chesterton has given us his.' It was perhaps an incautious suggestion to make to a person only too ready to write books upon the feeblest provocation. But after all, though Mr Street has inspired and created this book [*Orthodoxy*], he need not read it. If he does read it, he will find that in its pages I have attempted in a vague and personal way, in a set of mental pictures rather than in a series of deductions, to state the philosophy in which I have come to believe. I will not call it my philosophy; for I did not make it. God and humanity made it; and it made me.

I have often had a fancy for writing a romance about an English yachtsman who slightly miscalculated his course and discovered England under the impression that it was a new island in the South Seas. I always find, however, that I am either too busy or too lazy to write this fine work, so I may as well give it away for the purposes of philosophical illustration. There will probably be a general impression that the man who landed (armed to the teeth and talking by signs) to plant the British flag on that barbaric temple which turned out to be the pavilion at Brighton, felt rather a fool. I am not here concerned to deny that he looked a fool. But if you imagine that he felt a fool, or at any rate that the sense of folly was his sole or his dominant emotion, then you have not studied with sufficient delicacy the rich romantic nature of the hero of this tale. His mistake was really a most enviable mistake; and he knew it, if he was the man I take him for. What could have been more delightful than to have in the same few minutes all the fascinating terrors of going abroad combined with all the humane security of coming home again? What could be better than to have all the fun of discovering South Africa without the disgusting necessity of landing there? What could be more glorious than to brace one's self up to discover New South Wales and then realize, with a gush of happy tears, that it was really old South Wales. This at least seems to me the main problem of this book. How can we contrive to be at once astonished at the world and yet at home in it? How can this queer cosmic town, with its many legged citizens, with its monstrous and ancient lamps, how can this world give us at once the fascination of a strange town and the comfort and honour of being our own town?

To show that a faith or a philosophy is true from every standpoint would be too big an undertaking; it is necessary to follow one path of argument; and this is the path that I here propose to follow. I wish to set forth my faith as particularly answering this double spiritual need, the need for that mixture of the familiar and the unfamiliar which Christendom has rightly named romance. For the very word 'romance' has in it the mystery and ancient meaning of Rome. Any one setting out to dispute anything ought always to begin by saying what he does not dispute. Beyond stating what he proposes to prove he should always state what he does not propose to prove. The thing that I do not propose to prove, the thing I propose to take as common ground between myself and any average reader, is this desirability of an active and imaginative life, picturesque and full of a poetical curiosity, a life such as western man at any rate always seems to have desired. If a man says that extinction is better than existence or blank existence better than variety and adventure, then he is not one of the ordinary people to whom I am talking. If a man prefers nothing I can give him nothing. But nearly all people I have ever met in this western society in which I live would agree to the general proposition that we need this life of practical romance; the combination of something that is strange with something that is secure. We need so to view the world as to combine an idea of wonder and an idea of welcome. We need to be happy in this wonderland without once being merely comfortable. It is *this* achievement of my creed that I shall chiefly pursue.

But I have a peculiar reason for mentioning the man in a yacht, who discovered

England. For I am that man in a yacht. I discovered England. I do not see how this book can avoid being egotistical; and I do not quite see (to tell the truth) how it can avoid being dull. Dullness will, however, free me from the charge which I most lament; the charge of being flippant. Mere light sophistry is the thing that I happen to despise most of all things, and it is perhaps a wholesome fact that this is the thing of which I am generally accused. I know nothing so contemptible as a mere paradox; a mere ingenious defence of the indefensible. If it were true (as has been said) that Mr Bernard Shaw lived upon paradox, then he ought to be a mere common millionaire; for a man of his mental activity could invent a sophistry every six minutes. It is as easy as lying; because it is lying. The truth is, of course, that Mr Shaw is cruelly hampered by the fact that he cannot tell any lie unless he thinks it is the truth. I find myself under the same intolerable bondage. I never in my life said anything merely because I thought it funny; though, of course, I have had ordinary human vain-glory, and may have thought it funny because I had said it. It is one thing to describe an interview with a gorgon or a griffin, a creature who does not exist. It is another thing to discover that the rhinoceros does exist and then take pleasure in the fact that he looks as if he didn't. One searches for truth, but it may be that one pursues instinctively the more extraordinary truths. And I offer this with the heartiest sentiments to all the jolly people who hate what I write, and regard it (very justly, for all I know) as a piece of poor clowning or a single tiresome joke. For if this is a joke it is a joke against me. I am the man who with the utmost daring discovered what had been discovered before. If there is an element of farce in what follows, the farce is at my own expense; for this explains how I fancied I was the first to set foot in Brighton and then found I was the last. It recounts my elephantine adventures in pursuit of the obvious. No one can think my case more ludicrous than I think it myself; no reader can accuse me here of trying to make a fool of him: I am the fool of this story, and no rebel shall hurl me from my throne. I freely confess all the idiotic ambitions of the end of the nineteenth century. I did, like all other solemn little boys, try to be in advance of the age. Like them I tried to be some ten minutes in advance of the truth. And I found that I was eighteen hundred years behind it. I did strain my voice with a painfully juvenile exaggeration in uttering my truths. And I was punished in the fittest and funniest way, for I have kept my truths: but have discovered, not that they were not truths, but simply that they were not mine. When I fancied that I stood alone I was really in the ridiculous position of being backed up by all Christendom. It may be, Heaven forgive me, that I did try to be original; but I only succeeded in inventing all by myself an inferior copy of the existing traditions of civilized religion. The man from the yacht thought he was the first to find England; I thought I was the first to find Europe. I did try to found a heresy of my own; and when I had put the last touches to it, I discovered that it was orthodoxy. It may be that somebody will be entertained by the account of this happy fiasco. It might amuse a friend or an enemy to read how I gradually learnt from the truth of some stray legend or from the falsehood of some dominant philosophy, things that I might have learnt from my catechism – if I had ever learnt it. There may or may not be some entertainment in reading how I found at last in an anarchist club or a Babylonian temple what I might have found in the nearest parish church. If any one is entertained by learning how the flowers of the field or the phrases in an omnibus, the accidents of politics or the pains of youth came together in a certain order to produce a certain conviction of Christian orthodoxy, he may possibly read this book [*Orthodoxy*]. But there is in everything a reasonable division of labour. I have written the book, and nothing on earth would induce me to read it.

I add one purely pedantic note which comes, as a note naturally should, at the beginning. These essays are concerned only to discuss the actual fact that the central Christian theology (sufficiently summarized in the Apostles' Creed) is the best root of energy and sound ethics. They are intended to discuss the very fascinating but quite different question of what is the present seat of authority for the proclamation of that creed. When the word 'orthodoxy' is used here it means the Apostles' Creed, as understood by everybody calling himself Christian until a very short time ago and the general historic conduct of those who held such a creed. I have been forced by mere space to confine myself to what I have got from this creed; I do not touch the matter much disputed among modern Christians, of where we ourselves got it. This is not an ecclesiastical treatise but a sort of slovenly autobiography. But if any one wants my opinions about the actual nature of the authority, Mr G.S. Street has only to throw me another challenge, and I will write him another book.

*Orthodoxy*, London (Bodley Head) 1908, pp. 1–8.

# 8.

# A WEIGHTY PROBLEM

Once ensconced in Beaconsfield in October 1909, the Chestertons immersed themselves in the local community, with Gilbert walking his Aberdeen terrier, Winkle, as well as joining in amateur dramatic groups and supporting the Children's Convalescent Home by appearing in pageants, usually as Dr Johnson. Frances compiled a *Chesterton Calendar* (1911) and took to writing plays for production by local schools. Gilbert also had time to round off various projects on which he had been treading water for some years. His *George Bernard Shaw* had appeared in August 1909 much to Shaw's delight:

> This book is what everybody expected it to be: the best book of literary art I have yet provoked. It is a fascinating portrait study; and I am proud to have been the painter's model. It is in the great tradition of literary portraiture: it gives not only the figure, but the epoch. It makes the figure interesting and memorable by giving it the greatness and spaciousness of an epoch, and it makes it attractive by giving it the handsomest and friendliest personal qualities of the painter himself . . . All the same, it is in some respects quite a misleading book . . . Everything about me which Mr Chesterton had to divine, he has divined miraculously. But everything that he could have ascertained easily by reading my own plain directions on the bottle, as it was, remains for him a muddled and painful problem solved by a comically wrong guess.[1]

Chesterton had, of course, accused and convicted Shaw of being a Puritan. The book was generally well received, but Vivian Carter postulated 'the Shawterton':

It is by now surely general knowledge that Shaw and Chesterton are one and the same person. Shaw, tired of Socialism, weary of wearing Jaegers, and broken down by teetotalism and vegetarianism, sought some years ago an escape from them . . . therefore, he in order to taste the forbidden joys of Individualistic philosophy, meat food and strong drink, created 'Chesterton' . . . This mammoth myth should be beardless, large in girth, smiling of countenance, and he should be licensed to sell paradoxes only in essay and novel form, all stage and platform rights being reserved for Shaw. Emerging from his house plain, Jaeger-clad and saturnine Shaw, he entered the tunnel, in a cleft of which there was a cellar. Here he donned the Chesterton properties, the immense padding of chest, and so on, the Chesterton sombrero hat and cloak and pince-nez, and there he left the Shaw beard and the Shaw clothes, the Shaw expression of countenance, and all the Shaw theories. He emerged into the Strand 'GKC', in whose identity he visited all the cafés, ate all the meals, rode in all the cabs, and smiled on all the sinners. The day's work done . . . the giant figure returned to the tunnel, and once again was back in Adelphi the Shaw he was when he left it . . . However, I am not concerned with the Shaw-Chesterton theory, but only with the book as it reaches me . . . Seeing that it is a life of George Bernard Shaw, you will ask yourself whether it is a good or a bad one. And you will probably agree that it is a bad one, for it approaches the subject with the fatal purpose of seeking to explain it . . . to analyse Mr Shaw. He makes him out to be the creature of environment. He traces one of Mr Shaw's characteristics after another to the fact that he is, respectively, an Irishman, a Protestant, a Puritan, a rebel, a mathematician, a musician, and goodness knows what else . . . Mr Chesterton does not concede that Shaw is probably his own creation, that Irish birth, religious ancestry, and such habits of mind as mathematics and music are probably the barest accidents . . . Mr Chesterton is not content to contemplate Shaw, and to give us his critical estimate of the value of Shaw's art work. He does not sit at Shaw's feet save to inspect his boots. He does not put a laurel on his head, but examines the make of his hat . . . I never knew Chesterton so strangely analytical. The book, shorn of its paradoxical pyrotechnics, reads to me like a proposition of Euclid. It is all premises, and demonstrations and corollaries. The human man Shaw does not breathe in these pages. He is vivisected . . . Still, I intend to read this book.[2]

The friendly rivalry between Shaw and Chesterton went beyond the debating platform, and Shaw's efforts to tempt his friend to become a playwright, on one occasion involved J.M. Barrie who proposed to make a cowboy film:

It began by Bernard Shaw coming down to my house in Beaconsfield, in the heartiest spirits and proposing that we should appear together, disguised as Cowboys, in a film of some sort projected by Sir James Barrie. I will not describe the purpose or character of the performance; because nobody ever discovered it; presumably with the exception of Sir James Barrie. But throughout the proceedings, even Barrie had rather the appearance of concealing his secret from himself. All I could gather was that two other well-known persons, Lord Howard de Walden and Mr William Archer, the grave Scottish critic and translator of Ibsen had also consented to be Cowboys. 'Well,'

I said, after a somewhat blank pause of reflection. 'God forbid that anyone should say I did not see a joke, if William Archer could see it.' Then after a pause, I asked: 'But what is the joke?' Shaw replied with hilarious vagueness that nobody knew what the joke was. That was the joke.

I found that the mysterious proceeding . . . consisted of an appointment in a sort of abandoned brickfield somewhere in the wilds of Essex; in which spot, it was alleged, our cow punching costumes were already concealed . . . We went down to the waste land in Essex and found our Wild West equipment. But considerable indignation was felt against William Archer; who, with true Scottish foresight, arrived there first and put on the best pair of trousers. They were indeed a magnificent pair of fur trousers; while the other three riders of the prairie had to be content with canvas trousers. A running commentary upon this piece of individualism continued throughout the afternoon; while we were being rolled in barrels, roped over faked precipices and eventually turned loose in a field to lasso wild ponies, which were so tame that they ran after us instead of our running after them, and nosed in our pockets for pieces of sugar. Whatever may be the strain on credulity, it is also a fact that we all got on the same motor-bicycle; the wheels of which were spun round under us to produce the illusion of hurtling like a thunderbolt down the mountain-pass. When the rest finally vanished over the cliffs, clinging to the rope, they left me behind as a necessary weight to secure it; and Granville Barker kept on calling out to me to Register Self-Sacrifice and Register Resignation, which I did with such wild and sweeping gestures as occurred to me; not, I am proud to say, without general applause. And all this time Barrie, with his little figure behind his large pipe, was standing about in an impenetrable manner; and nothing could extract from him the faintest indication of why we were being put through these ordeals. Never had the silencing effects of the Arcadia Mixture appeared to me more powerful or more unscrupulous. It was as if the smoke that rose from that pipe was a vapour not only of magic, but of black magic . . . I only know that I received immediately afterwards a friendly and apologetic note from Sir James Barrie, saying that the whole scheme was going to be dropped.[3]

And yet, two years later on June 9th, 1916, the adventures of the fabulous four were shown under the title 'How Men Love' during a matinée performance at the London Coliseum in aid of the War Hospital. Shaw, who had been at the matinée wrote to William Archer: 'It wasn't in the least funny. Chesterton has possibilities as a comic film actor – or had before his illness spoilt his figure – But the rest of us were dismal failures as amateur Charlie Chaplins.'[4]

Publications poured forth as *The Ball and the Cross* serial publication, suspended in 1905 upon Knollys Blogg being committed to an asylum, now appeared in book form, followed by *What's Wrong With the World*, *William Blake*, and *The Ballad of the White Horse*. 'Lepanto' (a theme suggested by Father O'Connor) also belongs to this time, soon becoming a standard recitation piece. Comic and satirical verse was contributed to Belloc's newly founded *Eye Witness* (later *New Witness*), and material from the 1890s was reworked into *Manalive*. However, new directions had been taken, one when Father O'Connor was manhandled into an alter ego in the persona of Father Brown, and another when Chesterton began *The Return of Don Quixote*, his first chronologically arranged novel since *The Adventurous Abbot*, apparently for serialisation in the USA, and a third when Shaw at last goaded his friend into writing a play, *Magic*. All was on course until 1913 when Cecil became involved in the Marconi affair.

Once war had broken out in August, 1914 Charles Masterman, appointed to lead a Propaganda Office, had recruited a group of twenty-five authors including Chesterton to help contribute to the war effort; this seems to have involved the composition of short propaganda pamphlets, pep talks and recruiting campaigns.

One effect of the outbreak of war was an influx of refugees from Belgium. Walter Opsomer, nine years old at the beginning of the First World War, made Chesterton's acquaintance by the simple expedient of becoming the little refugee boy who lived next door. After the shelling of their town of Lier [the Lierre well known to GKC who had featured it in essay and ballade] by advancing German troops in the summer of 1914, the Belgian painter, Baron Isidoor Opsomer, together with his wife and son, headed for Ostend where they managed to board the last ferry for Dover.

'In England at that time', said Walter Opsomer, 'there was no greater accolade than that of "Belgian Refugees", as we were quickly to find. The refugees were received with great friendship, and people fought to do things for us. After eight days we were directed to Beaconsfield, a pleasant village with a thousand inhabitants. A lady put at our disposal for an unlimited time a big house with an immense garden. We arrived there at ten in the morning. At noon, just as we were sitting down to table, we heard someone calling out: Hello! hello! We looked out and saw two ladies and a gentleman on the other side of the hedge. Father went to meet them. They were our neighbours who spoke French quite well and identified themselves as Mr and Mrs Chesterton and Mrs Chesterton's sister [Ethel]. They showed a great deal of interest in us, asked how the journey had gone, and wanted to know where we had come from. The fate of the Belgians touched them very much. "As soon as you can, you must come and visit us," they said. Father, who was well up in artistic and literary matters, soon realised who our friendly neighbour was. Later I was to hear that Chesterton had written about the plight of Belgian refugees and about the German invasion of our country.

Chesterton, his wife and her sister actually lived not next door to us, but on the other side of the street. In a garden next to ours, they had what they called "a studio", where Chesterton came to work. It was a half-timbered kind of building with panelling, beams and leaded lights. The studio consisted of a large single room on one side of which

Chesterton had set up a toy theatre where he sometimes gave a Javanese puppet show with impressive silhouettes in black, red and yellow. In the middle of the studio was laid an open fire. The smoke in there would have cracked chestnuts. And everywhere I saw books, books, and yet more books.

The studio was situated in a beautiful garden arranged on formal lines. I marvelled at the great lawn, the huge flagstones, and the flowers such as I had never seen before. Chesterton kept two dogs [Winkle and Quoodle] which always smelt of the woodlands. Perhaps it is strange, but I don't recall our neighbour's appearance struck me in any way on first meeting him. He was a corpulent man, but that doesn't seem to have impressed me unduly. On the second day I felt completely at home in Beaconsfield. "Our Walter is really settling down," my people laughed. I used to go round to the Chestertons only too willingly for I was always given some sweets or asked for tea, and Mrs Chesterton was ever so nice.

"You will have to learn English." said Mrs Chesterton. And she sent round a young lady to give me lessons; a likeable and beautiful apparition, she was perhaps eighteen or nineteen years old and she was Chesterton's secretary [Freda Spencer]. She came every day from London. I was only a child, but I knew darned well how pretty she was. The first time she came to us, she said "Good Morning, Walter!" and with her she brought Chesterton's two dogs. Oh, how many pleasant days we passed! I learnt English as we played and rambled and romped through the dairy-like meadows and woodlands, the decor out of a miraculous play. The colour and the smells of that landscape have always stayed with me.'[5]

On November 25th, 1914 Chesterton was addressing an audience of undergraduates in Oxford 'In Defence of the English Declaration of War' when he was suddenly taken by a fit of dizziness which necessitated him leaving the platform unable to continue. He managed to return home to Beaconsfield where he took to his bed, falling so heavily upon it that it broke. Unable to rouse him, Frances sent for Dr Pocock who ordered complete rest for his patient on a water-bed under the supervision of two male nurses. Frances wrote the same day to Father O'Connor: 'You must pray for him. He is seriously ill and I have two nurses. It is mostly heart-trouble, but there are complications.'[6] Father O'Connor himself was to note the condition as 'exhausted beyond recovery . . . what can only be described as gout all over. Brain, stomach, lungs were affected.'[7] A week later Cecil wrote to Bernard Shaw: 'Gilbert has been pretty bad and we have all been anxious about him. He has been in bed with a complication of troubles, partly a sort of congestion of the larynx from which he has been suffering for some months but which had recently become worse, and partly from something wrong with his kidneys. However, I believe that he is seeing a specialist today.'[8] The specialist put him under sedation to induce a coma; the complications suggesting that the heart was no longer able to cope with the abuse it had received and was not strong enough to pump away the amount of fluid that had built up over many years. Kidneys and other organs were also on the point of shutting down.

Walter Opsomer resumes his account:

> I no longer know exactly when, but, as soon as I heard that our neighbour was so ill, I went to his house on the other side of the street where he was being nursed. On the door was a brass knocker in the shape of a bat with its wings spread and its feet uppermost. I made no use of it, for on a placard there was written: Please do not knock as *Mr Chesterton is badly ill.* A few weeks later, he was feeling better. He grew bored and he sent the young lady to come and get me. He was lying in a room on the first floor. Years later when I saw Rodin's statue of Balzac, I thought once more of Chesterton as I saw him that day when I found him in his sick bed. In that sculpture, I refound something of the effect that he had on me when he was dressed in a white nightshirt and lying, or rather more or less sitting up, against a heap of pillows. I must have looked somewhat taken aback, which was something that amused him. The door closed behind me, and I was left alone with him; he looked at me, but stayed silent for a while.
>
>    The room was whitewashed. Along the wall there were books piled high in stacks of a foot to over a foot and a half tall. I could find no stool. 'Sit down on the books,' was the first thing Chesterton said. I did what he said and took my place on one of the piles. 'Tell me,' he then asked, 'what do you really speak when you don't speak French?' 'Flemish,' I said. 'That's the same as Dutch,' he said. 'No, it isn't,' I protested. 'Oh yes, it is, it's the same,' he said. 'No,' I answered, 'Dutch is Dutch, but we speak Flemish.'

The quiet life of Beaconsfield did not suit Opsomer senior, and he looked round for work. The painter was unfamiliar with lithography and went to London to study that technique in a studio where other Flemish artists worked. Then, with the support of an English patron, it was proposed to open a house close to Hyde Park for the use of Belgian artists. And so in March 1915, the Opsomer family moved to London:

> Chesterton, of whom father had sketched a fair portrait, came there to see us on one occasion. We always kept in touch with him up until his death. Every year he sent us a Christmas card with a poem in it. We didn't see him again during the war, as at the end of May, 1915, we travelled to Holland.

When his health at last improved after several months of induced coma, Chesterton again took up his propaganda work, alongside his journalism and stories written for the US market to help fund the *New Witness*. His constitution was, however, no longer as sturdy as it had been prior to his collapse in

1914, and so in 1916 he was laid low first by the mumps and then by whooping cough. While confined to bed, he was still working on *The Return of Don Quixote*, as attested by the citing in chapter 16 of a phrase from a speech made by President Woodrow Wilson on May 10th, 1915: 'There is such a thing as a man being too proud to fight.' When he had again recovered, he took over editorship of the *New Witness* from Cecil in October, 1916, and in 1917 he was accompanying Winston Churchill (along with Churchill's cousin and GKC's secretary, Freda Spencer) to Warsash on the Solent to inspect seaplanes at Supermarine, Saunders-Roe and RNAS Calshot; Churchill had to rescue Freda when she fell into the Solent. It might be wondered what Gilbert's function was; possibly, together with more propaganda and recruiting speeches, he was also there in the capacity of a ghost-speechwriter for Churchill. The next year, 1918, saw more of the same when an invitation to Ireland from W.B. Yeats was combined with another recruitment drive which, given the then political situation in Ireland, was not overly successful. On October 10th, 1918 the RMS *Leinster* outward bound from Kingstown for Holyhead was sunk by three torpedoes from the German submarine U123 with the loss of five hundred lives. Chesterton travelled back on the next boat out. Articles on Ireland written during the trip were collected together in *Irish Expressions*.

The end of war with the Armistice of November 11th, 1918 and ensuing peace was all too soon clouded by Cecil's death, and certainly back in Beaconsfield Frances had not been feeling too happy with life, summing up her situation in her *Ballade of Difficulties*:

> I find it very hard to get a rest,
> I find it harder still to make ends meet,
> I often feel emotionally depressed
> Because I see my butcher in the street,
> And, though I don't believe he means to cheat,
> The matter is too serious for a jest:
> He charged me ten pence for a pound of meat.
>    Life is a trying business at the best.

> I'm envious of the way my neighbour's dressed,
> I hate the cold and long for Summer heat,
> I try to keep my silly temper lest
> My hair should turn out anything but neat.
> I summon up a sickly smile to greet
> A friend who enters obviously distressed,
> And this, I find, is not an easy feat.
>    Life is a trying business at the best.

I would set out upon that joyous quest
To find where peace dwells in her sure retreat
Where I may enter as a welcome guest,
The feast prepared for me to drink and eat,
Where from the far-off fields come very sweet
Low murmurs from the Kingdom of the Blest,
Yet my dull heart will worriedly repeat:
   Life is a trying business at the best.

#### ENVOY

Prince, it may rain or hail or sleet,
But keep this sentence safely in your breast,
It is a maxim very hard to beat:
   Life is a trying business at the best.

Frances' feelings went so far as to place her at variance with her husband's position in the matter of female suffrage:

#### BALLADE OF AN OPPRESSED WOMAN

Well here you are! Do take this comfy chair.
You like the fire? Do you take sugar? No?
At last the women's movement's in the air,
We must be strenuous now and strike a blow.
Where did you get that ravishing green bow?
Your sister never answered things I wrote.
My children went to see the Lord Mayor's show.
   I'm sure that women ought to have the vote.

I think that the police were most unfair.
Why does that woman spoil her figure so?
That bit of Chelsea is extremely rare.
The higher woman must evolve and grow.
Women have so much – never mind my toe!
I wish that I could brush my husband's coat.
When will the Beauchamp-Montmorencies go?
   I'm sure that women ought to have the vote.

They say the working woman does not care,
But the poor things have sunk so low.
Good heavens! Lady Margaret's dyed her hair.
And evolution proves – (That clock is slow!)
Lord Belper's speaking left me in a glow,
I almost felt inclined to make a note.

There's Mr Thompson with his wife in tow.
     I'm sure that women ought to have the vote.

L'Envoi
Princess, those men are talking still below,
They'll never come if they begin to quote.
Politics are so tiresome, don't you know.
     I'm sure that women ought to have the vote.

# 9.

# THE NORFOLK (OR WAS IT SUFFOLK?) DUMPLING

The collectively selective memories of Chesterton and Father John O'Connor were not in accord and indeed neither of them accurately recalled their first contacts. Father O'Connor wrote to the rising star of *The Speaker* and the *Daily News* on February 9th, 1903 to tell him that 'I like you, and advised by the Autocrat of the Breakfast Table [Canon Watson, his parish priest?] I make bold to tell you so . . . I am a Catholic priest, and though I may not find you quite orthodox in details, I first wish to thank you very heartily, or, shall I say, to thank God for having gifted you with the spirituality which alone makes literature immortal, as I think.'[1] At that time Father O'Connor was curate at Pugin's St. Anne's Church in Keighley in West Yorkshire, and it was later in 1903 that Chesterton was invited by Herbert Hugill to deliver an address on December 3rd on 'The Shyness of the Journalist' to the Keighley Literary and Scientific Society, a group which included 'the curate of the Roman Catholic Church, a small man with a smooth face and demure but elvish expression.' The lecturer and the priest met later at Herbert Hugill's house, and in his *Autobiography* Chesterton recalled 'something of a character . . . I liked him very much.' The next morning Chesterton was to return to Ilkley where he and Frances were staying with her erstwhile colleagues of the Parents' National Educational Union, Francis and Emmeline Steinthal,[2] in their house of St. John's and it was arranged that Father O'Connor accompany him on the five miles as the crow flies 'over Keighley Gate, the great wall of the moors that separates Keighley from Wharfedale, for I was visiting friends in Ilkley; and after a few hours' talk on the moors, it was a new friend whom

I introduced to my old friends at my journey's end. He stayed to lunch; he stayed to tea; he stayed to dinner. I am not sure that, under their pressing hospitality, he did not stay the night; and he stayed there many nights and days on later occasions; and it was there that we most often met.'[3]

However, on that first occasion, Fr. O'Connor did not stay overnight: 'The first evening I had to leave early, being under a certain green-eyed observation which passed away, as bad things do, some two years later.'[4] Two years later Father O'Connor was moved from his post as curate at Keighley to be parish priest at Heckmondwike.

Their walk over the moors is mentioned in a letter dated December 6th, 1903 from Fr. O'Connor to Frances Chesterton in which he relates how they 'walked together over the moor to Ilkley, favoured by the only two hours of sunshine in three days.' Their initial conversation as they walked the moors is conflated in Chesterton's *Autobiography* with a later occasion when Fr. O'Connor was at St. John's and met two undergraduates. Chesterton gives only a general outline of their conversation whereas Fr. O'Connor recalled precise details: 'As we crossed the [Leeds and Liverpool] Canal before breasting the steep Morton Bank, Zola happened to be a topic . . . We discussed as freely as the March wind blew such matters as the pros and cons of frequent Confession. If everyone frequented the Sacrament of penance as much as mere pious authors urge, it would soon kill off all the confessors, but the modern practice keeps the track smooth, open and safe. If people went to confess only great crimes, the CID might begin to haunt our churches after a murder or a burglary, and this would lead to heavier complications.

I had just seen Maria Monk, her book[5] still for sale on a Bradford Bookstall . . . We even got onto the burning of heretics . . . I instanced the famous heresy of the German Tyrol in the eighteenth century; how a Catholic peasantry became infatuated with the doctrine . . . that in order to be saved you had to die just as Jesus Christ had died. How whole families scourged and crucified one another, and over twenty thousand of all ages perished by crucifixion, protesting that they felt no pain but perfect delight . . . From this I went on to relate some of my adventures . . . Soon the exhilarating moorland air uplifted us out of these dark topics [vagrancy, lunacy, prostitution] and we cheered the way with singing. There is a point on the high moorland where everyone breaks into song. Not that Gilbert could sing then, he was tone-deaf, though most sensitive to musical rhythm or tempo . . . So came we just in time for lunch to St. John's, Ilkley, opposite the best-kept church in the world, St. Margaret's, unto a house of the open door, to the guest and the wanderer free. It was shepherd's pie for lunch . . . I am ashamed to think how little pressing I required to make me stay to dinner that evening, but so it was done. The master of the house came home from business, a man in ten thousand for charm and integrity, as we often proved in small things and in great; Francis Steinthal, Bradford born [1854], of Frankfurt ancestry and the Israel of God.[6] . . . His house was dedicated to the Beloved Disciple whose emblem surmounted the hearth . . . The house[7] was planned by Norman Shaw whilst he was engaged on St. Margaret's Church opposite.[8]

Chesterton was later to recall the circumstances which inspired him to launch his detective:

. . . a large number of my little crime stories were concerned with a person called Father Brown; a Catholic priest whose external simplicity and internal subtlety formed something near enough to a character . . . The notion that a character in a novel must be 'meant' for somebody or 'taken from' somebody is founded on a misunderstanding of the nature of narrative fantasy . . . Nevertheless, it has been generally said that Father Brown had an original in real life; and in one particular and rather personal sense, it is true . . . In Father Brown, it was the chief feature to be featureless. The point of him was to appear pointless; and one might say that his conspicuous quality was not being conspicuous. His commonplace exterior was meant to contrast with his unsuspected vigilance and intelligence; and that being so, of course, I made his appearance shabby and shapeless, his face round and expressionless, his manners clumsy, and so on. At the same time I did take some of his intellectual qualities from my friend, Father John O'Connor of Bradford, who has not . . . any of those external qualities. He is not shabby, but rather neat; he is not clumsy, but very delicate and dexterous; he not only is but looks amusing and amused. He is a sensitive and quick-witted Irishman, with the profound irony and some of the potential irritability of his race. My Father Brown was deliberately disguised as a Suffolk dumpling[9] from East Anglia . . . When we returned to the house we . . . fell into conversation . . . with two hearty and healthy young Cambridge undergraduates . . . and they began to discuss music and landscape with my friend Father O'Connor . . . when the priest had left the room, the two young men broke out into generous expressions of admiration, saying truly that he was a remarkable man . . . Then there fell a curious reflective silence, at the end of which one of the undergraduates suddenly burst out: 'All the same, I don't believe his sort of life is the right one. It's all very well to like religious music and so on, when you're all shut up in a sort of cloister and don't know anything about the real evil in the world.' . . . To me, still almost shivering with the appallingly practical facts of which the priest had warned me, this comment came with such a colossal and crushing irony, that I nearly burst into a loud harsh laugh in the drawing-room . . . And there sprang up in my mind the vague idea of making some artistic use of this comic yet tragic cross-purposes; and constructing a comedy in which a priest should appear to know nothing and in fact know more about crime than the criminals.[10]

Father O'Connor was well aware of what Chesterton was up to:

> My native talent for detection was of the slenderest, but it appealed to Chesterton's faculty for wonder; as thus: we discussed on the first day of our meeting, the pros and cons of mathematics versus literature in education. I pointed out in the spirit of gaiety, how a mathematician would put two and two together and the result would be four, whereas your writer or man of letters would put them together so as to make them twenty-two ... Gilbert's sense of wonder was thrilled to hear that I had twice been in touch with wilful murder, never proven ... The flat hat is true to life, but it perished in its prime, for it was wrong as wrong for my style of architecture. The large and cheap umbrella was my defence against wearing an overcoat ... Brown paper parcels! I carried them whenever I could, having no sense of style in deportment. [11]

The metamorphosis of Fr. O'Connor into Fr. Brown was a slow process over seven years before the clerical sleuth was to make his appearance on July 23rd, 1910 in Philadelphia in the *Saturday Evening Post*. Even then he was not to have primacy in the American market where the first of his adventures was entitled *Valentin Follows a Curious Trail*; it was only when Valentin himself was eliminated in *The Secret of the Sealed Garden* on September 3rd, 1910, that the first Father Brown story was re-entitled *The Blue Cross* for his introduction to the British market in the September issue of *The Story-Teller* magazine. By that time Father O'Connor was a long-established friend, especially of Frances Chesterton, and the Chestertons had become visitors to Heckmondwike as Father O'Connor had to Battersea and later Beaconsfield.

# 10.

# THE YOUNGER BROTHER

Cecil Edward Chesterton, born on November 12th in 1879 and five years Gilbert's junior, was greeted by his brother with the remark that now he would always have an audience. That was certainly true insofar as Gilbert could create fairy stories and poems for the new arrival, but misleading as the developing younger brother eventually became more of a heckler and at best a debating partner. Nonetheless, we should not forget the difference of five years in age in any assessment of the years before 1900. Cecil followed Gilbert to Colet Court and St. Paul's, but he only entered the senior school in the year that Gilbert left, and so his tenuous link with the JDC consisted of his being present at the family home when the JDC congregated there. Nor was he a welcome figure, for Bentley and Oldershaw among others seem to have taken a dislike to him. His years at St. Paul's were those that his elder brother spent on a gap year and at UCL, and the time that Gilbert spent in the employ of Redway's and T. Fisher Unwin was for Cecil taken up with his articles with Chesterton and Sons as he qualified to be a surveyor. Once qualified, Cecil took little interest in the family firm of estate agents and gravitated towards journalism in Fleet Street. Oddly enough, it does not seem to have been there but at one of the numerous then popular debating societies that he first met Ada Jones 'the Queen of Fleet Street.' Cecil at the time was twenty-one years old and would appear to have been quite smitten with a lady ten years his senior. Photos taken soon after that time explain her attraction for Cecil, and even in her seventies she was still a striking figure.

Ada Jones (1869–1962) had started her career in journalism as a cub reporter in 1885 when Cecil was six years old and even Gilbert was still at Colet Court. By the time Cecil met her around 1900 she was a well-known, even respected, figure in Fleet Street, working for several newspapers, contributing serial stories to magazines,[1] and the author of what she called 'preposterous' novels. She used several pseudonyms such as Sheridan Jones, Anne Turner and Margaret Hamilton, but her best known persona was as John Keith Prothero whom Bernard Shaw long believed to be an unfrocked priest. Indeed Ada Jones was far from masculine as is attested by her undertaking as an assignment for a newspaper in the 1890s, a stint as a chorus girl in pantomime, although it would be difficult to describe the donning of tights on stage as 'undercover' reporting. The very fact that she succeeded is itself testimony to presentable legs.

Cecil pursued Ada assiduously with offers of marriage which were always turned aside, but they formed what appears to have been a platonic relationship enduring over very many years as they both built up their careers in Fleet Street. Ada had met Gilbert at about the same time as she met Cecil, but she does not seem to have made the acquaintance of Frances Blogg until Gilbert married. Frances and Ada were predestined not to get on, Ada embodying everything that Frances disliked in 'print' and the social side of Fleet Street with its late hours and journalists' pubs; in other words everything that attracted Gilbert to it. Gilbert on the other hand seems to have respected Ada as a colleague and to have liked her as a friend. Ada in her turn found Frances parochial and parsimonious, and she joined Cecil in his belief that Frances wanted to point Gilbert's career in directions away from Fleet Street. Both of them also found Mrs Blanche Blogg unbearable.

The year 1908 saw not only the success of Gilbert's *The Man Who Was Thursday* and the publication of *Orthodoxy*, but also the appearance of Cecil's anonymously published *G.K. Chesterton: A Criticism* which gave some valuable insights into his subject while at the same time the disparity in their ages led Cecil to be misleading about events in Gilbert's early life.

With outside financial support Hilaire Belloc started the *Eye Witness* as a weekly review based in John Street, Adelphi in 1911 and was editor for about a year before he resigned in favour of Cecil Chesterton who carried on until November 1912 when it became clear that any real financial support had departed along with Belloc. Cecil then persuaded his father to put up the capital to take over what he proposed to re-entitle the *New Witness*, but hardly had this been agreed before bailiffs distrained for non-payment of rent on the John Street premises, and so the *New Witness* moved perforce to

Little Essex Street (where it would remain through its metamorphosis into *G.K.'s Weekly* until after Gilbert's death in 1936) close by the Cheshire Cheese pub on the corner of Milford Street; that was the pub which would become Chesterton's Cheshire Cheese, just as the pub of the same name in Bolt Court, off Fleet Street will always be associated with Dr Samuel Johnson. It is likely that Gilbert, beside his literary contributions, also gave financial support, as he became one of the directors of the *New Witness*'s board.

## Marconi

In a world in which the only communication was by mail-boat or by cable the Imperial Conference of 1911 agreed to the construction of a chain of wireless-telegraphy stations to link the far-flung British Empire. Tenders were invited and on July 17th, 1912 Sir Herbert (later Lord) Samuel, Postmaster General in the Liberal government, accepted the tender from the English Marconi Wireless-Telegraphy Company to the exclusion of those from Telefunken and other companies; a contract was drawn up and tabled in the House of Commons on July 19th. The acceptance of the tender brought a surge in the price of Marconi shares. The managing director of the English Marconi Company was Godfrey Isaacs, brother of Sir Rufus Isaacs, Attorney-General in the Liberal government; Godfrey Isaacs, who happened also to be managing director of the American Marconi Company in which the majority shareholder was the English Marconi Company, decided to float a new issue of two million shares in the American Marconi Company on the British market at a price of US$5.00 (then equivalent to £1.1s.3d in old money, or £1.06p in new money), the flotation to take place on April 19th, 1912. On April 9th Godfrey Isaacs suggested to his brothers, Harry and Rufus, that they should purchase shares. On April 10th Harry took 50,000, selling on 10,000 on April 17th to Rufus who in turn sold 1,000 each to David Lloyd George, Chancellor of the Exchequer [Finance Minister] and to the Master of Elibank (later Lord Murray), chief whip of the Liberal Party. Only on April 18th did the American Marconi Company authorise the issue. When the shares were floated, the shares at once soared to £3.5s.0d (now £3.25p) and later that day to £4.0.0 whereupon the three government ministers sold at a substantial profit: Rufus sold 2,856 shares averaging £3.6s.6d (now £3.33p) and also 357 each for Lloyd George and Elibank; the following day Lloyd George and Elibank sold a further 1,000 shares. By May 22nd the price had dropped by a pound and Lloyd George and Elibank bought a further 3,000 shares, while Elibank also bought 3,000 shares on behalf of the Liberal Party whose funds he controlled. Rumour was rife on the Stock Exchange and soon reached the press which condemned the bad contract, and eventually questions were asked in Parliament. Prime Minister Asquith promised that there would be full discussions when the House of Commons reassembled, and that ratification of the contract would be postponed until October. In September the *National Review* called attention to what would now be called insider dealing in American Marconi Company shares.

The promised debate took place on October 11th with Sir Rufus Isaacs denying that he had ever held any shares in a company negotiating with the government. This was, of course, true but disingenuous, for the negotiations were with the English Marconi Company and the shareholding in the American Marconi Company. Lloyd George ranted about the circulation of 'sinister rumours that have been passing from one foul lip to another behind the backs of the House'. The outcome was the nomination on October 29th of a Committee of Enquiry consisting of nine Liberal and six Conservative nominees, which sat until June 1913, but failed to call any of the ministers before it until March 1913. Cecil Chesterton appeared before the committee on January 2nd, 1913, followed on February 12th by L.J. Maxse, editor of the *National Review*, who noted the non-appearance of the three ministers: 'One might have conceived that they would have appeared at its first sitting clamouring to state in the most categorical and emphatic manner that neither directly nor indirectly, in their own names or in other people's names, have they had any transactions whatsoever, either in London, Dublin, New York, Brussels, Amsterdam, Paris, or any other financial centre, in any shares in any Marconi Company throughout the negotiations with the Government.' Two days later the Parisian paper *Le Matin* reported that Maxse had charged Samuel and the Isaacs brothers with buying shares in the English Marconi Company before any negotiations had been started and that they had resold at a profit of 400%. Of course, Maxse had not said that, so Samuel and Rufus Isaacs declared that they were going to sue and had briefed Sir Edward Carson and F.E. Smith. *Le Matin* withdrew and apologised within three days, but the hearing went ahead on March 19th, during which Sir Rufus Isaacs made a statement that he had bought 10,000 shares at market price, but did not mention from whom he had bought them or what price he had paid. Nonetheless, Sir Edward Carson declared that 'really the matter is so far removed from the charges made in the libel that I only go into it at all . . . because of the position of the Attorney-General and because he wishes in the fullest way to state this deal, so that it may not be said that he keeps anything whatsoever back.'

In the *New Witness* of February 27th, 1913 Gilbert Chesterton turned the *Le Matin* episode into a poem:

A SONG OF COSMOPOLITAN COURAGE

I am so swift to seize affronts
    My spirit is so high,
Whoever has insulted me
    Some foreigner must die.

I brought a libel action,
    For *The Times* had called me 'thief',
Against a paper in Bordeaux,
    A paper called *Le Juif*.

The *Nation* called me 'cannibal.'
    I could not let it pass –
I got a retraction
    From a journal in Alsace.

And when *The Morning Post* raked up
    Some murders I'd devised,
A Polish organ of finance
    At once apologised.

I know the charges varied much
    At times: I am afraid
The *Frankfurt Frank* withdrew a charge
    *The Outlook* had not made.

I know it sounds confusing –
    But as Mr Lammle[2] said,
The anger of a gentleman
    Is boiling in my head.

A week after the close of the *Le Matin* hearing Sir Rufus Isaacs appeared before the Parliamentary Committee to which he confided that his silence in the House of Commons about the American Marconi Company shares had been because his one concern at the time had been to answer the 'foul lies' for which he was 'quite unable to find any foundation for, quite unable to trace the source of, quite unable to understand how they were started.' When asked by Sir Arthur Spicer why he had failed to mention his shares in the American Marconi Company, 'because both being Marconis you could easily understand one might get confused with the other,' Sir Rufus was indignant. However, he admitted to Lord Robert Cecil that he had bought his shares at a price lower than that paid by the general public before they were available on the market.

David Lloyd George did not appear until March 28th when he explained that he had not mentioned his American Marconi Company shares in the House of Commons because there was limited time on a Friday afternoon and he felt he could not get up and take time from other members when two ministers had already spoken. Godfrey Isaacs told the Committee that half a million shares had been sold to him and that outright sale was in the minutes of the English Marconi Company; upon inspection of the relevant books, that minute was never found. The Committee concluded its hearings on May 7th. When its findings were published, the Committee split on party lines, issuing a majority report concluding that all those involved had acted in good faith, and a scathing minority report: pointing out that documents had been lost, competing tenders misinterpreted, and a sub-committee report shelved. An opposition motion was put forward in the House of Commons criticising the actions of those concerned, but this was again defeated in a vote split along party lines. The three ministers did not suffer in their careers: Rufus Isaacs was ennobled as Lord Reading and became Lord Chief Justice in 1913, and later in 1922 was appointed to be Viceroy of India; Lloyd George went on to succeed Asquith as Prime Minister in 1916; and Elibank was ennobled as Lord Murray of Elibank. A *Times* leading article on June 19th, 1913 declared: 'A man is not blamed of being splashed with mud. He is commiserated. But if he stepped into a puddle which he might easily have avoided, we say it is his own fault. If he protests that he did not know it was a puddle, we say he ought to know better, but if he says that it was after all quite a clean puddle, then we judge him deficient in the sense of cleanliness.' In *The Nation* H.W. Massingham, a strong supporter of the Liberal government, admitted that 'political corruption is the Achilles heel of Liberalism'.

Meanwhile on January 9th, 1913 Cecil accused Godfrey Isaacs of theft and gross dishonesty in his business affairs, listing twenty bankrupt companies with which Isaacs had been associated either as promoter or director. In Ada's words:

> Godfrey Isaacs' enterprises had not been registered under the Companies but under the Industrial and Provident Societies Act, which entails considerably less cost . . . under the I. and P. provisions it is possible to shelter failure from the fierce light

of publicity. The shareholders are not usually rich, or socially important, so that meetings are rarely reported in the press. As a consequence, the long list of Isaacs' short-lived concerns was not generally known, except of course to the unfortunate investors.

Isaacs' career included a large number and strange variety of activities, from gold-mining in Wales to motor car companies in Australasia, every one of which had gone phut. It was further discovered that Godfrey had broken the rules of the Act in that he had not made the annual return of balance sheets, etc., required of him. Altogether his past hardly seemed to justify his position as Managing Director of a company which had won the great Imperial Wireless Contract. Suspicions as to Brother Rufus increased.

We opened fire with the first instalment of Godfrey's financial history, written in Cecil's pellucid and damning style, with every point clarified and all leading up to the Marconi Contract and the Ministers chiefly interested. The article was incisive, the methods of publicity a stroke of genius.

On publishing day we bombarded the House of Commons with a squad of sandwich men who, selling quires of the *New Witness*, solemnly promenaded up and down outside the House, displaying posters in huge type, 'Godfrey Isaacs' Ghastly Record . . .'

And then one morning a policeman arrived at the *New Witness*, and served the Editor with a summons for criminal libel against Godfrey. This meant that, were he found guilty, Cecil would be liable to imprisonment, whereas an action for civil libel only carries the possibility of damages. The summons was duly framed and hung up in the office . . . and we solemnly drank to the Editor's success in champagne, which could be had on draught at the *El Vino*.[3]

Despite warnings from friends, even Belloc thinking that Cecil had gone too far, and a plea from Gilbert that he back down, after a preliminary hearing at Bow Street Police Court on February 28th, the case went forward on May 27th, 1913 to the Central Criminal Court at the Old Bailey where F.E. Smith and Sir Edward Carson were briefed to appear for Godfrey Isaacs. Ada, Frances, Gilbert, his uncle Arthur Chesterton and J.M. Barrie together with other friends were there, while Mr Ed. and Marie-Louise sat outside the court where they received reports of the proceedings from Gilbert and Arthur Chesterton. Opinions varied as to the performance of Cecil in the dock, Ada thinking that he made a good impression, Maisie Ward reporting that he was slow and hesitant. Either way, early in his trial he withdrew all charges of corruption against government ministers, together with any imputation of dishonesty by Sir Herbert Samuel, but maintained the accusation of double-dealing on the part of Godfrey Isaacs on grounds of justification and public interest:

> Sir Edward Carson: And do you now accuse [Godfrey Isaacs] of any abominable business – I mean in relation to the contract?

Cecil Chesterton: Yes, certainly; I now accuse Mr Isaacs of very abominable conduct between 7th March and 19th July.

Carson: Do you accuse the Postmaster-General [Samuel] of dishonesty or corruption?

Cecil Chesterton: What I accused the Postmaster-General of was of having given a contract which was a byword for laxity and thereby laying himself open reasonably to the suspicion that he was conferring a favour on Mr Godfrey Isaacs because he was the Attorney-General's brother.

Carson: I must repeat my question. Do you accuse the Postmaster-General of anything dishonest or dishonourable?

Cecil Chesterton: After the Postmaster-General's denials on oath I must leave the question; I will not accuse him of perjury.

Carson: And therefore you do not accuse him of anything dishonest or dishonourable?...

Cecil Chesterton: I have said 'No'.[4]

Sir Rufus Isaacs swore on oath that he had never discussed the Marconi Contract with his brother Godfrey, adding 'Never from the beginning have I had one single transaction with the shares of *that* company ... I did not know there was an American Marconi Company ... I had no notion at the moment that there was any business going to be transacted in America and that there was going to be any issue of capital.' On March 9th, 1913 Godfrey Isaacs had accompanied Guillielmo Marconi to New York where on March 16th a cable admittedly sent by Sir Rufus was read out at a luncheon given by the *New York Times*: PLEASE CONGRATULATE MARCONI AND MY BROTHER ON THE SUCCESSFUL DEVELOPMENT OF A MARVELLOUS ENTERPRISE.

Cecil Chesterton: My idea at that time was that Sir Rufus Isaacs had influenced Mr Samuel to benefit Godfrey Isaacs.

Carson: You do not have that opinion now?

Cecil Chesterton: Sir Rufus has denied it on oath and I accepted his denial.

On June 9th, 1913 Mr Justice Phillimore summed up against Cecil Chesterton and sent out the jury to consider their verdict; they returned after forty minutes to deliver a guilty verdict. Mr Justice Phillimore then gave Cecil Chesterton a severe dressing-down before imposing a £100 fine instead of the expected prison sentence. Cecil, Ada and their supporters took this to be a partial moral victory, but costs had also been awarded against Cecil who consequently incurred large debts paid off by his father, by Gilbert and possibly other supporters. Ironically the Isaacs and the Chestertons soon found themselves dining to celebrate in the same hotel restaurant. Gilbert had been shocked to the core by his brother's arraignment and was never to recover his lost confidence in politicians, especially when he witnessed Sir Rufus Isaacs appointed Lord Chief Justice and later Viceroy of India, and ennobled as Lord Reading:

### THE MAY QUEEN

(Adapted and set to music by Lord Reading of Earley)

If they take me, call me early, call me Earley, brother dear.
Tomorrow will be the rummiest start of all the glad New Year,
Of all the glad New Year, brother, so much the maddest day,
For I'm to be L.C.J. Chase me! I'm to be L.C.J.[5]

There's many a black, black eye, they say, but none so blacked as mine;
Samuel,[6] and George[7] and Murray[8] stood to be thumped in line,
Yet none so thumped as Rufus in all the land they say,
So I'm to be L.C.J. Rummy! I'm to be L.C.J.

I thought they'd hoof me out before, but still alive I am,
And all the Tories[9] round me are bleating like the lamb,
And now I think it can't be long before I find release,
And that good man, the Party Man, has told me words of peace.

To live and live in Parliament,[10] where rich men feel at home,
And there to wait a little while till you and Harry[11] come;
To live like old Boccaccio's boys[12] that camped beyond the Pest;
Where the honest cease from troubling, and the wicked are at rest.[13]

Somehow in the middle of all this Cecil, after taking instruction from Father Bowden at the Brompton Oratory on the suggestion of Elodie Belloc and Maurice Baring, had squeezed a few hours in which to be received into the Roman Catholic Church at Corpus Christi, Maiden Lane. In Ada's words: 'His decision had been taken swiftly and without any period of doubt. He sought a working philosophy, and his reason satisfied, he accepted the Catholic fundamentals quite simply.' It is possible that it was Cecil's conversion that caused him to withdraw his accusations at his trial. Once he was clear from that trial, Cecil set about organising a cross-party Clean Government League.

At the same time as Cecil's trial was taking place, Gilbert had also been threatened by a libel action over an answer he had given to a question after a lecture at the City Temple, in which he had described Lever Brothers' Port

Sunlight development as 'corresponding to a slave compound.'[14] Gilbert announced that 'Old Sun and Soap-suds' could sue until he burst, but, notwithstanding Cecil's lack of success as his own advocate, he prepared to conduct his own case despite being offered financial backing by Bernard Shaw. In the event Lever Brothers did not pursue the case, which might have also raised such contentious issues as cash for peerages and the Mental Deficiency Bill which in its original form conferred powers to sterilise any person thought to fall within its aegis. Even as late as the 1980s old ladies were being discovered in Mental Institutions, the only reason for whose incarceration was that when young they had become pregnant outside of wedlock, and in 2007 a lady of 85 was found who in 1937 had been sectioned under the 1890 Lunacy Act for allegedly stealing half-a-crown (now 12.5p, but then one eighth of a week's wages) from a doctor's surgery where she worked as a cleaner – the money was later found, but the girl had by then been lost in the system where she remained for seventy years until reunited with her younger brothers.[15]

At the start of the First World War (1914–18) both Gilbert and Cecil had been rejected for military service, Cecil on the grounds of his varicose veins. Gilbert was soon to be struck down by his long illness, but Cecil was asked to undertake a lecture tour in the United States that was to lead to his *History of the United States*. In his absence Ada took over the running of the *New Witness*. On his return Cecil resumed his attempts to join the army and eventually succeeded, probably because the need for more manpower dictated a lowering in standards of medical fitness. His eagerness to serve may have been to some extent influenced by Ada having earlier agreed to marry him if he went on active service. Much to Frances' dismay, in 1916 Gilbert took over the editorial chair of the *New Witness* when Cecil, in category B2 still considered unfit for active service, joined the East Surrey Regiment at Westgate in Kent. A few months of drill brought about a loss in weight and gain in fitness so Cecil was first reassessed as B1 and then as A1 fit for active service and, owing to his mother's Scottish blood, transferred to the Highland Light Infantry where he was issued with a kilt and bonnet. Armed with three days' embarkation leave, Cecil headed for London to hold Ada to her promise of marriage. They were married by special licence at Corpus Christi in Maiden Lane in June 1916, the bridegroom being 37 and the bride 47 years old, after which the wedding party retired to the Cheshire Cheese in Bolt Court.

Cecil was soon at the front near Ypres where he was three times withdrawn for medical conditions, but always volunteered to return. On the third occasion he was returned to Scotland with septicaemia resulting from a wound to his hand, but, despite a promise to Ada that he would not do so, he once again responded to an appeal for volunteers. He survived the war, refusing to go sick with nephritis (Bright's Disease) contracted from rats in the trenches until hostilities had ceased, and only then was treated at the 55th General Field Hospital at Wimereux near Bologne. His condition deteriorating rapidly, he was put on the danger list, but, as he was only a private soldier, his wife did not have the right to visit him that an officer's wife would have had; it was only after Gilbert had intervened to have Maurice Baring, by then a Wing Commander at the Air Ministry, use his influence, that Ada was granted permission to travel. She arrived barely in time for the next day, December 6th, 1918, Cecil Chesterton passed away to be buried with military honours as the Last Post echoed over the Channel to England. His grave (XII. B. 38) is in Terlincthun British Cemetery near Wimille. After Cecil's death a more strident and bitter tone appeared in Gilbert's attitude, giving rise to an *Open Letter to Lord Reading*:

> We cannot tell in what fashion you yourself feel your strange position, and how much you know it is a false position. I have sometimes thought I saw in the faces of such men as you that you felt the whole experience as unreal, a mere masquerade; as I myself might feel it if, by some fantastic luck in the old fantastic civilisation of China, I were raised from the Yellow Button to the Coral Button, or from the Coral Button to the Peacock's Feather. Precisely because these things would be grotesque, I might hardly feel them as incongruous. Precisely because they meant nothing to me I might be satisfied with them, I might enjoy them without any shame at my own impudence as an alien adventurer. Precisely because I could not feel them as dignified, I should not know what I had degraded. My fancy may be quite wrong; it is but one of many attempts I have made to imagine and allow for an alien psychology in this matter, and if you, and Jews far worthier than you, are wise they will not dismiss as Anti-semitism what may well prove to be the last serious attempt to sympathise with Semitism. I allow for your position more than most men allow for it; more, most assuredly, than most men *will* allow for it in the darker days that may yet come. It is utterly false to suggest that either I or a better man than I, whose work I now inherit, desired this disaster for you and yours. I wish you no such ghastly retribution. Daniel, son of Isaac, go in peace: but go.[16]

Again it was most probably his brother's death that inspired Gilbert to write with uncharacteristic bitterness directed against the continuing corruption of those in power and attending the Versailles Peace Conference:

ELEGY IN A COUNTRY CHURCHYARD

The men that worked for England
They have their graves at home:
And bees and birds of England
About the cross can roam.

But they that fought for England,
Following a falling star,
Alas, alas for England
They have their graves afar.

And they that rule in England
In stately conclave met,
Alas, alas for England
They have no graves as yet.[17]

Gilbert Chesterton had now to face the prospect that the editorial chair of the *New Witness*, taken over temporarily until Cecil should return from war, was to be his in perpetuity.

### *Witness* to the *Weekly*

The death of his brother faced Gilbert Chesterton with a dilemma concerning the *New Witness*: 'I must now either accept this duty entirely or abandon it entirely. I will not abandon it; for every instinct and nerve of intelligence I have tells me that this is a time when it must not be abandoned. I must accept a comparison that must be a contrast, and a crushing contrast; but though I can never be as good as my brother, I will see if I can be better than myself.'[18] Ada was also faced with the loss of Cecil: 'I could either endure familiar surroundings until time softened the sting of reiterated memory, or by a swift effort break from my previous way of life, and in new experience and fresh efforts try to retrieve a certain measure of peace.

I chose the latter course . . . I had to face the fact that the strongest tie of my life was broken, and to guard against ignominious collapse I had to go away.

I turned my eyes towards Poland.'[19]

Chesterton had, meanwhile, come to the conclusion that the best solution would be if Belloc took over the running of the 'Paper', but there was no chance of Belloc doing so if Ada were to continue as assistant editor. Writing to Belloc on May 3rd 1919 he explained 'My sister-in-law is my sister-in-law; and apart from my sympathy for her, she is not and never has been a person I could treat like an ordinary subordinate on what was after all, my brother's paper when he died. If it were a property, she would be the heiress . . .'[20] Ada's own decision solved the problem, 'The obstacle has removed herself with a gesture of considerable generosity; I feel under an obligation to her for the tone she takes . . . I should like to provide for her contributing something, preferably dramatic criticism; not because she stipulates for it, but rather because she does not. She is a curious and in some ways a very fine character; but she is not the sub-editor for the *New Witness*.'

In the event Chesterton's belief that Belloc would make a perfect editor and be better able to raise financial support proved to be wrong. His few attempts at editorship were never long-lived, and his fund-raising rarely successful; on more than one occasion his friends arranged functions intended to pay off his debts. Chesterton stayed as editor aided by W.R. Titterton, and Ada opened her Eastern European News Service; this remained the situation until Ada was summoned to Beaconsfield where:

we got together after dinner . . . Frances sat in her fireside chair, her pale delicate face set in the curious graven expression it wore for questions of finance . . . There was, Gilbert intimated, very little money in the *New Witness*, and he could see no possibility of raising more. This meant that there would be no salary available for an editorial assistant, and no fees for contributors . . . the *New Witness* must close down. It was a possibility that I had never visualised. I simply could not believe that the paper which had won through so many and such gallant fights was to end. I went straight to the main point. 'The sales ought to pay the printers?' I suggested. Gilbert agreed. 'And the rent,' I found myself arguing, 'the rent is not due for another three months.' My brother-in-law looked uncomfortable, and suggested that the manager felt the paper should not go on. 'But we must go on,' I protested. 'The paper *can't* stop.' Frances looked up. 'It's impossible for Gilbert to find the money to continue,' she said, and her voice had a finality I recognised. I urged that we could raise additional capital, cut down expenses, and that I would gladly work as Gilbert's assistant without salary while our contributors, I knew, would continue to write for us in sheer enthusiasm. I finally won the day. But Gilbert, though he consented, was not enthusiastic. I did not then realise why this was; I was at that moment too eager, too ardent – if I may use the word – for the *New Witness*, to analyse his motives or understand his attitude. And so the next week I wound up the News Service, and went back to [Little] Essex Street. It was hard work to keep things going, but the contributors were magnificently loyal, and I got additional financial backing and carried on with Gilbert, determined not to let go. I had to work overtime those days, writing articles for the general press after I left the office and reeling off preposterous serials for ready cash . . . [However] the harder I worked, the more the paper struggled . . . But – so I thought in my enthusiasm – like the Phoenix, it could live again, rising in new form from its ashes . . . I put the idea to my brother-in-law, and I could see that the notion appealed to him. He consulted friends and advisers who thought as we did – even Frances was not too discouraging . . . And so in May, 1923, the *New Witness* died . . .

Meanwhile, though the capital for *G.K.'s Weekly* was ready, nothing happened, apart from Gilbert's instructions to the manager [Mr Gander] to pay his own and Bunny's salary and the usual office expenses until such time as plans were matured . . . month followed month until over a year had passed, and still there was no sign. And then in the forest of procrastination something stirred. Gilbert . . . came to [Little]Essex Street and I went to see him. I was full of schemes and plans for the new project, which I eagerly poured out, unmindful at first of the absence of response. After a while Gilbert explained . . . and, in those lovely verbal undulations which flowed so easily, conveyed the impression that he was going to run *G.K.'s Weekly* by himself. I did not quite take this in for a moment. I forgot Gilbert's characteristic acceptance of service from others without question, and remembered only what I had done to raise the necessary capital . . . As, fascinated, I watched him trace the curves of a French cavalier on the blotting pad before him, he murmured: 'I think, do you know, that one Chesterton on the paper is enough.' I could not think that I had heard correctly. It seemed incredible that Gilbert, ignoring the years I had worked with him for mutual ideals, should have no further use for me . . . And then with a sudden incredible diversion to the family side of his temperament, he gave me a fraternal pat. That fraternal pat ended the matter for Gilbert . . . Remembering his proposal at Beaconsfield that the *New Witness* must end, and his lack of reciprocity when I showed him how it could be carried on, I have come to the conclusion that even then he was striving to break from certain old influences. In persuading him to continue I realise now that my first aim was to perpetuate those things for which Cecil had primarily stood, and that I regarded Gilbert somewhat in the light of a caretaker for him. It still seemed to me that the paper was the expression of Cecil's forceful personality, and perhaps Gilbert, too, felt something of this . . . Thus when later it came to his own paper, under his own initials, Gilbert perhaps felt that, if I still worked side by side with him, Cecil's ideals rather than his own must inevitably have been pushed to the front in the policy of *G.K.'s Weekly*.

This theory in the light of later happenings, must, I think, hold good. For under Gilbert's personal and sole editorship, the family journal gradually dimmed its torch and lost that challenge which had been the trumpet call of the lesser brother's crusade.'[21]

*G.K.'s Weekly* started with the *New Witness*'s existing staff, Mr Gander the manager, an office boy, and Miss 'Bunny' Dunham[22] who as sub-editor saw the paper through the press. Ada went off to work for the *Sunday Express* where, as an assignment, it was arranged, in her own words, that 'I would be a homeless woman – with all that it implied . . . But of all my experiences I think the first night as a down-and-out remains the most vital and discovering. It is a queer feeling to shed your habits, identity, clothes, customs, and without protective social covering emerge in the raw.

During that fortnight I went right down to the depths of penury and hunger, sampled filthy beds, met thieves and prostitutes, hard-working and respectable women, courageous women whose only crime was poverty. I found mere girls completely down and out, the bloom still on their cheeks, though hope was dead in their hearts.

I had to walk the streets when I could not get a bed, for I found there were too few beds for the destitute, and I tramped and tramped, until I was drugged with tramping and my sodden clothes clung to my tired body.'[23] Ada's articles, subsequently collected as *In Darkest London*, under the pseudonym Anne Travers, brought a torrent of attention, the Bishop of London preaching a sermon, the Lord Mayor allowing fund-raising in the Mansion House, and Queen Mary lending her support, with the result that 'In 1927 ideals became translated into bricks and mortar, and we opened our first Public Lodging House [in Devonshire Street, Bloomsbury], where any woman – no matter how lonely, how unfriended, could get a clean bed, with plenty of hot water for baths, tea and biscuits for 1s. [one shilling, i.e. 5p] a night. We had only one rule, that no questions should be asked of any applicant. The need of a bed was her passport, and if she could not pay the shilling she was to receive hospitality from the small fund specially set aside by friends for the purpose . . . So there came into being Cecil Houses [now Central and Cecil Housing Trust] of which pre-war [1939] we had five, and the spirit of comfort and human feeling pervades them all.'[24]

Charles Bennett, actor and screenwriter for Alfred Hitchcock, recalled

'a very smart, very dazzling, very bright-eyed lady. She helped me find direction and introduced me to London's most creative and successful society . . . Mrs Cecil "Keith" Chesterton had come into my life in 1923 . . . Keith Chesterton, whose middle name should have been compassion gave me infinitely more than the encouragement a budding writer needs. She gave me a belief in myself. Her friends, and they were legion, knew her as Keith. She was a Londoner bred and born. Her flat was on Fleet Street, opposite that big hanging clock at the Law Courts, and directly overlooking the original site of the old Temple Bar. To use a cliché, the printer's ink of Fleet Street was in her veins, and at that time she was probably the most successful and most highly paid woman journalist in London. Her frequent two-page feature spread in the *Sunday Express* was always exciting, and sometimes truly sensational. Keith was slim and chic and completely charming, and her laughter was spontaneous and tremendously catching. Her personality was so vital, her approach to life and people so vivid and bubbling with interest. On occasion she could be passionately eloquent, and her personal magnetism was such that her parties – those oh-so-frequent parties – drew most of the artistic and literary names of London. Not that names meant a thing to Keith Chesterton. Her all-consuming interest was in people, successful or not – it didn't mean a thing to her, so long as they were lacking in sham . . .

I remember it all so well: the Gay Twenties, the Roaring Twenties, the Hideous

Twenties. The starving, homeless women, contemptuously abraded as besotted and immoral pariahs, found all over London . . . the old broken women huddled in doorways in Central London, and when the police moved them on, as they frequently had to, because to sleep in the open through the bitter winter night was frequently to die . . . they would walk . . . and walk . . . and walk. Usually their frost-bitten feet were bleeding because their worn-out boots or shoes had ceased to offer protection. Some tied bundles of newspaper around their flapping, soleless footwear.

Keith was a woman of compassion. But she was also a journalist, a smart one, a top one. Thinking journalistically, she was looking for the story behind the horror that the rest of us accepted as the ordinary face of London. Keith started out to explore, and she was nothing if not thorough. She chose the bitterest months of the winter to eye the problem, donned her oldest clothes, and left that easy apartment in Fleet Street. She disappeared out of our lives and into the vastness of what was then the biggest city on earth. Keith was down at heel and ragged, selling matches, sleeping in flophouses and sometimes in the street, seeking pennies for her next cup of tea or her next piece of bread and margarine – but seeking a future for thousands of agonised souls. I recall the day when Keith returned to Fleet Street – out of the vast anonymity of London – filthy and ragged and more than half-starved, not because of what she had personally suffered, but because of what she had found and what she had seen.'[25]

In later years Ada, usually together with 'Bunny' who had left *G.K.'s Weekly*[26] to work for the Cecil Houses, travelled widely through Czechoslovakia, the Balkans, Soviet Russia and by sea to China and Japan until in August 1932 'Bunny' married Mark Phillips, an engineering officer off the SS *Menelaus*, the ship which had taken them to the Far East. Ada wrote books about her travels and continued her investigative journalism in *Women of the London Underworld* (1931) and *I Lived in a Slum* (1936); in 1938 her work was recognised by the award of an OBE. In 1941 she was received into the Roman Catholic Church by her friend Father Vincent McNabb, OP. She continued her work for the Cecil Houses until her death in 1962.

## 11.

## THE TRIP TO JERUSALEM

Gilbert was still very much grieving for the loss of his brother, Frances was suffering increasingly from her arthritis, so when an offer came from the *Daily Telegraph* (possibly at Bentley's suggestion or that of Hodder-Williams) of a fully funded tour of Egypt and Palestine, it was welcomed by both the Chestertons. By the end of May 1919 Gilbert was once again turning to Maurice Baring:

> could you possibly do me a great favour? It is very far from being the first great favour you have done me; and I should fear that anyone less magnanimous would fancy I only wrote to you about such things. But the situation is this. An excellent offer has been made to me to write a book about Jerusalem, not political but romantic and religious, so to speak; I conceive it as mostly about pilgrimages and crusades, in poetical prose, and working up to Allenby's great entrance. The offer includes money to go to Jerusalem but cannot include all the political or military permissions necessary to go there. I have another motive for wanting to go there, which is much stronger than the desire to write the book; though I do think I could do it in the right way and, what matters more, on the right side. Frances is to come with me, and all the doctors in creation tell her she can only get rid of her neuritis if she goes to some such place and misses part of an English winter. I would do anything to bring it off, for that reason alone. You are a man who knows everybody; do you know anybody on Allenby's staff; . . . or know anybody who would know anybody who would know anything about it?[1]

Maurice Baring, still a Wing Commander, did indeed have his contacts, and so in July Gilbert was able to ask Ada when she expected to return from Poland. She headed home almost at once, and Gilbert was able to make his travel

arrangements and arrange a lecture tour, the Chestertons leaving Charing
Cross at 8 o'clock on December 29th, 1919 for Folkestone, Boulogne and Paris,
Frances noting: 'Awful confusion at Boulogne, but eventually passed the
Customs and found our seats in the train – a good lunch and after a long wait a
good run to Paris. Much of the rolling stock on the line was German. Arrived
in Paris about 7. Terrible hunt for the big box – found finally with a damaged
lock, and at great expense landed at [Gare de] Lyons Palace Hotel – very nice
room – good dinner. December 30th. Very tired – stayed in all the morning.
Lunch at 12 and at the station at one o'clock where we found our seats on train
to Rome. Very comfortable Wagon-Lits – scenery not very interesting.' Gilbert
had, however, managed to take a stroll:

> I went out of the Gare de Lyon and walked along a row of cafés, until I saw again a
> distant column crowned with a dancing figure; The freedom that danced over the fall of
> the Bastille . . . an equal citizenship is quite the reverse of the reality in the modern world;
> but it is still the ideal in the modern world . . . As I looked at that sculptured goddess on
> that classical column, my mind went back another historic stage, and I asked myself where
> this classic and republican ideal came from, and the answer was equally clear: Rome.[2]

New Year's Eve at 9.30pm saw them in Rome where they 'again with
difficulty got to the Hotel Royal.' On New Year's Day after breakfast they 'saw
the Forum and Capitol where ancient Rome, Christian Rome and modern
Rome meet in a small space. After lunch another drive to the Coliseum and the
Baths of Caracalla and a view of Rome with St. Peter's in the distance. Tea in a
café and back to hotel for rest and dinner. Left by train at 10 pm. Wagon-Lits.'

> I saw the larger achievements of the later Romans . . . I saw the Coliseum, a monument of
> that love of looking on at athletic sports, which is noted as a sign of decadence in the
> Roman Empire and of energy in the British Empire. I saw the Baths of Caracalla,
> witnessing to a cult of cleanliness . . . which might indicate that Caracalla, like other
> Emperors, was a lunatic.

January 2nd. 'Not much sleep, but got up to see a lovely sunrise in South
Italy – orchards of olives and my first sight of oranges and lemons growing
in the open. Changed at Bari and arrived at Brindisi 12 o'clock. There met by
an excited representative of the Lloyd Triestino boat to say that the *Helouan*
would not be at Brindisi till the next day. He offered to take the luggage to his
office and deposited us finally at a hotel for lunch. No room to be had but the
energetic one found one in a private house. It rained and rained – terrible mud

and so depressing. The hotel full of strange people, Italian officers on the way to Albania, American Red Cross nurses returning, a French lady and child, a British officer, and a Roumanian ditto. Poked about the town a little, and went early to our room – a good Christian room with a statue of Our Lady and a crucifix and holy water. Two old ladies tried to converse with me in rapid Italian and we got on pretty well.'

> *The equality of men is a mystery I pondered as I stood in the corridor of the train going south from Rome. It was at daybreak, and (as it happened) before any one else had risen, that I looked out of the long row of windows across a great landscape grey with olives and still dark against the dawn . . . Yet the plantations were mostly marked out in private plots and bore every trace of the care of private owners . . . I remembered at last to what land I was going; and I knew the name of the magic which had made all these peasants out of pagan slaves, and had presented to the modern world a new problem of labour and liberty.*

January 3rd. A sunny morning and news that the boat would be in at one o'clock, which curiously enough proved to be true. Again much excitement and we safely got on board and the boat started at 5.30. A lovely boat and beautifully arranged. We had a very good cabin – However by dinner-time I was very seasick and so all night.

January 5th. Still rather sick, but up on deck all day – smooth sea – very blue lovely sky and clouds. Steamed past the coast of Greece and to Crete in the evening.

January 6th. No land now between us and Africa – a lovely day, blue sea, blue sky and a glorious sunset. Much better and able to go down to meals.

January 7th. Arrived at Alexandria 6.30, got up to see the sunrise over the East. We got into the harbour for landing about 10 o'clock and then the fun began. A dignified Egyptian gentleman took us under his protection, seated us in the shade while he secured the luggage, changed our money, settled the Customs and put us into a carriage. We went to Grand Hotel in the centre of the town and there on the verandah was the first chance of seeing the East. It is quite wonderful – Arabs, Egyptians, Sudanese, black Africans, all sorts of Europeans passing by every moment. We went into the Catholic Cathedral of St. Catherine – where Christmas was still being observed – a lovely crib, one of the most beautiful I have ever seen. After lunch we wandered about – found a café (had our boots cleaned).

January 8th. Decided to leave for Cairo by 12 o'clock train. Ismail (of the hotel) vowed eternal fealty for the time being and arranged everything and took us to the station and saw us off with oriental hand-kissing and salaams.

The journey to Cairo was most marvellous of all – Across the Nile Delta, flat as flat, with fields of cotton, or beans, or sugar cane – little Arab mud huts all along the way – here and there a small mosque – and by the road that runs beside the railway an unending procession of camels, mules, donkeys, goats, sheep, oxen, buffaloes, men, women, children. Every scene like some picture familiar from childhood from some illustrated Bible. The palm trees and date trees are the only things that rise any height above the ground. Then we saw the Nile and to our surprise in the distance the Pyramids! Arrived Cairo 3 pm. It looks like any other great cosmopolitan centre, though there are Eastern houses, and the vegetation is strange. Everyone talks a little English or French. Called at Cooks' office and decided on Hotel National. Pursued by a guide in a peacock kaftan who tried to arrange to take us to the Pyramids then and there! Had a bad headache and so stayed in room till dinner time.

January 9th. Not feeling very well and stayed in bed till 11 o'clock. Drove to Cooks' and then sat in public gardens.

January 10th. Stayed in bed till late, but went a little walk before lunch. After lunch hired a carriage and had a lovely drive out of town to the Gezirai or sporting ground.

January 11th. Went to church to St. Mary's (The chapel of the English Bishop of Jerusalem who was there) – choral Eucharist. Back to hotel for lunch. In the afternoon another drive on the road which leads to the Pyramids – saw all sorts of things – shepherds bringing in droves of Sudanese sheep – Mahomedans at prayers – sellers of sugar cane – water sellers, booths all along the route. The boats on the Nile are quite lovely, so is the view of the city from this further side. The citadel stands out very majestically against the background of the desert. The desert here is high like cliffs made of some alien substance – mud, I suppose.

January 12th. A Captain Keith-Roach tells us we are expected at Jerusalem and is to give us tips as to how the difficult journey is to be accomplished. After lunch went for a walk almost to native city – in search of a kettle (not to be had). Had tea at the fashionable resort *Grotti's [Groppi's]* – very good. Gilbert is to be given some official post (lecturing) in order to facilitate our means of getting to Jerusalem.

January 13th. We went for a prowl this morning, keeping mainly to the big thoroughfares and looked at the big shops oriental and European. In the afternoon went for a drive into the bazaars. Europeans are not allowed into the very inmost heart of the native quarter nor into the mosques, but accompanied by our faithful guide we had a marvellous view of the Eastern part of this remarkable city. It is impossible to describe the sights, the smells, the noise, the colour and movement in the narrowest and dirtiest of alleys – every craftsman at his craft – brass-workers, shoeing-smiths – bakers – woodcarvers – bead threaders, tabouch makers – rasqhili and a hundred others – crowds of women and children – barrows of fruit – sweets – copper ware – watersellers, scribes – readers of the Koran. We passed the great mosque, but it is considered inadvisable for Europeans to go into them just now.

January 14th. Such a glorious day. After lunch took Abdul and a carriage to the Pyramids. It's a wonderful drive about 6 miles mostly down a straight road or avenue of acacia trees. The Pyramids are visible all the time. At the end of the carriage drive you are requested to get on camels or donkeys, but we elected to walk – about 20 minutes up a steep road brings you to the base of the Great Cheops pyramid. It is really impressive though in a sense ugly – the landscape and colour quite unexpected. What is simply wonderful is coming on the Sphinx which you approach from behind. It is gigantic and weird, the face all hacked away by the Mamelukes who used it for a target. A new temple has been discovered quite near into which we looked: great granite pillars 60 feet long. We had not time to go into it. Tea at Mena House Hotel and drive home in the glow of a real Egyptian sunset. The desert is unlike anything else being hilly and almost mountainous. We hear there have been riots or rather demonstrations in Cairo today.

January 15th. A walk in the morning near the Mouski (native quarter) and then sat in the Ezbekiya gardens. After lunch engaged the rascally guide and went to the zoo – a very good one and noted for its famous hippopotamus who does tricks – opens his mouth and the keeper throws things in. Waited for a long time at the bridge and watched the boats pass through on their way up the Nile. These boats are a great feature with their one sail which looks blue in the shade. Lovely sunset. Tea at Groppi's.

January 16th. We went to GHQ in order to find out particulars re journey to Jerusalem . . . Gilbert lectured at 8 pm at GHQ to the military clerks, officers, etc. stationed there: 'Sightseeing for the Blind.' He was very good. I was asked to go too and was the only lady.

January 17th. Strolled up to the Sultan's Palace in the morning and came back by the Ezbekiya Gardens. After lunch took Abdul and went for a drive to the Citadel. That is the fortress on the height above the town built by the great Saladin (the enemy of our Richard Coeur de Lion) with stones taken from the Great Cheops Pyramid. The view from the wall is a splendid panorama of the whole country for miles. Pyramids, Nile, a hundred mosques with their minarets. We entered two mosques – the modern one of Mahomet Ali and the ancient one of Sultan Hassan. The former is like a very palatial dancing [hall] or state ballroom – hung with glass chandeliers – built of alabaster and very magnificent. The other very austere and very impressive. Home through the native quarter. Very cold for Cairo and some rain.

January 18th. Went to Church in the morning returning to lunch. After lunch began to pack – as it was too cold to go out. Gilbert gave an address at the Bishop's Chapel after Evensong, clad in cassock and surplice.

January 20th. Left Cairo at 11 accompanied by Captain Norton Griffiths and arrived Ismailia about 2.30. This is a perfectly beautiful little place, the headquarters of the Suez Canal Co., beautifully laid out and with masses of trees and real green grass. We were housed at the residency (Empress Eugenie's house when she stayed here. Saw Lesseps' bedroom. Very grand rooms), fetched in a motor and drove to HQ and had tea with General Palin. Gilbert then spoke to the English Club and we returned to General's hut to dine.

January 21st. A motor fetched us in the morning and took us to the far south of the camp where Gilbert spoke to officers and men in a large rush hut – so warm and beautiful. Returned and lunched with General Palin who then kindly dispatched us in his own motor launch up the Suez Canal to Kantara – a perfectly beautiful experience – saw camels returning to camp from Damascus – Turkish trenches and our own too, and where Turks tried to cross Canal. Landed at Kantara about 4 and were met by a motor and went to the Base Commandant's (Lord Stradbroke) who gave us tea. Immense camp, nine miles of tents they say. Gilbert spoke in camp theatre and we returned and dined with Lord Stradbroke. Then we went by motor to Kantara Station and arrived in Port Said 11.30.

January 22nd. Hotel Casino – overlooking the sea – strolled about the town – very warm, and after lunch drove about the town which is not very interesting except the native quarter. Gilbert lectured at 6, his most success-ful one.

January 23rd. Strolled about near the port and saw the great liners and the guard ship (*Caesar*). Left at 12.30 for Suez – lunched on train – a journey through the desert. The desert is quite extraordinarily beautiful especially where it is near the Canal which gives so much colour – arrived 4.30 and went to Hotel Bel Air – quite nice – dined there and then went to Port Tewfik (the Camp) where Gilbert spoke to officers and wives and a few civilians. Very nice place it seems.

January 24th. Wandered about Suez waiting orders. Base Commander

appeared and told us to return to beautiful Ismailia by 5.10. In the afternoon
had a lovely drive and saw Suez from Canal, very very beautiful . . . Caught
5.10 to Ismailia. Met there and taken to Officers' Mess for dinner, then sent by
motor to station and took train to Kantara. [ Over the railway bridge into Sinai
where] the train [track] made during the war was made practicable by laying
wire netting over sand, pegging it down and then laying sleepers and rails – a
simple device but never thought of before. It is a kind of cattle truck train, 'The
Milk and Honey Express', but not as terrible as had been made out. Managed
somehow and slept in fits and starts as the train slowly crossed the desert.

January 25th. Arrived Ludd [Lydda] 6.30 am. Met by RTO Officer who
took us to a tent for breakfast and then sent us to Jaffa [Joppa] by car. The
badness of the road is quite indescribable and I thought we should never reach
the hotel in safety. But so beautiful. My first glimpse of Palestine will always be
associated with great groves of orange trees (all in fruit) and fields of scarlet
anemones. Very fertile after the desert. Arrived Hotel Jerusalem. Lovely view
of Jaffa. Tomb of Tabitha as you enter Jaffa, interesting. Very cold and windy.
Had lunch – and a very perilous drive afterwards. In the evening Gilbert spoke
at Serona, the great camp outside the city.

January 26th. Fetched by car at 10 o'clock and motored back to Ludd.
Lunch YMCA hut where we met a Mr Evans, a great admirer of Gilbert's who
gave us a lovely Damascus lamp. Train to Jerusalem where we arrived 4.30.
It's a wonderful journey up the most perilous heights – very beautiful. We
were brought through the Jaffa Gate to this hotel, *Grand New*, in a Red Cross
ambulance, pouring with rain. Father Waggett came in. Quite comfortable
hotel – bed and sitting room.

[After four weeks the Chestertons had finally reached their goal, but it
seemed as if the English winter had followed them.]

January 27th. Very cold indeed and pouring rain. No chance of going out.
Dr Eder [President of the Zionist Commission and an old friend who had
written for the *New Witness*] called, and Father Waggett [the political officer
detailed to escort them]. In the evening we dined at the Governor's house
(Colonel Storrs). Very pleasant in spite of the bitter cold. Quite an adventure
getting there in a sort of carriage. I thought we should never find it, and the
chances of being upset every moment in the road were great.

January 28th. Finer but still cold. In the morning walked about and found
ourselves at the Zion Gate near the House of Caiaphas and the scene of the
Last Supper – also found David Street, one of the main streets – extraordinary
– all roofed in – in different quadrants – donkeys go up and down carrying

great weights. In the afternoon I wandered round the Citadel and saw 'the hills standing about Jerusalem'.

*As soon as I was walking inside the walls of Jerusalem, I had an overwhelming impression that I was walking in the town of Rye . . . It was not only a memory of Rye, it was mixed with a memory of Mont St. Michel . . . The first part of the sensation is that the traveller feels that he is inside a fortress . . . Then I remembered a steep hill crowned with a city of towers. And I knew I had the mystical and double pleasure of seeing such a hill and standing on it. A city that is set upon a hill cannot be hid.*

January 29th. Much finer, but cold. We went out in the morning and found the Holy Sepulchre – and went into the Christian quarter. A hopeless town to find one's way about in – no names or numbers anywhere. It rained after lunch so we stayed in and Gilbert worked. A stove was put in bedroom and sitting room! We dined at GHQ in the German Hospice, that wonderful building erected by the German Emperor. The chapel with his picture and that of the Kaiserin and the statue of himself as a crusader are of course a standing joke. We dined in his refectory and danced in his hall. The Officers' Mess have social gatherings every Thursday. The Hospice is on the Mount of Olives. It was a cold but beautiful drive (in a motor), even in the dark one could guess the beauty. We passed the slope on which 3,000 of our men on and around the Mt. of Olives are buried. The 3,000 little white crosses make me think of the three black crosses on the opposite hill of Golgotha, and those 3,000 that died that *one* cross might not be given over to shame.

January 30th. A fine morning at last and Jerusalem looks lovely . . . could watch the Jaffa Gate for hours. We went out through the wonderful arched and enclosed street which is the principal street in Jerusalem, David Street, and made our way out unexpectedly upon the great Mosque of Omar, the old site of the Temple and Hadrian's temple too. It stands on a massive platform, called the Haram or enclosure, and is entirely composed of coloured tiles, blues and greens – quite overwhelming. Got back by the Zion Gate at lunch time. Wrote for Gilbert all the afternoon.

January 31st. Went out by myself and discovered the Via Dolorosa, the road or rather arched little alley which leads from the corner of the Temple site to the Holy Sepulchre. There are no Stations to mark the way only numbers which are difficult to find. Also discovered the Damascus Gate. Went to lunch with Dr and Mrs Eder.

February 1st. After lunch went for a walk outside the city along the Jaffa road – very pretty and very busy.

February 2nd. Weather glorious – like June. We had the loveliest walk to the Mosque of Omar and saw the view of Mount of Olives and Garden of Gethsemane.

February 3rd. After tea I walked alone up the Jaffa road and along the further side of the Valley of Hinnon and saw Akeldama [the Potter's Field]. A wonderful view to the Mountains of Moab and the city complete in its height and walls. Moon and sunset together made a gorgeous effect. We have secured a typist and typewriter!

February 4th. Gilbert and I started this morning for the English Cathedral and College to leave a note for Canon Waddy. Through the Damascus Gate and by Gordon's Calvary, about half an hour's walk. Glorious sunset. Feast of Tabernacles. Saw the Jewish children returning from the hills.

February 5th. Glorious morning. We walked out through the Zion Gate and round the outer walls returning by Jaffa Gate. In the afternoon Captain Aaronsohn called and we had a long and interesting talk.

February 6th. Rather tired and stayed in all the morning. At one o'clock Colonel Popham sent his car and we went to lunch at his house which is the ex-German Consulate. He is Deputy Military Administrator. After lunch they took us a lovely car-ride on the only good road to see how the English troops advanced upon Jerusalem after taking Nebi-Samuel. We went right into the heart of the mountains and had a fine view all round and our first glimpse of the Dead Sea. We found red anemones growing everywhere.

February 7th. A cold morning and some rain. We went to the Holy Sepulchre and did the round with a guide which is unavoidable. But he was rather a nice guide, a Catholic, and he talked to us as if we had been small heathen children. I think the tombs of Godfrey de Bouillon and his brother thrilled us most. We must go again. A wet afternoon.

February 8th. A pouring wet day – as we both had colds did not attempt to go out. Wrote and read all day. When it rains in Jerusalem it does rain.

February 9th. Still raining and turning to snow. Only managed to get out to the Post Office.

February 10th. Woke up to find deep snow. It has not snowed in Jerusalem for ten years; snow in 1910 was six inches deep and considered a record then. Impossible to go out. We are quite cut off. The railway system has broken down from Jerusalem to Ludd and Ludd to Kantara– so no posts or wires. Snow over two feet deep. It looks very beautiful – but !!! not so very cold.

*When Jerusalem had been half buried in snow for two or three days, I remarked to a friend that I was prepared henceforward to justify all the Christmas cards. In this case it was not only snowed on, it was snowed up. If the snow had held for a sufficient number of days it might have been in a state of famine. The roads were impassable between Jerusalem and the nearest village, or even the nearest suburb. In some places the snow drifted deep enough to bury a man, and in some places, alas, it did actually bury little children; poor little Arabs whose bodies were stiff where they had fallen.*

February 11th. Still snow. On the level ground the snow is 29 inches deep. This is a record and never has such weather been recorded in Jerusalem. The dining-room is flooded and unusable, and there is no water – managing to keep warm, however, in fur coat all day. No typist can come and I hear all shops are shut. No attempts are made to clear the snow. Wolves appeared in the German Colony and a party had to go out to drive them off. About fifty houses had the roofs fall in and were flooded.

February 12th. Snow ceased at a depth of about 33 inches on the level. The actual snowfall was 43 inches. Had a violent headache and stayed in bed all day. Thaw began in the afternoon – paths have been cut through by the Yorkshire Regiment. Military orders issued to compel people to open their shops.

February 13th. Thaw commencing. Still feeling rather seedy. Stayed in and upstairs all day. Quite unfit for anyone to go out – Wrote for Gilbert and did some reading. Very depressing day.

February 14th. A slight improvement. Snow gradually disappearing but still very deep. Went as far as the P.O.

February 15th. The turn of the weather. Sun came out about 11.30. Gilbert and I went for a walk, if walk it could be called through snow and water. Bought goloshes! Very necessary.

February 16th. Much warmer though the streets are converted into rivers. It seems as if the snow would never get away. Went out by way of the Zion Gate round the outer wall up the path through prickly pears, through the Dung Gate to the Mosque of Omar. It is considerably damaged by the snow and some of the trees are broken down. The Turks' 'Hanging Tree' has come down – It was prophesied this tree would perish when the Turk left Palestine. In the afternoon I went as far as the Damascus Gate. The views were quite wonderful.

February 17th. Jerusalem herself again. Warm and sunny like a lovely May day. As Gilbert was busy, went alone by the Jaffa Gate along Jaffa Road to the Garden of Gethsemane. A small boy rang at a bell for me and obtained the key of the Garden. It is like a little cottage garden at home, just earth and little beds of marigolds, pansies, wallflowers, etc. One or two olives (one called the Tree of Agony) so old they *might* have been there in Our Lord's time. The old

Franciscan monk who let me in just waited quietly while I walked. He gave me a sprig of rosemary 'for remembrance'. Returned by Stephen's Gate and the Mosque. In the afternoon the bishop sent his car and we went to the English College where there was a sort of 'at home' tea party. Met lots of people among others the Grand Mufti (a delightful old man), Sir Louis Bols, Mrs Archibald Little (the traveller). Gilbert gave an address afterwards to the students of the English College and the assembled guests, which was very effective. The students made speeches of thanks in five languages, English, French, Greek, Hebrew and Arabic!

February 18th. Weather changed again to rain and cold. Only possible to get out in the morning for about three-quarters of an hour.

February 19th. Rather brighter but still cold. The Armenians predict snow (according to their calendar). At 10.30 Mr Legge fetched us in a car and took us to the Training College and School which are working under the OETA [Occupied Enemy Territory Administration] – very interesting. Boys are mostly Moslems but there are some Christians. The Arabic recitations were delightful, such fire and gesture. The work has been done under great difficulties but students and teachers are very keen. After lunch I went out, while Gilbert worked, through the bazaar to the Haram (the space around the Mosque of Omar).

February 20th. A little snow, so the Mahomedan and Armenian prediction was verified. An interesting call from Mr Khahlil Sakkahini, the head of the Training College here. He had been condemned to be hung by the Turks and only escaped at the last moment by the entry of the English into Jerusalem. We had a lovely walk as the weather improved a bit to the Garden of Gethsemane, St. Stephen's Gate, the Mosque, and home by David St.

Funeral of Boulos Inco – the big dealer who had a shop under this hotel. It was he who gave me coffee and flowers when I went in. Here they carry the corpse in an open coffin, dressed in everyday clothes. His funeral procession was quite imposing.

February 21st. Cold still, but fairly fine. We started out by the Zion Gate to the Mosque and penetrated the interior, The Dome of the Rock, supposed by Mahomedans to be the place where Mahomet ascended to Paradise, and by the Jews where Abraham was told to sacrifice Isaac. The inside work is very beautiful. Heard Moslems reading passages from the Koran.

February 22nd. Gilbert and I started out about 9 for service at St. George's. Went in to Canon Waddy's afterwards for a welcome cup of hot tea, for it is still cold.

February 23rd. Rather warmer. Went to Cooks' re return passage etc. and then had a walk round the inner walk of the Citadel. Went to lunch at the Popham's. The Grand Mufti and his son were there, Dr Glazebrook, the American Consul, and the Military Governor of Jaffa, Colonel Postlethwaite. Dr Glazebrook served in the North and South War under General Lee – also American-Spanish War – a delightful old man. After lunch we all went on to an 'at home' at Colonel Storrs. A wonderful party it was – all Jerusalem must have been present, Grand Mufti, the Greek patriarch, Armenian patriarch, Syrian patriarch, Coptic, Roman Catholic, Greek Orthodox priests, Jews, Arabs, Musulmen, British officers and their wives, and a good band and a good tea.

February 24th. A finer morning. We started off through the Zion Gate and saw the Upper Room, the traditional site of the Last Supper, which at any rate is just the sort of place one would expect it to be. Also the Tomb of David, which is only seen through an iron grating. We then went along a long walk through the Valley of Hennon to where it joins the Kedron valley – overlooking Akeldama. After lunch went to Canon Waddy's where he gave a very interesting lecture on the 1st crusade. Tea there. Dined in the evening with the Officers of the Governorate. The Governorate Buildings were the German Hospice for Pilgrims run by the Monks of St. Paul, not very beautiful, quite modern, but as all the German buildings, solidly and sensibly built. The damage done by the snowstorm, the Governorate people say, is incredible. Two hundred people had to be turned out of their crazy dwellings – a good many died. There is hardly a tree left in Jerusalem or outside. If not completely killed, they are broken off short.

February 25th. A lovely spring day. We started off to find the Pool of Siloam and the Virgin's Fount. The walk was lovely through the Valley of Hinnon to the point where it joins the Kedron Valley, about three miles, perhaps the most exquisite bit round Jerusalem. The Virgin's Fount is a spring and little rivulets run down the hillside and all is green between the patches of bare rock. After lunch I had a great hunt for the cigars which had arrived from Cairo at last. Found them at the Régie Tabac where I interviewed a charming Musulman in very bad French. In the evening dined at OETA, and after dinner Gilbert gave an address to officers there and their friends on the Arthurian legend – very good. He was a little embarrassed at having Herbert Samuel sitting opposite to him! Beautiful drive to Mount of Olives both going and returning.

February 26th. Lovely day. Went to Governorate with letter for Colonel Storrs and the Eders. We walked home in a lovely moonlight across the

Russian compound where we were challenged by the sentry, but Gilbert called out 'friends' and we were allowed to pass on.

February 27th. A lovely day again. Walked to Herod's Gate where we met Father Waggett who accompanied us to the Ashbees for lunch. Mr Ashbee, head of the Art Workers' Guild, is in charge of the town planning arrangements here and has done a lot of good work and is full of enthusiasm. They have a delightful house (quite new) outside the walls. Today is the great demonstration and protest against the Jews by the Christian and Mahomedan inhabitants of Jerusalem. The manifesto is fiery enough but the demonstrators seem fairly peaceful. The American Consul, Dr Glazebrook and his wife called and had tea with us – also Father Waggett. Worked in the evening.

February 28th. A fine morning, but turned into heavy rain about 11 o'clock and did not clear all day. Only got as far as the Russian compound and had to return.

Gilbert worked all the afternoon till 6.30.

February 29th. Went to church with Gilbert to St. George's, 9.30. Father Waggett preached – very good. After a cup of tea at the Waddy's went in Father Waggett's sort of lorry car to OETA. View of Dead Sea and all round quite glorious. After lunch I went by myself to the tomb of the Virgin and the Chapel of the Agony. Back by way of St. Stephen's Gate, Ecce Homo, Via Dolorosa. Gilbert then joined me and we had a cup of tea in the Municipality garden or what is supposed to be a garden here. Mrs Heron sent car for us and we dined at her house (Colonel and Mrs Heron) at 8.15. General Sir Thomas Yarr (who is here inspecting hospitals) went with us and we had a very pleasant evening.

March 1st. Such a lovely morning! We started about 9.30 with Dr Pool and Mrs Eder to see some of the houses of the poor Jews. Her servant, Rosa, accompanied us. She belongs to a strict sect of Jews called Keriem (I think) and cleanliness is its especial creed. Exquisite little rooms and roofs, no beds (they sleep on the ground) but wooden seats covered with beautiful wool rugs of traditional patterns. We ate preserved oranges. Saw synagogues (five leading into one another) and one underground of any age. Saw Book of the Law of great value. After school drove to the Belazel house. This is a wonderful collection of Palestine treasures of every description, which he, Dr Schaak, William Morris of Jerusalem, unaided has put together in the last twenty years. He has also started the local School of Arts and Crafts, and we saw the workers in metal and filigree, etc. pursuing their various trades. He had also some good etchings and paintings. Then we went on to the hospital which

1. Beatrice Chesterton (Birdie) 1878, aged 7.

2. Edward and Marie-Louise Chesterton with Gilbert aged 5, 1879.

3. Marie-Louise with Gilbert aged 6 and Cecil, 1880.

4. Gilbert and Cecil, *c*1881.

5. The Campden Hill water tower being demolished, 1990.

6. Gilbert Chesterton aged about 10, *c*1885.

7. Gilbert aged about 16, *c*1890.

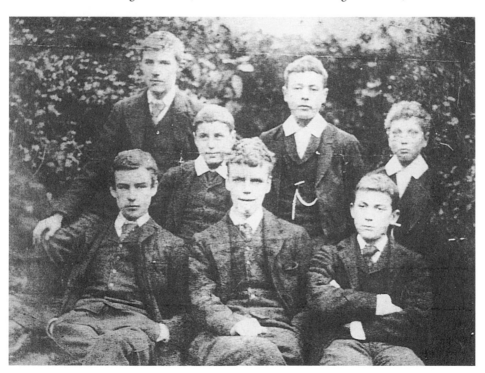

8. The Junior Debating Club, in 1890.

9. Gilbert possibly at Calderon's Art School, 1892.

10. The Junior Debating Club, in 1893.

11. Gilbert with Frances Blogg during their engagement.

12. Frances at the time of her marriage, *c*1901.

13. The Great Wheel at Earl's Court.

14. Gilbert beginning to put on weight, c1905.

15. Gilbert with Michael Braybrooke and Winkle, 1909.

16. GKC with Father O'Connor.

17. Fred(eric)a Elizabeth Spencer, (later 1919 Mrs Bayley) aged 18.

18. Cecil Chesterton with dog, *c*1896.

19. Ada 'Keith' Jones *c*1910.

20. Cecil Chesterton 'The Smiling Soldier' in
HLI uniform, 1917.

21. Ada, Mrs Cecil Chesterton, early 1920s.

22. Gilbert and Frances returning home abroad RMS *Aquitania* after the US tour, 1921.

23. GKC with three girls, possibly Hilary and Charity Gray on the right, *c*1920.

24. Frances Chesterton, Winifred Nicholl and GKC with Dorothy (holding fish) and Barbara Nicholl at Lyme Regis, 1925.

is run by the American Zionists. It had been started in the war under the greatest difficulty and is now a very creditable hospital indeed. There were five or six tiny babies and some very jolly children of all sorts. Went back to the Eders to lunch. Gilbert worked and I went for a short walk to see the sunset from the Citadel. Met General Yarr.

March 2nd. Mr Legge called for me about ten and I went to see the Girls' School here which is now under the British Education Department. The girls are about half Mahomedan and half Christian. Headmistress is Miss. Ridler. It was interesting, but obviously a very difficult school to conduct – some girls of 17 or 18 being quite unable to read or write, some smaller ones comparatively advanced. Saw beginnings of a kindergarten. Went on with Mr Legge in the car to Bethlehem where he wanted to see an orphanage (it had been German), 149 little Mahomedan boys who looked very well and happy. Best garden I've seen in Jerusalem. Just popped inside the Church of the Nativity, but am reserving it for a visit with Gilbert. The church door is so low you can hardly get in. This done to prevent the cattle from straying in. In the afternoon Gilbert lectured at St. George's on 'Dickens' England' which was much appreciated. Weather quite ideal now.

March 3rd. Very busy with article and letters all the morning, so did not go out until 12.45 when we left to lunch at the American Consulate. A very delightful time. Dr Glazebrook is a very interesting old man – he (I am told) was wonderful in looking after the English here when war broke out. It rained in the afternoon. A lady has arrived at the hotel (an American) whose husband has been murdered by the Turks somewhere near Aleppo. The two Syrians with him had their throats cut, and his fingers were chopped off for the rings. He and she were with the American Mission in Syria.

March 4th. A lovely day after the rain of yesterday. Gilbert and I walked outside the city to the fields on this side of the Mount of Olives. A very lovely view and I found a lot of wild flowers – the whole ground is powdered with small marigolds just as we have daisies and buttercups. They are pale yellow and orange. Also found anemones, forget-me-not, borage and ragged robin. After lunch I went through the market to the Church and Convent of Ecce Homo. A delightful English-speaking old nun showed me over. The church is exquisite, partly showing the scarp of bare rock behind the altar and the old arch which corresponds to the Ecce Homo arch which is outside in the street. The original street of the time of Our Lord is about thirty feet below the level of the church. The sister took me down and showed me the old street paving and the Roman tiling that still remains with the holes in the stones where the Roman soldiers played marbles. The Via Dolorosa starts in this underground crypt – 1st and 2nd Stations. 3rd, 4th, 5th, 6th, 7th and 8th are in the public street and the rest within the precincts of the Holy Sepulchre. Nash article sent to Watt, registered, and telegram.

March 5th. Still fine – short walk by Zion Gate to see the view. Went into Christ Church Shop and Bolous Pheo's. Story sent to Watt, registered. After lunch I walked with Mrs Little to the Syrian Orphanage where we were entertained to tea and music by members of the American Colony who are running the orphanage pro tem. There are nearly 500 orphans, boys and girls, Moslems and Christians. Like many charities here the orphanage was run by the Germans (no doubt with ulterior motives) and is therefore efficient and well built. Mr Schelling who had it before was so beloved and decent a man the English let him stay on in the place but he has nothing to do with the orphanage. A heavy thunderstorm and rain came on and we had to wait. It was a long and not very interesting walk along the Jaffa road, about two miles.

March 6th. Glorious day. Gilbert and I walked via David St. and St. Stephen's Gate to the Haram and from there to the Garden of Gethsemane. The old Franciscan gave me a bunch of violets and rosemary from the Garden. Then we wandered in the fields and I found anemones and grape hyacinths and ragged robin. After lunch Father Waggett came in a motor and took us off to Bethlehem – perfectly lovely all the way. The wild flowers are all out and the almond and cherries in blossom. We saw the Church of the Nativity, the Cave of the Manger, Jerome's Cave, the Catholic Church. As Father Waggett was responsible for taking over the church in the war he knows all about it and we had a truly sympathetic guide. At the place of the Nativity we said our Collect for Christmas Day. Service was going on and it looked so beautiful in the warm sunlight, and the women in their beautiful dress and lots of little children. We had tea presented to us in a shop where we bought a little Christmas manger. We then motored to Solomon's Pools, the great reservoirs which Solomon built, guarded by the ruins of an old Saracen fortress. The extraordinary stoniness of the ground is most remarkable, but, nevertheless, it is a smiling and pleasant land all round Bethlehem.

March 7th. Mr and Mrs Dana (Americans after oil here and very charming people) took us in their lovely car for a picnic to Nablus and beyond. It was gorgeous through most beautiful scenery. Right through the hills, a precipitous and even dangerous road, but Mr Dana is a wonderful driver. The distance is about forty miles. We went past the village of Bethel and Birch and Ramallah, Got a glimpse of Mount Hermon. We saw Jacob's Well, the traditional spot where Our Lord spoke with the woman of Samaria. A small modern church (quite beautiful) has been built over it. However, the priest in charge let down the bucket and we drank of the water. He also sent down lighted candles that we might see the immense depth. The property belongs to the Greek Church. Nablus is the old Shechem, one of the oldest cities in Palestine, situated between Mount Ebal and Mount Gerizim, the Samaritan Holy Mountain. It is surrounded by almonds and olives and looks very fertile. It is the city of the Samaritans. We had an excellent picnic lunch in blazing sunshine. Mrs Dana made coffee and the hotel had provided us with cold chicken, eggs, sardines, etc. On the way home we gathered masses of flowers, red, white, purple and pink anemones, cyclamen, iris, wild orchid, grape hyacinths and marigolds. Got back to hotel 5.30.

March 8th. A very warm day. In the morning I went to the Jewish Girls' school to see Miss Landau – a very good school and obviously very intelligent children. On the way home at the Damascus Gate I got into the crowd that was having another Anti-Jew demonstration. Rather excited. The leader had two drawn curved swords which he flourished about a great deal. We both saw the procession again outside the Jaffa Gate and listened to the speeches – no untoward incident occurred (as might easily have happened) though three Jews got their hats knocked off. Gilbert worked nearly all day. I spent the evening with Mrs Dana.

March 9th. Rather cool again. Started out with Gilbert but he went off and I went to Gordon's Calvary or as it is generally called the Garden Tomb. Whether it is the genuine tomb of Our Lord or not, it is an interesting spot and a perfect specimen of a Jewish tomb. The garden is supposed to be the Garden of St. Joseph of Arimathea, a very beautiful and peaceful little spot. After lunch to Cooks' to pay for tickets and then strolled down David St. and Christian St. to see the Holy Sepulchre again and to the Haram and at last found the Jews' Wailing Place. Several were wailing all right and many beggars doing a brisk trade. Saw an old Jew pelted with chestnuts. Dined at the Governorate Mess.

March 10th. At 8.30 Dr Pool (of the Zionist Committee) called with a car to take us to Richon and Rohobart, two of the most important of the sixty odd colonies that the Jews have founded in Judea and called the Jewish colonies. They lie south-west of Jerusalem towards Jaffa – about fifty miles away. The drive was glorious through the mountains on to the plain, with first glimpses of the sand dunes and the Mediterranean. The plain is a fertile part of the land, though a lot has been reclaimed by sheer hard labour, and near Richon the land is so sandy that the car could not plough through, and we had to walk. The drive was not an unmixed joy for the road is quite broken up in many places and we had violent shakings and nerve-racking escapes. The chauffeur, according to Dr Pool, was a reclaimed apache, anyhow he was a wonderful driver. At Richon we went to the Colony. Edmund de Rothschild is the great benefactor and capitalist of the colony. I saw Mr Moschovitch (I think) who had come from Russia as a refugee many years ago. A great quantity of wine is made and exported and we saw the great vats and cellars. They also grow oranges, almonds and olives. After sampling the wine (very strong) we drove to Rohobart where we first had lunch at a little restaurant. Food very amusing – sort of fish rissoles, poached eggs, sour cream and potatoes, very brown bread, a sort of cheese, coffee and oranges, but all very nice. Then on to see Mr Isenberg, one of the chief colonists and the Father of the community (talked German). Very like an early American township, or Dutch perhaps. There was one son a British officer, one a Russian prisoner (had been in Turkish army), one a chemist, one daughter a lawyer and one daughter a doctor! More strong drink and then we walked about the colony and I picked oranges and lemons!

On the way home we called at the Jewish Camp battalion (the 1st Judeans) and had tea in the Mess with a nice Jewish Colonel. It was very interesting to see the Arab tents pitched for the night, with the camels and donkeys outside. At the entrance to the mountain pass is an old inn, dating from the Crusaders (probably earlier) where men and beasts halt for the night. The journey home was varied by many halts as the tyres had to be often attended to, and the headlights continually gave out, but we got back eventually about 8.30, very tired but after a very wonderful day.

[Chesterton's support for Zionism has sometimes been quoted as evidence of his anti-Semitism, but he does seems to have had a genuine interest in the concept of the kibbutz which has so much in common with his ideas on Distributism.]

March 11th. We went in a garry (carriage) to Dr Wheeler's for lunch. Dr Wheeler has been here for twenty-eight years in charge of the English Hospital. After lunch we saw over the hospital which had been entirely denuded by the Turks and had been the HQ of the Turkish army. Allenby took it over when he arrived and stayed there with his staff. Had a rest in the afternoon, and then in the evening went to Miss Landau's Fancy Dress Ball, though not in fancy dress. A very entertaining night, everyone there, Jews, Turks, heretics and infidels! All Jerusalem turned out and the dresses were wonderful. We left about 12 pm.

March 12th. After breakfast Gilbert and I walked to the station to enquire about trains to Haifa and Nazareth. They go three times a week and three times to Kantara! Then on to the German colony to find HQ of the 8th

Brigade where Gilbert is to lecture before we leave. A number of Arab Sheiks (Bedouins) arrived at the hotel as a deputation to some British Arab. They looked so picturesque in their robes all dining at one table.

March 13th. Owing to a great influx of people into the hotel we were late getting breakfast, but we started out about 10.30 to walk to Bethany. It was coldish, a north wind, but very lovely. Bethany is about three miles out along the Jericho road. We had not time to get into the little town; in fact nothing remains except the reputed tomb of Lazarus. After lunch Gilbert worked and I did some shopping, but it came on to rain and I had to come in.

March 14th. A cold wet morning. Stayed in and wrote letters. At 2.30 Dr Wheeler came to take us to the Armenian Church of St. Gabriel's to witness a baptism. This is a church of the poorer people, but very beautiful and brightly decorated. After making a preliminary call at the home of the parents (a lovely little home – tiled floor, wool native rugs, the correct bench running along one wall – very dainty and clean). The baby had already preceded us. We went down little by-ways to the church and found three priests. One of the officials in a cope of white silk embroidered in gold and a wonderful crown (supposed to represent the Temple). The Armenians hold their type of vestments, etc. from the Jewish tradition. The church has a wonderful altar-hanging which came from India, quite unique. The godfather (a young man) was in a red velvet gown. After a good many prayers and chanting the babe (beautifully dressed) was taken to the font (which was in the side of the wall). There were more prayers and chanting, then cushions were laid on the floor and the child undressed, all of us assisting. At this point I was asked to stand godmother and gladly consented. The father is an Armenian carpenter by trade – very nice people – mother very pretty. The baby by this time quite naked was handed to the priest who immersed him completely under the water three times, giving him the name of Pedros (Peter). Before being re-clothed he was anointed with oil – the forehead, eyes, nose, mouth, ears, heart, hands and feet all being signed with the Cross. The child was by this time crying lustily and it was some business to get him dressed, especially as he was swaddled in bands very completely. When ready he was handed to me and he lay stiff in my arms whilst I held two very large lighted candles. I followed the priest from the font to the little altar, where a chain and a little gold cross were bound round his head (signifying that he was now a Christian). Then the priest touched his lips with sacramental wafer, and touched his nose with myrrh. After the blessing we left the church in a procession, the godfather carrying the baby. At the threshold of the house the priest took it and delivered it to the mother who sat waiting for it, also holding the two candles. Again the priests muttered a few prayers and blessed mother, child and godparents. The parents insisted that we should stay for refreshments and we were handed a very nice liquor in lovely little glasses and a very beautiful sort of pastry. Afterwards cups of weak tea and cakes. Dr Wheeler and the Armenian priests had a very interesting talk about political affairs as relating to Turkey and Armenia.

March 15th, Weather improving, still rather wet and cloudy. After lunch I started out and went to the top of the Mount of Olives. It is not a long walk but rather steep. I saw the little dome that covers the Rock of the Ascension (with Our Lord's footprint), the Church of the Pater Noster, and a little mosque. I also went up the mosque tower and got a lovely view of the Dead Sea, Jordan and Mounts of Moab, Bethany and Bethphage and Jerusalem itself.

March 16th. A lovely morning. Gilbert and I carried round a collection of presents, etc. to Ohan (familiarly known as Baron Ohan) who packed them in two parcels for England. It took a long time to write our list for Customs, etc. After lunch we walked to St. George's to hear Father Waggett's lecture on the Armenian Church. Tea at the Waddy's.

March 17th. Still lovely. In the morning I delivered my invitation cards about Jerusalem, calling at the Eders and on Mrs Storrs re Miss Trotter who is to accompany us to England – waited in for her in the afternoon but she failed to appear, so started out by myself for a long walk up to the windmill (Bethlehem Road) and the Valley of Gehenna. A glorious view and sunset. Gilbert very busy all day.

March 18th. At last I've done something I always meant to do! Walked right round Jerusalem. Started at the Jaffa Gate, through the Valley of Hennon to the Virgin's Fount and Pool of Siloam, through the village of Siloam which is on the Hill of Evil Counsel, up the steep Valley of the Kidron with tombs of Absolom, Zedekiah [Zechariah?], etc., coming out on Bethany Rd., past the Garden of Gethsemane, Virgin's Tomb, Herod's Gate, Solomon's Quarries, Damascus Gate and so round to Jaffa Gate. It is about 3–4 miles, very lovely all the way. Rested in the afternoon and then took a garry and went with Gilbert to tea with Mrs Sackville-West at the German Convent.

March 19th. A day of adventure. We had secured a car and started at 8.30 for Jericho, Jordan and the Dead Sea, taking lunch with us. It is impossible to describe the beauty of the scenery or the badness of the road. The continual bumping makes one feel like a jelly and the heat was intense. We went winding in and out of the wildest and barest mountain scenery, though the flowers everywhere are perfectly marvellous. We emerged on the great plain that borders the Dead Sea this side – the Moab mountains on the other. The greenish mountains gave place to the wildest, most fantastic shapes of hills imaginable, composed of apparently salt and sand. The composition is so soft that it melts like soap and is continually varying. The heat was great and we found it trying when the car broke down in the narrow ravine that leads directly on to the shore of the Dead Sea. There is no real road so the car bumped over sand hills and hollows until it reached the edge of the sea. We saw droves of goats and sheep with Arabs entirely naked. They are encamped on the edge but what they do I don't know. We bore the heat as long as we could and then drove over the plain on an even worse road to Jericho. This is not the Jericho of the Bible which lies a little higher up, but the Crusaders' Jericho. We found Elisha's Fount and there to the sound of running water in a plantation of palms (date and bananas) we ate our lunch. After lunch got into the car again and drove to the Jordan and saw the new bridge (Allenby Bridge), crossed it and so entered the rather hostile country of the Shereff of the Moabites. The Jordan is a pretty little stream, very muddy, fringed with tamarisk, not at all remarkable. Returned to Jericho where we had a puncture and waited at the Hotel Belle Vue, and about four o'clock started for Jerusalem. It seemed even more wonderful in the evening light, like a vision in the moon, or drawings by Blake of chaos emerging into order. Just outside Jerusalem we had another puncture and we waited half-an-hour on a wall overlooking the city and had a wonderful sight of the sunset succeeded by night. The stars in Palestine are always extraordinarily beautiful and the city looked like a jewelled picture. Reached hotel about 7 pm very tired and shaken.

March 20th. Felt so done up after yesterday that I did not attempt to go out at all. Stayed upstairs till after lunch. At 3 o'clock we went with Mr Dana to call on the Clarks (he is the American Vice-Consul, lived here thirty years). They have a very famous collection of archeological interest, the best in the city. Flint weapons, glass, iron weapons, vases, pottery, jewels, images, amulets, from the neolithic to the present age. Very interesting, and very nice people. Went to bed early.

March 21st. Still rather seedy so stayed in all the morning, especially as it has turned quite cold again. After lunch Captain Gladstone (Military Governor of Bethlehem) fetched us in his car and took us to our beloved Bethlehem again. We walked up some of the oldest streets and saw the Church of the Nativity, the Grotto, Jerome's Cave, Holy Innocents' Cave, Tomb of Jerome. He motored us back about 5.30. Troops on church parade looked fine entering through Jaffa Gate.

March 22nd. Cold again. Went with Gilbert to order cakes etc. for our 'at home' tomorrow. At 12 o'clock the Americans sent a car and we drove to the Syrian Orphanage (a longish way out) to lunch.

March 23rd. Started out on the Bethlehem Road to get some flowers for my tea-party tomorrow, but it was so bitterly cold I turned home again. Later on in the day it got a little warmer. About three o'clock we took a garry to St. George's to hear Dr Glazebrook's lecture on his recollections of the War and how he saved the British archives. It was most thrilling. He is a wonderful man and it was entirely owing to his exertions that the two hundred odd English people in the town finally got away from Jaffa. He said that one fifth of the population in Jerusalem died in the War. Tea at the Waddy's. After dinner to the Governorate for the meeting of the Palestine Oriental Society. Gilbert had to speak a few introductory words. The chairman was Abbé ——, a Dominican, one paper on some excavated house or other was by a French Franciscan, a Jew (Yellin) gave a long speech in Hebrew, another Jew had an account of fevers and their treatment in the Talmud also in French, and one interesting paper on Egyptian friezes was in English. It was amusing to find ourselves in that galère!

March 24th. Rather busy in the morning preparing for our party. We had a very successful party. Everyone seemed to turn up.

March 25th. Lady Day. Thinking it an appropriate occasion we walked this morning to the Virgin's Tomb. It is a very quiet spot, just opposite the Garden of Gethsemane. A long flight of stairs leads to the cave that contains the tomb itself. It is very dark and one has to be careful even with candles. After lunch I washed my hair. We then went out about 3.30 to call on Dr Glazebrook and had tea there. The old man full of stories and jokes. He is a most delightful man.

March 26th. A fine day. Gilbert and I started out about 10.30 to see the Church of the Ecce Homo. On the way we were overtaken by Mr Paterson who with another lady was in the company of Lady Allenby to whom he introduced us. She was very nice to us both and visited the church with us. In the afternoon we took a garry to the Garden Tomb. Then we walked to the Vester's house to tea (American Colony). About two hundred Americans live in the Colony which is entirely self-supporting. We had the supreme joy of seeing pigs, cows, chickens, mules, a lovely flower garden and vegetables. They do a good work amongst the poor, and during the war fed the starving population, nursed the Turks. They were ordered to go (when America came into the War) by General von Falkenhayn, but Jamal Pasha allowed them to stay, but they had very terrible experiences.

March 27th. Stayed in all the morning and sorted and packed. Went to lunch with the Eders to meet Dr Weitzmann, the famous Zionist [later to be in 1948 first President of Israel]. Gilbert went at 5.30 to HQ to speak and in his absence I went to see the models of the Tabernacle, Temples and Mosque at the American Colony and to hear the lecture, which though long is very interesting. The models are quite amazing, very large and done exactly to scale.

March 28th. Palm Sunday. Went to Christ Church (the Soldiers' Church) at ten. The Bishop preached. It's turned very wet and cold. After lunch we went to Benediction at the Ecce Homo Church – music very beautiful. Had a long walk back with the English sister, Sister Irene in Zion. Found Father Waggett here when we got back with Tiger. Met Dr Peters the great American archeologist who is staying here.

March 29th. Father Waggett called and took us to the Convent of the Holy Sepulchre where one of the priests met us. We went onto the Convent roofs where after ascending a high staircase we found two camels! An amazing sight. We looked over into the court of the Sepulchre and down into the church itself. We also saw the Chapel of St. James. After that to the Church of St. John Baptist where the relic of the saint is preserved in a wonderful chalice. The ikons in these Greek chapels are very interesting. There is another chapel below that of St. John, probably a Crusaders' chapel. Tea in the Bristol garden. many friends came to our room to say goodbye.

March 30th. Farewell to Jerusalem. We left at 5.30 am, met Miss Trotter and reached Ludd to find there had been an accident on the railway. Delayed there one and a half hours. A special was hurriedly put together and we went on to Kantara. Got the Cairo train all right and reached Benha 10.30 pm where we had to wait till 12.45. Got into train then and went on to Alexandria.

March 31st. Arrived Alexandria 5.30. Got to a little hotel (Grand Palais) where after waiting got quite decent rooms. Went to lunch with some charming people, Baron and Baroness Felix de Menasce, lovely house and garden. Took us to tea at Yacht Club. Dined at a little restaurant and then to bed.

April 1st. A tremendous morning at Consulates, Customs and police. We should not have got through had it not been for the kindness of Mr Menasce and the magic letters of Colonel Storrs with which Miss Trotter was supplied. Got on to the *Helouan* about 12.45 and she started about 3 pm. Herbert Samuels, Eders, Mr Lane, Mr Smith (Dr)

April 2nd. A spendid day on board.

April 3rd. ditto.

April 4th. Easter Day. Arrived at Brindisi about 7 am, got off the boat and went to hotel, had breakfast, went to Mass, lunches and got into train to Bari en route to Rome. Secured Wagon-Lits.

April 5th. Arrived in Rome. Hotel Russie. After some delay secured rooms. After lunch drove out and met Maisie Ward and Miss Trotter met her mother, both seemed miraculous.

[It would seem that Father Brown was not the only person trying to twitch a fishing-line. Maisie Ward and her family certainly thought of Chesterton as a 'catch': 'as we waved goodbye after their departing train my mother [Mrs (Josephine) Wilfred Ward] said thoughtfully, 'Frances did rather play off Jerusalem against Rome, didn't she?']³

April 6th. Spent morning trying to get passports visèd, a very difficult job. In the afternoon went to Capitol, Aracoeli, and the Forum and ruins, etc.

April 7th. Again Consulates. And then to St. Peter's and the Sistine Chapel. After lunch Gilbert and I had a lovely walk in the Pincio and saw Rome in the sunset. Wrenched my arm and went to Dr Philip Green, 7 via del piazza d'Espagna.

April 8th. Police and French Consulate and a walk in the Corso. In the afternoon with Lady Trotter and the girls to the Catacombs of Saint Calixtus, a lovely drive along the Appian Way. The catacombs are extraordinary, very lovely that of St. Cecilia. A delightful Franciscan showed us all over.

April 9th. Gilbert and I walked to Piazza Venezia and then up the long flight of stairs to the Aracoeli. Signor Cecchi came to lunch with us. About 4 o'clock Gilbert and I and Jacqueline Trotter went by carriage to the Castello dei Caesare where there is a wonderful view of Rome from the terrace of the Ristorante. Then to St.John Lateran and the Baptistry.

April 10th. I went with Lady Trotter and the girls to the Vatican Gallery to see the pictures – a lovely collection, especially the Primitives. After lunch all to the Borghese Palace (statues and pictures), tea and a lovely walk in the Borghese Gardens.

[Once the visas had been obtained it was on to Paris for London and finally once again Beaconsfield]:

> By the time I came to Beaconsfield itself, dusk was dropping over the beech woods and the white cross-roads. The distance seemed to grow deeper and richer with darkness as I went up the long lanes towards my home; and in that distance, as I drew nearer, I heard the barking of a dog.

# 12.

# NEW YORK AND THE MID WEST

In 1919 Dr Pocock who had been the Chestertons' doctor for many years, moved away from Beaconsfield and Dr George Bakewell took over as their general practitioner. Frances' problems were becoming worse and it was not long before she was referred for specialist advice:

18 Lower Seymour Street,
Portman Square, W.1.                                                        8th June 1920

Dear Dr Bakewell,
    I saw your patient Mrs Chesterton yesterday, I could find no evidence of any affection of the joints, and the pain seemed to me to be of nervous origin, and the difficulty she has in raising her arm probably due to the same source . . . I thought it wise to have her X-rayed, and took her round to Mr Coldwell's and had stereoscopic photographs taken. I have seen these this morning in the stereoscope and they show definite calcareous deposits in several of the cervical glands, and at the junction between the 6th and 7th cervical vertebrae on the right side there are blurred shadows and a general fuzziness of outline of the bones . . . I have very little doubt that she has had years ago some old tubercular trouble in the cervical glands: hence the calcification, and that there is some mischief, probably fibrous tissue round the exit of the 7th cervical nerve, possibly this may have been originally of a slow tubercular nature, but I do not think there is any active trouble there now . . . If my diagnosis is correct no medical treatment is likely to be much good, and all drugs would be futile . . . Of course, if the pain became very severe operative treatment to free the nerve might be discussed, though personally I should be inclined to consider it a great deal too grave a thing to advise unless the pain were really so severe as to absolutely make life not worth living.
    Yours sincerely, S. Russell Wills[1]

There had been little or no improvement by October when a trip to North America was contemplated:

1 Royal Crescent, W.8.                                                    Oct. 26, 1920

The story is a long one and dates back to the days of growth, when one leg grew somewhat longer than the other. This threw the transverse diameter of the pelvis out and compensating curves followed. The resulting pain has been regarded as a necessary evil and therefore neglected, till the condition is really very serious. I have advised raising the heel on the short side and am arranging a belt on Goldthwaite's pattern for supporting the sacro-iliac joints and lumbar spine. Meanwhile she is resting and I am trying by massage to allay the extreme sensitiveness and restore sleep . . . Two months' treatment should, I think, go far to restore her, if not to perfection, at least to comparative freedom from pain, and so enable her to pursue her life without undue suffering.

                                                    Yours sincerely, James B. Mennell[2]

                                                                          17.12.20
Your patient Mrs G.K. Chesterton has returned home this week. She is, I am glad to say, better in many ways. She is sleeping adequately, if not well. There is less tenderness and she looks less drawn and haggard. She is now able to wear a belt which I hope will help her considerably. I should have liked to continue the treatment for a little longer, but it could not be done and I think she is now safe for her trip to America. My experience of these cases, as regards the pain, is depressing. It seems to last off and on for about two years – but this I have not mentioned. It is possible to alleviate and to secure rest when near a breaking-point, and in this I hope we have succeeded.

                                                       Yours sincerely, James Mennell[3]

On Christmas Eve Gilbert in writing to Father O'Connor mentioned that 'Frances has not been well'[4] but nonetheless the Chestertons sailed from Liverpool on New Year's Day 1921 aboard the *Kaiserin Augusta Victoria* bound via Cobh for New York where a lecture tour was to begin. The ship headed west through 'fresh gales and rough seas', and even after January 8th on the run down the North American seaboard, Frances described the weather as 'squally'. Once alongside the pier on January 10th the 'World Famous Literary Genius and his wife' were greeted so enthusiastically that 'when . . . [he] first stepped off an Atlantic liner on to American soil, he discovered . . . that he was a much more important person than he had ever supposed . . . But America has a genius for the encouragement of fame . . . he found himself held up on the quay by a group of journalists, as by a gang of brigands, who asked him questions about all the subjects on which he was least likely to regard himself as an authority, such as the details of female dress and the criminal statistics of the country that he had only that moment clapped his eyes on.'[5]

The journalists in their turn tried to come to terms with GKC: 'The impression given by Mr Chesterton as he moved majestically along the pier or on the ship was one of huge bulk. To the ordinary sized people on the pier he seemed to blot out the liner and the river.' A little later the *New York Evening World* waylaid him at his hotel: 'I found . . . at the Biltmore, this big, gentle, leonine man of letters . . . he really doesn't look anything like as fat as his caricatures make him, however, and he has a head big enough to go with his massive tallness. His eyes are brilliant English blue behind the big-rimmed eyeglasses: his wavy hair, steel grey; his heavy moustache, bright yellow. Physically he is the crackling electric spark of the heaven-home-and-mother party, the only man who can give the cleverest radical debaters a Roland for their Oliver.'[6]

The constant pressure from reporters, especially the women reporters, trying for an interview outside their room door was unyielding with the result that both Chestertons wilted, with Frances taking to reconnoitring the corridor to see if the coast was clear before Gilbert would come out. Frances soon became exasperated with 'stupid letters' from female admirers 'who are splendid in their capacity for hero worship . . . Gilbert and I have the good fortune to be congenial, and our life is unostentatious, to say the least. I'm afraid that as an ideal adorer I should fail miserably . . . Of course my husband is intelligent, and I admire intelligence, but life is too short to put one's husband on a pedestal, and then it would prove unutterably boring.'[7] However, the press coverage did give publicity to the lecture tour and the *New York Herald* was to report that 'a large crowd stormed the doors of the Times Square Theatre to hear the British essayist.' Gilbert himself did appreciate his audiences: 'I find Americans a literary revelation, but they take my work absolutely too seriously, though they make the best audience to lecture to in the world. In England a lecture is a most dry affair. It is not a national sport. Here the good people are most appreciative of the individual's effort, whether that individual be Charlie Chaplin, Mr [Jack] Dempsey, or myself.'[8] The titles of the lectures were paradoxical: *The Ignorance of the Educated*, *The Perils of Health* and *Shall we abolish the inevitable?*, and the *New York Sun* commented that 'a superficial observer merely sees the Chestertonian paradox, the man who looks deeper sees the underlying truth.' The technique was not, however, to all tastes and in the *New York Herald* Edward Anthony wrote:

O Gilbert, I know there are many who like
Your talks on the darkness of light,
The shortness of length and the weakness of strength
And the one on the lowness of height.

My neighbour keeps telling me 'How I adore
His legality of the illicit.
And I've also a liking intense for his striking
Obscurity of the explicit.'

But I am unmoved. What's the reason? Oh, well,
The same I intend to expound
Some evening next week, when I'm going to speak
On the shallowness of the profound.[9]

Another sour note was struck by the presence outside the lectures of Jewish pickets who had taken exception to what they saw as anti-semitic comments in the articles sent back in 1919 from Palestine and collected in November 1920 under the title *The New Jerusalem*.

From New York the Chestertons moved on by train to Boston then New York again before Chicago, Philadelphia, Baltimore in Maryland, Nashville in Tennessee, Oklahoma City, Omaha and elsewhere, then back to Albany in New York State before crossing into Canada. The welcomes were always extremely warm and the fees reputedly up to $1,000 (then £200) per lecture, but it had all been exhausting and Frances was homesick: 'I care more for my dog, donkey and garden in the little English village where we live than for all the publicity in the world.'[10] In Boston Frances had consulted another eminent specialist, Dr Osgood, who sent a gloomy prognosis back to England. Aboard a train near Chicago she had given vent to her despair:

IN THE MIDDLE WEST
*Lines written in dejection near Chicago*
Along the unhedged, unhuman plains
The furrows stretch in ordered line,
Ocean to ocean roll the trains
Past little groups of oak or pine.
And in the little timber towns
Men live and struggle, laugh and die,
Frontierless, far from flags and crowns
Beneath no banner but the sky.

Deep hid in England's lovely heart
A cross is traced among the trees.
The rumble of the woodman's cart
Rolls with pre-Roman memories,
And little gardens stand ablaze
With our unstaled and startling Spring.
Veiled, I walk familiar ways,
And since I cannot see, I sing[11]

That it was not just a passing mood is shown by her continuing disquiet:

BALLADE OF A RESTLESS MIND[12]
I hear a lot about the cord that binds
This whirling country to my own quiet land,
And yesterday I met a man who finds
The Cause of Woman definitely fanned
By Lady Astor in her noble stand
'Gainst giving to the working men the kinds
Of drink they like. I do not understand.
Why have these people got such restless minds?

They say that in this sphere the husband grinds
So that his wife may look superb and grand
And also that our English wives are hinds
And only eat out of their husband's hand.
They tell me Woodrow Wilson really planned
To enter war much earlier, but declined
To yield to public clamour and demand.
Why have these people got such restless minds?

So hot their rooms I'd gladly suck the rinds
Of oranges, or ask for peaches (canned).
And then they say 'It's prejudice that blinds
You to the virtues of steam heating, and
The joys of ices and ice water fanned',
And then they often add 'Ah this reminds –
Why is Lord Reading's manner grave and bland?'
Why have these people got such restless minds?

Prince, Stars and Stripes float gaily o'er this land.
Our flag is by a little road that winds
By quiet ways to where a cross may stand,
And people there have not got restless minds.

Perhaps none too soon as far as Frances was concerned, on April 12th the Chestertons embarked on the SS *Aquitania* bound for Southampton. Back in Beaconsfield, the lecture fees went towards the cost of converting and extending the Top Meadow studio as a replacement for Overroads where the lease could not be extended any further. But even the prospect of a new house failed to raise Frances' spirits, and it was not long before she was again referred to a specialist:

1 Royal Crescent, W.8                                                        22.5.21

Perhaps you will remember that, some little time ago, you kindly consented that one of your patients, Mrs G.K. Chesterton, should place herself under my care for insomnia. I patched her up enough to get through her American tour somehow: but, when she returned home she again applied to me for help. I told her plainly that what I had done before was to treat symptoms and not the disease, and that this should now be investigated. Accordingly, I went all out. She has her blood and general bacteriology reports for you, and I now enclose X-ray reports. As you will see, the only flaw to be found is her teeth. I am sending a sterile tube, and if you could arrange for one of the teeth to be placed in this and sent off straight to me, I will have the vaccine prepared . . . In the meantime she is obviously trying to do much more than her condition warrants and, if she will not pull up, I am quite ready – any time you wish it – to advise that she goes into a Home for a regular rest-cure.

    The patient saw Dr Osgood – on my advice – in Boston, Mass. He sent me a most lugubrious report and I must say it was justified. I am sure that Mrs Chesterton can, and should, be made much better than she is; but it is a tough job and will need all our united efforts. But how far it is possible for her to live at home and get well I do not know . . .

                                                        Yours sincerely, James Mennell


Reports from X-Ray Department, St. Thomas's Home, 20.5.1921, were largely negative:
Spine: No evidence of Osteo-arthritis.
Teeth: Lower incisors show marked pyorrhocal absorbtion.
Chronic abscess at root of Right Upper 4th.
Left lower 5th and 6th show marked pyorrhocal absorbtion.
All teeth show heavy deposits of tartar below level of gum.
Stomach (Bismuth Meal): Some gastroptosis with an active stomach, but emptying at a normal rate. No other evidence of abnormality.


                                                                        19.5.22

Thank you for letting me see Mrs Chesterton again. I am afraid she is in the soup badly this time! The arthritis is very acute and I should refrain from all massage and movements. If surface stroking of the thigh will keep down some of the irritation, it might be tried – but it must not be ordinary massage. I have suggested a heat bath by day and anti-philogistine at night . . . If things quiet a little I should try plain galvanism

... The inoculation is obviously useless – at present at any rate. The right treatment, of course, is bed with extension or a walking calliper. I realise the impossibility of both. A poor substitute is a plaster gutter back splint, but I hope the strapping may help enough ... I have rarely met a woman I am more sorry for, and I can't help wondering if we are merely witnessing the onset of general osteo-arthritis. Heaven help them both, if we are!

Yours sincerely, James Mennell

P.S. I am only too willing to do anything I can to help, if you think it any good letting me see her again.

24th June 1922

I saw Mrs Chesterton again yesterday, and I cannot say that I was very pleased with the state of affairs, though the knee is certainly better than when I saw it last.

I think that there is no question that she is willing to undergo treatment if it can be provided, and the only people I can find out anything about are Miss Hessel and Miss Johnson whom Mrs Chesterton seems to know. There are two others down on the register ... Any of these should be able to carry out the treatment she really needs. This I think should consist of graduated Faradic contraction of her quadriceps for half an hour three days a week, and on the alternate days, a full Galvanic current through the knee, followed by Faradic foot-baths. After each treatment with the leg hanging over the side of a couch, the Tibia should be rotated on the femur as freely as it will go without pain. I am afraid that unless something of this sort is carried out she will take an intolerable time in recovering from her at present somewhat dilapidated condition.

Yours sincerely, James Mennell

Frances' condition had deteriorated so badly that the move to Top Meadow was left to Gilbert with Frances being lifted bodily from her bed in Overroads and carried across the street to her bed in their new house.

27th October 1922

Thank you for letting me see Mrs Chesterton again today. I was thankful to see how much better she was in general appearance ... It is, I am afraid, quite impossible for her to leave off her support yet, and it is a little difficult to see any active form of treatment that would be likely to help her at the present time. Of course your suggestion that she should go away for the winter, is really the ideal thing to do, though my choice of places would be limited to Morocco, Madeira or the West Indies. I have known such horrible catastrophes occur to these people in Egypt, that perhaps I am unduly prejudiced against it. I still hope that the time may come when I may be able to help her by active treatment, but I am sure it is not yet. If she pulls through the winter alright, perhaps we might be able to try at the beginning of the spring. It has been rather a dreadful case, has it not?

Yours sincerely, James Mennell

No further medical records survive for the next two years, but it would seem that Frances' health did not improve.

1st November, 1924

I saw Mrs Chesterton this afternoon as arranged, and certainly she seems to be in a very poor way. I gather that under no circumstances can she possibly leave England until Christmas, and I imagine that this too would fit in better with the season at Aquae than by going there just now.

In the meantime it struck me that it might be worth while to have her basal metabolism gone into, and if you agree, I will ask Gardiner-Hill to undertake it.

Certainly since the change she has put on a very considerable amount of weight, and the nature of the increase too made me think that perhaps her sugar tolerance was upset.

Another thing occurred to me as a vague possibility which I think we might go into. I do not know if you have heard anything about the work that Cumberbatch has been doing at Bart's lately on the subject of these obscure infections. There he has been doing a large amount of work on diathermy of the cervical canal . . . When you write it would help me a good deal if you could let me know whether you have ever heard of Mrs Chesterton having any vaginal discharge.

Yours sincerely, James Mennell

St. Thomas's Hospital Clinical Medical Unit

Westminster Bridge, London, S.E.1                                    9.12.24

Mrs G.K. Chesterton has asked me to write to you. Dr Mennell sent her to me a few days ago. She has apparently been putting on weight – chiefly about the hips – and getting rather easily fatigued. I think this is largely the result of the menopause. She appears to me to have been always an individual of the rather underdeveloped pituitary type – onset of menstruation late (ca. 17 – sterility – lack of genital development etc.), and I think these people often get more deficient at the menopause. I am going to suggest that she takes Thyroid and Pituitary Extracts in the form of HORMOTONE (with post pituitary) in gradually increasing doses for six months, starting with one tablet three times a day for six months and working up for a second month to 2 tablets three times a day. Continue at this dosage for the six months, Miss Carmride to make up the preparation. I think this should improve her general health. I suggested to Mrs Chesterton that if this did not benefit her, it would be wise to investigate her metabolism – as Dr Mennill (sic) originally suggested – and if necessary, start with more active treatment with dessicated Thyroid and whole Pituitary extracts.

Yours truly, H. Gardiner Hill

28, Circus, Bath                                                15th January 1925

Mrs G.K. Chesterton consulted me on her arrival in Bath, on account of debility and some general muscular rheumatism. On examining her, I found that her pulse was 140, blood pressure 180/100, that she had definite fine tremor, and she complained of palpitation on exertion and slight oedema of the feet. Her heart, though rapid, was regular, and there was no sign of valvular disease. Her electro-cardiogram shews a normal rhythm, and does not indicate any degenerative changes of the myocardium. I think her condition is due partly to the menopause, and partly to overwork. The symptoms appear to me to point to hyper-thyroidism, and I have warned her that it is very necessary to live very quietly and rest as much as possible for the next few weeks. I think really that her condition is, or will be, somewhat serious if she does not take this course. She should really have three or four weeks in bed to start with, but she appears to think that she must try and carry on, looking after her various household and other affairs as long as possible. I ordered her some mild massage baths for the rheumatism, which has somewhat improved under this treatment, and proscribed a medicine containing Bromide and *nux vomica*. I told her to see you on her return, as I am sure you will agree that she should be under regular medical supervision at the present time.

Yours truly, F.G. Thomson

19 Park Crescent                                                                          January 15th, 1926
Portland Place, W.1.

Thank you for your note about Mrs Chesterton. I am sorely afraid that there is little we can do to help her back, except support and encourage rest. How you ever got her into a Home for a decent spell of the latter, I cannot imagine, and therefore can only congratulate you. If, after a decent rest now, you can really get her away, as you propose, for several months, it might make all the difference in the world to her. I am not an expert in climatology, but from what I have heard from patients and others, the Mecca for people of this type is Biskra.[13] This, I gather, is some little distance inland, and is free from the ghastly storms which seem from time to time to ravage the coast, often for weeks and sometimes for months on end, and this apparently without any reason, and with very little respect to the time of year. Do not let her go to Egypt if you can possibly help it, but I am sure you are right to urge her to go somewhere.

Yours sincerely, James Mennell

# 13.

# A TWITCH ON THE THREAD

The somewhat vague Unitarianism of the Chestertons on Campden Hill never seemed to imprint itself on their eldest son who, when he showed any interest in religion, took himself off either to hear Stopford Brooke preaching at Bedford Chapel or R.J. Campbell at the City Temple. His eventual reaction was a surprising mixture of anticlericalism [*Ballad of the God Makers*] allied to a lifelong devotion to Mary the Mother of God which he retained from his schooldays right on throughout the 1890s as he debated at ethical, theosophical, philosophical and spiritual societies across the length and breadth of London. It was only late in 1896 or New Year 1897 when he met Frances Blogg, his future wife and a practising Anglo-Catholic, that he began to give any consideration to the religious position he would express definitively in 1908 in *Orthodoxy*:

> I never read a line of Christian apologetics. I read as little as I can of them now. It was Huxley and Herbert Spencer and Bradlaugh who brought me back to orthodox theology. They sowed in my mind my first wild doubts of doubt. Our grandmothers were quite right when they said that Tom Paine and the freethinkers unsettled the mind. They do. They unsettled mine horribly. The rationalist made me question whether reason was of any use whatever; and when I had finished Herbert Spencer I had got as far as doubting (for the first time) whether evolution had occurred at all. As I laid down the last of Colonel Ingersoll's atheistic lectures the dreadful thought broke across my mind, 'Almost thou persuades me to be a Christian.' I was in a desperate way.[1]

Once adopted, as it was, for life, his belief did not change even when in 1922 he converted from his Anglican allegiance to that of Rome, and indeed many were astounded that his Catholicism had not been of the Roman persuasion all along.

Chesterton was always to be of the opinion that no religion was worthwhile if it couldn't be made fun of,[2] and so from early on he could be found affectionately mocking the CSU of which he was an active member:

*The Christian Social Union, Nottingham*
The Christian Social Union here
Was very much annoyed;
It seems there is some duty
Which we never should avoid,
And so they sang a lot of hymns
To help the Unemployed.

Upon a platform at the end
The speakers were displayed,
And Bishop Hoskins stood in front
And hit a bell and said
That Mr Carter was to pray,
And Mr Carter prayed.

Then Bishop Gore of Birmingham
He stood upon one leg
And said he would be happier
If beggars didn't beg,
And that if they pinched his palace
It would take him down a peg.

He said that Unemployment
Was a horror and a blight,
He said that charities produced
Servility and spite,
And stood upon the other leg
And said it wasn't right.

And then a man named Chesterton
Got up and played with water.
He seemed to say that principles
Were nice and led to slaughter,
And how we always compromised
And how we didn't orter.

Then Canon Holland fired ahead
Like fifty cannons firing,
We tried to find out what he meant
With infinite enquiring,
But the way he made the windows jump
We couldn't help admiring.

I understood him to remark
(It seemed a little odd)
That half a dozen of his friends
Had never been in quod,
He said he was a Socialist
Himself, and so was God.

He said the human soul should be
Ashamed of every sham,
He said a man should constantly
Ejaculate 'I am'.
When he had done, I went outside
And got into a tram.
(1906)

A year later in *The Man Who Was Thursday* Gabriel Syme twists the words of Sir William Harcourt in 1885 into 'We are all Catholics now',[3] perhaps to gently mock Chesterton's brother-in-law, Knollys Blogg, recently converted to Roman Catholicism. Chesterton himself had been impressed when in 1903 he first met Father John O'Connor, a priest at Keighley in West Yorkshire, and they became life-long friends, a status which did not in 1910 bar Chesterton from taking him as the model for his clerical sleuth Father Brown. Another Roman Catholic, though this time a fictional character, to feature prominently was Evan MacIan, a fanatical but sympathetic Highlander in *The Ball and the Cross* (1905–1910): 'brought up in some loneliness and seclusion as a strict Roman Catholic, in the midst of that little wedge of Roman Catholics which is driven into the Western Highlands . . . He had uncovered himself for a few moments before the statue of Queen Anne, in front of St. Paul's Cathedral, under the firm impression that it was a figure of the Virgin Mary. He was somewhat surprised at the lack of deference shown to the figure by the people bustling by. He did not understand that their one essential historical principle, the one law truly graven on their hearts, was the great and comforting statement that Queen Anne is dead. This faith was as fundamental as his faith, that Our Lady was alive.' MacIan is ever keen to literally cross swords with the equally fanatical and sympathetic atheist Turnbull. In the course of the narrative both antagonists experience a dream embodying all their hopes for the future, a dream which gradually turns into nightmare. MacIan's dream of St. Paul's certainly gives an impression that the author was aware of excesses in the ultramontane tendency of Roman Catholicism:

> ... there sprang up, picked out in glittering silver, a dome and a cross. It seemed that it was really newly covered with silver, which in the strong moonlight was like white flame ... He saw the great thoroughfare that sloped upward to the base of its huge pedestal of steps ... he observed other alterations. The dome had been redecorated so as to give it a more solemn and somewhat more ecclesiastical note; the ball was draped or destroyed, and round the gallery, under the cross, ran what looked like a ring of silver statues, like the little leaden images that stood round the hat of Louis XI. Round the second gallery, at the base of the dome, ran a second rank of such images, and Evan thought there was another round the steps below ... he saw that they were figures in complete armour of steel or silver, each with a naked sword, point upward; and then he saw one of the swords move. These were not statues but an armed order of chivalry thrown in three circles round the cross. MacIan drew in his breath, as children do at anything they think utterly beautiful. For he could imagine nothing that so echoed his own visions of pontifical or chivalric art as this white dome sitting like a vast silver tiara over London, ringed with a triple crown of swords ... All the old black-coated bustle with its cockney vivacity and vulgarity had disappeared ... it required but a few mounted men to keep the streets in order. The mounted men were not common policemen, but knights with spur and plume whose smooth and splendid armour glittered like diamond rather than steel ... But one old grumbling man did not get out of the way quick enough, and the man on horseback struck him, not severely, across the shoulders with the flat of his sword.
>
> 'The soldier had no business to do that,' said MacIan, sharply. 'The old man was moving as quickly as he could.'
>
> 'We attach great importance to discipline in the streets,' said the man in white, with a slight smile.
>
> 'Discipline is not so important as justice,' said MacIan.
>
> '... Discipline for the whole society is surely more important than justice to an individual.'
>
> Evan, who was also leaning over the edge, swung round with startling suddenness and stared at the other's back.
>
> 'Discipline for society –' he repeated, very staccato, 'more important – justice to the individual? ... Who and what are you?'
>
> 'I am an angel,' said the white-robed figure, without turning round.
>
> 'You are not a Catholic,' said MacIan ... 'Why you great fool!' cried MacIan, rising to the top of his tremendous stature, 'did you think I would have doubted only for that rap with a sword? I know that noble orders have bad knights, that good knights have

bad tempers, that the Church has rough priests and coarse cardinals; I have known it ever since I was born. You fool! You had only to say, "Yes, it is rather a shame," and I should have forgotten the affair . . . Something is wrong . . . You are not an angel. That is not a church . . . You are not one of God's angels. But you were once."[4]

Nonetheless, in July 1909[5] Chesterton himself declared: 'I call myself both Catholic and Democrat; and if there were a specifically democratic wing of Catholicism, I would be with that wing . . . About the seat of Catholic authority I do not disguise from anyone that I am still in some doubt; and I agree much more with the high Anglicans than the Roman Modernists.' It was to take eleven more years, a change in Pope, and the death of Edward Chesterton before there was any sign of a further twitch on that thread:

Xmas Eve, 1920

Dear Father O'Connor,

I feel I must scribble you a line, with incongruous haste and crudity, to send you our love at Xmas and to ask for your prayers. Frances and I are going away to America for a month or two; and I am glad of it, for I shall at least be free from the load of periodical work that has prevented me from talking properly to anybody, even to her; and I want to talk very much. When it is over I shall probably want to talk to you, about very important things – the most important things there are. Frances has not been well, and though I think she is better, I have to do things in a considerate way, if you understand me; I feel it is also only right to consult with my Anglo-Catholic friends; but I have at present a feeling that it will be something like a farewell. Things have shaken me up a good deal lately – especially the persecution of Ireland. But of course there are even bigger things than that. Forgive this confused scrawl.

Yours always, G.K. Chesterton[6]

Two years later he had been discussing matters with Ronald Knox:

Undated [but 1922], Top Meadow, Beaconsfield

Dear Father Knox,

I had meant to make some attempt to finish the fuller reply I had actually begun to the very kind letter you sent me. I am ashamed to think how long ago, before my recent trouble,[7] and though the trail and tangle of those troubles will still, I fear, make this very inadequate, there were two things in your letter I feel I ought to acknowledge even so late.

I cannot tell you how much I was pleased and honoured even by the suggestion that you might possibly deal with the instruction yourself; it is something that I should value more vividly and personally than I can possibly express. But as this was so long ago, before so many delays and interruptions, I fear your margin of Sundays in London must now be very much narrowed. But I think there must be a Sunday or two left on your list; and with your permission, I propose to come up next Sunday, if I could have the pleasure of seeing you then. I have no doubt it could be arranged through Maurice Baring or somebody, supposing you have no arrangements of your own which you would prefer. Then we could see what could be done with that possibility, or finally make some arrangement about another one. I rather feel I should like to talk to you once more in either case. I hope it would not be an inconvenience.

For the other matter, I hope you do not really feel any need to apologise for what you said about private troubles dismounting a man from public platforms; for it is exactly what I am feeling most intensely myself. I am in a state now when I feel a monstrous charlatan, as if I wore a mask and were stuffed with cushions, whenever I see anything about the public GKC; it hurts me; for though the views I express are real, the image is horribly unreal compared with the real person who needs help just now.

I have as much vanity as anybody about any of these superficial successes while they are going on; but I never feel for a moment that they affect the reality of whether I am utterly rotten or not; so that any public comments on my religious position seem like a wind on the other side of the world; as if they were about somebody else – as indeed they are. I am not troubled about a great fat man who appears on platforms and in caricatures, even when he enjoys controversies on what I believe to be the right side. I am concerned about what has become of the little boy whose father showed him a toy theatre, and a schoolboy whom nobody ever heard of, with his brooding on doubts and dirt and day dreams of crude conscientiousness so insistent as to near hypocrisy; and all the morbid life of the lonely mind of a living person with whom I have lived. It is *that* story that so often came near to ending badly, that I want to end well. Forgive this scrawl; I think you will understand me.

Yours very sincerely, G.K. Chesterton

P.S. Forgive the disreputable haste of this letter, my normal chaos is increased by moving into a new house, which is still like a wastepaper basket. I am coming up to London tomorrow, and will try to fix something up with Maurice or somebody.[8]

[Postmark: July 11th, 1922]
Top Meadow, Beaconsfield.

Dear Father O'Connor,

I ought to have written to you long before to reply to your kind letter; but indeed I do not answer it now in order to agree with you about Ireland or disagree with you about France; if indeed we do disagree about anything. I write with a more personal motive; do you happen to have a holiday about the end of next week or thereabouts; and would it be possible for you to come south and see our new house – or old studio? This sounds a very abrupt invitation; but I write in great haste, and am troubled about many things. I want to talk to you about them; especially the most serious ones, religious and concerned with my own rather difficult position. Most of the difficulty has been my own fault, but not all; some of my difficulties would commonly be called duties; though I ought perhaps to have learned sooner to regard them as lesser duties. I mean that a Pagan or Protestant or Agnostic might even have excused me; but I have grown less and less of a Pagan or Protestant, and can no longer excuse myself. There are lots of things

for which I never did excuse myself; but I am thinking now of particular points that might really be casuistical. Anyhow, you are the person that Frances and I think of with most affection, of all who could help in such a matter. Could you let me know if any time such as I name, or after, could give us the joy of seeing you?
Yours always sincerely, G.K. Chesterton.[9]

GKC then extricated himself:

[July, 1922]

Dear Father Knox,
I ought to have written long ago to tell you what I have done about the most practical of business matters. I have again been torn in pieces by the wars of the *New Witness*; but I have managed to have another talk with my wife, after which I have written to our old friend Father O'Connor and asked him to come here, as he probably can, from what I hear. I doubt whether I can possibly put in words why I feel sure this is the right thing, not so much for my sake as for hers. We talk about misunderstandings; but I think it is possible to understand too well for comfort; certainly too well for my powers of psychological description. Frances is just at the point where Rome acts both as the positive and the negative magnet; a touch would turn her either way; almost (against her will) to hatred, but with the right touch to a faith far beyond my reach. I know Father O'Connor's would be the touch that does not startle, because she knows him and is fond of him; and the only thing she asked of me was to send for him. If he cannot come, of course I shall take other action and let you know. I doubt if most people could make head or tail of this hasty scrawl: but I think you will understand.[10]

Father Knox replied on July 17th, 1922: 'I'm awfully glad to hear that you've sent for Father O'Connor and that you think he's likely to be available. I must say that, in the story, Father Brown's powers of neglecting his parish always seemed to me even more admirable than Dr Watson's powers of neglecting his practice; so I hope this trait was drawn from life.'[11] On July 23rd Frances was concerned with more mundane but practical matters:

Dear Father O'Connor,
I just want to know if you can send *me* a line as to how long you can stay in Beaconsfield. I have a spare bed for Wednesday night [July 26th], but after that I must get a room out or at one of the inns for you. Please don't think me inhospitable, I am only too pleased that G. wants you – and I am sure that you will now be able to give him all the advice and help he wants.[12]

A few days later Father O'Connor was indeed in Beaconsfield:

On Thursday morning [July 27th], on one of our trips to the village, I told Mrs

Chesterton: 'There is only one thing troubling Gilbert about the great step – the effect it is going to have on you.' 'Oh! I shall be infinitely relieved. You cannot imagine how it fidgets Gilbert to have something on his mind. The last three months have been exceptionally trying. I should be only too glad to come with him, if God in His mercy would show the way clear, but up to now He has not made it clear enough to me to justify such a step.' So I was able to reassure Gilbert that afternoon.[13]

Three days later Gilbert's reception into the Roman Catholic Church took place in the wooden extension behind the pub where Mass was said, there being at that time no Catholic church in Beaconsfield:

The Railway Hotel [later the Earl of Beaconsfield and now demolished to make way for a supermarket] had its dance-room fitted up with Sir Philip Rose's chapel fixtures, fairly handsome they were; and Mrs Borlase was a buxom landlady from the west of Ireland and could be trusted to play up. So after lunch at Top Meadow on Sunday, July 30th, 1922, Gilbert and I set out for the Railway Hotel, Gilbert selecting from the stand with special solicitude, a rare and beautiful snakewood stick which the Knights of Columbus had just given him in America. The Creed of Pius the Fourth[14] was repeated very fervently – I recalled inwardly that at one time or another in our numerous encounters he had stoutly proclaimed his adherence to almost every clause.[15]

Father Ignatius Rice OSB had come over from Douai Abbey and he it was who reassured a weeping Frances while Gilbert made his confession to Father O'Connor. Later in the day Gilbert wrote a sonnet on his conversion:

THE CONVERT

After one moment when I bowed my head
And the whole world turned over and came upright,
And I came out where the old road shone white,
I walked the ways and heard what all men said,
Forests of tongues, like autumn leaves unshed,
Being not unlovable but strange and light;
Old riddles and new creeds, not in despite
But softly, as men smile about the dead.

The sages have a hundred maps to give
That trace their crawling cosmos like a tree,
They rattle reason out through many a sieve
That stores the sand and lets the gold go free:
And all these things are less than dust to me
Because my name is Lazarus and I live.

He then wrote to inform his mother:

> My Dearest Mother,
>
> I write this (with the worst pen in South Bucks) to tell you something before I write about it to anyone else; something about which we shall probably be in the position of the two bosom friends at Oxford, who 'never differed except in opinion.' You have always been so wise in not judging people by their opinions, but rather the opinions by the people. It is in one sense a long story by this time; but I have come to the same conclusion that Cecil did about needs of the modern world in religion and right dealing, and now I am a Catholic in the same sense as he, having long claimed the name in its Anglo-Catholic sense. I am not going to make a foolish fuss of reassuring you about things I am sure you never doubted; these things do not hurt any relations between people as fond of each other as we are; any more than they ever made any difference to the love between Cecil and ourselves. But there are two things, . . . in case you do not realize them through some other impression. I have thought about you, and all that I owe you and my father, not only in the way of affection, but of the ideals of honour and freedom and charity and all other good things you always taught me; and I am not conscious of the smallest break or difference in those ideals; but only of a new and necessary way of fighting for them. I think, as Cecil did, that the fight for the family and the free citizen and everything decent must now be waged by one fighting form of Christianity. The other is that I have thought this out for myself and not in a hurry of feeling. It is months since I saw my Catholic friends and years since I talked to them about it. I believe it is the truth. I must end now, you know with how much love; for the post is going.
>
> Always your loving son, Gilbert.[16]

Ada, looking back in 1942, the year of her own conversion, opined that:

> It was in this year of [his father's] death that Gilbert made his great decision. The final impetus which joined him to the Catholic faith was, I think, an increasing sense of family loss, and he had dwelt so long in spiritual uncertainty that he yearned to find himself anchored to a definite belief. His entry into the Church created world-wide interest, and from that time he seemed to find peace of mind.[17]

Father O'Connor later felt that Chesterton was taken advantage of by his new co-religionists: 'Gilbert had always been a skilled and keen defender of all Catholic ideals . . . He came into great demand on public occasions, and naturally was pulled to pieces by the "Oh let's" Brigade. I was much solicited by the obscure well-meaning to get him to do this, that and the other; and though I held out manfully I fear I let him be preyed upon to no-one's advantage but that of the would-be important.'[18]

Ada was more blunt: 'Gilbert, I always felt, was so impregnated with the super-natural power of the Church over her disciples, that he credited Catholics as such with an undue impeccability of motive and purpose in worldly affairs. I have known him impressed by the most obvious tricksters through the sheer fact of their Catholicism.'[19]

Gilbert explained what had occasioned the shift in his religious position:

The change I have made is from being an Anglo-Catholic to being a Roman Catholic. I have always believed, at least for twenty years, in the Catholic view of Christianity. Unless the Church of England was a branch of the Catholic Church I had no use for it. If it were a Protestant Church I did not believe in it in any case. The question always was whether the Church of England can claim to be in direct descent from the medieval Catholic Church. That is the question with every Anglo-Catholic or Higher Churchman.

Among the people who have most helped me to answer the question whether the Church of England is Catholic, and to whom I am most indebted, are the chief Protestant leaders in the Church of England, such as the Dean of St. Paul's [Dean Inge] and Bishop Hensley Henson. They have done me this good service, and I wish to express gratitude for it. They have done me the best service one man can do to another.

It appears to me quite clear that any church claiming to be authoritative, must be able to answer quite definitively when great questions of public morals are put. Can I go in for cannibalism, or murder babies to reduce the population, or any similar scientific and progressive reform? Any Church with authority to teach must be able to say whether it can be done. But Protestant churches are in utter bewilderment on these moral questions – for example on birth control, on divorce, and on Spiritualism.

You have people like Dean Inge coming out publicly and definitely to champion what I regard as a low and poisonous trick, not far removed from infanticide. It is perfectly true that there are in the Church of England and other Protestant bodies, men who would denounce these heathen vices as much as I can. Bishop Gore would speak about them as strongly as the Pope.

But the point is that the Church of England does not speak strongly. It has no united action. I have no use for a Church which is not a Church militant, which cannot order battle and fall in line and march in the same direction.[20]

Two months later in September 1922 Gilbert Chesterton was confirmed in his new faith, taking the confirmation name of Francis, the saint whose biography he wrote that year.

# 14.

# THE GIRLS THAT GO DANCING

## The Grays

The Chestertons always compensated for their childlessness by surrounding themselves with young people, some of whom they virtually adopted. Towards the end of the 1914–18 War the Gray family consisting of a widower and his daughters moved into Bourne House close to Overroads. Mr Gray, formerly a banker in Burma, had retired after losing his wife, and their household was organised by the eldest girl (Enid) Hilary born in 1901. They were to loom large in the Chesterton world and in Beaconsfield where Hilary featured in amateur dramatics and the newly formed Girl Guide movement. The developing relationship can be traced through the poems[1] and stories addressed to Hilary, Chillery, Harity and Enid (a name Hilary Gray sought to keep secret but which GKC had discovered). Mr Gray also is featured as involving himself in local social life in 'The Jazz':

> I have heard that modern dancing is barbaric,
>     Pagan, shameless, shocking, abominable.
> No such luck – I mean no such thing,
>     The dancers are singularly respectable
>     To the point of rigidity,
> With something of the rotatory perseverance
>     Of a monkey on a stick.
> But there is more stick than monkey
>     And not, as slanderers assert,
> More monkey than stick.
>     If Mr King stood on his head,

Or Mr Simon butted Mr Gray
   In the waistcoat,
There would then be a serene harmony,
   A calm unity and oneness
In the two arts.[2]

Mr Gray died in the early 1920s after which his daughters moved from Beaconsfield, Hilary marrying and returning to Burma.

## The Nicholls

In the late summer of 1925[3] Gilbert and Frances Chesterton were on a holiday tour of the English West Country which brought them to the Three Cups Hotel in Lyme Regis in Dorset, perhaps now best known for its Jurassic Coast and as the setting for the film of John Fowles' *The French Lieutenant's Woman*. Their intention had been to stay in the area for two days, although that stay was soon stretched to a couple of weeks by a chance encounter.

Stepping out of the Three Cups Hotel (a three storey Georgian building still standing though bordering on dereliction) the Chestertons descended Broad Street towards the harbour when they noticed two girls gazing disconsolately into the window of a toy shop upon discovering that their money would not stretch to the purchase of a very small teddy-bear. Gilbert was all for giving the young ladies half-a-crown (now 12.5p) to make up any deficit, but Frances had the good sense to dissuade him. The two girls were Barbara and Dorothy Nicholl, aged 12 and 10 respectively, and they too had observed the Chestertons and recognized GKC. Hurrying home, they poured out the news to their sister Clare (aged 19) who was a great fan. In Clare Nicholl's account:

> The children came rushing home even more urgently. They gasped and gulped and exclaimed almost simultaneously, 'You will NEVER GUESS who we saw in the village, standing outside Mr Isbell's toyshop.' Dorothy hinted: 'It's someone you like very much. Someone whose photograph you showed us in the paper . . . someone you taught us about in Literature lessons – THE MAN WHO WROTE *WHERE THE BEE SUCKS*.' 'Yes,' added Barbara, 'and that other poem, the one about the Donkey. I think he must be staying at the Three Cups Hotel.'
>
> I grabbed Barbara by the hand. 'Where are you going to now?' asked my mother.
>
> 'We are going to ask Mr Chesterton to tea . . .'
>
> The Three Cups has a bulging frontage that faces Lyme High Street. We peered through the revolving doors and saw G.K.C. sitting alone in the lounge, smoking the inevitable small cigar. We pushed through the doors and – our courage failed us: we walked straight past him to the reception desk and in loud unnatural voices asked to be shown rooms. 'We are enquiring for friends, who want to stay here . . .' we lied. We

were shown over the entire hotel (it is quite a large one), and finally landed back in the lounge. G.K.C. was still there. We explained to the receptionist that we would let her know . . . our friends were rather fussy . . . G.K.C. got up and revolved the doors for us: we bowed politely and murmured, 'Thank you.' We went out into the street.

'Well?' asked my mother, when we had trailed home, 'Is Mr Chesterton coming to tea?' 'We hadn't the nerve to speak to him,' we said flatly.

That night we wrote a letter instead. It would at least give him the chance to refuse the invitation . . . I added a postscript, asking him if he realised he was the Ghost of Shakespeare, and could the Ghost of Shakespeare drink tea? Barbara and I sneaked back to the hotel after supper and handed the note in at the desk. This time we stood our ground. 'Please tell Mr Chesterton we are waiting for an answer' we said.

We shall never forget the sight of G.K.C.'s large grey legs coming down those stairs: it was like watching the progress of a huge friendly elephant. He shook us by the hand as though we were long-lost friends. 'How JOLLY,' he said. 'I say, am I really Shakespeare's Ghost? May we really come to tea – my wife and I?'[4]

Mrs Winifred Mary Nicholl (née Ellis) was the widow of Bernard Vincent Nicholl (1867–1915), a District Commissioner in Assam and then a judge in the Indian Civil Service stationed at Dinajpur in Bengal until his death from pneumonia in 1915 had brought the family to England. There were seven children, Agnes (born 1898), Robert (1900), Cecilia (1901), Clare (1906), Joan (1912), Barbara (1913) and Dorothy (1915). At the time of the meeting with the Chestertons Agnes and Robert were already married with children, and Cecilia was working as a secretary to Osbert Sitwell. Bernard Nicholl came from a recusant family claiming descent from Charlemagne and Hugues Capet. In the early 1920s his son Robert had inherited from his grandmother Harbourstown House near Skerries, north of Dublin in Ireland, together with a considerable estate dependent on his changing his name to Nicholl-Cadell, but by 1925 the estate had been neglected and was requisitioned by the Irish government. Any nest egg had been squandered on fast cars and living; Robert was seeking to repair his fortunes in India, and the rest of the family were back in Lyme Regis.

And so it was that the Chestertons went to Woodmead Road to have tea with the Nicholls and struck up a ready rapport with them, returning to Lyme Regis for the following years until 1930 when, as Cecilia and Clare were working in London, the Nicholls were persuaded to move to Beaconsfield where they purchased Christmas Cottage, 22 Grove Road along the street from Top Meadow at number 1. The holiday time passed at Lyme Regis from 1925 to around 1929 was filled with walks and games and poems[5] and marked by the foundation of their very own secret society. The Nicholl children acquired

a surrogate 'unclet and auntlet' and Gilbert had a family of rumbustuous
teenagers to delight him until they one by one grew up.

> The Crier is crying in Lyme of the King
> Lost, Stolen or Strayed is the Marvellous Thing,
> I will ring for the sea-gulls that dance in the spray,
> But the girls that go dancing go dancing away,
> The girls that go dancing, go dancing, go dancing,
> The girls that go dancing, go dancing away.

The link with the Nicholls continued until long after Gilbert's death in 1936
and his influence is still felt among the family to this day. Barbara (nickname
Mike) recalled:

'I shall never be grateful enough for knowing him. It is not only what
he did and meant at the time, but what he meant later, remembering it in a
more grown-up way.[6] Joan expressed this in more detail: 'One of the things
I loved and honoured most in him and one of the things that made me feel
"exalted" and "humbled" together, as in the Magnificat, was his *deep* chivalry
and honour of women. And one felt and knew it was based on no whimsy and
namby-pamby ideas of colourless innocence and lack of temptation, but on
the contrary on a very profound and understanding experience.'[7]

Clare (Unicorn to GKC) added about 1950: 'Our friendship with G.K. was the daily
bread of life: he made one feel at home in the world and he himself was like a huge
comfortable house with great windows opening on to vistas and letting in the daylight.
Of all the things he said to us there is one remark that we remember with more happiness
and gratitude than all the rest. He came in one evening and told us, "I have just finished
writing my Memoirs [early 1936]. None of you are mentioned in my Memoirs: I had to
bring in most of my friends, but it delighted me not to have to bring in *all* my friends
– it is jolly to have friends who are just one's own private property." A house when it is
thrown open to the public is only too apt to look and feel like a museum rather than
a home, and therefore recorded stories about G.K. as we saw him and knew him take
on the character of 'exhibits', divorced from the personality which made them alive,
stripped of the casual intimacy which is the heart of friendship. For us he belongs (it is
impossible to think of him in the past tense) not to the limelight, but to the firelight.'[8]

Maisie Ward followed a habit of suppressing identities, particularly annoying
in the case of a girl (in fact Clare) thinking of trying her vocation in a convent,
to whom Chesterton wrote in a letter later destroyed:

If you are really For It (I use, not without justice, the jovial phrase commonly used about
people going to be jailed or flogged or hanged) – if you are For It, it is the grandest and

most glorious and deific thing that any human being can be For. It is far beyond my imagination. But never, for one instant, among all my sins, have I doubted that it was *above* my imagination. I have no more doubt that a man like Father McNabb is walking on a crystal floor over my head than I have that Quoodle[9] has a larger equipment of legs than I have: and (with all respect to his many virtues) a rather simpler intellectual plan of life. If that is your Way Out, then everybody must stand out of your way, as out of the way of a Celestial Fire-Engine. If one of my friends is caught up to Heaven in a fiery chariot – you will not think me capable of being a stout and stolid speed-Cop or Traffic Policeman to hold her up for enquiries. No: that is unanswerable. If that is so, nobody has the right to say anything except – 'God will love you even more than we do.'

But – there is still one little worrying thought left in the dregs of what I call my mind. You will be generous enough to forgive if the hesitation sounds personal. [Clare] I have often hailed as she rushed by: but I have met her rushing *from* places as well as to places. If you must rush, this is a place you must rush to and cannot rush from. I don't mean any material nonsense of the Walled-Up Nun – I mean that you yourself could not go from something greater to anything less great. Now you do have black fits, don't you? Reactions, scruples and the rest? What I want you to be quite clear about (I expect you are and grovel again) is that if you have one of those black reactions *after* this, it may do you what Professor Bobsky would call psychological harm, and those who talk English would call spiritual harm. It doesn't matter if you get tired of working for the Middlesex Mummies Exploration Fund and rush to the Ealing Ethical Dance Movement – because we all live in that world and laugh at it and earn our living in it. But if you have a reaction from this greater thing – you will feel quite differently. You may be in danger of religious melancholia: for you will say 'I have had the Best and it did not help.' Anyhow you may be hurt . . . and I hate your being hurt.

Reassure me on this one point and I am absolutely with you – if I am worthy to say so. Let me know (by a Wink or any recognized ritual) that you see what I mean, and have allowed for it, and I am at once a Trappist. Not your nearest and dearest – let alone a dubious acquaintance – have a right to speak. It is only in God that we all love each other.[10]

Early in 1936 Clare Nicholl did indeed join the noviciate of the Canonesses of St Augustine at Haywards Heath and took her first vows in 1939, but before the end of that year she had abandoned the religious life and was back at Christmas Cottage well in time for her sister Joan's wedding in February of 1940. According to Joan, Chesterton's letter has been filletted, for Clare was much comforted by one piece of advice omitted by Maisie Ward, to the effect that 'Remember that if you do jump in, it is always possible to jump out again'. Once home Clare took up Frances' old position as secretary to the PNEU at Murray House.[11]

Oddly enough, it was Chestertonians who showed a lack of interest in the Nicholls, a situation perhaps not helped by Mrs Nicholl's returning to

Lyme Regis in 1950 and the loss of the name when most of the girls married. Nonetheless, Nicholl grandchildren are still living in Beaconsfield unbeknown to local Chestertonians. Robert had died in the torpedoing of SS *Nerissa* in 1941, but his sisters survived him by many years, Barbara and Clare until the 1960s and Dorothy until 1971. The longest lived was Joan Nicholl (Mrs Edward Huffer) who passed away peacefully in her sleep on April 4th, 2012, just two months short of her hundredth birthday.

Joan was thirteen when the Chestertons first visited Lyme Regis. Her mother could only afford to send one child to school at a time and that at thirteen or fourteen years old, so the younger ones stayed at home and were educated by their elders. No consideration seems to have been given to enrolling them at the local schools, and so it was that Joan was away in Haywards Heath in Sussex when the Chestertons first met the Nicholls, but it was not long before she too made their acquaintance and became the recipient of poems and cartoons from GKC:

### NIGHTMARE NUPTUALS

> Steadfast, upstanding, magnanimous Joan
> Wed a brigand to whom the Albanian throne
> Descended by will:
> And she got it; but still
> Retained in addition a will of her own.

Joan recalled[12] that 'We used to meet in a horrible concrete shelter on the seafront and would then go for a walk with "Unclet" (GKC) who would give us tasks to perform as conspirators, such as bringing back hairs from a black cat that always sat in a cake-shop window.'

### SONG OF THE CONSPIRATORS

'We also rehearsed a dramatised version of Conan Doyle's *The Speckled Band* – we went out on the cliffs to practise the awful gurgling noises needed for the murders, much to the wonderment of the sundry walkers passing along the beach below.'

Joan's time with the Canonesses of St. Augustine in Sussex culminated in a period spent at the mother house (The English Convent) at Bruges in Belgium, after which she was accepted to read for a degree at the London School of Economics. To further improve her French she accepted a post *au pair* in France, deferring her studies for one and then more years. This enabled her younger sisters, Barbara and Dorothy, in their turn to attend the convent school at Haywards Heath: 'At that time it was a terrific adventure to go abroad.' Her employer, Edward Huffer, was an American widower with a daughter, Christiane, slightly younger than she and a son, Max,[13] somewhat older, and her duties were to act as companion to the daughter. Edward Huffer had been a military attaché in Paris in 1917–18, and had subsequently stayed on to represent his family's tobacco firm in Europe, becoming fluent in both French and German. His brother had been an American flying ace in 1917–1918 and the family, especially Max who had his own plane, kept up a keen interest in aviation. Joan recalled being taken aloft in the stringbags of those days. Christiane had been diagnosed as anaemic and Joan accompanied her to winter sports and in the mid 1930s took her to Lyme Regis during an extended visit to England. On their returning to France they took the ferry from Newhaven to Dieppe, the nearest French port to the Huffer's house. Max, who could be very foolhardy, decided to greet them with an aerobatic display over and about the ferry boat, a spectacle which ended tragically when he misjudged his height above the water and plunged into the waves, his sister and Joan watching from the boat, and his father observing everything from the quayside. Max had been killed outright. Joan took Christiane to a cabin and called a priest to comfort her, the priest also giving absolution when the ferry picked up the young man's body.

After Max's death there seemed little alternative but for Joan to stay on to support the bereaved family. She had already turned down several proposals of marriage from Edward who was almost twice her age, and it seems probable that this was a problem[14] on which she consulted GKC. She recalled there being no hint of any illness in GKC at the time, and left for France quite normally. Some time later she had a precognition dream in which she fought her way through a scurrying crowd towards 'Unclet' who was brandishing his stick at her, but she did not succeed in getting to him. On going down to breakfast, she took her continental edition of the *Daily Mail* from the table and immediately saw GKC's photograph and a notice of his death. This time the journey back to England for the memorial service in Westminster Cathedral was sad indeed.

# 15.

# THE ROLLING ROADS

**Barcelona.**

An invitation from the Polish Government for Gilbert Chesterton to visit Poland in 1926 was, in view of medical advice, considered too arduous a trip for Frances to undertake, and was postponed. However, another invitation to visit Spain was much more congenial to her and was eagerly accepted. No record seems to have been kept of whether the Chestertons travelled by train or by ship. The first surviving account has them in Madrid whither they had been invited by the Duke of Alba to stay at the Residentia des Estudiantes where Gilbert gave a series of lectures, one of which was attended by Queen Victoria Eugenia,[1] consort (1906–1931) of King Alfonso XIII. It is not clear whether it was this lecture or a later one which was attended by Luis Buñuel, Salvador Dali and Federico Garcia Lorca. The Chestertons stayed for a week in Madrid, visiting its environs including the Escorial and Toledo, before heading for Catalonia where Frances' cousin, Rhoda Bastable, was working at that time.

The Chestertons arrived in Barcelona on April 27th to stay at the Majestic Hotel on the Passeig de Gracia. The Catalan segment of the tour, arranged by the poet and writer Josep Maria Junoy, included on May 5th a lecture on 'England Seen from the Outside' at the University of Barcelona with the British Consul-General taking the chair. On the next day the PEN Club gave a dinner in GKC's honour at the Ritz Hotel where the poet and dramatist, Josep Maria de Saggara, drew a lively word-portrait of the guest:

Because of his height and size Chesterton seems to take on monstrous proportions compared to men in this country, although if he were seated amongst a group of Northern European men he would just appear to be tall and large and nothing more. At our table, however, he gives the impression of a legendary and jocular giant. During the meal he appears to be a drowsy man waking up from moment to moment, first to take a sip of his drink, then to utter a few words. If those words happen to be in French he has to struggle hard with them because Chesterton, like a good Englishman, travels the world with the magnificent impertinence of his own language. He has a shock of whitish hair and the sort of bushy mustache useful for catching bits of food and giving the person sporting it the look of a Franciscan walrus.[2]

On behalf of the local press Junoy took the opportunity to interview Chesterton at the Majestic Hotel; it would seem that either Frances was feeling the strain of travelling or felt she would like a quieter spot to spend time with her cousin, Rhoda Bastable, so Junoy took the Chesterton party south along the Costa Brava to Sitges where they spent a week at the Hotel Subur on the Passeig Maritim overlooking the sea, and Gilbert sat and wrote on the esplanade:

TO RHODA, otherwise called Rohda
*(Lines composed in contemplation of the statue of El Greco at Sitges)*

Greek Rose, if he men called the Greek
    Had chanced to pass your way
When Greek meets Greek – then, as you know,
    The band begins to play.

He would have drawn you on the spot,
    He liked them long and slim.
(How much more graceful I might seem,
    If I had sat for him!)

He would have splashed that sacred scene
    Across resplendent spaces
In the Acts of the Apostles (all
    With elongated faces.)

He over whom the Gates of Hell
    Shall tower but not prevail
Stood waiting at your Gate – and you
    (How like you!) did not fail.

How many doors you oped for us
  Quite different from Hell's –
Castles in Spain, cafés in France,
  Cathedrals and hotels.

He would have limned you in a blaze
  Bursting those golden locks,
Who know the keys of every door
  (if not of every box).

Whose Muse was Beauty in the Gate
  Had hailed you, not in vain,
Queen of the Catalonian port,
  Dear Door-keeper of Spain.

But what wild horror, what regret,
  What fury and what shame
Had filled the Greek who found the race
  That could not spell your name.

GKC was welcomed by the L'Amic de les Arts with a bouquet of carnations: 'Dear Mr Chesterton, In the name of Friends of Fine Arts I am giving you the most hearty welcome. Please accept, your wife and you, these carnations, characteristic of our village. It is highly pleasing for me to know you are among us. Sincerely, Josep Carbonell.' Chesterton replied: 'Dear Señor Carbonell i Gener, I really do not know how to thank you sufficiently for your most charming and generous gesture of welcome. You are kind enough to refer to my deplorable habit of writing; I only wish that anything I had ever written were half so beautiful as that bunch of flowers, or as likely to give anyone as much joy and encouragement as it gave to us.'[3] While in Sitges GKC wrote several articles for the *ILN*, but managed to fit in a visit to Tarragona, and was guest of honour at a dinner given at the Hotel Subur at which Señor Carbonell i Gener made a speech. On May 23rd the Chestertons left Sitges for Barcelona on their way back to England, but were still in Barcelona on 2nd June 1926 for the feast of Corpus Christi when GKC was spotted caught up in a procession of papier maché giants going through the Portal de l'Angel.

The time spent in Sitges was pleasant enough to draw the Chestertons back again in 1928 and 1935. Josep Maria Junoy was later to translate Chesterton into Catalan, and Chesterton made a strong enough impression on Sitges for the town council to discuss in 1936 the erection of a memorial to him. Sadly

the Spanish Civil War put an end to the proposals until 4th February 1976
when for the centenary of his birth it was decided to name a street in his
memory, a proposal later altered to the erection of a monument on the Passeig
Maritim which was inaugurated on 26th August 1976: 'To G.K. Chesterton,
lover of Sitges, who honoured Sitges's Springs with his noble presence.' There
his effigy gazes at the statue of El Greco.

The Chestertons had not been home from Spain for long when on June
20th Frances informed Father O'Connor: 'I want now, as soon as I can see
a few days clear before me, to place myself under instruction to enter the
Church. The whole position is full of difficulties and I pray you Padre to tell
me the first step to take. I *don't* want my instruction to be here. I don't want
to be the talk of Beaconsfield and for people to say I've only followed Gilbert.
It isn't true and I've had a hard fight not to let my love for him lead me to
the truth. I knew you would not accept me for such motives. But I am very
tired and very worried. Many things are difficult for me. My health included,
which makes strenuous attention a bit of a strain. I know you understand
– Tell me what I shall do.'[4] This was a long step indeed from her remarks to
then secretary Kathleen Chesshire when Gilbert had converted from Anglo to
Roman Catholicism: 'There are three things I shall never do: cut off my hair,
engage an efficient secretary, or become a Roman Catholic.'[5]

On June 28th, 1926 the Chestertons celebrated their silver wedding
anniversary and Frances' fifty-seventh birthday, and it was not until July 12th
that Frances was once again in touch with Father O'Connor:

> We have had such a week of alarums and excitements that I had not even time to thank
> you for the spoons. They are just what I like and incidentally just what I wanted. I
> feel so hopeless at getting out of this net of responsibilities in which I am at present
> enmeshed and to find time for instruction. I feel I have a lot to learn and I think after
> all I had better go quietly to Father Walker and talk to him. Gilbert is writing to you
> himself. I know he thinks I have made myself rather unhappy about things – and he
> is so involved with the paper (I pray he gives it up) we have not been able to talk over
> things sensibly . . .

In a second undated letter she wrote to him:

> I feel the paper must go, it is too much for Gilbert (4 days work always) and consequently
> too much for me who have to attend to everything else.[6]

Despite an annual holiday taken once again in Lyme Regis to see the
Nicholls, time was found for the instruction and on All Saints Day, 1st

November 1926, Frances Chesterton was received into the Catholic Church. An interesting coincidence is the fact that Chesterton only began to write for the Catholic newspaper *Universe* on 3rd November 1926. Frances had always involved her husband in activities to support the Anglican parish church, and now he was to be drawn into a similar round of fêtes and pageants in support of Beaconsfield's Catholic parish and nursing home, the latter soon becoming known as 'Frances's nuns'. No further medical report from Dr Mennell is extant until eighteen months later:

May 18th, 1928

It was very kind of you to let Mrs G.K. Chesterton come to see me again yesterday, and it was nicer still to see how immensely she seems to have improved from a general point of view. I cannot help thinking that her trouble is now entirely due to strain, or disease, in the left sacro-iliac joint.

The pain of which she complains is typical of pain referred from this joint, and her only chance of relief appears to me to lie in an adequate pelvic support. If we can manage to arrange this, I hope very much that the condition will quiet down very slowly during the course of the next two or three months, and on the whole I should feel inclined to take an optimistic view of the future.

I notice that she has put on a very considerable amount of weight, and once before I arranged for her to see Gardiner-Hill about the possibility of endocrine treatment, and in March 1925 he started her off on a definite course of pituitary and thyroid. I should think it is more than likely that it would be wise to start this again.

I do not think she is in a fit state to be racketing to and fro between Beaconsfield and London, so would you mind if she came to stay for a few days in London while I arrange for her support, and perhaps, if you agree, it might be worth while asking Gardiner-Hill to see her again with a view to resuming treatment.

Yours sincerely, James Mennell[7]

On July 18th, 1928 Frances, staying with her mother at the Queen's Hotel in Brighton, wrote to Dorothy Collins to thank her for some poems and mentioned that she would probably be seeing Dr Mennell on the following Monday or Tuesday. Unfortunately, further medical records are missing and so it is not possible to track the progress or otherwise of Frances' debilities any further until she arrived once more in North America some two and a half years later.

### An Eagle Whiter than a Dove[1]

The *New Witness* had always supported the principle of Polish independence, and early in 1919 after Cecil Chesterton's death his widow went to Poland as a special correspondent for the *Daily Express*, while at the same time filing articles on Polish affairs for the *New Witness* through the diplomatic bag:

Gilbert was very pleased with my descriptions of peasant life in Lublin, where everything for home use was produced by the people. The only things they lacked were agricultural implements, top boots, and great coats, which the cities, divested of machinery by the Germans, could not supply. With that rooted antagonism between rural and urban populations, the Lublin people, in retaliation, held up their grain, It was certainly an ideal opportunity for Distributism!

I stayed some weeks in Lublin, going from village to village, and always I was received with a charming courtesy. On Sundays the peasants were *en fête* in national costume – the Lublin colours were wine and green and flaming gold – and as they walked over the fields to church, emerging from the luminous grey mists which veiled the plains, it was as though fields of daffodils had come to worship.

But I not only enjoyed the peace and beauty of all that is real and enduring in Poland, I had my experiences in the fighting line.

At that time Lwow was besieged by the Ukrainians. All the young and able-bodied men were with the main Polish Army under Pilsudski at Kiev, and the defence was in the hands of old men, schoolboys, girls and women. I have never seen anything like the fighting spirit of Lwow. Munitions were very short; they had no artillery, not many rifles and insufficient cartridges. But the opposing forces were almost as badly commissioned, though they hopelessly outnumbered the besieged. There was hand-to-hand fighting in the streets, and, hard-pressed, the women helped to pour boiling water on the attackers from the housetops and the windows, with occasional ladles of molten metal. The indomitable courage, the inspired passion of the Polish women flamed above all else.

There was hardly any food left, but the city held on till Pilsudski arrived with his troops, when the Ukrainians retreated and Lwow breathed again.

From Lwow I went to Vilno [Vilnius] in the north . . . I found Vilno battered but not beaten. Here it was the Bolshevist invaders who had been driven back, leaving at their headquarters masses of papers and books – amongst them Russian translations of Gilbert's *The Man Who Was Thursday* and *The Club of Queer Trades* – a selection which greatly intrigued the Poles as well as me.

For twenty-four hours I went in an armoured car with the Polish army in pursuit of the retreating Bolshevists, and the landscape of long low-lying plains was lit up by flame from the burning forest which an advanced Polish guard was battling to put out. So close, so fierce was the fire, that as we sped through our car was scorched and blackened . . . It was towards the end of July . . . that G.K. wrote to ask me when I was returning . . . I put in my application for a seat in the diplomatic train, and started off for France at the end of the month. I arrived in Paris in time for the peace demonstrations, and saw the processions from a window overlooking the Place de la République.[2]

On her return Mrs Cecil took advantage of her experiences to start the East European News Service, while in the *New Witness* GKC continued to fight the Polish case for independence and access to the sea, eventually granted at Versailles by means of the so-called Polish Corridor: 'I saw something of that difficult statesmanship, enough to know that nothing but nonsense is talked in the newspapers which discuss what they call the Polish Corridor. The fairest generalisation is this: recent events would be better understood if everybody saw the self-evident fact that the Poles always have a choice of evils.'[3] Some time earlier he had sounded almost apocalyptic in tone:

> We know that a flood threatens the West from the meeting of two streams, the revenge of Germany and the anarchy of Russia; and we know . . . that without some such Christian and chivalric shield on that side, we shall have half Europe and perhaps half Asia on our backs . . . The Poles have raised revolution after revolution, when three colossal Empires prevented them from being a nation at all. It is not in the realm of sanity to suppose that, if we make them half a nation, they will not some day attempt to be a whole nation. But we shall come back to the place where we started, after another cycle of terror and torment and abominable butchery – and to a place where we might, in peace and perfect safety, stand firm today.[4]

Chesterton's life-long support for the Polish cause was appreciated and brought an invitation from the Polish government for him to visit, and so in April 1927 the Chestertons accompanied by Dorothy Collins set out via Berlin for Poland. The invitation had originally been made and accepted for them to go in 1926, but the journey had been deferred when Gilbert decided that Frances was in no fit state to travel. On April 27th en route to Berlin Dorothy wrote her first letter home to her mother: 'I was wondering whether in view of all the expense Mrs Chesterton would be regretting having taken me, but as we steamed out of Liverpool Street and I said 'How glorious. We are really off,' she said, 'I can't tell you how glad I am you are coming,' which makes a much nicer feeling . . . the trip will cost at the very least £160 I am afraid.'[5] April 28th 1927 saw them arriving in Warsaw where Miss Collins was struck by their welcome:

> Poland managed to regain her freedom in 1917 from the occupying powers of Russia, Germany and Austria which had dominated the country for 150 years. The government of the reconstructed country invited Chesterton to come and see what had been done in the ten years of freedom from Alien rule . . . He was fêted and lavishly entertained throughout the country. On arrival in Warsaw we were met at the station by an escort of Cavalry Officers [the Chevaux-Légers] and representatives of the PEN Club which had been made responsible by the Government for arranging the visit. This was during the time of Marshall Pilsudski, so everything in Warsaw was very dashing and military. A romantic speech in French was made by one of those gorgeously clad cavalry men, and we were driven with cavalry escort to the Europyski Hotel. The welcoming speech on the station extolled the callings of poet and cavalry officer as being the finest in the world for a layman, which amused G.K. and appealed to the romantic side of his nature. This officer said, 'I will not say you are the chief friend of Poland, for God is our chief friend', in those words summing up the spirit of the country.

A less romantic view was taken by Adam Harasowski, an engineering student acting as interpreter, who attended Chesterton throughout his visit:

> Due to my reasonable knowledge of English at the time I was selected as interpreter for G.K.C., translating for him all the Polish speeches that were made (far too many!) . . . Honesty compels me to admit that many Poles were annoyed and disgusted with the first speech of welcome made on 28 April, 1927 at the Warsaw Central Railway Station by the notorious *bon vivant*, drunkard and womaniser, Colonel Wieniawa-Dlugoszewski, who was then the 'blue-eyed boy' of Marshall Pilsudski, the strong man of Poland at that time. There was a reception committee of the Polish PEN Club, with many illustrious and distinguished men and women, all waiting at the station, but they did not get the chance to speak. The curious thing is that the colonel was not invited to greet Chesterton at the station; he just pushed himself forward, together with a group of Polish cavalry officers – and because he enjoyed the protection of Marshall Pilsudski, nobody dared to stop him. To give him his due, Colonel Wieniawa-Dlugoszewski made a witty speech, in passable French, welcoming Chesterton, not as a famous writer, not even as a friend of Poland, but as a born cavalry officer who just missed his profession. Chesterton was very amused and laughed his head off, but the representatives of the PEN Club were understandably not amused.
>
> The main Polish cities which G.K.C. visited were Warsaw, Poznan, Krakow [Francuski Hotel], Lwow and Wilno [now L'viv in Ukraine and Vilnius in Lithuania] in that order. From Krakow he made an excursion to the salt mines of Wieliczka; he also visited the beautiful mountain resort of Zakopane in the Tatra mountains . . . He asked me what Polish word would be most useful for him to remember. I told him he must learn to say 'psia krew,' which means 'dog's blood' and is really a mild swearword, but it is used often to express anger, as well as surprise or admiration. All the students roared with laughter and Chesterton laughed with us. Mrs Chesterton did not laugh and was far less at ease during the rest of her stay . . . I accompanied them everywhere during their two-and-a half day stay in Lwow . . . The programme of Chesterton's visit to Lwow was very varied; it included a 'must' for all visitors, namely a drive to the 'Kopiec Unii Lubelskeij,' a high mound on the outskirts of the town, erected to commemorate the union of Poland and Lithuania of 1569. From that mound one gets a magnificent view of Lwow. Visiting churches, museums, ands so on, filled the rest of their visit. A great crowd of students, with some professors, accompanied the honoured guests on May 20 to the main railway station of Lwow where they caught the train going north to Wilno [Vilnius].[6]

During the trip and its various excursions Miss Collins manages in her letters home to give an impression that there could have been a mild holiday romance:

> A nice young Polish barrister [Witold Chwalewik] and I had a car to ourselves for the drive. We got on very well; he spoke perfect English and I heard all about Poland. The roads are appalling and they drive at about forty-five miles an hour over everything,

so you may imagine one is shot sky high. It was very wet so we were covered in mud. Mrs C's hat is ruined, but luckily I foresaw something of the sort and wore an old felt.[7]

Miss Collins records Chwalewik's presence at the PEN dinner where they had 'great fun', and that she sat next to him at the visit to the Fukier wine cellar. On the afternoon of May 6th, after Chesterton's meeting with Marshall Jozef Pilsudski in Belweder, she wrote to her mother to mention how she went for a walk with the 'nice young Polish barrister' who then came the next morning to help with the luggage for their twelve hour railway trip onward to Poznan: 'Horror. Two people have just been heaved into our carriage; I hope they are not going far. There is no restaurant on the train so we have got our food for the day, and I do hate eating in trains when there are other people.' During a four day stay they met Roman Dmowski, leader of the National Democratic Party and Pilsudski's defeated rival: 'He is a brilliant man and talked most wittily about international things, telling us stories of our own politicians and summing them up in the shrewdest manner.' Of the excursion to Zakopane in the Tatra Mountains she writes that 'we only met three cars all day . . . one of which was in the ditch as a wheel had come off. We conveyed one of the occupants to hospital with a nasty head wound, but nothing very serious.' Encountering some peasants, they had to jump over a camp fire and at the same time drink a glass of whiskey with one hand and cut the top off a fir tree with the other. How GKC and Frances coped with the gymnastics is unknown. GKC was, however, impressed by the city of Chopin and Copernicus:

> What gives to Cracow a sort of sharp outline of spires and turrets against the background of history is the fact that it is a seat of culture on the edge of the uncultivated wilds . . . In Cracow can be seen all those crafts and schools of art with which we are familiar in the Western culture . . . But we see them there thrust up against the vast and vague hostility which is something altogether alien to us . . . For centuries the Tartars rolled around these towers a torrent of Asiatic barbarism. There is little change in the position today; except that the barbarism is called Bolshevism. Sections of the city wall are still shown, which were guarded by the guilds . . . Guilds of that type existed all over Europe; but when they went out to battle, it was commonly against other guilds or against the feudal nobility . . . but here in Cracow the guildsmen standing on the wall looked out across a wilderness that faced away into the formless east, where strange gods were worshipped under strange skies. Out of that mystery of the sunrise a strange horseman came riding . . . and from the tower of the city a trumpet is still blown every hour to the four winds of heaven, as if uttering the defiance of civilisation besieged. Only the trumpet peal breaks on the last note; to commemorate a medieval trumpeter slain by a Tartar arrow. And so odd and moving is the break that a man listening today can fancy that he hears not only the trumpet, but the bolt of the barbarian singing by.[8]

Miss Collins continued to take a romantic outlook: 'At Lwow [May 17th] we stayed at the Hotel George, where we were served by peasant women in their national costume and with bare feet – national costume as was worn daily and not put on for tourists.' On May 19th the local military commander put a car at their disposal and they drove over unrepaired roads to visit Count Tyszkiewicz round whose estate they drove in wooden carriages each pulled by two horses, GKC later recalling:

> I made the acquaintance of a young Count [Tyszkiewicz] whose huge and costly palace of a country house . . . had been burned and wrecked and left in ruins by the retreat of the Red Army after the Battle of Warsaw. Looking at such a mountain of shattered marbles and black and blasted tapestries one of our party said: 'It must be a terrible thing for you to see your old family home destroyed like this.' But the young man, who was very young in all his gestures, shrugged his shoulders and laughed, at the same time looking a little sad, 'Oh, I do not blame them for that,' he said. 'I have been a soldier myself and in the same campaign; and I know the temptations. I know what a fellow feels, dropping from fatigue and freezing with cold, when he asks himself what some other fellow's armchairs and curtains can matter, if he can only have fuel for the night. On the one side or the other, we were all soldiers; and it is a hard and horrible life. I don't resent at all what they did here. There is only one thing that I really resent. I will show it to you.'
>
> And he led us out into a long avenue lined with poplars; and at the end of it was a statue of the Blessed Virgin, with the head and the hands shot off. But the hands had been lifted; and it is a strange thing that the very mutilation seemed to give more meaning to the attitude of intercession; asking mercy for the merciless race of men.[9]

The next day it was back on the train for a ten hour journey to Warsaw on a 'kind of triumphal procession all along, with huge crowds at the stations to meet us and see us off, bouquets, speeches and so on.' On arrival in Warsaw 'the usual crowd and Chwalewik met us at the station.' On Sunday morning Chwalewik returned to lead a visit to the Botanical Gardens and the statue of Chopin. And then on Monday Miss Collins was taken to the Picture Gallery followed by a walk and 'afterwards to do some shopping with him.' Later at five minutes to midnight the party again left Warsaw:

> There were no air services in those days and we travelled all over the country in Wagon-Lits by night. From Warsaw to Vilna [Vilnius] on the Russian border, I had to share with a Russian lady and in advising me as to whether to take the upper or the lower berth, Gilbert remarked, 'What you have to consider is whether you prefer to be stabbed through the front or the back.' I decided for the back and took the upper berth. My companion turned out to be charming! At Vilna where there were still many signs of the oppressive Russian domination, we saw a procession in the Catholic [Ruthenian

Uniat] Cathedral and I have never seen such a collection of down and outs, led by an old priest with St. Vitus's Dance. It was a truly tragic sight.

In her diary she noted being moved at the sight of people kneeling in the street to pray at the shrine of the miraculous icon of the Madonna housed in the gateway in Vilnius known as Austros Vartai (Gate of Dawn) in Lithuanian and Ostra Brama (The Pointed Gate) in Polish, a sight that impressed itself on Chesterton too:

> I was driving with a Polish lady, who was very witty and well-acquainted with the whole character of Europe, and also of England . . . and I only noticed that her tone changed, if anything to a sort of coolness, as we stopped outside an archway leading into a side street, and she said: 'We can't drive in here'. I wondered; for the gateway was wide and the street apparently open. As we walked under the arch, she said in the same colourless tone: 'You take off your hat here'. And then I saw the open street. It was filled with a vast crowd, all facing me; and all on their knees on the ground. It were as if someone was walking behind me; or some strange bird were hovering over my head. I faced round, and saw in the centre of the arch great windows standing open, unsealing a chamber full of gold and colours; there was a picture behind; but parts of the whole picture were moving like a puppet-show, stirring strange double memories like the dream of a bridge in the puppet-show of my childhood; and then I realised that from those shifting groups there shone and sounded the ancient magnificence of the Mass.[10]

Miss Collins also mentioned a trip to Troki to visit the temple of the Karaim,[11] a dissident Jewish sect settled there since the 14th century, which rejected rabbinical tradition and interpreted Scripture literally: 'The Rabbi wore a bright yellow cloak for the service and a round hat of black and white velvet. He had a wonderful face, rather like the pictures one sees of the Old Testament characters – his hair and beard were quite auburn in colour and he had what we commonly call a Roman nose. In fact, there was no trace of Jew as we know it, in him.' Her familiarity with East European Jewry was obviously very limited.

Wherever they went the Chestertons were greeted with wild enthusiasm, but Frances had quickly found the hospitality overwhelming, as she mentioned in a letter to Marie-Louise:

> The P.E.N. Club Dinner was, I fancy, considered by the Poles a huge success. If numbers indicate anything, it certainly was. I found it a little embarrassing to have to eat hot kidneys and mushrooms standing about with hundreds of guests, and this was only the preliminary to a long dinner that followed and refreshments that apparently continued until two o'clock in the morning. The speeches were really perfectly marvellous and delivered in English quite colloquial and very witty, and showing a detailed knowledge

of Gilbert's works which no Englishman of my acquaintance possesses. Gilbert made an excellent, in fact, a very eloquent speech in reply, which drew forth thunders of applause.[12]

Gilbert enjoyed every minute, but Frances was also unlucky in the weather: 'very like England on a nasty day of east wind', for the Europyski Hotel did not have central heating and Frances had to manage with a small electric fire which could only warm a small part of their room. None the less she preferred to keep to her room in the evening to rest, unloading social engagements: 'I find Dorothy Collins the greatest possible help, and she is excellent with foreigners . . . In the evening [of May 4th] Gilbert and the energetic Dorothy Collins went off to have supper in the very famous wine-cellar of the Fukier family which dates from 1610. There apparently they drank Tokay and Mute (I think that is Mead) and there was a great deal of singing and national songs, both the peasant ones and the military ones and at the end, I am told, a sort of "He's a jolly good fellow" which is called "Live for a hundred years" in honour of Gilbert.'[13]

Wherever they went, there were tours of the attractions of the city and ever more receptions including on May 3rd the celebration of National Day at the former Royal Palace: 'Everybody in Warsaw was there, at least, so I was told and I think it must be true, because the crowd was enormous. It was an extraordinary sight; the old Royal Palace filled with lights and colour which the Poles for the first time were able to claim as their own Palace.'[14] And as they moved on Frances continued to dictate her impressions to Dorothy Collins for her to type up and send on to Marie-Louise: Poznan, which she found pleasant with 'all the German cleanliness and thoroughness which is not conspicuous perhaps in other parts of Poland'; Lwow – 'a busy and at present not a particularly interesting place.'

It is unknown what were Frances' reactions to the special performance of Stanislaw Wyspianski's prophetic drama *Acropolis* (1904) given in Gilbert's honour in Krakow where the manager of the theatre had come stage-front to thank him in the name of all the citizens of the city for his defence of Poland 'now and in the past.' Gilbert himself more than appreciated his welcome: 'When I visited Poland I was honoured by an invitation by the government; but all the hospitality I received was far too much alive to remind me of anything official. There is a sort of underground tavern in Warsaw, where men drink Tokay, which would cure any official of officialism; and there they sang the marching songs of the Poles.'[15] This may well be a reference to the 'Cellar of the Fukier family', but there is a painting displayed in the Warsaw Museum of a Caricature of GKC with Franc Fiszer in a tavern known as 'Under the Milky Way.'[16]

After another overnight train journey, the Chesterton party spent their last three days in Warsaw, extending a dinner invitation to Witold Chwalewik on their last evening. Miss Judith Lea believes that he was in love with Dorothy Collins as he visited her in England until the late 1950s; she thought Miss Collins was interested, but not interested enough. At 8.30 am on Tuesday, May 31st the Chestertons bade farewell and headed home, bypassing an invitation to Prague from Karel Capek (*R.U.R.* and *The Insect Play*), but breaking journey in Berlin and Aachen before stopping off to spend a week 'to recover from our fatigues' in Belgium at Ghent and Bruges. Arrived home in mid-June, Chesterton almost immediately was booked (it is to be wondered by whom) to lecture at the Essex Hall on 'What Poland Is', an occasion graced by the presence of the Archbishop of Westminster and the Ambassador together with a large delegation from the Polish Embassy. Chesterton began by saying that the title of the lecture was not just misleading, it was a lie as he could not even pretend to know the answer; 'I should be sorry if any brilliant Pole asked me what England is. I think it was Aristotle who said you cannot define a living thing, least of all such a living thing as Poland, one of the most living things in the world, because nothing can be so living as a thing which has risen from the dead.'[17] Little did he know that twice more within the twentieth century Poland would fall only to rise again.

### Where all Roads Lead

The last three months of 1929 found the Chestertons together with Dorothy Collins in Rome where they stayed at the Hassler Hotel overlooking the Spanish Steps which led down to the Piazza di Spagna and the house in which John Keats had lived and died. There Chesterton was to write perhaps one of the most disappointing of his books, *The Resurrection of Rome*, his reflections on history, literature and culture, in between his meetings with Benito Mussolini and other politicians and literary figures. There were also three audiences with Pope Pius XI. Chesterton seems to have been well aware that he could not quite grasp:

> . . . I suddenly saw lie open before me a book I cannot write. This book is the printed proof that I cannot write it. I could, I suppose, if I liked, go back and write another book, full of the details of Rome and the hundred accidents of travel . . . Or I might begin again and write a better book about the human contacts of the place, and the curious and interesting persons to be found there . . . the general historical or philosophical

notion I had in mind, as I looked on that luminous evening from the obelisk of the Trinità across to the dome of St. Peter's. Only the complete thing I had seen broke as I saw it; and all that follows here is but a litter of the fragments . . .[1]

## Chesterton had meant to interview Mussolini, but:

In short, to put it one way, I did not interview him because he interviewed me. He put a rapid succession of questions covering a wide field, but mostly concerned with my country and not his . . . Something I said about Imperialism and Internationalism seemed to arrest his attention sharply . . . I told him . . . I did desire England to be more self-supporting and less dependent on the ends of the earth, for I thought such dependence had become very perilous. Before I knew where I was, I found myself talking at large about my own fad of Distributism . . . I hated the idea of having talked too much, instead of listening to a more interesting person; but I could not quite get it out of my mind that the interesting person had possibly intended that I should talk a great deal about my politics, rather than he talk about his.[2]

Perhaps Mussolini, 'an alert, square-shouldered man in black', had been given an easy passage thanks to the kudos bestowed on him by Chesterton's co-religionists for having in 1929 made a *concordat* with the 'Prisoner of the Vatican' and the Church, which established the Vatican State. This vision of Mussolini, and later Franco, as a Catholic gentleman lingered well into the second half of the twentieth century in quarters perhaps best described as the Church Triumphant. Chesterton was in a muddle, his instincts telling him that all was not right, but he had a certain sympathy with the Fascist attack on capitalism:

I am well aware that two black shirts do not make a white. But I assure the reader that I am not, in this case, in the least trying to prove that black is white. I wish there were in the world a real white flag of freedom, that I could follow, independently of the red flag of Communist or the black flag of Fascist regimentation. By every instinct of my being, by every tradition of my blood, I should prefer English liberty to Latin discipline[3] . . . My motive in this matter is very simple to the point of violence; it is to point out, as emphatically as I can, that the whole political and financial world in which we live has been goading Fascism into revolt for the last fifty years. In this sense my remarks might rather be called a warning against Fascism, as a wise man in the early eighteenth century might have uttered a warning against the French Revolution.

The real centre of Chesterton's attention was elsewhere where his first sight of a Swiss Guard at the Vatican had taken him:

. . . As I watched him, and the pale light from one of Rome's stormy days striking his streaks of colour as he turned and shifted the hand upon the halberd, something else stirred within me, to which I could not as yet put a name . . . And then suddenly I remembered that long ago, in my older days of scribbling, I had written a ridiculous story about Notting Hill; of which the joke was that a man might die for a little suburb as if for a holy city; and that I had equipped the men fighting for it with the same sort of halberds and heraldic colours. The man standing on the great stairway was, among a myriad other more important things, one of my own little dreams come true. And I realised with something rather like alarm at the coincidence, that the comparison might really have been pressed further. For the Guard of the Vatican City really was defending a place almost parochial in size though the reverse of parochial in importance. That here in the heart of Christendom, on the high place of the whole world, on a plane above all earthly empires and under the white and awful light that strikes on an eternal town, was really a model state no larger than Notting Hill . . . I am particularly anxious to affirm, at the start, that though of course these shows and pageants meant immeasurably much to me, and profoundly affected my emotions, yet I do not base my belief on such emotions, still less on such pageants or shows. I was myself received into the Catholic Church in a small tin shed, painted brick-red, which stood among the sculleries and outhouses of a Railway Hotel . . . And the Pope would be the first to say that the step I took in entering that shed was inconceivably more important than the step of entering St. Peter's, or the Vatican, or his own presence.

I saw His Holiness Pius XI three times; the first time in private audience; the second in a semi-private assembly of various notables and the third time among the crowds that thronged St. Peter's on the day of the Beatification of the English Martyrs. On the first occasion a dignitary who was at the head of one of the National Colleges kindly helped to introduce me; and I have seldom been more grateful for human companionship. It is altogether inadequate to say I was nervous . . . He [Pius XI] came suddenly out of his study, a sturdy figure in a cape, with a square face and spectacles, and began speaking to me about what I had written, saying some very generous things about a sketch I wrote of St. Francis of Assisi . . . Then he made a motion and we all knelt; and in the words that followed I understood for the first time something that was once meant by the ceremonial use of the plural, and in a flash I saw the sense of something that had always seemed to me a senseless custom of kings. With a new strong voice, that was hardly even like his own, he began, 'Nous vous bénissons,' and I knew that something stood there infinitely greater than any individual; I knew that it was indeed 'We'; We, Peter and Gregory and Hildebrand and all the dynasty that does not die. Then as he passed on, we rose and found our way out of the Palace, through knots of Swiss and Papal Guards, till we were again under the open sky. I said to the clerical dignitary, 'That frightened me more than anything I have known in my life.'[4]

The Chestertons were also in St. Peter's to hear the Pope formally promulgate the Beatification of the forty English and Welsh Martyrs before a crowd of many thousands. After the ceremony in the milling confusion, Gilbert found it difficult to retrieve his trademark cloak. Fortunately, a group of girls from the Convent of the Holy Child where he had given several talks were at hand to plunge through the seething masses and bring it back to him. Not content with that triumph, the girls then found a taxi in St. Peter's Square, no small feat at the best of times, almost miraculous on that particular day. With his usual courtesy, Gilbert later wrote to acknowledge their help:

> *For the Young Ladies Suffering Education*
> *at the Convent of the Holy Child*
>
> To be a Real Prophet once
> For you alone did I desire,
> Who dragged the Prophet's Mantle down
> And brought the Chariot of Fire.

While Dorothy Collins had been taking Chesterton's dictation or Gilbert was visiting or lecturing, Frances was sometimes at a loose end. Fortunately, a fellow guest in the hotel, a pleasant American gentleman with a very large Packard limousine and his own chauffeur, was happy to put his car at Frances' disposal whenever it was not needed by himself. Gilbert would no doubt have delighted in the chauffeur's name, Dominic Cinderella, but it would have been interesting to have been able to note his reaction when some time later, after many kindnesses by the American, Frances introduced nice Mr Capone to Gilbert: Alphonse Capone was perhaps enjoying a quiet holiday after all the excitement of the previous February's St Valentine's Day massacre.[5]

The Italian trip concluded with a visit to renew acquaintance with Max Beerbohm at his villa in Rapallo where he had lived ever since going there for his honeymoon in 1910. The dining-room wall he had decorated with a fresco depicting his friends, Chesterton at their head, going in for a meal. While there Chesterton met Ezra Pound, already taken with Fascist ideas, and discussed the development of Social Credit in Canada. However, Christmas was at hand and the Chestertons returned to Top Meadow on December 20th, barely in time to stock their larder for the celebration.

# 16.

# THREE ACRES AND A COW

The Distributism propounded by Gilbert and Cecil Chesterton together with Hilaire Belloc was a social and to some extent a quasi-political pressure group rather than a political movement. Its main aims were to eliminate corruption¹ and to promote self-sufficiency on a basis of property and particularly land ownership. It took a good deal of its inspiration, certainly in Belloc's case, from Pope Leo XIII's encyclical *De Rerum Novarum* (1891), but there was also input in the case of Gilbert Chesterton from William Cobbett's *Rural Rides* and from the Anglican Christian Social Union. There was also influence from the Rochdale Pioneers of the Co-operative movement and from self-help Friendly Societies.

It had been the Enclosure movement which had brought about loss of common land holdings by the exercising of private property rights over customary rights, to drive what had been seen as a 'bold' independent peasantry from their land into the towns, thus depriving them of that independence. Those who did not become agricultural labourers were obliged to seek employment in the newly emerging industries in the towns. The 'bold peasantry' had been considered hopelessly inefficient and even subversive by the gentry, as the peasant or yeoman would produce a multiplicity of crops for his own survival whereas efficiency demanded that there be a single crop or at least a four-crop rotation system, together with the replacement of the strip system by ever larger fields. It was also an affront that a commoner could be as idle as he wished just as long as he produced enough to avoid starvation. The gentry viewed such independence as a threat, and as their class made up the Justices of the Peace, Members of Parliament and Knights of the Shire, statute law was used to override common law to evict the commoners so as to allow enclosures to replace them with sheep, railways, canals, textile and other mills or even large landscaped deer-parks. Some of the yeomanry might join the Army, some fishermen might find employment in the Navy, but most of the peasantry who did not become landless labourers became the 'sturdy beggars' whose only recourse was indeed to provide a work-force for the new industries. Land owning had then become the prerogative of a limited group of gentry who by clearances established large estates quite separate from the greater part of society; none of the Chestertons, estate agents (realtors) as they were, actually owned property until in 1914 Gilbert bought land in Grove Road, Beaconsfield[2] upon which Top Meadow was built in 1922. Common land not enclosed in the past has tended to fall under the control of district councils and is now largely confined at best to a cricket field often restricted in its use by its immediate neighbours. It is well nigh impossible to graze cattle thereon, not least because of the need to protect the cricket square.

Distributism's main aim was to ensure the return of independence based on private assets, principally a dwelling to give shelter and land sufficient to support a meagre living standard to avoid being beholden or 'tied' to any employer. The major flaw in the theory was that no real consideration was ever given to how the poor or even the working class were to acquire their property (often derided as three acres and a cow[3]). Once land had been acquired, how were the new proprietors to be retrained in husbandry? Above all, how were they to be prevented from selling on their property, for, if an owner does not have the right to sell, he is not really an independent proprietor; if he sells, land will return to the hands of the rich, and the merry-go-round will start up again.

After 1918 an impetus was given by a revulsion against wartime profiteers, and also the promise to build a land fit for heroes. Distributism took on a definite shape when on September 17th, 1926 various diverse groups came together at a meeting in the Essex Hall off the Strand under the auspices of G.K.'s Weekly to form the Distributist League. Now those various groups had their mouthpiece in G.K.'s Weekly, the print run doubled for a time. Chesterton was elected president and branches were founded throughout the country in very short order, but despite much effort there was really no common goal and a great deal of energy was expended in internal squabbles, some factions proving to be cranks of a neo-Luddite order inveighing against the use of any machinery whatsoever. Even Chesterton himself, constantly

travelling the length and breadth of the country to speak at League meetings
was constrained to lament the situation:

> I could only manage . . . to keep this paper in existence at all, by earning money in the
> open market; and more especially in that busy and happy market where corpses are
> sold in batches; I mean the mart of Murder and Mystery, the booth of the Detective
> Story. Many a squire has died in a dank, garden arbour, transfixed by a mysterious
> dagger, many a millionaire has perished silently though surrounded by a ring of private
> secretaries, . . . Many an imperial jewel has vanished from its golden setting, many a
> detective crawled about on the carpet for clues, before some of those little printer's bills
> could be settled which enabled the most distinguished and intelligent of Distributists
> to denounce each other as Capitalists and Communists . . . This being my humble
> and even highly irrelevant contribution to the common team-work, it is obvious that
> it could not be done at the same time as a close following of the various shades of
> thought in the Distributist debates . . . I have never belonged distinctively to any of the
> 43 different Distributist groups. I have never had time.[4]

Chesterton supported small against large, shop against multiple store, but
the intervening years have taken us through the realms of the supermarket
to the hypermarket and on to the multinational combine and just-in-time
provisioning, to massive credit card and mortgage debt in an era in which it
is no longer possible to say 'everyone knows what is meant by a peasantry',
for indeed they do not and would regard 'peasantry' as a pejorative term.
In the 1920s and 1930s Chesterton's dissenting voice could find resonances
elsewhere in the Social Credit theories of Major Clifford Hugh Douglas
(1879–1952) and echoes in films such as René Clair's *A Nous la Liberté*,
Charlie Chaplin's *Modern Times*, even Orson Welles's *Citizen Kane*. Now
Social Credit parties have disappeared along with the Distributist and Land
Leagues, the Art and Crafts inspired Guild of St. Joseph and St. Dominic at
Ditchling finally giving up the ghost in 1989; only one farming settlement
at Laxton had survived the Second World War (1939–1945), and that by the
adoption of modern farming practices. Once the Distributist League had
lost its leader in 1936, it was not long in disappearing as a serious movement,
quickly losing its voice as *G.K.'s Weekly* became the *Weekly Review* dependent on subsidies from the Polish government in exile until it at last expired
in the late 1940s.

The basis of Distributism was that ownership of property, especially a
house or land gives a modicum of independence in the tenure. However, the
development of a consumer society in the late twentieth century has often
seen the acquisition of property lead to crippling debt largely fed by negative

equity; and anyone thinking of keeping chickens in their garden would now most likely be faced by a noise abatement order.

Chesterton's own definitions were as follows:

**A.** Distributism stands for the restoration of liberty by the distribution of property. Its two primary principles are: 1. That the only way to preserve liberty is to preserve property; in order that the individual and the family may be independent of oppressive systems, official or unofficial. 2. That the only way to preserve property is through the better distribution of capital by individual ownership of the means and instruments of production. This can only be done by breaking up the great plutocratic concentration of our time. The commercial and industrial progress which began by professing individualism had ended with the complete swamping of the individual. The concentration of capital in large heaps controlled by little groups has now become equally obvious to those who defend and those who deplore it. But even those who deplore it seldom really try to reverse it. The problem of centralised wealth has produced proposals that what is centralised should be centralised even more by state ownership or nationalisation, but it has not produced the perfectly simple proposal that what is centralised should be decentralised by the voluntary co-operation of small owners.

**B.** Distributism is an approximate name for an approximate thing. That, to begin with, is where it is something more and less than socialism or the optimistic organising forms of capitalism. It aims at the more equal distribution of private property, especially in the primary forms of property such as land. But it does not necessarily expect to cut up the country in the precise pattern of a chess board, whereas the Utopian Capitalist or Collectivist does expect that his pattern of concentric rings will remain exactly as it is, with its rings unbroken. The difference between the ideas lies deep in the moral philosophies from which they sprang; the first Distributists in the modern English group, if not necessarily Catholics, were men of that sort of common sense which is actually produced by the complexity of Catholicism. For common sense does not come with simplicity, in the sense of mere simplification. Intellectual simplification is never far from fanaticism. It takes all sorts to make a church; it takes all sorts to make a Distributist state, in one sense it includes all those who are not Distributists. Just as we wish economic power balanced between various citizens, and not trusted blindly to one monopolist, so we want social and moral power balanced between different types and tenures, and not all blindly trusted to one monotonous ideal. We do not so much wish the world to be Distributist as wish it to be more Distributist, but not necessarily more and more and more Distributist.

I can perfectly well imagine a community in which there is too little Communism. Indeed there has actually been such a community since the destruction of the Monasteries. But the moral philosophy behind most modern experiments means one of two things; either the theory that a centralised plan can be so perfect that we never criticise the action of the centre; or else that some one idea, such as centralisation can be pushed further and further for ever. I do not say that Distributism can be pushed further and further for ever; I say it badly wants pushing now. And it wants pushing, not because it is the only idea that now needs to be considered, but because it is the only idea that is now blankly and utterly ignored.

We may begin any such explanation either at the live end or the dead end; but the duties of modern scientific discussion require us to begin at the dead end. I mean that there is now an unavoidable custom of describing all human beings in material or mathematical formulas; margins and multiples and mechanical reactions and the rest. Bowing my head to this ritual, I would explain with all solemnity that the Distributist believes that the modern movement should be centrifugal, and perceives that the modern movement is solely and exclusively centripetal. In an older and more human language, he is so eccentric as to feel more affection for a fountain than for a whirlpool. He recognises that the whirlpool is the most exact and exquisite spiral curve, very scientific when recorded in charts and diagrams; and that the fountain, in comparison, is liable to splash people rather indiscriminately. But he would rather be splashed than drowned; and he is firmly convinced that the heart of the modern whirlpool is hollow, and is the dwelling place of death.

To use a more homely and fitting figure, the Distributist, like his friend the peasant, begins with a profound suspicion about the wisdom of putting all his eggs in one basket. Like the peasant he is notably cold when it is made clear that it will not even be his own basket. He feels this is as equally true, whether it is the big basket of Capitalist or Communist organization. He does not believe that they are golden eggs laid by some silly goose of a politician or a plutocrat: he is quite willing to agree that many of them are rotten eggs, and do not so much come from the politician as return upon him in showers. But he wants the average output of eggs, good or bad, distributed into all the different baskets of different families; and not all trusted to the gigantic bag of the carpet-bagger. Or rather, to come to the core of the conception, he wishes as many families as possible to have their own eggs in the sense of keeping their own chickens. He wishes them to have, as far as possible, several ownership of the means of production. At the same time he says that this is not the same thing as buying eggs easily at the Stores or getting them from that great Store called the State. For the Store, if it is a Ring, may choose to sell small eggs; or bad eggs. The statesman, if he is a Higher Thinker, may think it immoral to eat anything except ducks' eggs; or the State may impose a law of total prohibition of eggs, because of the notorious excesses in stealing chickens.

In short in so far as most families, or many families, or even a few families, have access to actual production, independent of the new centralised organisations, those families alone are free. They are free in the perfectly practical sense that they cannot be instantly starved out if they oppose the powers of the world on any point of justice or self-respect. Now what we remark about this form of freedom is that the world has apparently forgotten all about it; not that the world fails to perfect it or universalise it, but that the world utterly despises and destroys it; that the world is engaged in strengthening and tightening up vast centralised systems under which it cannot exist at all, anywhere, anyhow, or for anybody. And we start by saying that the total loss of this true economic independence, as a basis for political and spiritual independence, is one vast blunder to which the world is bound and to which the world is blind.

But in all these things we recognise that we are in one sense supporting a relative truth, and we do not expect more than a relative triumph. It is for us a matter of proportion rather than perfection: but, if once we accept the real idea of property, we must agree that recent progress has not the very vaguest idea of proportion. It is making no attempt of any sort to preserve property from being entirely swallowed up in the whirlpools of commercial or civic centralisation. One of the queerest jests in human history is that in which a politician once described this extraordinary condition of Capitalism as 'normality'. It is almost as abnormal as anarchy. It is specially and peculiarly without the elements of balance, of criticism and a consideration of both sides. The Capitalists, or rather Monopolists, who are now maintaining it, are, in the most exact sense of the word, Extremists. But the Distributists are not Extremists. They recognise that there must be a gradation and a difference of application in their test of a state. The man who could live on his own eggs or vegetables is the standard of that state. He represents the ideal to which it approximates; but there are many other forms of property which, each in its degree, can be approximations. Property in houses and shops and tools counts for a good deal; even property in money for much, property in stocks and shares, if they are honest, for something. But the list is enough to show that property gets further and further from liberty as it gets nearer and nearer to the conveniences and conventions of current finance. The stocks are at the mercy of the Stock Exchange; even the coinage is at the mercy of the Crown or Government; only the kitchen garden and the fowl-run are held ultimately under the mercy of God.

Distributism, so far, is a tendency to reverse a tendency. But the Distributist does not necessarily think that one tendency is to be trusted for ever at the expense of everything else. He only points out that Centralisation is now in fact being trusted at the expense of everything else. This distinction must be kept in mind when we consider whether he has any chance of success; or how far he may already be succeeding.[5]

17.

# ST. FRANCIS, THE EVERLASTING MAN
# AND THE DUMB OX

## St. Francis

I had in my youth a huge admiration for Walt Whitman. I have it still, though balanced
with better things . . . At the same stage of my crude critical adventures I had already
made a picturesque romance of my own about St. Francis of Assisi. I knew nothing
about the most important part of him; I did not even know it was there to be known.
I no more thought of becoming a Catholic than of becoming a cannibal. It was an
entirely personal but perfectly spontaneous attraction towards a certain sort of poetry.
There was something in the few lines of the *Canticle of the Creatures* that there was
not, at least for me, in Shakespeare or in Shelley. It was the same gigantic firelight;
here it seemed that all sorts were welcome and I could see haloes round hundreds of
unconscious heads. Compared with these two, it seemed to me that most poets, and
much greater poets, were frozen with pessimism and with pride.

Now, as I have said, I note these two literary idols of mine to observe what has
happened to me, but still more what has happened to them. Ninety-nine men out
of a hundred would have said in that day: 'Whitman is the future; Francis is a mere
memory of the past. The world is going on to this wide democracy, this optimistic
camaraderie, this acceptance of everything. If this forgotten friar of yours has
something of it, he cannot hand it on.' Since then I have watched the way things really
happen, especially in art and poetry, and I have observed a curious thing. The poets
who have imitated Whitman have imitated everything except what is great about him.
His emotion of hospitality and human sympathy, because it was a mere emotion, has
not been perpetuated. The writers of Free Verse have followed him in being writers of
fragmentary prose. They have not followed him in being lovers of all men or acceptors
of all things. So far from priding themselves on digesting the most disgusting things,
they are disgusted with most ordinary things. They do not write poems about dung and
manure having a divine purpose; they write poems about hair or grass or the human

skin having a leprous and loathsome appearance. It is the very reverse of the poetry of acceptance and assimilation. It is the poetry of emetics. But, since emotion is the test, the one mood is as easily defended as the other. The modern poet has as much right to feel sick at the sight of a cutlet as the democratic poet had to feel affectionate at the sight of a cockroach. And it is *his* mood that he cannot hand on.

But when we come to the same sense of the mystery of a cockroach, or even of a common human being, as felt by St. Francis of Assisi, it is altogether different. St. Francis was as emotional and impulsive as anybody could be; but there was a reason for his emotion; there was a method in his madness. His mood of mysticism was connected with clear ideas that do endure; the idea that God made the cockroach; that God had died for the common person. It was part of the nature of the world, that could be urged on all men in all moods.

And the history of my own mind, so far as it can be shortly stated, might be summed up as the discovery of that doctrine that will justify that enthusiasm. The saint can support the intuitions of the poet, but without that support they fade away like any other fancies, and are often replaced by quite the opposite fancies. If I had in my youth flung myself entirely upon the future as unfolded by my favourite Walt Whitman, I should have found that in fact my favourite Whitman had no future. There was a future for his fad, but none for his faith. It was in the past that I had to look for the future, in something more enduring, and I am glad to end this note of it here upon the name of St. Francis.[1]

A sketch of St. Francis of Assisi . . . may be written in one of three ways. Between these the writer must make his selection; and the third way, which is adopted here, is in some respects the most difficult of all . . . First, he may deal with this great and most amazing man as a figure in secular history and a model of social virtues. He may describe this divine demagogue as being, as he probably was, the world's one quite sincere democrat. He may say (which means very little) that St. Francis was in advance of his age. He may say (what is quite true) that St. Francis anticipated all that is most liberal and sympathetic in the modern mood; the love of nature; the love of animals; the sense of social compassion; the sense of the spiritual dangers of prosperity and even of property. All those things that nobody understood before Wordsworth were familiar to St. Francis. All those things that were first discovered by Tolstoy had been taken for granted by St. Francis. He could be presented, not only as a human but a humanitarian hero; indeed as the first hero of humanism. He has been described as a sort of morning star of the Renaissance. And in comparison with all these things, his ascetical theology can be ignored or dismissed as a contemporary accident, which was fortunately not a fatal accident. His religion can be regarded as a superstition, but an inevitable superstition, from which not even genius could wholly free itself; in the consideration of which it would be unjust to condemn St. Francis for his self-denial or unduly chide him for his chastity. It is quite true that even from so detached a standpoint his stature would still appear heroic. There would still be a great deal to be said about the man who tried to end the Crusades by talking to the Saracens or who interceded with the Emperor for the birds. The writer might describe in a purely historical spirit the whole of that great Franciscan inspiration that was felt in the painting of Giotto, in the poetry of Dante, in the miracle plays that made possible the modern drama, and in so many other things that are already appreciated by the modern culture. He may try to do it, as others have done, almost without raising any religious question at all. In short, he may try to tell the story of a saint without God; which is like being told to write the life of Nansen and forbidden to mention the North Pole.

Second, he may go the the opposite extreme, and decide, as it were, to be defiantly devotional. He may make the theological enthusiasm as thoroughly the theme as it was the theme of the first Franciscans. He may treat religion as the real thing that it was to the real Francis of Assisi. He can find an austere joy, so to speak, in parading the common paradoxes of asceticism and all the holy topsy-turvydom of humility. He can stamp the whole history with the Stigmata,[2] record fasts like fights against a dragon; till in the vague modern mind St. Francis is as dark a figure as St. Dominic. In short he can produce what many in our world will regard as a sort of photographic negative, the reversal of all lights and shades; what the foolish will find as impenetrable as darkness and even many of the wise will find almost as invisible as if it were written in silver upon white. Such a study of St. Francis would be unintelligible to anyone who does nor share his religion, perhaps only partly intelligible to anyone who does not share his vocation. According to degrees of judgement, it will be regarded as something too bad or too good for the world. The only difficulty about doing the thing in this way is that it cannot be done. It would really require a saint to write the life of a saint . . .

Third, he may try to do what I have tried to do here; and, as I have already suggested, the course has peculiar problems of its own. The writer may put himself in the position of the ordinary modern outsider and enquirer . . . He may say to the modern English reader: 'Here is an historical character which is admittedly attractive to many of us already, by its gaiety, its romantic imagination, its spiritual courtesy and camaraderie, but which also contains elements (evidently equally sincere and emphatic) which seem to you quite remote and repulsive. But after all, this man was a man and not half a dozen men. What seems inconsistency to you did not seem inconsistency to him. Let us see whether we can understand, with the help of the existing understanding, these other things that now seem to be doubly dark, by their intrinsic gloom and their ironic contrast.' . . . by approaching it in this way, we may at least get a glimmering of why the poet who praised his lord the sun, often hid himself in a dark cavern, of why the saint who was so gentle with his Brother the Wolf was so harsh to his Brother the Ass (as he named his own body), of why the troubadour who said that love set his heart on fire separated himself from women, of why the singer who rejoiced in the strength and gaiety of the fire deliberately rolled himself in the snow, of why the very song which cries with all the passion of a pagan, 'Praised be God for our Sister, Mother Earth, which brings forth varied fruits and grass and glowing flowers,' ends almost with the words 'Praised be God for our Sister, the death of the body.'[3]

*St. Francis of Assisi* is not biography in the true sense of the word: it is no less than a critical study, a reverent critical study, to be sure, and, together with that object, travels a strenuous essay in apologetics. Chesterton wants

his readers to accept St. Francis for what he (Chesterton) thinks he was and
not as the ragged being who went about talking familiarly with animals
. . . Chesterton is obviously striving to reason to the nature of St. Francis
from the known data, and the bias of his own mind works unconsciously.
After all, every reader eventually makes up his own St. Francis, for the
great saint is one of those perplexing figures that lend themselves to this
personal shaping. It is interesting to note what Chesterton finds. His St.
Francis was a great lover, quite properly dubbed a *jongleur de Dieu*. He was a
troubadour singing before the courts of heaven, and Chesterton is quick to
point out that if we translate this divine love of Francis for God into the love
of a troubadour for his lady we shall see that many seemingly inexplicable
inconsistencies in the saint's life become immediately clear. Traced with this
analogy in mind, much of the life of St. Francis straightens itself out. His
attitude toward life becomes clearer when we view him as a man filled with
the ecstasy of love. And as a *jongleur*, a wandering minstrel (really a jester
in the old meaning of the word), it is easily seen why he should arrive at
the conclusion that monks should become migratory and nomadic instead
of concealing themselves in monasteries. The great teaching of Francis was
that the disciples of God should go out into the world, into the highways and
byways, instead of fleeing from the sins of the world and hiding behind the
buttress of the Church. The establishment of the three orders of Franciscans
changed the course of Church history.[4]

A perusal of *St. Francis of Assisi* reveals that it is inspirational rather than
factual, and that there is a possible lack of balance coming from reliance on
modern Franciscan sources. This means that the Fraticelli[5], and the Fraticelli
side of St. Francis, are not given a fair crack of the whip, and it also leads to the
conclusion that Chesterton had forgotten the original Greyfriars, and that he
was unaware that, for historical reasons, Franciscans in Europe and in parts of
the Americas wear black.

### The Everlasting Man

In late Victorian and early twentieth century times a popular children's
sweetmeat was called an everlasting stick; it was the size and shape of a twelve-
inch ruler and it did indeed last for the length of time that a child would
consider an eternity. Chesterton was no doubt familiar with the children's
favourite and when in 1925 he wrote the second of his great apologetic works
the title *The Everlasting Man* did not seem amiss for a book intended to
be a counter-balance to H.G. Wells's *Outline of History* (1919) and *A Short*

*History of the World* (1922), current ideas on evolution and then popular reinterpretations of Christ as a spiritual teacher.

Chesterton's book was divided into two halves, the first 'On the Creature Called Man' and the second 'On the Man called Christ'. In the first part he disputes Wells's history of early Man and argues a case that Man stands apart from the other animals insofar as Man has always expressed himself through art and other animals have not. In the second part he uses the argument *Aut Deus Aut Insanus Homo*, which translates as 'Either God or a Madman', by featuring all the claims that Christ Himself made:

> What should we feel at the first whisper of a certain suggestion about a certain man?
>
> Certainly it is not for us to blame anybody who should find that first wild whisper merely impious and insane. On the contrary, stumbling on that rock of scandal is the first step. Stark staring incredulity is a far more loyal tribute to that truth than a modernist metaphysic that would make it out merely a matter of degree. It were better to rend our robes with a great cry against blasphemy, like Caiaphas in the judgement, or to lay hold of the man as a maniac possessed of devils like the kinsmen and the crowd, rather than to stand stupidly debating fine shades of pantheism in the presence of so catastrophic a claim. There is more of the wisdom that is one with surprise in any simple person, full of the sensitiveness of simplicity, who would expect the grass to wither and the birds to drop dead out of the air, when a strolling carpenter's apprentice said calmly and almost carelessly, like one looking over his shoulder 'Before Abraham was, I am.'[6]

The book was well received, albeit in some quarters not without regret that 'Almost everything in *The Everlasting Man* – and that is not a little – would have had more chance of acceptance if urged in a work of the imagination than argued as it is, in a treatise. Mr Chesterton has a way of diving into dialectic much as a sea-lion takes a header into its tank.'[7]

> In the history of the world two inexplicable, miraculous events have occurred: the appearance of man and the appearance of Christ. These events, he [Chesterton] asserts, are inexplicable in the sense that nothing that preceded them would justify us in expecting them. In this connexion he discusses two branches of modern science, the theory of evolution, and the theory or theories of comparative religion . . . For Mr Chesterton's perceptions we have admiration and gratitude. He has certainly helped to make vivid to us the facts that man's history on the earth is very wonderful and that some 'Professors' are very silly. This is an important service to render, for, at the present time particularly, these are important facts to remember. But his theories so much more than cover his facts that we are left with the suspicion that they would cover an entirely different collection of facts equally well.[8]

> Mr Chesterton's new book is probably the best he has written. It is so rich in good sense, in wit, and in plain, profound and cheerful truth that almost every page deserves

a review to itself. He has no quarrel with the facts of science – who can quarrel with science on a point of observation? – but he has an utter disrespect for the conventional, materialistic interpretation of the facts. If anyone has forgotten that man is the image of God, he cannot refresh his memory better than by reading *The Everlasting Man*. If anyone has fallen into that lethargy of mind in which he feels, 'I know that man is inexplicable; but isn't materialism hard to refute?' – his doubts will be exorcised for him. Nor is Mr Chesterton's book only a debating manual: it is also a declaration of faith.[9]

## St. Thomas Aquinas – The Dumb Ox

It is often presumed on the evidence of Dorothy Collins that Chesterton wrote half of *St. Thomas Aquinas* without knowing anything about him, and then, when she had on Father O'Connor's advice procured a number of books, he 'flipped them rapidly through' before dictating the rest of the book, only by colossal luck producing a coherent and successful work. In fact Chesterton absorbed the *Summa* early in life and had been in the habit of frequently alluding to Aquinas, even writing a pastiche as a gentle reproof for a young boy late for dinner:

> 'Michael Angelorum dux in bellis primus ac
> clarisimus a domo tamen coelesti diu abest.'
> – St. Thomas Aquinas, *Summa Contra Gentes*.
>
> Translation (by a Person of Quality):
> Our Angel, Michael,[10] is a warrior good
> And kicks the ball about as angels should,
> But somewhat is he given to linger and roam,
> And come in late to his quite heavenly home.
> Those hours come round, when next the youth is seen,
> Like angels' visits few and far between. (c1912)

Chesterton also took a couple of other bites at the cherry, first in early papers[11] found in a box-file in the British Library and latterly in an article[12] published in *The Spectator* on February 27th, 1933:

The difficulty of dealing with St. Thomas Aquinas in [a] brief article is the difficulty of selecting that aspect of a many-sided mind which will best suggest its size and scale. Because of the massive body which carried his massive brain, he was called 'The Ox'; but any attempt to boil down such a brain into tabloid literature passes all possible jokes about an ox in a teacup. He was one of the two or three giants; one of the two or three greatest men who ever lived; and I should never be surprised if he turned out, quite apart from sanctity, to be the greatest of all. Another way of putting the problem is to say that the proportion alters according to what other men we are at the moment classing him with or pitting him against. We do not get the scale until we come to the few men in history who can be his rivals.

Thus, to begin with, we may compare him with the common life of his time: and tell the story of his adventures among his contemporaries. In this alone he shed a light on history, apart from the light he shed on philosophy. He was born in high station, related to the Imperial house, the son of a great noble of Aquino, not far from Naples, and, when he expressed a wish to be a monk, it is typical of his time that everything was made smooth for him – up to a point. A great gentleman could be decorously admitted into the now ancient routine of the Benedictines; like a squire's younger son becoming a parson. But the world had just been shaken by a religious revolution, and strange feet were on all the highways. And when young Thomas insisted on becoming a Dominican – that is a wandering and begging friar – his brothers pursued him, kidnapped him and shut him up in a gaol. It was as if the squire's son had become a gypsy or a communist. However, he managed to become a friar; and the favourite pupil of the great Albertus Magnus at Cologne. He afterwards proceeded to Paris, and was prominent in defending the new mendicant orders at the Sorbonne and elsewhere. From this he passed to the great central controversy on Averroes and Aristotle; in effect to the great reconciliation of Christian faith and Pagan philosophy. His external life was prodigiously preoccupied with these things. He was a big, burly, baldish man, patient and good-natured, but given to blank trances of absence of mind. When dining with St. Louis, the French king, he fell into a brown study and suddenly smote the table with a mighty fist, saying: 'And that will settle the Manichees!' The king, with his fine irony of innocence, sent a secretary to take down the line of argument, lest it be forgotten.

Then he could be compared with other saints or theologians, as mystic rather than dogmatic. For he was, like a sensible man, a mystic in private and a philosopher in public. He had religious experience all right; but he did not, in the modern manner, ask other people to reason from his experience. He only asked them to reason from their own experience. His experiences included well-attested cases of levitation in ecstasy; and the Blessed Virgin appeared to him, comforting him with the welcome news that he would never be Bishop. Similarly, we might compare the Thomist scheme with others, touching on the points in which Scotus or Bonaventura differed from it. There is no space for such distinctions here, beyond the general one; that St. Thomas tends at least relatively to the rational; the others to the mystic; we might almost say the romantic. In any case, there was certainly never a greater theologian, and probably never a greater saint. But saying that he was greater than Albertus or Scotus; even saying that he was greater than Dominic or Francis, would not (in the sense needed here) even hint at how great he was.

To understand his importance, we must pit him against the two or three alternative cosmic creeds: he is the whole Christian intellect speaking to Paganism or Pessimism. He is arguing across the ages with Plato or with Buddha: and he has the best of the argument. His mind was so broad, and its balance so beautiful, that to suggest it would be to discuss a million things. But perhaps the best simplification is this. St Thomas confronts other creeds of good or evil, without at all denying evil, with a theory of two levels of good. The supernatural order is the supreme good, as for any Eastern mystic; but the natural order is good; as solidly good as it is for any man in the street. That is what 'settles the Manichees.' Faith is higher than reason; but reason is higher than anything else, and has supreme rights in its own domain. That is where it anticipates and answers the anti-rational cry of Luther and the rest: as a highly Pagan poet said to me: 'The Reformation happened because people hadn't the brains to understand Aquinas.' The Church is more immortally important than the State; but the State has its rights, for all that. This Christian duality had always been implicit, as in Christ's distinction between God and Caesar, or the dogmatic distinction between the natures of Christ. But St. Thomas has the glory of having seized this double thread as the clue to a thousand things: and thereby created the only creed in which the saints can be sane. It presents itself chiefly, perhaps, to the modern world as the only creed in which the poets can be sane. For there is nobody now to settle the Manichees; and all culture is infected with a faint unclean sense that Nature and all things behind us and below us are bad; that there is only praise to the highbrow in the height. St Thomas exalted God without lowering Man: he exalted Man without lowering Nature. Therefore, he made a cosmos of common sense; *terra viventium*; a land of the living. His philosophy, like his theology, is that of common sense. He does not torture the brain with desperate attempts to explain existence by explaining it away. The first steps of his mind are the first steps of any honest mind; just as the first virtues of his creed could be those of any honest peasant. For he, who combined so many things, combined also intellectual subtlety and spiritual simplicity and the priest who attended the deathbed of this Titan of intellectual energy, whose brain had torn up the roots of the world and pierced every star and split every straw in the whole universe of thought and even of scepticism, said that in listening to the dying man's confession, he fancied suddenly that he was listening to the confession of a child of five.

This is better as an introduction for anyone knowing nothing of St. Thomas than the somewhat longer study[13] published in September of the same year which assumes a basic knowledge of history and philosophy, in fact being partly a popular summary of the *Summa* and partly placing St. Thomas against the background of his times. It does, nonetheless, give a readily understandable idea of how Aristotle entered the service of Catholic Christianity:

It was Aquinas who baptised Aristotle, when Aristotle could not have baptised Aquinas; it was a purely Christian miracle which raised the great Pagan from the dead. And this is proved in three ways (as St. Thomas himself might say) . . . First in the life of St. Thomas, it is proved in the fact that only his huge and solid orthodoxy could have supported so many things which then seemed to be unorthodox. Charity covers a multitude of sins; and in that sense orthodoxy covers a multitude of heresies; or things which are hastily mistaken for heresies. It was precisely because his personal Catholicism was so convincing, that his impersonal Aristotelianism was given the benefit of the doubt. He did not smell of the faggot because he did smell of the firebrand; of the firebrand he had so instantly and instinctively snatched up, under a real assault on essential Catholic ethics. A typically cynical modern phrase refers to the man who is so good that he is good for nothing. St. Thomas was so good that he was good for everything; that his warrant held good for what others considered the most wild and daring speculations, ending in the worship of nothing. Whether or no he baptised Aristotle, he was truly the godfather of Aristotle; he was his sponsor; he swore that the old Greek would do no harm; and the whole world trusted his word.

Second, in the philosophy of St. Thomas, it is proved by the fact that everything depended on the new Christian *motive* for the study of facts, as distinct from truths. The Thomist philosophy began with the lowest roots of thought, the senses and the truisms of the reason; and a Pagan sage might have scorned such things, as he scorned the servile arts. But the materialism, which is merely cynicism in a Pagan, can be Christian humility in a Christian. St. Thomas was willing to begin by recording the facts and sensations of the material world, just as he would have been willing to begin by washing up the plates and dishes in the monastery. The point of his Aristotelianism was that even if common sense about concrete things really was a sort of servile labour, he must not be ashamed to be *servus servorum Dei*. Among heathens the mere sceptic might become the mere cynic; Diogenes in his tub had always a touch of the tub-thumper; but even the dirt of the cynics was dignified into dust and ashes among the saints. If we miss that, we miss the whole meaning of the greatest revolution in history. There was a new *motive* for beginning with the most material, and even with the meanest things.

Third, in the theology of St. Thomas, it is proved by the tremendous truth that supports all that theology; or any other Christian theology. There really was a new reason for regarding the senses, and the sensations of the body, and the experiences of the common man, with a reverence at which great Aristotle would have stared, and no man in the ancient world could have begun to understand. The Body was no longer what it was when Plato and Porphyry and the old mystics had left it for dead. It had hung upon a gibbet. It had risen from a tomb. It was no longer possible for the soul to despise the senses, which had been the organs of something that was more than man. Plato might despise the flesh; but God had not despised it.[14]

Many thought Chesterton had failed to analyse the *Summa* deeply enough, but he was contributing to a short series; others appreciated it for what it was:

Mr Chesterton's little volume makes one of the pleasantest introductions to St. Thomas that could be desired, though it will be read more because it is by the wit of Beaconsfield than because it is about the Dumb Ox of Sicily; and, indeed, it tells us as much about the one as about the other . . . Mr Chesterton not only awakens the mind in this little volume but keeps it awake. He has extracted every paradox that can be obtained from the life of St. Thomas . . . That in St. Thomas's logic which most attracts Mr Chesterton is the fact that, under all its minutiae, it is a philosophy of common sense. But Mr Chesterton would be the first to admit that he has added little to the understanding of St. Thomas's metaphysic; and what he has to say on that subject has a traditional ring.

He is more at ease with St. Thomas the man, and gives a vivid picture of the diverse elements that went to the making of one of the greatest syntheses of all time.[15]

Etienne Gilson (1884–1978)[16], the leading Thomist scholar of the twentieth century, sent a letter to Sheed & Ward (Chesterton's publisher):

I consider it as being without possible comparison the best book ever written on St. Thomas. Nothing short of genius can account for such an achievement. Everybody will no doubt admit that it is a 'clever' book, but few readers who have spent twenty or thirty years in studying St. Thomas Aquinas, and who, perhaps, have themselves published two or three volumes on the subject, cannot fail to perceive that the so-called 'wit' of Chesterton has put their scholarship to shame. He has guessed all that they had tried to demonstrate, and he has said all that which they were more or less clumsily attempting to express in academic formulas. Chesterton was one of the deepest thinkers who ever existed; he was deep because he was right; and he could not help being right.

This was quoted in 1962 by Josef Pieper (1904–1997) in his *Guide to Thomas Aquinas*[17]: 'I think this praise somewhat exaggerated, but at any rate I feel no great embarrassment about recommending an "unscholarly" book.'

# 18.

## DAUGHTER OF DESIRE

By the middle of 1928 a warm rapport had been struck between Dorothy Collins and Frances Chesterton, so much so that before leaving to take her mother on vacation to Brighton, Frances addressed a poem to the secretary:

TO DOROTHY
In gratitude.

Did you dream there was a room in which
    Your heart might live?
That I was poor and you were rich
    With gifts to give?

Gifts from a countless store to load
    An empty shrine,
Flowers of sacrifice that glowed
    Like altar wine.

And did you know you had a hand
    To touch and heal,
Standing as a saint may stand
    At love's appeal?

And did you guess that comfort came
    In the dark night?
Because like some sure candle flame
    Burned sanctus light.

You did not know these haunting things,
    How should you know?
Unconscious love her treasure flings
    To earth below.

I took the gifts, I so hard driven
    The road I ride,
And saw the little door in heaven
    Stand open wide.

For these dear things you are confessed
    As one apart,
Whose purpose holds, whose soul is blessed,
    Who has my heart.

Dorothy responded almost at once with not one but two poems, possibly intended for Frances' birthday on June 28th of which this is the first:

THE ANSWER [I]
*'For these dear things you are confessed*
    *As one apart,*
*Whose purpose holds, whose soul is blessed,*
    *Who has my heart.'* F.C.

These verses bring to you my love
And thanks, O Lady fair,
For you have said I have your heart –
A gift more rare than minted gold,
A human heart to hold.

Your heart enshrined within my love
With joy is wrapt around,
I hold it close in secret strength,
A treasure without bound.

And when the years have come and gone
Shall I still have your heart?
The flower of love lives on and is
Of life itself a part.

This flower is mine, my joy will last,
Eternal as the Spring,
And so I think your heart will live
With me while I can sing.

My Lady fair, she has my heart,
And I have hers in thrall.
I sing her praise, her charming ways,
From morning to nightfall.

Frances replied on July 18th from the Queen's Hotel in Brighton:

My Dear Child,

I always suspected you were sometimes moved to write verse – and I do love yours and I wish you had given it to me in the home. They both please me, especially 'The Cloak' which is strong and original. Thank you, dear, and please write more. You know how much I care about you and all that concerns you. You have been such a help to me . . .

Yours Ever, Frances Chesterton

Frances appears studiously to avoid reference to 'The Answer', perhaps because it is indeed inferior to

### THE CLOAK

I strode on the Downs – desire came to me then
To create or make something anew,
So with air and with rain and the rays of the sun
I created a love-gift for you.

My gift is for you and in essence is pure,
Being made of the elements three.
It is boundless and vivid and virile and strong
And is made for you only by me.

It is hard and yet soft with a tenderness rare,
This gift which is grafted in me,
Composed as it is of the wind, rain and sun,
And the life-force within me set free.

You have nothing to hold or to see or to touch,
But my gift will enfold you with care,
This heart-woven cloak where you will find twined
All the love which I have to declare.

However, there must have been some further poem from Frances, as Dorothy in turn answers for a second time:

THE ANSWER [II]
How could I leave you? Did you know, dear heart,
A vast expanse, cold as the tomb,
Was empty for you; waiting till you came
To make my heart a well-filled room?

Now that I have you should I throw aside
Security which I have sought,
For whim or passing mood of fear,
And lose that big horizon you have brought?

For you are mine; I could not let you go,
Thus emptying on thirsty ground
The fullness which is consummate in you;
I could not, for you hold me bound.

Carissima, you bind me by your grace,
Your courage and humility,
Because you lean on me, and for your great
Fidelity and purity.

For all these things I know that we are one
In constant intercourse of mind;
My love for you is carefree, bold and strong;
Ahead are treasures still to find.

There are no further surviving poems from Frances until 1929:

TO D.E.C. – A DAUGHTER
My soul went groping all the past years through
Searching the barren deserts, for a dream,
A Mirage, some foreknowledge or a gleam
Of that long-waited day that should bring you.

Ready and warm, the chambers of my heart,
Garnished and 'broidered, treasuries in store;
Many had knocked upon the fast-closed door
But only came to question and depart.

Often I entered in that secret shrine,
Left there a thought, a vision or a word.
Sometimes I fancied that the silence stirred
Or that you answered a call of mine.

Where were you hiding, daughter of desire?
In some far convent hidden from the sun
Was I an Abbess, you perchance a nun
Wedded to charity, as flame to fire?

Was I your mother – sponsor to your vows
That held you captive to my clinging gown.
Did we together seek the heavenly crown
That poverty and chastity bestows?

Or am I Naomi, you my daughter Ruth,
Whither I travel will you also go?
My people yours – my God, it may be so,
Your vision too of unimagined truth.

No, these are dreams, and you are closer still
Than lovely Ruth, or any holy nun,
For you have made my very pulses run
With quickened beat, their purpose to fulfil.

And you have brought a long dead hope to birth
That I should hold a daughter by the hand
Like to myself – and I should see her stand
With serious eyes and answering smiles of mirth.

There is an empty space that must be filled
There is an empty room that needs a guest.
Enter my daughter, here you shall find rest,
All is for you, for so your mother willed.

Dorothy was not slow in taking up her new position[1]:

### MADRE MIA

I am your spirit daughter,
Conceived of thought and mind;
To your door my path has led,
I only look behind,
Remembering waiting months
Before this bond was grown,
For in that fallow season
A living seed was sown.
And did you feel the growing;
And did your conscious thought
Make the substance of a dream

This gift which time has wrought?
Slow in growth and deep of root,
Too strong to wither now;
So here, Oh Madre Mia,
A daughter's love I vow.
D.E.C.

Frances' letters over the period gradually changed their forms of address from Miss Collins to My Dear, then Dearest and Beloved D., while Dorothy progresses from Dearest to My Dearest to Dear Heart. An undated poem from Dorothy may belong to this period:

ST. VALENTINE'S DAY
If I wrote as a love, then
Would wit and words combine
To bring you this dull morning hour
    A lover's Valentine.

I cannot give the love you need,
I cannot play that part,
Yet out of its deep hiding place
    You have startled my heart.

Lovers have been, lovers may come,
Friendships may pass or stay,
But a deeper note is sounded
    This Valentine's Day.

For out of space, for out of home
You came to claim your own,
That neither you and, God grant, I
    Should ever be alone.

Frances' incomplete and undated sonnet could also find its place anywhere in those years:

TO DOROTHY: SONNET
Why did you call, Belovèd, in the night?
And I so near. The merest lift of breath
Had brought me to your arms. What sense of fright,
What sudden knowledge, what presage of death
Made all my world stand empty, and a cry
That cut the shadows as a hurtling knife
Flies from some tangled ditch where murderers lie
All keen to snap the little cord of life.

Had you aghast seen evil unashamed,
Naked and cruel – or some poor piteous ghost.
Caught with cold hands your breast, or Hell's mouth flamed
An instant sword – the heavy window post

. . .

(Last two lines lost)

In early April of 1929 illness seemed to have stricken all at Top Meadow. Dorothy Collins was incapacitated at her mother's in Ashtead with suspected Scarlet Fever and Gilbert was suffering from a recurrence of dropsy and also from dental pain. Frances wrote to Dorothy:

Top Meadow, Beaconsfield            Tea Time, April 8 [1929]

Dearest,

Your letter has just come. There is no doubt we must put off the start to Italy till next week anyhow. G. refuses to start for Paris – and that being the case we will wait and go all together. Of course I'm dreadfully disappointed about the Joan of Arc. I had rather set my heart on it. I hope Kathleen Chesshire[2] can get rid of the tickets. Let me hear how you go on – and don't attempt to do anything before you are quite fit. I am awfully, awfully sorry you've had such a bad time.

Dr Bakewell has been in today and insisted on a diet regime which will, I hope, do good, and the dentist managed to get out two bits of teeth without any anaesthetic, and he seems better. But you know what he is like – always glad to postpone any action – so I believe he's quite grateful to you for being ill. As for me, I live under a sense of frustration and don't expect things to go as planned . . . God bless you – I am so thankful you are better.

Yours ever, Frances Chesterton

Top Meadow, Beaconsfield            April 9 [1929]

Dearest,

I am quite sure that whatever happens you will not be fit to start for Italy on Thursday and I think we must make up our minds to wait a few days. It is so cold that it won't make such a vast amount of difference – all you can do is to take the greatest care of yourself and don't attempt to get about until you are absolutely fit, it is then that the damage is often done. Of course I am praying that the S.F. [Scarlet Fever] is only a scare, but I hear there is a good deal of it about in a very light form . . . I hope you are feeling better – I am so awfully sorry for you – it makes me miserable to think of you ill and worrying – but take heart of grace, 'more was lost at Mohac field' as your beloved Hungarians say. I do hope that I shall have good news in the morning.

Yours ever, Frances Chesterton

It was not long before Frances herself was struck by appendicitis, as reported by Gilbert in a letter to Mildred d'Avigdor:

My dear Mildred,

I cannot say how delighted I was to hear from you again and to hear that you might come down and see us next week. When you wrote at Christmas I, like a fool, carried off your letter and lost your address: and since then Frances and I have had a lot of bothers, fusses and frustrated schemes, which culminated in a way more dramatic than pleasant: when we had all our bags packed up to go to Rome, it was found that Frances had appendicitis and was operated on the day before we were to start. She got through splendidly but she is still recovering in the nursing home just around the corner, in Beaconsfield. She ought to be back here by the day you mention: but in any case do come – for she would love you to visit her there and it is but a step from our tea-table. Please come and see us then and whenever you like and it will do us good. I only forget addresses not names or faces or all that they bring with them. With love,

Yours always, G.K. Chesterton[3]

There are no surviving poems for nearly two years until 1931 when Dorothy marks Frances' birthday.

DOGGEREL FOR F.C. ON HER BIRTHDAY
28th June, 1931

Each bead a prayer for you, my love,
  On this your day of birth,
For Joy of spirit – precious gift,
For peace of soul and mirth;
For grace and health and length of days
  And you own wish come true,
Prayers in number as the beads
  I offer God for you.

Dorothy's conversion to Roman Catholicism is mentioned at the end of a letter from Paris dated September 10th, 1932: 'PRIVATE I am very glad I decided before I left England to join the Catholic Church. If I had not done so, I might have felt that I was influenced by the beauty of it all over here. It is such a peaceful atmosphere. I had almost forgotten the wranglings of the English Church until I saw *The Times* today which had three different references to it all – from different points of view. I think the easiest thing of all will be to go to Monsignor Smith.' Frances replied on September 13th: 'Of course I am more happy than I can say that you are going to be of the Faith. I have prayed for you and longed for it. I can hardly believe it is going to come true. I will help you all I can over the difficult road you've got to tread – but I believe you will think any sacrifice worthwhile. You will make a better Catholic than I ever could be, because you have come to it by such a process of hacking your way through the jungle to the clear light. God bless you, Christ fill you, the Holy Spirit guide you and Our Lady hold your dear hands.' Within weeks she was celebrating Dorothy's profession of faith:

ON THE VIGIL OF ALL SAINTS
To D.E.C. Oct. 31, 1932

I wondered as you sought the way,
  Is your inheritance in God?
Maybe the path the saints have trod
  Might prove too large a price to pay.

How will she stoop beneath the door
  That guards the knowledge from her eyes,
How see the golden shaft that lies
  Across the sanctuary floor?

The door so small, the world so wide,
  New heaven, new earth for mind to roam,
Yet in a tiny compass – home
  For the wanderer – satisfied.

Firm are the feet that scale the Rock,
  Proud is the head that humbly bows
Before the Godhead in His House,
  Holy the hands insistent knock.

As He has turned your heart's gold key,
  So you, impatient at His door,
Have asked for entrance: never more
  Is that door closed : bend but the knee.

Lift up the latch, throw wide the gate.
  Ten thousand saints at break of day
Welcome a pilgrim on the way
  That had no further strength to wait.

Frances had already on several occasions taken a nostalgic glance back at times she and Dorothy had spent together:

## MARIA IMMACULATA[4]
### A Sonnet to D.E.C.

Do you remember how we walked the streets
Of Rome and saw the Queen of Heaven high,
Raised and superb upon Her throne, and threw
Our roses to Her as we passed Her by?
The swinging bells rang out the Angelus,
Her head in glory with its starry crown.
You knew she stood for us and all the world,
Christ's kingdom regnant in the sacred town.
Of all my visions let this never fade,
Lady of Stars, the new moon at your feet.
Let us, Beloved, find Her once again
In her bright setting in the dusty street
Nearer and holier to us whose souls have met,
So that you too remember, and I may not forget.

## TECUM
### To D.E.C.

Sometimes my soul is sick for alien skies,
Skies that you know also, and knowing hold
In strong remembrance of our wandering there
When English skies are overcast and cold.

The velvet sky – star-dented over Rome,
Our Lady's mantle flung o'er dome and tower,
Those lifted witnesses to everlasting truth
Rooted in earth – the challenge tree of power.

That spire, crowned with a crown a queen may wear,
Tapering, a flame in buoyant-sunset gold
Where Cracow whispers of a nation's faith,
Young in her freedom – as her eagles old.

Or where the chimes rang to the silver sky
From the flat land of Flanders, looming large
The old high belfry set in a gold square
Rings in her depths the singing notes of Bruges.

Tho' Paris greeted us with strong tears,
She could not hide the rainbow; and we saw
The Sainte Chapelle, hoarding refracted light,
Spill her own jewels on tesselated floor.

I see again in Californian sky
How great Orion rode the vault of night,
And there aloft in your secluded tower
Your lamp shone out, one strong clear beam of light.

And there are other skies unvisited
Where we shall stand in sunshine or in rain
And cross perchance the Alcantara bridge
That reaches to the secret heart of Spain.

We have seen all these things and have been glad
Together; and have so crossed too; we roam
As weary exiles, prisoners in space
Needing that roof of cloud that is our home.

Out of your window here in England's sky,
Grey, holding, hiding as her mystery rare
Full rain or snow, high wind, or sudden sun
To fill our hearts with rapture or despair.

Here must we all in ultimate content
Return, as storm-worn eagle to the nest.
Each to his appointed place, at the world's end
The unimagined goal of every guest.

Stay here with me, dear heart, till forth we fare
From grey to gold, and back from gold to grey
Our pilgrimage goes on – we find our home
Who by God's mercy have not lost the way.

Dorothy continued to write verses for Frances' birthdays and on one occasion, sadly with no date indicated, made a fair attempt at a triolet:

### A TRIOLET

I've nothing to give you
But love with these roses.
It's sad but it's true
I have nothing to give you
But sweet buds that grow
That you might have posies
I have nothing to give you
But love with these roses.

A SECOND TRIOLET
A wine glass of sherry
Is the best I can offer:
Let that make you merry.
A wine glass of sherry
Is warming, yes very,
And you must not suffer.
A wine glass of sherry
Is the best I can offer.

These silly rhymes I write
Because it is your birthday night.
D.E.C.

The last extant poem which Frances dedicated on June 11th, 1933 to Dorothy Collins recalled a gypsy violinist who had played to them:

THE HAPPY FIDDLER
For D.E.C.

What does he play upon those happy strings
That he should smile at beggar's hat and coat
And ragged arm that music flings
Out to a toiling world, pure note on note;
    What does he play?

The music of ineffable content
Sings from the spirit of the curving bow;
Listen, oh listen, this is how it went,
Molto vivace, andante, adagio;
    Thus did he play.

First quick the air, as spring is light and keen
Then slower as the gathering years take toll
Of youth's bright hours, and all its tears unseen
From the worn body, calling forth the soul
    As he did play.

The long-drawn music of unfathomable peace,
Adagio of the restless heart of man,
Of heavy burdens bringing the surcease
Of length of living, and of death's short span;
    Of this he played.

And playing ever smiled, for well he knew
That he, poor fiddler from some summer shore,
When e'er the bow across the strings he drew
Eased the long exile of the homeless poor;
　　For them he played.

But not for them alone the moment rare,
The great enchantment of that happy smile;
For love he played upon the vibrant air
The world to harmony; yet all the while
　　For you he played.[5]

# 19.

# WESTWARD HO!

On 19th September 1930 the Chestertons were once again on the move, this time aboard the Cunard White Star liner SS *Doric* outward bound from Liverpool for Canada en route to the United States and the University of Notre Dame at South Bend, Indiana where Gilbert was to give a series of lectures on Victorian Literature and History over six weeks before undertaking a lecture tour the length and breadth of North America. Despite rough seas most of the way across the Atlantic, the tour started well with the SS *Doric* far from crowded, so Frances could write to her mother-in-law: 'We have a delightful suite on board (paid for by Gilbert's University People) – a bedroom with two beds, a sitting room and a bathroom, and Dorothy's room is quite near. We are fed like fighting cocks – as is always the way on these great liners.'[1] Gilbert threw himself into enjoying and helping organize the shipboard entertainment, and even Frances took great interest in the horse-racing games played in the evenings. As they sailed north there was the Aurora Borealis to admire, and, as they made landfall off Newfoundland and began to approach the Gulf of St. Lawrence through the Strait of Belle Isle, there were icebergs to spot and whales and porpoises at which to marvel. A short stop in Québec City gave opportunity for a fleeting tour of the city and of the Heights of Abraham to see the Wolfe and Montcalm memorials, but once arrived in Montréal and later Toronto, there commenced the long series of public lectures. Chesterton had liked the idea of giving lectures in one place instead of the incessant touring he had undertaken in 1921, but he had been persuaded by Lee Keedick, the leading US lecture agent, to agree to a so-called short tour. With the financial plight of *G.K.'s Weekly* in mind, and assured that the load would be light, Chesterton agreed only to find later that the tour was much longer and more onerous than expected. Another unexpected difficulty arose on arrival at South Bend, as the official Lecturer's quarters consisted of a bachelor apartment in a college where no women were admitted, and it was proposed to lodge Frances and Dorothy Collins with nuns in an Infirmary. A quick change of plan saw the Chesterton party move in with the Bixler family in South Bend. Frances described the household: 'There is a grandfather, a husband, and two small children – kindness itself, but so utterly unlike people of the same position at home. Here we have the true democracy at work and we shall all lead the family life I can see. Miss Collins is already nursing the baby and Gilbert is conversing with the grandfather about the Civil War and Lincoln, while I must help Mrs Bixler to clear the table.'[2] A far cry from the servants at home in Beaconsfield.

Mr Bixler was a Mid-Western Realtor [Estate Agent] and, as it was the time of Prohibition, maker of home-brew. Dorothy Collins is on record as saying that 'Chesterton observed [Prohibition] meticulously, saying that a visitor should always observe the laws of the country in which he found himself',[3] whereas Mrs Bixler recalled that Chesterton 'kept Daddy busy making home-brew for him' and Professor Engels at Notre Dame remembered that Chesterton 'would sit around consuming home-made ale by the quart. Truth, as ever, no doubt lies between the two extremes.

During the weekends, Chesterton fulfilled other engagements by lecturing as far away as Milwaukee, Detroit and Chicago, but on November 15th he left Notre Dame and his tour began in earnest in Cincinnati where they were given a royal suite vacated by Queen Marie of Roumania. Dorothy Collins remembered that 'the Union Jack was flying, and the entrance hall was decorated with Union Jacks and a large illuminated sign saying *Welcome G.K. Chesterton.*'[4] The welcomes soon became too much for Frances: 'Since we arrived in New York our life has been a nightmare. Publicity men, reporters, interviewers, photographers, even film producers, dog our uneasy footsteps.'[5] Thanksgiving was spent in New York, before forays by train throughout the north-east took him not only to lecture in Albany, Buffalo and Syracuse but on to Philadelphia and Cleveland, Ohio, and then back to Portland, Maine, and on into Canada to Ottawa. On December 12th Chesterton had given the winter inaugural lecture at Holy Cross College, Massachusetts, where he received a warm tribute from the then French ambassador to the United States, the poet and dramatist Paul Claudel:

I am delighted to bring my salutations to the great poet and the great Christian, G.K. Chesterton, during his tour of the United States. His books, for the past twenty years, have never failed to bring me joy and refreshment: and this feeling of regard is so tender and unusual that approbation is linked with admiration . . . He is the man that threw the doors wide open: and upon a world pallid and sick he sent floods of poetry, of joyousness, of noble sympathies, of radiant and thundering humour – all drawn from unfailing sources of orthodoxy. His onward march is the verification of that divine saying: 'The Truth will make you free.' If I were to state his essential quality, I would say that it is a sort of triumphant common sense – that *gaudium de veritate*, of which philosophers discourse; – a joyous acclaim towards the splendour and the powers of the soul, those faculties that were overburdened and numbed by a century of false science, of pedantic pessimism, and of *counterfeit* and *contra-fact*. In the sparkling and irresistible dialectics of a great poet, he keeps always bringing us back to that infallible promise of Christ: – And I will refresh you: *Et Ego reficiam vos.*[6]

Back in New York City for Christmas and the New Year, Chesterton took part in a debate at the Mecca Temple on 'Will the World return to Religion' with the Chicago lawyer Clarence Darrow (1857–1938) of the American Civil Liberties Union, famous for having appeared for the defence in the case of teenage thrill-killers Leopold and Loeb in 1924, and even better known for his part in the so-called Scopes Monkey Trial over the teaching of Darwin's Theory of Evolution in Dayton, Tennessee in July, 1925. Chesterton, who was adjudged to have won the debate by 2,359 to 1,022 votes, disconcerted Darrow by opening his reply with the words: 'It may come as a surprise to you, Mr Darrow, and perhaps to all of you in the audience, but I agree entirely with everything you have said.' No full transcript of the debate survives, but one who attended the debate, Frances Taylor Patterson, reported:

I have never heard Mr Darrow alone, but taken relatively, when that relativity is to Chesterton, he appears positively muddle-headed.
    As Chesterton summed it up, he felt as if Darrow had been arguing all afternoon with his fundamentalist aunt, and simply kept sparring with a dummy of his own mental making. When something went wrong with the microphone, Darrow sat back until it could be fixed. Whereupon G.K.C. jumped up and carried on in his natural voice, 'Science, you see, is not infallible!' . . . Chesterton had the audience with him from the start, and when it was over, everyone just sat there, not wishing to leave. They were loathe to let the light die![7]

On January 6th, 1931 the Chestertons headed south for Chattanooga. Suddenly, Frances began to take ill, no doubt because of the effect that the strain of travelling was having on her. At first her condition was thought to be due to exhaustion, and Gilbert left her in Dorothy's charge while he fulfilled his programme, for his contract with Lee Keedick required him to pay a penalty of £100 for every cancellation. Frances began to run a very high temperature and after six days she was admitted to hospital, where she had a private room with two nurses. Dorothy thought that 'it was quite doubtful whether she would get better,'[8] and two specialists were called in. Gilbert cancelled many lectures in the south and hurried back 'looking as if he had not undressed for a week.' He arrived without his tickets, his money and most of his clothes, and a considerable debt to Keedick. He was due to start lecturing on the West Coast on February 12th, so it was decided that Frances, now feeling much better and recovering from what had turned out to be influenza, should be left in a nursing home in Tennessee with the two nurses, while Gilbert accompanied by Dorothy should travel west to rescue what was left of the programme. Shortly before they reached the end of the three and a half days journey to Los Angeles on January 10th 'Gilbert was sitting in the Pullman car . . . [when] along came the fatherly old negro car-attendant to clean his shoes and brush his coat, as was the custom. G.K. waved him away, to be met with the remark, "Ho, Ho, young man, you'se getting old afore yer time, You must keep yerself nice for the gals." His day was made.'[9]

For the next week or so, 'we rushed up and down the Californian coast and Mr Chesterton gave a lecture every night' while receiving hospitality from the Matier family for whose eight-year old daughter, Sheila, he wrote and illustrated *The Three Conquistadors* in recompense:

> To Sheila's home Three Bravoes came
> Beyond the Angels' town,
> One Red, one Yellow and one White
> Or rather pinky-Brown.
>
> THE REDSKIN CHIEF
> Red Bison of the Hokum Tribe,
> His hunting and his fighting
> I write of in Red Indian style
> – Only in Picture Writing.
>
> JUAN THE DAGO
> From Mexico, where people drink
> Wild wine, the brew of shame,
> Came Juan to California, where
> The people do the same.

THE CHINESE PIRATE
Quong, who (unlike your father's friend)
    Was not a Buddhist monk,
A Chinese Pirate spoiled the ships
    And filled his Junk with junk.

But when they came to Sheila's home
    Those wild marauding three,
They felt her softening touch and grew
    Quite as polite as she.

Red Bison climbed to Sheila's house
    As goats that scale an Alp:
But though he much admired her hair,
    He did not take her scalp.

The Dago murdered nobody
    For days and days: and Quong
Found out, with tears, that he belonged
    To Mr Matier's Tong.

The Dog that up the Ladder goes
    He learned how to descry
With patient pleasure, and without
    One thought of Puppy-Pie.

'For O,' they cried, 'We come in peace
    Who walk the sunset strand
Far from that bleak but boiling sea
    That breaks on Eastern land,

'That swings and sways with dizzy tides
    Since first the ocean drank
Atlantis to the dregs: and left
    A whirlpool where she sank

'Of storms, Armadas, Vikings, Tars,
    That make its tides terrific:
But Sheila need not shrink from us:
    For we are all pacific.

Frances, still accompanied by a nurse, rejoined them on February 17th after which Dorothy managed to find a small Spanish hotel a few miles outside Los

Angeles, which she believed would be better for Frances' convalescence. Once there Gilbert found time to write to Clare Nicholl:

> The trouble is that she [Frances] got ill rather quickly and gets well rather slowly; two good doctors have told me there is nothing wrong and it is a matter of time . . . Frances is much better this morning and we shall probably resume normally the homeward march. For we are now really returning homeward, though so far away: we shall never, please God, go farther away. The idea is to lecture at San Francisco . . . and then work up the coast by Oregon . . . then pause by Vancouver where we have a friend or two [the Firmin sisters]: and then bang back to New York and Old England. Amen.[10]

Gilbert's optimism was ill-founded and Frances had to be left behind in the hotel to recuperate further while 'G.K . . . trekked up and down the country, worried about her but unable to cancel engagements.'[11] In Portland, Oregon there was a hold-up and killing outside their hotel, which they only missed by a couple of minutes, much to the chagrin of their taxi-driver. Then it was on into British Colombia and on again to Victoria on Vancouver Island where the *Victoria Daily Times* described his 'ruddy, somewhat rounded face with a high, broad forehead; thin slightly grey hair that embraced the upper part of his ears; a mustache of a sandier colour that hooked down below his mouth. His large eyes twinkled. They branded Chesterton as unavoidably genial, in spite of his heavy eyebrows, his aggressive nose. Layers of chin tapered down in to the folds of an ample winged collar. His skin was fair, delicate . . . His replies to the interviewers were often followed by a cavernous chortle, and his whole body shook and shifted around on the settee . . . Chesterton stood up to shake hands and was over six feet. His massive shoulders curved under his long cloak, and he walked with a slow amble. Not a man to be passed in a crowd – rather a Dr Samuel Johnson come to life in this twentieth century, able to talk on most things, dictatorially perhaps, but readily and optimistically.'

Back in California at the hotel in Palos Verdes not too far from Hollywood, Frances was writing to Marie-Louise that some film producers were 'very anxious to get hold of some Father Brown stories for filming. It would be splendid financially . . . and a great help, as naturally my illness has been a bit expensive. Everything out here is about four times as much as in England.'[12]

Chesterton thought Hollywood 'a remarkable place. It is like an explosion under an old English pantomime. Bits of Pierrot are joined with a tress or two of Columbine . . . A Punch and Judy nose is stuck upon a beautiful face.'[13] Dorothy negotiated hard with the film producers, as well as with American newspapers, but only one film was to result and that in 1935: *Father Brown,*

*Detective,* with Walter Connolly as Father Brown and Paul Lukas as Flambeau. On March 23rd the party of four finally left Los Angeles to drop off the nurse in Kansas City before reaching New York on the 29th. A final series of lectures had then to be given before they could take ship for home aboard the White Star liner SS *Majestic*, then the largest ship afloat.

A different point of view emerges in postcards Dorothy Collins sent home to her mother in Ashtead:

White Star Line                              On board s.s. 'Doric', Tuesday, 23/9/30
I will begin a letter today and finish it off before we can post at Quebec where I shall send you a cable . . . The sea has been rough all the time but no bad storms or mountainous seas, just a steady roll or pitch which becomes very monotonous and sickening. G.K. and I have not been sick. Mrs C. has once or twice but not to the point of incapacity. . .

Canadian National Railways        In train from Toronto to South Bend, nr. Chicago
                                             Saturday, 12.30 (your time 6.30 pm)
. . . Mrs C. is too dreary, chiefly I think because of her lumbago. I hope to goodness she will cheer up soon . . . G.K. is getting a very good press.

209 East Pokagon St., South Bend, Indiana, USA        Saturday 1 Oct. 1930
We are in the Middle West with a vengeance both here and at South Bend. It is an extraordinary country and gives one the impression of being totally unfinished. The good hotels are very good and there is one in nearly every town. The rest of the buildings I have seen so far are cheap and tawdry. Nearly all the houses are of wood, generally a grey colour and badly in need of paint – the country is one vast expanse of scrubby-looking grass with piles and piles of scrap iron and empty tins all over the place. There is practically no attempt at 'gardens'.
    The houses are just dumped down with no fences or hedges to enclose them. It all seems very ragged and uncivilized . . . There is practically no variation in the scenery and they go into ecstasies over the ugliest brick buildings if they happen to be 100 years old which is almost prehistoric in their reckoning of time. Still nothing has been decided about our future movements. I don't want to stay a bit. It is awful moving on from place to place with never more than 2 days in any one place, but it would be a pity to miss California and we are so far. The men sit about in their shirt sleeves in the best hotels. They have Funeral Homes in every town which are ordinary private houses where the undertaker embalms bodies. Everybody is embalmed in this country. Apparently the corpses and the undertaker and his family all live mixed up together in a most friendly way! I feel more as if I were in a foreign country than I have ever done in Europe. Chiefly, I suppose, because the differences do not please one and one is, therefore, very fully conscious of them all the time.

22nd October, 1930

... G.K. gave a very successful debate with the leader of the Ethical Society in Chicago on IS THE NEW WOMAN ENSLAVED? G.K. taking the affirmative. I was on the other side naturally, but G.K. makes out quite a good case for his old-fashioned ideas. He does not allow enough for modern economic conditions, or rather he does, saying that they are the causes of the enslavement. What he does not do is to suggest a working alternative to the present situation ...

2nd November, 1930

Delphine, aged 4[14] ... I am afraid that in her mind my destination is hell; she has never recovered from the shock she had when she saw me smoking. She thinks it simply awful. I very seldom do it as it worries her so. Her grandfather thinks it very wicked, but the rest of the family are a little more advanced in their outlook. That is the Middle West as it used to be 50 years ago ...

NEW YORK, Hotel St. Moritz. Sunday, 23/11 /30

... At Buffalo G.K. lectured on 'Culture and the Coming Peril' and was given another degree at the University there. Of course, these degrees are worth nothing, but he can't refuse them ... I cannot tell in any words how much I simply loathe this country and all it stands for. It is totally artificial and all their values are topsy-turvy... I am simply longing for the day when I land on English soil. I am not enjoying myself at all although it is a wonderful experience and if I were given the choice I should stay because it is an opportunity which will never come again.

The Providence Biltmore, Providence, R.I. Thursday, 11 Dec. 1930

Boston is easily the nicest place we have been so far. It is very European and has none of the ostentatious display and vulgarity of the other cities in this weird country.

Balfour is clearing up at Murray House [PNEU][15] for me and I have put it all into the hands of a solicitor. They are a swiney lot there ...

Last night I was rung up in the middle of the night 2a.m. to say that the C's had not locked their bedroom door. Meanwhile the police were hammering on that door and the hall porter was locking it from outside, so we were all wakened up. There is a police regulation that hotel doors must be locked at night and a policeman comes round to see that it is enforced. That is twice we have had this fuss. Most doors lock themselves with Yale locks, but when they don't G.K. would never dream of locking a door – if we gave him the key he would probably lose it! His vagueness is simply appalling, but nothing is worse than when he thinks he ought to be businesslike – the fussing that then ensues cannot be described. Luckily it only happens about once a week for a short time!! Mrs C. does not encourage it.

Hotel Bond, Hartford, Connecticut Monday, 15 Dec. 1930

... it is no exaggeration to say that I have not had a consecutive hour for my own affairs since we left South Bend. Interruptions are incessant. I am glad to say that I am to have a clear £200 out of proceeds in addition to all ex[pense]s and my salary. I shall invest it

I think for my old age. It would help towards buying an annuity later on which seems to be better with any savings I may have, than paying £40 or £50 a year insurance which so many people do to ensure an income for their old age. So far with expenses deducted we have made about £2,000 altogether, and shall probably clear another £2,000 after Xmas. Let us hope that it is not all swamped by that awful Oldershaw family[16] at Maidenhead. We are gradually paying off £800 for the paper's [G.K.'s Weekly] debts of last year and they are still losing £2 a week . . .

Three Arts Club                                     Saturday, December 19th, 1930
I hope that I shall never be abroad so long again, it certainly is not worth it. I hope that California will come up to expectations as some sort of payment for all this misery. They went off yesterday; she very reluctantly; he is a selfish creature like all men when it comes to big things, and she gives him his own way in everything. It makes me furious.

[The Three Arts Club] is quite all right as a place to stay for three weeks. It is run for art, drama and music students and the age limit is 30. They have all lived here for years and take no notice of a stranger. The rules for admission are waived at Christmas as the club is half empty owing to the art school holidays. Being run by coloured servants it inclines to be dirty – the first time I have seen any dirt in America which on the whole as far as hotels, stations, etc. are concerned is spotlessly clean. You would be amused to see these black girls as waitresses sidling about in the typical negro manner. I suppose they are cheaper than white servants. They are not employed in all the hotels but just a sprinkling in some of the hotels in smaller towns. The St. Moritz which is on a par with Browns or some such exclusive place in London would collapse from the foundations if one dared to put its nose inside the door.

Unlike most English people, we dislike the American food very much. Nearly all places serve à la carte meals and one has to pay 5/- [25p or US$0.50c] for a portion of meat without vegetables. For that one gets what looks like half a turkey – three-quarters of a chicken or an equal amount of beef or lamb as the case may be.

It is like attacking a mountain and puts one off altogether. Sometimes if we are feeling very brave Mrs C. and I order one portion between us – this suggestion is treated with scorn and the second plate is borne in with lofty disgust. However, we persist and are then able to go on to something else without overeating or ruining ourselves. G.K. has not the same objection as he does not mind whether he has a little or a lot and just munches through it.

It is cold but not damp cold. I am afraid Mrs C. will find Canada awful. It is two below zero and here we are 22 above. She has had an awful cold but dragged round with us all last week because he is incapable of getting into evening dress without her. I tell her she makes him more helpless than he need be. Like so many women I think she likes to feel that he is dependent on her.

c/o Mr Lee Keedick, 475 Fifth Ave., New York City.            Monday, January 5th.
. . . I had a very nice Christmas as I had both luncheon and dinner with English people . . . and had a jolly Christmas party with all the usual Christmas-in-England additions, such as caps, crackers, little candles, presents on the table and so on. I dare say they do the same in this country but I could not tell as I did not see an American family on

Christmas Day. I am afraid Americans would overdo it. At some parties they give such things as motor-cars and jewellery costing £100 each to every guest. Unfortunately, I have not been invited to such a party!! It seems rather vulgar to English ideas.

. . . The Chestertons went to Canada to stay with an old uncle of G.K.'s. I was very thankful to have the chance of two weeks alone.

. . . I cannot help feeling that the tremendous prosperity of the country has been very degrading to character. It is an established fact that America used to waste more than would keep one of the European countries alive. Of course things are rather different now as they say times are hard. Mr Rumpelmeyer. . . told me that on New Year's Eve they had 650 people for the Dinner and Dinner-dance. They were the richest people in New York and therefore the 'aristocracy' for that is all that counts here. He said that they behaved worse than pigs and their only idea of amusement was to make more noise than could be imagined and to get dead drunk (Prohibition!!). The noise at midnight made by all the sirens, motor-horns, trumpets, fireworks, etc., was so terrific that one could not hear the church bells. It all struck me as being appallingly vulgar.

. . . I do hope G.K. and Mrs C. will keep fit. She was very ill at Christmas with a bad cold and a general sort of collapse, but is better now.

6th January, 1931

. . . G.K. is a roaring success out here. Tremendously popular, and is given halls and theatres accommodating thousands. He often speaks in theatres the size of His Majesty's and completely fills them with an overflow standing. That is why we are going back to some of the places. The publicity is appalling; the reporters force their way into our bedrooms when we arrive at a place. G.K. is awfully good about giving them interviews and they treat him with a semblance of courtesy, but they have been known to break down the bedroom-door of someone who would not give them an interview. That is the sort of thing one is up against out here: no one in England could even imagine what it is like everywhere we go. The station is crowded with reporters, newspaper men, organisers of lectures, autograph hunters, etc, etc, etc. Mrs Chesterton and I get the most beautiful bouquets and presents of flowers. It all seems very futile and empty as we cannot help feeling that many of the people have never read his books and have not the remotest idea what he stands for.

In train Roanoke to Chattanooga.                          Wednesday, January 21, 1931

. . .. We are now trekking all over the country. Mrs C. has a mania against sleeping in the train so we have to break every journey and go to an hotel, which with seven pieces of luggage is, I think, much more tiring than having an occasional night in the train . . . Mrs C. has a cold – otherwise we are all flourishing. If she is not better by Friday I shall persuade her to stay in bed on Friday when we have a free day in Nashville.

. . . We are really in the South now. The waiting-rooms, etc. are all marked – White Men – Colored Men – White Women – Colored Women. The colored people are not allowed to mix with whites in trains, trams, restaurants, churches, etc. Most unchristian I think, but I suppose there *are* difficulties. There are no such divisions in the northern States but there are not so many of them there.

The Read House, Chattanooga, Tennessee.                              Saturday, 24.1.31

Whoever would have thought of staying in Chattanooga? Anyway here we have been since Wednesday and do not expect to get away till Monday. Mrs C. was laid low with an attack of 'grip' which the doctors here call a disease which is like 'flu but much quicker. She started it on Tuesday and we travelled all that day and on Wednesday she had a temperature and it got worse and was 103.5 on Thursday. I insisted on the doctor seeing her, and G.K. agreed. G.K. was for us all staying here and cancelling three lectures at St. Louis and Nashville. That seemed mad and he eventually agreed to go off on his own – a great adventure – I packed up his things, took him to the station and pushed him into the train with his tickets and pages of instructions – all of which he has probably long since lost. I tremble to think of the dirty dishevelled creature who is at present wandering the face of America. It was good to get rid of him though and thus avoid his catching the disease. I think as a matter of fact that he had it himself last Sunday, as he was choking and sneezing and had a temperature of 100. Mrs C. would always catch anything and have it worse than anyone else. I have escaped – the incubation time is over and she is no longer infectious. She will get up tomorrow. Luckily the hotel doctor is a very careful, capable person.

This is an awful place, a factory town but set in the most beautiful scenery on the Tennessee river.

Chattanooga                                                            25.1.31

All well. Mrs C. is better but frightfully depressed and lugubrious. We hope to leave tomorrow to join G.K. in New Orleans. Glorious warm sunny weather here. I wish you could enjoy it.

                                                            28 January, Wednesday

Mrs C. has finished the 'flu but has now got gastritis or its equivalent. We had to get a nurse yesterday as I could not manage alone with so much sickness, faintness and enemas to be given, and so on. Luckily a very nice nurse and a very good doctor.

G.K. came back today, a very roundabout journey, looking like <u>nothing on earth</u>. His hair had not been brushed for a week – he has slept in the train in his day clothes and his nails were filthy (as usual) and he needed a shave. He <u>can't</u> go about alone and I am at my wits end what to decide. She will be so upset if I leave her tomorrow when he is due to go south to New Orleans, and with so much moving about he can't go alone. All our luggage is at New Orleans and we are moving about so much she would never catch us up even if she were well enough to travel next week. It would cost us a fortune to cancel all these lectures which have been booked and advertised.

I heard Paderewski this evening. Very boring for anyone as unmusical as I am. I only stayed till half time.

                                                            Thurs. 29.1.31

Just a line further to my letter of last night to tell you that they took Mrs C. to the hospital in an ambulance this morning. The doctor thought it better that G.K. should cancel his engagements for the present which will be an enormous financial loss as we shall have to compensate for each one missed.

30 January 1931

Mrs Chesterton is dangerously ill – in fact I have never seen anyone so ill. As I told you in previous letters, she had 'flu and I was looking after her here from Wednesday to Tuesday. She got so much worse from Sunday onwards that on Tuesday the doctor found a nurse and I helped her until Thursday when they sent an ambulance and took here to a private room in the hospital, Now she has two nurses and two doctors and last night they called in a specialist. We quite expected to be called up in the night. I don't see any difference today, but the doctor says she is a tiny bit better. She certainly is not fighting for breath as she was yesterday. She is sick constantly and is retching all the time. They have been feeding her through the rectum and with intravenous injections but last night they started through the mouth again on the advice of the specialist. She has managed to retain some of it. They still give the injections. G.K. and I take it in turns to sit with her from 10 o'clock onwards – he from 1–4 and I from 4–7. It means that the nurse can get her lunch and supper and do things when necessary outside the room. She hardly recognizes us and cannot sit up even to be sick . . . There is no fear of infection with Mrs C. now as her temperature has been normal for some days until tonight when it has risen again. This worries the doctor but he says it is sometimes a sympton of starvation in which case it would be normal.

We have nothing to reproach ourselves with as we called the doctor in on the first day there was a rise of temperature. I suppose the only reproach is that she is too old [62] and delicate to have undertaken such a tour. I don't know what will happen now. We shall have tremendous compensation to pay if all the lectures have to be cancelled.

. . . It is very trying to have no one to talk to except G.K. as he is equally anxious. We should both be better if we had someone not so personally interested in her condition to talk to. He is marvellous though, and kindness and consideration itself to me.

31.1.31

They say at the hospital today that Mrs C. has pulled through the critical stage and is now off the danger list. She is appallingly weak but is managing to retain small quantities of food. I don't know what will happen. G.K. must keep his engagements in California beginning in Los Angeles on the 11th and I expect I shall have to stop here. All the papers in St Louis where G.K. went alone have stressed his untidy appearance, and if he was anything like when he arrived back here I don't wonder. I wish you could see him in the morning when he thinks he is ready for breakfast, his tie always on the outside of a turn-over loose collar – hair with no parting and his shoe laces undone. I always lead him back to his room and tidy him up a bit!! Also I cut his finger nails on Thursday which is the only way to keep them clean as he always cleans them with the point of a lead pencil which makes them a thousand times worse. The duties of a secretary are multitudinous!!

Wed. 4 Feb. 1931

Just a hasty line in the midst of mountains of work to say we are still here. G.K. and I go off at 5.45 pm. on Saturday and arrive Los Angeles 5 pm. Tuesday 10th, travelling all the time via New Orleans. Mrs Chesterton will follow us as soon as possible with the nurse who has been looking after her in the day . . . G.K. will keep the Californian engagements. It has cost us a fortune to cancel the others.

*Sunset Limited.* En route New Orleans – Los Angeles                    Sunday, 8 Feb. 1931
. . . There has been such a rush of work. G.K. has done twelve articles in a week and there have been all the letters and arrangements about this trip, packing and repacking and so on in addition to hospital visiting . . . Mrs C. . . . was seriously ill for a time but is progressing well now. We have had to leave her behind. It has been an awfully expensive business. The cancellation of the lectures cost over £200 to be paid out in addition to about £500 loss of fees. Her expenses are already £50.

I drag G.K. round like a good-tempered sack of potatoes. I pay everything and give him his pocket money. He seems to get rid of about £1 a day on detective stories and magazines and getting shaved – that is all he pays. I can't think what he does with it.

Biltmore Hotel, Los Angeles                    Tuesday, 10 Feb. 1931, 7 pm.
We have really arrived in this wonderful country of California after 3 days and nights from Chattanooga. We are not very tired; the trains are comfortable although I don't like their sleeping arrangements in long open coaches with curtains in front. . . you walk down the aisle between snoring men and women in top and bottom berths. The country is wonderful. The State of Texas takes 24 hours to cross and is very arid with scrub, yucca and cactus, and stony sandy soil and occasional negro encampments which are nothing but hovels. Today we went through Arizona and then California and went over a real desert with a salt inland sea – the Salton Sea. At Yuma the train stopped for 15 minutes and we all got out and found lining the platform a row of Red Indian women from one of the reservations, all with brilliant silk shawls on their heads. They were sitting quite immovable and silent and as if they belonged to a past age and possessed the wisdom of the ages. They took no apparent interest in anything we bought and did nothing to solicit buyers. Directly we got back on the train they packed up their things, took off their shawls and walked away quite silently and each one alone. Such a contrast to the babbling Americans.

. . . I hear that Mrs Chesterton walked a little bit today for the first time.

La Venta Inn, Palos Verdes, California                    Friday, 20th February, 1931
Mrs Chesterton arrived on Tuesday night from the long journey we had dreaded for her and which upset her dreadfully. She brought one of the nurses with her and had injections and strychnine etc. to boost her up with the result that they managed to get to Los Angeles without having to break the journey at some hospital en route as they almost expected. Today is the first day she is without a temperature so she really has taken a turn for the better . . .

I have, however, wired to the lecture agent to stop all bookings after Victoria as we do not know yet whether Mrs Chesterton will be well enough to travel or whether we shall have to leave her here and come back after the lectures and wait till she is fit. G.K. has had good offers from Hollywood for filming some of his detective stories; it does seem silly to refuse such offers but at the same time we are keen to get home. I have been offered £50 a week as English adviser for the production of a film they are starting quite soon . . . It is a good offer but I could not desert the Chestertons at this point of the proceedings.

Monday 23 Feb.

Mrs C. is much better and gradually gaining strength. I had an awful shock on Saturday as she started being sick again, but it was only temporary. We don't know yet whether she will come north or not. It is heavenly here and I am gloating over every minute. Ten days stolen from Summer in the middle of February.

La Venta, California                                    27th February, 1931

Just a line to tell you that all is going very well; I have gloated over every minute in this gorgeous colourful, sunshiny place and grudged every minute of the time I spent in Hollywood staying with the Patrick Macgills. I was away from here for 24 hours and went to a Hollywood dinner-party which was not at all Bohemian as I had expected . . . My time was not wasted though as I did some good business for G.K. which he could never have done for himself. I got into touch with an honest Hollywood agent and he is negotiating for the sale of film rights in *Magic* and some of the Father Brown stories. If anything comes of it, we need not bother any more about the small sums which lectures bring compared with the fabulous sums which Hollywood brings. They would pay him about £4,000 for the use of *Magic* whereas we only get £100 for a lecture and all our expenses to pay out of that.

Mrs C. has been very sensible and has consented to stay here with the nurse in order to get really strong. She could come with us but I think the strain would be too much for her as she has not had time to establish her strength. Of course, I would much rather she came but it might be rather an anxiety.

Southern Pacific Lines. *Lark.*                       Sunday, 9 am. 1 March [1931]

Here we are, G.K. and I, just arriving in San Francisco on a night journey. We left Mrs C. very dreary with nurse. I am thankful she is not coming. It is too much of a good thing. I don't look forward to the journey home.

. . . If Mrs C. is better we leave on the 21st. If not, we shall stay on. Galli-Curci[17] is coming to stay at the Inn on the 23rd. If our plans materialize we shall just miss her. She is building a house on the estate and says she has been all over the world (which is probably true) and has found <u>nowhere</u> so perfect as Palos Verdes.

In train to Vancouver.                                 Monday, 9th March [1931]

We are nearly at the end now. This time next week we shall be back in Palos Verdes and then in a few days we shall be leaving for the east and *home.*

We are going to keep the nurse anyway to accompany us as far as Kansas City in order to see how Mrs C. stands the journey. If she stands it badly I expect we shall take the nurse on to New York and hope for the best on the boat.

La Venta, Palos Verdes Estates, California.                    Friday. 19th March, 1931
Mrs C. is perfectly well again and it is £20 wasted to keep the nurse for an extra week.
She is coming to Kansas City with us and leaving us on Wednesday night.

I do hope your new maid has settled down well and that you are going to have a
little peace – anyway, if not entirely satisfactory, be free from the hugger-mugger and
misery of only one.

We leave here on Sunday the 22nd for the Grand Canyon which we shall reach on
Monday morning. We shall have the whole day and night there and leave at 8 am. on
Tuesday arriving at Chicago at 9.45 am. on Thursday morning. We shall sleep there
and meet Father O'Donnell, President of Notre Dame University . . . We shall probably
go through South Bend in the train and hope that the Bixlers will come to the station.
We sail on the 17th April on the *Majestic* (White Star) which comes into Southampton.

We went to Hollywood again yesterday and saw them making a film in the Meyer
studios. As I told you I have a definite offer of a good job at Hollywood but have decided
not to contemplate it at present. It might be worth it later on if one were able to save
£500 a year for a few years. The offer will hold good for two years.

I had a letter from Balfour, but I am not going to bind myself to live with her. I must
be quite independent. It seems silly to throw away the biggest advantage of not being
married by tying oneself to another woman.

St. Toras Hotel, Grand Canyon.                              Monday, 23rd March
This Canyon is the most wonderful thing that has ever been seen. It was 93 degrees
at Los Angeles yesterday, not a bit too hot for me though. I love it. We went to John
McCormack's house (the singer) for lunch on Saturday. He has a very lovely place at
Hollywood – also a castle in Ireland. He was paid £1,000 for half an hour's broadcasting
the other day, and £200,000 for that film work in 'Song of My Heart'.

Mrs C. stood the journey to here from 12.30 mid-day yesterday until this morning
*fairly* well. Nurse will be with us for two days and one more night and then we shall only
have one more night before reaching Chicago and then one more day to Toledo, and
one more night to New York. It is a huge country.

Hotel St. Moritz, New York City.                    Good Friday [27th March, 1931]
I have been frightfully busy since we got back here, as G.K. has developed a writing craze
and wants to be at it morning, noon and night. With our lack of office accommodation
it is very difficult, as he has to work in my room where all the things are and I never
seem to get rid of him. I go into Mrs Chesterton when he is correcting his work, but it
is difficult to settle down to letter-writing if she is anywhere about as she always talks.

I feel very hardly used when I work ordinary office hours when we are away!! It will
be difficult to settle down to ordinary ways. Mrs Chesterton is fairly well. She is not
sick but she has almost constant nausea and feels miserable in the mornings. It is partly
nervous I think, but whatever the cause it is very uncomfortable, Needless to say I am
not looking forward to the voyage, but we have chosen one of the quickest boats which
has a doctor and nurse and would be able to cope with the situation if she were taken
ill. I shall be thankful to get her onto English shores.

25. GKC with Clare Nicholl at Whitchurch Canonicorum, 1925–6.

26. GKC with a young friend in Sitges, Catalonia, 1926.

27. Gilbert and Frances with Frank Louis Halford and his wife (Helen) Margaret (née Busse), 1926.

28. George Bernard Shaw, Hilaire Belloc and GKC prior to a debate at Kingsway Hall, 1927.

29. GKC at Holy Cross College, Worcester, Massachusetts, December 1930.

30. Dorothy Collins, Sheila Matier (later Huxtable) and GKC, La Venta, California, 1931.

31. GKC in 1936.

32. Chesterton's gravestone designed by
Eric Gill, 1936.

33. Mrs Cecil (Ada) Chesterton OBE, 1941.

34. Mrs Joan Huffer (née Nicholl), 2011.

35. The JDC at Great Western Hotel, (now Hilton Paddington) in 1948, prior to presenting a bust of Chesterton to St Paul's School.

36. Israel Zangwill and GKC hail a taxi, September 24th, 1910.

**MIGUEL DE CERVANTES**

*The people of Spain think Cervantes
Equal to half-a-dozen Dantes:
An opinion resented most bitterly
By the people of Italy.*

1. Miguel de Cervantes.

2. St GKC.

3. Nymph *c*1894.

There were two little girls of Calcutta

Who used to eat white bread and butter,

One day it was dark,

So they said, " For a lark,

Now let us have brown bread and butter."

Cosmo Monkhouse

4. Two Little Girls from Calcutta, 1902.

5. The Beaconsfield Fancy Dress Fair.

I struck at working today and told G.K. that I thought as Christians we were entitled to a holiday on Good Friday. He had contemplated fitting in some work in the morning, but I did not!

The St. Moritz, New York                                   7th April, 1931

We have had Mrs C. in bed again. Her inside is very rocky. I had the Doctor on Saturday as she seemed to be going from bad to worse. He gave her a very thorough examination and took all tests again and could find nothing. At the same time she runs a daily temperature of 99.6 so one cannot be sure that there is nothing wrong. He thought it was largely nerves and gave her sedative medicine and Belladonna. She stayed in bed and is rather better now. Needless to state, I am not looking forward to the voyage. Luckily there are a doctor and two nurses on board. They tested for tubercular trouble in the lungs but the X-ray was negative. Of course there might be some trouble of that sort somewhere else to account for the temperature which is certainly very abnormal. It has been going on with a very short interlude, since January. Oh, how thankful we shall all be to get home.

# 20.

# LONDON CALLING

After his return from his American tour it was resolved that Chesterton's exhausting schedule had to be cut back, but an engagement book for what was left of 1931 reveals over forty lectures, not counting the Oxford Union debate, garden parties, rectoral campaigns, committee meetings, various dinners and mock trials, on top of which were added his work for *G.K.'s Weekly* and the Distributist League and his regular journalistic work for the *Illustrated London News* and elsewhere. Later in the year there were also sittings for *Conversation Piece*, the James Gunn's portrait of Chesterton, Belloc and Baring first shown at the Royal Academy Summer Exhibition in April 1932, although Marie-Louise cut that down to size: 'I fail to see anything remarkable in what is merely a picture of two fat men and one thin man.' Wilfrid Meynell went one better: 'Baring, over-bearing, and past all bearing.'[1]

Finally at the end of the year Chesterton was asked to make his first broadcast on Christmas Day on *Dickens and Christmas* for transmission to the U.S.A.:

> I have been asked to speak to you for a quarter of an hour on Dickens and Christmas; or, as I should prefer to say, on Christmas and Dickens. Why have I been asked to speak to you on Christmas and Dickens? Perhaps the official organisers do not know me very well. Perhaps they have a grudge against you. Why, on this day of a holiday, am I made to work? Why, on this day of rejoicing, are you made to suffer? Like everything connected with the mystery of suffering, it is profoundly mysterious. Perhaps, as my remarks proceed, the mystery will grow darker and deeper; and, at the end you will ask yet more wildly, 'Why, O why was he asked to speak about Christmas and Dickens?'

On the other hand, I, for my part, cannot help cherishing a faint hope that by the end of my remarks you may have some dim idea of what I am talking about, and why I am talking it. Anyhow, I am going to set myself to answer the question; or rather the two questions, Why Christmas and why Dickens? They are both things that many people think very old-fashioned. But nobody, just yet, thinks the Wireless old-fashioned. Why is it that the officials of the Wireless want to have somebody, anybody, even me, talking about Dickens on Christmas Day?

I will make two answers as simple as the two questions. We talk about Christmas because there is nothing else to talk about. We talk about Dickens because there is nobody else to talk about. I mean that there is no occasion, no date, no day, that has been able to do what Christmas does; and there is no writer, among all our brilliant modern writers, who has been able to do what Dickens did. There are any number of interesting institutions and social functions and so on, but nothing that can be a substitute for Christmas. There are any number of humorists, of witty writers and the rest, but nobody who can be a substitute for Dickens. That is the double proposition I propose to prove to you in fifteen minutes – or now rather less.

First, there is no other festival to keep except Christmas. No new religion has made a new festival. No new philosophy has been sufficiently popular to make a popular holiday. We all know that there are any number of pleasure-seekers in the world today, who think of nothing but amusement; but they do not count. They never have holidays, because they have nothing but holidays. But even they have never made a fixed occasion or form of festivity. It is often said that these pleasure-seekers are Pagans, and that all their life of jazz and cocktails is a life of Paganism. This seems to me a harsh judgment. I mean it seems to me very harsh to Paganism. The Pagan gods and poets of the past were never so cheap or tenth-rate as the fast sets and smart people of the present. Venus was never so vulgar as what they now call Sex Appeal. Cupid was never so coarse and common as a modern realistic novel. The old Pagans were imaginative and creative; they made things and built things. Somehow that habit went out of the world; the power of making feasts and shrines to Nature. Americans we know, are a nation of unadulterated water-drinkers; but it has never occurred to them to worship Niagara. If any ancient Greek had been a water-drinker, he would have worshipped Niagara on the spot. If we were Pagans, we should be content with nothing less than worship of Beauty. We shouldn't be content with photographs of Film Stars. If we were Pagans there would be a Temple of Venus at Hollywood. If we were Pagans, there would be a Temple of Bacchus; probably in Milwaukee. Even the financiers had a god in those days. There would be a Temple of Mercury, who was the god of commerce, at the end of Wall Street. I admit that, by a curious coincidence, he was also the god of theft. Perhaps that is why he is generally presented to us as the Flying Mercury. But anyhow, the point is that Paganism *could* make things; it could make festivals and festive days; it could make an alternative to Christmas, if it were still alive. But the modern Pagans cannot. The modern Pagans are merely atheists; who worship nothing and therefore create nothing. They could not, for instance, even make a substitute for Thanksgiving Day. For half of them are pessimists who say they have nothing to be thankful for; and the other half are atheists who have nobody to thank. Now you know all about those intellectual rebels who are called Radicals in your country and Revolutionists in mine. You know that they have their virtues as well as their vices, and that for certain destructive purposes they are often valuable. But they have no constructive purposes, and certainly no purpose of constructing anything like Christmas. Thus, for instance, I admire Mr Mencken in many ways and Mr Mencken admires Nietzsche in all sorts of ways; sometimes in quite extraordinary ways. But, if I may say so, Mr Mencken does not admire Nietzsche in a festive way. He does not admire him in a Christmas way. Mr Mencken does not go about singing carols in the snow, outside other people's houses, to celebrate the day when Nietzsche was born; or the day he went mad, or whatever is supposed to be the sacred date. Nietzsche said he was Anti-Christ. But Mr Mencken has not yet started giving presents to his family on a festival called Antichristmas. Or again, much has been said of late of Mr Dreiser; and many admire his very able work. But however jovial and rollicking Mr Dreiser's philosophy may be, we do not exactly expect him to come down the chimney, like Santa Claus. The modern Pagans have failed to do exactly what the ancient Pagans did. They have failed to make a feast. Therefore, I repeat, there is nothing to talk about except Christmas.

In the same way, there is nobody to talk about except Dickens. There are any number of other people to praise, for various powers of invention or imagination or satire. There are the Realists, for instance; and I hope nobody is so unfair to the Realists as to suppose that they describe real life; especially their own real life. Realists exaggerate, just as Dickens exaggerated. But Dickens is still absolutely the only man who exaggerates high spirits. Dickens is still the only man who exaggerates happiness. That is, he is the only person to be talked about at Christmas; because he was the only person who talked about Christmas as if it was Christmas; as if it was even more Christmas than it is. Now if you think of all the clever modern writers you admire, you will not admire them less, but you will see exactly what I mean. They do not exaggerate enjoyment. If they exaggerate anything, it is despair; it is the spirit of death. You have read, as I have read, countless current descriptions of gay young people dancing in night clubs and drinking cocktails. But you were not sure it made you happy. You were not even sure it made them happy. In Dickens you will find horrible hypocrites, degrading tricks and conspiracies; but they will make you happy. Let me take a parallel. Mr Sinclair Lewis in *Elmer Gantry* has described a scandalous Gospel minister. Dickens in *Pickwick* also described a scandalous Gospel minister; Mr Stiggins, known as The Red-Nosed Man. When Sam Weller is in prison, Mr Stiggins and Mrs Weller, his devout admirer, come to visit and console him. They sit on each side of the fire drinking rum, and uttering hollow groans at intervals. Old Mr Weller, the father, suddenly remarks: 'Vell, Samivel, I hope you feel your spirits rose by this 'ere friendly visit'. Now the extraordinary thing is that we *do* feel our spirits rose. Something in the utter idiocy of this form of consolation does really make us happy. The red-nosed man is a deplorable object; but we do not merely deplore. The rum he drinks does not seem to cheer him up; but it cheers us up. His red nose is ridiculous but not repulsive. Now turn from that to any modern novel in which, very probably, the heroine will be a restless spirit whose artistic temperament rebels against the ugliness of her surroundings. She will rebel against the ugliness of her Uncle William's red nose, which will be described in repulsive detail. You know the style of modern writing. 'What had life to offer her? Would that red nose be always there? Would that red nose thrust itself for ever between her and all delicate, all exquisite things?' Anyhow, the heroine is not happy. But, what is more important, the reader is not happy. The reader may see many aspects or take various sides. He may sympathise with the heroine, who, after all, cannot help having an artistic temperament. It is barely possible that he may sympathise with Uncle William; who, after all, cannot help having a red nose. The only point I emphasise is that in either case our sympathy will take the form of sorrow. Anyhow, it will not take the form of joy. No modern novel ever gives us joy of the uncle's nose or the niece's temperament. Nobody has discovered Dickens' secret of getting joy out of these things and I repeat that no other novelist exists at this season of enjoyment.

I will take another example. I will take a subject on which I trust I am not unduly sensitive; the subject of fat men. I have recently read in a modern novel a description of some indefensible old gentleman, some intolerable grandfather or unbearable great-uncle, gradually settling down into an armchair. Need I say that he presented to the artistic temperament the image of some shapeless monster of the slime? This is quite correct; it may even be quite artistic; but it is not gay. It does not especially cheer us up, even at Christmas. In a word, it is not funny. Now let me turn to Dickens; and make a perfectly fair comparison. Sam Weller tells a story entirely devoted to the subject of a Fat Man. After explaining that the gentleman had not seen his own legs for years, he adds with impressive solemnity: 'If you 'ad put an exact model of 'is legs on the table in front of 'im, 'e wouldn't 'ave known 'em by sight'.

Now that is a poem. It uplifts the heart. It might naturally add to the joy of Christmas Day; or any day. It is actually much more of an exaggeration than the pessimist exaggeration [which compares the old man to mud or a monster of the slime]. But it is not only exaggerative; it is also creative. It is a new angle; we might say a new artistic vision. There is something aboriginally absurd in the idea of the old gentleman staring wild-eyed at his own legs; and half recalling something familiar about them; as if he were revisiting the landscape of his youth. Now that is the essential quality that made Dickens great. He exaggerated, in the sense of making things more laughable than they were; more enjoyable than they were. It makes the reader happier; just as if one of the lost and visionary legs had actually been thrust into his own Christmas stocking. Now I defy anybody to say that even the best of the modern satirical writers makes the reader happier. I deny that *Elmer Gantry* is a Christmas present. I deny that anybody wants Mr Dreiser thrust into his Christmas stocking. These works and these authors have all sorts of other valuable qualities, no doubt, but I am talking about Christmas; and why it is that people want to talk about Dickens at Christmas. The reason is in two sentences. The thing he did may or may not be suitable for all purposes; but it is suitable for Christmas. The thing he did may or may not be superior in all respects; but it has never been done since.

I apologise. That is why this dreadful accident has occurred. That is why there has been this disgusting interruption of your Christmas Day; and, I will add, this equally disgusting interruption of my Christmas Day. It is because the most modern of modern people, wielding the most modern and amazing of all forms of scientific machinery – the magic machine which can even do without a machine – is here set to work to carry for so many thousands of miles these two familiar or antiquated names: the name of a feast founded nearly two thousand years ago; the name of a man born more than a hundred years ago. The answer is the answer I have given. It is not because they are superior to their rivals. It is because they have no rivals. The particular achievement they represent has not since been achieved, or even attempted. The particular thing they did men are not even trying to do. If a man wants other things, no doubt he will look for other things; and in these days have no difficulty in finding them. If a man wants to worship the Life Force merely because it is a Force, he may very naturally worship it in the electric battery. I am tempted to say it will serve him right if he eventually worships the life force in the electric chair. But if he wants to worship life because it is living, he will find nothing in history so living as that little life that began in the cave at Bethlehem and now visibly lives for ever. And if he is looking, in a lighter sense, for what is living in all literature – then he may find many descriptions of life more exact or subtle or analytical than that of Dickens; but he will find nothing in all literature so utterly alive. Dickens was separated by centuries of misunderstanding from that mysterious revelation that brought joy upon the earth; but at least he was resolved to enjoy it. It is because Dickens did hand on that tradition of joy, even if it was only traditional, that his name can never be separated from that greater name to which he also was loyal, in an uncongenial time, by an instinct that was almost inspiration. He knew enough about it to enjoy it; and to enjoy himself; and now in the name of all such things, let us all go and do the same.[2]

The experiment was a resounding success and his audience charmed by the way he managed to convey the warmth of his personality. Those who expressed surprise were not aware that when he was a boy in Warwick Gardens his father had rigged up a toy telephone which enabled him to broadcast from the house to the end of the garden or back; he was also on record as saying: 'I have often thanked God for the telephone.'[3] Above all, since he had broken his arm in 1912 he had adopted dictation as his chief tool in expressing himself, so he was practised in speaking to a single individual, the most basic technique in radio. This was actually done in reality, for he took Frances and Dorothy with him to Broadcasting House and his talk was delivered to them. 'He liked it best that way and talked direct to us, which gave his talks the intimate character the public so much enjoyed . . . He would watch the green light turn to red and with an agonised glance at us, he would begin, and immediately be oblivious of his surroundings as he read and improvised his script as he went along . . . 'You are a born broadcaster and we must have much more of it,' wrote the Director of Talks.[4] Have it they did, and on 31st October 1932 Chesterton began the first of a series with 'Some Famous Historical Characters' in which he reviewed recently published biographies. 'The Building rings with your praises! I knew I was not alone in my delight at your first talk. I think even you in your modesty will find some pleasure in hearing what widespread interest there is in what you are doing. You bring us something very rare to the microphone. I am most anxious that you should be with us till after Christmas. You will have a vast public by Christmas and it is good that they should hear you. Would you undertake six further fortnightly talks from January 16th onwards.'[5] He did, most of the talks being published in *The Listener*, and continued to address that vast new public until the end of his life when in a series entitled *The Spice of Life* he said (*pace* T.S. Eliot's *The Hollow Men*): 'I will defend the spiritual appetite of my own age, I will even be so indecently frivolous as to burst into song and say to the young pessimists:

> Some sneer, some snigger, some simper,
> In the youth where we laughed and sang;
> And *they* may end with a whimper,
> But we will end with a bang.

Dorothy Collins expressed a 'Beaconsfield' point of view: 'Frances and I thought he spent too much time on journalism and on his paper, *G.K.'s Weekly*. Many did not agree with us, but this certainly put much pressure on him and time and energy were spent on extra work, which was necessary to finance his paper and keep it going. Even so, he never satisfied all the requests for books, and from the newspaper and magazine editors.'[6] There is much truth in what she said, for certainly after 1930 if not before, journalism had taken over and the 1930s saw only two books published, other than collections of essays and stories. A reawakened interest in the theatre did not run, in the case of *The Surprise* (1932), as far as stage productions, although it is possible that *The Ages Are Passing* was put upon the amateur stage somewhere among the Distributist Movement, as the surviving text is based upon parts of more than one stage script found in the effects of that movement's members. Another constant pressure was the ill health of both the Chestertons. Frances had always been far from strong and over the years lumbago, rheumatoid arthritis and later osteoporosis had worsened the curvature of the spine for which she wore a metal support; whenever possible she sought a warmer climate further south in Europe to escape damp and even seaside air which she felt aggravated her condition. Gilbert, still exhausted from the length and breadth tour of North America, gradually began to exhibit symptoms of ill-health similar to those of 1914–15, photographs revealing a transition from a healthy-looking big man to someone bloated in appearance. Photographers seemed to rush to record the latter stage.

In June 1932 the Chestertons attended the Eucharistic Congress in Dublin as official guests at the Viceregal Lodge where they were pleased to learn that John MacCormack the tenor, whom they had met previously in California, was a fellow guest; MacCormack sang at the Pontifical High Mass in Phoenix Park to which Chesterton wore his robes as a Doctor of Letters of the National University of Ireland.

By the time GKC was feeling better his mother was beginning to fail. Frances too was kept busy by her own mother, Blanche Blogg, who, now almost totally blind, had left the care of the Oldershaws for The Yews, a nursing home in Beaconsfield, so it was largely left to Ada, Cecil's widow, to keep an eye on Marie-Louise:

> It was the little things that made me realise that life was becoming an effort for Marie-Louise. She would say good-night to me from her small upright chair, instead of coming to the front door as she had done for years. She did not talk much as to the future, but she still looked forward to seeing Gilbert, though his visits came at rarer intervals . . . One Sunday evening she did not seem quite herself. That is to say, she spoke very little. The marvel was that she kept going at all . . . persistent questioning of her maid gained the information that, a few hours previously, Marie-Louise had missed her footing and fallen down the stairs. She had forbidden Thirza to tell me what had happened . . . It was the next Sunday that she told me quite quietly that I must forgive her but she did not want to go on any longer . . . She went to bed that night and did not get up again, but it was by no means an immediate death scene . . . Her passage was slow but dreadfully sure . . . one afternoon I brought some early tulips. She looked up at me and laughed. 'Darling,' she said, holding the flowers in her kindly hands. 'You're too early for the funeral . . . please don't cry . . . I *want* to go.' . . . She grew worse that evening and I sat up all night dreading the dawn. Gilbert and Frances arrived early in the morning [February 21st, 1933], and later, a smile on her face, a last tender look in her eyes, Marie-Louise fell asleep – and did not waken.[7]

> With the passing of Marie-Louise the house at Warwick Gardens went also . . . the gaunt board 'To Let' put *finis* to the old home.

> The den at the end of the passage . . . had remained almost untouched since Mister's death [in 1922] . . . family documents, diaries, correspondence, including some of the Regency Chesterton, with records of a more modern date, packets of Gilbert's and Cecil's letters and early manuscripts which Marie-Louise had faithfully treasured.

> From the point of view of the biography of both the brothers some of these papers would have been of considerable value, but one day Gilbert drifted into Warwick Gardens on his own and the worst happened . . . before Dorothy Collins could catch him up he got into the den and launched on prodigies of destruction . . . the dustman's somewhat untimely arrival aided Gilbert's design, and he swept Edward's neat sheaves, together with priceless data, to the rapacious bins. By the time the guardian angel Dorothy arrived irreparable damage had been done.

> What was left from the holocaust was taken to Beaconsfield.[8]

And in Beaconsfield it lay until, after Chesterton's death, some small part was used in *The Coloured Lands*, a two volume compilation the first of which appeared in November 1938 and the second was abandoned after the loss of all the stock together with some manuscript material in the incendiary bomb raid upon Sheed & Ward's London premises during the 1940 blitz. At the outbreak of the Second World War Top Meadow Cottage became an annexe to St. Joseph's Nursing Home, whereupon the rest of Mr Ed's collection had been crammed into an old chest and put into a loft where the papers lay until, on the death of Miss Collins in 1988, they were acquired by the British Library for a reputed £200,000 with funds taken from the bequest of GKC's old debating opponent, Bernard Shaw.

Soon after Marie-Louise's days drew to a close in Warwick Gardens, so did those of Frances' mother, Blanche Blogg in The Yews in Beaconsfield, though she lingered until August 26th, 1933. Maisie Ward once drove Frances between the two sick beds and heard of difficulties in comforting her agnostic mother. Frances also confided that she knew her mother-in-law had never really liked her, but had of late said that she accepted that Frances had been the right wife for Gilbert. It is a moot point whether Frances knew the reason Marie-Louise told to her cousin, Nora Grosjean: 'I always respect Frances – she kept Gilbert out of debt.' Forty years earlier when Gilbert had been a student, Marie-Louise had said: 'I always give a penny to a pavement artist; because that's what Gilbert would have become, if he had not been shielded.'

Gilbert Chesterton was still on the treadmill with ever disastrous effect on his health. The closing week of 1933 found him telling H.G. Wells that he had been 'temporarily laid out in bed',[9] and early in the New Year of 1934 he was suffering from a jaundice probably caused by infectious hepatitis.[10] On his mother's death Gilbert had received a legacy in her will, but much more from the residue of the trust set up by his father: Mr Ed's will had specified that his estate be split between Gilbert, Frances and Ada. A great deal was set aside to provide legacies for the nieces, nephews and cousins on Frances' side of the family, plus a donation towards the building of St. Theresa's Church in Beaconsfield, a project only brought to completion as a memorial to him after his death.

## Ignorance Is Bliss
It is unlikely that Gilbert Chesterton was ever aware that in 1934 he had been nominated for the 1935 Nobel Prize for Literature by one of the members of the Nobel Committee, Torsten Fogelqvist, a Christian writer and member of the Swedish Academy. In that year there were thirty-seven nominees of whom

Chesterton was numbered thirty-three. After discussion in the Committee, an expert report was written by another Committee and Academy member, Per Hallstrom:

> The expert report willingly and cordially recognizes the genius of this writer, but has decided to recommend the rejection of the proposal, due to Chesterton's many eccentricities. There is high value in much of his preaching and almost unique critical acumen, yet on the other hand he has expressed a very heavy load of frantically nervous, rash and absurd judgements and views. As an educator in a time when nobody like Chesterton has realized tentative helplessness in all essentials, his writings cannot always be considered helpful. A Nobel Prize for Mr Chesterton would only be justified as an admiration of his eminent intelligence, not the effect of that same intelligence. All Committee members basically agree that Mr Chesterton should not receive the Nobel Prize.[11]

In the event the Nobel Prize for Literature was not awarded in 1935, and Chesterton joined a long list of distinguished authors not so rewarded. The reference to Chesterton's *preaching* suggests that the report was based on the collections of essays and did not include the poetry, novels, drama and short stories; Hallstrom's citation of 'frantically nervous, rash and absurd judgements and views' further suggests that he was singularly lacking in sense of humour and did not appreciate the use of paradox. Not that the 'obese mountebank who crucified truth upside-down'[12] would have been particularly worried if he had known.

The only books to have been translated into Swedish by 1935 were *The Innocence of Father Brown* (1912), *The Barbarism of Berlin* (1915), *The Wisdom of Father Brown* (1921), *The Flying Inn* (1922), *Manalive* (1926), *The Everlasting Man* (1926), *St. Francis of Assisi* (1926), *The Secret of Father Brown* (1928) and *Charles Dickens* (1933).

# 21.

# NUNC DIMITTIS SERVUM TUUM, DOMINE

In 1934 both Chesterton and Belloc were inducted by Cardinal Bourne as Knights Commander with Star into the Papal Order of St. Gregory the Great. Anecdote has it that Belloc muttered against receiving cheap trinkets from a greasy Italian monsignor, but Chesterton resolved in gratitude that, as it was Holy Year, he would make a pilgrimage to both Rome and Jerusalem. Setting out on March 20th the Chestertons' party travelled by train, all going well until they reached Sicily where in Syracuse Gilbert began to suffer inflammation of the nerves of the neck and shoulders [shingles?], a condition which took five weeks to improve. The trip to the Holy Land was then abandoned in favour of a return by sea via Malta where they stayed at the Osborne Hotel. The state of Gilbert's health remained far from good and he was unable to accept an invitation from Admiral Lord Fisher to dine at Admiralty House. On the voyage home via Marseilles and Morocco the Chestertons made the acquaintance of André Maurois. Once back in June the fortnightly broadcasts for the BBC did not resume until September but then continued until March of 1935. One notable landmark along the way was the appearance on October 11th, 1934 of the 500th issue of *G.K.'s Weekly* complete with Thomas Derrick's cartoon depicting GKC as St. George slaying the dragon.

Early in 1935 Dorothy Collins consulted Maisie Ward about an autobiography which Gilbert had begun some years previously: 'She had she said, a superstitious feeling about urging him to get on with it – as though the survey of his life and the end of his life would somehow be tied together. I urged her to get over this feeling because of all the book would mean to the world.' Miss Collins took out the existing manuscript and laid it before GKC who immediately read what he had written and thereupon started to dictate what was to be the rest of the book. About a year later GKC mentioned to a group of his friends (at the *G.K.'s Weekly* office?) that he had completed it. One quipped *Nunc dimittis*, but Edward Macdonald found that 'the words were chilling, though he seemed to be in fairly good health. But certainly he was tired . . .'[1] Indeed in September 1935 Frances had been concerned enough to write to Dorothy (on holiday in France) who in turn replied on September 15th from Carcassone: 'It seems almost inevitable that he should have these attacks at stated intervals. I suppose it is Nature's warning to him that he is not made of cast-iron and that he must be careful.' Within three days she was writing again this time from Avignon: 'It was lovely to find your dear letter waiting for me and to hear that he is going on well. Is the doctor going to be very severe about a future regime for him? He is generally so good after he has been ill for a little while. I do hope he will be careful. It would be so awful if he got properly ill again. I always wonder that he does not . . . Give him my love and best wishes for a speedy recovery.'[2] The letter crossed with one from Frances to say that Gilbert was better, but that she thought the problem had been that he was drinking again to keep going. Dorothy took up this point: 'I am glad that he is really better, but sorry to hear that your feelings do not entirely coincide with the doctor's opinions. What is worrying you now? I can't help feeling that possibly his nervousness is bound to react on you and you may worry in sympathy with him when there is not any cause. It will do you both a lot of good to get away.'[3]

And away they got, as Dorothy had not long returned before she was once again on her way as she drove the Chestertons through France to Avignon, Nîmes and Perpignan then on into Spain to Barcelona and Sitges where, in Dorothy's words, 'we spent several happy weeks and did a great deal of work' before reversing towards Italy where, still on a supposedly non-working holiday achieved only by preparing all the newspaper contributions in advance, GKC lectured in Florence on English Literature and the Latin Tradition, at the International Festival. Even Dorothy Collins had expressed doubts about the workload she imposed on GKC: 'I am glad that he feels that I am moderately reasonable, because so often I feel he would be much happier with someone who was more haphazard about the work and did not bother him about dates, and getting letters answered, and so on. It could be done on those lines I realise quite well, and I often wonder if I try to drive it too much along a road instead of letting it wander in the woods. He is more than patient with me, whatever he thinks.'[4] Their return was via Switzerland and Belgium: 'The trip was a great success as they were wonderful passengers. Gilbert did once remark rather plaintively, 'Frances, I wish you wouldn't keep telling Dorothy to admire the view when we are hanging over precipices', but on the whole they had no fears.' One lasting souvenir of their incursion into Spain was a toy theatre with electric lighting in which Gilbert delighted.

Mid-November saw the Chestertons back in England for Gilbert to resume his radio broadcasts, but after just one broadcast on November 16th he was indisposed and was not heard again until March 15th, 1936. Although not up to broadcasting, GKC still tended to visit the Nicholls' Christmas Cottage in the evenings where he would sit by the fire and chat to the girls until the early hours. Dorothy Collins somewhat ruefully recalled that Frances 'liked to think of him enjoying himself with them. Her best self felt that way. But other times it was too hard.'[5]

Frances had certainly disapproved when Gilbert and a group of young people disrupted the showing of a film in the local cinema, even though it was unlikely to have been *Father Brown, Detective* (1935) with Walter Connolly and Paul Lukas. The Nicholls received GKC's hand-drawn cards for Christmas 1935: 'Bringing in the Bore's head' and 'The Wait Who Would Not Wait', and thereupon invited the Chestertons for Twelfth Night:

> This particular Christmas the table was a concerted family effort. We made them wait in the hall while we arranged the final dramatic effect. When the door to the dining room was opened, the room was in darkness except for the firelight. In the middle of the table was a seascape (the big looking-glass from the hall) and a ship in full sail towards a high rocky harbour (representing the Cobb at Lyme). On the edge of the harbour wall was a toy lighthouse. The windows revolved and a night-light inside made miniature beams shoot through the darkness and lit up the sea and the ship, its sails full set for home.
>
> We of course expected pleasure and surprise and plenty of appreciation of our labours. What we were not prepared for was G.K.'s reaction. He came in at last, being 'taken into dinner' by one of us. He said no word at all, but paused in the doorway and stared and stared. And the sister whose arm was in his was stirred out of all proportion and heard herself muttering her thoughts aloud to G.K. (one of his rarest qualities was that one could literally think aloud to him without fear or self-consciousness). 'It reminds me,' she said, 'of the *Salve Regina*.' And G.K. said below his breath, 'Yes – *nobis, post exilium ostende*' . . .[6]

By the time of his last two broadcasts on March 15th and 27th a decision had been taken to visit Lisieux and Lourdes in the hope that the pilgrimage would restore his health. On the evening before his departure he once again joined two (Barbara and Dorothy) of the Nicholl sisters for supper at Christmas Cottage:

> Two of us only were at home. It was a particularly beautiful night, flower-scented, sunlit and enchanted, as only a May [probably April] night in England can be. G.K. arrived looking for the first time in our memory dreadfully tired. We made the excuse of drinking him *Bon Voyage* to produce brandy, which brought some colour, but not much, back into his face.
>
> For some reason on this one occasion we stood together in the porch to see him off, and neither walked to the gate. The dusk was still gold in a lingering and splendid sunset. G.K. went through the wooden gate and turned, his hand still on the latch. He looked back at us; then he stretched out his hand in the strangest prolonged gesture – it was like a mixture of benediction and farewell. He stood still, for quite five minutes; then the latch clicked and we heard his footsteps crunching down the road. We stood together in silence and my sister said, whispering, 'Do you feel horribly strange? Did you see how he stood and looked and looked, as though he were looking for the last time? I don't like it – I don't like it at all.'[7]

Ada also found cause for anxiety: 'I always thought that Top Meadow was at its best in the spring and early summer. It certainly looked most attractive when one afternoon in May I went down to speak at a local function, run by an enterprising group of players who had fitted up a big barn into a quite well decorated theatre. They were reviving *Magic* . . . I was so fond of the play that I was very pleased to do it . . . when I arrived at Top Meadow . . . Gilbert was distrait and in bad spirits. He did not cheer up at all during dinner and ate very little. His eyes, focussed on space, did not seem to see, and his hands looked strangely gaunt. He hardly spoke throughout the meal and, when I said good-bye, barely roused himself to give me a brotherly kiss – the last he ever gave me . . .'[8]

Chesterton was not much taken by Lisieux, but found Lourdes, as it then was:

> A nice little Pyrenean town, full of poor people drinking very cheap wine: much *less* transformed by touts and trippers than older shrines . . . Lourdes is *not* spoilt: Our Lady came here to the very humblest, to a ragged child almost barefoot: and perhaps that is why there is a sense that she left this rocky place in a naked purity like stone: as if there were health but not wealth to be got out of it. By comparison, I hope that I shall not lose the intercession of a Saint I have come to honour and understand better – and who presides in my own English town – if I say there was something a little *bourgeoise* about St. Theresa of Lisieux – or rather her social setting. At Lourdes the framework is hard rock and Holy Poverty – all that Assisi ought to be. Of course there are shops that sell souvenirs: that is inevitable; for we must all sympathise with those who buy if not with those who sell . . . The Grotto is not a 'blaze of gold and tinsel' as it is its

duty to be for the sake of Baptist tourists from Tennessee. The Grotto is a grey forest of crutches and wooden legs hung up by ex-cripples who could only afford such things in honest wood.[9]

No mention was made of another trip to Sitges, but on May 5th Chesterton had picked up his mail in Menton near the Italian border and was answering a request from Barbara Nicholl for a reference:

> Gd. Café de Paris,
> 2 Rue Saint-Michel,
> Menton, Alpes Maritimes

Some Wednesday or Other – or is it Tuesday? [Postmark 5th May 1936]
My Dear Barbara,

The application for a testimonial to your flaming virtues and charms (from the Hospital authorities) followed us here and arrived when I was wandering elsewhere [Florence]: so Frances, rightly I think, filled it up at once and sent it back lest it should be late, or appear so, by the delay. I only write to add that of course anything I could write myself is at your service.

But the things I could write, especially after a holiday in the Mediterranean, would perhaps overflow the formal limits of the form. Would it really help you, would it in this cold world truly help if I broke into song, for instance, and wrote across the form:

> When first I saw dear Barbara
> Rush like a sea-wind to the sea,
> She woke it with a wild ozone
> Not of the sea but all her own:
> That blast of blessing blown and hurled
> Will heal the Wards of all the world;
> The sick will leap from lying flat
> (If you will let her rush like that)
> And wake them as she wakened me.

But would this testimonial be well received? Would the doctors and officials think it of close and cogent relevance? . . . I doubt it. I doubt if they would yield even if I tried another metre. As

> Blow before Barbara, blow the horn for the Rider of Horses:
> As for Hector Hippodromio uprose the shout:
> For she is the tamer of horses, if sometimes they toss her
> And throw her all over the district and leave her lying about.
> But she that did so in implacable purpose persist
> To break every bone in her body will surely exist
> To be an expert experienced practised Anatomist.

This you will note, is more in the rugged modern manner: but would this soothe the modern medical authorities? It is doubtful. There is so much red tape about. Or even in quieter vein –

> Health follows where she goes: and in her track
> Hospitals rise in Bucks behind her back:
> Sweden is swept with gusts of youth and sport:
> And even Bournemouth is a Health resort.

Forgive me. I send off all this nonsense now because I have a faint fear that my own signature may be needed in some fussy official way in your affair. Unfortunately, we have no fixed address, even in this town, except 'Cooks', whatever that may mean. Why Mr Cook should guard all our private correspondence, I do not know. Qu'est-ce qu'il est, ce Monsieur Cook? Why should he have the key of our secrets, this mysterious intimacy with our intimate affairs . . . Anyhow, we escape from Cook in a few days and the only other fixed address is Poste Restante, Bourges: in case of emergency: but we shall be home about the end of next week. Will you please tell Clare that I am half-way through a letter I began to her in Lourdes: it got longer and longer under the influence of the subject: which is tremendous. But I will send it after this in a day or so. Meanwhile, I do hope our disgraceful flight has not embarrassed your more practical affair. You know I would do anything.

> Yours with love always, G.K. CHESTERTON[10]

Whether or not the post was collected in Bourges, his letter to Clare was to remain unfinished. Although in 1974 Dorothy Collins recalled that 'He had sung songs from Gilbert and Sullivan with much gusto and less tune on our long drive home from the coast, and had shown no signs of illness', she had thirty years earlier told Maisie Ward that before reaching Bourges 'the first signs of his illness showed at a Mass on Ascension Day at Clermont Ferrand when he had to come out before the Mass was finished and did not feel well enough to enjoy his breakfast.' Once home in Beaconsfield about May 24th, a little later than forecast, not only was he still retaining fluid, but he found it difficult to keep concentration and began to doze off at his desk while working. When Dr George Bakewell was at last called he expressed concern over the condition of the patient's heart and confined him to bed where he drifted in and out of consciousness under the care of two male nurses. Dorothy said 'Frances was devastated and unable to attend to anything' other than a bedside vigil. On June 12th the parish priest, Monsignor Smith, came to anoint Gilbert Chesterton with the Extreme Unction of the Last Sacraments. Father Vincent McNabb, O.P. also came to intone the *Salve Regina*:

I went to see him as he died. I asked to be alone with the dying man. There that great frame was in the heat of death, the great mind getting ready, no doubt, in its own way, for the sight of God. It was Saturday, and I think that perhaps in another thousand years Gilbert Chesterton might be known as one of the sweetest singers to that ever-blessed daughter of Sion, Mary of Nazareth. I knew that the very finest qualities of the Crusaders was one of the endowments of his great heart, and then I remembered the song of the Crusaders, which we Blackfriars sing every night the Lady of our love. I said to Gilbert Chesterton: 'You shall hear your mother's love song.' And I sang to Gilbert Chesterton the Crusaders' Song: *Salve, Regina (mater) misericordiae, vita, dulcedo, et spes nostra, salve. Ad te clamamus exsules filii Hevae, ad te suspiramus, gementes et flentes in hac lacrimarum valle. eia, ergo, advocate nostra, illos tuos misericordes oculos ad nos converte; et Jesum, benedictum fructum ventris tui, nobis post hoc exsilium ostende. O clemens, O pia, O dulcis (Virgo) Maria.* [Hail (Holy) Queen (mother) of mercy, hail! Our life, our sweetness and our hope, to thee do we cry, poor banished children of Eve; to thee do we send up our sighs, mourning and weeping in this veil of tears. Turn then, most gracious advocate, thine eyes of mercy towards us, and after this, our exile, show unto us the blessed fruit of thy womb, Jesus. O clement, O loving, O sweet (Virgin) Mary.][11]

E.C. Bentley was not permitted by Frances to see his old school friend so he sat with Dorothy in the study. A journalist from the *Daily Mail* rang to confirm a rumour that Chesterton was seriously ill. Dorothy did confirm the news but extracted a promise that the illness would not be publicised, and, despite Bentley's doubts, that promise was kept. Chesterton only briefly emerged from his reverie, once to repeat a remark that he had made several times: 'The issue is now quite clear. it is between light and darkness and every one must choose his side,' and on the evening of June 13th when, regaining consciousness and seeming more alert than for several days, he turned to Frances and said, 'Hello, my darling' and realising Dorothy was also there added 'Hello, my dear.' Soon afterwards he lapsed once more into unconsciousness and then breathed laboriously through the night until the next morning at a little after ten o'clock on June 14th, 1936, Sunday in the Octave of Corpus Christi, he breathed his last. Frances took up her pen and wrote an in memoriam poem.

IN MEMORY OF G.K.C., 14th JUNE, 1936

'Fair Shine The Day On The House With Open Door' (R.L. Stevenson)

In the sure sanctuary of your spreading roof-tree
Each restless thought was folded into peace
And all my heart's nostalgia would cease,
Assuaged in your great house of charity.

Your hand was stretched to all who knocked: 'Hail, friend!'
And which of those who hungered was not fed
With wine of your warm mirth, with wisdom's bread?
The door stood wide: the hearth glowed to the end.
In the third watch when the slow hours tramp
On heavy, heavy feet towards the light,
The last guest entered . . . every pane was bright,
And the slow, kind hand of death turned out the lamp.

The day is fair . . . but will your house put off
Its firelit front of hospitality?
Rooted in peace and reared in light, your tree,
And all my prayers rest in the boughs thereof.

The word of welcome may be left unsaid,
Strongest in silence. Shall I find
Your shining morning face less kind
Than when at twilight while the logs burned red
We shared the sacramental wine and bread? . . .
The door stands wide and I am comforted.

Later she was to write to Father O'Connor that 'Our Lady's answer to my prayers for him . . . was not what I expected – but right, I know, however hard.'[12]

The death, certified by Dr G.V. Bakewell OBE, was attributed to I. (a) Anasarca [Generalised oedema or dropsy]. (b) Fatty degeneration myocardial [Congestive cardiac failure due to ischaemic heart disease], and to II. Cirrhosis of liver [possibly caused by the jaundice or viral hepatitis suffered in 1934], the death registered at Amersham Registry Office on Monday June 15th by J. O'Callaghan, one of the nurses in attendance at the time of death.

Arrangements for the funeral must have already been in hand, with the Requiem Mass at 10.30 on Wednesday June 17th, followed by interment in the cemetery on Shepherd's Lane. Gilbert had always been incommoded by the narrowness of the stairs and passages in Top Meadow; in death the size of the coffin was such that it could not be taken up or brought down the stairs, so a window-frame had to be removed to allow Gilbert's mortal remains to be lowered by block and tackle. June 17th was sunny and warm, and despite the short notice a crowd of over four hundred overflowed outside St. Teresa's Church, and the specially arranged circuitous route of the funeral procession through Beaconsfield old and new towns was lined with others wishing to pay tribute. There were wreathes in abundance and atop the coffin Frances' cross of *Red Roses full of rain, for you – as you would wish.*

The Nicholls recalled: 'There was not one candle socket empty in the Beaconsfield church during G.K.'s Requiem Mass. One of us said afterwards with truth that at the moment of the Consecration of the Mass she had a sudden and most strong sense of festival and an inrush of joy – there was nothing of mourning in that requiem – it was part of a huge birthday party in Heaven.'[13]

Ada, Mrs Cecil Chesterton's, viewpoint was, as usual, slightly different:

A solemn Requiem Mass was celebrated at the Beaconsfield Catholic Church, in the building of which G.K. had been personally interested. The service started at 10.30a.m., but this early hour did not deter those who admired him from paying their last tribute, though to many this involved a long journey. I do not think that Top Meadow anticipated that, apart from in-laws and personal friends, Gilbert's funeral would gather a large crowd. But there was a considerable congregation in the church that overflowed into the porch, following every word of the long ritual . . . From the church intimate friends and relations were taken in cars to the cemetery, while the rest of the crowd followed on foot to the graveside . . . We finally reached Top Meadow after two o'clock suffering, as might be expected, both from emotional strain and physical sinking. Gilbert had always appreciated the classic tradition of funeral baked meats, and had frequently praised the understanding of the poor, who always provide sustaining ham for the burial of their nearest and dearest. But in her secluded vision of Gilbert, Frances had not anticipated the attendant throng of sincere and loving followers. There was no banquet of the dead. The idea of solid provision for those ravaged by long journeying and sense of loss had not occurred to a household which, in its outlook, was dominantly feminine.

Frances was not in the studio to receive the condolences of her husband's friends. She went straight to her room, and downstairs there was a sense of utter emptiness, accentuated by a quite inadequate supply of food. A few ladylike sandwiches, with sherry, spread on a long table, disappeared with the first arrivals. Forlorn little groups stood about the gardens, others crowded the hall and inner rooms, and I was sorry for Belloc, who tired and hungry was looking vainly for refreshment. But nothing further was forthcoming and, gradually, hunger overcoming the desire to linger in the hope of seeing Frances, to express their sorrow in the place where Gilbert had lived so long and worked so arduously, the crowd finally departed . . .

I had a short talk with Frances before I left . . . She was very quiet and very brave, but it seemed to me that underlying all her grief and desolation there was a sense of relief from temporal anxiety. Now, after long, long years of safeguarding, yearning, wondering over Gilbert, she could rest secure; she knew that he was safe.[14]

Fr. O'Connor had been too ill in bed to attend, but was invited to celebrate the Mass at a Memorial Service held ten days later in Westminster Cathedral, with a panegyric being delivered later by Fr. Ronald Knox in Westminster Hall. Joan (Nicholl) Huffer recalled picking out Shaw in his trademark Jaeger knickerbockers among the vast congregation. In Fr. Knox's words:

The man whom we laid to rest the other day in the cemetery of Beaconsfield was one of the very greatest men, certainly be remembered as a great and solitary figure in literature, an artist in words and in ideas with an astounding fecundity of imaginative vision. He will almost certainly be remembered as a prophet in an age of false prophets. He warned us, in spacious times that human liberties were threatened, and today human liberties are in debate. He warned us, in times of prosperity, against the perils of industrialism, and industrialism is labouring for breath. He warned us, when imperialism was a fashion, that nationalism was a force not easily destroyed; today nationalism is the shadow over men's hearts . . .'[15]

Other tributes included a telegram from Cardinal Eugenio Pacelli (Vatican Secretary of State and later Pope Pius XII) on behalf of Pope Pius XI. It was read out by the then Cardinal Archbishop of Westminster Arthur Hinsley: 'Holy Father deeply grieved death Mr Gilbert Chesterton, devoted son Holy Church, gifted Defender of the Catholic Faith. His Holiness offers paternal sympathy people of England, assures prayers dear departed, bestows Apostolic Benediction.' Fleet Street in the main did not report the phrase Defender of the Catholic Faith: *Fidei Defensor* being considered to be a royal title (albeit one originally bestowed on Henry VIII by the Pope).

Back at Top Meadow there was the grim prospect of life without Gilbert and the need to cancel all engagements including a passage to Australia booked to leave on P & O's RMS *Narkunda* in July in good time to arrive for the Catholic Educational Congress in November 1936. In view of Chesterton's ill health over the previous twelve months, and considering Frances' previous record of severe indispositions whenever she travelled, it is to be wondered whoever contemplated such arrangements in the first place.

# 22.

# AFTERMATH

To the surprise of many Gilbert Chesterton left an estate of £28,389 gross and net £23,300 (now the equivalent of almost a million pounds). George Bernard Shaw had been so concerned about Frances Chesterton's well-being that he had written to offer a then very generous three figure sum to tide her over; like most other people he was obviously unaware that Frances was wealthy in her own right by the terms of Edward Chesterton's will which gave her one third of the trust fund on Marie-Louise's death, the other beneficiaries being Ada and Gilbert himself. Gilbert now left her extremely well provided for, although copyright royalties were given to the Royal Literary Fund and Dorothy Collins was appointed as literary executrix to administer his literary works. It would seem that Miss Collins always kept the control of copyright and presumably of royalties in her own hands until her death in 1988, although the actual administrative control was left in the hands of A.P. Watt.

Once Frances had recovered from the immediate shock of losing her husband she followed her usual practice of seeking solace on the continent, this time in Rome and Rapallo (with Max Beerbohm) and later with her cousins in Germany even though Nazi Germany in 1936 would hardly have appealed to the late Gilbert. By early 1937 Frances had returned to Beaconsfield upon the death of Frau Margaret Arndt (née Heaton) because the Arndts were considering their own situation in Germany under Hitler's rule, and because she was beginning to experience the onset of the illness eventually diagnosed as a cancer which was to prove terminal. Nonetheless, plans went ahead for publication of the collection of stories to be called *The Paradoxes of Mr Pond* and for two volumes of miscellaneous collected pieces to be known as *The Coloured Lands*, only one of which was ever to reach publication and both to experience a chequered career as the entire stock would be destroyed in an incendiary bomb attack in 1940.

As her illness progressed Frances stayed at home enjoying her garden. The fate of her donkey, Trotsky (so-called as he couldn't runsky), went unrecorded, no doubt as once again everybody knew. At last, however, palliative medicine reached its limits and Frances was taken into the St. Joseph's Nursing Home opened by Gilbert only a couple of years previously where her friends considered her final agony to have been bravely borne. Winifred Nicholl saw Frances shortly before her end:

> Just before she died I saw her in the hospital. She didn't see me, but the nuns had left her door open. Her arms were spread out and there was a lovely expression of happiness on her face. I felt that Gilbert had come to tell her everything was all right and to welcome her.[1]

Frances died on December 12th, 1938 and was buried alongside Gilbert under the stone designed by Eric Gill after a requiem in the new St. Teresa's Church built as a memorial to him. Her estate was even greater than Gilbert's (£30,000) with Top Meadow being left to the Parish of St. Teresa's with the wish expressed that it be used as a college as Gilbert had desired, and with provision made for part of the grounds of Top Meadow on Station Road to go to Dorothy together with sufficient funds for her to build herself a residence in which to undertake her duties as literary executrix. There on Station Road Dorothy built Top Meadow Cottage, perhaps best described as a stock-broker style house in which she was to reside until her death in 1988. In fact Top Meadow Cottage was only completed shortly before the outbreak of the Second World War on September 3rd, 1939 and soon was being used along with Top Meadow as a refuge for pregnant ladies to escape the London Blitz and have their babies in relatively peaceful conditions; Dorothy Collins acted as an ambulance driver and when petrol was in short supply wheeled her charges down the road in a bath chair to St. Joseph's Nursing Home for their confinement.

Chesterton had long had a strong following in the United States and in 1938 Orson Welles' Mercury Theater of the Air broadcast Welles' production of *The Man Who Was Thursday*. In his introductory remarks Welles recorded:

> Gilbert Keith Chesterton, great, greatly articulate Roman convert, liberal, has been

dead now for two years. For a unique brand of common sense enthusiasm, for a singular gift of paradox, for a deep reverence and a high wit, and most of all for a free and shamelessly beautiful English prose, he will never be forgotten.[2]

It is idle to speculate about a transfer to the cinema screen by Welles, but it is certainly one of the great might-have-beens; suffice it to point out that the following month saw the production of H. G. Wells' *War of the Worlds* with the furore that followed. The young Welles was to drive nails into his Hollywood coffin with *Citizen Kane* and *The Magnificent Ambersons* and so he was never to get the opportunity to bring Chesterton to the screen, although later in life he may have found inspiration in GKC for the brigand's cloak and hat which he wore on television in his Domecq Sherry advertisements. He certainly looked like Chesterton.

After *Father Brown, Detective* (1935) Chesterton did not come to the silver screen again for many years, although many film rights had been bought up, and it has occasionally been suggested that they were bought to prevent any films being made. Be that as it may, Father Brown once more appeared in 1954 in a film directed by Robert Hamer with Alec Guinness as Father Brown and Peter Finch as Flambeau. The plot was a loose combination of 'The Blue Cross' and 'The Flying Stars' and is probably the best version of Father Brown yet made; sadly Alec Guinness, although influenced by his role to convert to Roman Catholicism, was not sure that he was the ideal person for the part and no sequels were to follow. But in 1960 a similar plot appeared on television in a BBC series called 'The Detectives' with Mervyn Johns as Father Brown. What may have been intended as a pilot episode was not followed up until the BBC's rivals ABC launched a prize-winning series with Kenneth More as Father Brown. It was reported that More had been reluctant to take on the role, but he gave a good portrayal of the part for thirteen episodes until it was at first suspended and then abandoned after More was diagnosed with the Parkinson's Disease from which he died. Father Brown had appeared on radio in both Britain and the United States but his next transatlantic trip was to be for a television movie now variously known as *The Girl in the Park* (1979) or *Father Brown – Detective* or *Sanctuary of Fear*, with a much modernised Irish-American Brown worried about repairs to his church roof until he goes out jogging in Manhattan's Central Park and finds himself involved in the murder of the eponymous girl, a plot-line not obviously derived from Chesterton's stories. Many years were to pass before a new Father Brown television series was launched in 2013 on BBC2 with Mark

Williams as the priest, though once again plot lines were only tenuously based on the original stories.

In her later years Dorothy Collins came at times to be very forgetful, possibly as the result of an at first unrecognized onset of dementia. She could be very helpful or obstructive, often changing from one to the other in quick succession, but always very protective of what she saw as Chesterton's reputation and heritage and on occasion eager to stress that as literary executrix she had the right to destroy original material. It will never be certain whether she did or did not, but, fortunately, the old exercise books in the trunk were to be forgotten over many years. It does appear that she continued the practice of disposing of original holographs once they had been published even when not all of the original had been included. It is on record[3] that *The Surprise* only escaped revision of its ending on the insistence of Dorothy L. Sayers, and several of the essays published posthumously were rearranged in format or only published in part. In fact, apart from *The Surprise*, very little previously uncollected material was to appear, either because Miss. Collins considered it to be unworthy of GKC or because it would have been, as she put it, scraping the barrel. Her attitude is evident in a letter sent to Mildred d'Avigdor (née Wain) on March 19, 1938:

> Dear Mrs d'Avigdor,
>
> Thank you so much for sending your letters which I have copied and now return. I am also sending you the book we talked about [*Shipwrecked off Fairyland*]. You certainly ought to have it. Will you arrange for it to be destroyed or cared for after your death, as we do not want all these jokes bandied about in salerooms. It has already happened in a good many cases I am sorry to say. A lot of things have been sold to America. Max Beerbohm was talking about the horrors of this when we saw him at Rapallo where we were for a week after leaving Rome. We had a very nice time and Frances is much better for her holiday.[4]

Some manuscript material does seem to have been given away as souvenirs of GKC's handwriting, and the bookseller Sims Rare Books was at times given free rein to help himself to such samples in return for help in cataloguing; what was taken appears to have been largely the opening and closing pages of pieces where GKC had sketched a rubric or signed. In many instances this has resulted in the loss of the title Chesterton gave to the work, but it is, of course, quite impossible to establish whether any complete poems or stories were taken or not.

As soon as was practicable after the Second World War was over and when financial exchange controls had at last been eased after 1952, Miss Collins and Miss Judith Lea had resumed the pre-war routine of trips to the Continent. In view of Miss Collins' insistence that Chesterton had no knowledge of foreign languages and always relied on her for communication, it is interesting to find that Miss Lea in her turn insisted that Miss Collins had no such knowledge and she herself always acted as interpreter.[5]

The end of war in 1945 had also raised the question of what was to happen to Top Meadow. The parish would seem to have shown no interest in using it as a college or a school and seems to have been glad to unload it onto the Convert's Aid Society which was to use it until 1999 as a home for Anglican and other clergymen who had converted to Roman Catholicism and were suffering the loss of their benefices and stipends.

Miss Collins continued to reside in some style at Top Meadow Cottage with maids and a cook until 1988 when she was 94 years old, only going into St. Joseph's for the last weeks of her life. She died on September 8th, 1988 leaving a net estate of £962,682 (considerably more in current value). Subsequently in 1994 the Chesterton papers from the attic were sold to the British Library for a reputed £200,000 taken from the Shaw Fund. It then transpired that in the fifty-three years since Chesterton's death precious little effort had gone into collating the surviving manuscript material and what had been done in the late nineteen-thirties had been largely misdirected with dates and titles on some notebooks indicating that the contents either had not been read or had been misconstrued; nor did it appear that there had ever been any attempt to publish the unpublished work or to trace what had been sent to long-forgotten magazines. Some of the papers had deteriorated over the years and a good many could not be identified due to the number of title pages which had been removed. Top Meadow Cottage and its contents were left to the Roman Catholic diocese of Northampton with Miss Judith Lea receiving rights of tenure for her lifetime or until such time as she decided to relinquish those rights. She did so in 2004 and moved into secure residential accommodation in Oxford whereupon Top Meadow Cottage reverted to the Northampton Diocese which subsequently sold it; its value in 2005 being well in excess of £700,000. The residue of Miss Collins' estate had previously been distributed by her executors and trustees, Miss Lea and Miss Collins' solicitor (Brendan Lawrence Garry), the beneficiaries being The Royal Literary Fund for Authors, The Cecil Houses, The Cheshire Foundation Homes for the Sick and The Distressed Gentlefolks Aid Association, each of which received an equal share.

All attempts to acquire either Top Meadow or Top Meadow Cottage as a location for some sort of Chesterton Study Centre proved futile, foundering largely on lack of available funds. Top Meadow was sold by the Society of St. Barnabas (previously The Converts' Aid Society) into private hands; it would appear that the purchase was in some measure funded by the subsequent sale of building plots from the acreage of Top Meadow, with at least one large house (Chesterton Gardens) and an apartment block (Chesterton Park Management Ltd.) now standing where Trotsky grazed. With that sale the last links of Chesterton with Beaconsfield were broken, apart from his grave where the original gravestone has been replaced by a replica. The original carved by Eric Gill had been damaged by Miss Collins' gardener using caustic materials to clean it; it is now bolted to the exterior wall of St. Teresa's Church. Subsequently, Top Meadow Cottage appears to have been demolished and replaced with an apartment block known as Willington Court. Top Meadow itself has been extended into what little is left of its original garden.

In 1941 Ada (Mrs Cecil Chesterton) brought out *The Chestertons*, possibly a very partial account, but nevertheless a primary source dating back to 1901. By then Ada was living on Kingsway, having been bombed out of 3 Fleet Street, and her book burst like another bomb with her journalistic highlighting of Gilbert and Frances' alleged marital difficulties which resulted in their marriage never being consummated. She had apparently heard the story from Cecil in whom Gilbert is supposed to have confided, but, whatever the basis for it, it does seem unlikely that Cecil at his then age of twenty-one would have proved to be an ideal marriage guidance consultant. Nonetheless, Ada's book caused consternation in Chestertonian circles with Maisie Ward making space in her forthcoming Chesterton biography (1944) to refute the suggestion. The allegation still rankles in certain quarters, but at this distance in time there does not appear to have been an excess of malice on Ada's part, and it is possible that she believed the story on Cecil's word. Neither Cecil nor Ada liked Frances and that fact, allied to their penchant for sensational journalism, no doubt caused them to propagate a story which Gilbert had implicitly denied in *Orthodoxy*: 'I have not myself any instinctive kinship with that enthusiasm for physical virginity, which has certainly been a note of historic Christianity . . . It takes all sorts to make a church; she does not ask me to be celibate. But the fact that I have no appreciation of the celibates, I accept like the fact that I have no ear for music . . . celibacy is one flower in my father's garden, of which I have not been told the sweet or terrible name.'[6]

Maisie Ward's biography (1944) taken together with her sequel *Return to*

*Chesterton* (1953), was in many ways exhaustive, even exhausting in its detail. Its over-riding virtue lies in her having known Chesterton so that wool could not always be pulled over her eyes as seems to have happened when some later biographers took information from Miss Collins whose knowledge of events prior to late 1926 was in its turn based on what Frances had chosen to tell her. The general effect was that they were fed a Top Meadow Cottage point of view which consciously or unconsciously discounted those parts of Chesterton's career of which Frances and Dorothy Collins had disapproved and denigrated the work of Chesterton's earlier secretaries,[7] not all of whom were the dummies they were made out to be. Although Frances could move heaven and earth to appoint an incompetent, several professionals slipped through her net. There also seems to have been a different relationship between Chesterton and Dorothy Collins compared to those he had with his other secretaries, certainly not unfriendly but more distant and less jolly. This difference in tone can be discerned in the poems he addressed to them.[8]

The fear that Top Meadow Cottage might well influence and mislead biographers underlies Harold Robbins' *Chesterton: Last of the Realists*[9] intended for publication in the late 1940s but denied an allocation of paper at that time of rationing with the result that it appeared in serial instalments in the limited circulation Land League magazine *The Plough and the Stars* and thus not having the impact it might have had in book form. Robbins' text, announced in book form by IHS Press since 2004, had still not appeared at the end of 2014.

## The Cause for Canonization

In 1994 it was reported that Señor Miguel Angel Espeche Gil (sometime Argentinian ambassador to Thailand and later in 2005 nominated for the Nobel Peace Prize), abetted by Count John de Salis (1947–2014),[10] a 'sharp sword in the Order of Malta', had collected signatures in Argentina from diplomats, politicians, and others including an archbishop, to help further the cause for Chesterton's beatification. Subsequently, an approach was made to the Archbishop of Westminster, then Cardinal Basil Hume, who indicated that any process would have to be initiated by the Bishop of Northampton. There appears to have been little progress since that time, although both the American and British Chesterton Societies have lent their support. Obstacles raised include the financial burden of seeing a cause successfully through investigation by the Vatican, and also the establishment of 'heroic sanctity' on the part of the nominee, it being considered that, although GKC was a good man, his reputation for enjoying food and drink would not fit well into the ascetic frame traditionally associated with sanctity; in short a saint should not be fat, jolly, nor should he or she enjoy the fruits of the earth. It seems redundant to point to St. Thomas Aquinas when others are all too keen to cite Friar Tuck, and indeed how many fat saints are there? However, it might be possible to count on the support of the Mother and Son responsible for providing forty water-pots full of the best quality wine at a wedding feast in Cana of Galilee.[11]

More recently in 2005 a Chesterton conference was opened in Argentina with a Mass concelebrated by Fr. Ian Boyd of the Chesterton Institute, The Archbishop of La Plata Mons, Hector Aguera, and Cardinal Jorge Mario Borgoglio (now Pope Francis I). It is reported that Pope Francis was indeed a member of the Argentinian Chesterton Society who on March 10th, 2013 had approved a prayer (for private devotional use) asking for Chesterton's intercession, so perhaps there is some chance of success for a cause for Chesterton's canonisation brought forward in 2013 by Bishop Peter Doyle of Northampton who appointed Canon John Udris, Spiritual Director of Oscott College, as Devil's Advocate to review Chesterton's cause and determine whether he lived a life of heroic virtue.

# PART TWO

# THE MAN OF LETTERS

# THE NOVELIST

Chesterton's early interest in the telling of tales developed into the composition of Stevensonian-style novellas, but the first indication that he was drawn to the longer form of the novel is a narrative written in the early mature handwriting replaced when he adopted an italic hand soon after he began his studies at University College, London in 1893–94; this suggests a date of composition in late 1893 or early 1894. The two notebooks containing that narrative had been classified, apparently without reading them, by Dorothy Collins as separate stories entitled 'Valentine Amiens' and 'The History of Three Babies'. As the title page had been lost, the present author chose to call Chesterton's first novel *Basil Howe*.[1] Like many other first novels Chesterton's account of developing love between a gauche and lanky young man and a fiery, free-spirited red-headed girl seems to have a strong autobiographical undertow. Both date and autobiographical content are confirmed by *Our Future Prospects*, a fictitious tale of what happened to the members of the Junior Debating Society after they had left their alma mater, that tale being firmly dated June 16th, 1894. Each member was to contribute a chapter that guyed the others and confronted the one writing the following chapter with a problem which could only be solved by his ensuing literary effort. The part of *Our Future Prospects* relevant to *Basil Howe*, is the meeting, love affair and marriage of Gilbert Chesterton and a red-headed cousin of Bentley's called Gertrude Grey. The thrust of the narrative and their adventures in Russia is, of course, nonsense but it is obvious that the JDC members were familiar with Gertrude Grey and did not find it amiss that she should marry a tall shy young man (as he then was) called Chesterton. In other words, they had all read *Basil Howe* when it was pedalled around the JDC.

Ada Chesterton, Gilbert's sister-in-law and colleague, noted[2] that 'the fugitive heroines who occasionally flit through his stories are inevitably red-headed . . . red hair signified to Gilbert beauty and romance.' Early in the 1890s he had described the Vivian sisters who lived down the street at 80 Warwick Gardens: 'I have never been able, in fact I have never tried to tell which of the three I really liked best, and if the severer usefulness and domesticity of the eldest girl, with her quiet art colours, and broad brave forehead as pale as the white roses that clouded the garden, if these mature qualities in Nina demanded my respect more than the levity of the others, I fear they did not prevent me feeling an almost equal tide of affection towards the sleepy acumen and ingrained sense of humour of Ida, the second girl and book-reader for the family; or Violet, a veritably delightful child with a temper as formless and erratic as her tempest of red hair.' Within a couple of years Chesterton was describing that self-same temper and hair in the person of Gertrude Grey in *Basil Howe*, in which it is worth noting that the first encounter takes place in Walton-on-the-Naze, a resort for which he always retained fond memories.[3]

Chesterton would appear to have been drafting other novels for we have his brother's assurance that 'The cold fact is that Mr Chesterton . . . has had this story [*The Napoleon of Notting Hill*] by him in a more or less developed form since his schooldays . . . that this story was cast and, in essence, completed before Mr H.G. Wells (say) had published his first story . . . Its introductory chapter is a dozen years younger than the book itself.'[4] Members of the JDC remembered a master at St. Paul's School whose appearance was similar to that of Auberon Quin, and recalled that masters did tend to walk in pairs with their frockcoat tails flying in the wind like Barker's and Lambert's did as they were metamorphosed into a pair of dragons. In his *Autobiography* (1936) GKC himself 'remember[ed] an interminable romance, for which I was always drawing pictures, and which I still think had a touch of wild fancy. It arose merely from our walking behind three of the masters; two of them, who were young and tall, had between them a third, who was old and very small; so that there seemed a vague suggestion that they were supporting him. On this was based the great constructive theory that the elder master (who was one of the most important persons in the school) was in fact only a clockwork figure, which they carried about with them and wound up to go through his daily round. The dummy and the two conspirators were dragged through an endless reel of long-drawn (and badly drawn) adventures, some scraps of which must still be kicking about the world somewhere.'[5]

As indicated elsewhere (p. 90), it is likely that an early version of *The Napoleon of Notting Hill* had to be revised and rewritten to circumvent copyright problems before John Lane could publish it at the Bodley Head in 1904. Chesterton marshalled material that drew on his school days, on his personal solipsist crisis in 1893–94, and on the political position he had taken up in opposition to the South African War; he is quite explicit in his dedicatory verses that he is really playing war-games in the streets of his childhood:

> I saw the dream; the streets I trod,
> The lit straight streets shot out and met
> The starry streets that point to God.
> This legend of an epic hour
> A child I dreamed, and dream it still,
> Under the great grey water-tower
> That strikes the stars on Campden Hill.

And so we are taken back not just to the 1890s but to the 1880s when the little boy from Sheffield Terrace looked up at the Campden Hill water-tower and walked nearly every one of the streets of Holland Park and Notting Hill, every one except Pump Street, for that he could walk only in his imagination.

Part of the scenario of the action in *The Napoleon of Notting Hill* is the creation of a fool, perhaps a bloody fool, but in many ways a holy fool, someone completely irresponsible who becomes beyond all control when elected absolute monarch in a world eighty years after 1904 and therefore, the world of 1984.[6] Chesterton takes no account of possible technological developments, leaving such things for H.G. Wells and his ilk, and so his 1984 is little different from 1904 except for one thing, King Auberon Quin's Charter of the Cities. King Auberon's joke, possibly a sick joke, has created a ridiculous backdrop for his obsession of making all his acquaintances dress up in a monstrous game of charades, but, upon meeting a red-headed little boy in Notting Hill, he encourages the child to love and defend his insalubrious district. Without Auberon either knowing it or intending it, 'I am King of the Castle' thereupon ceases to be the game of a child and becomes a mission, for Adam Wayne, with the total solemnity of a child, believes heart and soul and cap-à-pié in the task entrusted to him by the irresponsible King, and for ever and aye he will defend his Hill of Notting. Like most children, he believes that promises must be kept, and again like most children, he may have a sense of fun but lacks the very adult quality of a sense of humour. Chesterton has defined it: 'If we take out of the mind of a man an essential human quality, it may often happen that what we leave behind is sometimes like inspiration. A prophet may sometimes be an ordinary man minus an ordinary quality.'[7] For twenty years the boy lacking in a sense of humour will grow to manhood, when he will emerge full of common sense but devoid of common nonsense, King Auberon's time-bomb waiting to explode.

Auberon Quin may be a fool, may even be mad nor'-nor'-west, but his proposals that everyone should dress in a manner that reveals trade, derivations, and even personality was one very close to Chesterton's heart.[8] It may seem redolent of the Imperial Chinese court, but it prefigures many ideas of existentialist thinkers such as Sartre and Camus – you are what you make of yourself and so it is logical that you accept that situation, in Chesterton's opinion, by not only wearing your heart upon your sleeve but also by declaring your identity in the way a medieval knight did by wearing his escutcheon on his tabard and his shield. Chesterton's own identity and his very roots on Campden Hill are paraded throughout *The Napoleon of Notting Hill*, but so are those aspects of himself that so troubled him during his student years: was it all a dream? Did anything exist outside himself? Was it all a joke? That line of thought had culminated in an identity crisis, a schizophrenic dream with which he eventually came to terms by recognising and accepting it, and then rebuilding the different parts of himself into a single whole. Like Auberon Quin he had bordered on madness; like Adam Wayne he had been a fanatic; like them the logical and illogical spheres of his brain had come apart for a while. Now that he was again whole and wholesome the situation could be acknowledged in Adam Wayne's words:

> We are mad, because we are two lobes of the same brain, and that brain has been cloven in two. And if you ask for the proof of it, it is not hard to find. It is not merely that you, the humorist, have been in these dark days stripped of the joy of gravity. It is not merely that I, the fanatic, have had to grope without humour. It is that, though we seem to be opposite in everything, we have been opposite like man and woman aiming at the same moment at the same practical thing . . . in healthy people there is no war between us.[9]

Oddly enough Chesterton throughout the whole extent of his career found it difficult to convince many of his readers that when at his most serious he would illustrate his arguments with a joke, that solemn kind of hilarious joke akin to the 'laughter on the secret face of God.'[10] In *The Napoleon of Notting*

*Hill* Chesterton is utterly serious in telling the story of a joke played on an almost cosmic scale, a joke that in the end man has no choice but to take seriously, for he must accept his lot and fight for justice. The underlying message is that Nicaragua is ridiculous, Notting Hill is ridiculous, and all the cities with all their charters are supremely ridiculous, but Adam Wayne, Buck, Barker, Lambert, et al., and even Auberon Quin, are not ridiculous, for the reason that they have given their lives meaning. Fools or fanatics they might well be, solemnity and frivolity personified, but they are the two sides of one problem, of the one conflict and ultimately of each human personality. The real adventure is to stand firm and balance the two halves so they form an integrated whole, and that is in some measure what Gilbert Chesterton did in the 1890s and is in part the story he finally published in 1904.

About 1895, still in his pre-italic hand, Chesterton wrote *The Adventurous Abbot* (aka *The Face of Brass*), a historical novel about Abbot Stephen Ironcross of Beaulieu and his struggles against Earl Hugh Brassface of Beaulieu.

Chesterton's work, written in two parts, was certainly finished, but it is unclear whether it was ever submitted to a publisher. Early in his career Chesterton tended to sell copyrights for cash, so it is possible that it appeared without mention of his name in a serial magazine or one of the then popular annual compendiums of stories. Part of the surviving text is written on the back of publisher's copy for *Charles Dickens* so it appears that Frances Chesterton, ever careful, may have provided her husband with paper by recycling whatever was to hand:

*THE ADVENTUROUS ABBOT*
*Chapter 1, The Face of Brass.*
The hand of Hugh Brassface, Earl of Beaulieu, was heavy upon the sons of Adam. He dwelt in an endless summer of success that seemed to eclipse moral distinctions, so that when King Henry III, a pious king, came through that part of the country with a small retinue, Hugh Brassface, after a chronicle of impieties, rode at the right hand of the King, but those that saw them pass would have said rather that the King rode at the left hand of Brassface. The Earl was taller than the King by a head and a half, and stouter by God knows how many girths, for he was the most monstrously fat man of his time, and yet more dignified for his corpulence, and in spite of it one of the strongest knights alive in war and tournament. Henry Plantagenet bore himself well in the saddle, like most of his blood, and carried his gold head and beard high as he rode. But Hugh of Beaulieu rode like an emperor, and his head was set on his great shoulders like a tower on a mighty building. And his face, heavy and handsome and yellow, stared before him unendingly with great arched eyebrows and a little smile, as though his large Norman features were, as his nickname suggested, carven out of eternal brass . . .

Prince Edward was struck rigid with astonishment, and the King had gone pale with fear. Then amid the earthquake and eclipse of the wrath of Brassface, a small clear voice answered him. The Abbot stood erect in the open space, like a single tree left by a cyclone.

'You have blundered, Brassface of Beaulieu.' And the one word in a bright cutting tone brought the Earl up short like a bridled horse. 'You have gone too far. I am in some poor sense the host here, and I will protect, under your favour, the peace of the presence of the King. Cut down your own oppressed vassals, proud Earl, strut and bellow in your own gloomy castle, but by St. George of England, if I were a nameless hind instead of a mitred Abbot of the Eternal Church, it would be shame to me if I let the King's own gift be snatched from me in the King's own presence. If I were a beggar by the roadside and His Majesty had flung me a crown, do you think I would let all the Beaulieus between France and Hell rob me of the sovereign's own token? You crow too loud, Brassface of Beaulieu, but crow on your dunghill! Your barons think perhaps that the King is but one of you, a captain of earthly armies. We of the Church know better: if Henry Plantagenet stood before you as I stood but now, lonely and a prisoner, I would say 'Our oil is on his head: he is the anointed of the Lord".

*Chapter 12, The Battle in the Woods.*
*Chapter 13, The End of the Great Battle of Beaulieu.*
*Chapter 14, The Four-Headed Lion.*

*Epilogue. Whatever illusion may be mingled with the conception of the march of progress, some horrors we hope, at least, are buried for ever, like vampires with a stake through the heart: tortures like the Iron Virgin, doctrines like the Hell of Infants. And buried under mountain upon mountain, stifled for ever, let us pray, is the noise of the laughter of Brassface.*

The last three chapters of Part I and the first eight chapters of Part II are missing, perhaps consigned to the incinerator or land-fill by GKC when he cleared papers from Warwick Gardens in 1933. One short story, a spin-off from *The Adventurous Abbot*, entitled 'The Free Man' later appeared in the 1911 Christmas Number of *T.P.'s Weekly*.

Various outlines and sketches were written during the closing years of the nineteenth century under the title *The Man With Two Legs*, a project which began as a development of *The Human Club*. It is far from clear whether or not any of the varying versions were ever submitted to publishers, but the constant rewriting might well indicate that that was so. A synopsis undated but written on the notepaper of the publisher T. Fisher Unwin, Chesterton's employer from 1896–1901, gives us some idea of his intentions:

I think this might be called a new kind of novel, approximately defined as the romantically inclined philosophic: i.e. a story in which modern thoughts are typified, not by long arguments, but by rapid, symbolic incidents – an allegorical comedy.

*Prologue* A fantastic detective incident containing a new theoretic motive for crime. A quiet suburban family are invaded by an eccentric professor with insane high spirits and childish amusements. One night he walks home with another visitor and the family are informed that he has been arrested by the police for attempting his companion's life with a pistol. The host and a theorising friend plunge into the mystery, and after much light detective story business find in the professor's poems and other works hints of the principle on which he acted. At last it dawns upon them that the companion must have had an intention and idly declared himself averse to existence; the professor with a kind of philosophical fanaticism of the opportunist resolved at all cost to suddenly and dramatically test the sincerity of the other's nihilism with the pistol point.

*Book I.* The book then goes back and narrates the psychical history of the professor in which he learnt this mania for playing death to the woodman. The scene opens in Paris where the professor, then a young man of depraved life and hopeless philosophy, finds the last remaining pleasure of life in the excitement of fighting duels in which he is the terror of the city. He loves jesting with the heraldry of death, sleeping in a coffin, etc. At last he hears that another duelist has arisen as deadly as himself and takes a dark aesthetic pleasure in imagining a moral monstrosity more mystic than his own. To his surprise, however, he finds that the other is a boy and a rustic, with nothing to distinguish him but the eccentricity of carrying a feather and a sword. After losing himself for some time in wonder at the unlettered innocence of this man of blood he discovers him to be a mysteriously elemental type, who has founded his life upon the fairy tales, gone out to seek his fortune, and kills wicked men as princes killed giants, without parley or remorse. The freshness of the elfin view of this world intoxicates the professor. He is strangely refreshed by the powerful simplicity which sees in his own artistic disorder only a definite balance of evil to be killed. The boy sees men in strong sunlight, black and white: the professor sees for a while through his eyes, and sees himself unquestionably 'black'. There is a mysterious relief in the knowledge: a sense of the boy and the world going forward.

A duel takes place between them. Before it is halfway through the professor, who has drunk from skulls and jested with the tomb so often, feels for the first time *Death* – his own possible death. He suddenly realises a hundred simple experiments and pleasures he has neglected: he sees a tree half-way up the hill he would like to climb. He realises the great vision of the whole world, blazing with possibilities, just as the sword is through his body. The boy leans on the sword in the sunset like an executioner who has beheaded another tyrant. But the tyrant lies on his back with his hands full of flowers, like a child asleep.

*Book II.* Shaving death by a hair, the professor recovers slowly: surprising all who knew him by his new studious and simple life. Gradually, however, it dawns on his adoring decadents that a secret occupation steals dark hours from his time. They conceive some strange sin, and abound in loathly imaginations. Finally, he is tracked down to a small and dark toyshop, and it is discovered that he 'plays' like an actual infant: having now always before him that vision of the small excitements and enterprises which he had at the moment of losing consciousness. He expounds his new theory of endless hide and seek of life and it becomes an aesthetic fashion: the jaded pessimists of his circle limping after his own joyous capers. Gradually, his sense of the *multum in parvo*[12] overwhelms him and he tries to throw into a poetical play for a little toy theatre for which he gilds, paints, carpenters and composes, his sense of the play-box character of life. After rejecting many epics Norse and Eastern, as subjects, he settles on the biblical story of creation. He takes six days to build it: exulting in the qualities of light, darkness, water, fire, and clay. They find him among doll-angels and archangels, wearing a crown as he works.

Having thus satisfied his joy of life by rehearsing the principal joys of God, he comes to the dusk of the seventh day, and a thought smites him. He has now to face the Fall–evil–death. Snatching up his duelling sword, he cries out to the angel of death to descend and answer. The room is dark. The door is slowly opened and he sees a figure, sword in hand. It is the boy with the feather in his cap come to visit him and enquire after his wound. The boy finds him fallen to the ground, struck down by a gleam of the meaning of death.

Part I. The Eye of the Pistol
1. How a great wind arose.
2. Hunt-the-slipper.
3. The Wisdom of Terence Quain.
4. The Brothers in Arms.

Part II. The Toy Universe
1. The Seven Epitaphs of Eric Petersen.


It is a sufficiently well-known fact that some years ago in Paris two of the most notorious and ruthless duellists, veritable destroyers of their species, crossed swords, and one was thought to have killed the other. The meeting was considered sensational: but only one who knows the spiritual and internal history of it, knows how extraordinary it was. No word was said, but one of them made a discovery about the other which amounted almost to an epoch in the history of the human mind. It is the inner story of that duel that we have to tell.

There must be a certain unholy interest attaching to the causes which lead any two men in an age of refinement and compassion to lightly make themselves responsible for rivers of blood, and with regard to the first of these two bravoes, we can easily satisfy our curiosity.

Professor Petersen was a well-known figure in Paris. He was a Norwegian by birth, but a thorough Parisian by habit: he lectured on Roman history and it was said that the constant exercise of his powerful and luminous intellect on the corruption and fall of the first great civilization of the world had bred in him that utter pessimism and unbelief in the future of civilized Europe to which he constantly gave expression. Wiser men however thought that his hopelessness lay deeper: for they saw at times looking out his great pale blue eyes that awful thing for which no power of intellect is a consolation, the mood which would find the flowers of Paradise coarse and the wings of the angels gaudy.

He was a handsome man, of enormous stature and physical prowess. His great fair features, aquiline in type, seemed those of a good man as well as a wise one, his open forehead had the look of some generous and sagacious King. It was only when men saw the back of his head that they knew suddenly that he was a wicked man. A glimpse of the great bull neck and big ears, seeming to dwarf the skull, gave some men a feeling of physical sickness. Some declared that when they saw it they had the shocking fancy that he was not a man at all, but an animal in human clothes. But men were morbid on this subject: and I have heard one man utter a more detestable notion still: that walking behind Petersen quietly for a half mile, he was suddenly made to jump with blinding horror, for the idea came upon him that Petersen's face in front was but an intellectual mask and that the neck and head before him, where the flaxen hair ceased high up, was the great blind featureless jeering face of a figure walking backwards.

But all this was a tribute not so much to Petersen himself, but to the mental anarchy of fear which he contrived to inspire in the weak of the earth. For with the sword of the duellist he had established something like a physical autocracy in the city.

Petersen, despite these horrible fables, was no mere animal. Though only thirty two, he had grown grey in many successive philosophies. He himself used to say that there had been six Eric Petersens before the present one. In his witty mood, he would make little tombstones for them inscribed with sarcastic epitaphs – each commemorating the end of some faith or practice of his life. These he set up in his garden among the flowers.

The first Eric Petersen was a blatantly moral atheist and republican, who lived on bread, coffee and hard work and wrote a tract called 'The Late Lamented Jehovah' and a poem called 'The Damnation of Christ.' He was the youngest, the most solemn, the most needy, the most funereal and probably the happiest of the series. His epitaph is the single word 'Raka'.

This gentleman and his ideal, however, soon vanished and the second tombstone commemorated the Eric Petersen who was devoted to Art, and had outlived morality. His frock-coat was of a curious green for which no name was ever found; though sonnets were written to express it. This was a silly but not altogether ignoble period of his life. Perhaps more courage was shown in facing the gamins in that coat than in all his after duels. His epitaph was 'The Coat Remains'.

The next Eric Petersen is one about whom the less said the better. A man may have ten mistresses in a year and yet be emotionally a monogamist. But Petersen was emotionally a polygamist. Repellent stories were told of the shameless ceremonialism and discipline of his seraglios. For a good year he was certainly the wickedest man in Paris. Then he tired of that form of wickedness, and by a repulsive irony, reformed. This epitaph is not for publication.

Then he started again, hungrily and madly, as a man must who has desecrated and exhausted sex, the only universal source of poetry, and fell into strange places. Some say he went with the Devil-worshippers – it is certain that he became a sort of indecent imitation of a Freemason: he declared that he had found the Kabalistic secret and could conjure with all the souls in heaven and hell. The excitement given him by the mystics and spiritualists lasted, however, but a short time. His intellect, always keen and sceptical, turned upon them and rent them. Few more dramatic scenes had been witnessed in Paris society than the great public lecture in which the fourth Eric Petersen closed his career with a sensational exposure of the whole of French Spiritualism full of murderous satire and telling examples. His epitaph ran 'On the third day he rose again from the dead'.

The fifth Eric Petersen was an uglier and shabbier figure. For the first time, he took to drinking, seriously. But although he talked with tipsy pathos and scorn of the folly of those who went after women when a bottle of cognac would give them a vision of Helen, this intemperate period was the first hint of his intellectual tragedy. He had discovered his doom – to tire of the thing he could get always. He drank sometimes with a diabolical moderation, in order to keep the taste for drinking. But the end came. He became a sober man. His epitaph was 'He often took the Sacrament'.

Then came the sixth Eric Petersen, who kept his head as clear as glass, for he was a gambler. He was refreshed as with a new boyhood to discover what new emotions there were in risking money on the turn of a card. But this was also only for a time. He became callous to the loss of money – generous people called it. A train of hypocritical imps dressed as virtues always followed him. The epitaph on Petersen the gambler was 'Now he plays Consequences' – or its French equivalent.

Lastly at the age of thirty the grey Ulysses of pleasure found the one supreme and remaining physical ecstasy, fighting. To be a destroyer was to be a god – the nearest to a creator to which a mortal can arrive. And the moment that his sword slipped under another and slid through a man's body still had a thrill. But year by year, as he added to the red list of his victims, he felt that the day was coming nearer when this artificial excitement would also fail him – and he would fall back on an honourable old age amid the loathsome respect and plaudits of mankind, hideously humane, hideously chaste, hideously temperate, a caricature of virtue so subtly filthy that even his brazenness blinked at it.

From this fading of this last and most monstrous of his religions he was saved for a [time] by the appearance in Parisian circles of the second duellist, a mysterious figure even more destructive than himself. This man seemed to be a perfect cannibal. He had killed three brothers successively before breakfast, the three merchants of the firm of Latude Brothers. He had killed a father before his son and the son afterwards, the old Marquis de Gerone and his heir. And Petersen, who seemed to have reached the highest and loneliest peak of human infamy, suddenly found a new interest in life as he saw this new figure, like a gigantic shadow of himself, cast upon the void. One night as he made his way along the line of glittering cafes to the one which he affected, among the sea of bewildering faces, faces of women that looked like mosaics seen too close, faces of stunted students, monkey-like and fringed with effeminate black hair, faces of blond young men with curled beards, at once . . .[13]

The answer to the question of which novel Chesterton was working on in the 1890s is that he was working on all of them, for there is also 'The Fight on the Towpath', an early version of *The Ball and the Cross* to be taken into account. It is all too often forgotten that he was brought up in a Unitarian and largely freethinking family, that his first encounter with a human being who seriously practised a religion was when he met his Anglican future wife, and that *pace* Father Brown, he became a convert to Roman Catholicism only in 1922 at the age of forty-eight, when he had only fourteen years to live. It must, therefore, have appeared somewhat odd when in 1905 in *The Commonwealth*, the magazine of the Christian Social Union, he began to publish a serial in which one of the protagonists was a Highland Scottish Roman Catholic, Ewan MacIan, and the other the freethinking Lowland Scottish editor of *The Atheist*, John Turnbull. Once again Chesterton melded together tales from the 1890s, that of the Bulgarian monk, Michael, whose conflict with (Professor) Lucifer is used as prologue and epilogue to the story of two men who hold sincere and diametrically opposed beliefs, which they are willing to uphold in all circumstances even unto death in a duel. Both have red hair, though

MacIan's is brighter than Turnbull's, a colour code which in Chesterton's works always suggested that the personalities concerned were on the side of the angels; it was also the colour of the hair of Archie MacGregor and of Bernard Shaw with both of whom Chesterton enjoyed arguing and debating and with both of whom he would have a life long friendship based on a deep mutual respect for the beliefs and opinions of each other. This respect for other people's opinions went back to the Junior Debating Club at St. Paul's and to heated arguments in Bedford Park and at the Fabian Society and the Pharos Club, arguments which often concerned belief and non-belief in many subjects, also included the opposition of materialism and deism, in Christian terms of *The Ball and the Cross*. It is now usually presumed that Chesterton was always an adherent of the Cross, but his conversion to Anglicanism only came about gradually after his meeting Frances Blogg early in 1897, and he might well have at times taken up a variety of freethinking positions. He was to think and argue himself into an entirely new philosophical position only then to make the final discovery that it was in fact the orthodoxy of which he was to write in 1908, but that process took some time. Even then it was to remain Anglo-Catholic orthodoxy for many a long year, and Gilbert was not averse to poking sly fun at his brother-in-law, Knollys Blogg (before 1905), and his own brother Cecil (1912) when they became Roman Catholics. The secret of success in balancing the two sides of the quarrel between MacIan and Turnbull was that he supported or had supported both. What emerges from the adventures of the two is empathy and personal liking between two individuals who find that they have more common ground than they could possibly have imagined, and that they stand together in opposition to a series of people who for various reasons of their own wish to bring their quarrel to an end or pervert it for their own purposes. However, MacIan and Turnbull are willing to fight for their ideals because they believe in them and know what they involve, and so when those ideals are perverted each man can recognize that something has gone wrong with his dream and he wakes from what has become a nightmare. Turnbull will reject revolutionary brutality and MacIan will spurn Catholic fascism; Chesterton's description of the dome of St. Paul's Cathedral swathed to make it resemble a papal tiara and surrounded by knights akin to the Swiss and Palatine Guards is written very much by an Anglican with his tongue in his cheek and is a dreadful warning to those of overly ultramontane persuasion. The narrative eventually shows MacIan and Turnbull, like d'Artagnan and the Musketeers, putting aside their fight but not their quarrel to unite in a moral cause; as a result they are consigned to Professor Lucifer's lunatic asylum which they find to hold everybody they have encountered since their first meeting. When the asylum is burnt to the ground after being set ablaze by a logical Frenchman, the inmates are led to safety by Michael the Bulgarian monk released from captivity by the conflagration and Lucifer's plans are foiled.

Faced, like those creatures in Carroll's *Alice in Wonderland*, with the dilemma expressed in 'Will you, won't you join the dance?' Chesterton has opted for MacIan's doctrine but also for Turnbull's command of logic and reason. His sympathies for the other side of the argument are beautifully expressed elsewhere in 'A Party Question':

> We know the tale; half truth and double treason,
> Borgia and Torquemada in the throng,
> Bad men who had no right to their right reason,
> Good men who had good reason to be wrong.

What did the freethinkers of 1910 think of it all? They loved it, which suggests that Chesterton must really have achieved some measure of impartiality:

Armed in motley and banging a bladder Mr G.K. Chesterton has for some years haunted the camp fires of the army of Liberty. Although identified with the enemy, his personality is so jolly, his quips and cranks so amusing, that he is always a welcome guest. In return he often displays a quiet fondness for Freethought traditions, and in his writings his flights of fancy are often barbed with iconoclastic points which are as disconcerting to his own side as they are diverting to Freethinkers. In a recent work, *The Ball and the Cross*, Mr Chesterton has introduced an Atheist as one of the principal characters. Of course, the author 'wears his rue with a difference,' and his Atheist is unlike the traditional iconoclast of orthodox publications. He is Chestertonian; but we think we recognise some of the lineaments as being borrowed from life . . . Mr Chesterton cannot simply keep humanity out of his books. His big, breezy, jolly nature, refuses to be cribb'd, cabin'd, and confined within the narrow limits of ecclesiasticism. Let him write what he will, he is always sure of an audience. He is a licensed jester. ('Minermus': A Licensed Jester, *Freethinker*, October 16th, 1910).

In 1896 'A Picture of Tuesday' [see pp. 46–48] appeared in the first issue of the Slade magazine *The Quarto*, a story to which GKC referred in a letter to E.C. Bentley: 'There is that confounded 'Picture of Tuesday' which I have been scribbling at the whole evening, and have at last got it presentable.' Presentable it certainly was insofar as one of the main themes of *The Man Who Was Thursday* was at its centre. Other variations followed:

The president of the sketching club, a lean, dark, fiery man with restless eyes, ascended the platform. 'I will give out the subject for competition,' he said. 'The studies are to be sent in next Thursday.'

Patrick Staunton regarded him tranquilly, like an experienced hunter regarding a lion about to spring. He it was who had interpreted the subject of 'The Old, Old Story' by a sketch of two pterodactyls with their heads together in a defiant spirit.

'The subject,' went on Professor Jackson in a loud clear voice, 'will be a picture of Tuesday.'

There was a silence and Plumtree broke his charcoal.

'I beg your pardon, sir?' asked Staunton.

'A picture of Tuesday, Mr Staunton,' replied the professor, composedly, 'to be shown up next week,' and gathering up his papers, he left the classroom.

'I say, Plumtree, is our excellent professor off his head?'

'I don't know,' replied Plumtree, but his dark face was knitted. He was a very promising impressionist. His impression of 'Gaslight on Westminster Bridge' was unlike anybody else's. It bore no inconsiderable resemblance to the child's impression of the earthquake at Lisbon. He was a hard-working modest man of great talents. He was never overbearing, though crowds of knots of the cultured gathered round his pictures and bathed solemnly – bathed in their entire absence of meaning.

'Thomas, be kind enough to lend me a piece of india-rubber,' said Staunton. 'Man shall not live by bread alone. As for the picture – india-rubber is also necessary. As for the picture of Tuesday, I think the man's mad.'

'Are you going to yield the contest?' asked Thomas.

'Yield,' cried Staunton, jutting his chest, 'to bow at knee before old Jackson's feet and to be bated with a rabble's curse? Certainly not!'

The carpet was torn off the large picture. It seemed as if from being large, it had become colossal. It filled the room and dominated it. It was a dark picture, not with dust and greys, but with an intricate density of dim rich colours, blending in a sort of gorgeous twilight of blue and purple. At first one could detect nothing but a chaos of monstrous waters wrapping the canvas like dragons. Then there grew upon you the presence of a gigantic central figure, rising with his back to the observer, a figure huge, grey and mysterious, only clearly seen where a rift of fitful dawn brought his colossal thighs into relief. As far as his vast outlines could be traced, he had one hand above his head driving up the upper load of waters, his feet moved below a great solemn infinite sea. It was a blue form, but it blinded like a light. Above was written 'Tuesday,' and underneath was written 'And the Lord divided the waters that were above the firmament from the waters that were below the firmament, and that evening and morning were the second day.'[14]

How many versions sprang from Chesterton's pen we can never know, but three pages (the last marked Page 11) survive from a dramatized version, one that is different from any episode of the published novel:

SMITH:    What a significant back!

GOGOL:    A back teeming with modern thought.

SMITH:    And humour.

GOGOL:    A back which accuses the civilization of Europe.

SMITH:    And yet a tactful back.

GOGOL:    There is sadness in it, Smith. Perhaps we are looking at the real side of him. Perhaps this is the side that he does not show to the world.

SMITH:    Well, I imagine that he does not always enter a drawing-room backwards if that is what you mean . . .

GOGOL:    Why do his shoulders shake in that curious way? Is he weeping for the sorrows of suffering humanity?

SMITH:    (*turning away rather sharply*) No, he is laughing at us.

GOGOL:    Well, we have now accounted for three of our little committee. Here are you, here is the President, here am I. Who is the fourth and where is he?

SMITH:    I do not know him. He is not a member of our Inner Council, the Council of Five, but I believe the President wants him elected to it. He is standing as a candidate in the West London branch. He wrote a little brochure on dynamite which was very graceful and pretty. But . . . I don't think there will be another myself . . . this young anarchist the President's so fond of seems to me to be too poetical for practical politics.

GOGOL:    What is his name?

SMITH:    His name is Nickel and here he comes. (*Enter Nickel*)

Page 11

(NICKEL *sits down suddenly . . . and weeps.*)

NICKEL:    Here snaps the last tie between me and humanity. What shall I do? What shall I do?

SMITH:    Oh, if you have pity and a human heart, nothing.

GOGOL:    I know you are very clever, Mr Nickel. But I think you could best help us by – by – by a sort of passive strength. A silent pervasive influence, you know.

NICKEL:    (*starting up suddenly*) I have it! I will consult the President. Where is the President?

GOGOL:    (*in a hollow voice – pointing to the window*) There is the President.

NICKEL:    (*stands for a moment staring*) But why does he sit in front of the window like that?

SMITH:    He says he won't be noticed.

NICKEL:    In the front of the window!

SMITH:    Well, have you noticed him up to now?

NICKEL:    (*suddenly throwing his policeman's helmet on the ground*) No, by God, that's true! He must be a clever fellow. But why does he write up in his window 'Charitable contributions received'?

SMITH:    Oh, he says he does that so as not to be disturbed.

NICKEL:    (*firmly*) He is a great man. I throw myself at his feet. I give in. Perhaps my own ideas were a little crude. (*He steps towards the window*) Mr President. (*There is no answer*) Mr President.

GOGOL: Has he gone to sleep?

SMITH: He doesn't seem to take any notice.

NICKEL: (*suddenly and very loud*) What the devil is the matter with his shoulders!

SMITH: (*sharply*) He's always laughing at us. Mr President! Mr President![15]

This dramatic dialogue with its reference to a Council of Five links with a novella version, *The Appalling Five*,[16] dating from after 1897 as the surviving copy is written in Frances Blogg's hand. There is also recycling of material, evidenced by the reworking of the female lead around the persona of Frances: 'She had a mass of brown hair, too soft and delicate perhaps to secure conventional admirations, but eyes particularly bright and significant which produced a remarkable and not easily explained effect upon the mind.'

All these efforts only came to fruition in 1907 with the publication of *The Man Who Was Thursday* in which we are taken once again on a trip to a slightly disguised Bedford Park and thence on a nightmare journey around Chesterton's old stamping grounds, especially at points where he seems to be indulging in fantasy. The party in Saffron (Bedford) Park could well have been held in the Bloggs' garden at 8 Bath Road or in that of the Yeats family at 3 Blenheim Road, for the meeting of Syme, poet of order, and Gregory, poet of anarchy, is yet another stage in the ongoing dichotomy previously represented in *Napoleon* by Quin/Wayne, in *The Ball and the Cross* by Michael/Lucifer and MacIan/Turnbull, but now with an added dimension in that they also represent Gabriel (Syme) versus Lucifer (Lucien Gregory). General Booth of the Salvation Army maintained that the devil should not be allowed to have all the best tunes, but Chesterton does ensure that Lucien Gregory at least has a fair hearing; if he appears to be sidelined after his initial impact, it is because Gabriel Syme, logical poet and philosophical detective dedicated to the extinction of dynamiters and philosophical heretics, does have the advantage of his logical reasoning and can, therefore, appear to be bigger and better in his anarchy than the real anarchist, and so is elected in his place to the General Anarchist Council under the codename Thursday. Equipped with all the paraphernalia of Chesterton's daily life[17], Syme/Thursday goes forth to pursue his investigations among the Council of the Days headed by the dreaded Sunday. It seems a truism to remark that seven days make a week just as it is to say that a week consists of seven days, but Thursday is in some ways a profoundly religious novel in which Chesterton gives some idea of how he first encountered the Bible and came to terms with the concept of God. Reading and thinking through the Bible story, all was fresh and marvellous and terrible, be it the Genesis account of Creation over six days, Job's encounter with God in the Whirlwind, or Exodus' account of Moses seeing God: 'And the Lord said, "Behold, there is a place by me where you shall stand upon the rock; and while my glory passes by I will put you in a cleft of the rock, and I will cover you with my hand until I have passed by; then I will take away my hand, and you shall see my back; but my face shall not be seen." (*Exodus* 33. 21–23). These images had stuck hard and in 1904 in *G.F. Watts* he took up this 'most awful and mysterious thing in the universe, it is impossible to speak about it', and then did the impossible: 'To walk behind anyone along a lane is a thing that, properly speaking, touches the oldest nerve of awe. Watts has realised this as no-one in art or letters has realised it in the whole history of the world: it has made him great. There is one exception to his monopoly of this magnificent craze. Two thousand years before, in the dark scripture of a nomad people, it had been said that their prophet saw the immense creator of all things, but only saw Him from behind.'

It would indeed be as well to begin at the beginning. Saffron Park is far beyond the start: the start is the dynamite outrage that is followed by Syme's thinking of throwing himself from the Thames Embankment into the river and his subsequent recruitment as a detective by the philosophical policeman. Syme wishes to pursue the anarchist dynamiters, so he is all too willing to hunt down philosophical heretics on behalf of the Chief of Detectives, the man in the dark room at Scotland Yard. Is he qualified to do so? Yes, he is told, anyone can be a martyr to a cause. And so Gabriel Syme goes to Saffron Park, presumably to find heretical dynamiters. Find one he does in Lucien Gregory, a parody of everything an anarchist should be to the extent that nobody can take his anarchism seriously. Stung by Syme's jibes, Gregory, out of hurt vanity, decides to reveal his credentials as a true anarchist to the one man from whom he should keep them concealed. Bound by mutual undertakings of secrecy, binding in 1907 but almost preposterous today, Gregory introduces the logical poet-detective into the local anarchist lodge, only to find himself outwitted by logic and reason to the point that Syme is elected to the General Anarchist Council of Days as Thursday; Syme accordingly goes forth to give battle in a six-day war on his own in the face of his enemies.

Now *The Man Who Was Thursday* is an onion with a great many skins, some still unpeeled, a book that has puzzled many and infuriated some because they could not or would not plumb its depths, a book that both comments on the ideas and trends of its era and investigates problems of human identity. Syme first meets Monday, secretary of the Council of Days, whose 'sad and beautiful

face smiled and his smile was a shock, for it was all on one side, going up
in the right cheek and down in the left.' As he leaves behind the normal
human world to climb up to the hotel[18] balcony in Leicester Square where
the monstrous Sunday with a face like the mask of Memnon in the British
Museum addresses his fellow conspirators, he is entering a nightmare world.
Sunday suddenly levels an accusation that there is a traitor among them: Syme
grips his revolver, but it is Tuesday, Gogol, who leaps to his feet to defiantly
acknowledge that he is a Scotland Yard detective. Syme can breathe again,
but is once more isolated; if only he had known that Gogol, that parody of a
revolutionary, was really a friend among enemies! Impelled to flee, he is tailed
by Friday, the disgusting Professor Worms, and harried close to the point of
desperation before that individual also reveals that he is a detective. From
that moment on it is really no surprise to discover that most of the members
of the Council of Days are policemen, but Chesterton is everywhere strewing
clues to more subtle intentions: only Syme can start the car; darkness falls as
Monday is knocked to the ground. It must all mean something, but what?
Syme eventually comes up with an answer when he realises that six men are
going to ask Sunday what they mean.

When Sunday is eventually run, or lets himself be run to earth he
reveals the secret of their identities by dressing them up as the six days
of Creation: Monday is Light, so it follows that darkness falls when he is
knocked down; Syme is Enlightenment and so it follows that he can start the
car, and so on. But there is also a deeper parallel imagery in which Syme's
nightmare and Chesterton's personal nightmare from the 1890s merge:
Syme undergoes his nightmare because he is a fragmented multi-schizoid
personality, perhaps blown to pieces by the dynamiters' bomb or broken up
like light in an Impressionist painting. Perhaps he did leave part of himself
in Saffron Park, a part that will only return when he has gathered together
and come to terms with yet other parts of himself, when he has put the
days together to make a week. He had feared the other days for what they
seemed to represent: Monday may well be light, lucidity, and clarity, but also
seeing things in black and white, and his sardonic, twisted smile implies
intellectual doubt; Tuesday may represent the limitless firmament, but also
fanaticism and unreason; Wednesday is earth, but also earthy passions hard
to control; Thursday, Syme himself, is Man's logical powers of reasoning as
represented by the great lights that rule day and night; Friday represents the
monstrousness of the waters which, like a cold shower, can bring despair
– a despair that can come from the self-disgust associated with personal

appearance; Saturday is animal life, vibrant but often coldly inimical, rational but devoid of perception. Syme had feared them all, but once they are stripped of their masks, disguise and dark glasses, they are revealed as friends, for indeed people and things are not always what they seem. Just as Gilbert Chesterton in his own personal crisis learned to come to terms with his own doubts, fanaticism, sexuality, reason, despairs and perception of good and evil, so in a fully integrated personality each can be viewed as a friend struggling to prevent anarchy.

For Syme and his fellow conspirator-detectives, there remains just one piece of the puzzle to slot into place, Sunday the arch-anarchist now revealed as the chief officer of law and order, the man in the dark room at Scotland Yard. Is Sunday a sort of proto-Fu-Manchu whose tentacles stretch far and wide to subvert politics, business, both the police and the forces of anarchy? He is most certainly a larger-than-life figure, topsy-turvy, black and white, good and evil, alpha and omega, the beginning and the end, and when the conspirator-detectives go to ask him for an explanation all he does is give them a good run for their money. That pursuit of Sunday is perplexing in being devoid of any point unless one finds a key or a clue to the wild goose chase. That may once again be found in Chesterton's encounter or confrontation with what he called the darkest book of the Bible, Job[19] ; Job is maltreated, abused and tormented, apparently for no reason, until he demands an explanation and a chance to justify himself. Chesterton's own discussions on *The Book of Job* is where we can seek that very explanation:

> The one thing which would make our agony infamous would be the idea that it was deserved. On the other hand, the doctrine which makes it most endurable is exactly the opposite doctrine, that life is a battle in which the best put their bodies in the front, in which God sends only his holiest into the hail of the arrows of hell. In the book of Job is foreshadowed that better doctrine full of a dark chivalry that he that bore the worst that men can suffer was the best that bore the form of man.
>
> There is one central conception of the book of Job, which literally makes it immortal, which will make it survive our modern time and our modern philosophies as it has survived many better times and many better philosophies. That is the conception that the universe, if it is to be admired, is to be admired for its strangeness and not for its rationality, for its splendid unreason and not for its reason. Job's friends attempt to comfort him with philosophical optimism, like the intellectuals of the eighteenth century. Job tries to comfort himself with philosophical pessimism like the intellectuals of the nineteenth century. But God comforts Job with indecipherable mystery, and for the first time Job is comforted. Eliphaz gives one answer, Job gives another answer, and the question still remains an open wound. God simply refuses to answer, and

somehow the question is answered. Job flings at God one riddle, God flings back at Job a hundred riddles, and Job is at peace. He is comforted with conundrums. For the grand and enduring idea in the poem, as suggested above, is that if we are to be reconciled to this great cosmic experience it must be as something divinely strange and divinely violent, a quest, or a conspiracy, or some sacred joke. The last chapters of the colossal monologue of the Almighty are devoted in a style superficially queer enough to the detailed description of two monsters. Behemoth and Leviathan may, or may not be, the hippopotamus and the crocodile. But, whatever they are, they are evidently embodiments of the enormous absurdity of nature. They typify that cosmic trait which anyone may see in the Zoological Gardens, the folly of the Lord, which is wisdom. And in connection with one of them, God is made to utter a splendid satire upon the prim and orderly piety of the vulgar optimist. 'Wilt thou play with him as with a bird? Wilt thou bind him for thy maidens?' That is the main message of the book of Job. Whatever this cosmic monster may be, a good animal or a bad animal, he is at least a wild animal and not a tame animal; it is a wild world and not a tame world.[19]

## A further discussion followed two years later:

The Old Testament idea was . . . what may be called the common-sense idea, that strength is strength, that cunning is cunning, that worldly success is worldly success, and that Jehovah uses these things for His own ultimate purpose, just as He uses natural forces or physical elements. He uses the strength of a hero as He uses that of a Mammoth – without any particular respect for the Mammoth . . .

. . . Everywhere . . . the Old Testament positively rejoices in the obliteration of man in comparison with the divine purpose. The Book of Job stands definitely alone because the Book of Job definitely asks, 'But what is the purpose of God? Is it worth the sacrifice even of our miserable humanity? Of course it is easy enough to wipe out our own paltry wills for the sake of a will that is grander and kinder. But is it grander and kinder? Let God use His tools; let God break His tools. But what is He doing and what are they being broken for?' It is because of this question that we have to attack as a philosophical riddle the riddle of the Book of Job . . .

When, at the end of the poem, God enters (somewhat abruptly), is struck the sudden and splendid note which makes the thing as great as it is. All the human beings through the story, and Job especially, have been asking questions of God . . . By a touch truly to be called inspired, when God enters, it is to ask a number more questions on His own account. In this drama of scepticism God Himself takes up the role of sceptic. He does what all the great voices defending religion have always done. He does, for instance, what Socrates did. He turns rationalism against itself. He seems to say that if it comes to asking questions, He can ask some questions which will fling down and flatten out all conceivable human questioners. The poet by an exquisite intuition has made God ironically accept a kind of controversial equality with His accusers. He is willing to regard it as if it were a fair intellectual duel: 'Gird up now thy loins like a man; for I will demand of thee, and answer thou me.' The everlasting adopts an enormous and sardonic humility. He is quite willing to be prosecuted. He only asks for the right which every prosecuted person possesses; He asks to be allowed to cross-examine the witness for the prosecution. And He carries yet further the correctness of the legal parallel. For the first question, essentially speaking, which He asks of Job is the question that any criminal accused by Job would be most entitled to ask. He asks Job who he is. And Job, being a man of candid intellect, takes a little time to consider, and comes to the conclusion that he does not know.

God comes in at the end, not to answer riddles, but to propound them. The other great fact which, taken together with this one, makes the whole work religious instead of merely philosophical, is that other great surprise which makes Job suddenly satisfied with the mere presentation of something impenetrable. Verbally speaking the enigmas of Jehovah seem darker and more desolate than the enigmas of Job, yet Job was comfortless before the speech of Jehovah and is comforted after it. He has been told nothing, but he feels the terrible and tingling atmosphere of something which is too good to be told. The refusal of God to explain His design is itself a burning hint of His design. The riddles of God are more satisfying than the solutions of man.

. . . Of course, it is one of the splendid strokes that God rebukes alike the man who accused, and the men who defended Him; that He knocks down pessimists and optimists with the same hammer. And it is in connection with the mechanical and supercilious comforters of Job that there occurs the still deeper and finer inversion of which I have spoken. The mechanical optimist endeavours to justify the universe avowedly upon the ground that it is a rational and consecutive pattern. He points out that the fine thing about the world is that it can all be explained. That is the one point, if I may put it so, on which God, in return, is explicit to the point of violence. God says, in effect, that if there is one fine thing about the world, as far as men are concerned, it is that it cannot be explained. He insists on the inexplicableness of everything; 'Hath the rain a father? . . . Out of whose womb came the ice?' He goes farther, and insists on the positive and palpable unreason of things; 'Hast thou sent the rain upon the desert where no man is, and upon the wilderness wherein there is no man?' God will make men see things, if it is only against the Black background of nonentity. God will make Job see a startling universe if He can only do it by making Job see an idiotic universe. To startle man God becomes for an instant a blasphemer; one might almost say that God becomes for an instant an atheist. He unrolls before Job a long panorama of created things; the horse, the eagle, the raven, the wild ass, the peacock, the ostrich, the crocodile. He so describes each of them that it sounds like a monster walking in the sun. The whole is a sort of psalm or rhapsody of the sense of wonder. The maker of all things is astonished at the things He has Himself made . . .

The Book of Job is chiefly remarkable, as I have insisted throughout, for the fact that it does not end in a way that is conventionally satisfactory. Job is not told that his misfortunes were due to his sins or a part of any plan for his improvement. But in the prologue we see Job tormented not because he was the worst of men, but because he was the best. It is the lesson of the whole work that man is most comforted by paradoxes. Here is the very darkest and strangest of the paradoxes; and it is by all human testimony the most reassuring. I need not suggest what a high and strange history awaited this paradox of the best man in the worst fortune. I need not say that in the freest and most philosophical sense there is one Old Testament figure who is truly a type; or say who is pre-figured in the wounds of Job.[20]

Sunday runs away and then poses conundrums to his pursuers while he is on the run. A cross between Job's riddling God in the whirlwind and *Deus absconditus*, he shows off his modern Leviathans, the hansom cab, the omnibus and the fire-engine, then tiring of riddles displays the oddities of Creation in Regent's Park Zoo before escaping again on an elephant whose special etymology must have been *Behemoth>mammoth>elephant*, only to take refuge in a balloon that climbs higher than the Great Wheel of Earl's Court. When his pursuers catch up with him, they have been through thick and thin, rough and smooth, and have some idea of how Job must have felt when he asked for an explanation. Like Job, they do not receive one other than to have the mythology of the Days explained by the new clothes offered to replace those reduced to rags by being put to the test, although they will also see Creation revealed when all its parts turn to show their faces instead of their backs at the fancy-dress ball held in their honour. One might be forgiven for wondering whether Chesterton had any real explanation to give for he too seemed to find it a problem:

Mr Herbert Skimpole's book, *Bernard Shaw: The Man and His Work* [1918] . . . suggests that all the active figures in my idle fictions are made as fat as I am; though I cannot recall that any of them are fat at all, except a semi-supernatural monster in a nightmare called *The Man Who Was Thursday*. ('Ego et Shavius Meus' collected in *The Uses of Diversity*, 1920, p. 160).

You ask me who Sunday is? Well, you may call him Nature if you like. But you will notice that I hold that when the mask of Nature is lifted you find God behind. All that wild exuberance of Nature, all its strange pranks, all its seeming indifference to the events and feelings of men, all that is only a mask. (*Illustrated Sunday Herald*, January 24, 1926).

I wrote 'The Man Who Was Thursday' . . . with reference to notions that lay behind nationalism, and concerned not a country but a cosmos. And it is a very good example of how difficult I find it to describe my writing without boring everybody else about my thinking. The peculiarity of that period was that while we were expected to be optimistic about Empire, we were also expected to be pessimistic about existence. The people who were painting the map red were also painting the universe black, and I was early moved to the heresy that the universe was not so black as it was painted. Even that brilliant pessimist, the Shropshire Lad [A.E. Housman, GKC's Latin tutor at UCL], was sardonically confident that 'God would save the Queen' while thinking it rather unusual for God to save anybody. Now among those pessimists I was an optimist; and in 'The Man Who Was Thursday' I tried to justify that phase of my optimism. I suggested that perhaps much of the apparent evil of the world was meant as a trial to our courage, and that many foes if they were faced might turn out to be friends. I expressed this in a grotesque fantasia of masked anarchists who turn out to be all of them policemen. But I suggest that even optimism can hardly hold that everything is for the best, since one of the best things is a good fight.

'In the Days of My Youth', *T.P.'s and Cassell's Weekly*, January 23rd, 1926.

People have asked me whom I meant by Sunday . . . I think you can take him to stand for Nature as distinguished from God. Huge, boisterous, full of vitality, dancing with a hundred legs, bright with the glare of the sun, and at first sight, somewhat regardless of us and our desires. There is a phrase used at the end, spoken by Sunday: 'Can ye drink from the cup that I drink of?' which seems to mean that Sunday is God. That is the only serious note in the book, the face of Sunday changes, you tear off the mask of Nature and you find God. (Introduction to Ralph Neale's and Mrs Cecil Chesterton's play 1929)

I have often been asked what I meant by the monstrous pantomime ogre who was called Sunday . . . some have suggested, and in one sense not untruly, that he was meant for a blasphemous version of the Creator. But the point is that the whole story is a nightmare of things . . . and the ogre who appears brutal but is also cryptically benevolent is not so much God, in the sense of religion or irreligion, but rather Nature as it appears to the pantheist . . .

(*Autobiography*, 1936)

*The Man Who Was Thursday* . . . was a very melodramatic sort of moonshine, but it had a kind of notion in it; and the point is that it described, first a band of the last champions of order fighting against what appeared to be a world of anarchy, and then the discovery that the mysterious master of both the order and the anarchy was the same sort of elemental elf who had appeared to be rather too like a pantomime ogre. This line of logic, or lunacy, led many to infer that this equivocal being was meant for a serious description of the Deity; and my work even enjoyed a temporary respect among those who like the Deity to be so described. But this error was entirely due to the fact that they had read the book but not read the title-page . . . the book was called *The Man Who Was Thursday: A Nightmare*. It was not intended to describe the real world as it was, or as I thought it was, even when my thoughts were considerably less settled than they are now.

(*Illustrated London News*, June 13, 1936).

Was Chesterton in the 1890s inclining to gnosticism or even to Manichaean beliefs? There could be a strong streak of either in Victorian religious thought, with Browning and Hopkins along with many others not escaping the tendency, and, although it is clear that Chesterton is ducking and bobbing and weaving and that he ends with a Chaucerian recantation, he never brought himself to say that Sunday was *not* God. Perhaps in later life he was no longer all that sure of what he had meant in the 1890s. Could Sunday have been an *un*serious description of the Deity? When challenged Sunday uses Christ's reply[21] to the request of the mother of the sons of Zebedee: 'Can ye drink of the cup I drink of?', but he also declares 'I am the peace of God.' Possibly Sunday is the God Chesterton found in the 1890s, far different from the One he worshipped at the time of his death. Perhaps Sunday is 'the laughter on the secret face of God', but, if so, that is very close to identifying him with that most flamboyant person of the Trinity, the Holy Ghost. Once that piece of the puzzle is in its place, the nightmare is over and Syme returns at dawn to Saffron Park after 'a very entertaining evening' to find himself again in the company of the poet Lucien Gregory, the one loose end in the tale. Gregory has been 'the real anarchist', the Accuser of the Book of Job, and indeed there is something of a whiff of brimstone about him. It is well to recall Chesterton's interest in William Blake's *Marriage of Heaven and Hell* where there is written: 'In the *Book of Job* Milton's Messiah is call'd Satan.' So exactly who is it taking Gabriel Syme home to breakfast?

The British Library copy of *The Ball and the Cross* was deposited with copyright claimed from 1906 in December 1909 at the time of the American publication three months before that in Britain, suggesting that the novel had been complete when serialisation was discontinued after Knollys Blogg was committed to Holloway Sanitorium. Possibly the latter part of the narrative set in Professor Lucifer's asylum was thought too sensitive until after Knollys' death in 1908. No further novel followed until 1912 when *Manalive* was reconstructed from remnants of stories from the 1890s such as *The Man With Two Legs* and *Homesick at Home*, though Eric Petersen and White Wynd had been dropped in favour of Innocent Smith; in many ways Smith is even more exasperating than his predecessors in reliving their adventures with the Great Wind, the Pistol, the Housebreaking and the alleged Bigamy. In the list of scenarios it is called 'Crimes of a Philanthropist':

> It is intended while containing some serious ideas to be somewhat brisker and more popular sensational reading than any other attempt except 'Queer Trades'. It describes the entrance of a character who impresses every one with his hilarity and magnanimity, who is to everyone's surprise convicted of an apparently infamous attempt at murder, and an investigation into whose life brings to light an extraordinary series of dubious and indefensible acts.[22]

Perhaps it deserved the accolade of 'a Good Bad Book' given it by John Wain, but it has long been popular as a cheerful romp, and in an odd way Innocent Smith's bigamy can be seen as a forerunner of themes taken up by Harold Pinter. At worst Chesterton does make his readers take a fresh view of the world around them:

> A wind sprang high in the west, like a wave of unreasonable happiness, and tore eastward across England, trailing with it the frosty scent of forests and the cold intoxication of the sea. In a million holes and corners it refreshed a man like a flagon and astonished him like a blow. In the inmost chambers of intricate and embowered houses it woke like a domestic explosion, littering the floor with some professor's papers till they seemed as precious as fugitive, or blowing out the candle by which a boy read *Treasure Island* and wrapping him in roaring dark. But everywhere it bore drama into undramatic lives, and carried the trump of crisis across the world. Many a harassed mother in a mean backyard had looked at five dwarfish shirts on the clothes-line as at some small, sick tragedy; it was as if she had hanged her five children. The wind came, and they were full and kicking as if five fat imps had sprung into them; and far down in her oppressed subconscious she half-remembered those coarse comedies of her fathers when the elves still dwelt in the homes of men. Many an unnoticed girl in a dank walled garden had tossed herself into the hammock with the same intolerant gesture with which she might have tossed herself into the Thames; and that wind rent the waving wall of woods and lifted the hammock like a balloon, and showed her shapes of quaint clouds far beyond, and pictures of bright villages far below, as if she rode heaven in a fairy boat. Many a dusty clerk or curate, plodding a telescopic road of poplars, thought for the hundredth time that they were like the plumes of a hearse; when this invisible energy caught and swung and clashed them round his head like a wreath or salutation of seraphic wings. There was in it something more inspired and authoritative even than the old wind of the proverb; for this was the good wind that blows nobody harm.[23]

## Parables for Social Reformers
The years preceding the Great War of 1914 to 1918 and culminating in his major illness in December 1914 were years in which Gilbert Chesterton saw political hopes based on the Liberal Party landslide of 1906 sadly disappointed; men he thought to be politicians of good will were shown to be little better than fools, charlatans, and mountebanks. The Marconi scandal of 1912 to 1913 and the libel case later brought against Cecil Chesterton are usually considered to be the blow that shattered the elder brother's illusions, but an examination of Gilbert Chesterton's novels of that period, and even of his dramatic works, reveals that he had long been aware of creeping corruption and had given clear and unequivocal warning that there were dangers to personal freedom, not only from those who wielded power, be it in Parliament, in the

press, in bureaucracy, in industry or commerce, but also from the growing number of people attracted by the ideas propounded by Chesterton himself, in fact from that group eventually to support the Distributist movement and party in the 1920s. The early date of GKC's awareness of a peril from within only becomes apparent when the true chronology of his later novels, none of which was begun later than 1913, is established. Suffice it to say that we accept that *The Return of Don Quixote* up to the end of the Dr Hendry and his Old Illumination Colours[24] theme predates *The Flying Inn*,[25] with the subsequent part of *The Return of Don Quixote*[26] being revised or completed in separate bursts of creativity in 1926 to 1927. In his usual fashion Chesterton was specific about what he was up to and when he was up to it, but in their usual fashion his readers and critics have tended to ignore what he said and to read into what he said what they wanted him to say.

Chesterton's disgust at the way public life was then developing and political power being wielded led to his being very pointed indeed when he came to tilt at targets in his novels. It should never be forgotten that he knew most of the people involved in the Liberal administrations of 1906 and 1911, often on social terms as in the cases of Charles Masterman and Prime Minister Asquith, who had even appeared in a film along with Chesterton, Shaw, and Barrie,[27] and as a journalist Chesterton had an entrée into all those press circles where daily gossip was exchanged. When in *The Return of Don Quixote* he describes a house party gathered to perform *Blondel the Troubadour* at Seawood Abbey, an ancient pile now owned by a government minister, Lord Seawood, and frequented by the Prime Minister and other politicians such as the ubiquitous but hapless Julian Archer, we would do well to give Chesterton credit for knowing the milieu he is writing about. However aimless the lives and attitudes of the guests and hosts at that house party may be, it is very certain that they belong to a leisured caste with time enough on its hands to provide the cast for the play which will later inspire the League of the Lion. One unexpected vacancy in the cast has been offered to Jack Braintree, a Trade Unionist, whose proposed participation causes what Chesterton calls (in his chapter heading[28]) 'A Hole in the Caste'. Braintree, who is leading a miners' strike on the principle of the miners owning the mine just as the painters of stage scenery own their own paintbrushes, is affronted when it is put to him by Douglas Murrel that he must take a part in the play because

'There really and truly aren't any other men at all.' Braintree still looked at him. 'There is a man in the next room,' he said, 'there is a man in the passage; there is a man in the garden; there is a man at the front door; there is a man in the stables; there is a man in the kitchen; there is a man in the cellar. What sort of palace of lies have you built for yourselves, when you see all these round you every day and do not even know that they are men? . . .' Murrel stepped back from his canvas . . .: 'I think his idea about the servants is first rate,' he observed placidly . . . 'Don't talk nonsense,' said Archer irritably, 'it's a small part, but he has to do all sorts of things. Why, he has to kiss the princess's hand.'[29]

In fact Chesterton uses both Braintree and Murrel as mouthpieces, while at the same time never hesitating to use his privileged position as narrator to intervene whenever necessary with a barbed comment. Nevertheless, Braintree seems to put over the social arguments and to win them, even to carry the day on literary and artistic matters in which he is inexpert although well read, but it is 'Monkey' Murrel who holds the moral centre ground:

He was a man of wide culture and had failed in all subjects. He had especially failed in politics; having once been called the future leader of his party, whichever it was. But he had failed at the supreme moment to seize the logical connection between the principle of taxing deer-forests and that of retaining an old pattern of rifle for the Indian Army: and the nephew of an Alsatian pawnbroker, to whose clear brain the connection was more apparent, had slipped into his place. Since then he had shown that taste for low company which has kept so many aristocrats out of mischief and their country out of peril, and shown it incongruously (as they sometimes do) by having something vaguely slangy and horsey about his very dress and appearance, as of an objectless ostler.[30]

It is this same objectless ostler who is tuned into mainstream humanity, an ironic *honnête homme* with a twisted smile, someone who can balance Olive Ashley's romantic idealism with rueful digs about leprosy and who, by taking Braintree out for an evening on the town, reveals that the latter is really more at home arguing in the drawing rooms of the rich than in the public bars with the poor. But whereas Murrel's ease, intimacy, and urbanity are in strong contrast to Archer's brashness and over-familiarity, he tends to complement Braintree's earnestness and social awareness; in fact, and taken together with Michael Herne and possibly even Dr Hendry, they represent another of Chesterton's multi-schizoid personalities in which the sum of the constituent parts has a health and vigour lacking in the individual personalities.[31] It is, of course, Murrel who, as *Meneur du jeu*, is instrumental in bringing Braintree, Herne, and Hendry into the action where their various talents can be deployed.

In Herne, Chesterton has created a visionary, a man touched by poetry, perhaps a simple soul;[32] a man who, for those very reasons is tainted by fanaticism and is in the nicest possible way quite mad:

The librarian was certainly of the sort that is remote from the daylight, and suited to be a shade among the shades of a great library . . . His face was lean and his lineaments long and straight; but his wan blue eyes were a shade wider apart than other men's; increasing the effect of having one eye off. . . . the eyes of the learned librarian, like the eyes of a fool, were in the ends of the earth . . . on Herne's face that expression of shrewdness that is the final proof of simplicity.[33]

Above all, Herne has all the virtues of a scholar allied to the sad disadvantage of being totally lacking in a sense of humour. This lack gives him a single-mindedness of purpose akin to that of Adam Wayne's as displayed in *The Napoleon of Notting Hill*, and so Herne can also take up medieval life and dress to the point of assuming the role of the lost leader and that of the king who has returned. It is significant that, when Herne is first induced to take an interest in the twelfth century, the house party with the exceptions of Murrel and Braintree have already donned their costumes for the play; all that is needed before Olive Ashley has control of her play taken from her, is that Braintree should return to his responsibilities in organising a strike, and Murrel be sent on his quest for the illumination colours. The one's red tie and the other's tweeds are links with reality, while Olive Ashley's wish that Herne really were King of England will prove to be a dream, or possibly a nightmare, come true. Oddly enough, Chesterton puts a warning into Herne's own mouth:

'I can't help thinking . . . that it might give rather an interesting scope . . . to act exactly that sort of high and yet hollow romance. I say hollow not as a condemnation, you understand, but as an approximate artistic description. In a sense its beauty is in its being hollow, like a golden shell or an exquisitely gilded mask. Nay, it boasts of being hollow, as the drum and the trumpet both boast of being hollow. For that sort of poetic pleasure was and is stretched over a void of night and negation. I can imagine it might be interesting for an actor to wear the mask of that masquerade. There is a kind of dance that expresses contempt for the body. You can see it running like a pattern through any number of Asiatic traceries and arabesques. That dance was the dance of the Albigensian troubadours; and it was a dance of death. For that spirit can scorn the body in either of two ways; mutilating it like a fakir or pampering it like a sultan; but never doing it honour. For to that mind the body of man, like the sun and moon and the whole material order, were a sort of snare set by an evil spirit. Man was trapped; he was caught, so to speak, in a net of stars. Surely it will be rather interesting for you to interpret that ironic pride and bitter hedonism, the high and wild cries, the horns and hooting of the old heathen revel, along with the underlying pessimism.'[34]

For a brief moment it is as if Herne the Hunter has appeared at the side of Michael Herne the librarian who voices all the heresies that were anathema to

Chesterton: the hollowness and emptiness of decadence, the void of solipsism, the sterility of the Cathars, the rejection of the physical in Eastern mysticism, proud hedonism, and most especially that underlying pessimism. All the dangers are adumbrated as the voice of sanity in the person of Murrel strides away 'into the labyrinth of commonplace and cockney towns; and his plain and pleasant and shrewd face was wrinkled with a laugh of irony.'[35] It is to be in his absence that corrupting forces will take Olive Ashley's vision and twist it into the superficially attractive League of the Lion.

Murrel leaves a world that is speeding back through time to the reign of Richard Coeur-de-Lion and enters the world of Selfridge's and 'the long line of Babylonian buildings that bore the title 'The Imperial Stores' in gold letters rather larger than the windows.'[36] He is in 1911 after the House of Lords has had its powers limited, after the passing of the Mentally Deficient Bill and the Health Insurance Bill, after Chesterton has written 'The Song of the Wheels' and 'The Silent People'[37]; and his misadventures in town are more immediately social and political against Selfridge's or the other department stores that have taken over the High Street, and against Dr Gambrel, the Prussian psychiatrist from Berlin,[38] and beyond him the Liberal administration. The delicious parody offered by Chesterton is in many ways disarming, but there can be little doubt that he intends to depict the diminution and even the grinding down of the individual:

He approached . . . 'The Imperial Stores' . . . deliberately; but it would have been rather difficult to approach anything else, for it occupied the whole of one side of the High Street and some part of the other. There were crowds of people inside trying to get out and crowds of people outside trying to get in, reinforced by more crowds of people not trying to get in, but standing and staring in at the windows without the least ambition to get anywhere.

At intervals in the crawling crush he came on big bland men who waved him on with beautifully curved motions of the hand; so that he felt a boiling impulse to hit these highly courteous bounders a furious blow on the head with his heavy walking-stick . . . Every now and then they came on the huge shaft or a well of a lift; and the congestion was slightly relieved by some people being swallowed up by the earth and others vanishing into the ceiling. Eventually he himself found he was one of those fated, like Æneas, to descend into the lower world . . .

Gripping his piece of paper firmly in his hand, he confronted the shop girl with the eye of a lion-tamer, and said: 'Have you got Hendry's Old Illumination Colours?' The young woman gazed at him for a few seconds; and there was on her face exactly the same expression as if he had spoken to her in Russian or Chinese . . . How should rapid narrative describe how Big Business dealt with the problem? How she said they had got illumination colours and produced water colours in a shilling box. How she then said they had not got illumination colours and implied there were no such things in the world; that they were a fevered dream of the customer's fancy. How she pressed pastels upon him, assuring him that they were just the same. How she said, in a disinterested manner, that certain brands of green and purple ink were being sold very much just now. How she asked abruptly if it was for children, and made a faint effort to pass him on to the Toy Department. How she finally relapsed into an acid agnosticism, even assuming a certain dignity, which had the curious effect of appearing to give her a cold in the head, and causing her to answer all further remarks by saying: 'Dote know, I'be sure.'[39]

It transpires that it was from this madhouse that Dr Hendry disappeared, dismissed by the affable manager, Mr Harker, for not living in, for lunching at the Spotted Dog, and, in a final fit of exasperation, for throwing the manager of the department through a great picture on an easel and belabouring him with a mahl-stick, after his illumination colours had been replaced by the Empire Illuminator as produced by a manufacturer of chemical dyes, which is a subsidiary of the mining industry in which Braintree is leading a strike. As luck has it, Murrel rediscovers Dr Hendry's tracks at the Spotted Dog and heads for a coastal town only to discover that he has exchanged one kind of nightmare world for yet another:

He came to the beginning of a much sharper descent, where the road suddenly shot downwards into the still whirlpool of the town. It looked rather like a still whirlpool and still more perhaps like a still earthquake. For the rows and rows of roofs rose and fell like waves upon a wildly unequal ground, the chimneys of one street being often close against the railings and pavement of another, and the whole gave an almost weird impression of the whole town turning over or being sucked into the sea in a sort of silent and eternal catastrophe. Rolling and sprawling as was the whole green landscape behind him, no casual rise and fall of turf or heath could possibly give that strange sense of almost dizzy movement that was given by the straight and prosaic streets thus tilted and toppling over each other . . . Murrel had almost a sense of nightmare in this combination of monochrome dullness with that wild sky-line . . . It seemed as if the whole town were writhing in death and he had come just in time to see it die. It was in this dark if fanciful mood that he looked up and saw the name of the street; and it was the name that had been given him as a clue to the man he sought.[40]

In this topsy-turvy town Murrel finds a hansom cab that will become his Rosinante, Dr Hendry and his daughter, and Dr Gambrel and the effects of the Mental Deficiency Bill, the latter providing the first of the giants against whom he must tilt with the help of his trusty steed. In short order Murrel acquires the hansom cab, loses his heart to Dr Hendry's daughter, finds that Dr Hendry is but mad nor' nor' west and misjudged because of his theory that the world has become colour-blind; just as it can no longer tell the difference between his illumination colours and the Empire Illuminator, it can no longer tell the difference between good and evil or between anything. As Dr Hendry says:

> 'Colouring is in its nature opaque. So many people confuse the fact that it is brilliant with some notion of its being transparent. I myself have always seen that the confusion arose through the parallel of stained glass. Both, of course, were typically medieval crafts, and Morris was very keen on both of them. But I remember how wild he used to be if anybody forgot that glass is transparent. "If anybody paints a single thing in a window that looks really solid," he used to say, "he ought to be made to sit on it." Now in this business the red has got to be red, but it's got to be solid; like a red apple or . . .'
> 'A red-hot poker,' murmured Murrel, 'I believe you really feel that to be solid.'[41]

This is of little account when faced with the power of Dr Gambrel under the Mental Deficiency Bill of 1913:

> Dr Gambrel had the power of the modern state, which is perhaps greater than that of any state, at least, so far as the departments over which it ranges are concerned. He had the power to invade this house and break up this family and do what he liked with this member of it . . .[42]

However, the requirements of the law defining the Commission for Lunacy demanded that at least two doctors, one a magistrate, should certify any lunatic, and Murrel, seizing his opportunity, locks Dr Gambrel in a waiting room:

> The official, finding himself trapped, had behaved as very full-blooded and confident people often behave when something happens to them which they never believe to be possible . . . The consequence was that while the official doctor gasped and snorted and swore in unintelligible manner, the certified lunatic stood with his head gracefully on one side, making a soft clucking noise in his throat to indicate sorrow over the downfall of the human mind.[43]

And so, 'Dr Hendry, once famous in the artistic world, walked out between the dark pillars of the porch that stood out against the sea; as free as the seagull that was swerving along the line of the cliff.'[44] And Chesterton for one reason or another slipped his manuscript into a drawer where it was to remain for nearly fifteen years.

We do not know who had commissioned the novel in serial form, but it seems obvious that Chesterton's severing of his long relationship with Cadbury's *Daily News*,[45] his disillusionment with the Liberal Party, together with the Marconi scandal,[46] must have had some effect on his decisions at that period of his life. There was certainly a hardening in his attitude as he condemned the mock-Tudor workers' estates at Port Sunlight[47] as little better than the gingerbread house in which Hansel and Gretel were imprisoned by a witch, slave compounds erected by a false sense of paternalism which merely restricted the workers' right to withdraw labour without losing their homes. He likewise viewed with jaundiced eye parallel developments at Bourneville by the Cadburys who, Quakers like so many chocolate manufacturers, had sponsored the Inebriate Bill and were to establish hostelries at Bourneville which were only permitted to sell milk and cocoa:

> Cocoa is a cad and coward,
> Cocoa is a vulgar beast.[48]

Chesterton was also to denounce the Guinness interests which also provided tied housing at their brewery in Dublin, but his attack has been cloaked by the very process of change of name to which he objected most vociferously, for the name *Guinness* had been ennobled as the Earl of Iveagh, and it is on that name that Chesterton launched his assault:

> The Druids waved their golden knives
> And danced around the Oak
> When they had sacrificed a man . . .
> But though they cut the throats of men
> They cut not down the tree,
> And from the blood the saplings sprang
> Of Oak-woods yet to be.
> But Ivywood, Lord Ivywood,
> He clings and crawls as ivy would [Iveagh would]
> About the sacred tree.[49]

In the preceding and ensuing narrative of both versions of *The Flying Inn*[50] it is made clear that Lord (Iveagh would) Ivywood has been prepared to sacrifice many a man, even though the cutting of throats may have been as often commercial or spiritual as literal.

This identification can be easily confirmed by the comparison of Ivywood House with Lord Iveagh's house on the borders of Suffolk and Norfolk at

Elveden where he entertained royalty and politicians of all hues. Elveden with its Italianate facades had been purchased in 1863 by Duleep Singh, Maharajah of Lahore, who gutted the interior to replace it with the complete reconstruction of a Mogul palace with all its elaborate plasterwork crafted by workmen specially brought from the East to undertake the task. Lord Iveagh subsequently purchased Elveden from his executors for £159,000.[51]

Within his poisonous palace, Lord Ivywood is invested by Chesterton with many of the best but also most of the worst characteristics of his class. At our peril do we neglect the influence of Cobbett on Chesterton, who had become all too aware of what Cobbett called 'The Thing,' a sort of old-boy network manipulated by all sides in politics to look after their own and ensure that the interests of the governing classes were always paramount. He does not represent Lord Ivywood as a crook or a charlatan; on the contrary he shows him to be honest, sincere, and fanatically civil, but nevertheless, so wrong that he is akin to a perfect gemstone riven by a flaw that is undetectable in normal circumstances, a flaw that consists of defending the totally indefensible with all the honesty, sincerity, and eloquence at his command:

> Lord Ivywood, the English Minister, was probably the handsomest man in England; save that he was almost colourless both in hair and complexion . . . It seemed a mere matter of the luck of lighting whether his hair looked dull silver or pale brown; and his splendid mask never changed in colour or expression. He was one of the last of the old Parliamentary orators; and yet he was probably a comparatively young man: he could make anything he had to mention blossom into verbal beauty: yet his face remained dead while his lips were alive.[52]

This is the man who is found in the company of Dr Gluck, the Prussian minister; Oman Pasha, the Turkish general; Mysisra Ammon, the prophet of militant Islam; and Dr Moses Meadowes, founder and proprietor of Peaceways;[53] ever and even willing to defend the forcible carrying-off of young women to harems:

> 'The Ithacan Ambassador asks that the girls taken to harems after the capture of Pylos be restored to their families. This cannot be granted . . . I will admit I am sufficiently old-fashioned to think any interference with the interior life of the family a precedent of no little peril. Nor will I be so illiberal as not to extend to the ancient customs of Islam what I would extend to the ancient customs of Christianity. A suggestion had been brought before us that we should enter into a renewed war or recrimination as to whether certain women have left their homes with or without their own consent. I can conceive no controversy more perilous to begin or more impossible to conclude. I will venture to say that I express all your thoughts when I say that, whatever wrongs may

have been wrought on either side, the homes, the marriages, the family arrangements of this great Ottoman Empire shall remain as they are today.'

Ready to further the economic interests of his dubious associates by the importation of coolie labour,[55] willing to burn vineyards and prohibit the sale of alcoholic beverages in public houses,[56] Ivywood will espouse any cause that is to his own advantage, and in pursuit of it will stoop to any form of meanness and dishonesty, because he cannot see that cause being anything other than noble. In fact, Ivywood is devoid of taste, judgment, and common sense, as becomes all too evident at the Futurist exhibition at the Tate Gallery, and particularly at the Vegetarian Congress:

(*Lord Ivywood enters, accompanied by a crowd of Vegetarians, who disperse themselves among the benches. Lord Ivywood detaches himself from the crowd in complete unconsciousness and going up to the platform takes the chair as if it were his ordinary place.*)

IVYWOOD.    Ladies and Gentlemen, I will not at this stage state what you all know: the great ideals of humanity and intellectual purity to which this Congress is devoted, as I am merely presiding at its preliminary ceremonies and shall have to address you later . . . I am pleased to announce the first item on the programme will be a song by the Duchess of Battle-axe. I understand it is entitled, 'Whorls'.

DUCHESS.    Well this is only a little trifle written for me by my dear friend Binns, of the Earthquake School, you know. It was really much more rugged and stark when he wrote it; but I persuaded him to make the lines a little bit more the same length, so that it could be sung. (*Sings*)

Is our ugliness utterly, utterly lovely,
Can we hair-split our hells?
Is it worse to grow sick of green noises
Or be torn by triangular smells,
To be deafened by daylight
Or throttled with bells?

Is toothache as truly a purple
As Tuesday is pink?
Can we choose between dung and dried hair?
—Can we think? Can we think? Can we think?
Is it worse, the weak whisper of thunder,
Or the snigger of ink?

(*Decorous applause . . . Lord Ivywood rises, in the same automatic manner and speaks in the same level voice.*)

# HISTORY OF THE HUSBANDS OF RHODA.

These suitors rolled upon the sand.
Asking for Rhoda's heart & hand

(1) Professor Piff, whose "Tuscan Rome"
Is loved in every English home
Bits from his "British Trace in Gaul"
Bring down the house at the music hall.

(2) Roy Beauchamp, you observe to follow
A god, an artist, an Apollo —
What little cash, I am aware,
He had to spare, he did not spare.

(3). Sbolsky: an Anarchist, still alive:
Politically known as "5."
He blew up thousands, it was said.
Married & was blown up instead.

(4). Through Major Bumper's pleasant oaths
Moustaches, and delightful clothes
He was M.P. for Gallowglass.
To represent the working class ——

(5) Giles Rosethorn was an actor free
Who with romantic mystery.
Buttoned that cape about his throat
Because he had not got a coat.

(6.) And Mummer! Music he in sum!
He played the fiddle, fife and drum
He played the fool, when all was spent,
It was his favourite instrument.

(7.) Good Captain Cubby then began,
A fine old country gentleman,
With him our Rhoda lived at ease
Perpetually shelling peas. —

(8) Then came the Rev. Ehud Boe
("The Battle-Blast of Pimlico")
He turned a Mormon later on
And married ten. But One had gone.

(9.) Living with Philip William Trevor
One had no sentiments whatever.

(10.) Swarra Nagilos naphey after worldly
Which, let me tell you, rhymes to "boots"
His ways were somewhat savage: he
Ate his papa .... but reverently.

(11) Of COLONEL BROWN. —
the writer begs
To utter nothing but the legs.

6. History of the Husbands of Rhoda, c1898–9.

7. Mr Winston Churchill inspecting Sea-planes.

8. The Mystery of the Boots.

9. The Sitwells arrive bearing manuscripts.

## THE CHINESE PIRATE

Quong, who (unlike your father's friend)
 Was *not* a Buddhist monk,
A Chinese Pirate spoiled the ships
 And filled his Junk with junk.

But when they came to Sheila's home
 Those wild marauding three
They felt her softening touch and grew
 Quite as polite as she.

Red Bison climbed to Sheila's house
 As goats that scale an Alp:
But though he much admired her hair,
 He did not take her scalp.

The Dago murdered nobody
 For days and days: and Quong
Found out, with tears, that he belonged
 To Mr. Matier's Tong.

The Dog that up the Ladder goes
 He learned how to descry
With patient pleasure, and without
 One thought of Puppy-Pie.

"For O," they cried, "We come in peace
 Who walk the sunset strand
Far from that bleak but boiling sea
 That breaks on Eastern land,

"That swings and sways with dizzy tides
 Since first the ocean drank
Atlantis to the dregs: and left
 A whirlpool where she sank

"Of storms, Armadas, Vikings, Tars,
 That make its tides terrific:
But Sheila need not shrink from us:
 For we are all Pacific.

(1931)

10. The Chinese Pirate.

11. The Wait Who Would Not Wait.

12. Three Acres and a Cow.

IVYWOOD. The beautiful lyric to which we have just listened forms, as I feel sure you will agree, a fitting prelude to the more severe intellectual pleasures of the evening. It is a great gratification to me on this occasion to welcome to the Vegetarian Congress one of the most remarkable intellectual reformers of modern times. The great religion of Islam, which our guest represents, has not indeed in its beginnings laid any veto upon meat, though it foresaw the future course of the path of progress in laying a definite veto upon pork. Where the world owes it most, we must all agree is in the fact of having laid a veto upon wine. (*Loud Applause, especially from those who have already had dinner.*)[57]

Lord Ivywood is in all this a composite figure representing everything Chesterton thought wrong in political life and had pilloried in *Time's Abstract and Brief Chronicle*[58] as far back as 1905 and was continuing to do in his political writing in *What's Wrong with the World?*,[59] work in which he was supported by Hilaire Belloc's *The Servile State* (1912).[60] Even though there is a great deal of fun to be had from Lord Ivywood 'pulling down beershops right and left'[61] and being frustrated by an Irish adventurer, an English Tory of the old school, and a donkey and cart together with an inn sign, a keg of rum, and a Cheddar cheese, Chesterton's intent is always serious. Ivywood personifies that type of intellectual, as often as not a clergyman, whose latitudinarianism goes so far as to look for a full unity between Christianity and Islam, or 'something called Chrislam', as Captain Patrick Dalroy puts it, with 'some sort of double emblem, you know, combining cross and crescent – and called the Croscent'.[62] It is such a hybrid and hypocritical creed that destroys The Saracen's Head and makes Dalroy and Humphrey Pump take to the roads. Their flight and semi-guerrilla campaign waged when The Old Ship becomes The Flying Inn is against a personality who 'stood for hours on the lawn, watching the smashing of bottles and the breaking up of casks, and feeding on fanatical pleasure: the pleasure which his strange, cold, courageous nature could not get from food or wine or woman'.[63] There is a touch of icy rage in Chesterton's unusually explicit descriptions of Ivywood's pleasure taking, a note that occurs elsewhere only when he wishes to castigate an idea he finds twisted to its roots:

The song of the fury of Fragolette is a florid song and a torrid song,
The Song of the sorrow of Tara is sung to a harp unstrung,
The Song of the cheerful Shropshire Lad I consider a perfectly horrid song,
And the song of the happy Futurist is a song that can't be sung . . .
But the song of Beauty and Art and Love
Is simply an utterly stinking song,
To double you up and drag you down
And damn your soul alive.[64]

Celtic Twilight, Futurism, Decadence, Aestheticism join Vegetarianism and Total Abstinence as movements that are suspect, for it is on them that Lord Ivywood and his ilk feed. Once started, Ivywood advances all too languidly to the Higher Polygamy with its consequent downgrading of women to mere playthings in a harem, to prohibition for the poor but not for the rich, the undermining of established religion, and the sellout to foreign interests by those entrusted with the defence of the realm. All this manipulated through an uncaring Parliament which receives its own share of condemnation from Dorian Wimpole in the smoking room of the Palace of Westminster:

> 'Take care Englishmen don't sit in judgment on you as they do on many another corpse at an inquest – at a common public-house! Take care that the one tavern that is really neglected and shut up and passed like a house of pestilence, is not the tavern in which I drink to-night; and that merely because it is the worst tavern on the king's highway. Take care this place where we sit does not get a name like any pub where sailors are hocussed or girls debauched.'[65]

Within the context of *The Flying Inn* this is to no avail:

> Philip Ivywood raised himself on his crutch . . . Then he and his crutch trailed out of the long room . . . He also left behind an unlighted cigarette and his honour and all the England of his fathers – everything that could really distinguish that high house beside the river from any tavern for the hocussing of sailors . . . And from that hour forth he was the naked fanatic; and could feed on nothing but the future.[66]

Lord Ivywood will go on to face defeat and to achieve a madness more peaceful than his megalomania, but his *alter egos* in real life have not always been so easily defeated.

Chesterton was never to commence another full-length novel; a combination of factors including serious illness,[67] the assumption of the editorial chair of the *New Witness*,[68] his conversion to Catholicism,[69] and the launching and editing of *G.K.'s Weekly*[70] were to see to that. Shorter works such as the stories collected in *The Man Who Knew Too Much*[71] reveal disillusionment with the political scene, but one would have then expected the 1920s, which brought the great flowering of the Distributist League, to have brought an upsurge of hope. This proved not to be the case, for, when seeking a suitable serial for *G.K.'s Weekly*, Chesterton rifled the drawers and took out *The Return of Don Quixote*, and began the rewriting or completion with a hardening of attitudes, as becomes apparent when we contrast his description of Dr Gambrel:

This was Dr Gambrel, who spoke perfectly good English, but never lost a faint air of being foreign; which, among his poorer patients, was perhaps merely due to his being fussy, not to say impatient and irritable.[72]

After the passage of years this was changed in 1925:

This was Dr Gambrel, who spoke perfectly good English, but stumbled on the steep stairs and swore softly in some other speech.[73]

After this point, unfortunately, we have no standard of comparison, but the development of the story suggests that Seawood Abbey and its inhabitants are now firmly planted in 1926, or perhaps in the twelfth century, for Michael Herne has taken his decision to adopt medieval dress and lifestyle:

'The old society was truthful and . . . you are in a tangle of lies', answered Herne. 'I don't mean that it was perfect or painless. I mean that it called pain and imperfection by their names. You talk about despots and vassals and all the rest; well, you also have coercion and inequality; but you dare not call anything by its own Christian name. You defend every single thing by saying it is something else. You have a King and then explain that he is not allowed to be a King. You have a House of Lords and say it is the same as a House of Commons. When you do want to flatter a workman or a peasant you say he is a true gentleman; which is like saying he is a veritable viscount. When you want to flatter the gentleman you say he does not use his own title. You leave a millionaire his millions and then praise him because he is "simple" – otherwise mean and not magnificent; as if there were any good in gold except to glitter! You excuse priests by saying they are not priestly and assure us eagerly that clergymen can play cricket. You have teachers who refuse doctrine, which only means teaching; and doctors of divinity disavowing anything divine. It is all false and cowardly and shamefully full of shame. Everything is prolonging its existence by denying that it exists.'

'What you say may be true of such things or some of them', answered Braintree. 'But I do not want to prolong their existence at all. And if it comes to cursing and prophesying, by God, you will see some of them dead before you die.'

'Perhaps', said Herne looking at him with his large pale eyes, 'you may see them die and then live; which is a very different thing from existing. I am not sure that the King may not be a King once more.'

The Syndicalist seemed to see something in the staring eyes of the librarian that changed and almost chilled his mood.[74]

Braintree may oppose the heart of a man to the League of the Lion, but in Olive Ashley's words: 'The madness is infectious. The infection is spreading. None of you can get out . . . of my poor little play'.[75] Unfortunately, there are those who are trying to get into the act in the persons of Lord Seawood and his Prime Minister, Lord Eden,[76] who is eager to seize an opportunity:

> 'Wasn't I actually saying that we must have something new because the poor old Empire has gone stale? Wasn't I saying we wanted a new positive thing to back up against Braintree and the New Democracy? Well, then . . . It's got to be backed up with horse, foot, and artillery; or what's a damn sight more important, pounds, shillings, and pence. It's got to be backed up as we never backed anything in our lives.'
>
>     . . . And stepping across the threshold he strode across the garden . . . [and] the Prime Minister's voice in the distance lifted like a trumpet, like the voice of the great orators of fifty years ago.
>
>     Thus did the librarian who refused to change his clothes contrive to change his country.[77]

Flawed from its inception, the revolution takes place; Michael Herne is elected King-at-Arms and 'sat on his high throne above all the coloured crowd, and his eyes seemed to inhabit the horizons and the high places. So have many fanatics ridden high on clouds over scenes as preposterous; so Robespierre walked in his blue coat at the Feast of the Supreme Being.'[78] The feeling is infectious, indeed, for Olive Ashley speculates:

> 'On an evening like this . . . can't you imagine the culmination coming, and our seeing some knight of the Round Table pricking along the road, ever so far away, bringing us a message from the King'
>
>     '. . . there really is somebody coming along [said Rosamund Severne]; and I believe he's on a horse, too.'
>
>     The knight-errant from King Arthur's Court certainly was a very queer shape; for as the equipage came nearer and nearer, it took on to the amazed eyes of the medieval crowd the appearance of a dilapidated hansom cab, surmounted by a cabman in a dilapidated top-hat. He removed his battered headgear with a polite salutation and revealed the unpretentious features of Douglas Murrel . . .
>
>     '. . . I say, Olive, is your play *still* going on? . . .'
>
>     'It isn't a play', she answered, staring at him in a stony fashion. 'It began as a play; but we aren't playing any longer.'
>
>     'Sorry to hear that', he said.[79]

Murrel has returned out of time and out of sympathy with The Movement, as it is now known. His collar and tie and trousers no longer fit in and, as Archer says: 'Odd thing is he can't *see* he's out of it. Always so difficult to manage fellows who can't *see* when they're out of it.'[80] And yet Murrel has brought along with the illumination colours a beam of sanity that touches Herne enough for him to reward the man who 'has avenged one wrong upon at least one ruffian and saved a woman in distress.'[81] Unfortunately, that beam of sanity is not strong enough to contain the extremes of medieval theory which have strange overtones of extreme Distributist thinking, and so Herne declares:

'Let us tell John Braintree to his teeth that we have had enough of science, enough of enlightenment, enough of education, enough of all his social order with its mantrap of machinery and its death-ray of knowledge. Take this message to John Braintree; all things come to an end and these things are ended.'[82]

And in 1926 many a Distributist would have thought that the General Strike[83] should be brought to an end just as John Braintree's Great Strike was due to be, despite the latter's bravado in the last episode to be serialised in *G.K.'s Weekly*.[84]

'For nearly a hundred years', he said, 'they have thundered at us about our duty to respect the Constitution: the King and the House of Lords – and even the House of Commons. We had to respect that too . . . We were to be the perfect Constitutionalists. Yes, my friends, we were to be the only Constitutionalists. We were the quiet people, the loyal subjects, the people who took the King and the lords seriously. But they were to be free enough. Whenever the fancy took them to upset the Constitution, they were to be indulged in all the pleasures of revolution. They could in twenty-four hours turn the Government of England upside down; and tell us that we were all to be ruled not by a constitutional monarchy but by a fancy dress ball . . . We would not submit to lawful Toryism. We will not now submit to lawless Toryism. And if this Wardour Street curiosity shop sends us a message that we must attend its court – our answer is in four words "We will not come." '[85]

Of course, Braintree is arraigned and, rather like Charles I, compelled to come to his trial, and there is a final confrontation between King-at-Arms and Trade Unionist. There can be little doubt of Chesterton's own intentions in his text:

The triumph of the lunatic, otherwise the librarian, is crowned by his betrothal to the great lady [Rosamund Severne] and his enthronement as a Dictator, in the Mussolini manner, to settle the Strike. He retires to refer it to all the mysteries of medieval law; and comes out to the cheers of the partisans of law and order; he is himself quite shocked and shaken; and he decides against them. He lays down the theory of the Guild which justifies Braintree and the theory of Forestalling which condemns the whole world which supports him and especially the father of his betrothed. Even he is not such a lunatic as not to know that he has broken his own life and leadership; the whole of that world deserts him . . .[86]

This is made more explicit in the words given to Murrel:

> 'I should say that the one place where we have never wanted a strong man is England. I can only remember one person who went into the profession, poor old Cromwell; and the consequence was that we dug him up to hang him after he was dead and went mad with joy for a month because the throne was going back to a weak man – or one we thought was a weak man. These high-handed ways don't suit us a bit, either revolutionary or reactionary . . . we are not democratic enough to have a dictator. Our people like to be ruled by gentlemen, in a general sort of way. But nobody could stand being ruled by one gentleman. The idea is too horrible . . . When you see Braintree condemned . . . you won't understand how much is being condemned with him . . .'
>
> 'Are you a Socialist?' inquired his friend, staring at him in a puzzled fashion.
>
> 'I am the last Liberal', said Monkey. 'Partial friends have described me as a Grand Old Man.'[87]

Herne's decision does go for Braintree and against Lord Eden, the industrialists and the League of the Lion, and there is little else for him to do except to depart in the hansom cab with Murrel accompanying him as his Sancho Panza. Yet Chesterton must still make a matter of precedence quite clear:

> 'Don't you see?' he [Herne] cried, '. . . All your machinery has become so unhuman that it has become natural. In becoming a second nature, it has become as remote and indifferent and cruel as nature . . . You have made your dead system on so large a scale that you do not yourselves know how or where it will hit. That's the paradox! Things have grown incalculable by being calculated. You have tied men to tools so gigantic that they do not know on whom the strokes descend. You have justified the nightmare of Don Quixote. The mills really *are* giants.'
>
> 'Is there any method in that case?' demanded the other.
>
> 'Yes; and you found it,' replied Herne. 'You did not bother about systems, when you saw a mad doctor was madder than the madman. It is you who lead and I who follow. You are not Sancho Panza. You are the other . . . You are the knight that has returned.'[88]

Murrel is, of course, the voice of sanity and individualism, always ready to fight abuse, and 'this parable for social reformers, . . . planned and partly written long ago . . . was [and perhaps still is] a quiet unintentional prophecy.'[89] The canker is within, and we are our own worst enemies, but the answer is not to dress up and posture.

# THE PLAYWRIGHT

O ne of the most puzzling aspects of the long friendship and rivalry between George Bernard Shaw and Chesterton was Shaw's insistence over some thirty years that Chesterton was admirably and pre-eminently fitted to be a playwright:

> Circumstances led to my seeing *Magic* performed several times, and I enjoyed it more and more every time. Mr Chesterton was born with not only brains enough to see something more in the world than sexual intrigue, but with all the essential tricks of the stage at his fingers' ends, and it was delightful to find that the characters which seem so fantastic and rag dolly (stage characters are usually wax dolly) in his romances become credible and solid behind the footlights . . . Mr Chesterton is in the English tradition of Shakespear [sic] and Fielding and Scott and Dickens, in which you but grip your character so masterfully that you can play with it in the most extravagant fashion . . . The Duke in *Magic* is much better than Micawber or Mrs Wilfer, neither of whom can bear the footlights because, like piping bullfinches, they have only one tune, whilst the Duke sets everything in the universe to his ridiculous music. That is the Shakespearean touch. Is it grateful to ask for more?[1]

Chesterton's writing technique was always essentially dramatic and based on the interplay of ideas expressed through dialogue and confrontation; however, biographer and critic alike have tended to largely ignore Chesterton's work for the stage even in the face of Shaw's continuing admiration for his friend's work: 'There is, of course, a born genius for dialogue which needs no training. Moliere, Goldsmith, Chesterton, Lady Gregory are the first highly literary names that occur to me.'[2] The sincerity of his tribute was genuine enough, for Shaw had decided very early in their friendship that Chesterton was squandering his talents in not writing for the stage. However, it has always been presumed that Shaw spent several years goading Chesterton into dramatic activity before he saw the first fruit of his efforts in *Magic*, and then continued his encouragement with renewed zest for another seventeen years before *The Judgement of Dr Johnson* appeared. One might be forgiven for wondering why Shaw was prepared to waste time on such a fruitless campaign, but, if in the light of his perseverance and the continuing friendly exchange of ideas between the two men, one takes another look at the known facts, another picture emerges.

Maisie Ward[3] states that quite early in their friendship Shaw proposed that Chesterton write a play. No date was given, as the beginnings of that friendship remain vague; even the memories of the two parties were never reliable enough to establish the when and where with any certainty, and it is usual to cite Shaw's comments on 'A Generous Opponent' made in 1937 (after Chesterton's death and thirty-six years after the event): 'I cannot remember when I first met Chesterton. I was so much struck by a review of Scott's *Ivanhoe* which he wrote for the *Daily News* in the course of his earliest notable job as a feuilletonist to that paper that I wrote to him asking who he was and where he came from, as he was evidently a new star in literature. He was either too shy or too lazy to answer. The next thing I remember is his lunching with us on quite intimate terms accompanied by Belloc.[4] Chesterton's 'The Position of Sir Walter Scott' appeared on August 10th, 1901, but it is possible that they had met at the Moderns in Hampstead or the Pharos Club in Covent Garden where both were members; in the case of the latter, Shaw's connection was strong enough for him to arrange for the first copyright performance of *The Admiral Bashville* to be held there on December 14th, 1902. There are also accounts of Shaw heckling Chesterton when he addressed the Arts and Crafts Group in 1902, enquiring whether he believed in the miracle of St. Januarius's blood liquefying twice a year in Naples.

There were reports of Chesterton writing a play in 1903; one in a good position to be sure of his information was Charles Masterman who in the February issue of *The Bookman* noted that Chesterton 'has at present on hand a play bearing the attractive title of *The Devil among the Cattle*.' However, no play appeared, as also happened with the plays for George Alexander and Harvey Granville Barker mentioned in Frances' diary.[5] What Shaw is almost certain to have read was *Time's Abstract and Brief Chronicle* (published in *The Fortnightly Review* in five parts between October 1904 and 1905)[6], a mature work postdating *The Napoleon of Notting Hill* in which there was a mastery of dialogue which fully explained Shaw's enthusiasm. It took the form of an ongoing debate about contemporary affairs delivered through the mouths of three politicians of widely different views: Patrick Desmond, Irish Nationalist M.P. for N.W. Kilkenny, Colonel Harry Bartram, Tory M.P. for Wimbledon Common, and Dr Paul, leader of the Dacotah [sic] Labour Party. Appearing more or less monthly, it was a political commentary in a modern idiom and with a good deal of bite, a debate in which no one party won all the arguments. No holds were barred, no topic excluded and no persons sacred as Chesterton emerged as a political thinker of the first order, as his own man and nobody's stooge. It was this man whom Shaw thought was letting his great talents go to waste in Battersea: 'A hybrid Superman, and Grand Transmogrifier of ideas, a great force in danger of being wasted.'[7] This was followed up by the first of a series of personal letters:

> Ayot St. Lawrence, Welwyn, Herts.
> 1st March 1908
>
> My Dear G.K.C.,
> What about that play? It is no good trying to answer me in *The New Age*: the real answer . . . is the play. I have tried fair means: *The New Age* article was the inauguration of an assault below the belt. I shall deliberately destroy your credit as an essayist, as a journalist, as a critic, as a Liberal, as everything that offers your laziness a refuge, until starvation and shame drive you to serious dramatic parturition. I shall repeat my public challenge to you; vaunt my superiority; insult your corpulence; torture Belloc; if necessary, call on you and steal your wife's affections by intellectual and athletic displays, until you contribute something to the British drama . . . Nothing can save you now except a rebirth as a dramatist. I have done my turn; and I now call on you to take yours and do a man's work.[8]

Chesterton was preoccupied by Knollys Blogg's mental breakdown and subsequent suicide, but once the Chestertons had made their move to Beaconsfield, Shaw returned to the attack:

> 10 Adelphi Terrace, W.C.
> 30th October 1909
>
> CHESTERTON. SHAW SPEAKS. ATTENTION!
> . . . I still think that you could write a useful sort of play if you were started. When I was in Kerry last month I had occasionally a few moments to spare; and it seemed to me quite unendurable that you should be wasting your time writing books about me . . . Now to business. When one breathes Irish air, one becomes a practical man. In England I used to say what a pity it was you did not write a play. In Ireland I sat down and began

writing a scenario for you. But before I could finish it I had to come back to London; and now it is all up with the scenario: in England I can do nothing but talk. I therefore now send you the thing as far as I scribbled it; and I leave you to invent what escapades you please for the hero, and to devise some sensational means of getting him back to heaven again, unless you prefer to end with the millennium in full swing.[9]

Chesterton still did not take up the gauntlet, but none the less Shaw persevered, although he now redirected his attack via Chesterton's wife:

> 10 Adelphi Terrace, W.C.
> 5th April 1912
>
> Dear Mrs Chesterton,
>     I have promised to drive somebody to Beaconsfield on Sunday morning; and I shall be in that district more or less for the rest of the day. If you are spending Easter at Overrroads, and have no visitors who couldn't stand us, we should like to call on you at any time that would be convenient.
>     The convenience of time depends on a design of my own which I wish to impart to you first. I want to read a play to Gilbert. It began by way of being a music-hall sketch; so it is not 3½ hours long as usual: I can get through it in an hour and a half. I want to insult and taunt and stimulate Gilbert with it. It is the sort of thing he could write and ought to write: a religious harlequinade [*Androcles and the Lion*]. In fact, he could do it better if a sufficient number of pins were stuck into him. My proposal is that I read the play to him on Sunday (or at the next convenient date), and that you fall into transports of admiration of it; declare that you can never love a man who cannot write things like that; and definitely announce that if Gilbert has not finished a worthy successor to it before the end of the third week next ensuing, you will go out like the lady in A Doll's House, and live your own life – whatever that dark threat may mean . . .
>     Forgive this long rigmarole: it is only to put you in possession of what *may* happen if you approve, and your invitations and domestic circumstances are propitious.
>                                                   Yours sincerely, G. Bernard Shaw[10]

Shaw's efforts were at last rewarded when, eighteen months later on November 7th, 1913, *Magic* was produced in London at the Little Theatre following a preview on November 3rd at the Devonshire Park Theatre in Eastbourne. The play was well received and was to run for 165 performances. Shaw admired it, and then contributed a curtain-raiser, *The Music Cure*, which ran in pair with *Magic* after its hundredth performance.

Chesterton took every opportunity to ride his familiar hobbyhorses, but his sorties against prohibition, vegetarianism, mental deficiency in the aristocracy, unbelieving clergymen, scientific agnosticism, and perhaps mild guying of the Celtic twilight associated with Yeats and Lady Gregory, are all subordinated to the main theme dealing with the very real existence of evil. It should never be forgotten that at one time Chesterton worked for a publisher of spiritualist tracts and himself had dabbled in spiritualism; in his *Autobiography* he states: 'I saw quite enough of the thing to . . . testify, with complete certainty, that something happens which is not in the ordinary sense natural, or produced by the normal and conscious human will. Whether it is produced by some subconscious but still human force, or by some powers, good, bad or indifferent, which are external to humanity, I would not myself attempt to decide. The only thing I will say with complete confidence, about that mystic and invisible power, is that it tells lies.' It is against such a background and against Chesterton's wide knowledge of the opinion of Yeats, Crowley and others that *Magic* must be interpreted. In his play he takes his thinking on good and evil a little further than he did in *Orthodoxy* by arguing the case for an unfashionable belief in the power of evil. In fact, he argues the case for any kind of belief, as, with the exception of Patricia and the Conjurer, nobody in the play believes in anything; the Doctor is a sceptic, Morris is hysterically so, the Vicar may have a belief in social service but none in religion, and the Duke never expresses an opinion either way about anything. The comment is a wry one, for, although Morris and the Doctor will not believe the truth, they are all too willing to believe a lie provided it enables them to preserve preconceptions and prejudices undamaged. Chesterton presumes that his audience, like Morris Carleon, does not believe that a magician can use real magic; it is suggested that magic as opposed to trickery is used three times as the picture dances on the wall, the chair falls over, and the lamp changes in colour from red to blue and back again. No audience does believe that, even though they may suspend their disbelief for the course of the play; if they did begin to suspect that supernatural powers are at work in the world, then they would find, like Morris, that doubt can be a madness. And so the audience also implicitly accepts the lie; and Chesterton has said that it is a mystic and invisible power that tells lies.

Among those to praise Chesterton's play were Frank Harris and George Moore, who wrote to Foster Bovill:

24th November 1913

I followed the comedy of *Magic* from the first line to the last with interest and appreciation, and I am not exaggerating when I say that I think of all modern plays I like it the best. Mr Chesterton wished to express an idea and his construction and dialogue are the best that he could have chosen for the expression of that idea: therefore, I look upon the play as practically perfect. The prologue seems unnecessary, likewise the magician's love for the young lady. That she should love the magician is well enough, but it materialises him a little too much if he returns that love. I would have preferred her to love him more and he to love her less. But this spot, if it be a spot, is a very small one on a spotless surface of excellence.[11]

Chesterton even contributed a criticism of his own play to a symposium, 'Notes on Recent Books by Their Writers' in the *Dublin Review* in January 1914:

The author of *Magic* ought to be told plainly that his play, like most other efforts of that person, has been treated with far too much indulgence in the public press. I will glide mercifully over the most glaring errors, which the critics have overlooked – that no Irishman could become so complete a cad merely by going to America – that no young lady would walk about in the rain so soon before it was necessary to dress for dinner – that no young man, however American, could run round a Duke's grounds in the time between one bad epigram and another – that Dukes never allow the middle classes to encroach on their gardens so as to permit a doctor's lamp to be seen there – that no sister, however eccentric, could conduct a slightly frivolous love-scene with a brother going mad in the next room – that the secretary disappears half way through the play without explaining himself; and the conjurer disappears at the end, with almost equal dignity. Such are the candid criticisms I should address to Mr G.K. Chesterton, were he my friend. But as I have always found him my worst enemy, I will confine myself to the criticism which seems to me most fundamental and final.

Of course I shall not differ from any of the dramatic critics; I am bursting with pride to think that I am (for the first time) a dramatic critic myself. Besides, I never argue except when I am right. It is rather a curious coincidence that in every controversy in which I have been hitherto, I have always been entirely right. But if I pretended for one moment that *Magic* was not a pretty badly written play, I should be entirely wrong. I may be allowed to point out the secret of its badness. By the exercise of that knowledge of all human hearts which descends on any man (however unworthy) the moment he is a dramatic critic, I perceive that the author of *Magic* originally wrote it as a short story. It is a bad play, because it was a good short story. In a short story or mystery, as in a Sherlock Holmes story, the author and the hero (or villain) keep the reader out of the secret. Conan Doyle and Sherlock Holmes knew all about it; and everybody else feels as silly as Watson. But the drama is built upon that grander secrecy which was called Greek irony. In the drama, the audience must know the truth when the actors do not know it. That is where the drama is truly democratic: not because the audience shouts, but because it knows – and is silent. Now I do seriously think it is a weakness in a play like *Magic* that the audience is into the central secret from the start. Mr G.S. Street put the point with his unerring simplicity by saying he could not help feeling disappointed with the conjurer because he had hoped that he would turn into the Devil. If anyone knows any real answer to this genuine and germane criticism, I will see that it is conveyed to the author.

At the time it must have seemed that Shaw had at last aroused Chesterton's interest in the theatre; yet there was considerably irony in the situation, for he had been preaching to a man who had an obsession with theatre. Almost all Chesterton's work had been cast in a dramatic form and his father, an enthusiast for the toy-theatre had passed it on in an even more intense form:

> I will not say positively that a toy-theatre is the best of theatres; though I have had more fun out of it than out of any other . . . Now the first rule may seem rather contradictory; but it is quite true and really quite simple. In a small theatre, because it is a small theatre, you cannot deal with small things. Because it is a small theatre it can only deal with large things. You can introduce a dragon; but you cannot really introduce an earwig; it is too small for a small theatre. And this is true not only of small creatures, but of small actions, small gestures and small details of any kind . . . All your effects must be made to depend on things like scenery and background. The sky and the clouds and the castles and the mountains and so on must be exciting things; along with other things that move all of a piece such as regiments and processions; great and glorious things can be done with processions . . . In a real comedy the whole excitement may consist in the nervous curate dropping his tea-cup; though I do not recommend the incident for the drama of the drawing-room. But if he were nervous, let us say, about a thunderstorm, the toy-theatre could hardly represent the nervousness, but it might mange the thunderstorm. It might be quite sensational and yet entirely simple; it would largely consist of darkening the stage and making horrible noises behind the scenes . . . The second and smaller rule, that really follows from this, is that everything dramatic should depend not on a character's action, but simply on his appearance. Shakespeare said of actors that they have their exits and their entrances; but these actors ought really to have nothing else except exits and entrances. The trick is to so arrange the tale that the mere appearance of a person tells the important truth about him. Thus, supposing the drama to be about St. George, let us say, the mere abrupt appearance of the dragon's head (if of a proper ferocity) will be enough to explain that he intends to eat people; and it will not be necessary for the dragon to explain at length, with animated gestures and playful conversation, that his nature is carnivorous and that he has not just dropped in to tea.[12]

These rules for the toy-theatre were not entirely abandoned when Chesterton wrote for the larger stage, and it might well be argued that they played an important role in all his work. Now pleased with the success of *Magic* and in close contact with Shaw in the theatre, he began work on a musical play, *The Flying Inn*[13]; poems published in *The New Witness* and in the novel version of *The Flying Inn* appear as lyrics in the typescript of this musical. Unfortunately, Chesterton was taken ill in November 1914 and was largely incapacitated until May 1915 by when the First World War was well under way; no doubt the wartime atmosphere was unfavourable to a musical play pillorying a conspiracy against the British people by their ruling classes in alliance with the Turk (at that time an enemy power), and so the play was laid aside[14] . Both the novel and the play deal with topics very alive in the early years of the twentieth century but now no longer political or philosophical issues. Chesterton was writing when there was a very definite possibility of prohibition being introduced in Britain, as it was indeed introduced into the United States, and when the influence of eastern thought and mysticism was gaining ground. It is now difficult to comprehend the influence of mental attitudes of Empire, of an Anglo-Japanese alliance, and of the ever-present threat in Europe of a Turkey that then ranked as a world power. Above all, the social divide between nobility and working class, landlord and tenant, employer and employee, rulers and ruled, although it has not disappeared, has blurred beyond recognition. What has not changed is the ongoing challenge to traditional morality and the invasion of privacy by misguided bureaucrats and other well-meaning meddlers from the nanny state. Dalroy's crusade to save the English inn from prohibition is a forthright statement of the rights of ordinary people to the personal human dignity they usually preserve so well while their so-called betters are busy climbing aboard bandwagons or taking up fads and fetishes; it ends in a victory not so much for sanity as for common sense.

In 1925 St. George was taken out of Chesterton's toy-theatre as he created a remarkable pastiche of the traditional Christmas mummers' play. In *The Turkey and the Turk* he uses the confrontation of St. George and the Turkish Knight without sacrificing the simple characterization and other elements of mumming. The oriental fatalism and mores of the Turkish Knight are contrasted with the more European virtues of St. George and Father Christmas. The knock-about is played for all its worth, with most of the knocks aimed at the Doctor who embodies Prussian militarism, international intrigue and spare-part surgery of the monkey-gland type. When a slighter piece, *What You Won't*, followed within the month, it became obvious that Chesterton was amusing himself by having a thinly disguised Shakespeare meet his agent in Tiger's Tidy Teashop on Twelfth Night, followed as it was by *At the Back of Methuselah* and then *The Tragic Women*[15] written for Barbara West's 21st birthday. But more serious work was afoot in Beaconsfield. In 1911 Chesterton noted that the 'essential comedy of Johnson's character has never, oddly enough, been put upon the stage.'[16] He was a great admirer of Dr Johnson's common sense, enjoyed impersonating him in pageants, and had long been attracted by the idea of wedding the republican libertarianism of John Wilkes to the religious position of Johnson. It is hardly surprising that, when he looked around for a plot for another play, he chose to undertake the difficult balancing act of mixing traditional ethics with very revolutionary politics. What is surprising is that he should succeed in doing so and at the same time give as good an exposition of his own point of view as he ever gave, and this done quite often by putting Johnson's own words in Johnson's mouth. The thread of plot which takes an American colonist and his wife first to Scotland and then to London to become embroiled in revolutionary clubs, spying and a hint of Hell Fire Club wife-swapping is slight although pleasant enough, but it is merely a peg on which Chesterton can hang Wilkes and Johnson and their world. There are some surprises, notably in the portrayal of Wilkes who emerges as a well-balanced character instead of the degenerate one might have expected (and with whose private life Chesterton disagreed). In the portrayal of Dr Johnson (with whose politics Chesterton likewise disagreed) one sees not the explosive pedant of legend but the Chestertonian Johnson of the pageants, quite tolerant of extremes, someone who respects even when he does not approve of Wilkes, even accepting bloodshed and revolution as long as they are based on a sound moral foundation. Unfortunately, *The Judgement of Dr Johnson* was not the type of play fashionable in 1925, was not published until 1927 and not produced until 1932[17]. The critical reaction was quite good with the main reservation being its wordiness; the meaning of wordiness then and now, however, is not the same, and the play seems to have worn well. Nonetheless, after its limited run of six performances at the Arts Theatre Club, it failed to find a commercial management to take it up.

Shaw once again whipped his old hobbyhorse into action in May 1930 when again he wrote to Mrs Chesterton: 'There is a new play wanted for the Malvern festival this year and I do not see how I can possibly find time to write it. A chance for Gilbert, who ought to have written *The Apple Cart*. He leaves everything to me nowadays.'[18] Dates are not clear[19], but Chesterton's *The Surprise* was written between 1929 and 1932, ostensibly for production by Patricia R. Burke to whom he had already dedicated *The Incredulity of Father Brown* in 1926. Once finished, the play was never typed up and the rough papers deteriorated until the early 1950s when Dorothy Collins, who had denied its existence for years to Patricia R. Burke[20], consulted Dorothy L. Sayers about it. Sayers was enthusiastic and insisted on Chesterton's text being respected where Dorothy Collins considered it sacrilegious. It is possible that Shaw was unaware that his friend had written *The Surprise* which was not staged until June 5th, 1953, three years after Shaw's death, by the Hull University Dramatic Society;

Patricia Burke was horrified as she had been planning a London production.

Typically Chestertonian in the sense that he tended to be least solemn when he was most serious, under the cloak of a round of apparently romantic nonsense, *The Surprise* is a profoundly religious play dealing with the problem of free will in the context of the Creation, the Fall of Man, and the Incarnation. Chesterton certainly had no wish to belittle the biblical accounts, but he did consider that the most wonderful events for a Christian in the history of mankind were often ignored because their significance had been forgotten. He attempts to shake the scales from the eyes of his audience and by 'rewriting' the Bible, to share with them the immense excitement in the discovery of the greatest surprise of them all – the Incarnation. The repetitiveness of the action, in itself no small technical feat, presents us with lifelike puppets who present a play so well that they are given the gift of life, whereupon they react to the same situations so differently that the disastrous outcome causes their creator to intervene in their now human lives.

Dates are as ever vague but *The Cottage*[21] incomplete as it is, does contain references to television and Croydon airport which probably places it in the early 1930s, and the remnants of *The Ages (Centuries) Are Passing*,[22] a celebration of priesthood, have been reconstructed from play parts used by Distributist groups, so a similar date is indicated.

### THE DEVIL AMONG THE CATTLE (a Scenario)

A somewhat grotesque mystical play in rhyme, gathering round the spiritual idea of the two ways of looking at moral evil, the view which sees in it a bottomless and supernatural terror almost equal to God, and that which sees in it a kind of brute blunder, a muddling of existence, a manifest inferiority. The first act is in heaven. Satan comes before the Lord as in the Book of Job and delivers a speech full of the usual eloquent blasphemy business. God whose remarks are throughout characterised by a certain mysterious amusement as if He knew more than He talked about, agrees to accept the challenge of Satan and sends St. George after him to fight him. A second act devoted to some wild adventures of St. George during the pursuit terminates with a momentary encounter with Satan who again flies and cannot be found. The third act (which may be called the second part of the play) opens in a farm house in which an old farmer and his wife discuss a certain stampede and disorder which has appeared among their cattle. After much investigation this is eventually traced to one ox who perpetually eludes capture. Later it is discovered that the quadruped, though it has horns and tail of an ox, is not exactly an ox; finally that it is not a quadruped. It is brought into the farm kitchen as a poor monstrosity and mongrel and carefully tended by the old couple as if it were an idiot child. It is, of course, Satan. The more Satan goes off into blasphemous tantrums, the more his protectors insist on treating him medicinally. Finally at the last point of exasperation he rises and delivers the same tremendous speech which he made in heaven, and when at last his voice fails him, he is soothed and stroked. The old couple have just begun to say how silly the poor thing is, and how few people would have been nice enough to take any trouble about him, when there is a thundering upon the door with a sword hilt and a great voice calling out challenges in the name of God and the Angels. After a certain amount of dramatic scurry and delay the door is burst open and St. George rushes in sword in hand, and flies at the Devil, and is hurled back by the farmer. Finally, the couple explain their attitude, and it gradually dawns upon St. George that [he] is in the presence of a new and strange victory over evil. 'Was God laughing at me?' he asked. 'He laughs at all of us,' said the Devil.[23]

# THE STORY TELLER

A large percentage of the population can quote, probably inaccurately, Chesterton's frantic telegram: 'Am at Market Harborough. Where ought I to be?' In fact, as he travelled the railway network, consuming pies and ale in station buffets, he did tend to lose track of his whereabouts because his mind was occupied elsewhere, often on several levels, for the funny man with the sword-stick and brigand's hat and cloak was capable of writing and dictating two separate works at the same time. A professional writer to his fingertips, almost always working to a deadline, he tended to forget yesterday's work in a rush of enthusiasm for what he was to do today. Stories were sent off to magazines without a copy kept for the file, and all too often Chesterton had no file and relied on others to compile the many collections for which he is known. Without any shadow of a doubt he wrote for too many magazines on too many occasions for it to be easy to trace his work. The situation was not helped when he sent cartloads of papers to the municipal dump. Where an original survives as in the case of *Child Street* (surely the first literary instance of cloning?), *The House of Stars* or *The Sky Thief*, the narrative can be startling in its inventiveness, and it would appear that Chesterton was writing parables for popular consumption which were later continued in his *Daily News* columns in squibs such as *How I found the Superman*, *The Long Bow* and *A Somewhat Improbable Story*.

Many early stories written while he was still at St. Paul's School survive in fragmentary form in his notebooks and scrapbooks, often foreshadowing later work. An example of this is the development of *The Club of Queer Trades* from its beginnings as *The Human Club* in the mid-1890s until it finally began to appear in print in 1903, first in the USA and then in Britain; this tendency to target work to the American market continued up to and after the years of the First World War, perhaps because that market was not on a war footing until 1917–18. Late examples include *The Trees of Pride*, *Garden of Smoke*, *Five of Swords*, *Tower of Treason*, and *The Man Who Shot the Fox*, but it is often overlooked that Father Brown made his debut on July 23rd, 1910 in Philadelphia in the *Saturday Evening Post* which did not even give him top billing in 'Valentin Follows a Curious Trail [The Blue Cross]'. The priest did not really establish himself until Chesterton had dispatched Valentin in 'The Secret of the Sealed Garden [The Secret Garden]' to give his clergyman-detective primacy alone with Flambeau in 'Why the True Fishermen Wear Green Evening Coats [The Queer Feet]'; by the time the stories were collected in 1911 in *The Innocence of Father Brown* the little priest remained unchallenged through *The Wisdom of Father Brown* (1914) until he was returned to his parish duties as the Great War raged and Chesterton took over the editorial chair of *The New Witness* from his brother in 1916.

Eventually, the need to support financially the magazine he saw as his brother's memorial caused Chesterton to emulate Conan Doyle by resurrecting his own detective in 'The Oracle of the Dog' in *Nash's Magazine* in December 1923, and then keep him busy indeed, for Father Brown was to continue his investigations throughout more than fifty cases[1]. Attempts to replace his sleuth by Horne Fisher in *The Man Who Knew Too Much* and by the bureaucrat Mr Pond were not entirely successful, although the latter was to continue his paradoxes in a story left unfinished upon Chesterton's death. There was occasionally an attempt to collect stories within a frame tale, successfully in *The Man Who Knew Too Much*, less so in *Tales of the Long Bow* and *Four Faultless Felons*. One odd man out is *The Poet and the Lunatics* featuring Gabriel Gale throughout a series of tales whose magazine publication began in 1920 but only collected in 1929; the narratives somehow suggest that this collection is a novel *manqué* which never came to fruition, was set aside, and then was tied up with a final story so as to once again provide financial support for *G.K.'s Weekly* and the Distributist League.

There is evidence that Chesterton wrote about a hundred other fairy tales and weird and wonderful stories (see Bibliography, pp. 429–431); if Father Brown could take up the case, he would prove invaluable in uncovering the missing parts of those which are incomplete. In Chesterton's own words: 'I have never taken my novels or short stories very seriously,' but then as Muriel Spark said: 'How well he could tell a story!'

The narrow confines within which a short story writer works tend to restrict the manner and form in which he tells his tale: economy in words and in description, discretion and clarity become of prime importance in style. Despite such restricting influences a skilful storyteller can fashion endless variations in the way material is presented, and, if a writer is endowed with genius, he can throw away the conventions and still produce a masterpiece of the genre. Chesterton often did throw away all the conventions, but that touch of genius was always there to save him: 'Chesterton wrote too sincerely and vigorously to earn a mere niche in a museum . . . To teach and please at the same time is given to few. In the twentieth century only Shaw, Wells, Aldous Huxley and Chesterton have had the faculty.' (Anthony Burgess).

It was the torture chamber of the gnomes, and the glimmering cells were filled with ghastly instruments of torment. There was the Albert Chevalier[2] barrel organ, invented by that unscrupulous statesman, who was himself one of the first to perish by its handle; there was the Scorcher's Wheel and the horrible Masher's Collar[3], sufficient in its very form to strike terror into the victim's soul. The dais at the other end of the hall was ranged with masked and hooded figures in the centre of whom sat the Wizard, crowned with a tiara of twelve iron crowns. 'Prisoner,' thundered the Inquisitor, 'You are charged by this Holy Court with the crime of being a were-wolf. What do you have to say in your defence?'

'Hypocrite!' replied the undaunted Williamson, 'I am no were-wolf. The lady has released me.'

The Judge turned pale with wrath and fear, and Williamson saw that he had conquered.

'In the name of the ten moons of Saturn (*he was much too excited to mind astronomy*) I command you to give me back the lady and let me go.'

With an oath, at which the sky blushed red for three days, the Wizard threw down his sceptre, and in a moment the Lady was at his side. They went back together and were married, and became two of the most zealous members of the Wesleyan Communion.

(Fragment of a story dating from *c*1889. GKC aged 15.)

Chesterton not only went on to be a master practitioner of the art of the short story, he became acknowledged as such by his contemporaries who were glad to seek his advice:

All men have what is called the artistic temperament; though those who talk most about it have it least. But whether any given person with the artistic temperament ought to be an artist is one of those all-important problems of proportion and judgment about which there is no rule. The only thing approaching to a practical hint was given by Stevenson, when he said (I forget the words) that a man could weigh his vocation by asking himself if he found something pleasant even in the unpleasant part of his work.

There is really something valuable in the test. An intelligent man who thinks at some moment that he would like to write a particular story often only means that he would like a particular story to be written. If he can imagine himself as continuously, day after day, by setting his wits to the considerable worry of putting it together, it is likely enough that he is the man really meant to write it. But if all he would enjoy would be the accomplished thing, then probably he is not meant to write it, but to read it. His status as a reader will be probably spiritually and almost certainly economically higher than that of the writer.

But when we come to certain negative warnings about the work, something practical may perhaps be said. It would be rather ungracious to put the truth by saying that the only advice we can really give a writer is to tell him to disregard nearly all the advice which it would be wiser to criticise than to accept as authoritative criticism. The warning against the *cliché*, for instance, is now almost a *cliché* itself. But the greater part of these errors work back, as most things do, to moral questions; and the first line of attack upon them lies through the question of that literary element which is talked about as truth, and what is very much less talked about, courage. It is especially desirable to be honest when demanding honesty. It is therefore necessary to admit, to start with, that truth in any courageous sense in modern English writing may not lead to success, and may sometimes lead to ruin. It does not become anybody who, by luck and the loyalty of friends, has been moderately successful without consciously selling his pen, to be pharisaical about anyone whom the most tragic necessities have forced into selling it. But it is certain that to recommend a young writer to tell the truth is to recommend something risky. It is my purpose here to point out that there is another side to the speculation; that it has certain genuine chances of success like many risky speculations in commerce or finance, as well as being a risk more worthy of what is respectable in human nature. The question of truth in literature is confused by sexual controversies; but that element in the affair is here irrelevant and is everywhere exaggerated. The things conventionally hidden are only conventionally hidden; that is, they are not really hidden at all. Sex is a *secret de Polichinelle*; and the phrase is appropriate, for the facts in themselves are mostly as coarse and healthy as Punch and Judy. Real courage is only called out in dealing with facts that are really hidden from the man in the street, even when he is not in the street; and these are almost always political or financial, or generally both. To give a true picture of modern England in relation to these things is, it must be repeated, risky. Yet it is the only possible course for a man whose motive is conviction; for conviction of its nature requires him not only to practise, but to preach.[4]

In 1903 at the time *The Napoleon of Notting Hill* was dispatched to the printer GKC made a fair copy of a Stevensonian-type novella in six chapters. The six chapter format seems to have appealed to him for he used the form from the early 1890s until *Four Faultless Felons* in 1930. In almost every case a large part or a small part of these novellas is missing and it is not known where they may have been published. *Dead Man's Drum* shows GKC at the height of his literary prowess, taking a phrase that RLS had suggested in 1894 would form an ideal opening for a story, and then following his own imagination through restoration Paris.

DEAD MAN'S DRUM

Chapter 1. The Old Cockade.

Snow had covered Paris with caps and hoods and crowns of white for all its varied towers, which made the parts below seem blacker in contrast, and above the highest of these elvish crests the skies were like an empty house of stars.

Jean Rossignol, the lawyer, descended by jagged streets, sometimes growing so steep that they tumbled down hill in the form of irregular steps, until he reached the main level of the city. But all the time he trod even the craziest stairs or slimiest steps of stone, the lantern swung aimlessly in his hand and his face was turned to the stars.

Jean Rossignol, though not more than twenty-five, had the full legal gravity. He was black as a crow in garb and solemn as an owl in countenance; but there is nothing so secret, I had almost said, so hypocritical, as youth, and under this dry and methodic exterior his heart was singing like a bird, smarting like a wound, raging like a battle and melting like an old song. It is hardly necessary to name his disease. To fall in love with Adrienne de Salçy, daughter of the King's own Minister of Finance, was for a young scholar who boiled his own chestnuts, a grotesque feat. Towards the end of the reign of the restored king, Louis XVIII, the extreme Royalists, with all their fierce feudal memories and traditions of scorn and hatred, had gained the upper hand, the court was fenced with the most pompous and oriental etiquette, and the idea of a *mésalliance* had the ring of a blasphemy. As Jean Rossignol crossed the end of one of the broad roads of the fashionable quarter, the long line of carriages, seen only in the darkness, a line of mocking goblin eyes of gold, green and crimson fire, seemed to stretch away up the steep road, a symbol of the chain of derisive obstacles that stretched far away into the paradise of his proud lady's company.

Jean Rossignol was neither a coward nor a snob: if Adrienne had been his washerwoman he would have reverenced her; though she was a count's daughter he did not fear her: but to him as to almost all men similarly placed, the worldly luxury and distinction of his lady were impressive as a half poetic materialisation of her superiority to him, and its gorgeousness deepened his sense of tragedy, for there is nothing so desperately pathetic as the world of frivolity and passion.

As he was crossing the pale and desolate Place de la Concorde thinly floored with snow, he heard a sound that brought his feet to a standstill and started his heart galloping, as the crack of a pistol starts a race. From the centre of that wan and wintry open space came a sound of all earthly sounds the most vivid, terrible, maddeningly alive, like the laughter of devils – the sound which Heine called 'The Dance of the French Drums'. Rossignol's first thought was by what lunacy, military drums were beating in the centre of the Place de la Concorde at midnight, but a moment's attention made him drop that idea with a gasp. The roll was not the same as that to which the King's troops marched: and the next moment he had remembered an awful thing, an old wives' tale that he had heard pass from mouth to mouth, but always laughed at, that on many a dark night had been heard louder than the wind and rain, a drum that played the infernal tattoo which had never been heard save from the army of the Great Revolution.

Rossignol was a strong man: one could almost have told that if one had seen him there in that starlight with his square shoulders set back and his great chin set forward: and he did not flinch. He had formed his conclusion. It was the phenomenon, whatever its cause, which the gossips of the city had called 'Dead Man's Drum'. Such being the case he would investigate it.

As he drew near the spot, he heard a big voice booming through the darkness, 'Left turn! March. Halt – attention.' 'Good heavens,' thought Rossignol, 'An army being drilled – a spectre army.'

Then he ran wildly forward and in the centre of the square he saw, not a ghostly army, but two ghosts, standing alone face to face. Both were strapped and buttoned tight in the uniform of the old Republican Guard, which no man had seen since the Revolution. The taller of the two, who was shouting the orders, had only a sword at his side: the other was saluting at the word of command with a musket and bayonet. It was as if this were the only one of a drilling battalion who was visible to human eyes. And behind, seen now for the first time was a boy in the dress of a drummer who from time to time broke the stillness with a rolling peal.

Jean Rossignol accepted them as ghosts, and should have been frozen with terror: but he was not. The fears were swept away on the racing flood of a new emotion. The two stiff, archaic and fantastic figures in tricolour cockades did not fit into any scheme of possibilities, or any aspect of contemporary Paris. But into Jean's own thoughts they fitted with a sudden and sensational appropriateness, like a tale ended in a picture.

As we have said, he recognised his love as hopeless: he accepted the ring within ring of stately ritual that kept him from the Count's daughter as an ordained mystery: the fashion and splendour of her circle to some degree intoxicated him with a poetry as of the Arabian Nights, but he turned his back on it with a chivalrous fatalism, and went deeper and deeper into the dark.

And now the rattle of the old drum turned his blood to wine. For it reminded him, as in a blasphemous yet blissful vision, that he came of a people that had once at least overturned this huge tower of hopeless caste, so that the noise of its falling filled the earth: that with an army of ruffians and a government of debating-clubs, they had fought and conquered, not merely Europe, but the plainest logic of destiny: that for some three years at least amid the crash of guns and the roar of torchlight meetings, there had ruled a triumphant Republic in which he and Lucille would have stood on the same level of humanity. By a confusion, as in an amorous dream, he seemed to see the Jacobins hurling back the invaders solely to protect his own wedding, he and Adrienne standing on the rocking tower and Danton and Napoleon fighting round them as their servants.

Rossignol stood there a few seconds: then the taller figure, he as clearly the officer, started, wheeled round and put his hand to his sword.

'Who goes there?' he cried.

And Rossignol, boiling with his own thoughts, snatched off his hat without knowing what he was doing. 'Vive la République!' he cried, wildly.

'Ah,' cried the other, joyfully, 'Are you a brother?'

And as he advanced into the light, Rossignol saw that he was no ghost, but a solid and athletic human being, dressed with pedantic accuracy in the old uniform as if he were going to a masquerade ball. It was not easy to study his face, for the old cocked hat jutting forward almost on the nose and the old stock almost bandaging the mouth, left little to be seen by starlight except the big nose like an eagle's. In figure the man was tall, spare and elegant.

'But, Monsieur,' said Jean, 'What are you doing here?'

The officer looked thoughtfully at him for a few moments and then said with apparent irrelevance, 'Do you think the drum is a musical instrument?'

'I suppose so,' said Jean, all abroad.

'Mine' said the other in a low voice, 'is an instrument of torture.'

'Oh, not at all,' said Jean with vague politeness.

'You do not understand,' hissed the officer. 'With this I torture and scourge this degenerate city. I will not let them sleep. They shall not forget what they have been. Look at me – you think a carnival dress, but it is my own. I fought for France under Hoche and Dumouriez and Buonaparte; I commanded a regiment. But of all that regiment one only will still follow me. We live the life of hunted hares. We hide ourselves in a cellar of this city and on dark nights sally out to startle the city with the old brave signals, the hymn of liberty and the drum of glory. Every sleek sycophant who has made his place with Capet shall hear over the card table the accusing voice which is the voice of his own youth. Every fat rhetorician, happy in a mild official patriotism, shall remember that there was a time when France did not lick the feet of the foreigner. It may be that the world has lost its youth, but by God, sir, it shall know what it had lost.'

'It must be sad for you,' assented Rossignol, 'to see the old order restored.'

'No, by God,' cried the other, 'you pay it too high a compliment. The old order was oppressive, but it was strong, it meant something. The despotism of Louis XIV, let us say, was the living embodiment of an ideal, good or bad. But this drivelling vacation and half-holiday, this fat compromise as blind as a bat, this idiotic reign of oblivion – this pretence that what has occurred has not occurred – what ideal could live in it? Any ideal that wakes in any mind must be what my drum is – an instrument of torture.'

Jean thought of his own ideal of love, and started at the truth of the words. In a fairly varied social experience he had never met before such a monster as a philosophical soldier. 'Is it uncivil to ask your name?' enquired Jean.

'I am Citizen Castagnac,' said the other, proudly.

'Castagnac,' repeated the lawyer. 'Are you De Castagnac, Marquis de St. Ouen?'

'It is not generous, sir,' said the Republican, fiercely, 'to allude to misfortunes of birth.'

'I beg your pardon, Citizen,' said the lawyer, with a slight smile, 'but your history is not unknown. You were distinguished, I think, in the wars of the republic.'

Castagnac touched the medals on his breast.

'This I gained at Valmy,' he said, 'and this at Fleury. This was given to me by the champion of the Republic, the great General Buonaparte, three days before his fall.'

'His fall?' said Jean. 'Do you mean his first abdication?'

'No, sir,' said the officer, 'I mean his coronation.'

During the conversation the private soldier, sole remnant of the hosts that once conquered Europe, had stood as motionless as a statue . . .

# THE POET

Speaking on January 11th, 1934 to the Distributist League at Gatti's Restaurant in London Gilbert Chesterton summed up what he called his moral, mental and spiritual condition in a triolet:

> My writing is bad,
> And my speaking is worse;
> They were all that I had,
> My writing is bad;
> It is frightfully sad,
> And I don't care a curse.
> My writing is bad,
> And my speaking is worse.[1]

Chesterton, recognised as one of the greatest speakers of the century, was indulging his habit of digging the grave of his literary reputation. Ironically, he did so in an off-the-cuff verse form that many poets have found almost impossible to tackle at leisure, but it is a late example of him denigrating his own work quite typical of his attitude from the beginning of his career when in 1898 he wrote, 'I do not feel as if things like the Fish poem are really worth publishing. I know they are better than many books that are published, but Heaven knows that is not saying much ... with regard to this occasional verse I feel a humbug. To publish a book of my nonsense verses seems to me exactly like summoning the whole of the people of Kensington to see me smoke cigarettes.'[2] His self-effacement coupled with a tendency to lose poems and a penchant for publishing them in obscure, now long forgotten, magazines ensured that much of his work was lost or at best mislaid; other poems were given to friends and only re-emerged years later after his death, and Frances kept the poems addressed to her strictly to herself, ordering their destruction after her own death. Chesterton was, of course, a power-house pouring forth poetry, and his prodigious memory, not to be confused with his forgetfulness, could at the drop of a hat recreate, or more correctly rewrite missing verses. New versions proliferated as they were conjured up as occasion demanded, one example among many being 'The Nativity' which appeared in differing forms over many years.

The poetic muse descended early on Chesterton who well before the age of ten was writing competent pastiches, after which he found his own voice, rapidly developing precocious solemnity alongside light hearted and eclectic tones. His output from the late 1880s throughout the 1890s was phenomenal, as he experienced first love, began to run the gamut of a variety of religious positions, and took up interest in politics; after 1900 his poetry turned in the direction of the social or political lampoon and ballade. Nonetheless, he was able to retain a lightness of touch which ensured that even the bitterest satirical attack was always acclaimed as a comic masterpiece. On a more solemn note he found time to undertake great recitation pieces such as *The People of England (The Secret People)* and *Lepanto*, to which he added his tribute to King Alfred in *The Ballad of the White Horse*.

The great outpouring continued until in the 1920s he took on more and more editorial duties on *G.K.'s Weekly* alongside other journalistic work, and undertook lecture tours overseas. His light-hearted banter became more confined to the private poems he exchanged with groups of young people with whom he had ready rapport, a rapport that did not always extend to the parties to which they invited him (*The Jazz* and *All Through the Night*). Eventually in the 1930s his work load together with health problems did restrict him so that poems appeared far less regularly, but Gilbert Chesterton was almost certainly the most prolific poet of his age, one whose poems so entered the public consciousness that they became part of the *bric à brac* of the mind. Soon after his death Herbert Palmer found 'his verse full of preachings, politics and arresting hymns of hate . . . Chesterton, in spite of his frequent blare and bombast, has been extraordinarily successful in infusing true poetry into his thundering orchestra. God speaking through him, he knows no restraint, but comes at you, marches up the street and round the corner, a rage of music and colour that seeks to hold up the traffic . . .But poetry that is merely like that does not necessarily contain the enduring line, the wonderful stanza, and it is astonishing that in the verse of Chesterton there is so much that is really fine . . . There is plenty of magic in Chesterton's verse, not exactly the delicate elvish magic of Yeats or Walter de la Mare, a rather flick-in-the-eye magic if you like, but none the less evident. Sometimes, indeed, he achieves it when flying right in the jaws of bombast he steers miraculously clear, or when formulating a paradox he gets beyond the truth of paradox to the creation of the rose that shines upon the lips of truth. Then there is the Chesterton who is memorable because he says something very droll, even though it be penetratingly satirical . . . But Chesterton was a sort of God's fool, the Almighty's chosen jester, who fearlessly took liberty, secure in most instances beneath his cap and bells.'[3]

HOW TO READ POETRY

There is only one piece of information or talent that is the least necessary for the purpose of reading poetry. That is, to realise that it is poetry and to realise what poetry is. This is not necessarily a thing that requires to be taught at all. An enormous number of simple and straightforward people know by instinct quite well what poetry is, and understand it a great deal better than they do prose. The greater part of humanity in all ages and countries would know much better what was really meant by a song than what was really meant by a leading article, for poetry is not an artificial or ingenious or highly civilised thing; it is older than every other literary form. Moderns put their poetry into poems, and the rude and ancient peoples put their history and politics, and sporting news, and advice to gardeners, into poems. If our society were in a healthy state, it would not be necessary to tell anybody how to read or write poetry, for they would go naturally to the poetical form whenever they wished to write a column on dressmaking, or a history of temperance legislation.

As it is, however, it is in some degree necessary to point out to people who have to read poetry, what poetry is. For if you approach even the finest poem with a vitally wrong notion of the nature of poetry, it is quite evident that the better the poem really is, the worse you will think of it, you will be judging it by the excellence of something quite different, much as if you criticised a chisel as a bad razor. Now there are really two things only that have to be remembered about the nature of poetry, before we read any sort of poem. The first is that the nature of poetry is, so to speak, exclamatory. It is the relieving of human emotion by means of some outburst of words which shall express that emotion better because it consists of much bigger and nobler words than the common words we use. The real feelings inside us are too great, too precious and painful to be conveyed by our daily phraseology. Therefore, we have to cry out suddenly to something great – to the stars, or to humanity, or to the beauty of woman. The thing which is really most like poetry in ordinary life is some such phrase as 'Thank God,' or 'Mercy on us.' In these you perceive the emotion of the speaker is such that he is obliged, in order to express his own feelings about catching a train or receiving a telegram, to use the tremendous vocabulary of the great religious idea. Our feelings even about small things, when these feelings are sufficiently intense, demand a haughty and heroic language, and, sometimes, a supernatural language. This is the first point to remember about poetry; it is a splendid exclamation.

The second thing to remember about poetry is that it is a splendid exclamation uttered under what is called conventions. That is to say, every poet when he asks you to join with him in his burst of noble words, asks you to agree with him (a convention of course means an agreement) that certain things shall be understood between you, that certain assumptions shall be made, that certain objections shall not be made. When Burns, let us say, writes a love-song, he practically says 'If I manage to get expressed the unmistakable feelings of a man in love, you on your part will not object to my rhyming every second line with every fourth, which certainly no man declaring his passion would have the patience to do.' So long as the exclamation really gets rid of the dumb emotion, we are not to mind the exclamation itself being artificial. Thus again, if a man really conveys his astonishment in the words 'By Jove,' we do not reproach him with assuming the existence of a pagan and discredited deity. Innumerable examples might be given; perhaps the reader may as well be referred, for instance, to the dying speech of John of Gaunt in *Richard II*. In that scene, an old man at the point of death rolls out a rich and elaborate rhetorical speech, full of metaphors and music on the decline of England. As a matter of material fact, of course, the old man would only have mumbled 'The country's going to the dogs' about half a dozen times. But the real pride and agony of insulted patriotism would really be pent up in his heart without an outlet. Shakespeare gives it an outlet, and by reading a column of blank verse we feel what John of Gaunt felt. That is the triumph and that is the definition of poetry.[4]

# THE ESSAYIST

Although it has now become unfashionable, throughout Chesterton's lifetime and indeed long afterwards the essay was a popular form of entertainment in newspapers and magazines, one intended to divert and interest the readership, rarely didactic and even refraining from any form of preaching. The topics of Chesterton's essays were usually quite ephemeral and the form adopted that of a first person narrative, communicating personal judgments and experiences in a train of thought that more often than not surprised in its use of paradox and its unusual point of view. Chesterton was very conscious of the form of writing to which he most frequently turned and which was the very foundation of his popularity, and on several occasions he was glad to define it:

[E]ditors, publishers, and the public are really hungry, not to say starving, for what is called 'good copy.' They will pay a great deal, and they will tolerate a great deal for anything that is as a fact interesting. Men as different, for instance, as Mr Rudyard Kipling and Mr Bernard Shaw undoubtedly really shocked the rather shapeless conventions of the later Victorians; but clove their way through such prejudices by the very fact that there was something tart and disconcerting about their tone. And whatever we may think of their opinions, they earned the public place they gained by the simple fact that their matter was so much more interesting than the corresponding mass of printed matter they displaced. It is here necessary to enter the *caveat* referred to above against one of the cant phrases of advice addressed to the young writer. I mean the insistence on the necessity of suiting any journalism to the exact tone and habit of the journal. This advice has spoilt much more good journalism than it has ever made. It has left many a man earning a little money by writing dull things for a dull paper, when he might have earned a lot by being the only bright spot on it. I do not say that this principle can be safely carried to its final and somewhat fantastic extreme. It might be unwise to contribute the most trenchant refutation of Darwin or Karl Marx to lend solidity to *The Winning-Post*, or to save the more racy of the points from a French farce to sparkle in the setting of *The British Weekly*. But it is quite equally true that many a man has become the chief feature of a frivolous paper by writing the one article that was worth reading; and has created the popularity of a serious paper by refusing to be entirely serious. And it will really be worth while considering the superior chances of a good argument even in the pink paper, or a good joke even in the Puritan paper, over those of a bad argument or a bad joke anywhere. For the first fact, as I have said, is that good arguments and good jokes are really wanted, not only by newspaper readers, but by the much more ignorant class of newspaper proprietors. I have here considered the commercial problem merely in its relation to journalism; but it is evident that the same general principle applies to the young book writer when he is told to suit the taste of the public, or more often of the publisher. The general truth involved here concerns the first of the practical advantages of conviction – the fact that a man saying what he has really seen and really thinks, whatever the quality of his brains may be, is quite certain to be showing those brains at their brightest and best. The staleness of much modern journalism does not consist, as the supercilious so often suggest, of stupid men trying to be clever; it largely consists of clever men trying to be stupid. They do it well; but it is a mistake.

But the case for conviction is even stronger and sharper than this. It is a matter that nobody adequately notices in the modern world; because complete and connected beliefs have been discouraged by a sceptical temper. But complete and connected beliefs are an incomparable help to quickness in wit and words. There is a vague idea that a man will be freer in his fancies and have larger licence for his humour if he keeps what some would call an open mind and I should call an empty head. It is supposed that a man like Mr Bernard Shaw gains his reputation as a wit by saying anything that comes into his head. To suppose this is as stupid as to suppose that a mob can manoeuvre more quickly than an army. The very fact that a mere mob can go anywhere is the reason why it goes nowhere. The kind of man who will say whatever comes into his head generally has a long while to wait before anything comes into it. The quickest mind is that which knows where to find all its thoughts; which can put every problem promptly to a test; and the sparks of whose wit come from the collision of a fact like flint upon a creed like steel. Therefore the most important of all admonitions to a writer, for the most popular or even the most playful purposes, is to tell him to possess himself of a positive view of things and to apply it boldly until it breaks down. The process will not narrow him; on the contrary, it will broaden him very much. To put in its simplest form, if he believes something that applies to everything, he will always have something to say.[1]

The Essay is the only literary form which confesses, in its very name, that the rash act of writing is really a leap in the dark. When men try to write a tragedy, they do not call the tragedy a try-on. Those who have toiled through the twelve books of an epic, writing it with their own hands, have seldom pretended that they have tossed off an epic as an experiment. A man does not really write an essay. He does really essay to write an essay. One result is that, while there are many famous essays, there is fortunately no model essay. The perfect essay has never been written, for the simple reason that the essay has never really been written. Men have tried to write something, to find out what it was supposed to be. In this respect the essay is a typically modern product, and is full of the future and the praise of experiment and adventure. In itself it remains somewhat elusive, and I will own that I am haunted with a faint suspicion that the essay will probably become rather more cogent and dramatic, merely because of the deep and deadly divisions which ethical and economic problems may force upon us. But let us hope there will always be a place for the essay that is really an essay. St. Thomas Aquinas, with his usual common sense, said that neither the active nor the contemplative life could be lived without relaxation, in the form of jokes and games. The drama or the epic might be called the active life of literature; the sonnet or the ode the contemplative life. The essay is the joke.[2]

Certainly in Chesterton's case his essays were often jokes because they were always entertaining.

### LONDON

There is an old London story that has never lost its loveliness for me. It was about a stout old lady from the country, who travelled round and round the Underground Railway in a circle, because at each station she tried to get out backwards, and at each station the guard pitched her in again, under the impression that she was trying to get in. It is a beautiful story; doing honour alike to the patience of the female sex and the prompt courtesy of the male; it is a song without words. But there is another and milder version (perhaps we might dare to say a more probable version) of the same story. It describes an aged farmer and his daughter travelling the same sad circle, and failing to alight anywhere, partly because of the impediments of country parcels, but partly also because they were almost satisfied with the staring names of the places set up on the Underground Railway. They thought the 'Mansion House' was rather a dark place for the Lord Mayor to live in. They could detect no bridges through the twilight of 'Westminster Bridge', nor any promising park in 'St. James' Park Station'. They could only suppose that they were in the crypts of 'The Temple', or buried under the foundations of 'The Tower'.

Nevertheless, I am not quite so certain that this cockney tale against countrymen scores so much as is supposed. The rustic saw the names at least; and nine times out of ten the names are nobler than the things. Let us suppose him as starting westward from the Mansion House, where he commiserated the dim captivity of the Lord Mayor. He would come to another gloomy vault in which he would read the word 'Blackfriars'. It is not a specially cheery word; but it goes back, I imagine, to that great movement, at once dogmatic and democratic, which gave to its followers the fierce and fine name of the 'Dogs of God'. But at worst, the mere name of Blackfriars Station is more dignified than the Blackfriars Road. He would pass on to the Temple; and surely the mere word 'Temple' is more essential and eternal than either the rich lawyers in its courts, or the poor vagabonds on its embankment. He will go on to Charing Cross, where the noblest of English knights and kings set up a cross to his dead queen. But unless his rustic erudition informs him of the fact, he will gain little by getting out of the train and going to the larger station. Neither porters carrying luggage nor trippers carrying babies, will encourage any conversation about the original sacredness of the spot. He will stop next at a yet more sacred spot, the station called Westminster Bridge, from which he can visit, as Macaulay says, 'the place where five generations of statesmen have striven, and the place where they sleep together.' By walking across the street from this station he can enter the House of Commons. But, if he is wise, he will stop in the train. He will then arrive at St. James' Park; and (as Mr Max Beerbohm has truly remarked) he will not meet St. James there.

Yet these mere names that he has seen on a dingy wall, like advertisements, are really the foundation stones of London; and it is right that they should (as it were) be underground. The mere fact that these five names, in a row along the riverside, all bear witness to an ancient religion and would tell the rustic in the railway train (supposing him to be of elaborate culture and lightning deduction) the great part of the history of London. The old Temple Church still stands, full of the tombs of those great and doubtful heroes who signed themselves with the sign of Christ, but who came, rightly or wrongly, to be stamped with the seal of Antichrist. The old Charing Cross is gone; but its very absence is as much of a historical monument as itself. For the Puritans pulled it down merely for being a cross; though (as it says in a humorous song of the period) Charing Cross had always refrained from uttering a word against the authority of the Parliament. But these old things, though fundamental, are fragmentary; and whether as ruins or merely as records, will tell the stranger little of what London has been and is, as distinct from Paris or Berlin or Chicago. London is a mediaeval town, as these names testify; but its soul has been sunk deeper under other things than any other town that remembers mediaevalism at all. It is very hard to find London in London.

There is a story (one among many) that there was a settlement before the Romans came, which occupied about the same space that is now occupied by Canon Street Station. In any case, it is probable that the seed of the city was sown somewhere about that slope of the riverside. The Romans made it a great town but hardly their greatest town, and the barbarians of the ninth century left it bare. Its second or third foundation as a predominant city belongs, like many such things, to the genius and tenacity of Alfred. He did not indeed hold it as a capital of England, but rather as an outpost of Wessex. From his point of view, London was a suburb of Wantage. But he saw the practical importance of its position towards the river mouth; and he held it tight. The Norman Conquest clinched the condition, which was roughly symbolised by the Tower of London, which for many centuries was a trophy captured and recaptured by opposite factions. But, in the main, London had one political character from first to last. It was always, for good or evil, on the side of the Parliament and against the King. Six hundred years ago, it was the citizens of London who had to stand the charge of the strongest of the Plantagenets, on the downs round Lewes. Four hundred years afterwards, it was the citizens of London who held the high places of Buckinghamshire, when the army of Charles I threatened London from Oxford. Later still, the Londoners stood solidly against James II and splendidly against George III. Whether Parliament was worth such fidelity, whether the merchants of the Thames were wise to tie themselves so entirely to the grandees of the counties, is no subject for this place. But that the tradition of the town was sincere and continuous cannot be doubted. To this day the Lord Mayor of London is probably proud that the King of England can only enter London by his leave. That fact is as close a summary of the purely political history of London as one could want. It exactly expresses the victory of the merchants over the central power. It is often observed that the French think the Lord Mayor of London more important than the King. They are an acute people. This rather surly love of liberty (or rather of independence) is written in the straggling map of London, and proclaimed in its patchwork architecture. There is in it something that every Englishman feels in himself, though he does not always feel it to be good; something of the amateur; something of the eccentric. The nearest phrase is the negative one of 'unofficial.' London is so English, that it can hardly be called even the capital of England. It is not even the county town of the county in which it stands. That title, I believe, belongs to Brentford, which legend credits with two kings at once, like Lacedaemon. It is just London. As his French friend said about Browning, its centre is not in the middle. The Parliament sits in London, but not in the City of London; the City of London is not under the London County Council; and in spite of the opinion of General Choke[3], the Sovereign does not live in the Tower. Crowded and noisy as it is, there is something shy about London: it is full of secrets and anomalies; and it does not like to be asked what it is for. In this, there is not a little of its history as a sort of half-rebel through so many centuries. Hence it is a city of side streets that only lead into side streets; a city of short cuts – that take a long time. There have been recent changes in the other direction, of course; but the very name of one of them, unintentionally illustrates something not native to the place. A more broad and sweeping thoroughfare, in the Continental manner, was opened between the Strand and Holborn, and called Kingsway. The phrase will serve for a symbol. Through all those creative and characteristic epochs, there was no King's Way through London. There was nothing Napoleonic; no roads that could be properly decorated with his victories or properly cleared with his cannon. It had something of the licence and privilege of that Alsatia[4] that was its sore; the little impenetrable kingdom of rascals that revelled down in Whitefriars, where now rascals of a more mournful kind write imperialist newspapers. One might call mediaeval London a rabbit warren; save that the trainbands who took their pikes, and 'prentices who caught up their clubs at a bell or a beacon, were certainly anything but rabbits. I have said that this eccentricity, amounting to secrecy, remains in the very building of London. Some of the finest glimpses of it are got as through a crack in a door. Our fathers gained freedom of vision through the gap in the fence; just as they often gained freedom of speech through a flaw in an Act of Parliament. In their glorious visions of height or distance, there is always something of the keyhole; just as in their glorious fights for law or liberty, there was always something of a quibble. There is no finer effect than that of St. Paul's from the foot of its hill in delicate and native weather; for the English climate (I may remark) is the finest in the world. I assume, of course, that the spectator is a serious mystic (that is, a materialist also) and appreciates the bodily beauty of heights, which should always be seen from below. The Devil takes us to the top of an exceeding high mountain, and makes us dizzy; but God lets us look at the mountain. Yet this mountain made by man can only be seen in London by 'sighting'; by getting it between two houses, as a pilot steers between two rocks. Get the sighting wrong and you will see only a public-house, or (which is much worse) a shop full of newspapers. Had either a French or a Prussian temple commanded such an eminence, the whole hill would have been swept bare as with a sabre and studded with statues and gardens, that it might be seen from afar. Only I should not like it so much. But then I was born in London.[5]

# THE CRITIC

O ne of the lesser known episodes in Chesterton's life was the offer made to him in 1904 by Sir Oliver Lodge of the foundation chair of English Literature in the University of Birmingham. In the event that offer was rejected and the chair went to John Churton Collins, Tennyson's 'louse upon the locks of Literature.' Chesterton was later to boast: 'If I have had a profession, at least I have never been a professor,' but he spent a great deal of time either lecturing or writing literary criticism of a quality which brought Geoffrey Tillotson (1905–69) to say that 'it is surely becoming plain that G.K. Chesterton is one of the best critics of the first half of the twentieth century . . . perhaps his criticism will last longer than any other section of his work,' a view supported by William Empson's (1906–84) comment that 'G.K. Chesterton . . . has great powers as a verbal critic.' T.S. Eliot's assertion in 1927 that 'there is no better critic of Dickens than Mr Chesterton' received later support in 1974 from Sir Victor S. Pritchett (1900–97): 'It is conventional to say that Chesterton's book on Dickens is the best thing he ever wrote. I read it again this week. It is not merely good; it is a masterpiece and contains, amongst other things, the most enlightening portrait of Dickens himself that I have ever read.' Of course, there were dissenting voices such as that of Anthony Burgess, 'As a critic he is best left alone' in 1958, but time has seen the rehabilitation of Chesterton as a critic by figures such as W.H. Auden:

> Our day has seen the emergence of two kinds of literary critic, the documentator and the cryptologist. The former with meticulous accuracy collects and publishes every

unearthable fact about an author's life, from his love letters to his dinner invitations and laundry bills, on the assumption that any fact, however trivial, about the man may throw light upon his writings. The latter approaches his work as if it were an anonymous and immensely difficult text, written in a private language which the ordinary reader cannot hope to understand until it is deciphered for him by experts. Both such critics will no doubt dismiss Chesterton's literary criticism as out-of-date, inaccurate and superficial, but if one were to ask any living novelist or poet which kind of critic he would personally prefer to write about his work, I have no doubt as to the answer.

Perhaps we should apply the adage that 'it takes one to know one' and consult Chesterton himself:

> Criticism does not exist to say about authors the things they knew themselves. It exists to say the things about them which they did not know themselves. If a critic says that the *Iliad* has a pagan rather than a Christian pity, or that it is full of pictures made by one epithet, of course he does not mean that Homer could have said that. If Homer could have said that, the critic would leave Homer to say it. The function of criticism, if it has a legitimate function at all, can only be one function – that of dealing with the subconscious part of the author's mind, which only the critic can express. Either criticism is no good at all (a very defensible position) or else criticism means saying about an author the very things that would have made him jump out of his boots.[1]

Nobody was better than Chesterton at making authors and even critics jump out of their boots. It has never done him much good, for he has always been singularly missing from recommended reading lists. That omission has led, over several generations, to him being practically unknown and unread in academic circles with but few exceptions:

> As a critic Mr Chesterton has been underrated. It is true that he is not a 'scientific' critic; his criticism is a series of acute impressions on individual authors, rather than a logical, intellectual system, complete with its own categories and catchwords. But it is none the worse for that. After all the aim of criticism is to make one appreciate good writing. And the peculiar, essential qualification of the critic is a just and catholic taste: the power to detect what is good, and to isolate, and convey to the reader, the particular qualities that go to make it so. Without this flair no amount of systemic logic or original theory is of any value, because it is founded on the wrong premises. There is no more value in a criticism, however logical and brilliant, that sets out to prove that *Paradise Lost* was a bad poem than there is in a medical diagnosis that sets out to prove that cancer is a mild disease. It is the distinguishing mark of the great English critics, Dryden, Lamb, Hazlitt, that they had this flair; and to a greater degree than almost any modern critic it is the distinguishing mark of Mr Chesterton. Like them he has evolved no new system of incomprehensible critical values and unpleasing critical terminology; but, like them, he knows a good thing when he sees it. Of course, his sympathies have their limitations: his dislike of pessimism did, for a time at least, make him blind to the splendour of

Hardy's genius. But on the whole his appreciation is extraordinarily catholic; his little book on Victorian Literature is equally and discriminatingly appreciative of Carlyle and Arnold, Tennyson, Swinburne and Fitzgerald. And he does not only appreciate them; he picks out to praise exactly those qualities of style and standpoint which give each his especial place in the temple of letters. If all their works were lost, anyone who had read Mr Chesterton's brief sentences on them would have caught an authentic whiff of their individuality . . . [A] page of Mr Chesterton's is far more illuminating than most of the books of Chaucer's other critics put together. He brings out more forcibly than anyone has before the scale of Chaucer's genius: the fact that with all his playfulness and simplicity he was a poet in the grand manner, as much in that profound, sunlit philosophy which is the foundation of his humour as in his moments of stark, massive tragedy: and if he chose the level trodden causeway through the midst of life, it was not for want of realising the heights and depths above and below him. It is in this combination of common sense point of view with literary genius on the grand scale that Mr Chesterton rightly sees the peculiar secret of Chaucer's greatness.[2]

Mr Chesterton is to other writers one of the most highly dangerous men living. I sometimes think that authors should not read him at all, because he is so fatally easy to imitate. He is one of our very greatest writers. He has made an imperishable contribution to English letters. But he is a strongly individual writer, such as Sterne was or Ruskin, to take two completely dissimilar men; and individual writers are traps and snares for ordinary writers. They must not be read for their style. One can learn from them, and one can watch the performance of their tricks with admiration; but they are to be imitated only in private and only at great risk of falling into their own bad habits. For let this be said, a strongly individual style is a style of many bad habits which are endured for other reasons. Sterne's inconsequence, Ruskin's eloquence, and Chesterton's paradoxes and alliterations are tolerable in their own pages; but not anywhere else . . . All the same, young writers should read Chesterton; but they must read him for his matter. His matter is always alive. If the writers of our age could catch Chesterton's spirit, what a different world of books we should have! What a transformation would be made in the world we live in! Chesterton's spirit is that of the poet who has the courage to touch every thing with poetic truth. There is no subject on which he writes that he does not illuminate. There is no living writer who can rightly be held in more honour.[3]

It was in 1932 that Richard de la Mare dangled £1,000, GKC's largest ever retainer, as a bait for a study of Chaucer; the matching of the fourteenth and twentieth century humourist and satirist poets certainly was inspired and Chesterton gave fair value for the money. He was sometimes adjudged to be a neo-medievalist, but not in the mould of Rossetti, as from *Basil Howe* (1894) through to *The Return of Don Quixote* (1912–27) he had always eschewed and even condemned any dream-world based on overly romantic notions. He was also strongly opposed to the type of criticism that saw in Chaucer some harbinger of the Reformation:

Some critics have vaguely suspected Chaucer of being a Lollard . . . Nobody can begin to suggest that Chaucer was a Lollard, unless he can prove either or both of two propositions about him. First, that he held any Lollard doctrine that can be proved to be heretical by exact and authoritative definition: the sort of precise thing not very likely to be found in such poetry. And, second, that if he did hold it as a private opinion, he would in the last resort have preferred that private opinion to membership of the Body of Christ. I need not say that there is not the wildest suggestion of a reason for supposing that Chaucer was a Lollard either in one sense or the other . . . He was unquestionably and even passionately devoted to the particular parts of Catholicism that have been most condemned by Protestantism. He had a devotion to Our Lady perhaps greater than that of Dante; as great as that of St. Bernard in his great oration in Dante . . . Modern critics have congratulated Chaucer, or congratulated themselves, on the fact that he was so enlightened a reformer as to satirise the Monk and the Friar. Curiously enough, they have neglected to notice what he satirised them for . . . And the simple truth is Chaucer satirises the Monk for not being sufficiently Monastic . . . The point is rather practical; because nearly all studies of this period are full of the suggestion that Chaucer, like his contemporary Wycliffe, was a sort of morning star of the Reformation. We can only answer that in that case he was an eccentric star who wanted the sun to move backwards instead of forwards. In the whole of his satirical sketch of the Monk, the point is, not that the Monk is sunk in monkish superstition, but simply that the Monk is not monkish enough.[4]

Although there was a general feeling that Chesterton, not being a Chaucerian scholar, was not fitted to write such a book, he had powerful defenders:

His new book on the poet *Chaucer* displays his best qualities. It is the most solid piece of work he has ever done. Chaucer is, indeed, a solid subject; and Mr Chesterton has put his whole heart into the writing of this book. He makes a modest claim for it. He has, he says, aimed at describing 'only the effect of a particular poet on a particular person.' And he has tried to be popular, writing the book 'for people who know even less about Chaucer than I do.' But the book is the result of real study of the poet and of his time by a man wholly in sympathy with his subject.[5]

But one thing is certain, Chesterton as critic had undoubtedly enjoyed himself:

Bob-Up-And-Down[6]
*Irresponsible outbreak of one who, having completed a book of enormous length on the Poet Chaucer, feels himself freed from all bonds of intellectual self-respect and proposes to do no work for an indefinite period.*

> 'Woot ye nat wher ther stant a litel town,
> Which that ycleped is Bobbe-up-and-down[7]
> Under the Blee, in Caunterbury Weye?'
> *The Canterbury Tales*

They babble on of Babylon,
They tire me out with Tyre,
And Sidon putting side on,
I do not much admire.
But the little town Bob-up-and-Down,
That lies beyond the Blee,
Along the road our fathers rode,
O that's the road for me.

In dome and spire and cupola
It bubbles up and swells
For the company that canter
To the Canterbury Bells.
But when the Land-Surveyors come
With maps and books to write,
The little town Bob-up-and-Down
It bobs down out of sight.

I cannot live in Liverpool,
O lead me not to Leeds,
I'm not a Man in Manchester,
Though men be cheap as weeds;
But the little town Bob-up-and-Down,
That bobs towards the sea,
And knew its name when Chaucer came,
O that's the town for me.

I'll go and eat my Christmas meat
In that resurgent town,
And pledge to fame our Father's name
Till the sky bobs up and down;
And join in sport of every sort
That's played beside the Blee,
Bob-Apple in Bob-up-and-Down,
O that's the game for me.

Now Huddersfield is Shuddersfield,
And Hull is nearly Hell,
Where a Daisy would go crazy
Or a Canterbury Bell,
The little town Bob-up-and-Down
Alone is fair and free,
For it can't be found above the ground,
O that's the place for me.

# PART THREE

# NEW AND ORIGINAL VIEWS

# CHESTERTON AND THE JEWS

*Nebuchadnezzar the King of the Jews*
*Bought his wife a pair of shoes.*
*When the shoes began to wear*
*Nebuchadnezzar began to swear.*
*When the shoes got worse and worse,*
*Nebuchadnezzar began to curse.*
*When the shoes were quite worn out,*
*Nebuchadnezzar began to shout.*
*When the swearing began to stop,*
*Nebuchadnezzar bought a shop;*
*When the shop began to sell,*
*Nebuchadnezzar bought a bell;*
*When the bell began to ring,*
*Nebuchadnezzar began to sing:*
*Do ray me fa so la tee do!*

So sang the urchins skipping in the street, and presumably so sang the girls who skipped in the Chestertons' garden; the refrain is inescapable as it has been passed down by the strongest of oral traditions. On January 30th, 1913 Chesterton took the traditional children's skipping rhyme and wrote his own version known as 'The Song of the Happy Vegetarian', a title later replaced by 'Pioneers, O Pioneers' borrowed from Walt Whitman:

Nebuchadnezzar the King of the Jews
Suffered from new and original views,
He crawled on his hands and knees, it's said,

With grass in his mouth and a crown on his head.
Those in traditional paths that trod
Thought the thing was a curse from God
But a pioneer men always abuse
Like Nebuchadnezzar the King of the Jews.

Neither the skipping children nor Chesterton seem to have been unduly worried that Nebuchadnezzar (604–562BC) was not King of the Jews, but the King of Babylon who in 586BC drove the Jews into their Babylonian exile and captivity; the rhyme was easy and it went with a swing, but many easy rhymes were to return to dog Chesterton's footsteps over subsequent years until in 1935 in a passage from his *Autobiography* he lamented:

> Oddly enough, I lived to have later on the name of an Anti-Semite; whereas from my first days at school I very largely had the name of a Pro-Semite. I made many friends among the Jews, and some of these I have retained as lifelong friends; nor have our relations ever been disturbed by differences upon the political or social problem . . . I was criticised in early days for quixotry and priggishness in protecting Jews; and I remember once extricating a strange swarthy little creature with a hooked nose from being bullied . . . I made many friends among the Jews, and some of these I have retained as lifelong friends; nor have our relations ever been disturbed by differences upon the political or social problem. I am glad that I began at this end; but I have not really ended any differently from the way in which I began. I held by instinct then, and I hold by knowledge now, that the right way is to be interested in Jews as Jews; and then to bring into greater prominence the very much neglected Jewish virtues, which are the complement and sometimes even the cause of what the world feels to be the Jewish faults.[1]

The unidentified schoolfellow at Colet House (Bewsher's) was in all probability one of the Jewish boys who in 1890 became members of the Junior Debating Club, and were later always fondly remembered and recorded in poems and dedications. A little later on January 5th, 1891 Chesterton noted in his diary: 'Read in *Review of Reviews* [ ii, no. 10, October 1890, p.350] various revelations of Jews in Russia. Brutal falsehood and cruelty to a Jewish girl. Made me feel strongly inclined to knock somebody down, but refrained.' The case involved 'a respectable young girl of honest parents seduced by a Christian who promised to marry her.' Reminded of his promise he used relatives in the Police to have her exiled as 'a disorderly Jewess'. Two years later Chesterton imagines himself in 'Our Future Prospects'[2] as being in St. Petersburg in support of 'the old soldiers' children as well as the Jews' Quarter'. Also dating from the early 1890s is his 'Before a Statue of Cromwell', Cromwell 'who set the Hebrew free':

Little need we search for causes 'neath the charnel and the sod
While a brave and tortured people cry the shame of men to God!
You that work the will of Russia, howling Christ against the few,
He will take some crowd of heathen ere He opes the gates to you.
Christ has borne from you more insult than from Israel He has borne.
Ye have placed the scourge of murder where they placed the reed of scorn.[3]

Chesterton was not quite his own worst enemy when he failed on occasion to resist a facile rhyme about noses, for either his wife or his editor was always prepared to step in to take on that role. Chesterton was always ready to name names, but his wife, over-anxious after his brother's trial to avoid libel-suits, cut out names and inadvertently turned a complaint by a dog locked out of the park at Lyons' Cadby Hall by Isidore Gluckstein into an attack on a Jew:

THE SONG OF THE DOG QUOODLE

They haven't got no noses,
The fallen sons of Eve;
Even the smell of roses
Is not what they supposes,
But more than mind discloses
And more than men believe.

They haven't got no noses,
They cannot even tell
When door and darkness closes
The park Old Gluck encloses,
Where even the law of Moses
Will let you steal a smell. (1911)

The change to 'The park a Jew encloses' was made during Chesterton's long illness in 1914 by Frances Chesterton for a collected edition of poems. Reversing the process neither proves nor disproves whether Chesterton was anti-Semitic or not. Likewise, listing his Jewish friends, who were many, is a pointless exercise. A glance at his file in the Weiner Library will find it very thin indeed compared with most of his contemporaries, political and literary. Nonetheless, it is probably best to examine all of his opinions, writings and social contacts, and then leave it to the readers to draw their own conclusions.

Chesterton's first recorded contacts with those of Jewish race were made at St. Paul's School and were members of the Junior Debating Club, Lawrence and Maurice Solomon, Digby and Waldo d'Avigdor, Leonard Magnus and

Humbert Woolf. Albeit that the Solomons were on occasion referred to as the 'sons of Abraham', the bonds of friendship were lifelong with the Solomons later moving to Beaconsfield, and Chesterton dedicating *The Innocence of Father Brown* to Waldo d'Avigdor, and in other poems extolling their virtues and the beauty of Waldo d'Avigdor's sweetheart, Mildred Wain:

> Lawrence, with quiet face, scarcely lit
> With mock maliciousness of wit,
> Legal and formal: praise the Lord
> For one man true as a steel sword.
>
> And Waldo, tumbled in the press
> Who in divine fastidiousness
> Chose stars, and stood out from the mire,
> Alone with his own soul's desire.
>
> Mildred, one face for everyone,
> Whom God made happier than the sun,
> Who flashed and fluttered, singing by,
> The ribbons of life's bravery. (late 1890s)

During this period Chesterton often spent time with the Solomon family when they were on holiday at Broadstairs on the Isle of Thanet where he first encountered Moses Montefiore, a very flamboyant Jewish gentleman who tended to exotically ornate taste in clothing; this meeting may have been the origin of Chesterton's opinion that Jews often wore purple ties with yellow spats:

### BALLADE OF AN INTERESTING PEOPLE

> They put on hats to praise the Lord,
> They bleed their meat till it is dry,
> They scorn the ploughshare and the sword,
> And pass the pig severely by;
> Nor do I see a reason why
> They should not do so if they choose
> – They also are a German spy –
> Such are the customs of the Jews.
>
> They bargain till they can afford
> To sit and make the money fly,
> They like to give out of a hoard
> And – if the interest is high –
> They like to lend it. And they cry

Whenever customers refuse:
'I'm persecuted. Hi! Hi! Hi!',
Such are the customs of the Jews.

Lord Rothschild ruled the Gare du Nord,
King Solomon the Genii,
Samuel, the Education Board,
And Joseph, Egypt's corn supply.
Reinach remodels history,
And Baron Reuter alters news,
And Bloch was pained that people die.
Such are the customs of the Jews.

   Envoy.
Prince, stick to it and don't be shy,
And wear white spats with yellow shoes,
Pink waistcoats and a purple tie
– Such are the customs of the Jews.

Given his reaction to anti-Semitism, Chesterton's imagination was bound to be caught by the Dreyfus Affair in France which in 1894 involved the accusation, court martial and sentencing of a Jewish officer, Captain Alfred Dreyfus (1859–1935) to imprisonment on Devil's Island in French Guiana on a charge of being a German spy. The matter split the French nation and divided opinion in England as well. Those who, like Colonel Georges Picquart (1854–1914) uncovered forgeries and revealed the identity of the real spy, Major Esterhazy, were likewise punished. Chesterton was incensed by the injustice and wrote an address to an appeal court martial, and when there was indeed an appeal he sent a letter to the court in Rennes:

### DREYFUS

On the vast mass of the matter at issue, the prosecution has simply no evidence at all. But the more remarkable and startling fact is this, that wherever and whenever they have any evidence of any kind – we have better. Wherever, I repeat, they have evidence we have better. It is the same all the way along.

   They, as I have said, can quote the declaration of the distinguished French officers on behalf of themselves. But we can quote the declarations of distinguished French officers against themselves – confessions of error, renunciations of personal interests. To show that Maurel was right in condemning Dreyfus, they can quote Maurel. But to show that Freystaelter was wrong in condemning Dreyfus, we can quote Freystaelter himself. Their testimony, if they be human, must be biassed. But our witnesses, if they be human, must, if biassed at all, be biassed against the testimony they give.

Again, they have quoted expert evidence as to the handwriting. They have told us to listen to an anthropologist and criminologist who is not a handwriting expert at all. But we have shown you not only a real handwriting expert, but the best handwriting expert in France – the expert of the Bank of France. The very man, Messieurs, who holds in his hand the financial honour and the financial destiny of thousands. The voice to whose arbitrament we submit questions involving millions of the national property, on the correctness of whose eye and brain depends the fate of sums at which the brain reels – this man, the most terribly trusted of the sons of France, declares promptly and clearly, that this is not the work of Dreyfus. After that, where is Bertillon, the amateur who thinks that letters are to be measured like the skulls of burglars? He is crushed. Everywhere, I say, where they have evidence, we have better.

But one thing [about] the Dreyfus case is beyond question: it is the most startling and dramatic vindication of the old idea of moral principle as against the new idea of philosophic optimism, that anyone could have dreamed of. There came an hour when, to all appearance the whole weight of statesmanship, tradition, tact, experience and national credit were in one scale, in the other a single man with a single scruple. This man was Picquart. The Generals, not fiends as they have been depicted, but gentlemen, men of the world and fathers of families, professing the purely official cynicism of diplomatic Europe, reasoned with him and implored him in vain: it is evident that many of them liked him and even admired him, but they put forth every conceivable effort to prevent him bringing about, as it seemed, the certain ruin of the new hope of France, for the sake of the doubtful vindication of an obscure convict. That spirit, the spirit of good-humoured alarm and benevolent broad hints, is their attitude as we see it first, in the almost affectionate letters of Gouse to Picquart. But these veterans who had considered the signs of the sky, the delicacies of politics, the secrets of discipline, the necessities of popularity, had left one thing out of their considerations, a thing destined to reappear dramatically in their midst – the soul of man. That too has its laws, and one of them is this. That if any man, from whatever motives, fights with a view lower than his own, he will grow in nobility in that process. Gouse and Picquart when they conducted that correspondence were neither of them remarkable – they were merely well-intentioned officers. But they parted where the roads forked. And no possible visions of social ruin, such as the political opportunist paints so luridly, could equal, as a calamity, the nameless corruption which was slowly generated in the minds of those once honourable men by the process of having, even from patriotic motives, to dodge the blunt questions and hoodwink the accusing eyes of one younger man. It is a monstrosity fit for Dante, and it is this alone, this spiritual law of advance and retrogression, that makes the Dreyfus case, in the long run, worth narrating at all. It is better that a man or a nation plunge into the maddest war, with great armies, than with any one who, they feel in their heart of hearts, is really right. If this consuming fire of sincerity be kindled, no nation need ever rot.

As for Picquart, they could not prevent him becoming one of the world's heroes: he could not prevent himself becoming one. He set out as a simple officer, docketing bills and documents. But he got onto the right road, which is marked on the eternal map of the spiritual universe as leading to the mountains – where man may perhaps still hear an ancient voice: and can at least tolerate the ancient silence.

And where were the chiefs, the wise men who had challenged their own consciences to single combat? The story is pathetic enough: it comes home with sudden poignancy when we read of little courtesies that remind us that these men had once been chivalrous gentlemen. But in the war against the inward light they had lost even the military silence and obedience for which they had fought so hard. Grubbing in the dust hole for documents, insulting their superiors, tub-thumping like demagogues and chattering like old women, they had sunk from an army into a rabble, and by a supreme and avenging irony, it was no judge or moralist or philanthropist, but the old queller of the rabble of the Commune that trod out their embers with his iron feet. Yet we are indignant that the French do not hail the hypothesis with joy when it is first propounded by a novelist! [Emile Zola].

But the whole thing is a mistake. It is not true that if Dreyfus is innocent, the ex-Ministers must have lied. Nor is it true that, if the ex-Ministers are men of honour, Dreyfus must be guilty. When they swore that they had knowledge of his guilt they were of course referring to the secret dossier; which contains many documents – which, if genuine, would prove that guilt.

Therefore, it was a mere matter of the authenticity of documents, a legitimate matter of opinion, on which they may have been deceived. And here comes in the plain historical fact: but everyone seems to have forgotten it. Not only do we know that they may have been deceived: we know that they were deceived. M. Cavaignac, certainly not the least acute of them, and obviously the least military, published to the eyes of friends and foes, as a picked instance of the proofs that had convinced him, a document that he himself afterwards discovered to be a forgery. And if he could be deceived by a forgery, why not the others by other forgeries? With the story of Henry and Cavaignac staring me in the face, I consider two types of men sufficiently unreasonable: one is the fanatical Revisionist who says that Cavaignac must be a dark deceiver because the document he flaunted for criticism turned out to be a forgery. And the even more ridiculous figure is the fanatical anti-Revisionist, who declares that as Cavaignac, after being deceived by a forgery, swore that Dreyfus was guilty, it must be true.

My excuse for this arid reasoning must be my firm conviction that if the French public could once grasp this simple idea – that to call Dreyfus innocent is not to call France and her politics a hell upon earth – I believe the unhappy man would lose his last enemies. It may be true of course that certain generals, Mercier in particular, have surrounded themselves with 'an atmosphere of suspicion' in the moral sense as well. But let us be cautious. If this appalling national error has not taught us to be sick of gossip and bias, of preconceived fantasies and partisan rumours, of the 'bad name' that hangs, and the idle word that lives for ever, it has taught little indeed.

I am, yours etc. G.K. Chesterton[4]

The Rennes inquiry did not exculpate Dreyfus, although his sentence was reduced. The military courts never admitted their mistake and it was only in 1903 that the civilian Cour de Cassation [Court of Appeal] declared Dreyfus innocent. He was promoted in 1906 to Major and reinstated, together with Picquart who was to reach the rank of Brigadier General and become Minister for War; both men were later appointed to the Légion d'Honeur. The matter had brought great discredit to the reputation of the French military authorities.

In two poems in 1898 Chesterton showed his indignation towards the French nation:

### TO A CERTAIN NATION

We will not let thee be, for thou art ours.
We thank thee still, though thou forget these things,
For that hour's sake when thou didst wake all powers
With a great cry that God was sick of kings.

Leave thee there grovelling at their rusted greaves,
These hulking cowards on a painted stage,
Who, with imperial pomp and laurel leaves,
Show their Marengo – one man in a cage.

These, for whom stands no type or title given
In all the squalid tales of gore and pelf;
Though cowed by crashing thunders from all heaven,
Cain never said, 'My brother slew himself.'

Tear you the truth out of your drivelling spy,
The maniac whom you set to swing death's scythe.
Nay; torture not the torturer – let him lie:
What need of racks to teach a worm to writhe?

Bear with us, O our sister. Not in pride
Nor any scorn we see thee spoiled of knaves,
But only shame to hear, where Danton died,
Thy foul dead kings all laughing in their graves.

Thou hast a right to rule thyself; to be
The thing thou wilt; to grin, to fawn, to creep,
To crown these clumsy liars; ay, and we
Who knew thee once, we have a right to weep.

And as a tribute to the one military man who sought justice for Dreyfus:

## PICQUART

Pour we our dark oblation
With all goodwill we can,
God's price in dogs and devils –
For the making of a man.

Buy with a whole land's havoc
In putrid passions hurled
One man that walked like a hero
In the morning of the world.

Though the altar-steps ran bloody,
And throned to the topmost star
Glared high and grinned above him
The brainless god of War.

He was brave in the world's old fashion
And he walked to the world's old song
That a host is a heap of weapons
And only a man is strong.

And he set the light of his anger
As naked as his steel's,
Alone in an earth of armies,
Alive in a world of wheels.

To the guards that sat by the secret,
To the lords of the shameful thing,
To them that were peers and captains,
Here is a hymn to sing –

Pour we the foul oblation
With all fair will we can,
God's price in swine and devils
For the making of a man.

With this litter of beasts we bought him;
One face through the prison bars
With the pride of the House of Adam,
And all its scorn of the stars.

Oddly enough in later years these somewhat opaque poems were to be mis-interpreted as evidence of Chesterton's anti-semitism.[5] After being influenced by Hilaire Belloc (who on the basis of his year's military service supported the French military and was never to admit Dreyfus's innocence) Chesterton in 1905 came to place blame on the reporting by the English press: 'In the matter of the Dreyfus case, while not having been able to reach my final conclusion about the proper verdict on the individual, I have come largely to attribute the difficulty of doing so to the acrid and irrational unanimity of the English Press. My position may be roughly stated thus: There may have been a fog of injustice in the French courts; I knew that there was a fog of injustice in the English newspapers.'[6] It may also have been Belloc's influence which caused Chesterton not to continue with a study of the whole Dreyfus Affair which he had sketched out:

DREYFUS

Part I. Alfred Dreyfus. A Paragraph.
  1. The Third Republic and the Man on the Black Horse.
  2. Sketches in the General Staff.
  3. Infamy.

Part II. The Paragraph Read Again.
  1. A Horrible Idea.
  2. The Remarkable Adventure of Colonel Picquart.
  3. The Fête of Esterhazy.
  4. J'Accuse.
  5. The Trial of Zola.
  6. The Campaign against Dreyfusards.
  7. A Thunderbolt.

Part III. The Paragraph Interpreted.
  1. Madame Dreyfus.
  2. The Coup of the Generals
  3. The Criminal Chamber.
  4. M. Q[uesnay] De Beaurepaire.
  5. Unanimity.
  6. The Return of Captain Dreyfus.
  7. What it all meant.

Chesterton's next involvement with matters Jewish was during the Second South African War (1899–1902) when he supported the Boer cause against that of the so-called Rand Lords and their financiers such as Albert and Otto Beit, Herman Eckstein and Marcus Goldman. Ever afterwards he was to have an aversion to what he named 'cosmopolitan' and we now call multinational enterprises, especially when they involved finance and money lending. Ironically the greater part of Chesterton's pro-Boer support was given through the pages of *The Speaker*, an organ which turned down much of his work because his italic handwriting looked too Jewish. However, it was on March 2nd, 1901 in *The Speaker* that Chesterton wrote a review:

Mr David Baron has written an interesting book called *The Ancient Scriptures and the Modern Jew* [London, Hodder & Stoughton, 1901] in the whole course of which it never seems to strike him for a moment that he is dealing with a riddle of ethics and history compared with which squaring the circle would be trivial; that if there is one thing that is more dark and remote to us then even the Ancient Scriptures, that thing is the Modern Jew. He never seems to realise, even for one dazzling instant, the idea that a bland, black-coated Aryan gentleman sitting in his armchair with a creed formulated at the Reformation and a political system diluted from the ideas of 1790, may possibly not be in complete possession of all the abysmal spiritual divisions and eternal spiritual energies which alone could finally throw light on the destiny of an immemorable people, whose strange discoveries in the world of the soul, discoveries embedded whole and often undeciphered in our later systems, were made under strange stars and lost temples, as alien as the landscapes of another planet.

The first part of Mr Baron's work deals with the ancient writings, on which he argues ingeniously enough, but about which he ignores two small points – first, that they are ancient, and, secondly, that they are writings. A man cannot comprehend even the form and language of the Psalms without a literary sense. For what are the essential facts? A great though rude and wandering people lived thousands of years ago who had, by what, from any point of view, may truly be called an inspiration, a sudden and startling glimpse of an enormous philosophical truth. These bloodthirsty Bedouins realised the last word of scientific thought, the unity of creation. Opulent empires and brilliant republics all round them were still in the nets of polytheism; but this band of outlaws knew better. This is the immortality of the Jews. Them we can never dethrone: they discovered the one central thing no modern man can help believing: whatever we think, or do, or say, we are all bound to the wheel of the stars which can only have a single centre.

This awful simplification of things they discovered, as it has since been discovered by innumerable sages. But their unique historic interest lies in this: that by a strange circumstance, that has every resemblance to a miracle, they discovered it in the morning of the world, in an age when man had needed no philosophical language. Hence they threw it into poetical language. They spoke of this startling speculative theory with the same bold, brisk, plain-coloured imagery with which primitive ballads commonly speak of war and hunting, women and gold. If we imagine Spinoza's philosophy written with enormous vividness in the literary style of 'Chevy Chase,' we shall have some idea of that confounding marvel which is called the Old Testament . . .

. . . The second part of Mr Baron's work, that which deals with the modern Jew, is infinitely more satisfactory. It would be quite unfair to Mr Baron to say that this was because it contains two very interesting articles contributed by other people, for his own remarks on the Semitic problem of today are genuinely good in themselves. But he has certainly elucidated the problem in no small degree by including two chapters in quotation marks, one by a distinguished Jew, and another by a distinguished Christian. The modern Jew is unpopular in Europe, but chiefly, we fear, for his virtues. No one has the pleasure of the friendship of any Jews who has not noticed that almost weird domesticity, that terrible contentment which makes the life of parlour and nursery quite satisfactory to a Jew of the calibre and spirit which, if he were a Gentile, would make it a devouring necessity to him to 'see life.'

It is this formidable normality that constitutes the real power of the Jew. It is the survival of the blinding simplification of existence of which we have spoken. It is no mere accident that the most brilliant Jew of this age is Dr Max Nordau; a man with whom, to speak paradoxically, sanity has become a madness. He spares nothing in his application of the religion of commonsense, the law that is written in men's bones. Neither the hardness of Tolstoi nor the fragility of Maeterlinck; neither the bitter simplicity of Ibsen nor the drunken glory of Whitman can lure this old Hebrew from the straight path of Judgment. Dr Max Nordau (1849–1923), in a passage which Mr Baron quotes, speaks with splendid scorn of decadents even of his own race – and the decadents of his own race are, in his opinion, the Jewish millionaires. No Gentile certainly would dare speak of them as they are spoken of by a Jew: – 'These money-pots who despise what we honour and honour what we despise . . . Many of them forsake Judaism and we wish them God-speed, only regretting that they are all of Jewish blood, though but of the dregs.' . . . There is one lesson that remains to be drawn, more especially from the case of those Semitic plutocrats of whom Dr Max Nordau speaks so disdainfully: – 'In an ordinary independent Jewish community,' . . . he says with sharp. but just sarcasm, 'they would not receive titles of honour such as those by which they are decorated by Christian societies.' But the real lesson of the Jewish plutocratic problem seems to us a simple one, and one very much needed at present. It is the utter futility of attempting to crush a fine race. In science men know that no force is ever destroyed; but the fact has yet to be learnt in politics. There are a thousand things that a wronged people may become – a rival, like America; a clog, like Ireland; an internal disease, like Jewish commerce; but it always becomes something. We forbade to the Jews all natural callings except commerce, and today commerce is what might be expected from being eternally recruited with all the most intellectual sons of a most intellectual people. We pray that the error may not be repeated in certain corners of the earth.To avoid a repetition of it would be far worthier than the frivolous Continental anti-Semitism which can find no answer to Jewish triumphs, except to flourish tauntingly the image of a martyred Jew upon an Aryan gibbet.[7]

Yet about the same time he wrote in condemnation of Jewish influence in South Africa:

### LINES SUITABLE TO A LADY'S ALBUM

So Cecil Rhodes has gone to Hell,
– Not there by faithful Beit forsook –
Eckstein's feeling far from well,
And Goldtmann is not yet a Duke:
They lent their aid when England shook,
At five per cent or even ten,
Yet Death and Shame their shame rebuke:
Where are the Empire's choicest men?

And Kipling's skull's an empty shell
Just haunted by his bleating spook,
Who brought such aid to . . . Israel. (c1902)

### TO LORD CLAUDE HAMILTON AND ANOTHER

*'General Botha is a man. Such men are wanted in the United Kingdom.'*
Lord Claud Hamilton

. . . For you, New Tory of the ink-soiled trade,
Whom foreign foes bid call a spear a spade,
Who on Dutch kicks and Yiddish bribes have thriven,
Whose trembling fingers have torn down and given
The Union Jack up to this first of foes
To wipe his bloody knife and blow his nose –
Lie down; curl up; do anything you can,
You will not be mistaken for a man. (c1903)

Any Jew who changed his name or hid it behind a title was mocked as 'that old salted Viking called Sassoon' or lambasted in a lampoon:

### BALLADE OF BACON (to Lucy Masterman)

Our Saxon Earl, Lord Cedric Westlandehaugh,
Still blinks and shrinks from pork before him placed,
His taste in dress is somewhat rich and raw,
His taste in smiles is ponderous and unchaste;
A sleek old sneering, sniggering, blubber-faced
Fat old Phoenicean thief and thimblerig –
For finding out the race from which he raced
I know few things more pleasing than a pig. (1911)

About the same time in *The Logical Vegetarian* a remarkably similar view was expressed:

> Oh, I knew a Doctor Gluck
> And his nose it had a hook,
> And his attitudes were anything but Aryan;
> So I gave him all the pork
> That I had, upon a fork,
> Because I am myself a Vegetarian.

However, Chesterton was not always right in his interpretation. For instance in *The Ball and the Cross* (1905) he wrongly presumed that the Mr Gordon who ran a curio emporium in St. Martin's Lane, had usurped a Scottish name, whereas Gordon is quite a common Ashkanazim name originating in Russia.

> The keeper of the curiosity shop . . . was a Jew of another and much less admirable type; a Jew with a very well-sounding name. For though there are no hard tests for separating the tares and wheat of any people; one rude but efficient guide is that the nice Jew is called Moses Solomon, and the nasty Jew is called Thornton Percy. The keeper of the curiosity shop was of the Thornton Percy branch of the chosen people; he belonged to those Lost Ten Tribes whose industrious object is to lose themselves. He was a man still young, but already corpulent, with sleek dark hair, . . . and a full, fat permanent smile, which looked at the first glance kindly, and at the second cowardly. The name over his shop was Henry Gordon, but two Scotchmen who were in his shop that evening could come upon no trace of a Scotch accent.[8]

Such a faux pas, noted by Julius West as early as 1912 may have been due to Chesterton's Jewish friends being Sephardic rather than from the more recently arrived Ashkanazim community. Even to this day there is a tendency for Sephardic and Ashkanazim groups to live in different areas. Perhaps Chesterton should just have stuck to Thornton Percy.

On July 13th, 1907 writing in the *Illustrated London News* on sport, Chesterton noted 'It is, broadly speaking, true that the Jews are, as a race pacific, intellectual, indifferent to war, like the Indians, or perhaps, contemptuous of war, like the Chinese: nevertheless, of the very good prize-fighters, one or two have been Jews.' He had obviously forgotten to refer to the Old Testament.

Another reference in the same year in 'The People of England' (also known as 'The Secret People') had the persona of the bent lawyer or manipulative money-lender looming large:

But the squire seemed stuck in the saddle; he was foolish, as if in pain.
He leaned on a staggering lawyer, he clutched a cringing Jew,
He was stricken; it may be, after all, he was stricken at Waterloo.
Or perhaps the shades of the shaven men, whose spoil is in his house,
Come back in shining shapes at last to spoil his last carouse:
We only know the last sad squires ride slowly towards the sea,
And a new people takes the land: and still it is not we.

However, it was in 1909 or before (*The Ball and the Cross* having been begun in 1905) in Turnbull's Dream that Chesterton outlined his principles when faced with a situation very reminiscent of 'Arbeit Macht Frei':

Turnbull looked down and saw that the polished car was literally lit up from underneath by the far-flung fires from below. Underneath whole squares and solid districts were in flames, like prairies or forests on fire.

'Dr Hertz has convinced everybody,' said Turnbull's cicerone in a smooth voice, 'that nothing can really be done with the real slums. His celebrated maxim has been quite adopted. I mean the three celebrated sentences: 'No man should be unemployed. Employ the employables. Destroy the unemployables.'

There was a silence, and then Turnbull said in a rather strained voice: 'And do I understand that this good work is going on under here?'

'Going on splendidly,' replied his companion in the heartiest voice. 'You see, these people were much too tired and weak even to join the social war. They were a definite hindrance to it.'

'And so you are simply burning them out?'

'It *does* seem absurdly simple,' said the man, with a beaming smile, 'when one thinks of all the worry and talk about helping a hopeless slave population, when the future was only crying to be rid of them. There are happy babes unborn ready to burst the doors when these drivellers are swept away.'

'Will you permit me to say,' said Turnbull, after reflection, 'that I don't like all this?' . . . 'I think I should always have said that I don't like this. These people have rights.'

'Rights!' repeated the unknown in a tone quite indescribable. Then he added with a more open sneer: 'Perhaps they also have souls.'

'They have lives!' said Turnbull, sternly; 'that is quite enough for me. I understood you to say that you thought life sacred.'

'Yes, indeed!' cried his mentor with a sort of idealistic animation. 'Yes, indeed! Life is sacred – but lives are not sacred. We are improving Life by removing lives. Can you, as a freethinker, find any fault in that?'

'Yes,' said Turnbull with brevity.

'Yet you applaud tyrannicide,' said the stranger with rationalistic gaiety. 'How inconsistent! It really comes to this: You approve of taking away life from those to whom it is a triumph and a pleasure. But you will not take away life from those to whom it is a burden and a toil.'

Turnbull rose to his feet in the car with considerable deliberation, but his face seemed oddly pale. The other went on with enthusiasm.

'Life, yes, Life is indeed sacred!' he cried; 'but new lives for old! Good lives for bad! On that very place where now there sprawls one drunken wastrel of a pavement artist more or less wishing he were dead – on that very spot there shall in the future be living pictures; there shall be golden girls and boys leaping in the sun.'

Turnbull, still standing up, opened his lips. 'Will you put me down, please?' he said, quite calmly, like one stopping an omnibus.

'Put you down – what do you mean?' cried his leader. 'I am taking you to the front of the revolutionary war, where you will be one of the first of the revolutionary leaders.'

'Thank you,' replied Turnbull with the same painful constraint. 'I have heard about your revolutionary war, and I think on the whole that I would rather be anywhere else.'[9]

Although there is no specific identification, It seems that Turnbull would have included Jewish lives among those he thought sacred.

On March 11th, 1911 Samuel Montagu (born Montagu Samuel), Lord Swaythling (1832–1911) was criticised in *The Nation* (successor to *The Speaker*) because his will demanded that his children keep to the orthodox Jewish religion, refrain from marrying outside the Jewish faith and promoting any kind of liberal Judaism on pain of losing bequests from the said will. In the following issue on March 18th Chesterton dashed in where angels might have feared to tread to defend Lord Swaythling's right to dispose of his estate on the terms he wished:

Sir, I venture to ask you to give a more liberal consideration to the right of Jews. As an old-fashioned Radical, I was brought up in the tradition of doing justice to another man's religion. But it is only his irreligion that the moderns seem disposed to respect. In a note to your last issue, you severely blame the late Lord Swaythling because (as he saw the thing) he left money to such Jews as should remain Jews and not become apostates. It is, I think, the first time you have ever blamed Lord Swaythling, as it is the first time that I have ever very specially admired him. Why on earth should not a man love a cause, and leave money to a cause, and leave it on condition of the maintenance of the cause? You say he is controlling the spiritual liberty of his relatives; but how could he? His relatives retain complete spiritual liberty: the spiritual liberty to refuse the money. And if, (as you say) the unorthodox Jews are 'the best minds and lives' in the society, how can there be an instant's doubt about their decision . . .

Many Englishmen, and I am one of them, do seriously think that the international and largely secret power of the great Jewish houses is a problem and a peril. To all this, however, you are indifferent. You allow Jews to be monopolists and wire-pullers, war-makers and strike-breakers, buyers of national honours and sellers of national honour. The one thing apparently that you won't allow Jews to be is Jews. You don't mind their managing our affairs; it is when they venture to manage their own affairs that you interfere with them. You would think me a horrible 'anti-Semite' if I denounced the Jew who really works underground, who commands the sweat of Whitechapel and blood of Spion Kop, who is a traitor in France and a tyrant in England; but you passionately protest against the Jew who leaves some of his own money to his own family in accordance with his own religion. The wealthy Semite sits in the inmost chamber of the State; he controls it by a million filaments of politics and finance. But the only pebble you throw at the poor old man, you throw at his one most honorable moment, when his schemes are over and his riches vain, and with a gesture, momentarily sublime, he bears witness to the God of his fathers. This does not strike me as respecting a religion – or even as tolerating it. Yours &c., G.K. Chesterton, Beaconsfield.

The editor of *The Nation* responded: *Mr Chesterton is true to his faith, as we to ours. He believes in penning a man in the spiritual paddock into which he was born; we believe in enlarging the bonds of the paddock. Mr Chesterton praises a Jew only when he does an illiberal act. The late Lord Swaythling did not, as he says, merely leave money on condition that the recipients remained Jews and did not become apostates. He practically disinherited two of his children unless they consented to take precisely the same view of Judaism as he took. This is the act we criticised, and Mr Chesterton approves . . . Ed. Nation [H.W. Massingham].*

## On March 15th, 1911 Chesterton again took up his pen:

I want . . . to protest against being summarised in your note as holding the exact opposite of what I really hold. You say I hold that a man must remain in the paddock where he was born. I don't hold this: and I have not said or done it. If I had remained in the paddock where I was born, I should be in your paddock. I was brought up in your modernism and new Theology; and I should not dream of such blasphemy against reason and freedom as to say that a man must stay in such a narrow corner. I never said that, if a man ceases to believe in his creed, he must not quit it. What I said was that as long as he does believe it, I don't think the worse of him for acting on it. Some reflections upon Saul of Tarsus might be permitted here.

. . . My sympathies are with the masses that really believe in the several creeds. I do not like your aristocracy of doubt. I think a Dervish dying on the bayonets is not only nearer to God, but nearer to Christianity, than a young Turk talking in French or thinking in German. I think a poor Jew keeping the feast of Tabernacles [Succoth] in Petticoat Lane is not only more Jewish, but more psychologically Christian than a rich Jew 'extending the borders' of his mind, his income and the British Empire all at once. And I complain that the modern mind permits men like Lord Swaythling to achieve economic omnipotence and hereditary sanctity, but denies them the rights of conscience. It allows Lord Swaythling to create a Jewish oligarchy. It only rebukes him for the one thing that may be shared by the Jewish democracy.

Yours, &c., G.K. Chesterton, Beaconsfield.

[*We should like to hear Mr Chesterton develop the grounds of his religious preference for a 'Dervish dying on the bayonets' to a 'Young Turk talking in French.' Is it that the Dervish is not, while the other is, a thinking human being? – Ed., Nation*]

## The editor of the *Nation* did not have longer to wait than three days:

Sir, – Do you mean it? May I really? At the end of my last letter you append the madly tempting phrase: 'We should like to hear Mr Chesterton develop the grounds of his religious preference for a Dervish dying on the bayonets to a Young Turk talking in French. Is it that the Dervish is not, while the other is, a thinking human being?' Would you really like to hear me? Well (in the words of one of your Hebrew apostles of Liberalism), the time will come when you shall hear me (Disraeli). It will come now in fact. It will come before the end of this letter. But before I accept so uproarious an invitation, you may allow me to answer some positive challenges that you have printed. For convenience I will put my opponents in paragraphs.

(1) First comes Mr Levy, who points out, with some wealth of metaphor, that the fruit of my imagination is a herring across your contention. He says that a legatee receiving money on a religious condition is merely like a man who must choose between recantation and the rack. Surely the answer is very simple. Is it a common human custom to leave instructions with your lawyer that your children are to be racked? Plainly, it is a common human custom to leave estates conditionally, to promote causes. I never claimed for Lord Swaything more than this common conventional sympathy. I never said it was the best thing he could have done or the precise thing that I should have done. I only said it was much the most dignified thing that I had ever heard about him.

(2) I have so real a respect for the intellect of Dr Warschauer that I looked him up in 'Who's Who' to see whether he could be the same Warschauer. What can Dr Warschauer mean by saying that what I resent is the use of private judgment? He might as well say I resent the use of private property. Does he think that the Thirty-Nine Articles decree that I sympathise with Lord Swaything? Does he think the Pope told me to congratulate Jews on being Jews? Doesn't he know private judgment when he sees it?

(3) The letter of Mr Lucian Wolf I have read four or five times, wondering whether it was hypocrisy or simplicity. By the fifth reading I am sure it is simplicity: so the friendliest feeling can now prevail. But what a letter! He asks me, with monstrous solemnity, for the names of any Jews concerned in effecting the Transvaal War. Does he want you to publish a special supplement? Does he mean that Mr Beit was a Scottish Highlander by blood and an English High Churchman by education? Or does he mean that Mr Beit happened to be thinking about the Atomic Theory all through the intrigues that made the war? If Mr Wolf talks like that, I can only say that while I have the highest respect for him, I have not the faintest patience with him. I happen to prefer to exist among realities and to walk in the land of the living.

Mr Wolf's letter might suggest to some that I said that 'Jews' were traitors in France and tyrants in England. Some of my oldest and dearest friends are Jews; and none of my friends are tyrants or traitors. I said that there was one particular kind of Jew who is a traitor in France and a tyrant in England. I cannot believe that a sensible Jew would deny this, any more than I should deny that there is a kind of Englishman who is a black sheep in South Africa, but a bully in Ireland. As Mr Wolf acutely says, there are bad Jews as there are bad Christians. My complaint is that the bad Jews are never denounced except for being good Jews.

The case of Dreyfus is an unfortunate choice for the purpose of convincing me. For I happen to be quite certain that in that case the British public was systematically and despotically duped by some power – and I naturally wonder what power. Whether or no Dreyfus betrayed his country, the English journalist certainly betrayed his readers. Gigantic and glaring facts, huge chapters of the story, were totally blacked out by the Dreyfusard censor. The Rennes trial was so mutilated that it scarcely made grammatical sense. I can only guess about the traitor in France; but I know about the tyrant in England.

As to Mr Wolf's general challenge, my reply is simple. I will write what I think about the Semite financiers if you will print it. But as a paper was recently fined nearly a thousand pounds for saying 'Blumenfeldt,' I rather doubt if you can be expected to.

(4) Mr Dell's notions of persuasion are even quainter. He tries to prove to me that I am wrong by telling me how many of the ablest men in France have come to my conclusion. He seems to suppose I shall be horrified at the prospect of agreeing with some of the most celebrated French men of letters. I think I can face it. Of course, it would be absurd to say that there are no oppressive capitalists who are not Jews. But it is much more absurd to say that the capitalist belonging to a wandering and detached nation, not to the nations in which he wanders, is a fact that makes no difference. It must make a difference, in common sense. Suppose Lord Kitchener had a brother at the head of of the French army, another at the head of the German army, a cousin at the head of the Russian, and a nephew at the head of the Austrian, should we not look doubtfully at the Kitchener family? Yet this is the exact condition in finance.

Mr Dell also asks me if I know of some other economic solution than the collectivising of all capital. The answer is, 'Yes.' But the only part of it relevant here is that we should begin to talk plainly about Lord Swaythling and everybody else. But Mr Dell says with true Fabian caution, 'We do not denounce capitalists or monopolists, but Capitalism and Monopoly.' It is safer.

(5) I want to thank Mr Sacher for his extremely sensible letter, and assure him that I never meant to interfere with the Jews' own definitions of Judaism. I only objected to such interference when it took the form of rebuke.

(6) That thing you want to hear me develop. When you asked if my meaning was not really that the Dervish is not, but the young Turk is 'a thinking human being,' I felt as if the Statue of Liberty had fallen in New York Harbour. The whole edifice of democracy came down with a crash. Don't you see that all possible democracy, brotherhood, or rights of man rests on the fact that every man alive is a thinking human being? Don't you see that all aristocracy and exclusiveness is built on your idea that a man only begins to 'think' when he learns French – or some such thing? The Dervish is not a thinking human being! The Jingoes, sir, may live to thank you for that word. When next

it is convenient to the 'Capitalists' to mow down men like grass in the Soudan, to steal their land and desecrate their tombs, it may be remembered that you said they were not really thinking human beings. It may be quoted and recalled that a Liberal paper classed the Arabs with the brutes that perish because they do not know French . . .

This correspondance was quick to draw the attention of *The Jewish Chronicle*, which on April 28th, 1911 interviewed Mr G.K. Chesterton:

The *Outlook* is not the only journal that has commented unfavourably on certain provisions in the will of the late Lord Swaythling. *The Nation*, of which Mr H.W. Massingham is the distinguished editor, has also had a good deal to say about what it complains of as the exclusive narrowness which dictated what it terms the offending clauses. Thereupon Mr G.K. Chesterton rushed into the little fray with a letter to *The Nation*, in which he asked for 'a more liberal consideration to the right of Jews' to maintain a continuity of their faith among their relatives by withholding money from those who apostasised. 'Why on earth should not man love a cause and leave money to a cause, and leave it on condition of the maintenance of the cause? asked Mr Chesterton. He denied that Lord Swaythling controlled by his testament 'the spiritual liberty of his relatives' because he argued they retained 'complete spiritual liberty' to refuse the money. Mr Chesterton, however, before concluding his letter to the *Nation*, had some remarkable things to say about Jews and Jewish influence generally, and it was in reference to this pronouncement of his that a representative of the Jewish Chronicle called upon him at his charming retreat in the Buckinghamshire village, the name of which was made for ever famous by the Jew who became England's Prime Minister.

*Tell me, Mr Chesterton, what on earth, to use your own expletive, do you mean by daring to suggest in your letter to the Nation, that there is a problem, and, above all, a peril, in 'the international and largely secret power of the great Jewish houses." I am surprised to find you afflicted with such a bogey?*

'I can only look at things as they are,' humbly pleaded Mr Chesterton, 'indeed this is the métier in life I am constantly endeavouring to fulfil, and, of course, it gets me into no end of troubles. When I find a great banking house, controlling vast financial resources, has branches in every capital, I think I am correct in calling the power it possesses "international".'

*But no more than in the case of many another business?*

'It is the same family, whether you are in London or Paris or Vienna, and, of course, the power is a "secret" one. One such firm, and there is more than one among Jews, is able to wield an influence altogether independent of the countries in which these houses operate.'

*I confess I do not follow you unless you are referring to the power of money in general which to my mind has at least as good counterpoise in the power of organised labour on international lines?*

'But I was speaking of Jews,' put in Mr Chesterton 'and . . .'

*Exactly and then?*

'That to my mind makes all the difference and I should call any international Jewish organisation of labour just as much a problem and a peril.'

*Then religion with you governs the whole matter?*

'Not religion, but civilisation. No one can regard Jews as otherwise than a separate civlisation, a separate people with a separate tradition through many ages.'

*This will be news to the Jewish bankers?*

'Oh, yes. I know they call themselves, for instance, in this country Englishmen, and they are patriots and loyal, and hold land and give liberally to English institutions, subsidise party funds, become Peers and Members of Parliament, entertain, hunt, shoot, and all the rest of it. Still the Jew is not an Englishman, because his nationality is not English. They are something different, and in many ways very much better. Still, being better, they cannot be the same. They are allied, and rightly and justifiably, to their own people of their own race who are not English even in point of view of citizenship – Jews in Germany, Russia, France, everywhere.'

*That is why you rush to the conclusion that Jews are 'monopolists and wire-pullers, war-makers and strike-breakers, buyers of national honour and sellers of national honour'?*

'Jews have not the exclusive right to these distinctions' replied Mr Chesterton lustily shaking his leonine locks. 'Not by any means. All that I wanted to point out in my letter to the *Nation* was the horrible inconsistency of this organ of public opinion. It raises no sort of objection to Jews being all that I said, to their oppression, by power of capital, of the peoples of the world, to their doing the most un-Jewish things according to the Old Testament as so many non-Jews do the most un-Christian according to the New Testament, and yet when a man like Lord Swaythling, a rich capitalist, does something to defend his creed, something in the cause of Judaism, then and only then does the *Nation* demur. Don't mistake me,' went on Mr Chesterton, 'I am no anti-Semite. I respect and have the deepest regard for Jews, for their wonderful history, for their wonderful faith, and for their remarkably fine qualities, mental and moral, which the Jew evinces in his natural state. Of course, I can't stand the Jew who, having struck oil, oils himself all over; he is only a little more repugnant in my eyes than the non-Jew who does likewise, because he is a Jew with infinite potentialities. The sort of Jew that I am against is the one who is unfaithful to his race, who, saying he is proud about being a Jew, strives his utmost to assimilate. That is why, as I said, that it occurred to me as intolerable that the *Nation* should have thrown its only pebble at Lord Swaythling just, as I remarked, 'At his one most honourable moment, when his schemes are over and his riches vain, and, with a gesture momentarily sublime, he bears witness to the God of his fathers."

*That is all very well, Mr Chesterton, but as Jews are, they are in the aggregate the poorest people on earth. Why deny us our handful of capitalists – your English Christians reek with wealth?*

'Because to my mind, a Jewish capitalist is different from an ordinary capitalist. The latter is restrained by nationality. Jews are not, say what you will. For instance,' proceeded Mr Chesterton, 'the great English landowners are tied to England in a way that no Jewish capitalist can be tied – by something more than his land, by association with his past. You see I believe that England is in danger of a real smash-up, of a great national disaster. When such an event happens, our wealthy people will remain here and bear the burden of the nation's sorrow. The Jews won't, and we can't expect them to.'

*Why?*

'Because they are not historically fixed to the soil as are Englishmen. Jews have many great qualities – a marked thing I have often noticed about them is that they are, as it were, born civilised. You don't get among Jews anything like the 'yokel' type. That is because they are not Englishmen, or Frenchmen, or Germans, or Russians, all of whom produce their 'yokels', but belong to a much more ancient strain of civilisation which tells in their heredity. What would, of course, happen if England encountered a smash-up is that the Jews would leave as they did when Spain ceased to be a first-class power . . .'

*'Leave' is good – I beg pardon, Chestertonian – in the case of Spain!*

'Exactly. I know what you are thinking of; they were made to leave, and, therefore, as a fact they did leave. But why were they made to leave? Because Spain when she became nationally weak was not strong enough any longer to harbour a people like the Jews, ethnologically and historically a people separate from the Spanish. When countries are weak, their peoples are naturally prone to look with suspicion and even honest fear upon any elements that make for national disintegration, which means national undoing. It is, I believe, the same in Russia today, and I see the possibility, mutatis mutandis, of the same sort of thing coming about in England.'

*Truly you have spun a supreme paradox, Mr Chesterton, pleaded our representative. You will not have the Jew assimilate, and you regard him as a national danger because he doesn't – unless, perhaps, he is always and everywhere ground down by poverty. Must, then, the Jew always be burnt?*

'No human brain could spin such a paradox as the Jew actually is,' declared Mr Chesterton, with an emphasis which with him means weight: 'it is a paradox he has woven for himself through generations, and so he will remain always in danger of being "burnt", as you put it, until . . .?'

*He loses himself . . .?*

'No, no, no,' interrupted Mr Chesterton. 'Exactly the contrary – till he finds himself! Till the Jew discovers he is of a separate race, with a history of his own, and a future which to be worthy he must make his own. Till thus finding himself the Jew perceives the necessity for a habitat, a centrum, wherein he can develop that which he now lacks, naturally. You see I am not an anti-Semite. I am a Zionist . . .'

*Terms which some people declare to be identical?*

'That is arrant nonsense. It is equivalent to saying that a man who is anxious of the preservation of the supremacy of the English race is an Anglophobe, or that a mountain is a valley.'

*Surely the realisation of the Zionist plan would accentuate our separateness and so pro tanto does its advocacy?*

'But no one grumbles at separateness. The average Englishman does not dislike a foreigner so long as he is the real thing. Its the sham they object to – they dislike the German who with raucous gutturality shouts, "Alles Beritisch" and not the Teuton, who, with a bad cigar between the fingers of one hand and a half-yard high glass of lager in the other sings the "*Wacht am Rhein.*" The Jew, as member of a separate nationality – frankly and openly so – would disarm dislike. Besides, he would gain respect in the world were he one of a nation and not one of a wandering tribe. Anyway the Jew would then be taking up his rightful position which he doesn't today. Today he is like a master key, plunged into every keyhole upside down. He may open the door but he deranges the lock. I want the Jew to form a key that will fit into his own door. I believe Zionism would bring to the Jew territorial patriotism, which he now lacks. It would assuredly allow him to develop his own culture in arts, in literature, in science, and it would put an end to the eternal entanglement of mutual wrong of which he is the unhappy cause between himself and the nations among whom he lives.'

*But Palestine will not absorb all the Jews, and all the Jews won't go.*

'It will not absorb all the Jews, but it will absorb all the Judaism, so that the Jews of the rest of the world could then quite safely and conscientiously, without, I should think, any disloyalty, allow themselves to be absorbed. You would have secured the continuity of the race, its traditions and its history by those who went to form the nation in

Palestine. As to the rest of the Jews, it would not matter then if they were lost. Nay, I think it might be an advantage.'

*That is all very well in theory, Mr Chesterton. But, I fancy in practice, a Jewish State notwithstanding, Jews would find assimilation by intermarriage impracticable?*

'Of course, it would not be all done at once. You could not, for instant, expect the Russian Jew to assimilate by intermarriage with the Russian Moujik. But the Jews as a nation, instead of a wandering society in a chaotic state of disorganisation, their status would be so raised that classes higher in the social scale would not disdain marital alliance with the Jew, so that Jewish assimilation outside the Jewish State would be more rapid than is possible under present conditions. Besides,' continues Mr Chesterton, 'I don't see why people need bother their heads about "solving" questions. You can't do that as it were in a go. You can't solve the Jewish question by any preconceived, definite, set plan. The most and best you can do is to put it upon lines whereby it will have the best opportunity of its solving itself. Zionism, I believe to be the right line, and the Jews who are anxious to see the Jewish question solved should do their utmost to shunt it on that line. Otherwise . . .'

*Otherwise?*

'Well, history will go on repeating itself for the Jew. As has been his past, so his future. My point is this: That the Jews, being landless, unnaturally, alternate between too much power and too little, that the Jew Millionaire is too safe and the Jew pedlar too harassed. It is not likely that millionaires amongst you will be otherwise than the very few. Therefore, for the many, I am afraid the future will be as the past has been – murder, outrage, persecution, insult, moral and physical torture, wandering unrest, oscillations of comfortless abasing and uncertain toleration with grinding, enervating, cramping disabilities; in short, the Jew – at least for the most part always burnt.'

*Unkind history!*

'It is not the fault of history that it repeats itself,' said Mr Chesterton, bringing an end to the interview, 'when you keep on giving it nothing but the same material to work upon. If you supply an artisan with hides, hides, nothing but hides, you must not grumble if he produces none but leather goods. If you want jewellery and plate, you must supply your worker not with leather, but with gold and silver and precious stones!'[10]

Chesterton's next foray was in 'The Aristocratic 'Arry', *Daily News*, June 15th, 1912, reprinted in *Miscellany of Men* 1912:

The thing that is really vulgar, the thing that is really vile, is to live in a good place without becoming part of it, without living by its life. Anyone who settles down in a place without becoming part of it is (barring peculiar personal cases, of course) a tripper or wandering cad. For instance the Jew is a genuine peculiar case. The Wandering

Jew is not a wandering cad. He is a highly civilised man in a highly difficult position; the world being divided, and his own nation being divided, about whether he can do anything else except wander.

## This was followed, again in 1912 in *Manalive*, Part 2, Chapter 2

'. . . I believe the maniac was one of those who do not merely come, but are sent; sent like a great gale upon ships by Him who made His angels winds and His messengers a flaming fire. This, at least, I known for certain. Whether such men have laughed or wept, we have laughed at their laughter as much as at their weeping. Whether they cursed or blessed the world, they have never fitted it. It is true that men have shrunk from the sting of a great satirist, as if from the sting of an adder. But it is equally true that men flee from the embrace of a great optimist as from the embrace of a bear. Nothing brings down more curses than a real benediction. For the goodness of good things, like the badness of bad things, is a prodigy past speech; it is to be pictured rather than spoken. We shall have gone deeper than the deeps of heaven and grown older than the oldest angels before we feel, even in its first faint vibrations, the everlasting violence of that double passion with which God hates and loves the world. – I am, yours faithfully, 'Raymond Percy'

'Oh, 'oly, 'oly, 'oly!' said Mr Moses Gould.

The instant he had spoken all the rest knew they had been in an almost religious state of submission and assent. Something had bound them all together, something in the sacred tradition of the last two words of the letter; something also in the touching and boyish embarrassment with which Inglewood had read them – for he had all the thin-skinned reverence of the agnostic. Moses Gould was as good a fellow in his way as ever lived; far kinder to his family than more refined men of pleasure, simple and steadfast in his admirations, a thoroughly wholesome animal and a thoroughly genuine character. But wherever there is conflict, crises come in which any soul, personal or racial, unconsciously turns on the world the most hateful of its hundred faces. English reverence, Irish mysticism, American idealism, looked up and saw on the face of Moses a certain smile. It was that smile of the Cynic Triumphant, which has been the tocsin for many a cruel riot in Russian villages or mediaeval towns.

'Oh, 'oly, 'oly, 'oly!' said Moses Gould.

Finding that this was not well received, he explained further, exuberance deepening on his dark exuberant features.

'Always fun to see a bloke swallow a wasp when 'e's corfin' up a fly,' he said pleasantly.[11]

What is usually missed by those who quote this passage as evidence of Chesterton's anti-Semitism, is that, cynic or sceptic as he may be, Moses Gould is right in his reactions, and English reverence, Irish mysticism and American idealism are wrong in their reactions to 'Raymond Percy'. Of course, being right has never spared anyone in a riot.

In 1912 Chesterton fell over a plant-pot and badly broke his right arm which was never set properly, leaving him unable to lift it above shoulder height. His doctor asked him to take a pen and write in order to assess the extent of his disability. Chesterton wrote down the name of a particular prominent individual followed by a triolet.

> I am fond of Jews,
> Jews are fond of money:
> Never mind of whose,
> I am fond of Jews.
> Oh, but when they lose,
> Damn it all, it's funny.
> [I am fond, of Jews,
> Jews are fond of money.]

Maisie Ward noted, 'The name at the head (which wild horses would not drag from me) is the key to this impromptu'.[12] The paper was either lost when Sheed & Ward's offices were hit by a German bomb in 1941, or it was thrown away once published in Ward's biography, as seems to have become common practice.

A year later Chesterton was advocating a variation on his idea that everyone should wear clothes to distinguish their trade:

'What Shall We Do With Our Jews?

> I am a Liberal; and I dislike the idea of Jews being excluded from any civic order. By all means let a Jew be Prime Minister. But what a good taste Disraeli might have had in Oriental dress! And what a damnable taste he had in English dress! By all means let a Jew [Rufus Isaacs] be Lord Chief Justice. I cannot quite grasp why the most discredited Jew should be specially selected for that post; but in this precisely what puzzles me is the existence of so many more worthy Jewish lawyers. By all means let him be Lord Chief Justice; but let him not sit in wig and gown, but in turban and flowing robes.[13]

This was further compounded by:

> ... the man sitting next to him ... never spoke at all but whose face seemed to speak for him. This man was Dr Gluck, the German Minister, whose face had nothing German about it; neither the German vision nor the German sleep. His face was as vivid as a highly coloured photograph and altered like a cinema: but his scarlet lips never moved in speech. His almond eyes seemed to shine with all the shifting fires of the opal; his

small curled moustache seemed sometimes almost to twist itself afresh, like a live black snake: but there came from him no sound. [14]

Of course, it is now largely forgotten what an influence Ottoman power had at the time Chesterton was writing just before the First World War when the Axis alliance brought a real threat from Turkish forces. The year 1914 also brought a reprise of the Dreyfus Case by Father Brown:

'What was it then? Treason?' asked Flambeau, resuming his dinner.

'I don't know that either,' answered Brown, with a face of blank bewilderment.

'The only thing I can think of . . . Well, I never understood that Dreyfus case. I can always grasp moral evidence easier than other sorts. I go by a man's eyes and voice, don't you know, and whether his family seems happy, and by what subjects he chooses and avoids. Well, I was puzzled in the Dreyfus case. Not by the horrible things imputed both ways; I know (though it's not modern to say so) that human nature in the highest places is still capable of being Cenci or Borgia. No; what puzzled me was the *sincerity* of both parties. I don't mean the political parties; the rank and file are always roughly honest, and often duped. I mean the persons of the play. I mean the conspirators, if they were conspirators. I mean the traitor, if he was a traitor. I mean the men who must have known the truth. Now Dreyfus went on like a man who knew he was a wronged man. And yet the French statesmen and soldiers went on as if they knew he wasn't a wronged man but simply a wrong 'un.

I don't mean they behaved well; I mean they behaved as if they were sure. I can't describe these things; I know what I mean.'

. . . 'I believe it's some plot!' snapped Valognes – 'some plot of the Jews and Freemasons.'[15]

Then in 'The Five of Swords', *Hearst's International*, February 1919:

Monk had long felt that his friend was more and more disposed to let the opposite group off lightly; he had long been speaking of them soberly as sober merchants. But whether or no it was the anti-climax of safety, he had a sense that the figures opposite had shrunk, and were more commonplace and ugly. The eagle nose of Le Caron looked more like a common hook; his fine clothes seemed to sit more uneasily on him, as on a hastily dressed doll; and even the solid and solemn baron somehow looked more like a large dummy outside a tailor's shop. But the strangest thing of all was that the baron's other colleague, Valence, of the shaven head, was standing astraddle in the background, wearing a broad though a bitter grin. As the baron and the defeated duellist made their way rather sullenly through the garden door to the car beyond, Forain went up to this last member of the strange group, and (much to Monk's surprise) talked quickly and quietly for several minutes. It was only when Bruno's great voice was heard calling his name from without that this last figure also turned and left the garden.

'*Exeunt* brigands!' said Forain, with a cheerful change in his voice . . .

'You know the château, Monsieur Lorraine?' repeated Forain, looking at him steadily and even sternly. 'I think that's where the locket came from.' And he tossed it on the many-coloured heap in the drawer . . . 'There are valuable things here, Monsieur Lorraine, and I believe that you're a judge of them . . . There was a ring too, I suspect,' said Forain. 'I have put back the locket. Would you, Monsieur Lorraine, kindly put back the ring?'

Lorraine rose, the smile still on his lips; he put two fingers in his waistcoat pocket and drew out a small circlet of wrought gold with a green stone. The next moment Forain's arm, shot across the table trying to catch his wrist; but his motion, though swift as his sword-thrust, was yet too late. Young Mr Waldo Lorraine stood with the smile on his lips and the Renascence ring on his finger while one could count five. Then his feet slipped on the smooth floor and he fell dead across the table, with his black ringlets among the rich refuse of the drawer . . .

'Strange' he [Forain] said at last, 'that he should die just here, with his head in all that dustbin of curiosities that he was born among and had such a taste for. You saw that he was a Jew, of course, but, my God, what a genius! Like your young Disraeli – and he might have succeeded too and filled the world with his fame. Just a mistake or two, breaking a cucumber frame in the dark, and he lies dead in all that dead bric-à-brac, as if in the pawn-shop where he was born . . . Oh, how little you rich masters of the modern world know about the modern world! What do you know about Miller, Moss and Hartman, *except* that they have branches all over the world and are as big as the Bank of England? You know they go to the ends of the earth, but where do they come from? Is there any check on businesses changing hands or men changing names? Miller may be twenty years dead, if he was ever alive. Miller may stand for Muller, or Muller for Moses. The back-doors of every business to-day are open to such newcomers, and do you ever ask from what gutters they come? And then you think your son lost if he goes into a music-hall, and you want to shut up all the taverns to keep him from bad company. Believe me, you had better shut up the banks . . .'

The investigator turned slightly in his chair and made a movement, as of somewhat sombre introduction, towards Valance, who sat looking at the table with a face like coloured stone . . . There was a long silence, and the stony lips of the shaven Apollo curled and moved at last. 'Well,' he said, 'I won't trouble you with much about these men I had to serve. Their real names were not Lorraine, Le Caron, etc., any more than they were Miller, Moss, etc., though they went by the first in society and the second in business. Just now we need not trouble about their real names; I'm sure they never did. They were cosmopolitan moneylenders mostly; I was in their power . . .

This was very much in accordance with the atmosphere of novels and cinema of the time. What stepped further and even over the bounds of good manners on December 13th, 1918 was Chesterton's open letter in the *New Witness* to Rufus Isaacs, Lord Reading:

My Lord,
    I address to you a public letter as it is upon a public question: it is unlikely that I

should ever trouble you with any private letter on any private question; and least of all on the private question that now fills my mind. It would be impossible altogether to ignore the irony that has in the last few days brought to an end the great Marconi duel in which you and I in some sense played the part of seconds; that personal part of the matter ended when Cecil Chesterton was found dead in the trenches to which he had freely gone; and Godfrey Isaacs found dismissal in the very courts to which he once successfully appealed. But believe me I do not write on any personal matter; nor do I write, strangely enough perhaps, with any personal acrimony. On the contrary, there is something in these tragedies that almost unnaturally clarifies and enlarges the mind; and I think I write partly because I may never feel so magnanimous again. It would be irrational to ask you for sympathy; but I am sincerely moved to offer it. You are far more unhappy; for your brother is still alive.[16]

In 1919–20 during his trip to Jerusalem Chesterton contributed a series of articles to the *Daily Telegraph*, but his final article was rejected for publication and did not appear until collected in *The New Jerusalem*, London (Hodder and Stoughton) 1920, Chapter XIII, pp. 264–301.[17]

There is an attitude for which my friends and I were for a long period rebuked and even reviled; and of which at the present period we are less likely than ever to repent. It was always called Anti-Semitism; but it was always much more true to call it Zionism. At any rate it was much nearer to the nature of the thing to call it Zionism, whether or no it can find its geographical concentration in Zion. The substance of this heresy was exceedingly simple. It consisted entirely in saying that Jews are Jews; and as a logical consequence that they are not Russians or Roumanians or Italians or Frenchmen or Englishmen. During the war the newspapers commonly referred to them as Russians; but the ritual wore so singularly thin that I remember one newspaper paragraph saying that the Russians in the East End complained of the food regulations, because their religion forbade them to eat pork. My own brief contact with the Greek priests of the Orthodox Church in Jerusalem did not permit me to discover any trace of this detail of their discipline; and even the Russian pilgrims were said to be equally negligent in the matter. The point for the moment, however, is that if I was violently opposed to anything, it was not to Jews, but to that sort of remark about Jews; or rather to the silly and craven fear of making it a remark about Jews. But my friends and I had in some general sense a policy in the matter; and it was in substance the desire to give Jews the dignity and status of a separate nation. We desired that in some fashion, and so far as possible, Jews should be represented by Jews, should live in a society of Jews, should be judged by Jews and ruled by Jews. I am an Anti-Semite if that is Anti-Semitism. It would seem more rational to call it Semitism.

Of this attitude, I repeat, I am now less likely than ever to repent. I have lived to see the thing that was dismissed as a fad discussed everywhere as a fact; and one of the most menacing facts of the age. I have lived to see people who accused me of Anti-Semitism become far more Anti-Semitic than I am or ever was. I have heard people talking with real injustice about the Jews, who once seemed to think it an injustice to talk about them at all. But, above all, I have seen with my own eyes wild mobs marching through a great city, raving not only against Jews, but against the English for identifying themselves with the Jews. I have seen the whole prestige of England brought into peril, merely by the trick of talking about two nations as if they were one. I have seen an Englishman arriving in Jerusalem with somebody he had been taught to regard as his fellow countryman and political colleague, and received as if he had come arm-in-arm with a flaming dragon. So do our frosty fictions fare when they come under that burning sun.

Twice in my life, and twice lately, I have seen a piece of English pedantry bring us within an inch of an enormous English peril. The first was when all the Victorian historians and philosophers had told us that our German cousin was a cousin german and even germane; something naturally near and sympathetic. That also was an identification; that also was an assimilation; that also was a union of hearts. For the second time in a few short years, English politicians and journalists have discovered the dreadful revenge of reality. To pretend that something is what it is not is business that can easily be fashionable and sometimes popular. But the thing we have agreed to regard as what it is not will always abruptly punish and pulverise us, merely by being what it is. For years we were told that the Germans were a sort of Englishman because they were Teutons; but it was all the worse for us when we found out what Teutons really were. For years we were told that Jews were a sort of Englishman because they were British subjects. It is all the worse for us now we have to regard them, not subjectively as subjects, but objectively as objects; as objects of a fierce hatred among the Moslems and the Greeks. We are in the absurd position of introducing to these people a new friend whom they instantly recognise as an old enemy. It is an absurd position because it is a false position; but it is merely the penalty of falsehood.

Whether this Eastern anger is reasonable or not may be discussed in a moment; but what is utterly unreasonable is not the anger but the astonishment; at least it is our astonishment at their astonishment. We might believe ourselves in the view that a Jew is an Englishman; but there was no reason why they should regard him as an Englishman, since they already recognised him as a Jew. This is the whole present problem of the Jew in Palestine; and it must be solved either by the logic of Zionism or the logic of purely English supremacy and impartiality and not by what seems to everybody in Palestine a monstrous muddle of the two. But of course it is not only the peril in Palestine that has made the realisation of the Jewish problem, which once suffered all the dangers of a fad, suffer the opposite dangers of a fashion. The same journalists who politely describe Jews as Russians are now very impolitely describing certain Russians who are Jews. Many who had no particular objection to Jews as Capitalists have a very great objection to them as Bolshevists. Those who had an innocent unconsciousness of the nationality of Eckstein, even when he called himself Eckstein, have managed to discover the nationality of Braunstein, even when he calls himself Trotsky. And much of this peril also might easily have been lessened, by the simple proposal to call men and things by their own names.

I will confess, however, that I have no very full sympathy with the new Anti-Semitism which is merely Anti-Socialism. There are good, honourable and magnanimous Jews of every type and rank, there are many to whom I am greatly attached among my own friends in my own rank; but if I have to make a general choice on a general chance among different types of Jews, I have much more sympathy with the Jew who is revolutionary than the Jew who is plutocratic. In other words, I have much more sympathy for the Israelite we are beginning to reject, than for the Israelite we have already accepted. I have more respect for him when he leads some sort of revolt, however narrow and anarchic, against the oppression of the poor, than when he is safe at the head of a great money-lending business oppressing the poor himself. It is not the poor aliens, but the rich aliens I wish we had excluded. I myself wholly reject Bolshevism, not because its actions are violent, but because its very thought is materialistic and mean. And if this preference is true even of Bolshevism, it is ten times truer of Zionism. It really seems to me rather hard that the full storm of fury should have burst about the Jews, at the very moment when some of them at least have felt the call of a far cleaner ideal; and that when we have tolerated their tricks with our country, we should turn on them precisely when they seek in sincerity for their own.

But in order to judge this Jewish possibility, we must understand more fully the nature of the Jewish problem. We must consider it from the start, because there are still many who do not know that there is a Jewish problem. That problem has its proof, of course, in the history of the Jew, and the fact that he came from the East. A Jew will sometimes complain of the injustice of describing him as a man of the East; but in truth another very real injustice may be involved in treating him as a man of the West. Very often even the joke against the Jew is rather a joke against those who have made the joke; that is, a joke against what they have made out of the Jew. This is true especially, for instance, of many points of religion and ritual. Thus we cannot help feeling, for instance, that there is something a little grotesque about the Hebrew habit of putting on a top-hat as an act of worship. It is vaguely mixed up with another line of humour, about another class of Jew, who wears a large number of hats; and who must not therefore be credited with an extreme or extravagant religious zeal, leading him to pile up a pagoda of hats towards heaven. To Western eyes, in Western conditions, there really is something inevitably fantastic about this formality of the synagogue. But we ought to remember that we have made the Western conditions which startle the Western eyes. It seems odd to wear a modern top-hat as if it were a mitre or a biretta; it seems quainter still when the hat is worn even for the momentary purpose of saying grace before lunch. It seems quaintest of all when, at some Jewish luncheon parties, a tray of hats is actually handed round, and each guest helps himself to a hat as a sort of *hors d'œuvre*. All this could easily be turned into a joke; but we ought to realise that the joke is against ourselves. It is not merely we who make fun of it, but we who have made it funny. For, after all, nobody can pretend that this particular type of head-dress is a part of that uncouth imagery 'setting painting and sculpture at defiance' which Renan remarked in the tradition of Hebrew civilisation. Nobody can say that a top-hat was among the strange symbolic utensils dedicated to the obscure service of the Ark; nobody can suppose that a top-hat descended from heaven among the wings and wheels of the flying visions of the Prophets. For this wild vision the West is entirely responsible. Europe has created the Tower of Giotto; but it has also created the topper. We of the West must bear the burden, as best we may, both of the responsibility and of the hat. It is solely the special type and shape of hat that makes the Hebrew ritual seem ridiculous. Performed in the old original Hebrew fashion it is not ridiculous, but rather if anything sublime. For the original fashion was an oriental fashion; and the Jews are orientals; and the mark of all such orientals is the wearing of long and loose draperies. To throw those loose draperies over the head is decidedly a dignified and even poetic gesture. One can imagine something like justice done to its majesty and mystery in one of the great dark drawings of William Blake. It may be true, and personally I think it is true, that the Hebrew covering of the head signifies a certain stress on the fear of God, which is the beginning of wisdom, while the Christian uncovering of the head suggests rather the love of God that is the end of wisdom. But this has nothing to do with the taste and dignity of the ceremony; and to do justice to these we must treat the Jew as an oriental; we must even dress him as an oriental.

I have only taken this as one working example out of many that would point to the same conclusion. A number of points upon which the unfortunate alien is blamed would be much improved if he were, not less of an alien, but rather more of an alien. They arise from his being too like us, and too little like himself. It is obviously the case, for instance, touching that vivid vulgarity in clothes, and especially the colours of clothes, with which a certain sort of Jews brighten the landscape or seascape at Margate or many holiday resorts. When we see a foreign gentleman on Brighton Pier wearing yellow spats, a magenta waistcoat, and an emerald green tie, we feel that he has somehow missed certain fine shades of social sensibility and fitness. It might considerably surprise the company on Brighton Pier, if he were to reply by solemnly unwinding his green necktie from round his neck, and winding it round his head. Yet the reply would be the right one; and would be equally logical and artistic. As soon as the green tie had become a green turban, it might look as appropriate and even attractive as the green turban of any pilgrim of Mecca or any descendant of Mahomet, who walks with a stately air through the streets of Jaffa or Jerusalem. The bright colours that make the Margate Jews hideous are no brighter than those that make the Moslem crowd picturesque. They are only worn in the wrong place, in the wrong way, and in conjunction with a type and cut of clothing that is meant to be more sober and restrained. Little can really be urged against him, in that respect, except that his artistic instinct is rather for colour than form, especially of the kind that we ourselves have labelled good form.

This is a mere symbol, but it is so suitable a symbol that I have often offered it symbolically as a solution of the Jewish problem. I have felt disposed to say: let all liberal legislation stand, let all literal and legal civic equality stand; let a Jew occupy any political or social position which he can gain in open competition; let us not listen for a moment to any suggestions of reactionary restrictions or racial privilege. Let a Jew be Lord Chief Justice, if his exceptional veracity and reliability have clearly marked him out for that post. Let a Jew be Archbishop of Canterbury, if our national religion has attained to that receptive breadth that would render such a transition unobjectionable and even unconscious. But let there be one single-clause bill; one simple and sweeping law about Jews, and no other. Be it enacted, by the King's Most Excellent Majesty, by and with the advice of the Lords Spiritual and Temporal and the Commons in Parliament assembled, that every Jew must be dressed like an Arab. Let him sit on the Woolsack, but let him sit there dressed as an Arab. Let him preach in St. Paul's Cathedral, but let him preach there dressed as an Arab. It is not my point at present to dwell on the pleasing if flippant fancy of how much this would transform the political scene; of the dapper figure of Sir Herbert Samuel swathed as a Bedouin, or Sir Alfred Mond gaining a yet greater grandeur from the gorgeous and trailing robes of the East. If my image is quaint my intention is quite serious; and the point of it is not personal to any particular Jew. The point applies to any Jew, and to our own recovery of healthier relations with him. The point is that we should know where we are; and he would know where he is, which is in a foreign land.

This is but a parenthesis and a parable, but it brings us to the concrete controversial matter which is the Jewish problem. Only a few years ago it was regarded as a mark of a blood-thirsty disposition to admit that the Jewish problem was a problem, or even that the Jew was a Jew. Through much misunderstanding certain friends of mine and myself have persisted in disregarding the silence thus imposed; but facts have fought for us more effectively than words. By this time nobody is more conscious of the Jewish problem than the most intelligent and idealistic of the Jews. The folly of the fashion by which Jews often concealed their Jewish names, must surely be manifest by this time even to those who concealed them. To mention but one example of the way in which this fiction falsified the relations of everybody and everything, it is enough to note that it involved the Jews themselves in a quite new and quite needless unpopularity in the first years of the war. A poor little Jewish tailor, who called himself by a German name merely because he lived for a short time in a German town, was instantly mobbed in Whitechapel for his share in the invasion of Belgium. He was cross-examined about why he had damaged the tower of Rheims; and talked to as if he had killed Nurse Cavell with his own pair of shears. It was very unjust; quite as unjust as it would be to ask Bethmann Hollweg[18] why he had stabbed Eglon or hewn Agag in pieces. But it was partly at least the fault of the Jew himself, and of the whole of that futile and unworthy policy which had led him to call himself Bernstein when his name was Benjamin.

In such cases the Jews are accused of all sorts of faults they have not got; but there are faults that they have got. Some of the charges against them, as in the cases I have quoted concerning religious ritual and artistic taste, are due merely to the false light in which they are regarded. Other faults may also be due to the false position in which they are placed. But the faults exist; and nothing was ever more dangerous to everybody concerned than the recent fashion of denying or ignoring them. It was done simply by the snobbish habit of suppressing the experience and evidence of the majority of people, and especially of the majority of poor people. It was done by confining the controversy to a small world of wealth and refinement, remote from all the real facts involved. For the rich are the most ignorant people on earth, and the best that can be said for them, in cases like these, is that their ignorance often reaches the point of innocence.

I will take a typical case, which sums up the whole of this absurd fashion. There was a controversy in the columns of an important daily paper, some time ago, on the subject of the character of Shylock in Shakespeare. Actors and authors of distinction, including some of the most brilliant of living Jews, argued the matter from the most varied points of view. Some said that Shakespeare was prevented by the prejudices of his time from having a complete sympathy with Shylock. Some said that Shakespeare was only restrained by fear of the powers of his time from expressing his complete sympathy with Shylock. Some wondered how or why Shakespeare had got hold of such a queer story as that of the pound of flesh, and what it could possibly have to do with so dignified and intellectual a character as Shylock. In short, some wondered why a man of genius should be so much of an Anti-Semite, and some stoutly declared that he must have been a Pro-Semite. But all of them in a sense admitted that they were puzzled as to what the play was about. The correspondence filled column after column and went on for weeks. And from one end of that correspondence to the other, no human being even so much as mentioned the word 'usury.' It is exactly as if twenty clever critics were set down to talk for a month about the play of Macbeth, and were all strictly forbidden to mention the word 'murder.'

The play called *The Merchant of Venice* happens to be about usury, and its story is a medieval satire on usury. It is the fashion to say that it is a clumsy and grotesque story; but as a fact it is an exceedingly good story. It is a perfect and pointed story for its purpose, which is to convey the moral of the story. And the moral is that the logic of usury is in its nature at war with life, and might logically end in breaking into the bloody house of life. In other words, if a creditor can always claim a man's tools or a man's home, he might quite as justly claim one of his arms or legs. This principle was not only embodied in medieval satires but in very sound medieval laws, which set a limit on the usurer who was trying to take away a man's livelihood, as the usurer in the play is trying to take away a man's life. And if anybody thinks that usury can never go to lengths wicked enough to be worthy of so wild an image, then that person either knows nothing about it or knows too much. He is either one of the innocent rich who have never been the victims of money-lenders, or else one of the more powerful and influential rich who are money-lenders themselves.

All this, I say, is a fact that must be faced, but there is another side to the case, and it is this that the genius of Shakespeare discovered. What he did do, and what the medieval satirist did not do, was to attempt to understand Shylock; in the true sense to sympathise with Shylock the money-lender, as he sympathised with Macbeth the murderer. It was not to deny that the man was an usurer, but to assert that the usurer was a man. And the Elizabethan dramatist does make him a man, where the medieval satirist made him a monster. Shakespeare not only makes him a man but a perfectly sincere and self-respecting man. But the point is this: that he is a sincere man who sincerely believes in usury. He is a self-respecting man who does not despise himself for being a usurer. In one word, he regards usury as normal. In that word is the whole problem of the popular impression of the Jews. What Shakespeare suggested about the Jew in a subtle and sympathetic way, millions of plain men everywhere would suggest about him in a rough and ready way. Regarding the Jew in relation to his ideas about interest, they think either that he is simply immoral, or that if he is moral, then he has a different morality. There is a great deal more to be said about how far this is true, and about what are its causes and excuses if it is true. But it is an old story, surely, that the worst of all cures is to deny the disease.

To recognise the reality of the Jewish problem is very vital for everybody and especially vital for Jews. To pretend that there is no problem is to precipitate the expression of a rational impatience, which unfortunately can only express itself in the rather irrational form of Anti-Semitism. In the controversies of Palestine and Syria, for instance, it is very common to hear the answer that the Jew is no worse than the Armenian. The Armenian also is said to be unpopular as a money-lender and a mercantile upstart; yet the Armenian figures as a martyr for the Christian faith and a victim of the Moslem fury. But this is one of those arguments which really carry their own answer. It is like the sceptical saying that man is only an animal, which of itself provokes the retort, 'But what an animal!' The very similarity only emphasises the contrast. Is it seriously suggested that we can substitute the Armenian for the Jew in the study of a world-wide problem like that of the Jews? Could we talk of the competition of Armenians among Welsh shop-keepers, or of the crowd of Armenians on Brighton Parade? Can Armenian usury be a common topic of talk in a camp in California and in a club in Piccadilly? Does Shakespeare show us a tragic Armenian towering over the great Venice of the Renascence? Does Dickens show us a realistic Armenian teaching in the thieves' kitchens of the slums? When we meet Mr Vernon Vavasour, that brilliant financier, do we speculate on the probability of his really having an Armenian name to match his Armenian nose? Is it true, in short, that all sorts of people, from the peasants of Poland to the peasants of Portugal, can agree more or less upon the special subject of Armenia? Obviously it is not in the least true; obviously the Armenian question is only a local question of certain Christians, who may be more avaricious than other Christians. But it is the truth about the Jews. It is only half the truth, and one which by itself would be very unjust to the Jews. But it is the truth, and we must realise it as sharply and clearly as we can. The truth is that it is rather strange that the Jews should be so anxious for international agreements. For one of the few really international agreements is a suspicion of the Jews.

A more practical comparison would be one between the Jews and gypsies; for the latter at least cover several countries, and can be tested by the impressions of very different districts. And in some preliminary respects the comparison is really useful. Both races are in different ways landless, and therefore in different ways lawless. For the fundamental laws are land laws. In both cases a reasonable man will see reasons for unpopularity, without wishing to indulge any task for persecution. In both cases he will probably recognise the reality of a racial fault, while admitting that it may be largely a racial misfortune. That is to say, the drifting and detached condition may be largely the cause of Jewish usury or gypsy pilfering; but it is not common sense to contradict the general experience of gypsy pilfering or Jewish usury. The comparison helps us to clear away some of the cloudy evasions by which modern men have tried to escape from that experience. It is absurd to say that people are only prejudiced against the money methods of the Jews because the medieval church has left behind a hatred of their religion. We might as well say that people only protect the chickens from the gypsies because the medieval church undoubtedly condemned fortune-telling. It is unreasonable for a Jew to complain that Shakespeare makes Shylock and not Antonio the ruthless money-lender; or that Dickens makes Fagin and not Sikes the receiver of stolen goods. It is as if a gypsy were to complain when a novelist describes a child as stolen by the gypsies, and not by the curate or the mothers' meeting. It is to complain of facts and probabilities. There may be good gypsies; there may be good qualities which specially belong to them as gypsies; many students of the strange race have, for instance, praised a certain dignity and self-respect among the women of the Romany. But no student ever praised them for an exaggerated respect for private property, and the whole argument about gypsy theft can be roughly repeated about Hebrew usury. Above all, there is one other respect in which the comparison is even more to the point. It is the essential fact of the whole business, that the Jews do not become national merely by becoming a political part of any nation. We might as well say that the gypsies had villas in Clapham, when their caravans stood on Clapham Common.

But, of course, even this comparison between the two wandering peoples fails in the presence of the greater problem. Here again even the attempt at a parallel leaves the primary thing more unique. The gypsies do not become municipal merely by passing through a number of parishes, and it would seem equally obvious that a Jew need not become English merely by passing through England on his way from Germany to America. But the gypsy not only is not municipal, but he is not called municipal. His caravan is not immediately painted outside with the number and name of 123 Laburnam Road, Clapham. The municipal authorities generally notice the wheels attached to the new cottage, and therefore do not fall into the error. The gypsy may halt in a particular parish, but he is not as a rule immediately made a parish councillor. The cases in which a travelling tinker has been suddenly made the mayor of an important industrial town must be comparatively rare. And if the poor vagabonds of the Romany blood are bullied by mayors and magistrates, kicked off the land by landlords, pursued by policemen and generally knocked about from pillar to post, nobody raises an outcry that *they* are the victims of religious persecution; nobody summons meetings in public halls, collects subscriptions or sends petitions to parliament; nobody threatens anybody else with the organised indignation of the gypsies all over the world. The case of the Jew in the nation is very different from that of the tinker in the town. The moral elements that can be appealed to are of a very different style and scale. No gypsies are millionaires.

In short, the Jewish problem differs from anything like the gypsy problem in two highly practical respects. First, the Jews already exercise colossal cosmopolitan financial power. And second, the modern societies they live in also grant them vital forms of national political power. Here the vagrant is already as rich as a miser, and the vagrant is actually made a mayor. As will be seen shortly, there is a Jewish side of the story which leads really to the same ending of the story; but the truth stated here is quite independent of any sympathetic or unsympathetic view of the race in question. It is a question of fact, which a sensible Jew can afford to recognise, and which the most sensible Jews do very definitely recognise. It is really irrational for anybody to pretend that the Jews are only a curious sect of Englishmen, like the Plymouth Brothers or the Seventh Day Baptists, in the face of such a simple fact as the family of Rothschild. Nobody can pretend that such an English sect can establish five brothers, or even cousins, in the five great capitals of Europe. Nobody can pretend that the Seventh Day Baptists are the seven grandchildren of one grandfather, scattered systematically among the warring nations of the earth. Nobody thinks the Plymouth Brothers are literally brothers, or that they are likely to be quite as powerful in Paris or in Petrograd as in Plymouth.

The Jewish problem can be stated very simply after all. It is normal for the nation to contain the family. With the Jews the family is generally divided among the nations. This may not appear to matter to those who do not believe in nations, those who really think there ought not to be any nations. But I literally fail to understand anybody who does believe in patriotism thinking that this state of affairs can be consistent with it. It is in its nature intolerable, from a national standpoint, that a man admittedly powerful in one nation should be bound to a man equally powerful in another nation, by ties more private and personal even than nationality. Even when the purpose is not any sort of treachery, the very position is a sort of treason. Given the passionately patriotic peoples of the west of Europe especially, the state of things cannot conceivably be satisfactory to a patriot. But least of all can it conceivably be satisfactory to a Jewish patriot; by which I do not mean a sham Englishman or a sham Frenchman, but a man who is sincerely patriotic for the historic and highly civilised nation of the Jews.

For what may be criticised here as Anti-Semitism is only the negative side of Zionism. For the sake of convenience I have begun by stating it in terms of the universal popular impression which some call a popular prejudice. But such a truth of differentiation is equally true on both its different sides. Suppose somebody proposes to mix up England and America, under some absurd name like the Anglo-Saxon Empire. One man may say, 'Why should the jolly English inns and villages be swamped by these priggish provincial Yankees?' Another may say, 'Why should the real democracy of a young country be tied to your snobbish old squirearchy?' But both these views are only versions of the same view of a great American:[19] 'God never made one people good enough to rule another.'

The primary point about Zionism is that, whether it is right or wrong, it does offer a real and reasonable answer both to Anti-Semitism and to the charge of Anti-Semitism. The usual phrases about religious persecution and racial hatred are not reasonable answers, or answers at all. These Jews do not deny that they are Jews; they do not deny that Jews may be unpopular; they do not deny that there may be other than superstitious reasons for their unpopularity. They are not obliged to maintain that when a Piccadilly dandy talks about being in the hands of the Jews he is moved by the theological fanaticism that prevails in Piccadilly; or that when a silly youth on Derby Day says he was done by a dirty Jew, he is merely conforming to that Christian orthodoxy which is one of the strict traditions of the Turf. They are not, like some other Jews, forced to pay so extravagant a compliment to the Christian religion as to suppose it the ruling motive of half the discontented talk in clubs and public-houses, of nearly every business man who suspects a foreign financier, or nearly every working man who grumbles against the local pawn-broker. Religious mania, unfortunately, is not so common. The Zionists do not need to deny any of these things; what they offer is not a denial but a diagnosis and a remedy. Whether their diagnosis is correct, whether their remedy is practicable, we will try to consider later, with something like a fair summary of what is to be said on both sides. But their theory, on the face of it, is perfectly reasonable. It is the theory that any abnormal qualities in the Jews are due to the abnormal position of the Jews. They are traders rather than producers because they have no land of their own from which to produce, and they are cosmopolitans rather than patriots because they have no country of their own for which to be patriotic. They can no more become farmers while they are vagrant than they could have built the Temple of Solomon while they were building the Pyramids of Egypt. They can no more feel the full stream of nationalism while they wander in the desert of nomadism than they could bathe in the waters of Jordan while they were weeping by the waters of Babylon. For exile is the worst kind of bondage. In insisting upon that at least the Zionists have insisted upon a profound truth, with many applications to many other moral issues. It is true that for any one whose heart is set on a particular home or shrine, to be locked out is to be locked in. The narrowest possible prison for him is the whole world.

It will be well to notice briefly, however, how the principle applies to the two Anti-Semitic arguments already considered. The first is the charge of usury and unproductive loans, the second the charge either of treason or of unpatriotic detachment. The charge of usury is regarded, not unreasonably, as only a specially dangerous development of the general charge of uncreative commerce and the refusal of creative manual exercise; the unproductive loan is only a minor form of the unproductive labour. It is certainly true that the latter complaint is, if possible, commoner than the former, especially in comparatively simple communities like those of Palestine. A very honest Moslem Arab said to me, with a singular blend of simplicity and humour, 'A Jew does not work; but he grows rich. You never see a Jew working; and yet they grow rich. What I want to know is, why do we not all do the same? Why do we not also do this and become rich?' This is, I need hardly say, an over-simplification. Jews often work hard at some things, especially intellectual things. But the same experience which tells us that we have known many industrious Jewish scholars, Jewish lawyers, Jewish doctors, Jewish pianists, chess-players and so on, is an experience which cuts both ways. The same experience, if carefully consulted, will probably tell us that we have not known personally many patient Jewish ploughmen, many laborious Jewish blacksmiths, many active Jewish hedgers and ditchers, or even many energetic Jewish hunters and fishermen. In short, the popular impression is tolerably true to life, as popular impressions very often are; though it is not fashionable to say so in these days of democracy and self-determination. Jews do not generally work on the land, or in any of the handicrafts that are akin to the land; but the Zionists reply that this is because it can never really be their own land. That is Zionism, and that has really a practical place in the past and future of Zion.

Patriotism is not merely dying for the nation. It is dying with the nation. It is regarding the fatherland not merely as a real resting-place like an inn, but as a final resting-place, like a house or even a grave. Even the most Jingo of the Jews do not feel like this about their adopted country; and I doubt if the most intelligent of the Jews would pretend that they did. Even if we can bring ourselves to believe that Disraeli lived for England, we cannot think that he would have died with her. If England had sunk in the Atlantic he would not have sunk with her, but easily floated over to America to stand for the Presidency. Even if we are profoundly convinced that Mr Beit or Mr Eckstein had patriotic tears in his eyes when he obtained a gold concession from

Queen Victoria, we cannot believe that in her absence he would have refused a similar concession from the German Emperor. When the Jew in France or in England says he is a good patriot he only means that he is a good citizen, and he would put it more truly if he said he was a good exile. Sometimes indeed he is an abominably bad citizen, and a most exasperating and execrable exile, but I am not talking of that side of the case. I am assuming that a man like Disraeli did really make a romance of England, that a man like Dernburg did really make a romance of Germany, and it is still true that though it was a romance, they would not have allowed it to be a tragedy. They would have seen that the story had a happy ending, especially for themselves. These Jews would not have died with any Christian nation.

But the Jews did die with Jerusalem. That is the first and last great truth in Zionism. Jerusalem was destroyed and Jews were destroyed with it, men who cared no longer to live because the city of their faith had fallen. It may be questioned whether all the Zionists have all the sublime insanity of the Zealots. But at least it is not nonsense to suggest that the Zionists might feel like this about Zion. It is nonsense to suggest that they would ever feel like this about Dublin or Moscow. And so far at least the truth both in Semitism and Anti-Semitism is included in Zionism.

It is a commonplace that the infamous are more famous than the famous. Byron noted, with his own misanthropic moral, that we think more of Nero the monster who killed his mother than of Nero the noble Roman who defeated Hannibal. The name of Julian more often suggests Julian the Apostate than Julian the Saint; though the latter crowned his canonisation with the sacred glory of being the patron saint of inn-keepers. But the best example of this unjust historical habit is the most famous of all and the most infamous of all. If there is one proper noun which has become a common noun, if there is one name which has been generalised till it means a thing, it is certainly the name of Judas. We should hesitate perhaps to call it a Christian name, except in the more evasive form of Jude. And even that, as the name of a more faithful apostle, is another illustration of the same injustice; for, by comparison with the other, Jude the faithful might almost be called Jude the obscure. The critic who said, whether innocently or ironically, 'What wicked men these early Christians were!' was certainly more successful in innocence than in irony; for he seems to have been innocent or ignorant of the whole idea of the Christian communion. Judas Iscariot was one of the very earliest of all possible early Christians. And the whole point about him was that his hand was in the same dish; the traitor is always a friend, or he could never be a foe. But the point for the moment is merely that the name is known everywhere merely as the name of a traitor. The name of Judas nearly always means Judas Iscariot; it hardly ever means Judas Maccabaeus. And if you shout out 'Judas' to a politician in the thick of a political tumult, you will have some difficulty in soothing him afterwards, with the assurance that you had merely traced in him something of that splendid zeal and valour which dragged down the tyranny of Antiochus, in the day of the great deliverance of Israel.

Those two possible uses of the name of Judas would give us yet another compact embodiment of the case for Zionism. Numberless international Jews have gained the bad name of Judas, and some have certainly earned it. If you have gained or earned the good name of Judas, it can quite fairly and intelligently be affirmed that this was not the fault of the Jews, but of the peculiar position of the Jews. A man can betray like Judas Iscariot in another man's house; but a man cannot fight like Judas Maccabaeus for another man's temple. There is no more truly rousing revolutionary story amid all the stories of mankind, there is no more perfect type of the element of chivalry in rebellion, than that magnificent tale of the Maccabee who stabbed from underneath the elephant of Antiochus and died under the fall of that huge and living castle. But it would be unreasonable to ask Mr Montagu to stick a knife into the elephant on which Lord Curzon, let us say, was riding in all the pomp of Asiatic imperialism. For Mr Montagu would not be liberating his own land; and therefore he naturally prefers to interest himself either in operations in silver or in somewhat slower and less efficient methods of liberation. In short, whatever we may think of the financial or social services such as were rendered to England in the affair of Marconi, or to France in the affair of Panama, it must be admitted that these exhibit a humbler and more humdrum type of civic duty, and do not remind us of the more reckless virtues of the Maccabees or the Zealots. A man may be a good citizen of anywhere, but he cannot be a national hero of nowhere; and for this particular type of patriotic passion it is necessary to have a *patria*. The Zionists therefore are maintaining a perfectly reasonable proposition, both about the charge of usury and the charge of treason, if they claim that both could be cured by the return to a national soil as promised in Zionism.

Unfortunately they are not always reasonable about their own reasonable proposition. Some of them have a most unlucky habit of ignoring, and therefore implicitly denying, the very evil that they are wisely trying to cure. I have already remarked this irritating innocence in the first of the two questions; the criticism that sees everything in Shylock except the point of him, or the point of his knife. How in the politics of Palestine at this moment this first question is in every sense the primary question. Palestine has hardly as yet a patriotism to be betrayed; but it certainly has a peasantry to be oppressed, and especially to be oppressed as so many peasantries have been with usury and forestalling. The Syrians and Arabs and all the agricultural and pastoral populations of Palestine are, rightly or wrongly, alarmed and angered at the advent of the Jews to power; for the perfectly practical and simple reason of the reputation which the Jews have all over the world. It is really ridiculous in people so intelligent as the Jews, and especially so intelligent as the Zionists, to ignore so enormous and elementary a fact as that reputation and its natural results. It may or may not in this case be unjust; but in any case it is not unnatural. It may be the result of persecution, but it is one that has definitely resulted. It may be the consequence of a misunderstanding; but it is a misunderstanding that must itself be understood. Rightly or wrongly, certain people in Palestine fear the coming of the Jews as they fear the coming of the locusts; they regard them as parasites that feed on a community by a thousand methods of financial intrigue and economic exploitation. I could understand the Jews indignantly denying this, or eagerly disproving it, or best of all, explaining what is true in it while exposing what is untrue. What is strange, I might almost say weird, about the attitude of some quite intelligent and sincere Zionists, is that they talk, write and apparently think as if there were no such thing in the world.

I will give one curious example from one of the best and most brilliant of the

Zionists. Dr Weizmann is a man of large mind and human sympathies; and it is difficult
to believe that any one with so fine a sense of humanity can be entirely empty of anything
like a sense of humour. Yet, in the middle of a very temperate and magnanimous
address on 'Zionist Policy,' he can actually say a thing like this; 'The Arabs need us with
our knowledge, and our experience and our money. If they do not have us they will fall
into the hands of others, they will fall among sharks.' One is tempted for the moment
to doubt whether any one else in the world could have said that, except the Jew with his
strange mixture of brilliancy and blindness, of subtlety and simplicity. It is much as if
President Wilson were to say, 'Unless America deals with Mexico, it will be dealt with
by some modern commercial power, that has trust-magnates and hustling millionaires.'
But would President Wilson say it? It is as if the German Chancellor had said, 'We must
rush to the rescue of the poor Belgians, or they may be put under some system with a
rigid militarism and a bullying bureaucracy.' But would even a German Chancellor put
it exactly like that? Would anybody put it in the exact order of words and structure of
sentence in which Dr Weizmann has put it? Would even the Turks say, 'The Armenians
need us with our order and our discipline and our arms. If they do not have us they will
fall into the hands of others, they will perhaps be in danger of massacres.' I suspect that
a Turk would see the joke, even if it were as grim a joke as the massacres themselves. If
the Zionists wish to quiet the fears of the Arabs, surely the first thing to do is to discover
what the Arabs are afraid of. And very little investigation will reveal the simple truth
that they are very much afraid of sharks; and that in their book of symbolic or heraldic
zoology it is the Jew who is adorned with the dorsal fin and the crescent of cruel teeth.
This may be a fairy-tale about a fabulous animal; but it is one which all sorts of races
believe, and certainly one which these races believe.

But the case is yet more curious than that. These simple tribes are afraid, not only
of the dorsal fin and dental arrangements which Dr Weizmann may say (with some
justice) that he has not got; they are also afraid of the other things which he says he
has got. They may be in error, at the first superficial glance, in mistaking a respectable
professor for a shark. But they can hardly be mistaken in attributing to the respectable
professor what he himself considers as his claims to respect. And as the imagery about
the shark may be too metaphorical or almost mythological, there is not the smallest
difficulty in stating in plain words what the Arabs fear in the Jews. They fear, in exact
terms, their knowledge and their experience and their money. The Arabs fear exactly
the three things which he says they need. Only the Arabs would call it a knowledge of
financial trickery and an experience of political intrigue, and the power given by hoards
of money not only of their own but of other peoples. About Dr Weizmann and the true
Zionists this is self-evidently unjust; but about Jewish influence of the more visible and
vulgar kind it has to be proved to be unjust. Feeling as I do the force of the real case for
Zionism, I venture most earnestly to implore the Jews to disprove it, and not to dismiss
it. But above all I implore them not to be content with assuring us again and again of
their knowledge and their experience and their money. That is what people dread like
a pestilence or an earthquake; their knowledge and their experience and their money.
It is needless for Dr Weizmann to tell us that he does not desire to enter Palestine like
a Junker or drive thousands of Arabs forcibly out of the land; nobody supposes that

Dr Weizmann looks like a Junker; and nobody among the enemies of the Jews says that they have driven their foes in that fashion since the wars with the Canaanites. But for the Jews to reassure us by insisting on their own economic culture or commercial education is exactly like the Junkers reassuring us by insisting on the unquestioned supremacy of their Kaiser or the unquestioned obedience of their soldiers. Men bar themselves in their houses, or even hide themselves in their cellars, when such virtues are abroad in the land.

In short, the fear of the Jews in Palestine, reasonable or unreasonable, is a thing that must be answered by reason. It is idle for the unpopular thing to answer with boasts, especially boasts of the very quality that makes it unpopular. But I think it could be answered by reason, or at any rate tested by reason; and the tests by consideration. The principle is still as stated above; that the tests must not merely insist on the virtues the Jews do show, but rather deal with the particular virtues which they are generally accused of not showing. It is necessary to understand this more thoroughly than it is generally understood, and especially better than it is usually stated in the language of fashionable controversy. For the question involves the whole success or failure of Zionism. Many of the Zionists know it; but I rather doubt whether most of the Anti-Zionists know that they know it. And some of the phrases of the Zionists, such as those that I have noted, too often tend to produce the impression that they ignore when they are not ignorant. They are not ignorant; and they do not ignore in practice; even when an intellectual habit makes them seem to ignore in theory. Nobody who has seen a Jewish rural settlement, such as Rishon, can doubt that some Jews are sincerely filled with the vision of sitting under their own vine and fig-tree, and even with its accompanying lesson that it is first necessary to grow the fig-tree and the vine.

The true test of Zionism may seem a topsy-turvy test. It will not succeed by the number of successes, but rather by the number of failures, or what the world (and certainly not least the Jewish world) has generally called failures. It will be tested, not by whether Jews can climb to the top of the ladder, but by whether Jews can remain at the bottom; not by whether they have a hundred arts of becoming important, but by whether they have any skill in the art of remaining insignificant. It is often noted that the intelligent Israelite can rise to positions of power and trust outside Israel, like Witte in Russia or Rufus Isaacs in England. It is generally bad, I think, for their adopted country; but in any case it is no good for the particular problem of their own country. Palestine cannot have a population of Prime Ministers and Chief Justices; and if those they rule and judge are not Jews, then we have not established a commonwealth but only an oligarchy. It is said again that the ancient Jews turned their enemies into hewers of wood and drawers of water. The modern Jews have to turn themselves into hewers of wood and drawers of water. If they cannot do that, they cannot turn themselves into citizens, but only into a kind of alien bureaucrats, of all kinds the most perilous and the most imperilled. Hence a Jewish state will not be a success when the Jews in it are successful, or even when the Jews in it are statesmen. It will be a success when the Jews in it are scavengers, when the Jews in it are sweeps, when they are dockers and ditchers and porters and hodmen. When the Zionist can point proudly to a Jewish navvy who has *not* risen in the world, an under-gardener who is not now taking his ease as an upper-gardener, a yokel who is still a yokel, or even a village idiot at least sufficiently idiotic to remain in his village, then indeed the world will come to blow the trumpets and lift up the heads of the everlasting gates; for God will have turned the captivity of Zion.

Zionists of whose sincerity I am personally convinced, and of whose intelligence anybody would be convinced, have told me that there really is, in places like Rishon, something like a beginning of this spirit; the love of the peasant for his land. One lady, even in expressing her conviction of it, called it 'this very un-Jewish characteristic.' She was perfectly well aware both of the need of it in the Jewish land, and the lack of it in the Jewish race. In short she was well aware of the truth of that seemingly topsy-turvy test I have suggested; that of whether men are worthy to be drudges. When a humorous and humane Jew thus accepts the test, and honestly expects the Jewish people to pass it, then I think the claim is very serious indeed, and one not lightly to be set aside. I do certainly think it a very serious responsibility under the circumstances to set it altogether aside. It is our whole complaint against the Jew that he does not till the soil or toil with the spade; it is very hard on him to refuse him if he really says, 'Give me a soil and I will till it; give me a spade and I will use it.' It is our whole reason for distrusting him that he cannot really love any of the lands in which he wanders; it seems rather indefensible to be deaf to him if he really says, 'Give me a land and I will love it.' I would certainly give him a land, or some instalment of the land, (in what general sense I will try to suggest a little later) so long as his conduct on it was watched and tested according to the principles I have suggested. If he asks for the spade he must use the spade, and not merely employ the spade, in the sense of hiring half a hundred men to use spades. If he asks for the soil he must till the soil; that is, he must belong to the soil and not merely make the soil belong to him. He must have the simplicity, and what many would call the stupidity of the peasant. He must not only call a spade a spade, but regard it as a spade and not as a speculation. By some true conversion the urban and modern man must be not only on the soil, but of the soil, and free from our urban trick of inventing the word dirt for the dust to which we shall return. He must be washed in mud, that he may be clean.

How far this can really happen it is very hard for anybody, especially a casual visitor, to discover in the present crisis. It is admitted that there is much Arab and Syrian labour employed; and this in itself would leave all the danger of the Jew as a mere capitalist. The Jews explain it, however, by saying that the Arabs will work for a lower wage, and that this is necessarily a great temptation to the struggling colonists. In this they may be acting naturally as colonists, but it is none the less clear that they are not yet acting literally as labourers. It may not be their fault that they are not proving themselves to be peasants; but it is none the less clear that this situation in itself does not prove them to be peasants. So far as that is concerned, it still remains to be decided finally whether a Jew will be an agricultural labourer, if he is a decently paid agricultural labourer. On the other hand, the leaders of these local experiments, if they have not yet shown the higher materialism of peasants, most certainly do not show the lower materialism of capitalists. There can be no doubt of the patriotic and even poetic spirit in which many of them hope to make their ancient wilderness blossom like the rose. They at least would still stand among the great prophets of Israel, and none the less though they prophesied in vain.

I have tried to state fairly the case for Zionism, for the reason already stated: that I think it intellectually unjust that any attempt of the Jews to regularise their position should merely be rejected as one of their irregularities. But I do not disguise the enormous difficulties of doing it in the particular conditions of Palestine. In fact the greatest of the real difficulties of Zionism is that it has to take place in Zion. There are other difficulties, however, which when they are not specially the fault of Zionists are very much the fault of Jews. The worst is the general impression of a business pressure from the more brutal and businesslike type of Jew, which arouses very violent and very just indignation. When I was in Jerusalem it was openly said that Jewish financiers had complained of the low rate of interest at which loans were made by the government to the peasantry, and even that the government had yielded to them. If this were true it was a heavier reproach to the government even than to the Jews. But the general truth is that such a state of feeling seems to make the simple and solid patriotism of a Palestinian Jewish nation practically impossible, and forces us to consider some alternative or some compromise. The most sensible statement of a compromise I heard among the Zionists was suggested to me by Dr Weizmann, who is a man not only highly intelligent but ardent and sympathetic. And the phrase he used gives the key to my own rough conception of a possible solution, though he himself would probably, not accept that solution.

Dr Weizmann suggested, if I understood him rightly, that he did not think Palestine could be a single and simple national territory quite in the sense of France; but he did not see why it should not be a commonwealth of cantons after the manner of Switzerland. Some of these could be Jewish cantons, others Arab cantons, and so on according to the type of population. This is in itself more reasonable than much that is suggested on the same side; but the point of it for my own purpose is more particular. This idea, whether it correctly represents Dr Weizmann's meaning or no, clearly involves the abandonment of the solidarity of Palestine, and tolerates the idea of groups of Jews being separated from each other by populations of a different type. Now if once this notion be considered admissible, it seems to me capable of considerable extension. It seems possible that there might be not only Jewish cantons in Palestine but Jewish cantons outside Palestine, Jewish colonies in suitable and selected places in adjacent parts or in many other parts of the world. They might be affiliated to some official centre in Palestine, or even in Jerusalem, where there would naturally be at least some great religious headquarters of the scattered race and religion. The nature of that religious centre it must be for Jews to decide; but I think if I were a Jew I would build the Temple without bothering about the site of the Temple. That they should have the old site, of course, is not to be thought of; it would raise a Holy War from Morocco to the marches of China. But seeing that some of the greatest of the deeds of Israel were done, and some of the most glorious of the songs of Israel sung, when their only temple was a box carried about in the desert, I cannot think that the mere moving of the situation of the place of sacrifice need even mean so much to that historic tradition as it would to many others. That the Jews should have some high place of dignity and ritual in Palestine, such as a great building like the Mosque of Omar, is certainly right and reasonable; for upon no theory can their historic connection be dismissed. I think it is sophistry to say, as do some Anti-Semites, that the Jews have no more right there than the Jebusites. If there are Jebusites they are Jebusites without knowing it. I think it sufficiently answered in the fine phrase of an English priest, in many ways more Anti-Semitic than I: 'The people that remembers has a right.' The very worst of the Jews, as well as the very best, do in some sense remember. They are hated and persecuted and frightened into false names and double lives; but they remember. They lie, they swindle, they betray, they oppress; but they remember. The more we happen to hate such elements among the Hebrews, the more we admire the manly and magnificent elements among the more vague and vagrant tribes of Palestine, the more we must admit that paradox. The unheroic have the heroic memory; and the heroic people have no memory.

But whatever the Jewish nation might wish to do about a national shrine or other supreme centre, the suggestion for the moment is that something like a Jewish territorial scheme might really be attempted, if we permit the Jews to be scattered no longer as individuals but as groups. It seems possible that by some such extension of the definition of Zionism we might ultimately overcome even the greatest difficulty of Zionism, the difficulty of resettling a sufficient number of so large a race on so small a land. For if the advantage of the ideal to the Jews is to gain the promised land, the advantage to the Gentiles is to get rid of the Jewish problem, and I do not see why we should obtain all their advantage and none of our own. Therefore I would leave as few Jews as possible in other established nations, and to these I would give a special position best described as privilege; some sort of self-governing enclave with special laws and exemptions; for instance, I would certainly excuse them from conscription, which I think a gross injustice in their case. [Footnote: Of course, the privileged exile would also lose the rights of a native.] A Jew might be treated as respectfully as a foreign ambassador, but a foreign ambassador is a foreigner. Finally, I would give the same privileged position to all Jews everywhere, as an alternative policy to Zionism, if Zionism failed by the test I have named; the only true and the only tolerable test; if the Jews had not so much failed as peasants as succeeded as capitalists.

There is one word to be added; it will be noted that inevitably and even against some of my own desires, the argument has returned to that recurrent conclusion which was found in the Roman Empire and the Crusades. The European can do justice to the Jew; but it must be the European who does it. Such a possibility as I have thrown out, and any other possibility that any one can think of, becomes at once impossible without some idea of a general suzerainty of Christendom over the lands of the Moslem and the Jew. Personally, I think it would be better if it were a general suzerainty of Christendom, rather than a particular supremacy of England. And I feel this, not from a desire to restrain the English power, but rather from a desire to defend it. I think there is not a little danger to England in the diplomatic situation involved; but that is a diplomatic question that it is neither within my power nor duty to discuss adequately. But if I think it would be wiser for France and England together to hold Syria and Palestine together rather than separately, that only completes and clinches the conclusion that has haunted me, with almost uncanny recurrence, since I first saw Jerusalem sitting on the hill like a turreted town in England or in France; and for one moment the dark dome of it was again the Templum Domini, and the tower on it was the Tower of Tancred.

Anyhow, with the failure of Zionism would fall the last and best attempt at a rationalistic theory of the Jew. We should be left facing a mystery which no other rationalism has ever come so near to providing within rational cause and cure. Whatever we do, we shall not return to that insular innocence and comfortable unconsciousness of Christendom, in which the Victorian agnostics could suppose that the Semitic problem was a brief medieval insanity. In this as in greater things, even if we lost our faith we could not recover our agnosticism. We can never recover agnosticism, any more than any other kind of ignorance. We know that there is a Jewish problem; we only hope that there is a Jewish solution. If there is not, there is no other. We cannot believe again that the Jew is an Englishman with certain theological theories, any more than we can believe again any other part of the optimistic materialism whose temple is the Albert Memorial. A scheme of guilds may be attempted and may be a failure; but never again can we respect mere Capitalism for its success. An attack may be made on political corruption, and it may be a failure; but never again can we believe that our politics are not corrupt. And so Zionism may be attempted and may be a failure; but never again can we ourselves be at ease in Zion. Or rather, I should say, if the Jew cannot be at ease in Zion we can never again persuade ourselves that he is at ease out of Zion. We can only salute as it passes that restless and mysterious figure, knowing at last that there must be in him something mystical as well as mysterious; that whether in the sense of the sorrows of Christ or of the sorrows of Cain, he must pass by, for he belongs to God.

On July 14th, 1921 Chesterton took the part of Theseus in *A Midsummer Night's Dream* produced by The Players' Club in Beaconsfield. Puck was played by Margaret Halford, a Jewish friend and former West-End actress who had felt a certain restraint when first meeting the Chestertons: 'I'm a stiff-necked viper on the Jewish question. I wasn't really "afraid" about my own welcome, but though I had for years been an enthralled admirer of G.K.'s, I'd have foregone the pleasure of a personal friendship, if his true attitude . . . had not become so manifest.'[20] Mrs Halford appeared frequently in entertainments at the Chestertons' studio and was showered with verses.[21]

A MIDWINTER NIGHT'S DREAM

Midsummer Night, whose dream we knew,
Is gone with that great Summer's gleams,
And better words could better show
Midwinter has its nights and dreams;
Memories of many friends could bring
Not I alone, the clumsiest,
But better mummers of our masque
This tribute to the best.

. . .

> Yet, as you bear with lenient laughter,
> The clowns that to your portals come,
> The waits who will not wait for Christmas,
> The mummers who are far from mum;
> Take with such tolerance of these rhymes
> Our love, that equals art with art;
> You, who in better things than mumming,
> Can choose the better part. (Christmas, 1921)

By 1926 Chesterton was president of The Players' Club at Hale's Barn and at Christmas wrote to Margaret Halford:

> Far from the Players' Club but not in play,
> For many months I have wandered far away . . .
> I missed your brightest shows; I cannot tell . . .
> . . . how Maurice Solomon, they say,
> Romped through Goliath in the Scripture play,
> But I have not forgotten and to you
> For all your works I yield my thanks anew.

In 'The Tower of Treason', *Popular Magazine*, February 7th, 1920 yet another Jewish doctor is introduced as a red herring:

'You know that sort of château that some French nobleman, an exiled prince I believe, built upon the wooded ridge over there beyond the crucifix – you can see its turrets from here. I'm not sure who owns it now; but it's been rented for some years by Dr Amiel, a famous physician, a Frenchman, or, rather, a French Jew. He is supposed to have high humanitarian ideals, including the idealization of this small nationality here, which, of course, suits our Foreign Office very well. Perhaps it's unfair to say he's only "supposed" to be this; and the plain truth is I'm not a fair judge of the man, for a reason you may soon guess. But apart from sentiment, I think somehow I am in two minds about him. It sounds absurd to say that like or dislike of a man could depend on his wearing a red smoking-cap. But that's the nearest I can get to it; bare-headed and just a little bald-headed, he seems only a dark, rather distinguished-looking French man of science, with a pointed beard. When he puts that red fez on he is suddenly something much lower than a Turk; and I see all Asia sneering and leering at me across the Levant. Well, perhaps it's a fancy of the fit I'm in; and it's only just to say that people believe in him, who are really devoted to this people or to our policy here . . .'

'I cannot see that you have much reason to be jealous of the poor Jewish gentleman, as you seem to be, even if he is so base and perfidious as to wear a smoking-cap . . . it is perfectly true that the Jews have woven over these nations a net that is not only international, but anti-national; and it is quite true that inhuman as is their usury and inhuman as is often their oppression of the poor, some of them are never so inhuman as when they are idealistic; never so inhuman as when they are humane . . . I could take your hint about the scarlet smoking-cap, and say it was a signal and the symbol of a secret society; that a hundred Jews in a hundred smoking-caps were plotting everywhere, as many of them really are; I could show a conspiracy ramifying from the red cap of Amiel as it did from the *Bonnet Rouge* of Almereyda . . . But what corrects all this is the concrete difficulty I defined at the beginning. I still do not see how wearing a red fez could conjure very small gems out of a steel box at the top of a tower.' Then there came anew a noise of death from the tower; and the hermit fell all his length crashing among the undergrowth, and lay still as a stone. Bertram Drake stood up . . .

In a sort of tumbled dream he saw Dr Amiel lift the body on to the pedestal, producing surgical instruments for the last hopeless surgical tests. The doctor had his back to Drake, who did not trouble to look over his shoulder, but stared at the ground until the doctor said:

'I fear he is quite dead. But I have extracted the bullet.'

There was something odd about his quiet voice, and the group seemed suddenly, if silently, seething with new emotions. The girl gave an exclamation of wonder, and it seemed of joy, which Drake could not comprehend.

'I am glad I extracted the bullet,' said Dr Amiel. 'I fancy that's what Drake's friend with the sabre was trying to extract.'

. . . Drake thrust his head over the other's shoulder, and saw what they were all staring at. The shot that had struck Stephen in the heart lay a few inches from his body, and it not only glittered but sparkled. It sparkled as only one stone can sparkle in the world . . . For Stephen the hermit had died indeed with the truth in his heart; and the truth had been taken out of his heart by the forceps of a wondering Jew; and it lay there on the pedestal of the cross, like the soul drawn out of his body.

## SONGS OF EDUCATION
*New Witness*, July 11th, 1919, p. 117:

### II. Geography
. . . Gibraltar's a rock that you see very plain,
And attached to its base is the district of Spain.
And the island of Malta is marked further on,
Where some natives were known as the Knights of St. John.
Then Cyprus, and east to the Suez Canal,
That was conquered by Dizzy and Rothschild his pal
With the Sword of the Lord in the old English way;
And that is the meaning of Empire Day.

Our principal imports come far as Cape Horn;
For necessities, cocoa; for luxuries, corn;
Thus Brahmins are born for the rice-field, and thus,
The Gods made the Greeks to grow currants for us;
Of earth's other tributes are plenty to choose,

Tobacco and petrol and Jazzing and Jews:
The Jazzing will pass but the Jews they will stay,
And that is the meaning of Empire Day . . .[21]

## *What I saw in America*, (Dodd Mead) 1922, pp. 48–50:

There was a time when English poets and other publicists could always be inspired with instantaneous indignation about the persecuted Jews in Russia. We have heard less about them since we heard more about the persecuting Jews in Russia. I fear there are a great many middle-class Englishmen already who wish that Trotsky [Braunstein] had been persecuted a little more. But even in those days Englishmen divided their minds in a curious fashion and unconsciously distinguished between the Jews whom they had never seen, in Warsaw, and the Jew whom they had often seen in Whitechapel. It seemed to be assumed that, by a curious coincidence, Russia possessed not only the very worst anti-Semites but the very best Semites. A moneylender in London might be like Judas Iscariot; but a moneylender in Moscow must be like Judas Maccabaeus.

Nevertheless there remained in our common sense an unconscious but fundamental comprehension of the unity of Israel; a sense that some things could be said, and some could not be said, about the Jews as a whole. Suppose that even in those days, to say nothing of these, an English protest against Russian Anti-semitism had been answered by the Russian Anti-semites, and suppose the answer had been somewhat as follows:

– 'It is all very well for foreigners to complain of our denying civic rights to our Jewish subjects; but we know the Jews better than they do. They are a barbarous people, entirely primitive, and very like the simple savages who cannot count beyond five on their fingers. It is quite impossible to make them understand ordinary numbers, to say nothing of simple economics. They do not realise the meaning of the value of money. No Jew anywhere in the world can get into his stupid head the notion of a bargain, or of exchanging one thing for another. Their hopeless incapacity for commerce or finance would retard the progress of our people, would prevent the spread of any sort of economic education, would keep the whole country on a lower level than that of the most prehistoric methods of barter. What Russia needs most is a mercantile middle class; and it is unjust to ask us to swamp its small beginnings in thousands of these rude tribesmen, who cannot do a sum of simple addition, or understand the symbolic character of a threepenny bit. We might as well be asked to give civic rights to cows and pigs as to this unhappy half-witted race who can no more count than the beasts of the field. In every intellectual exercise they are hopelessly incompetent; no Jew can play chess; no Jew can learn languages; no Jew has ever appeared in the smallest part in any theatrical performance; no Jew can give or take any pleasure connected with any musical instrument. These people are our subjects; and we must understand them. We accept full responsibility for treating such troglodytes on our own terms.'

It would not be entirely convincing. It would sound a little far-fetched and unreal. But it would sound exactly like our utterances about the Irish, as they sound to all Americans, and rather especially to Anti-Irish Americans. That is exactly the impression we produce on the people of the United States when we say, as we do say in substance, something like this: 'We mean no harm to the poor dear Irish, so dreamy, so irresponsible, so incapable of order or organisation . . .'

Now the point is not only that this view of the Irish is false, but that it is the particular view that the Americans know to be false. While we are saying that the Irish could not organise, the Americans are complaining, often very bitterly, of the power of Irish organisation. While we say that the Irishman could not rule himself, the Americans are saying, more or less humorously, that the Irishman rules them.

1921   'The Bottomless Well', *Harper's*, March 1921, pp. 50–15. Collected in *The Man Who Knew Too Much*, New York (Harper & Bros.) October 1922.

It's bad enough that a gang of infernal Jews should plant us here, where there's no earthly English interest to serve, and all hell beating up against us, simply because Nosey Zimmern has lent money to half the Cabinet. It's bad enough that an old pawnbroker from Bagdad [*sic*] should make us fight his battles; we can't fight with our right hand cut off . . . But if you think I am going to let the Union Jack go down and down eternally, like the bottomless well, down into the blackness of the bottomless pit, down in defeat and derision, amid the jeers of the very Jews who have sucked us dry – no, I won't, and that's flat; not if the Chancellor were blackmailed by twenty millionaires with their gutter rags, not if the Prime Minister married twenty Yankee Jewesses, not if Woodville and Carstairs had shares in twenty swindling mines. If the thing is really tottering, God help it, it mustn't be we who tip it over.'

Hawker, the old squire, had been a loose unsatisfactory sort of person; had been on bad terms with his first wife . . . and had then married a flashy South American Jewess with a fortune. But he must have worked his way through this fortune also with marvellous rapidity, for he had been compelled to sell the estate to Verner . . . Who is Verner? Where does he come from? His name sounds old, but I never heard of it before, as the man said of the Crucifixion. Why talk about his blue blood? His blood may be gamboge yellow with green spots for all anybody knows. All we know is that the old squire, Hawker, somehow ran through his money (and his second wife's, I suppose, for she was rich enough) and sold the estate to a man called Verner. What did he make his money in? Oil? Army contracts?'

('The Fool of the Family', *The Man Who Knew Too Much*, 1922.)

1925   *The Unobtrusive Traffic of Captain Pierce*, Collected in *Tales of the Long Bow*, 1925.

'What was the change?' asked the colonel.

'Old Oates has gone into another business,' answered Pierce quietly.

'What on earth has old Oates got to do with it?' asked Hood staring. 'Do you mean that Yankee mooning about over mediaeval ruins?'

'Oh, I know,' sad Pierce wearily, 'I thought he had nothing to do with it; I thought it was the Jews and vegetarians, and the rest; but they're very innocent instruments. The truth is Enoch Oates is the biggest pork-packer and importer in the world, and he didn't want any competition from our cottagers. And what he says goes, as he would express it. Now, thank God, he's taken up another line.

1929    *The Poet & the Lunatics* – Dr Simeon Wolfe, psychologist. Page 260: 'Wolfe's face was still wrinkled with its Semitic sneer, but his olive tint had turned to a sort of loathsome yellow.'

1930    *Four Faultless Felons*. The Loyal Traitor – II. The Procession of the Plotters., pp. 175–76: the quiet and intelligent banker, to whom they all owed money, was most powerful of all . . . The last was a slight, refined little figure with straight, grey hair and a hooked nose rather large for his attenuated features. He was dressed in dark grey so that his streaks of limbs seemed to repeat his streaks of hair, and only when he carefully fitted on a pair of tortoise-shell goggles, did his eyes seem suddenly to stand out and and come to life, as if he were a monster who put his eyes on and off like a mask. This was Isidor Simon, the banker, and he had never taken any title though many had been offered to him.

pp. 177–78: 'this pawnbroker; he is little Loeb, who calls himself Lobb and lives at the corner of the Old Market, in the poorest part of town. He's a Jew, of course, but not so much disliked as some Jews of his trade, and such thousands of people do business with him that we were rather led to look into the matter. The result of our inquiries points to the man being quite incredibly rich, all the more because he lives like a poor man. The general belief is that he is a miser.' . . . 'He isn't a miser,' said Simon, 'and if he's a millionaire, then my question is answered.'

'Do you know him?' asked the King, speaking for the first time. 'Why do you say he isn't a miser?'

'Because no Jew was ever a miser,' answered the banker. 'Avarice is not a Jewish vice; it is a peasant's vice, a vice of people who want to protect themselves with personal possessions in perpetuity. Greed is the Jewish vice: greed for luxury; greed for vulgarity; greed for gambling; greed for throwing away other people's money and their own on a harem or a theatre or a grand hotel or some harlotry – or possibly on a grand revolution. But not hoarding it. That is the madness of sane men; of men who have a soil.'

'How do you know?' asked the King with mild curiosity. 'How did you come to make a study of Jews?'

'Only by being one myself,' replied the banker.

p. 188: III. The Princess Intervenes. '. . . And yet the last is the most typical of all. How absolutely characteristic of the little Jew to have a little champagne, but very expensive, and to have black coffee, the proper digestive, after it. Ah, he understands health better than the health-faddist does! But there's something blood-curdling about these cultured Jews, with their delicate and cautious art of pleasure. Some say it's because they don't believe in a future life.'

The turn of the decade into the 1930s did bring a change of direction, as Chesterton once again confronted his old Prussian enemy in a letter in *The Times*, 8th April, 1933:

'The Return of Prussianism'

There are some who wonder how I came to pick up the strange fancy that Hitler and his colleagues are as warlike as they say they are; as narrowly nationalist and imperialist as they say they are, and as proud of the great period of Prussian victories as every sane man knows them to be. I have seen a vast number of statements coming from their side; and the nearest to any note of peace, or even international justice, was an account of Hitler repudiating German War-Guilt over the tomb of Frederick the Great. Humour can hardly be his strong point; anyhow some of us are but little reassured by a man abjuring piracy over the bones of Captain Kidd or perjury upon the holy relics of Titus Oates.

But apart from Hitler's hero, who waded in war-guilt all his life, and scarcely pretended anything else, it would be easy for me to make a whole dossier of what Prussians and Pro-Prussian Germans are saying now. It is only a matter of looking up a lot of files; but I will mention two indications merely from memory. Hindenburg himself is reported as saying, 'What has been German land must be German once more.' Which means, and can only conceivably mean, that all the land that Prussia ever stole, in her most piratical and imperialistic period, Prussia now intends to steal again. Prussia will generously give back to the Poles all that Austria and Russia stole from them, on condition that she can keep all that she stole herself. Does anyone in his five wits fancy this policy can be pursued without a World War? Or to take a small popular indication, the streets are hung with banners inscribed 'No honour without battle'; a very neat abbreviation of the well-known epigram of the German philosopher [ Nietzsche ]; 'You say a good cause justifies any war; but I tell you a good war justifies any cause.'

Nor need we look only among Prussians or Prussianists for these evidences of Prussianism. Count Montgelas, a Bavarian, a Catholic, a man writing like a cultured and humane gentleman, a man professing even to repudiate the old Prussianism of Prussia, yet himself offers something like its most extreme programme, as if it were a moderate programme? I do not quite follow the reasoning by which he desires the reunion of Austria with the Reich, when he should surely desire rather the reunion of the Reich with Austria. But anyhow, he then calmly goes on to treat it as an equal tragedy that 'The Germans of Lorraine' – the province of Joan of Arc – should be cut off from the Reich. Bismark himself doubted the annexations of 1870. In this sort of thing, Count Montgelas seems to be more Prussianist than Bismark. The French word Lorraine is traditional in all Western Europe; indeed he instinctively uses it himself. Outside the strict Prussian State Schools, not one man in a thousand even knows the German name for Lorraine [Lotharingen]. But there are supposed to be 'Germans' there; and wherever there are Germans he will wander with a drawn sword to recover them. We shall soon hear of his besieging Bradford.

I am not defending the bunch of politicians who made the last Treaty; and I can assure Count Montgelas that I have always denounced it for its stupid and shameful destruction of Austria. I am defending a historic fact; for which thousands of the most thoughtful Englishmen and Frenchmen, as well as the bravest, died for the fact that Prussia had distorted the whole destiny of Germany and Europe.

We may all be wrong; God can bring good out of evil; and the new Bismarkian may complete his resemblance to Bismark; he may go to Canossa. But if or when the New Germany moves one inch towards infringing on the present ancient frontiers of the Polish realm – then I shall know that I was right.

## G.K.'s Weekly, 'The Judaism of Hitler', July 20th, 1933, pp. 311–312.

Hitlerism is almost entirely of Jewish origin. This truth, if inscribed in the noble old German lettering on a large banner and lifted in sight of an excited mob in a modern German town, might or might not have the soothing effect which I desire. The simple historical explanation, if written on a post-card or a telegraph-form, and addressed to Herr Hitler's private address, might or might not cause him to pause in his political career, and reconsider all human history in the light of the blazing illumination with which I have furnished him in these words. Finally, these words, placed even where they stand at the beginning of this paragraph, may not be wholly comprehended or connected with their true historical origins; but they are none the less strictly historical.

It is a horrible shame to say I was ever unkind to a Nordic Man. I have had many of these innocent creatures of God gambolling round my house from time to time, and I have always found them faithful and affectionate; when treated and trusted, as they should be, with faith and affection. I am very fond of the real Nordic Man, especially when he does really look like a Nordic Man; as, for example, when he is Scandinavian. I think the Scandinavian is a thoroughly nice fellow; and probably a much better man than I. Hitler does not look in the least like a Nordic man; but that is another question, and need not discredit his personal good qualities. But, when it comes to the reading of history, there is one thing that I can never for the life of me see. I can easily believe that a nice large Scandinavian may have brought great elements of strength or simplicity into any family into which he married; and what is true of the Scandinavian may be quite often true of the German. But what I frankly and flatly deny, in history as a whole, is that the Nordic Men have excelled in bringing *ideas* into the world. The Germans came in due course to describe their piracy as imperialism; but they borrowed the idea of imperialism from the Romans. They produced a sort of Prussianism that was praised or blamed as militarism; but they borrowed the idea of militarism from the French. The German Emperors modelled themselves on the Austrian Emperors, who had modelled themselves on the Greek Emperors and the Roman Emperors. The greatest of the Prussians did not even conceal his contempt for Prussia. He refused to talk anything but French or to exchange ideas with anybody, except somebody of the type of Voltaire. Then came the liberal ideas of the French Revolution, and the whole movement of German Unity was originally a liberal movement on the lines of the French Revolution. Then came the more modern and more mortally dangerous idea of Race, which the Germans borrowed from a Frenchman named Gobineau. And on top of that idea of

Race, came the grand, imperial idea of a Chosen Race, of a sacred seed that is, as the Kaiser said, the salt of the earth; of a people that is God's favourite and guided by Him, in a sense in which He does not guide other and lesser peoples. And if anybody asks where anybody got that idea, there is only one possible or conceivable answer. He got it from the Jews.

It is perfectly true that the Jews have been very powerful in Germany. It is only just to Hitler to say that they have been too powerful in Germany, but the Germans will find it very hard to cut up their culture on a principle of Anti-Semite amputation.

They will find it difficult to persuade any German, let alone any European who is fond of Germany, that Schiller is a poet and Heine is not; that Goethe is a critic and Lessing is not; that Beethoven is a composer and Mendelssohn is not; or that Bach is a musician and Brahms is not. But again, it is but just to Hitlerism to say that the Jews did infect Germany with a good many things less harmless than the lyrics of Heine or the melodies of Mendelssohn. It is true that many Jews toiled at that obscure conspiracy against Christendom, which some of them can never abandon; and sometimes it was marked not by obscurity but obscenity. It is true that they were financiers, or in other words usurers; it is true that they fattened on the worst forms of Capitalism; and it is inevitable that, on losing these advantages of Capitalism, they naturally took refuge in its other form, which is Communism. For both Capitalism and Communism rest on the same idea: a centralisation of wealth which destroys private property. But among the thousand and one ways in which Semitism affected Germanism is in this mystical idea, which came through Protestantism. Here the Nordic Men, who are never thinkers, were entirely at the mercy of the Jews who are always thinkers. When the Reformation had rent away the more Nordic sort of German from the old idea of human fellowship in a faith open to all, they obviously needed some other idea that would at least look equally large and towering and transcendental. They began to get it through the passionate devotion of historical Protestants to the Old Testament. That, of course, is where the joke comes in; that the Protestants now wish to select for destruction what nobody else except the Protestant had ever wanted to select and set apart for idolatry. But that is a later stage of the story. By concentrating on the ancient story of the Covenant with Israel, and losing the counterweight of the idea of the universal Church of Christendom, they grew more and more into the mood of seeing their religion as a mystical religion of Race. And then, by the same modern processes, their education fell into the hands of the Jews. There are Jewish mystics and Jewish sceptics; but about this one matter of the strange sacredness of his own race, almost every Jewish sceptic is a Jewish mystic. When they insinuated their ideals into German culture, they doubtless very often acted, not only as sceptics, but as cynics. But, even if they were only pretending to be mystics, they could only pretend to understand one kind of mysticism. This German mysticism became more and more like Jewish mysticism: a thing not thinking much of ordinary human beings, the hewers of wood and drawers of water, the Gentiles or the strangers; but thinking with intense imagination of the idea of a holy house or family, alone dedicated to heaven and therefore to triumph. This is the great Prussian illusion of pride, for which thousands of Jews have recently been rabbled or ruined or driven from their homes. I am certainly not enough of an Anti-Semite to say that it served them right.

But it is true that it all began with the power of the Jews; which has now ended with the persecution of the Jews. People like the Hitlerites never had any ideas of their own; they got this idea indirectly through the Protestants, that is primarily through the Prussians, but they got it originally from the Jews. In the Jews it has even a certain tragic grandeur; as of men separated and sealed and waiting for a unique destiny. But until we have utterly destroyed it among Christians, we shall never restore Christendom.

This attempt to link the Master Race with the Chosen People brought another request for an interview from *The Jewish Chronicle*, to which Chesterton as usual acceded, unlike contemporaries such as Shaw and others.

In our early days Hilaire Belloc and myself were accused of being uncompromisingly anti-Semites. Today, although I still think there is a Jewish problem, I am appalled by the Hitlerite atrocities. They have absolutely no reason or logic behind them. It is quite obviously the expedient of a man who has been driven to seek a scapegoat, and has found with relief the most famous scapegoat in European history, the Jewish people. I am quite ready to believe now that Belloc and I will die defending the last Jew in Europe.

The Prussian spirit . . . is fraught with . . . danger to harmless people . . . By [badly] treating harmless, and in scores of cases, valuable and distinguished Jewish citizens of the German Reich . . . [Hitler] has forfeited all claim to the label statesman.[22]

## G.K.'s Weekly, 1934:

### GENTLEMEN PREFER BLONDES

*'My leader wishes me to marry. I shall therefore seek a Protestant, pure Aryan girl, blonde, slim and possessed of private means.'*

– Quoted in *Hail Hitler*

Not the wild Walkyr maid alone
In her tremendous teens
Drags men with ropes of golden hair
And also private means.

For us that second golden string
Is known behind the scenes;
We too rejoice in public men
Who know what 'private' means.

Still the poor German has the worst
When Nazi might unscreens
Such rather private matters on
The way to private means.

And If he seeks the Dark Lady,
Judith or Sheba's Queens,
The public power may shoot him dead
By very private means.

## G.K.'s *Weekly*, March 19th, 1936, pp. 1–2:

### 'HITLER VERSUS HISTORY'

*German troops entered the demilitarized Rhineland on March 7th, 1936 with Hitler denouncing the Treaty of Locarno signed in 1925.*

At the time of writing, most people are rushing to the bookstalls to read about Hitler's violation of Locarno in the evening editions and stop-press news. They would be much wiser to rush to the library and read volumes half a century old, about what their fathers and grandfathers thought of things now mostly forgotten. A famous scholar and humorist said somewhere, 'When a new book comes out, read an old one.' It is even more practically true to say, 'When the latest news arrives, then go back to the oldest you can get hold of.'

For there is now a cultural controversy far more fundamental than that between those who are pro-French or those who are pro-German; and it is the quarrel between those who are historical and those who are unhistorical. Those who would teach men how to hustle have only taught them how to forget. The effort to get the latest information means not so much information as ignorance; ignorance even of the origin of the information. So that there must be thousands of people today who really imagine that Hitler invented the racial arrogance now prevalent in Germany; or that his warlike demonstration without warning is something new in the international action of the tribe he leads; or that the situation is 'unprecedented', which is exactly what the sensational newsvendors love to call it, and exactly what it is not. The process is now nearly two hundred years old; and it began when Frederick the Great, by whose tomb Hitler like Hannibal dedicated himself to his heathen gods, shocked his own age by attacking Austria without a declaration of war.

The most piteous case is that of the Prussian Prime Minister, Goering, who seems to have said, 'They say we do not observe our treaties; look at our treaty with Poland.' This treaty had actually been running for more than a year; and the suggestion is that Goering has searched the whole history of Prussia for any other example of a treaty that was not broken. But I rather doubt whether the Poles even now draw deep breaths of confidence from the past memories of the attitude of Prussia towards them. But anyhow, the essential point to realise is that, whoever else is right, the person who is perilously and pestilently wrong is the person who says, 'Oh don't ask me to go back on all that old business about Frederick the Great and Bismark; really, it's almost as remote as the invasion of Belgium!' He is building a somewhat insecure efficiency upon the mere fact that he forgets what other people remember.

In *The Storyteller*, February, 1936. 'A Tall Story,' later included in 1937 in *The Paradoxes of Mr Pond*, highlighted the plight of Jews in Germany:

They had been discussing the new troubles in Germany: the three old friends, Sir Hubert Wotton, the famous official; Mr Pond, the obscure official; and Captain Gahagan . . .

. . . 'It's an infernal shame,' Wotton was saying, 'the way these fellows have treated the Jews; perfectly decent and harmless Jews, who were no more Communists than I am; little men who'd worked their way up by merit and industry, all kicked out of their posts without a penny of compensation. Surely you agree with that, Gahagan?'

'Of course I do,' replied Gahagan. 'I never kicked a Jew. I can definitely remember three and a half occasions on which I definitely refrained from doing so. As for all those hundreds and thousands of poor little fiddlers and actors and chess-players, I think that it was a damned shame that they should be kicked out or kicked at all. But I fancy they must be kicking themselves, for having been so faithful to Germany and even, everywhere else, pretty generally pro-German.'

'Even that can be exaggerated,' said Mr Pond. 'Do you remember the case of Carl Schiller, that happened during the war? It was all kept rather quiet, as I have reason to know; for the thing happened, in some sense, in my department . . .

Mr Pond himself always spent several hours in the office . . . Immediately outside his door . . . there was an old curiosity shop opposite, with a display of ancient Asiatic weapons; and there was Mrs Hartog-Haggard next door, more alarming than all the weapons of the world . . .

'Mr Pond, do you know what is right opposite your own house?'

'Well, I think so,' said Mr Pond, doubtfully, 'more or less.'

'I never read the name over the shop before!' cried the lady. 'You know it is all dark and dirty and obliterated – that curiosity shop, I mean; with all the spears and daggers. Think of the impudence of the man! He's actually written up his name there: "C. Schiller" '.

'He's written up C. Schiller; I'm not so sure he's written up his name,' said Mr Pond.

'Do you mean,' she cried, 'that you actually know he goes by two names? Why, that makes it worse than ever!'

And for the third time did Mr Pond take some steps to verify the Hartog-Haggard revelations. He took the ten or twelve steps necessary to take him across the road and into the shop of C. Schiller, amid all the shining sabres and yataghans. It was a very peaceable-looking person who waited behind all this array of arms; not to say a rather smooth and sleek one; and Pond, leaning across the counter, addressed him in a low and confidential voice.

'Why the dickens do you people do it? It will be more than half your own fault if there's a row of some kind and a Jingo mob comes here and breaks your windows for your absurd German name. I know very well this is no quarrel of yours. I am well aware,' Mr Pond continued with an earnest gaze, 'that you never invaded Belgium. I am fully conscious that your national tastes do not lie in that direction. I know you had nothing to do with burning the Louvain Library or sinking the *Lusitania*. Then why the devil can't you say so? Why can't you call yourself Levy like your fathers before you – your fathers who go back to the most ancient priesthood of the world? . . .'

'There'th a lot of prejudith againth my rathe,' said the warden of the armoury.

'There'll be a lot more, unless you take my advice,' said Mr Pond with unusual brevity; and left the shop to return to the office.

. . . Mr Levy was certainly not a German; and it was very improbable that he was a real enthusiast for Germany; but it was not altogether impossible to suppose, in the tangle and distraction of all the modern international muddle, that he might be some sort of tool, conscious or unconscious, of a real German conspiracy. So long as that was possible, he must be watched. Mr Pond was very glad that Mr Levy lived in the shop exactly opposite.

However, Mr Schiller-Levy is a complete red herring, as the spy turns out to be Signor Tizzi, a stilt-walker from the pantomime.

German or Jewish derivation did not necessarily condemn the party concerned. Maurice Baring, a convert to Roman Catholicism, was one of Chesterton's closest friends; and a strong continuing friendship had sprung up between the Chestertons and the Steinthals of Ilkley in whose house in 1903 Chesterton was staying when he first met Father John O'Connor, the model for Father Brown. The Steinthals were high-church Anglicans. The following year (for Francis Steinthal's fiftieth birthday on August, 1904) Chesterton wrote 'The Queen of the Green Elves,'[23] a pastoral romp, as a tribute to him:

> Upon this place in after time shall stand
> A splendid house that shall be called St. John's . . .
> Here, on this barren glade on which we tread
> STEINTHAL shall have a garden; possibly
> Children of Steinthal may herein enact
> The very battle between you and me
> Which now we end: I know not. But the doom
> Which I pronounce on you is terrible . . .
> Since you are King of England, you shall make
> All Englishmen as excellent as Steinthal.

GKC always appears to have been at ease discussing Jews and Jewish matters, although it became clear that those discussed were not always comfortable with his benign intentions, for, as with the candid friend in the deodorant advertisement, uncomfortable news is not always welcomed and the well-intentioned messenger blamed for the message, just as any outsider intervening in a domestic argument is almost sure to end up reconciling the quarrelling parties only in so far as they unite against the intruder.

We can be sure that Chesterton was at times offensive, patronising and snobbish to an extent that at times can make us wince. In this he was very much of his times. It is little excuse to say that he compares well with many contemporaries such as Shaw,[24] Buchan, Eliot and Christie and predecessors like Dickens and Trollope and Voltaire. Winston Churchill's views on what he termed international and terrorist Jews[25] are as strong, if not stronger, than anything said by Chesterton. Nonetheless he suggested that Jews should wear traditional distinctive clothing, but then he wanted everybody to wear distinctive clothing.[26] In an odd way he was ahead of his time, as with the development of fundamentalism in later years many did in fact come to do so. A further irony was that many of his colleagues were Jewish printers and journalists from Whitechapel, the majority working on newspapers far more anti-semitic than Chesterton ever was.

Above all else, Chesterton was one of the first to spring to the defence of German Jews. He died on July 14th, 1936 three days before the start of the Spanish Civil War and two weeks before the Berlin Olympics, long before the excesses of Kristallnacht in November 1938 and the demands for *Lebensraum*, let alone the obscenities of the final solution. He condemned the Nuremberg laws of 1935 which reduced Jews to second-class citizens or worse. But was he anti-Jew as sometimes accused? On a personal or racial level probably not, as attested by his friends. Nevertheless, guilty as charged? Possibly, but with extenuating circumstances. He meant well by the Jews, although we must acknowledge that the road to hell is paved with good intentions. He is also unfortunate that since his death he has often to his detriment been confused with his second cousin, Arthur Kenneth Chesterton (1896–1973) born in South Africa, who joined the British Union of Fascists in 1933 and edited the BUF newspaper *Blackshirt*. A friend of William Joyce and member of The Right Club, after the Second World War A.K. founded the League of Empire Loyalists and co-founded the National Front. However, A.K. Chesterton was not G.K. Chesterton.

# CRITICAL JUDGEMENTS

**Gilbert Adair** (1944–2011)

It is, at any rate, his flesh-creeping proximity to Poe and Kafka and indeed Borges that makes him not just still readable but still curiously modern. *The Guardian*, October 20th, 2007.

**Kingsley Amis** (1922–1995)

No writer has ever excelled Chesterton.

He achieves some of the finest, and least regarded, descriptive writing of this century. And it is not just description; it is atmosphere, it anticipates and underlines mood and feeling, usually of the more nervous sort, in terms of sky and water and shadow, the eye that sees and the hand that records acting as one. The result is unmistakable: 'That singular smoky sparkle, at once a confusion and a transparency, which is the strange secret of the Thames, was changing more and more from its grey to its glittering extreme . . .' Even apart from the alliteration, who else could that be?

*The Man Who Was Thursday* is not quite a political bad dream, nor a metaphysical thriller, nor a cosmic joke in the form of a spy novel, but it is something of all three . . . it remains the most thrilling book I have ever read.

**John Atkins** (1916–2009)

Some of the old pros say that the best spy book ever written was Chesterton's *The Man Who Was Thursday* . . . McCormack actually claims that Thursday still provides a model for aspiring spy writers, to prevent them from 'keeling over too far in the direction of fantasy'. This is in itself a Chesterton-type paradox which means it must be treated seriously. *The British Spy Novel* (1984).

**W.H. Auden** (1907–1973)

I can always enjoy reading him.

Both in his prose and his verse, [Chesterton] sees, as few writers have, the world about him as full of sacramental signs or symbols. I would not call him a mystic like Blake . . .

Chesterton never disregards the actual visible appearance of things. Then, unlike Wordsworth, his imagination is stirred to wonder, not only by natural objects, but by human artefacts as well. Probably most young children possess this imaginative gift, but most of us lose it when we grow up as a consequence, Chesterton would say, of the Fall.

I cannot think of a single comic poem by Chesterton that is not a triumphant success.

### J.L. Borges (1899–1986)

I believe that Chesterton is one of the foremost writers of our time, not only because of his happy inventiveness, visual imagination and childlike or godlike cheer so evident in all his writing, but also because of his rhetorical skill and the sheer brilliance of his craft.

Chesterton restrained himself from being Edgar Allan Poe or Franz Kafka, but something in the makeup of his personality leaned toward the nightmarish, something secret and blind, and central.

### Ray Bradbury (1920–2012)

'The RB, GKC and GBS Direct Orient Express' is not a story, per se, but more a story poem, and it is a perfect demonstration of my complete love for the library and its authors from the time I was eight years old. I didn't make it to college so the library became my meeting place with people like G.K. Chesterton and Shaw and the rest of that fabulous group who inhabited the stacks. My dream was to one day walk into the library and see one of my books leaning against one of theirs.

### Anthony Burgess (1917–1993)

Chesterton – his novels are excellent.

He wrote too well, too sincerely and vigorously, to earn a mere niche in a museum. His best novels – *The Napoleon of Notting Hill. The Man Who Was Thursday* and *The Flying Inn* – are as entertaining as when they were first written, and the substructure of the farce and fantasy – a concern with free will, Western civilization, and the ultimate mysteries of religion – is not less valid in an age of superstates and nuclear deterrents and brainwashing than it was in Chesterton's more innocent heyday. To teach and please at the same time is given to few. In the twentieth century, perhaps only Shaw, Wells, Aldous Huxley, and Chesterton have had the faculty.

### Agatha Christie (1890–1976)

Father Brown has always been one of my favourite sleuths . . . He is one of the few figures in detective fiction who can be enjoyed for his own sake, whether you are a detective fan or not.

### John Stewart Collis (1900–84)

I esteem Chesterton more than any 20th-Century writer, because almost everything you are told, almost everything which people take for granted, turns out to be the exact opposite of the truth. Chesterton was on to this.

### Jim Crace (1946–)

A favourite of mine is G. K. Chesterton's *The Man Who Was Thursday*. It has weathered well, and still seems as mischievous and clever as ever.

### Clarence Darrow (1857–1938)

I was favourably impressed, warmly attached to G.K. Chesterton. I enjoyed my debates with him, and found him a man of culture and fine sensibilities. If he and I had lived where we could have become better acquainted, eventually we would have ceased to debate, I firmly believe.

### Colin Dexter (1930–)

The unassuming, unpretentious, retiring (though never diffident) priest had one great thumping advantage over his fellow workers in the business of detection: he had the ear of the Almighty – or perhaps, more accurately, the Almighty had the ear of Father Brown. Certainly the pair of them shared a direct line; and this, it will be agreed, is ever likely to be a decided asset when the terrestrial subscriber is faced with some complex and seemingly impossible case – *The Insoluble Problem*, say – and puts him a few furlongs ahead of the rest of the field (including one of his co-investigators, the low-church atheist, Morse).

### Stephen Fry (1957–)

His profundity may have been disguised by his rotundity. That roast-beef complexion and par-adoxical style hid a great thinker, a great Englishman, a genuine theologian and a passionate lover of the human race.

### T.S. Eliot (1888–1965)

His disappearance, from a world such as we live in, is one of those which give even to us who did not know the man, a sense of personal loss and isolation . . . Behind the Johnsonian fancy-dress, so reassuring to the British public, he concealed the most serious and revolutionary designs – concealing them by exposure, as his anarchist conspirators chose to hold their meetings on a balcony in Leicester Square. (The real Johnson, indeed, with his theology, politics and morals, would be quite as alien to the modern world of public opinion as Chesterton himself.) Even if Chesterton's social and economic ideas appear to be totally without effect, even if they should be demonstrated to be wrong – which would perhaps only mean that men have not the goodwill to carry them out – they were the ideas for his time that were fundamentally Christian and Catholic. He did more, I think, than any man of his time – and was able to do more than anyone else, because of his particular background, development and abilities as a public performer – to maintain the existence of the important minority in the modern world. He leaves behind a permanent claim upon our loyalty, to see that the work he did in his time is continued in ours.

### Neil Gaiman (1960–)

It was in the school library that I discovered Chesterton . . . I was always aware, reading Chesterton, that there was someone writing this who rejoiced in words, who deployed them on the page as an artist deploys his paints upon his palette. Behind every Chesterton sentence there was someone painting with words, and it seemed to me that at the end of any particularly good sentence or any perfectly-put paradox, you could hear the author, somewhere behind the scenes, giggling with delight. Father Brown, that prince of humanity and empathy, was a gateway drug into the harder stuff, this being a one-volume collection of three novels: *The Napoleon of Notting Hill* (my favourite piece of predictive 1984 fiction, and one that hugely informed my own novel *Neverwhere*), *The Man Who was Thursday* (the prototype of all Twentieth Century spy stories, as well as being a Nightmare and a theological delight) and lastly *The Flying Inn* (which had some excellent poetry in it, but which struck me, as an eleven-year old, as being oddly small-minded. I suspected that Father Brown would have found it so as well.) Then there were the poems and the essays and the art.

Chesterton and Tolkien and Lewis were not the only writers I read between the ages of six and thirteen, but they were the authors I read over and over again; each of them played a part in building me. Without them, I cannot imagine that I would have become a writer, and certainly not a writer of fantastic fiction.

### Mahatma Mohandas Gandhi (1869–1948)
Mr G.K. Chesterton is one of the great writers here. He is an Englishman of a liberal temper. Such is the perfection of his style that his writings are read by millions with great avidity. To *The Illustrated London News* of September 18th, 1909 he has contributed an article on Indian awakening, which is worth studying. I believe that what he has said is reasonable. *Indian Opinion*, January 1910.

### André Gide (1868–1951)
J'ai pour les écrits critiques de Chesterton une admiration des plus vives. Je tiens son Dickens en particulier, et plus encore son *Browning* pour des chefs-d'oeuvre d'intelligence et de pénétration psychologiques, tout en souffrant parfois de son affectation de mépris pour ses lecteurs. Certains chapitres de son *Orthodoxy* m'ont profondément secoué. Je goute un peu moins ses oeuvres d'imagination (*Le Nommé Jeudi*, etc.) tout en les trouvant encore fort remarquables.

(I have the greatest admiration for Chesterton's critical writings. In particular I consider his *Dickens*, and more so his Browning to be masterpieces of comprehension and psychological insight, whilst occasionally exhibiting his pretence of contempt for his readers. Some chapters of his *Orthodoxy* startled me deeply. I appreciate his imaginative works (*The Man Who Was Thursday*, etc.) a little less, while still finding them astonishing.) Letter to Cyril Clemens, Mark Twain's nephew.

### Graham Greene (1904–1991)
*Orthodoxy, The Thing*, and *The Everlasting Man* are among the great books of the age. Much else, of course. It will be disappointing if time does not preserve out of that weight of work: *The Ballad of the White Horse*, the satirical poems, such prose fantasies as *The Man Who Was Thursday* and *The Napoleon of Notting Hill*, the early critical books on Browning and Dickens.

Put *The Ballad of the White Horse* against *The Waste Land*. If I had to lose one of them, I'm not sure that . . . well, anyhow, let's just say that I re-read The Ballad more often! *The Observer*, March 12th, 1978.

### John Gross (1935–2011)
His critical writings are still widely known, although they have long been excluded from the official canon of modern literary criticism. The reasons are plain enough. His methods are everything that our schoolmasters have brought us up to abjure. He wanders from the text and generalizes lavishly. He is too excited by large conceptions to pay very much attention to accuracy in small ones. He is often content to make his point through a mere phrase, or a joke or

an unexpected adjective. He would hardly have known how to begin 'erecting his impressions into laws'. He is extravagant, and he relished extravagance in others. Much of what he wrote was unashamed popularization. He is casual, unguarded, unsystematic. He plays with words, and he would rather parody an author than tabulate his faults. He contradicts himself. While he is working out his own ideas he is never afraid to get in the way of his author. In a word he is a stimulating and at times an inspired critic.

**Ernest Hemingway** (1899–1961)
Chesterton's a classic.

**Richard Ingrams** (1937–)
Chesterton was the natural champion of the patriotism of small groups. It is a curious fact that his best known book, *The Napoleon of Notting Hill*, a fantasy set in the future, begins in the year 1984. And it tells, among other things, how the citizens of Notting Hill go to war against the rest of London in order to save a small street of shops, which is being knocked down in order to build a motorway. The idea has often been dismissed as ridiculous but, as a prophecy, written in 1904, it stands up better than George Orwell's.

**P.D. James** (1920–2014)
Unlike most of the Golden Age heroes of detective fiction he [Father Brown] works alone. He has no professional supporter to do the routine legwork or provide additional support when required as has Lord Peter Wimsey in Inspector Parker. He is not bizarrely eccentric, as is Agatha Christie's Poirot. Unlike Sherlock Holmes, he has no Watson to ask questions which the more simple-minded readers might like to put and whose purpose is to demonstrate the great detective's brilliance and superior intellect. Naturally, given the decades in which he operates, he has no scientific advice available, indeed no official person whose help he can readily enlist in moments of crisis. He solves crime by a mixture of common sense, observation and deduction, and by his knowledge of the human heart. After years of hearing confessions, he knows the best and worst of which human beings are capable even though those secrets are locked in his heart. As he says to Flambeau, the master thief whom he outwits in 'The Blue Cross' and whom he restores to honesty, 'Has it never struck you that a man who does next to nothing but hear men's real sins is not likely to be wholly unaware of human evil?' We read the Father Brown stories for a variety of reasons including their ingenuity, their wit and intelligence, and for the brilliance of their writing. But they provide more. Chesterton was concerned with the greatest of all problems, the vagaries of the human heart . . . In one respect G.K. Chesterton was ahead of his times. He was one of the first writers of detective fiction to realize that this popular genre could be a vehicle for exploring and exposing the condition of society and of saying something true about human nature. Introduction to *Father Brown, The Essential Tales*, New York (Modern Library Classics) 2005, pp. xiii-xvi.

**C.S. Lewis** (1898–1963)
Read again *The Man Who Was Thursday*. Compare it with another good writer, Kafka. Is the difference simply that one is 'dated' and the other contemporary? Or is it rather that while

both give a powerful picture of the loneliness and bewilderment which each one of us encounters in his (apparently) single-handed struggle with the universe, Chesterton, attributing to the universe a more complicated disguise and admitting the exhilaration as well as the terror of the struggle, has got in rather more; is more balanced: in that sense, more classical, more permanent?

His humour was of the kind which I like best – not 'jokes' embedded in the page like currants in a cake, still less (what I cannot endure), a general tone of flippancy and jocularity, but the humour which is not in any way inseparable from the argument but is rather (as Aristotle would say) the 'bloom' on dialectic itself. The sword glitters not because the swordsman has set out to make it glitter but because he is fighting for his life and therefore moving it very quickly. For the critics who think Chesterton frivolous or 'paradoxical' I have to work hard to feel even pity; sympathy is out of the question.

### Herbert Marshall McLuhan (1911–1980)
*What's Wrong* changed my life in terms of ideas and religion.

### Vincent McNabb, OP (1868–1943)
I looked upon this child of London Town as one of the greatest sons born to England for four centuries. Londoners at their best like More and Chesterton do not look down on England; they look round on England and see its central place in Europe and the world. Their London River (as all seamen call it) after its long and quiet sauntering through England's smiling meadow-land welcomes with a smile all nations of the earth. Londoner of Londoners, English of the English, Gilbert Chesterton towered shoulder high above his contemporaries. His massive body, crowned with a massive head, struck me as being only the well-proportioned outward sign of the massive intellectual, spiritual reality within. And this inward reality was in the sphere of memory, mind and heart. His memory was not just beyond the average. Had it not been balanced by equal powers of mind it would have been, as in lesser minds, a danger or even a disease. But Gilbert Chesterton's memory was a storehouse of such ordered facts that from it, almost at will and always at need, he could bring forth things old and new. In control of this vast, densely filled memory was a mind of more than average power. It was not just a power of reason – though few could reason better – it was an unusual power of instant intuition; which, the philosophies say, is to be found only in a few men; and, as the theologians say, is found in all the angels.

### André Maurois (1885–1967)
Let us apply to Chesterton what he himself said about Dickens. There are critics who wish that Dickens had been different; and there are visitors to the Zoo who gaze at the hippopotamus or the elephant and think that these giant creatures would be more nearly perfect if they were different. But the hippopotamus and the elephant are facts. Dickens and Chesterton are facts. Without his paradoxes, without his jokes, without his rhetorical switchbacks, Chesterton might perhaps be a clearer philosopher. But he would not be Chesterton. It has often been supposed that he is not serious, because he is funny; actually he is funny because he is serious. Confident in his truth, he can afford to joke.

**George Orwell*** (1903–1950)

Chesterton's Introductions to Dickens are about the best thing he ever wrote.

Chesterton's vision of life was false in some ways, and he was hampered by enormous ignorance, but at least he had courage. He was ready to attack the rich and powerful, and he damaged his career by doing so.

[*Orwell's first work for the British press appeared in *G.K.'s Weekly* in 1928. His *Down and Out in Paris and London* (1933) took up the pioneering work of Ada Chesterton's *In Darkest London* (1926).]


**Terry Pratchett** (1948–)

It's worth pointing out that in *The Man Who Was Thursday* and *The Napoleon of Notting Hill* [Chesterton] gave us two of the most emotionally charged plots of the twentieth century: one being that both sides are actually the same side; it doesn't matter which sides we are talking about, both sides are actually the same side. This has been the motor of half the spy novels of this century. The other plot can't be summarized so succinctly, but the basic plot of *The Napoleon of Notting Hill* is that someone takes seriously an idea that wasn't intended to be taken seriously and gives it some kind of nobility by so doing. He was a good 'sunsets' man, G.K. Chesterton: when it came to sunsets no-one could describe one better than him – he just used to spill a paint box on the page and that was it. If you read lots and lots of Chesterton after a while it becomes extremely tedious, but in small doses taken regularly he's good for the soul.

My grandmother had a shelf of books that was all of two feet long, but which seemed in retrospect to contain some remarkably important volumes. That was where I first found GKC . . . She lived in Beaconsfield, just opposite Chesterton Green and a short walk from the Saracen's Head. I'm sure that made everything more immediate. He was real. I've read most of the better-known works, and I suspect now that he has been a major influence. I consider myself an atheist but, I think, a Chestertonian one.


**V.S. Pritchard** (1900–1997)

It is conventional to say that Chesterton's book on Dickens is the best thing he ever wrote. I read it again this week. It is not merely good; it is a masterpiece and contains, among other things, the most enlightening portrait of Dickens himself that I have ever read.


**Ellery Queen** (Frederic Dannay, 1905–1982, and Manfred Lee, 1905–1971)

The miracle book of 1911 introduced Father Brown to an eternally grateful public. You will find in *The Innocence of Father Brown* all the wondrous qualities of Chesterton's genius: his extraordinary cleverness of plot, his unique style, and his brilliant use of paradox both in language and in the counterplay of the supernatural and the natural. Father Brown is one of the few characters in all fiction who, through his humanity, sagacity, personal charm and credible genius, is likely to survive the fickle years.


**President Theodore 'Teddy' Roosevelt** (1858–1919)

What a supreme genius Chesterton is! I never met a man who could talk so brilliantly and interestingly.

**Barnaby Ross** (Fredric Dannay and Manfred Lee)
If there is one character in detective fiction who possesses the innocence and wisdom to sit beside the immortal Holmes, it is that apotheosis of incredulity, Father Brown.

**Dorothy L. Sayers** (1893–1967)
To the young people of my generation, GKC was a kind of Christian liberator. Like a beneficent bomb, he blew out of the Church a quantity of stained glass of a very poor period, and let in gusts of fresh air, in which the dead leaves of doctrine danced with all the energy of Our Lady's Tumbler.

**Will Self** (1961–)
Chesterton's *The Man Who Was Thursday* is a great book to give to a young person.

**George Bernard Shaw** (1856–1950)
He was a man of colossal genius. The sort of man England can produce when she is doing her best. The world is not thankful enough for Chesterton.

**Muriel Spark** (1918–2006)
How well he could tell a story and how deep was his Englishness.

**Julian Symons** (1912–1994)
[In] Chesterton's detective stories reality is made to seem like fantasy and Flambeau the great criminal soon becomes a detective, like Vidocq. The stories also embody a principle, that 'the only thrill, even of a common thriller, is concerned somehow with the conscience and the will'. This is true at least of his own very uncommon thrillers, which almost always exemplify a witty paradox about the condition of society or the nature of man. The effect of the Father Brown stories rests partly on the moral point that many of them bring home, yet this might appear anodyne but for the witty and subtle way in which Chesterton makes it. He fairly spilled over with good ideas, and they are as evident in his detective stories as in the novels that were the product of his verbal and mental dexterity, like *The Napoleon of Notting Hill* or his metaphysical thriller, *The Man Who Was Thursday* . . . A reading of Chesterton reinforces the truth that the best detective stories have been written by artists and not by artisans.

**John Wain** (1925–1994)
*Manalive* was the first 'novel of ideas' I had ever come across. I must have been aware that the characters were unconvincing and the action incredible; after all it is part of the charm of the book that Chesterton doesn't even try to make them anything else. And the story has vitality because, for all the artificiality of its people, it is about something real, the struggle between denial and affirmation in which Chesterton believed with all his might. I had already taken sides in the struggle, although I didn't even know it had been formally joined. When Innocent Smith declared 'I don't deny that there should be priests to remind men that they will one day die, I only say that at certain strange epochs it is necessary to have another kind of priests called poets, actually to remind men that they are not dead yet' – the effect on me was of a revelation. All at once I knew that my instinctive, unformulated feelings could be put into words, that

they had the dignity of a 'philosophy of life', that other people, too, wanted what I wanted: to push down the blank walls behind which we were hiding and step out boldly to larger feelings, broader perspectives, and life more abundant. *Punch*, April 4th, 1962

### Auberon Waugh (1939–2001)
The poems remain the best way to approach an understanding of Chesterton's prodigious vision and enormous generosity of spirit. In life, he was a semi-heroic, semi-preposterous figure with his enormous girth, his flapping, broad-brimmed hat, his cape and sword stick. The spirit that lives on is similarly heroic, only very occasionally preposterous. He is still remembered in Fleet Street.

### Orson Welles (1915–1985)
Gilbert Keith Chesterton, great, greatly articulate Roman convert and liberal, has been dead now for two years. For a unique brand of common sense enthusiasm, for a singular gift of paradox, for a deep reverence and a high wit, and most of all, for a free and shamelessly beautiful English prose, he will never be forgotten. September 5th, 1938.

### Katherine Whitehorn (1928–)
Chesterton wasn't the first person to suggest that there is order in the universe, or that the poor get pushed around by the rich, or that the more you look at things the less you see them, unless you continually jolt yourself into a new awareness – which he was singularly good at doing . . . I still occasionally find that the last word on something I'm writing about was said by this blasted man before the First World War.

# CHRONOLOGY

1874 (May 29th) G.K. Chesterton born at 14 (later renumbered 32) Sheffield Terrace, Campden Hill, London W8.

1877 (September 8th) Elder sister Beatrice dies from typhoid fever aged eight.

1879 (November 12th) Cecil Edward Chesterton born.

1880 The Chestertons move to 11 Warwick Gardens, London W14.

1883 Gilbert Chesterton begins to attend Colet Court (Bewsher's) School.

1887 Transfers to St. Paul's School.

1890 Foundation of the Junior Debating Club.

1892 'The Song of Labour' published in *The Speaker*. GKC leaves St. Paul's School for Calderon's Art School in St. John's Wood, and tours Europe.

1893 Completes his first novel [*Basil Howe*]. Follows English, French and Latin courses at University College London with one course in Fine Art at the Slade School of Art.

1894 Drops Latin and Fine Art in favour of History and Political Economy.

1895 Leaves UCL to take employment as a reader at the Spiritualist publishers Redway near the British Museum.

1896 In November moves to T. Fisher Unwin's in Paternoster Row as a reader.

1897 In January meets Frances Blogg in Bedford Park.

1898 Proposes and becomes engaged to Frances Blogg.

1899 Death of Gertrude Blogg, Frances' youngest sister, in a road accident.

1900 Regular work for *The Speaker*. First books, *Greybeards at Play* and *The Wild Knight*. Meets Hilaire Belloc. Member of the Pharos Club and the Christian Social Union.

1901  Begins his association with the *Daily News*. On June 28th marries Frances
      Blogg and after a few months in Edwardes Square moves to Overstrand
      Mansions, Battersea. Publishes *The Defendant*.

1903/4  *Robert Browning*. Meets Father O'Connor in Keighley. *The Club of Queer
      Trades, Dead Man's Drum, G.F. Watts* and *The Napoleon of Notting Hill*.

1905  *Heretics*. Begins to write 'Our Notebook' in *The Illustrated London News*.
      Serialisation of *The Ball and the Cross* in *Commonwealth* and much
      other work abandoned when Knollys Blogg is committed to Holloway
      Sanitorium.

1906  *Charles Dickens*. Begins to write prefaces to Dickens' novels.

1907  *The Man Who Was Thursday*.

1908  *All Things Considered. Orthodoxy. The People of England (The Secret
      People)*. Knollys Blogg dies in mysterious circumstances. Frances
      Chesterton has a nervous breakdown.

1909  The Chestertons leave London for 'Overroads', Station Road,
      Beaconsfield. *George Bernard Shaw* and *Tremendous Trifles*.

1910  *The Ball and the Cross* appears in book form in Britain. *What's Wrong
      with the World* and *William Blake*. First Father Brown story published
      in the USA.

1911  Begins to contribute to the *Eye-Witness* (later *New Witness*). *Appreciations
      and Criticisms of the Works of Charles Dickens* (collected prefaces), *The
      Innocence of Father Brown, The Ballad of the White Horse* and *Lepanto*.

1912  *Manalive* and *A Miscellany of Men*. Begins *The Return of Don Quixote*.

1913  *The Victorian Age in Literature* and *Magic*. GKC helps to reveal the
      Marconi scandal and is embittered by politics and politicians.

1914  *The Flying Inn, The Wisdom of Father Brown* and *The Barbarism of
      Berlin*. Undertakes propaganda for the government. In November taken
      seriously ill and is kept under sedation for three months.

1915  Recovers from his illness which was a heart problem induced by dropsy.

1916  In October takes over from his brother as editor of the *New Witness*
      when Cecil joins the army.

1917  *A Short History of England*.

1918  The Gray family, a widower and his daughters, moves into Bourne House
      in Grove Road. GKC visits Ireland. Cecil Chesterton dies.

1919  *Irish Impressions*. GKC and Frances visit Palestine.

1920  *The New Jerusalem*. GKC undertakes a lecture tour in the United States.
      Begins magazine publication of stories later collected in *The Poet and
      the Lunatics*.

1922 *What I Saw in America, Eugenics and Other Evils* and *The Man Who Knew Too Much*. Building of Top Meadow completed. GKC's father dies. GKC visits Holland. Received into the Roman Catholic Church.

1923 *St. Francis of Assisi*. The *New Witness* folds.

1924 Mr Gray dies. His daughters move from Beaconsfield.

1925 On March 21st GKC relaunches the *New Witness* as *G.K.'s Weekly*. *Tales of the Long Bow*, *The Everlasting Man* and *William Cobbett*. GKC meets the Nicholl family in Lyme Regis. Begins serialisation of *The Return of Don Quixote*.

1926 *The Incredulity of Father Brown*, *The Outline of Sanity* and *The Queen of Seven Swords*. Start of the Distributist League. Lecture tour to Spain.

1927 Invited to visit Poland. *The Catholic Church and Conversion*, *The Return of Don Quixote* (in an abridged version), *Collected Poems*, *The Secret of Father Brown*, *The Judgement of Dr Johnson*, *Robert Louis Stevenson*.

1928 *Generally Speaking. Do We Agree?* (a debate with Bernard Shaw).

1929 Visits Rome. *The Poet and the Lunatics* and *The Thing*.

1930–1 *The Resurrection of Rome, Four Faultless Felons* and *Come to Think of it*. Visiting lecturer at University of Notre Dame, South Bend, Illinois, then undertakes a second lecture tour of North America.

1932 *Sidelights of New London* and *Newer York* and *Chaucer*. Visits Dublin for the Eucharistic Conference (*Christendom in Dublin*). Death of Marie Louise Chesterton, GKC's mother. Begins to broadcast regularly on the BBC. Blanche Blogg, Frances' mother, dies.

1933 *St Thomas Aquinas*.

1934 Appointed Knight Commander with Star of the Papal Order of St. Gregory the Great. Sets out on a second trip to Jerusalem but after Rome falls ill in Sicily and returns home from Malta by sea. Meets André Maurois on the voyage to Marseille. Nominated for the Nobel Prize for Literature, but no prize is awarded for 1934.

1935 *The Scandal of Father Brown* and *The Well and the Shallows*. Revisits Catalonia, returning via France, Italy and Switzerland

1936 Not Well. Visits Lisieux, Lourdes and Menton in May. Returns but falls ill and dies at home on June 14th to be buried three days later. Memorial Service at Westminster Cathedral on June 27th. *Autobiography*.

1938 Death of Frances Chesterton on December 12th.

1962 Death of Mrs Cecil Chesterton (Ada Jones) also known as John Keith Prothero and by other pseudonyms.

# BIBLIOGRAPHY

## A: Works by G. K. Chesterton

### Chesterton's History and Philosophy
*Heretics,* London (Bodley Head) 1905
*Orthodoxy,* London (Bodley Head) 1908
*A Short History of England,* London (Chatto & Windus) 1917
*The Everlasting Man,* London (Hodder) 1925
*St. Thomas Aquinas – The Dumb Ox,* London (Hodder) 1933

### Chesterton's Novels
*Basil Howe* (1894), London (New City) 2001
*The Man With Two Legs* (1896–98), Collected Works XIV, San Francisco (Ignatius) 1993
*The Adventurous Abbot Stephen* (Face of Brass) (1896–98), Collected Works XIV, 1993
*The Napoleon of Notting Hill,* London (Bodley Head) 1904
*The Ball and the Cross* (1905–09), 'Commonwealth' 1905; New York 1909 and London (Wells Gardner Darton) 1910
*The Man Who Was Thursday,* London (Simpkin Marshall) & Bristol (Arrowsmith) 1907
*Manalive,* London (Nelson) 1912
*The Flying Inn,* London (Methuen) 1914
*The Return of Don Quixote* (1912), 'G.K.'s Weekly' December 5th, (1925–November 13th, 1926; New York (Dodd Mead) 1926; London (Chatto & Windus) 1927
*Collected Works,* Volumes VI, VII, and VIII, San Fancisco (Ignatius) 1991, 2004, 1999

## Chesterton's Plays

Three Priests, a scene, c1889

Dialogue between Our Lord and St. Joseph (The Carpenter's Son, a miracle play, c1890?)

JDC Play, 1892

Consistency, 1893

Recognition, 1893

A Shipwreck off Fairyland, 1895

The Wild Knight, 1896

PNEU, 1897

The Devil amongst the Cattle, c1903. Scenario.

The End of Fleur-de-Lys, c1903. A romantic play in rhyme about St. Francis and the Troubadours.

The Mad Innkeepers, c1903. Scenario.

The Soul of Polyphemus, c1903. Scenario.

Queen of the Green Elves, 1904

The Almighty Man, 1904. Frances Chesterton's Diary, December 8th, 1904 (Chesterton Review): George Alexander has an idea that he wants Gilbert to write a play for him, and sent for him to come and see him. He was apparently taken with the notion of a play on the Crusades.

Time's Abstract and Brief Chronicle, I–V, 'The Fortnightly Review', October 1904–May 1905

The Flying Inn, 1912 and 1929

Magic, London (Martin Secker) 1913

Christian Science Comic Opera, c1914

The Tragic Women (1925)

At The Back of Methuselah. No.1. – From our series of Modified Modern Dramas, G.K.'s Weekly, March 28th, 1925, pp. 12–14

The Disconnected Drama for the Bottomless Pittite, GK's Weekly, August 29th, 1925

The Temptation of St. Anthony, G.K.'s Weekly, September 19th, 1925

The Turkey and the Turk, G.K.'s Weekly, December 5th, 1925

What You Won't, G.K.'s Weekly, January 9th, 1926

The Judgement of Dr Johnson, London (Sheed & Ward) 1927

The Flying Inn Libretto (1929)

The Surprise (1929*–1932), London (Sheed & Ward) 1953 (*Fr. Kevin Scannell (Fr. O'Connor's friend) claimed to have a manuscript written in Rome in 1929)

The Cottage (early 1930s)

The Centuries (Ages) are Passing (1930s)

Collected Works, Volume XI, San Francisco (Ignatius)1989; Volume X part 2 (2008);
    Volume X part 3 (2010)

**Chesterton's Short Stories and Novellas**
Queen of the Evening Star
The Wild Roses
The Black Friar
The Bells of St. Cuthbert
Half Hours in Hades
The Wild Goose Chase
The Taming of the Nightmare
Twilight
A Fragment
The White Cockade
Prince Wildfire
Man and His Image
The Wages of Sin
Dick Featherhead
The Ghost
The Black Crow
Princess Esmeralda
The Maiden of Windsor
Dumb Show
Wreckage
In 1661
A Traveller's Tale
Why the Moon Was Made
My Uncle the Professor
The Moderate Country
Child Street
The Picture of Tuesday
Consistency
Gods, 'The Speaker' 1897
Homesick at Home
A Fable in Bricks and Mortar, *Parents' Review*, March 1904
Elf of Brixton
Apotheosis or The House of Stars
Le Jongleur de Dieu

Earthquake Esquire

A Crazy Tale

The Snail Boy

The Headsman's Heads

The Human Club

Quoodle (Lost)

The Appalling Five

The Mystery of Three

*The Club of Queer Trades,* 'Harper's Weekly' 1903–04; 'The Idler' June/December, 1904; New York and London (Harper Bros.) 1905

Dead Man's Drum (*c*1904)

Crimes of a Philanthropist

Magic (Lost)

*The Innocence of Father Brown,* London (Cassell) 1911

*The Wisdom of Father Brown,* London (Cassell) 1914

A Free Man 1914

The Shop of Ghosts

A Nightmare

A Somewhat Improbable Story

The Long Bow

How I found the Superman

The Modern Scrooge

The Coloured Lands

Conversion of an Anarchist, New York (Paget) 1912

Liberty Hall (Conversion of an Anarchist), 'London Opinion', Summer issue 1912

Father Brown and the Donnington Mystery 1914

The Sword of Wood 1917

The Trees of Pride *c*1917

The Garden of Smoke

The Five of Swords

The Tower of Treason

The Man Who Shot The Fox 1919

Gabriel Gale stories, 'Harper's Bazaar' and 'Nash's' 1920–1922 (Collected in *The Poet and the Lunatics* 1929)

England in 1919

The End of the Roman Road 1919

*The Man Who Knew Too Much,* 'Harper's' 1920–1922; London (Cassell) 1922

The Dragon at Hide and Seek

Concerning Grocers as Gods
A Real Discovery
The Paradise of Human Fishes
The Fish
*Tales of the Long Bow,* London (Cassell) 1925
*The Incredulity of Father Brown,* London (Cassell) 1926
Dr Hyde, Detective, and The White Pillars Murder
The New Christmas
The Professor and the Cook, I, II and III
*The Secret of Father Brown,* London (Cassell) 1927
The End of Wisdom 1927
*The Poet and the Lunatics,* London (Cassell) 1929
*Four Faultless Felons,* London (Cassell) 1930
*The Scandal of Father Brown,* London (Cassell) 1935
*The Paradoxes of Mr Pond,* London (Cassell) 1937
The Vampire of the Village 1936
The Mask of Midas 1936
Incomplete Mr Pond story 1936
*Chesterton Collected Works,* XIV, San Francisco (Ignatius) 1993

**Chesterton's Poetry**
*Greybeards at Play,* London (Brimley Johnson) 1901
*The Wild Knight and Other Poems,* London (Grant Richards) 1901
*The Ballad of the White Horse,* London (Methuen) 1911
*Wine, Water and Song,* London (Methuen) 1915
*Poems,* London (Burns & Oates) 1915
*The Ballad of St. Barbara and Other Poems,* London (Cecil Palmer) 1922
*The Queen of the Seven Swords,* London (Sheed & Ward) 1927
*Collected Poems,* London (Cecil Palmer) 1927, 3rd Edition (Methuen) 1933
*Collected Works: Poetry Part 1, Edited by Aidan Mackey,* San Francisco (Ignatius) 1994
*Collected Works: Poetry Part 2, Edited by Denis Conlon,* San Francisco (Ignatius) 2008
*Collected Works: Poetry Part 3, Edited by Denis Conlon,* San Francisco (Ignatius) 2010

**Chesterton's Biography and Criticism**
*Robert Browning,* London (Macmillan) 1903
*G.F. Watts,* London (Duckworth) 1904
*Charles Dickens,* London (Methuen) 1906
*George Bernard Shaw,* London (Bodley Head) 1909

*William Blake*, London (Duckworth) 1910

*Appreciations and Criticisms of Charles Dickens*, London (Dent) 1911

*The Victorian Age in Literature*, London (Williams & Norgate) 1913

*St. Francis of Assisi*, London (Hodder & Stoughton) 1923

*William Cobbett*, London (Hodder & Stoughton) 1925

*Robert Louis Stevenson*, London (Hodder & Stoughton) 1927

*Chaucer*, London (Faber & Faber) 1932

*St. Thomas Aquinas*, London (Hodder & Stoughton) 1933

**Collected Works**

Ignatius Press, San Francisco, USA. Volumes 1–8, 10A, 10B, 10C, 11–16, 18–21, 27–39.

## B: Works about G. K. Chesterton

**Bibliography**

Sullivan, John J.: *Chesterton, a Bibliography*, London (ULP) 1958

Sullivan, John J.: *Chesterton Continued*, London (ULP) 1968

Sullivan, John J.: *Chesterton Bibliography Continued*, 'Chesterton Review', Vol.2, No 2, 1976; Vol IV, No 2, 1978, collected as *Chesterton 3*, Bedford (Vintage Publications) 1980

Sprugg, Joseph W.: *Index to Chesterton*, Washington (CUA Press) 1968

Christophers, Richard: *British Library Catalogue of Additions to the Manuscripts: The G.K. Chesterton Papers*, London (British Library) 2001

Geir Hasnes: *G.K. Chesterton – A Bibliography*, Kongsberg, Norway (Classica Forlag AS) 2014.

**Biography**

Chesterton, Mrs Cecil (née Ada Jones): *The Chestertons*, London (Chapman & Hall) 1941

Ward, Maisie: *G.K. Chesterton*, London (Sheed & Ward) 1944, New York (Sheed & Ward) 1943

Robbins Harold: *G.K. Chesterton: Last of the Realists*, 'The Sword and the Plough' 1948; Reprint long announced by IHS Press but not published by end 2014

Ward, Maisie: *Return to Chesterton*, London (Sheed & Ward) 1954, New York (Sheed & Ward) 1953

Barker, Dudley: *G.K. Chesterton*, London (Constable) 1973

Canovan, Margaret: *G.K.Chesterton, Radical Popularist*, New York (Harcourt Brace) 1977

Dale, Alzina Stone: *The Outline of Sanity*, Grand Rapids, Mich. (Eerdmans) 1982

Dale, Alzina Stone: *The Art of G.K. Chesterton*, Chicago (Loyola U.P.) 1985

Ffinch, Michael: *G.K. Chesterton*, London (Weidenfeld and Nicolson) 1986

Coren, Michael: *Gilbert, The Man who was G.K. Chesterton*, London (Jonathan Cape) 1989

Pearce, Joseph: *Wisdom and Innocence*, London (Hodder & Stoughton) 1995

Oddie, William: *The Romance of Orthodoxy – The Making of G.K. Chesterton*, Oxford (OUP) 2008

Ker, Ian: *G.K. Chesterton*, Oxford (OUP) 2011


**Secondary Literature**

[Blogg] George Knollys: *Ledgers and Literature*, London (Bodley Head) 1907

[Chesterton, Cecil]: *G.K. Chesterton – A Criticism*, London (Alston Rivers) 1908

Chesterton, Frances: *Poems*, Beaconsfield (Sheed & Ward), Christmas 1915

West, Julius: *G.K. Chesterton: A Critical Study*, London (Martin Secker) 1915

Braybrooke, Patrick: *G.K. Chesterton*, Philadelphia (Lippincott) 1922 and London (C.W. Daniel) 1926

Titterton, W.R.: *Chesterton, a Portrait*, London (Ousley) 1936

O'Connor, Fr. John: *Father Brown on Chesterton*, London (Martin Secker) 1938

Belloc, Hilaire: *On the Place of Gilbert Chesterton in English Letters*, London (Sheed & Ward) 1940

Bentley, E.C.: *Those Days*, London (Constable) 1940

Kenner, Hugh: *Paradox in Chesterton*, New York (Sheed & Ward) 1948

McLuhan, Marshall: Introduction to Hugh Kenner's *Paradox in Chesterton*, 1948

Wills, Gary: *Chesterton: Man and Mask*, New York (Sheed & Ward) 1961; Revised edition, New York (Doubleday) 2001

Pieper, Josef: *Guide to Thomas Aquinas*, Chapter 1, pp. 6-7, London (Faber & Faber) 1962, reissued San Francisco (Ignatius Insight) 1991.

Maycock, A.L.: *The Man Who Was Orthodox*, London (Dobson) 1963

Hollis, Christopher: *The Mind of Chesterton*, London (Hollis & Carter) 1970

Clipper, Lawrence J.: *G.K. Chesterton*, New York (Twayne) 1974

Boyd, Ian: *The Novels of G.K. Chesterton*, London (Elek) 1975

Sewell, Brocard: *Cecil Chesterton*, Faversham (Saint Albert's Press) 1975

Conlon, D.J.: *Chesterton: The Critical Judgements 1900–1937*, Antwerp (Antwerp Studies in English Literature) 1975

Hunter, Lynette: *Chesterton, Explorations in Allegory*, London (Macmillan Press) 1976

Ribstein, Max: *G.K. Chesterton (1874–1936) Création romanesque et imagination*, Paris (Klincksieck) 1981

Coates, John D.: *Chesterton and the Edwardian Cultural Crisis*, Hull (HUP) 1984

Conlon, D.J.: *G.K. Chesterton: A Half Century of Views*, Oxford (OUP) 1987

Lauer, Quentin: G.K. Chesterton, *Philosopher without Portfolio*, Bronx, NY (Fordham UP) 1988

Ahlquist, Dale: *Chesterton: Apostle of Common Sense*, San Francisco (Ignatius) 2003

Armitage, Mark: 'Chesterton on St. Thomas Aquinas. Some newly Discovered Pages'. *Chesterton Review*, Vol. 30, 1/2, Spring/Summer 2004, pp. 27-49

Knight, Mark: *Chesterton and Evil*, New York (Fordham U.P.) 2004

Maxence, Philippe: *Pour le réenchantement du monde, une introduction à Chesterton*, Paris (Editions Ad Solem) 2004

Morris, Kevin L: *The Truest Fairy Tale, A Religious Anthology of G.K. Chesterton*, with foreword by Eamon Duffy, Cambridge (Lutterworth Press) 2007

Maxence, Philippe: *L'Univers de G.K. Chesterton, petit dictionnaire raisonné*, Paris (Via Romana) 2008

Nichols O.P., Aidan: *Chesterton Theologian*, London (Darton, Longman & Todd) 2009

Hillier, Bevis:*The Wit and Wisdom of G.K. Chesterton*, London (Continuum) 2010

Julius, Anthony: *Trials of the Diaspora: A History of Anti-Semitism in England*, Oxford (OUP) 2010

Belamonte, Kevin: *Defiant Joy*, Nashville (Thos. Nelson) 2011

Wood, Ralph C.: *Chesterton: The Nightmare Goodness of God*, Waco Texas (Baylor U.P.) 2011

Brown, Nancy: *How Far is it to Bethlehem? The poems and plays of Frances Chesterton*, Charleston S.C. (Chesterton & Brown) 2012

Mayers, Simon: *Chesterton's Jews*, London (Create Space) 2013

Beaumont & Ingleby, Matthew (Eds.): *G.K. Chesterton, London and Modernity*, London (Bloomsbury), 2013

Farmer, Ann: *Chesterton and the Jews: A Fully-rounded Portrait*, Tacoma WA (Angelico) 2014

Brown, Nancy: *Frances, The Woman Who Was Chesterton*, (ACS) forthcoming 2015

## Magazines devoted to G.K. Chesterton

*The Defendant* (1952–1954), Great Britain

*The Chesterton Review* (1974–), Canada and USA

*The Chesterton Quarterly* (1992–2006), Great Britain

*The Defendant*, Australia

*All Things Considered*, Ontario, Canada

*Mid-West Chesterton News*, USA

*The Flying Inn*, British Columbia, Canada

*Gilbert* (which has absorbed the latter three titles above), USA

**Magazines partially devoted to G.K. Chesterton**
*SEVEN*
*Second Spring*

**Societies devoted to G.K. Chesterton**
The Chesterton Society
The American Chesterton Society
The Australian Chesterton Society
The Chesterton Institute for Faith and Culture
Chesterton in the Chilterns

# NOTES

**Chapter 1 (Under the Great Grey Water-Tower)**

1. *Chesterton Quarterly*, No. 1, October 1996.
2. *Chesterton: Collected Works* [hereafter *CW*] Vol. 10, parts A, B and C, San Francisco (Ignatius) 1994, 2008 and 2010. All poems quoted throughout this volume can be found therein.
3. *Daily News*, December 19th, 1908 reprised in *Autobiography*, London (Hutchinson) 1936, Chapter I, p. 15: 'And it is also recorded of me that, at the age of six or seven, I tumbled down in the street in the act of excitedly reciting the words:

> Good Hamlet, cast thy nightly colour off,
> And let thine eye look like a friend on Denmark,
> Do not for ever with thy vailed lids
> Seek for thy noble father in the dust.'

4. Stolen from Top Meadow in the 1930s.
5. The late Mrs Margaret Smith recalled being taught as a girl by GKC to skate a figure of eight on the frozen dykes at Tewkesbury prior to the First World War.
6. *Daily News*, October 18th, 1901 and *What's Wrong With the World*, London, New York (Cassell) 1910.
7. Marie-Louise has been alleged to be one of 21 siblings of a family of Swiss origin on her father's side and Scottish (Keith) on her mother's. It seems more likely that she was one of seven surviving children of which she was the fifth. Her father, Pierre Frederic J. Grosjean (1806–77), was a merchant tailor well known in Regent Street for 'Grosjean's Celebrated Trowsers' at sixteen shillings (80p) a pair.

8. *T.P.'s and Cassell's Weekly*, January 23rd, 1926.

9. Besides being an artist manqué, Edward Chesterton was a regular contributor to *Academy* and other magazines as well as the author of *The Wonderful Story of Dunder Van Haeden*, London (R. Brimley Johnson) 1902.

10. Maisie Ward, *Gilbert Keith Chesterton*, London (Sheed & Ward) 1944 [hereafter: Ward, *GKC*], p. 16.

11. *Autobiography*, Chapter 2, p. 35.

12. Mrs Cecil Chesterton, *The Chestertons*, London (Chapman & Hall) 1941, [hereafter: *The Chestertons*], pp. 19–21

13. 'In the Days of my Youth', *T.P.'s and Cassell's Weekly*, January 23rd 1926.

14. BL, Add. MS 73316C, ff. 62v–52 volume reversed; *Chesterton Quarterly*, No. 23, Summer 2002, pp. 3–5.

### Chapter 2 (A Lump of White Fat)

1. Ward, *GKC*, pp. 19–20.

2. Ibid., pp. 36–7.

3. *Autobiography*, Chapter 3, p. 58; Ward, *GKC*, p. 25.

4. Maisie Ward, *Return to Chesterton*, London and New York (Sheed & Ward) 1952 [hereafter: Ward, *RTC*], p.12.

5. Ward, *GKC*, p. 91.

6. Ward, *RTC*, p. 16.

7. Ward, *GKC*, pp. 91–2.

8. *CW*, Vol. 14, 1993.

9. Ward, *GKC*, p. 28.

10. 'When I Was Young', *Strand Magazine*, Vol. 69, April 1925, pp. 347–51.

11. Milton was St. Paul's most famous alumnus. GKC's view of his own achievement is interesting: 'I went to St. Paul's School where I did no work but wrote a lot of bad poetry, which has, fortunately, perished with the almost equally bad exercises. I got a prize for one of those prize-poems which stand as the salutary humiliations at the head of so many paths of journalism and literature. Golly! What a poem! It had a sturdy Protestant tone. It was about St. Francis Xavier, of whom I had never heard.' 'How I Began', *T.P.'s Weekly*, March 21st, 1913, p. 355.

12. This promotion was short lived as Chesterton left St. Paul's at the end of term after receiving his Milton prize on Apposition Day when he recited his poem.

### Chapter 3 (The Wheel of Stars)

1. *The Debater*, June 1893.

2. *Autobiography*, London (Hutchinson) 1936, p. 59.

3. Ibid., p. 63–4.

4. Some thirty poems and songs devoted to the JDC can be found in *CW*, Volumes 10A, 10B and 10C.

5. E.C. Bentley, having failed to continue the narrative, returned it with the following rather fanciful note: 'The gentleman introduced above as Mr Chesterton is one of those people who have a habit of being clever, and was by way of being a genius. From his earliest years he had talents for drawing and writing poetry, which manifested themselves at the opening stages of his career at St. Paul's School on his lesson book and writing-paper. He had then become chairman of the Junior Debating Club. It was at this point that his literary work came to be regarded as promising, a series of his contributions to a small private magazine, the 'Debater', attracted the notice of several persons, who strongly advised him to send his poetry to magazines which would make it public. He had then left St. Paul's School and gone to various art-schools, and at the time of writing this story he was regarded as an artist of exceptionally brilliant prospects, and his papers upon various subjects in magazines, as well as two small volumes of poetry, had awakened enthusiastic feelings in the bosoms of many reviewers. In fact, Mr Chesterton came dangerously near to being a "coming man", and only escaped that stigma by his offensive and overweening modesty, which forbade him to publish more than one-tenth part of what he wrote, while it caused him to be affected in the most painful manner when anybody ventured to speak of his work. His praises, at the outset, had been mainly chanted by two of his friends, one of whom we already know as Mr Bentley, who was a Barrister, and who occasionally disgraced his nature and his name by writing articles in papers and reviewing books. The other was a Mr Oldershaw, who had begun a journalistic career of great promise, and, who, together with Mr Bentley, started what the latter called "the G.K.C. Riots"; in other words, they succeeded in producing an immense enthusiasm about the aforesaid volumes of poems, which had left Mr Chesterton with a reputation; this Mr Bentley occasionally stimulated by inserting in the reviews, such as, "We hear on good authority that Mr Chesterton, the New Poet, has in preparation an important work, which is to deal with", etc., etc. The "New Poet's" poems were eagerly sought after, and Mr Oldershaw published long critical articles entitled "Gilbert Chesterton, Poet and Artist", "Gilbert Chesterton and his Work", and similar headings.'

6. British Library, Additional MS [hereafter: BL, Add. MS] 73325A, f. 35v.

7. Now BL Add. MS 73324A.

8. Richard A. Christophers: *The British Library Catalogue of Additions to the Manuscripts: The G.K. Chesterton Papers*, London (British Library) 2001, p. 110 (BL, Add. MS 73334, f. 70).

9. Ffinch, *G.K. Chesterton*, London (Weidenfeld & Nicolson) 1986, p. 33.

10. Ward, *GKC*, p. 51.

11. Ibid., p. 52.

12. Archives of Chesterton Humbert quoted in Oliver Chesterton's obituary, *Daily Telegraph*, November 6th, 2007.

13. Republished in *The First Clerihews*, Oxford (OUP) 1982.

14. The identifying symbols were Bentley (a Dodo), GKC (a Gavel), Oldershaw (a Stag's Head), Edward Chesterton (a Pipe), Waldo d'Avigdor (double Pi) and Maurice Solomon (666).

15. Michael Coren: *Gilbert: The Man Who Was Chesterton*, London (Jonathan Cape) 1989 [hereafter: Coren, *Gilbert*], p. 39.

16. *CW*, Vol. 10B, pp. 200–18.

17. Calderon's, founded in 1880 as the St. John's Wood Art School by the Peruvian artist (Eliseo) Abelardo Alvarez-Calderon.

### Chapter 4 (The Devil and the GKC)

1. 'The Song Against Songs', 1911.

2. BL, Add. MS 73197, ff. 14–15.

3. *Autobiography*, Chapter 4, pp. 99–100.

4. 'When I Was Young', *T.P.' s Weekly*, January 23rd, 1926, p. 350.

5. Ward, *GKC*, p. 48.

6. *Autobiography*, Chapter 4, pp. 81–93 *passim*.

7. 'Apotheosis', *CW*, Vol. 14, p. 624.

8. *The Poet and the Lunatics*, London (Cassell) 1929.

9. Slade's steps are steeper but not higher than those of St. Paul's Cathedral.

10. *Daily News*, November 9th, 1907.

11. *T.P.' s Weekly* op. cit., 1926, pp. 347–51.

12. *Autobiography*, Chapter 4, pp. 82–5 *passim*.

13. Ward, *GKC*, p. 66–7.

14. *The Quarto*, 1896, reprinted in *CW*, Vol. 14, p. 60.

15. Ibid., p. 769.

16. Ibid., pp. 769–803.

17. Ibid., p. 779.

18. *Autobiography*, Chapter 15.

19. *Parent's Review*, 1904, reprinted in *Chesterton Society Newsletter*, No. 45, March 1996.

20. *Autobiography*, Chapter 6, p. 139.

21. *CW*, Vol. 14, p. 665.

22. *The Man Who Was Thursday*, London (Simpkin Marshall) & Bristol (Arrowsmith) 1907, Chapter 1.
23. *Autobiography*, Chapter 6, pp. 153–4.

**Chapter 5 (The Satisfaction of Satan)**
 1. After the separation George Blogg resided at various London clubs. His correspondence with his daughter Frances (BL, Add. MS 73454, ff. 1–6v, 9–13v.) relating to his military adventures guarding Queen Victoria would appear to be a pleasant fiction designed to help explain an awkward situation.
 2. *The Chestertons*, pp. 9–10.
 3. *Autobiography*, Chapter 6, p. 151.
 4. Ward, *GKC*, p. 80.
 5. Ibid., pp. 93–4.
 6. *Chesterton Quarterly*, No. 20, Autumn 2001, pp. 4–5.
 7. *CW*, Vol. 10B, pp. xxi–xxiv.
 8. Ibid., p. 157.
 9. Frances' colleagues at the PNEU are featured.
10. *Autobiography*, Chapter 6, p. 155.
11. Ward: *RTC*, p. 36.
12. Ward, *GKC*, p. 98; see also BL, Add. MS 73193, ff. 9 seq.: 'All other letters not quoted [in Maisie Ward's biography] have been destroyed according to a promise made to Frances. D.E. Collins.' 'Cut according to a promise made to Frances. DEC.' 'Beautiful love paragraphs. Cut according to a promise made to Frances. D.E. Collins.'
13. Ward, *GKC*, pp. 81–3.
14. Ibid., p. 97.
15. Ibid., pp. 98–9.
16. Ibid., p. 99.
17. Ibid., p. 100.
18. *CW*, Vol. 10B, pp. 297–303.
19. Ward, *GKC*, pp. 100–1.
20. Ibid., p. 101.
21. Ibid., p. 104.
22. Ibid., pp. 105–6.
23. Ibid., pp. 122–3.
24. Ibid., p. 70.
25. Ward, *RTC*, pp. 44–5.
26. *The Speaker*, September 29th, 1900.

27. D. J. Conlon, *G.K. Chesterton, The Critical Judgments* 1900–1937 Antwerp (Antwerp Studies in English Literature) 1975, p. 30.

28. Ward, *GKC*, p. 124.

29. Ibid., p. 128.

30. Ibid., p. 129.

31. Ibid., pp. 130–2

32. *The Chestertons*, p. 27.

### Chapter 6 (Lucifer Meets His Match)

1. With the loss of Frances' and imminently Ethel's income, the Bloggs had down-sized and moved to 38 Chepstow Place, Kensington where Blanche Blogg was advertising her services as a dressmaker.

2. Conrad Noel (1869–1942) was from 1910 Vicar of Thaxted where he flew both the red flag and the flag of Sinn Fein, leading to clashes with groups of students from Cambridge. He was known as the 'Red Vicar'.

3. Belloc kept a boat on the Broads and was known to make it available. A letter dated August 31, 1899 from GKC to Frances' sister Ethel records that 'Jack is away with Oldershaw at the time I write, sailing on the Norfolk Broads in Belloc's boat. You probably know more than I do about all that, but he is, I fancy, coming back about Monday, when I hope to see a good deal of him and console him as far as possible for your absence.' BL, Add. MS 73193, f.4.

4. *Autobiography*, Chapter 2, p. 37; Ward, *GKC*, p. 133.

5. *The Chestertons*, pp. 170–1.

6. In *What's Wrong With the World*, Part 1, Chapter 7 'The Free Family', GKC insists 'that in everything worth having, even in every pleasure, there is a point of pain or tedium that must be survived, so that the pleasure may revive and endure . . . and the success of the marriage comes after the failure of the honeymoon.'

   Sometime in 1904 or 1905 Frances went into a nursing-home at Battersea Bridge connected with the Clapham Maternity Hospital where a procedure was performed by the surgeon Frances Ivens Knowles, to try to cure Frances' sterility. Clapham was the first hospital to offer guaranteed treatment by women doctors and surgeons, but it is not clear what sort of operations were then available, other than treatment for an unperforated hymen or realignment of the uterus. In the event the operation was not a success.

7. *The Man Who Was Thursday*, Chapter I. GKC is playing with the words 'We are all Socialists now' attributed to Sir William Vernon Harcourt (1827–1904), Liberal statesman, sometime Home Secretary and Chancellor of the Exchequer.

8. I am indebted to Dr Richard A. Christophers and to his article 'The Death of

Knollys Blogg' in the *Chesterton Quarterly*, No. 9, Winter 1998, p. 10.

9. Dudley Barker, *G.K. Chesterton*, London (Constable) 1973, Chapter 15, p. 155.
10. There is no evidence that Frances ever left Lowestoft. Ian Ker seems to presume that the Chestertons' stay in Rye in 1905 took place in 1908.
11. Ward, *GKC*, p. 220–1.
12. *The Chestertons*, p. 69.
13. 'Diary of Frances Chesterton, 1904–1905', *Chesterton Review, XXV*, No.3, August 1999.

## Chapter 7 (Towards a Slovenly Biography)

1. 'When the midnight of Jingoism had passed, and the *Daily News* had been recovered for the older liberal tradition, the new editor, Mr R.C. Lehmann, gave me a place upon that paper. In that paper I have written a vast amount of nonsense and also, I happen to think, a great deal of sense. As the more fanciful parts of the work, the tales and the parables, do not easily lend themselves to any logical exposition, I will confine myself to stating one principle upon which I went in the abstract or controversial passages – a principle, I think, of some genuine value. I was and am a Liberal; though the Liberal Party has seceded from Liberalism. But while that danger was only threatening I took a certain view of the nature of that danger, which led me into a large number of extremely agreeable rows. I found that in official and editorial circles there was a strong notion that we must prevent the Liberal Party being split by a controversy. I was quite convinced that it was, in sober truth, being split by the absence of a controversy. I do not mind you calling this phrase paradoxical: the Party was really being split by silence and unanimity. It is really a very simple truth, and it is related to the admitted truth about the danger of allowing uncontradicted rumours or unpurged slanders to proceed. The two sections of our party would not have minded their leaders differing in public. What they minded was the leader they disagreed with making a speech, and the leader they agreed with not being allowed to answer him. A reasonable Imperialist speech from Sir Edward Grey, directly answered by a reasonable pro-Boer speech from Sir Henry Campbell-Bannerman, would have united the Liberal Party. It was on this principle that I proceeded in all my own controversies: that nothing could pull us together except public division and debate . . . It did no harm to socialism or revolution that Blatchford, a secularist, should wrangle with Chesterton, an orthodox person. It did great harm that Blatchford should wrangle all by himself: it simply meant the secession of all Socialists who were not secularists. This absolute conviction that a controversy not only clears the air, but solidifies the real sympathies I have followed persistently on the 'Daily News,'

until I left it a week ago.' 'How I Began', *T.P.'s Weekly*, March 21st, 1913, p. 355.

2. Coren, *Gilbert*, p. 138.

3. Various illustrations can be found among the Chesterton papers in the British Library.

4. It was, of course, GKC's first novel to be published, although not the first written.

5. Robert Barr (1849–1912), editor of *The Idler*, welcomed the stories very warmly: 'Just a year ago I read in manuscript "The Tremendous Adventures of Major Brown," by Mr Chesterton, and I knew that if the author could write a series of tales even fifty per cent as good, and let me have them, I should be possessed of a literary gold mine . . . I now have five of the stories in hand. Incredible as it may seem, each appears more striking than the one that preceded it. They form the most remarkable set of stories that any magazine has ever been privileged to print since magazines were first published.'

6. A term used to describe the three Persons of the Trinity. In the Nicene Creed it is used to mean 'consubstantial' or 'of one substance' with the Father.

7. *Charles Dickens*, London (Methuen) 1906, Chapter 5.

### Chapter 8 (A Weighty Problem)

1. *The Nation*, August 25th, 1909.

2. *The Bystander*, September, 1909.

3. *Autobiography*, Chapter 10, pp. 231–4 *passim*.

4. Denis Mackail, *The Story of J.M.B.*, New York (Charles Scribner's Sons) 1941.

5. D.J. Conlon, *Chesterton Review, XIV*, No. 4, November 1988, pp. 630–4.

6. Ward, *GKC*, p. 329.

7. John O'Connor, *Father Brown on Chesterton*, London (Frederick Muller) 1937 [hereafter: O'Connor], p. 94.

8. *G.K. Chesterton*, p. 227.

### Chapter 9 (The Norfolk, or was it Suffolk? Dumpling)

1. Mgr. John O'Connor T.P., D.D, (1870–1952) was born at Clonmel, County Tipperary. He trained for the priesthood in Douai, France and at the English College in Rome before being appointed to St. Bede's Grammar School in Bradford as assistant master. After three years as curate at St. Anne's in Keighley, he became parish priest at Heckmondwike in 1905, building the new church of the Holy Spirit there in 1914 and staying until 1919 when he moved to St. Cuthbert's at Manningham in Bradford where he was involved in fund-raising and planning for Our Lady and the First Martyrs, first of the new generation of 'in the round' churches which opened in 1935. He took a great interest in Education,

especially in St. Joseph's College which lay within his parish boundaries:

'We had many priest visitors, but probably the most familiar was Father John O'Connor, when he was parish priest at St. Cuthbert's. He came at all times of the day, but most often just before lunch, and when he arrived he might ask to speak to the Sixth Form. Maybe the topic was English poetry or perhaps French carols, or a Latin author, or travels to Rome, or the Holy Shroud, or some point of Theology, or the appreciation of art or music ... [He] had a very salutary effect on girls' minds in those days; he scotched any tendency to prudery or religious sentimentality and his theories were much more suitable to post-Vatican Two than to these earlier times.' (*The Story of St. Joseph's College 1908–1978*)

Mgr. O'Connor remained at St. Cuthbert's until 1952. He died in St. Joseph's Nursing Home, Horsforth, Bradford after a prolonged illness and was buried in Scholemoor Cemetery. BL, Add. MS 73196, ff. 31–4v.

2. Coren, *Gilbert*, p. 147.

3. *Autobiography*, Chapter 16, p. 325.

4. O'Connor, p. 32.

5. *The Awful Disclosures of Maria Monk*.

6. Francis Steinthal (August 23rd, 1854–April 6th, 1934) might well have been of Jewish ancestry, but he was certainly a devout Anglican. He was the son of Charles Augustavus Steinthal (whose names do not seem to indicate that he was Jewish as has been suggested) who did hail from Frankfurt-am-Main and who established Steinthal & Company, woollen merchants at 55 Leeds Road in Bradford. Francis Frederick was educated at Bradford High School and London International College, Spring Grove, Bradford. He became a member of the Bradford Chamber of Commerce and was later well-known both as an industrialist and philanthropist. His wife (m. April 5th, 1882), née Emmeline Petrie (1855–1921), eldest daughter of George Petrie J.P. of Rochdale, had been trained as a painter and sculptor at the Slade and in Paris, and she long continued to give art lessons. Both of the Steinthals took an interest in Education in association with Charlotte Mason of Ambleside with whom Mrs Steinthal had trained, and were instrumental in the founding of the Parents' National Educational Union and its magazine *The Parents' Review*. Emmeline Steinthal exhibited at the Royal Academy and undertook a marble bust of John Bright for Oldham Town Hall. The Steinthals' children included Cornelius Peter (188?–1930); Francis Eric (1886– 1934), master at Durham School and later at Abbot Holme, Staffordshire, who represented England at Rugby Union Football against Wales and France and was a Captain in the Royal Fusiliers; and Dorothy Dulcia (1884–1978) who took a Diploma in Public Service at the University of Leeds and then moved to Burgess

Hill in Sussex where she was later joined by her father after his wife's death.

During the 1914–18 War it was found expedient along with many, to change the German family name, so males of the Steinthal family adopted their mother's name of Petrie; Dorothea keeping the name of Steinthal. Other children were Dr Telford Petrie (1883–1930) and Major Paul Cuthbert Petrie, DSO, MC, (1888–1970), a partner in Hoffman & Co. of Bradford with whom Steinthal & Co. had amalgamated. Grandchildren included Flying Officer Ronald Anthony George Petrie RAF (1915–1939) killed in an air crash on April 28th, and Martin (Manfred) Alfred Petrie (1913–1941) who died on active service in Kenya.

In 1926 Maria Petrie (1887–1972), née Zimmern, wife of Francis Eric Petrie and mother of Martin (Manfred) Alfred Petrie made a bronze bust of Chesterton now in the National Portrait Gallery; she was an art teacher who exhibited at the Royal Academy and the Glasgow Institute. In 1934 she designed a reclining nude for Wedgwood which was sold widely.

7. The magnificent four-storey gentleman's mansion known as St. John's still stands on Queen's Road, Ilkley, although it has in recent years been converted into flats with one wing demolished and rebuilt somewhat unsympathetically in an out of character way. St. John's, designed by Norman Shaw when he was working on St. Margaret's Church opposite with the same stone used for both buildings, was commissioned for himself by John William Atkinson and completed in 1879, complete with a large stained-glass window bearing the motto *This is the House that Jack built*. It did not pass into the ownership of Francis Steinthal until 1901 when he and his wife returned from London to oversee the family firm of Steinthal & Company, woollen merchants in Bradford.

8. O'Connor, pp. 5–32 *passim*.

9. Fr. Brown was first described in The Blue Cross as a Norfolk dumpling, but later Chesterton was to vacillate between Norfolk and Suffolk.

10. O'Connor, pp. 38–9, 167.

11. Ibid.

### Chapter 10 (The Younger Brother)

1. Ada would seem to have worked for D.C. Thomson of Dundee. GKC recounts one incident in *Autobiography*, Chapter 8, p. 189: 'You have left your hero and heroine tied up in a cavern under the Thames for a week, and they are not married!'

2. A character in Dickens' *Our Mutual Friend*.

3. *The Chestertons*, pp. 93–5.

4. Ward, *GKC*, pp. 300–1.

5. Lord Chief Justice, head of the English legal system.

6. Herbert Samuel (1870–1963), Post-Master General responsible for awarding contracts for the establishment of a British Empire-wide Telegraph service.

7. David Lloyd George (1863–1945), Liberal politician and later Prime Minister 1916–22.

8. Lord Murray of Elibank, Chief Whip of the British Liberal Party.

9. Members of the British Conservative Party.

10. The Lord Chief Justice does not have rooms in the Houses of Parliament although the Lord Chancellor did and now the Lord Speaker does.

11. Godfrey and Harry Isaacs, Rufus's brothers.

12. In Boccacio's *Decamerone* tales are told by a group camping outside Florence to escape the effects of the plague then rampant in the city.

13. *New Witness*, April 16th, 1914.

14. Ward, *GKC*, p. 319. Other opinion at that time regarded the development as an advance in social housing.

15. *The Daily Telegraph*, Saturday, September 29th, 2007, 'Woman locked up for 'stealing' 2s 6d [12.5p] freed after 70 years.'

16. *New Witness*, December 13th, 1918.

17. A reference to the Peace Conference in Versailles attended by Lloyd George and Lord Reading (Rufus Isaacs).

18. *New Witness*, Dec. 20th, 1918.

19. *The Chestertons*, p. 241.

20. Letters from GKC to Belloc, May 3rd 1919 seq. (John J. Burns Library, Boston College, Mass.).

21. *The Chestertons*, pp. 257–63 *passim*.

22. Miss Eleanor Dunham, later Mrs Mark Phillips, had on her first day with the *New Witness* been 'christened' Bunny by Cecil Chesterton with his usual tact once he had noted her prominent front teeth.

23. *The Chestertons*, pp. 271–2.

24. Ibid., p. 274.

25. Charles Bennett: *Keith Chesterton, My Most Unforgettable Character*, 1923.

26. Miss 'Bunny' Dunham had felt vulnerable being responsible for financial situations over which she did not believe she had any proper control.

## Chapter 11 (The Trip to Jerusalem)

1. Ward, *GKC*, p. 377.

2. All quotations are from Gilbert's *The New Jerusalem*, Hodder & Stoughton (London) 1920 and Frances' diary, BL, Add. MS 73468.

3. Ward, *GKC*, p. 378.

## Chapter 12 (New York and the Mid-West)

1. Frances' fragmentary medical reports are to be found in BL, Add. MS 73470, ff. 7–40.
2. Ward, *GKC*, pp. 478–9 seq.
3. Ibid., p. 479.
4. O'Connor, p. 125.
5. G.K. Chesterton, 'The Arrow of Heaven', *The Incredulity of Father Brown*, London (Cassell and Company) 1926, pp. 32–3.
6. Ward, *GKC*, p. 479.
7. Ffinch, p. 271.
8. Ibid.
9. Ward, *GKC*, p. 483.
10. Ffinch, p. 271.
11. How Far Is It to Bethelem, (Nancy C. Brown, ed.), 2013.
12. Ibid.
13. Biskra was and remains a winter resort at the end of the Algerian railway system. It is situated in NE Algeria on the edge of the Sahara Desert. In the 1920s it had a population of some 20,000 but is now much larger at 300,000. It was used as a setting in André Gide's novel *L'Immoraliste* (1902).

## Chapter 13 (A Twitch on the Thread)

1. *Orthodoxy*, p. 137.
2. 'It is the test of a good philosophy whether you can defend it grotesquely. It is the test of a good religion whether you can joke about it.' 'Spiritualism' collected in *All Things Considered*, London (Methuen) 1908.
3. 'We are all Socialists now.' Attributed to Sir William Vernon Harcourt (1827–1904), Liberal Statesman, Home Secretary and later Chancellor of the Exchequer.
4. *The Ball and the Cross*, London (Wells Gardner, Darton) 1910, Chapter 15, pp. 298–304 *passim*.
5. 'The Staleness of Modernism,' *The Church Socialist Quarterly*, July 1909, pp. 199–200.
6. O'Connor, pp. 124–5.
7. The death of Chesterton's father.
8. *The Chesterton Society* Newsletter No. 43, February 1995, p.4.
9. O'Connor, pp. 126–7.
10. Ward, *GKC*, p. 395.
11. Ibid., p. 395.
12. O'Connor, pp. 127–8.

13. Ward, *GKC*, p. 395.
14. The Creed of Pius the Fourth promulgates the conclusions of the Council of Trent.
15. O'Connor, pp. 130–1; see also Ward, *GKC*, pp. 396–7. Chesterton's own later account is to be found in pages 387–95 of the typescript of his *Autobiography* (BL, Add. MS 73268A) 'taken out' of the published book after one manuscript page (between 388 and 389) had been lost.
16. Ward, *GKC*, p. 396–7.
17. *The Chestertons*, pp. 264–5.
18. O'Connor, p. 133.
19. *The Chestertons*, pp. 97–8.
20. *Toronto Daily Star*, cited in O'Connor, pp. 139–41.

## Chapter 14 (The Girls That Go Dancing)

1. Poems addressed to the Grays can be found in *CW* 10A, B and C. 'The Case of the Vanishing Car', a story written for Hilary Gray after she crashed her father's car, is featured in Michael Ffinch's Biography, p. 180.
2. *CW*, Vol. 10C, pp. 310–12.
3. Joan Nicholl recalled that she was thirteen years old when the Chestertons came to Lyme Regis in 1925. The third summer after that meeting Clare Nicholl, then living in Notting Hill, on a visit to Top Meadow asked to borrow Chesterton's new book, *The Return of Don Quixote* published in May, 1927. Joan reported that it was Mr Hatton's toyshop, whereas Clare thought it was Mr Isbell's toyshop. Both could have been correct if the ownership had varied, but neither of them was there at the time, only Barbara and Dorothy being involved.
4. BL, Add. MS 73481A, f. 152.
5. More than thirty poems were dedicated to the Nicholl family, most of them to be found in *CW*, Vols. 10A, 10B and 10C. Various games can be found in Lyme Regis Library.
6. Ward, *RTC*, p. 200.
7. Ibid., p. 201.
8. Ibid., pp. 161–2.
9. Quoodle was the name given to a succession of Scottish Terriers, the first of which joined Winkle about 1911. The dog referred to here must have been the second to bear the name.
10. Ward, *RTC*, pp. 206–7.
11. Murray House was situated in Vandon Street just off Victoria Street, close to Petty France.
12. A conversation recorded in Joan's home in Sorel Moussel in 2009.

13. Some of Joan's relations suspect that Joan was in love with Max.
14. Ward, *RTC*, p. 201.

## Chapter 15 (The Rolling Roads)
### Barcelona

1. Queen Victoria Eugenia (Ena) von Battenberg (1887–1969), consort of King Alphonso XIII of Spain, granddaughter of Queen Victoria and grandmother of King Juan Carlos. The lecture on April 22nd, 1926 was 'The Romance of History'. Frances felt too unwell to attend.
2. 'El Hombre que fu G.K. Chesterton', *Archipiélago* 65, Barcelona, April 2005.
3. op. cit.
4. Ward, *GKC*, p. 457.
5. Ward, *RTC*, p. 153.
6. Ward, *GKC*, p. 458.
7. BL, Add. MS 73470, f. 30.

### An Eagle Whiter Than a Dove

1. This is a line taken from Chesterton's poem on Poland.
2. *The Chestertons*, pp. 249–52.
3. *Autobiography*, Chapter 15, p. 317.
4. Ward, *GKC*, p. 365.
5. All Miss Collins's comments are quoted from her nephew Giles Darvill, 'With the Chestertons in Poland', *Chesterton Review*, XXII, No. 4, November 1996, pp. 475–85.
6. *Chesterton Review*, III, No. 2, pp. 300–4.
7. Darvill, op. cit.
8. 'On New Capitals', *Generally Speaking*, London (Methuen & Co) 1928, pp. 42–3.
9. *Autobiography*, Chapter 15, pp. 318–9.
10. Ibid., pp. 317–8.
11. The Chestertons had previously encountered the Karaim in Palestine.
12. Ward, *GKC*, pp. 488–9.
13. Ffinch, p. 311.
14. Ibid., p. 310.
15. *Autobiography*, Chapter 15, pp. 316–7.
16. In 1937 Jerry Zaruba painted this portrait to commemorate GKC's visit ten years previously.
17. *Chesterton Review*, XI, No. 3, August 1985, p. 320.

## Where All Roads Lead

1. *The Resurrection of Rome*, London (Hodder & Stoughton) 1930, pp. 34–6 *passim*.
2. Ibid., pp. 232–5 *passim*.
3. Ibid., p. 283.
4. Ibid., pp. 299–301, 317–9.
5. Neville Braybrooke, 'The Poet of Fleet Street', *John o'London's Weekly*, February 8th, 1962.

## Chapter 16 (Three Acres and a Cow)

1. The anti-corruption campaigns derived from the *New Witness* and *G.K.'s Weekly*'s Clean Government League.
2. The land was purchased from the Burkes to prevent its possible redevelopment into a commercial laundry business.
3. The slogan was first used by Jesse Collings for a land reform campaign in 1885.
4. Ward, *GKC*, pp. 438–9.
5. G.K. Chesterton: 'The Distributist', Leaflets for Leaguers, 1927, reprinted in *The Defendant*, 1, No. 7, July, 1953.

## Chapter 17 (St. Francis, The Everlasting Man and The Dumb Ox)
### St. Francis of Assisi

1. 'In the Days of My Youth', *T.P.'s and Cassell's Weekly*, January 23rd, 1926, reprinted in *The Chesterton Society Newsletter*, No. 43, February 1995.
2. Marks of Christ's five wounds that appear without physical cause on a body. The first to receive them would appear to have been St. Francis of Assisi.
3. *St. Francis of Assisi*, London (Hodder & Stoughton) 1923, Chapter 1, pp. 7–11.
4. *The New York Times*, March 2nd, 1924.
5. The Fraticelli (Little Brothers) or Spiritual Franciscans favoured a strict interpretation of the Rule of St. Francis, especially in regard to poverty and the ownership of property. This brought them into conflict with Church authorities and they were condemned as heretics after 1226. Umberto Eco's novel *The Name of the Rose* is set against persecution of the Fraticelli.

### The Everlasting Man

6. *The Everlasting Man*, London (Hodder & Stoughton) 1925, Part 2, end of Chapter 2.
7. *Punch*, October 28th, 1925.
8. *The Times Literary Supplement*, October 15th, 1925.
9. Alan Porter, *The Spectator*, October 17th, 1925.

**St. Thomas Aquinas – The Dumb Ox**

10. Michael Braybrooke, a young cousin of Frances Chesterton, was from 1909 semi-adopted by the Chestertons until he left school in the course of the Great War to join the Royal Naval Air Service.

11. *Chesterton Review*, XXX, Issue 1/2, Spring/Summer 2004, pp. 27 seq.

12. 'St. Thomas Aquinas (1225–74)', *The Spectator*, February 27th, 1933, then collected in *The Spectator's Gallery*, London (Jonathan Cape) 1933.

13. *St. Thomas Aquinas*, London (Hodder & Stoughton) 1933.

14. Ibid., Chapter 4, 'A Meditation on the Manichees.'

15. *The Times Literary Supplement*, October 5th, 1933.

16. Congregation of St. Basil.

17. New York (Pantheon Books) 1962.


**Chapter 18 (Daughter of Desire)**

1. It would seem that it was about this time that Dorothy Collins moved out of the rooms she had in Beaconsfield and into Top Meadow.

2. Kathleen Chesshire was Chesterton's previous secretary but one. The tickets were possibly for the celebrations to mark the 5th century of Joan of Arc at the Grand Palais in Paris.

3. Original in the possession of Mildred Wain's granddaughter.

4. Maria Immaculata. The statue of Our Lady in the Piazza di Spagna in Rome decorated for the feast of the Immaculate Conception on December 8th, 1929.

5. Letters and poems between Frances and Dorothy Collins derive from BL, Add. MS 73456, ff. 1–28v.


**Chapter 19 (Westward Ho!)**

1. Frances Chesterton's letters home. BL, Add. MS 73456, ff. 29–68v.

2. Ibid.

3. Dorothy Collins, 'Recollections' in J. Sullivan (ed), *Chesterton, A Centenary Appraisal*, London (Elek) 1974, p. 165; Ward, *RTC*, p. 252; *GKC*, p. 494.

4. Dorothy Collins, op. cit.

5. Frances Chesterton, op. cit.

6. Paul Claudel, BL, Add. MS 73403, folio 71.

7. Ward, *GKC*, p. 497.

8. A postcard home to Dorothy Collins's mother, BL, Add. MS 73471.

9. This story also appears in *Autobiography*, Chapter 15, p. 310.

10. Ward, *RTC*, pp. 247–8.

11. Dorothy Collins, op. cit.

12. Cited by Ffinch, p. 325.
13. *Sidelights: On New London and Newer York*, London (Sheed & Ward) 1932.
14. The daughter of the Bixler family at South Bend.
15. Dorothy Collins reserved accommodation at Murray House, Vandon Street, London SW 1, but objected to paying for meals she had not taken.
16. GKC's old schoolfriend and Frances' sister Ethel.
17. Amelita Galli-Curci (1882–1963), Italian coloratura soprano.

### Chapter 20 (London Calling)

1. In recent years Meynell's jibe has sometimes been mistakenly attributed to GKC himself.
2. This first broadcast was not reprinted in *The Listener*. It finally appeared in John J. Sullivan, *Chesterton Continued, a Bibliographical Supplement*, London (ULP) 1968, pp. 98–104.
3. *What's Wrong With the World*, Part 3, Chapter II, 'The Universal Stick'.
4. Dorothy Collins: 'Recollections', p. 159.
5. Chesterton is wrongly adjudged to have had a high-pitched, squeaky voice. This may have been because his size suggested that he should have been a *basso profundo*. All archive recordings from the BBC and cinema newsreels reveal that he had the well-modulated voice one would expect from a man of his class, education and era, not dissimilar to those of Neville Chamberlain, Clement Attlee, William Beveridge and many others.
6. Dorothy Collins, op. cit., p. 161.
7. *The Chestertons*, pp. 288–91.
8. Ibid., p. 292–3.
9. Ward, *GKC*, p. 513.
10. His condition casts doubt on the purity of water supply either at Beaconsfield or when he was on his travels.

### Ignorance Is Bliss

11. *Chesterton Quarterly*, Nos. 34 & 35, Spring/Summer 2005, p. 14.
12. This is usually attributed to Dean Inge.

### Chapter 21 (Nunc Dimittis Servum Tuum, Domine)

1. Ward, *GKC*, p. 548.
2. Letter from Dorothy Collins to Frances; Ffinch, p. 330.
3. Ibid., p. 330.
4. Ibid., pp. 330–1.

5. Ward, *RTC*, p. 265.
6. Ibid., p. 258.
7. Ibid., p. 268.
8. *The Chestertons*, pp. 299–300.
9. Unfinished letter to Clare Nicholl; Ward, *RTC*, pp. 268–9.
10. Letter to Barbara Nicholl.
11. Wikipedia, *Vincent McNabb, Quotes*. It seems likely that Fr. McNabb, O.P. sang the original version of the *Salve Regina* without the brief additions from the sixteenth century.
12. Ward, *RTC*, p. 269.
13. Ward, *RTC*, p. 267.
14. *The Chestertons*, pp. 304–6.
15. Ronald Knox, *Pastoral and Occasional Sermons*, San Francisco (Ignatius) 2002, p. 1059.

## Chapter 22 (Aftermath)

1. Ward, *RTC*, p. 270.
2. Mercury Theater of the Air, *The Man Who Was Thursday*, September 5th, 1938.
3. Introduction, G. K. Chesterton, *The Surprise*, London & New York (Sheed & Ward) 1952.
4. Letter in the possession of Mildred Wain's granddaughter.
5. 'I came to live at Top Meadow Cottage in 1952. Each year, we went to Europe in the car for about three weeks . . . I supplied the foreign language; she had no ear or interest in learning a language.' *Chesterton Review*, XIV, No. 4, November 1988. Her words almost re-echo Dorothy Collins's contention that Gilbert had no knowledge of any foreign languages, despite much evidence to the contrary.
6. *Orthodoxy*, pp. 269–70.
7. Some of the secretaries in chronological order were as follows:
   Marjorie Biggs (1906–1909). Later PA to chairman of Cassells.
   Nellie Allport (1910–1920). Could not type or take shorthand. Part-time?
   Mrs Meredith (1911–1914). Learnt to type with two fingers. Part-time?
   Frederica Spenser (1914–1918). Left to be secretary at Godolphin School.
   Winifred Pierpoint (1914–21). Part-time?
   Mrs Maddock Jones (c1915).
   Mrs Walpole (c1916–1918). Could not type. Part-time?
   Kathleen Chesshire (c1919–1925). Could type well and was efficient.
   Miss Stevens (c1925–1926). Far too efficient for Frances? Left by mutual consent.
   Dorothy Collins (1926–1988).

8. Poems addressed to Dorothy Collins are to be found in *CW*, Vol. 10A, and poems for Marjory Biggs, Freda Spenser and Kathleen Chesshire in *CW*, Vols. 10A, 10B and 10C.

9. *The Cross and the Plough*, Vol. 15, Nos. 1–4, 1948.

10. 9th Count de Salis of the Holy Roman Empire, hereditary Knight of the Golden Spur, ambassador of the Order of Malta to Thailand, 1996–9.

11. John, 2.1.


## PART 2 (The Man of Letters).
### The Novelist

1. *Collected Works*, Volume 14, p. 439, and full version in *Basil Howe*, London (New City) 2001.

2. *The Chestertons*, p. 38.

3. His poem dedicated to Walton-on-the-Naze can be found in *CW*, Vol. 10A, p. 487.

4. Review, *Vanity Fair*, April 7th, 1904.

5. *Autobiography*, Chapter 3, p. 62.

6. Orwell was familiar with Chesterton's work, having contributed his first publications in English to *G.K.'s Weekly* in 1929. His *Down and Out in Paris and London* (1933) took up what Ada Chesterton (pseudonym Anne Turner) had started in 1926 in *In Darkest London* and in 1936 *I Lived in a Slum*.

7. 'The Great Shawkspear Mystery', *Daily News*, April 15th, 1905.

8. *The Napoleon of Notting Hill*, *passim*.

9. Ibid., Book V, Chapter 3.

10. *CW*, Vol. 10A, 'The Fish.'

11. *CW*, Vol. 14, pp. 769–802; *Chesterton Quarterly*, No. 20, Autumn 2001.

12. Much in little.

13. *CW*, Vol. 14, pp. 772–5.

14. *CW*, Vol. 14, p. 60.

15. BL, Add. MS 73306, ff. 72–74.

16. *CW*, Vol. 14, p. 695.

17. The sword-stick, revolver and cloak.

18. Possibly the Hotel de l'Europe later known as Victory House.

19. 'Leviathan and the Hook'. *The Speaker*, September 9th, 1905.

20. Introduction to the *Book of Job*, London (Wellwood) 1907.

21. Mark, 10.38.

22. BL, Add. MS 73229.

23. *Manalive*, London (Nelson) 1912, Chapter 1.

24. Chesterton stated quite clearly ('The Return of Don Quixote – An Explanation',

*G.K.'s Weekly*, 20 November 1926, p. 135) that 'It was started at another stage of our career on the advice of those who specially asked for a serial . . . It is unfortunately planned on a larger scale than most of the same writer's stories; and the climax of its various issues is yet to come.' This he confirmed in his dedication to W.R. Titterton (managing editor of *G.K.'s Weekly*) of the 1927 edition: 'My Dear Titterton, This parable for social reformers, as you know, was planned and partly written long ago before the War [1914 to 1918]; so that, touching some things from Fascism to rag-time dance, it was a quite unintentional prophecy. It was your too generous confidence that dragged it from its dusty drawer; whether the world has any reason to thank you I doubt . . . Yours always, G.K. Chesterton.' The original version was published, probably for reasons of copyright (New York: Dodd Mead & Company, 1926), and also formed the basis of the narrative up to the entry of Dr Gambrel into Dr Hendry's house in chapter 9 as serialised in *G.K.'s Weekly* (12 December 1925). A further part was serialised until 11 November 1926 when it was discontinued in the middle of chapter 14. The novel was subsequently revised, completed, and published on 8 May 1927 (London: Chatto & Windus) with Dodd Mead then issuing the revised version in the same year.

25. The novel *The Flying Inn* was first published on 22 January 1914, but the songs included in it had appeared in the *New Witness* between 14 November 1912 and 27 November 1913. The dramatised version (Chesterton's musical) probably predates the novel; it omits the Peaceways episode, which has all the signs of being an interpolation, but includes some characters who, like the Duchess of Battle-axe, were later found redundant. The dramatised version is included in *CW*, Vol. XI, ed. D.J. Conlon– San Francisco (Ignatius Press), 1989.

26. It seems likely from internal evidence and a feeling of hasty composition that chapters 18 and 19 were written after November 1926. Certainly, the sequence of Catholic marriages and the presentation of Seawood Abbey to a community of monks indicate a date of composition after Chesterton's conversion in 1922.

27. Incredible as it may seem, stills depicting the quartet-wearing Stetsons still exist.

28. There are discrepancies between the 1926 and 1927 editions as to when a chapter begins and when it ends. The 1926 edition seems more logical in its division.

29. *The Return of Don Quixote* , New York (Dodd Mead), 1926, p. 17; London (Darwen Finlayson) 1963, pp. 18–19.

30. Ibid., p. 4; p. 9.

31. One can cite Wayne/Quin with their complementary fanaticism and humour in *The Napoleon of Notting Hill*, MacIan/Turnbull in *The Ball and the Cross*, the diverse ladies in *Manalive* who are revealed to be one, and especially the

personality shattered into seven days who can only be at peace when it is realised that the feverish days can find the peace of God on the Sabbath and become as one in a week (*The Man Who Was Thursday*).

32. Cf. The Simple Souls, a group of gullible fools in *The Flying Inn* (op. cit.) who meet in a low shed of corrugated iron they call the Universal Hall for enlightenment by lecturers such as Mysisra Ammon.

33. *The Return of Don Quixote*, p. 24 seq.

34. Ibid., p. 99; pp. 71–2.

35. Ibid., p. 110; p. 79.

36. Ibid., p. 110; p. 79.

37. An early version of 'The Secret People' which appeared in *A Chesterton Calendar*, London (Kegan Paul) 1911, and *Wit and Wisdom of G.K. Chesterton*, New York (Dodd Mead & Company) 1911.

38. One of several lampoons concerning psychiatrists, especially the German variety, in Chesterton's works. One can cite the lunatic asylum in *The Ball and the Cross* and the Doctor from Berlin in *The Turkey and the Turk*, but there is also 'On Professor Freud,' *G.K.'s Weekly*, 28 March 1925:

> The Ignorant pronounce it Frood,
>> To Cavil or applaud.
> The well-informed pronounce it Froyd,
>> But I pronounce it Fraud.

39. *The Return of Don Quixote*, p. 116; p. 83.

40. Ibid., p. 131; p. 91 seq.

41. Ibid., p. 141; pp. 197–8.

42. Ibid. (1926 edition), p. 103.

43. Ibid., p. 111.

44. Ibid., p. 113. It should be noted that there is evidence in the 1926 text that Dr Hendry in some earlier version had been called Lorne.

45. Chesterton's last *Daily News* article appeared on 1 February 1913.

46. The affair lasted from 7 March 1912 to 9 June 1913.

47. A. Stone Dale, *The Outline of Sanity: a biography of G. K. Chesterton*, Grand Rapids, Mich. (Eerdmans), 1982, p. 180.

48. 'A Song of Strange Drinks,' *New Witness*, 23 January 1913; 'The Song of Right and Wrong,' *The Flying Inn* (London: Methuen, 1914), Chapter 18.

49. 'The Song of the Oak.' Chapter 23.

50. See note 25 above.

51. Elveden Hall has stood empty since the present Earl of Iveagh sold off its contents in 1984 after it had been unused for many years. It has frequently been featured in

films which use its oriental interiors. The descendants of the third Earl of Iveagh have continued their interest in politics and his grandson, Paul Channon, was Secretary of State for Transport in the third Thatcher government.

52. *The Flying Inn*, Chapter 2.

53. Peaceways, with its milk product and thatched cottages, may owe something to the image of the Ovaltine factory and egg farm at King's Langley, long a feature to be noticed from the railway line running north from London, Euston. It has now been redeveloped.

54. *The Flying Inn*, Chapter 2.

55. One of the aggravating factors in South Africa prior to the outbreak of the Boer War.

56. Lord Ivywood seems to have forestalled the Volstead Act and the 18th Amendment, but the Total Abstinence Movement was quite vociferous at the time.

57. *The Flying Inn – a Play*, Scene III. See note 2 above.

58. *The Fortnightly Review*, October 1904, pp. 705–14; December 1904, pp. 1096–1103; February 1905, pp. 341–7; May 1905, pp. 732–9.

59. London (Cassell), 1910.

60. London (T. N. Foulis), 1912.

61. *The Flying Inn*, Chapter 3.

62. Ibid., Chapter 4.

63. Ibid., Chapter 4.

64. *New Witness*, 19 December 1912; 'The Song against Songs', *The Flying Inn*, Chapter 6.

65. Ibid., Chapter 17.

66. Ibid., Chapter 17.

67. November 1914 for some three months.

68. October 1916. The magazine folded on 21 April 1923.

69. 1922.

70. The first issue was on 21 March 1925, but Chesterton had been planning its launch for many years.

71. London (Cassell), 1922. The stories had previously appeared in *The Storyteller* and *Cassell's Magazine* from October 1919.

72. *The Return of Don Quixote*, New York (Dodd Mead & Company) 1926, p. 149.

73. Ibid., London (Darwen Finlayson) 1963, p. 102.

74. Ibid., pp. 127–8.

75. Ibid., p. 130.

76. Lord Eden first appeared in Chesterton's fiction as a Prime Minister in *Tales of the Long Bow* (London: Cassell, 1925), although the constituent stories had earlier

appeared in 1924 and 1925 in *The Storyteller*. His presence in *The Return of Don Quixote* is evidence that this part of the narrative was rewritten to suit the circumstances of 1926.

77. *The Return of Don Quixote*, p. 147.

78. Ibid., p. 156.

79. Ibid., pp. 159–60

80. Ibid., p. 162.

81. Ibid., p. 168.

82. Ibid., p. 168.

83. The General Strike lasted for ten days in May 1926. When the strike took place Chesterton was away in Spain, but in his absence Titterton decided to support the striking workers, much to the anger of many readers of *G.K.'s Weekly*. This action was endorsed by Chesterton on his return in an article 'The Pride of England', *G.K.'s Weekly*, 22 May 1926, p. 162. His readers' reactions can be found in the issues of May and June 1926.

84. 11 November 1926.

85. *The Return of Don Quixote*, pp. 177–8.

86. 'The Return of Don Quixote – An Explanation', *G.K.'s Weekly*, 20 November 1926, p. 135.

87. *The Return of Don Quixote*, p. 189.

88. Ibid., pp. 218–9.

89. Dedication to W.R. Titterton, *The Return of Don Quixote*, London (Chatto & Windus), 1927, p. v.

## The Playwright

1. 'The Case against Chesterton', *The New Statesman*, May 13th, 1916, p. 136.

2. *Shaw on Theater*, E.J. West (ed.), New York 1961, p. 161.

3. Ward, *GKC*, London and New York (Sheed & Ward) 1944, p. 196 or 226. Books of the same date vary in pagination and even content, the result of resetting after a German bombing raid.

4. *The Mark Twain Quarterly*, I, Spring 1937, p. 9.

5. Ward, *GKC*, p. 149 and in *Chesterton Review*, XXV, No. 3, August, 1999.

6. Parts I–IV reprinted in *CW*, Vol. 9, San Francisco (Ignatius) 1989, pp. 53–96, with Part V reprinted in the *Chesterton Quarterly*, No. 11, Summer 1998.

7. Ward, *GKC*.

8. Ibid., p. 196 or 226.

9. Ibid., p. 203 or 234.

10. Ibid., pp. 207–08 or 239.

11. Ibid., p. 315.

12. 'The Best Game in the World', *Merry-Go-Round*, December 1923 and January 1924.

13. See *CW*, Vol. 11, San Francisco (Ignatius) 1989.

14. A similar fate awaited an attempt to use the text as a comic opera libretto in 1929 when the Great Depression intervened.

15. *Chesterton Quarterly*, No. 18, Spring 2001.

16. Introduction to Alice Meynell's *Samuel Johnson*, London (Herbert & Daniel) 1911, pp. vi-xx.

17. Chesterton gave outright several copyrights including *The Queen of Seven Swords* and *The Judgement of Dr Johnson* to Frank Sheed and Maisie Ward to help them (re)launch their publishing house. However, there were delays.

18. Barker, *Chesterton, a Biography*, p. 272.

19. Father Kevin Scannell, Monsignor O'Connor's curate, claimed to have a manuscript written in Rome in 1929, a claim disputed by Dorothy Collins who dated *The Surprise* to 1932. After Father Scannell's death his Chesterton collection was bequeathed to St. Michael's University in Toronto, Canada, but as yet the manuscript has not been unearthed.

20. BL, Add. MS 73231C, ff. 34–38v.

21. *Chesterton Quarterly*, No. 9, Summer 2001.

22. *Chesterton Quarterly*, Nos. 6, 7, 8 and 9, 1998.

23. BL, Add. MS 73229.

### The Story Teller

1. Forty-eight as originally collected, plus *The Donnington Affair*, *The Vampire of the Village* and *The Mask of Midas*.

2. Albert Chevalier (1861–1923) was actually an actor, music hall comedian and singer, now best remembered for his rendition of Cockney songs including 'My Old Dutch'.

3. A Scorcher was an aggressive cyclist who had little regard for pedestrians. A Masher was someone who forced his unwelcome attentions on women, usually depicted in early cinema with oiled hair parted in the middle, grotesque frequently twirled moustache, and prominent collar.

4. 'Sincerity and Success', in Walter Scott Liddell (ed.), *Short-Story Writing*, London (Author's Advice Bureau) 1916, pp. 65–76.

5. BL, Add. MS 73353A, ff 50v–41v, pages reversed.

### The Poet

1. *The Times*, January 12th, 1934. There exists a *Triolet of the Self-Examining Journalist* dating from February 27th, 1912 in which the third line reads 'I have lost all I had.' See JOT, 101, July 14th, 2013.
2. Preface, *Greybeards at Play*, London (Elek) 1974, p. 9.
3. 'G.K. Chesterton and His School', in Herbert Palmer, *Post-Victorian Poetry*, London (Dent) 1938.
4. *The University Extension Journal*, Cambridge, March 1904, pp. 85–6.

### The Essayist

1. 'On the Essay', *Illustrated London News*, February 16th, 1929.
2. Introduction to F. J. H. Darton (ed.), *Essays of the Year 1931–1932*, London (Argonaut Press) 1932.
3. General Cyrus Choke, a character in the American episode of Dickens' *Martin Chuzzlewit*.
4. An area of sanctuary from the law situated where the Whitefriars Abbey once stood at the west end of Fleet Street between the Temple and the River Thames. From the fifteenth century until its privileges were withdrawn in the eighteenth century it was a haven for debtors and other lawbreakers.
5. *London* (G. Foy) 1914.

### The Critic

1. Introduction to Dickens' *The Old Curiosity Shop*, London (Everyman Library) 1907, as collected in G. K. Chesterton, *Appreciations and Criticisms of the Works of Charles Dickens*, London (Dent) 1911, pp. 51–2.
2. Lord David Cecil, *New Statesman and Nation*, May 3rd, 1932.
3. Unsigned review, *Everyman*, April 14th, 1932.
4. *Chaucer*, London (Faber) 1932, Chapter VIII, pp. 251–3.
5. Unsigned review, *Everyman*, op. cit.
6. G. K. Chesterton, *The Coloured Lands*, London & New York (Sheed & Ward) 1938.
7. Chaucer's Bob-up-and-Down was based on Harbledown which, though now bisected by a new road, still stands very much up-and-down by Blean Woods just to the north of Canterbury.

### PART 3 (New and Original Views)

1. *Autobiography*, Chapter 3, pp. 74–5.
2. *Basil Howe*, London (New City) 2001, p. 46.
3. BL, Add. MS 73321B, ff. 41v–45v.

4. BL, Add. MS 73307, ff. 171–251.
5. Gerald Kaufman, 'Chesterton's Final Solution', *Times Higher Educational Supplement*, January 2nd, 1998.
6. *The Complete Poems of G. K. Chesterton*, 3rd Edition, London (Methuen) 1933, p. 318.
7. *The Speaker*, March 2nd, 1901.
8. *The Ball and the Cross* (1909), Chapter 3.
9. Ibid., Chapter 16.
10. *Jewish Chronicle*, April 28th, 1911; reprinted in *Chesterton Review*, XIII, No. 2, May, 1987, pp. 143–59.
11. *Manalive*, Part 2, Chapter 2.
12. Ward, *GKC*, p. 227.
13. *New Witness*, July 24th, 1913, p. 37.
14. *The Flying Inn*, 1914, Chapter 2.
15. 'The Duel of Dr Hirsch', *Pall Mall Magazine*, August 1914; Collected in *The Wisdom of Father Brown*, 1914.
16. *New Witness*, December 13th, 1918; reprinted in Ward, *GKC*, pp. 359–62.
17. *The New Jerusalem*, London (Hodder and Stoughton) 1920, Chapter XIII, 'The Problem of Zionism', pp. 264–301.
18. Theobald von Bethmann-Hollweg (1856–1921), German Chancellor (1909–17). Eglon and Agag were kings of the Amalekites.
19. Abraham Lincoln.
20. Ward, *RTC*, p. 116.
21. *New Witness*, July 11th, 1919, p. 217.
22. *Jewish Chronicle*, September 22nd, 1933, p. 14.
23. *CW*, Vol. 10B, op. cit.
24. Shaw: 'This is the real enemy, the invader from the East, the Druze, the ruffian, the oriental parasite; in a word: the Jew.' *Morning Post*, December 3rd, 1925. 'This craving for bouquets by Jews is a symptom of racial degeneration. The Jews are worse than my own people. Those Jews who still want to be the Chosen Race (chosen by the late Lord Balfour) can go to Palestine and stew in their own juice. The rest had better stop being Jews and start being human beings.' *Literary Digest*, October 12th, 1932. Buchan: 'The Jew is everywhere but you have to go far down the backstairs to find him. Take any big Teutonic business concern. If you have dealings with it, the first man you meet is Prince von und zu Something, an elegant young man who talks Eton-and-Harrow English. But he cuts no ice. If your business is big, you get behind him and find a prognathous Westphalian with a retreating brow and the manners of a hog . . . But if you're on the biggest kind of job and are bound to get

to the real boss, ten to one you are brought up against a little, white-faced Jew in a Bath-chair, with an eye like a rattlesnake. Yes, sir, he is the man who is ruling the world just now.' *The Thirty-Nine Steps*, 1915.

Eliot: 'My house is a decayed house,

> And the Jew squats on the window sill, the owner,
> Spawned in some estaminet of Antwerp,
> Blistered in Brussels, patched and peeled in London. *Gerontion*, 1920.

Christie: 'men of Hebraic extraction, sallow men with hooked noses, wearing flamboyant jewellery.'

Voltaire considered Jews 'deadly to the human race.' *Lettres de Memmius à Ciceron* (1771).

25. 'Zionism versus Bolshevism, a Struggle for the Soul of the Jewish People', *Illustrated Sunday Herald*, February 20th, 1920, p. 5. See also 'How the Jews can combat Persecution', an unpublished 3,000 word article from 1937 in Cambridge University's Churchill archives: [Their] 'aloofness and separateness means they have been partly responsible for the antagonism from which they suffer.'

26. See *The Napoleon of Notting Hill*, 1904, *passim*.

# INDEX